WORLD TRADE ORGANIZATION

Dispute Settlement Reports

1999

Volume III

Pages 949-1439

CAMBRIDGE
UNIVERSITY PRESS

PUBLISHED BY THE PRESS SYNDICATE OF THE UNIVERSITY OF CAMBRIDGE
The Pitt Building, Trumpington Street, Cambridge, United Kingdom

CAMBRIDGE UNIVERSITY PRESS
The Edinburgh Building, Cambridge CB2 2RU, UK
40 West 20th Street, New York, NY 10011–4211, USA
477 Williamstown Road, Port Melbourne, VIC 3207, Australia
Ruiz de Alarcón 13, 28014 Madrid, Spain
Dock House, The Waterfront, Cape Town 8001, South Africa

http://www.cambridge.org

Printed in the United Kingdom at the University Press, Cambridge

French edition and Spanish edition paperbacks of this title are both available directly from WTO Publications, World Trade Organization, Centre William Rappard, 154 rue de Lausanne, CH-1211 Geneva 21, Switzerland http://www.wto.org

ISBN 0 521 80322 5 hardback
ISBN 0 521 00565 5 paperback

THE WTO DISPUTE SETTLEMENT REPORTS

The *Dispute Settlement Reports* of the World Trade Organization (the "WTO") include panel and Appellate Body reports, as well as arbitration awards, in disputes concerning the rights and obligations of WTO Members under the provisions of the *Marrakesh Agreement Establishing the World Trade Organization*. The *Dispute Settlement Reports* are available in English, French and Spanish. Starting with 1999, the first volume of each year contains a cumulative index of published disputes.

This volume may be cited as DSR 1999:III

TABLE OF CONTENTS

AUSTRALIA - SUBSIDIES PROVIDED TO PRODUCERS AND EXPORTERS OF AUTOMOTIVE LEATHER

Report of the Panel

WT/DS126/R

Adopted by the Dispute Settlement Body on 16 June 1999

TABLE OF CONTENTS

I. INTRODUCTION

1.1 On 4 May 1998, the United States requested consultations with Australia under Articles 1 and 4 of the Understanding on Rules and Procedures Governing the Settlement of Disputes ("DSU") and Articles 4.1 and 30 (to the extent that it incorporates by reference Article XXIII:1 of the General Agreement on Tariffs and Trade 1994) of the Agreement on Subsidies and Countervailing Measures (the "SCM Agreement") regarding allegedly prohibited subsidies provided to an Australian producer and exporter of automotive leather, Howe and Company Proprietary Ltd. ("Howe"), or any of its affiliated and/or parent companies (WT/DS126/1).

1.2 The United States and Australia met on 4 June 1998.[1]

1.3 On 11 June 1998, pursuant to Article 4.4 of the SCM Agreement and Article 1.2 of the DSU, the United States requested the immediate establishment of a panel to examine the consistency of the subsidies provided to Howe with Australia's obligations under the Marrakesh Agreement Establishing the World Trade Organization (the "WTO Agreement"), in particular those contained in the SCM Agreement (WT/DS126/2).

1.4 At the meeting of the Dispute Settlement Body ("DSB") on 22 June 1998, the DSB established a panel in accordance with Article 4.4 of the SCM Agreement and Article 6 of the DSU with standard terms of reference. The terms of reference were:

> To examine, in the light of the relevant provisions of the covered agreements cited by the United States in document

[1] Australia does not consider that this meeting constituted "consultations" under the DSU. *See* WT/DS126/3, 19 June 1998.

> WT/DS126/2, the matter referred to the DSB by the United States in that document and to make such findings as will assist the DSB in making the recommendations or in giving the rulings provided for in those agreements. (WT/DS126/4)

1.5 On 27 October 1998, the United States requested the Director-General to determine the composition of the Panel, pursuant to paragraph 7 of Article 8 of the DSU. On 2 November 1998, the Director-General composed the Panel as follows:

Chairperson: H. E. Carmen Luz Guarda

Members: Mr. Jean-François Bellis

Mr. Wieslaw Karsz

1.6 The Panel met with the parties on 9-10 December 1998 and 13-14 January 1999.

1.7 The Panel submitted its interim report to the parties on 8 March 1999. On 15 March 1999, Australia and the United States submitted written requests for the Panel to review precise aspects of the interim report. The Panel submitted its final report to the parties on 23 March 1999.

II. FACTUAL ASPECTS

2.1 This dispute concerns certain assistance provided by the government of Australia to Howe, a wholly-owned subsidiary of Australian Leather Upholstery Pty. Ltd., which is owned by Australian Leather Holdings, Limited ("ALH"), part of which is owned by Schaffer Corporation, Ltd. Howe is the only dedicated producer and exporter of automotive leather in Australia. Automotive leather is primarily used for seat coverings and other interior components of automobiles, such as head and armrests, centre consoles and door trim.

2.2 On 9 March 1997, the Australian government signed two contracts with ALH and Howe: a grant contract (the "grant contract") and a loan contract (the "loan contract") providing for funding for an assistance package. The Australian Department of State of Industry, Science and Resources[2] is the governmental authority responsible for administering the contracts and disbursing the payments thereunder.

2.3 The grant contract provides for a series of three grant payments totalling up to a maximum of A$30 million. The aggregate of payments under the grant contract was capped at A$30 million to limit the overall level of *ad valorem*

[2] Before October 1998, this Department was known as the Department of Industry, Science and Tourism.

subsidization of sales over the period to mid-2000 to approximately 5 percent.[3] The payments were scheduled to occur in three instalments: the first payment of A$5 million was to paid upon conclusion of the grant contract; the second payment of up to A$12.5 million was to be paid in July 1997 on the basis of Howe's performance against the performance targets set out in the grant contract for the period 1 April 1997 to 30 June 1997, as well as due diligence considerations such as whether the company was functioning properly; the third payment of up to A$12.5 million was to be paid in July 1998 on the basis of Howe's performance against the performance targets set out in the grant contract for the period 1 July 1997 to 30 June 1998, as well as due diligence considerations such as whether the company was functioning properly. The performance targets consisted of sales targets and capital expenditure targets for certain specified periods: 1 April - 30 June 1997; 1 July 1997 - 30 June 1998; 1 July 1998 - 30 June 1999; and 1 July 1999 - 30 June 2000. Under the grant contract, Howe was required to use its best endeavours to achieve the performance targets. With regard to capital expenditure under the grant contract, the aggregate target for approved capital expenditure was $22.8 million over the four-year period in question.[4] The maximum amount of A$30 million was essentially paid out in the three grant payments, in accordance with the grant contract.[5]

2.4 The loan contract provides for a fifteen-year loan of $A25 million by the government of Australia to ALH/Howe. For the first five-year period of this loan, ALH/Howe is not required to pay principal or interest. After the expiration of this five-year period, interest on the loan is to be based on the rate for Australian Commonwealth Bonds with a ten-year maturity, plus two percentage points. The loan is secured by a second lien over the assets and undertakings of ALH.

2.5 These arrangements were put in place by the Australian government in compensation[6] for the excision, as of 1 April 1997, of automotive leather from the Australian Textiles, Clothing and Footwear Import Credit Scheme[7] (the

---

3 *See* para. 123 of Australia's first written submission; *infra*, para 7.191.

4 Howe constructed a new tannery at Rosedale and a new finishing plant at Thomastown. The latter was commissioned during February/March 1998 and commenced operating in April 1998. It replaced the old plant in Preston which was decommissioned during the same period and closed in May 1998.

5 A portion of the third payment of A$12.5 million was held back pending completion of the audit process.

6 In response to questioning by the Panel, Australia stated that this was not "compensation" in the sense of off-setting a legal obligation on the part of the government of Australia, nor in the sense of trying to achieve an equivalent outcome, nor in the sense of it being an equivalent amount of assistance. Australia stated, however, that there was a political commitment to help maintain the commercial viability of Howe in the light of the settlement reached between Australia and the United States in November 1996.

7 The ICS has been in effect from 1 July 1991, and remains in effect through 30 June 2000. Under this programme, exporters of eligible textile, clothing and footwear products can earn import credits that may be used to reduce the import duties payable on eligible textile, clothing and foot-

"ICS") and the Export Facilitation Scheme for Automotive Products[8] (the "EFS") pursuant to a settlement agreement with the United States reached in November 1996. This excision was enacted on 26 March 1997 by Australian Customs Notice No. 97/29. Automotive leather will be part of the general textile, industry and clothing arrangements due to come into force in Australia on 1 July 2000.

III. PREVIOUS WTO DISPUTE SETTLEMENT PROCEDURES BETWEEN THE PARTIES WITH RESPECT TO THE SAME OR RELATED MATTERS

3.1 On 7 October 1996, the United States requested consultations with Australia concerning subsidies available to leather under the ICS and any other subsidies to leather granted or maintained in Australia which were prohibited under Article 3 of the SCM Agreement.[9] Following one round of consultations, the United States and Australia reached a settlement on 24 November 1996. This settlement was announced on 25 November 1996. Under the terms of settlement, the government of Australia would excise automotive leather from eligibility under the ICS, as well as under the EFS, by 1 April 1997. On 26 March 1997, Australian Customs Notice No. 97/29 excised automotive leather from the ICS and EFS, effective 1 April 1997.

3.2 On 10 November 1997, the United States requested consultations regarding "prohibited subsidies provided to Australian producers and exporters of automotive leather, including subsidies provided to Howe Leather" which the United States understood to "include the provision by the government of Australia of an $A25 million loan on preferential and non-commercial terms and

---

wear items by an amount up to the value of the credits held. Exporters are not required to use their credits as offsets against import duties, but may transfer them to another holder in exchange for a cash payment. The value of import credits that can be earned is calculated as the F.O.B. value of an eligible export sale, multiplied by the Australian value-added content of the export sale. This total is multiplied by a specified "Export Phasing Rate". *TCF Import Credit Scheme: Administrative Arrangements* (March 1995), United States Exhibit 7. The ICS is managed by the Australian Customs Service on behalf of the Australian Textiles, Clothing and Footwear Authority.

[8] The EFS has been in its current form since 1991, and remains in effect until 31 December 2000. The EFS allows Australian manufacturers to earn A$1 of export credit for every dollar of eligible exports of covered automotive items. The value of exports eligible to earn exports credits is equal to the Australian value-added content of eligible exports, calculated as the F.O.B. sales price less the value of any imported components and raw materials. Export credits earned under this programme can be used to obtain rebates on the duties payable on eligible imports of automotive vehicles and automotive components or may be sold for cash to any importer of eligible goods who may similarly seek such rebates. The amount of import duty that can be rebated under this programme is determined by a tariff reduction schedule that varies depending on the year in which the export credit is used. Australian Department of Industry, Science &Technology, *Report on the State of the Automotive Industry 1994* (June 1995), United States Exhibit 13.

[9] WT/DS57/1, G/SCM/D7/1, 9 October 1996.

grants amounting potentially to another $A30 million."[10] Consultations held between the United States and Australia on 16 December 1997 failed to resolve the dispute. At its meeting of 22 January 1998, the DSB established a panel in accordance with Article 4.4 of the SCM Agreement and Article 6 of the DSU pursuant to the request made by the United States on 9 January 1998. That panel was never composed.

IV. PROCEDURES ADOPTED BY THE PANEL GOVERNING "BUSINESS CONFIDENTIAL INFORMATION"

4.1 Due to concern expressed by one of the parties concerning the submission to the Panel of sensitive business information, the Panel adopted "Procedures Governing Business Confidential Information" at its first meeting with the parties. Pursuant to these procedures, only "approved persons" - i.e. a Panel member, representative, Secretariat employee or a member of the Permanent Group of Experts (the "PGE") - having filed with the Chairperson of the Panel a Declaration of Non-Disclosure were permitted to view or hear information designated by a party as business confidential information in the course of the Panel proceedings. Such approved persons were under an obligation not to disclose that information, or allow it to be disclosed, to any other person other than another approved person, except in accordance with the Procedures. The Panel was under an obligation not to disclose business confidential information in its interim and final reports, but could make statements of conclusion drawn from such information. Accordingly, the Panel has taken steps to ensure that all information designated by a party as business confidential information has been omitted from this Panel Report. Where the Panel deemed it necessary, a description of the type of information concerned has been provided.

V. FINDINGS AND RECOMMENDATIONS REQUESTED BY THE PARTIES

5.1 The **United States** asks the Panel to make the following preliminary requests and rulings:

(a) that Australia produce, by 30 November 1998, authentic copies of certain documents[11] for review by the Panel and the United States;

(b) "rejecting Australia's argument that any further proceedings before this Panel should be terminated";

[10] WT/DS106/1, G/SCM/D17/1, 17 November 1997.

[11] These documents are listed *infra*, para. 6.1.

(c) "that the United States has met its obligations under Article 4.2 of the Subsidies Agreement"; and

(d) "rejecting Australia's argument that the Panel should disregard those facts and argument not explicitly set forth in the consultation request".

5.2 With respect to the merits of the case, the United States requests the Panel to find that "Australia is in violation of its obligations under Article 3.1 of the SCM Agreement", and asks the Panel to "recommend that Australia withdraw the subsidy to Howe without delay".

5.3 **Australia** asks the Panel to make the following preliminary rulings:

(a) that "the establishment of the Panel was inconsistent with the DSU and that as a consequence the Panel should terminate its work";

(b) that "in WT/DS126/1 the United States did not meet its disclosure obligations under Article 4 of the Subsidies Agreement and that consequently the establishment of the Panel and the basis for the United States case before the Panel are irremediably flawed. Australia asks that, as a consequence, the Panel terminate the proceedings, or rule immediately that the United States has not demonstrated its claims before the Panel"; and

(c) "If the Panel does not agree to the requests in subparagraphs [(a) and (b)] above, then Australia asks that the Panel rule that, as a result of the failure of the United States to fulfil its disclosure obligations under Article 4 of the Subsidies Agreement, all facts and arguments not explicitly spelled out in the request for the Panel (WT/DS126/1) will be disregarded for the purpose of the proceedings of the Panel. Of this evidence, Australia asks in addition that information acquired in the context of consultations under WT/DS106/1 be ruled to be confidential to that process [footnote omitted] and not admissible before this Panel, including Exhibit 2 of the United States First Submission."

5.4 In the event that the Panel does not terminate the proceedings on the basis of Australia's requests for preliminary rulings, Australia requests the Panel to find that:

(a) "the Loan does not fall under Article 3.1(a) of the Subsidies Agreement";

(b) "the two first payments under the Grant contract do not fall under Article 3.1(a) of the Subsidies Agreement"; or

(c) "if the Panel decides to consider subsequent payments or the Grant contract itself, none of the payments or the Grant contract itself falls under Article 3.1(a) of the Subsidies Agreement".

5.5 In addition, if the Panel finds that any measure before it is inconsistent with Article 3.1(a) of the SCM Agreement, then Australia requests that:

(a) "consistent with Article 19.2 of the DSU, the Panel make no recommendation or suggestion regarding the way in which Australia should bring itself into conformity"; and

(b) "consistent with Article 4.12 of the Subsidies Agreement, recommend that Australia have at least 7.5 months for implementation from the adoption of the Panel or Appellate Body report, i.e. at least half of that provided as a benchmark period in Article 21.3(c) of the DSU, but that this issue be addressed by the Panel and the parties after the circulation of the Interim Report setting out the Panel's draft findings on the nature of the measures before the Panel".

VI. PRELIMINARY ISSUES AND REQUESTS FOR PRELIMINARY RULINGS

A. *Request for Documents by the United States*

6.1 In its first written submission to the Panel, the **United States** asked the Panel to request that Australia produce, by 30 November 1998, authentic copies of the following documents for review by the Panel and the United States:

(a) "Any document which provides the grant from the Australian government to Howe, and any related documents;

(b) The loan contract between the Australian government and Howe, and any documents related to that contract;

(c) The report prepared by the accounting firm commissioned by the Australian government and used in devising the replacement package;

(d) Financial statements of Howe (or related corporate entities) for the period 1989 to present;

(e) Internal business plans or strategic plans of Howe (or related corporate entities) for the period 1995 to present;

(f) Any correspondence between the Australian government and Howe (or corporate entities related to Howe), or vice versa, regarding the replacement subsidy package;

(g) Annual reports of Howe (or related corporate entities) for the period 1989 to present; and

(h) Any analysis or forecast of the Australian automotive leather market in the custody or control of the Australian government, Howe, or any entity related to Howe."

6.2 The United States indicated that it was prepared to agree to appropriate procedures necessary to protect any business confidential information contained in the documents. The United States asserted that it had requested most of this information in consultations with Australia, but the Australian government had to date been unwilling to provide it. The United States recalled that the Appellate Body Report in *India - Patent Protection for Pharmaceutical and Agricultural Chemical Products* ("*India - Patents*") stated:

> All parties engaged in dispute settlement under the DSU must be fully forthcoming from the very beginning both as to the claims involved in a dispute and as to the facts relating to those claims. Claims must be stated clearly. Facts must be disclosed freely. This must be so in consultations as well as in the more formal setting of panel proceedings. In fact, the demands of due process that are implicit in the DSU make this especially necessary during consultations. For the claims that are made and the facts that are established during consultations do much to shape the substance and the scope of subsequent panel proceedings. If, in the aftermath of consultations, any party believes that all the pertinent facts relating to a claim are, for any reason, not before the panel, then that party should ask the panel in that case to engage in additional fact-finding.[12]

6.3 **Australia** responded that the obligation is upon the complainant, the United States, to come forward with the facts on which its case is based. There is no obligation upon Australia to provide the information sought by the United States. The United States could at any time have used the procedures of the SCM Agreement to seek information about the measures in question. Specifically, Australia pointed out, Article 25.8 of the SCM Agreement is the means by which a Member can seek information about measures of another Member. The United States chose not to use this procedural provision under the relevant agreement and so cannot expect that the information will be provided at its request in the Panel process.

6.4 The **United States** indicated that it had requested information, including information concerning notification of the subsidies as provided in Article 25.8 of the SCM Agreement, during consultations. According to the United States, at that time, Australia did not provide any of the requested information.

6.5 In **Australia**'s view, the United States was misrepresenting the situation in implying that it was analogous to that before the Appellate Body in *India - Patents*.[13] While the statement of the Appellate Body may have wider application, it was made in respect of a particular situation where the analogy for this case would be that there had been a substantial change affecting the measures before the Panel. Of course, it is within the scope of a Panel's working proce-

[12] WT/DS50/AB/R, adopted 16 January 1998, para. 94.

[13] *Ibid.*

dures to seek additional information from parties. However, that is for the Panel to do in the light of whether the admissible evidence from the United States has made a case that warrants further investigation by the Panel. It is up to the complainant to make a case that there has been a breach of the rules.

6.6 Australia asserted that if the Panel were to rule against Australia's requests to terminate the Panel proceedings, then Australia wanted to cooperate with the Panel to enable it to reach its conclusions. Accordingly, if the Panel considered that the two contracts (i.e. the grant contract and the loan contract) were necessary for its deliberations, Australia was willing to provide the Panel with the two contracts, without the more sensitive commercial-in-confidence numbers that, in Australia's view, are not pertinent to issues under Article 3 of the SCM Agreement. However, Australia would look for assurances that the contracts would be treated as confidential information by both the Panel and the United States. There is only one medium-sized Australian company involved in this dispute and the mere fact of the United States' action has placed a great deal of commercial pressure and uncertainty on this company in the market place. This is a situation where a single company is involved and any information about its business is potentially valuable to its competitors. It is essential, therefore, that Howe's competitors do not gain further advantage from the disclosure of commercially sensitive information. Australia expressed its regret that statements by the United States to the Panel regarding Howe could only be understood as being driven by commercial considerations rather than legal argumentation for this Panel. It would be inappropriate for the government of Australia to provide further information on the contracts that would find its way quickly into the commercial domain.

6.7 Australia submitted redacted versions of the grant contract and the loan contract at the first substantive meeting of the Panel with the parties.

6.8 The **United States** expressed its appreciation for Australia's willingness to provide redacted copies of the grant contract and the loan contract and assured Australia that it would treat the information as confidential. At the first substantive meeting of the Panel with the parties, the United States urged the Panel to request that Australia provide the remaining information it had requested, in the belief that this information would better enable the Panel to make an objective assessment of the facts and their applicability under the SCM Agreement. The United States assured Australia that all information would be treated as confidential.

6.9 As noted below[14], on 10 December 1998, the Panel ruled as follows with respect to the United States request that the Panel ask Australia to produce certain documents:

---

[14] *Infra*, para. 9.9 and note 182.

> "... we note that Australia has already submitted redacted versions of the loan and grant contracts. In addition, among the questions from the Panel to the parties are certain requests for information and documents which we have concluded are relevant to our consideration of the issues in this dispute, and therefore have asked Australia to submit."

6.10 On 10 December 1998, as part of the written questions posed to the parties by the Panel after its first substantive meeting with the parties, the **Panel** asked Australia to provide the following to the Panel and the United States:

(a) "the report prepared by the accounting firm commissioned by the Australian government and used in devising the compensation arrangements to Howe;

(b) any correspondence between the Australian government and Howe (or corporate entities related to Howe) regarding the compensation arrangements to Howe and any documents relating to payments made under the grant contract which would indicate precisely what facts were taken into account in determining that Howe was in compliance with the performance criteria of the grant contract in order to make the grant payments to date, including the report for the year ending 30 June 1997 showing performance against the performance targets and the report for the year ending 30 June 1998 showing performance against the performance targets;

(c) in the schedule of the grant contract, the numbers relating to performance targets (these could be indicated in indexed form, or as a range), the headings for categories of capital expenditure and the numbers for capital expenditure (these could be indicated in indexed form, or as a range);

(d) any documents indicating the legal basis for the grant(s) and the loan in Australian law (for example, budget documentation); and

(e) any records or reports of discussions in the Australian Parliament relating to the grant(s) and the loan."

6.11 On 17 December 1998, **Australia** responded, with respect to the report by the accounting firm commissioned by the Australian government and used in devising the compensation arrangements to Howe that:

> "As part of the development of this compensation arrangements, the then Department of Industry Science and Tourism (DIST) engaged the firm of KPMG, Chartered Accountants, to assess the financial viability of Howe as a result of the removal of automotive leather from the ICS and EFS schemes. Under the terms of the engagement KPMG was required to examine certain information provided by Howe Leather and report to the Government of

Australia. The report was to be strictly confidential between the Government of Australia and KPMG. In fact, KPMG agreed to undertake the engagement on the pre-understanding that "our report is solely ... for the information of the Australian Government and *is not to be used for any other purpose or distributed to any other party*". (emphasis supplied by Australia)

The Government of Australia often engages firms to carry out such reviews as part of its industry policy development. It is critical that these reports be completely candid and this means that confidentiality must be absolute. It is only to be expected in this case that the Government would require an independent assessment of the viability of the company."

6.12 Australia submitted, as business confidential information, redacted versions of the letters from ALH to the Department of Industry, Science and Tourism in July 1997 and July 1998 reporting on Howe's actual performance against the interim performance targets for the periods 1 April-30 June 1997 and 1 July 1997-30 June 1998, as well as a non-business-confidential attachment explaining the domestic law on "best endeavours" as it applied in this case. With respect to the Panel's request for the numbers relating to performance targets, the headings for categories of capital expenditure and the numbers for capital expenditure, Australia stated: "Any financial data provided either in indexed form or as a range would be amenable to deductive manipulation which could unfairly breach the commercial confidentiality of any data so provided in good faith. Similarly, provision of any further details of the categories of capital investment undertaken by Howe could endow its competitors with an unfair commercial advantage. Accordingly, Australia regrets that it is unable to respond to this request by the panel." Australia asserted that the fundamental legal basis for the grant and loan is in the 1996/97 Portfolio Additional Estimates Statements for the Industry, Science and Tourism Portfolio of the Australian Government, in particular in the section entitled "Explanation of additional estimates 1996/97". Australia submitted a copy of this, as well as a digest of Appropriation Bill (No. 4) 1996/97 and extracts from the 1997-98 and 1998-99 Budget papers. Australia further stated that there had been no discussions in the Australian Parliament relating to the grant(s) and the loan.

6.13 On 12 January 1999, the **Panel** reiterated its request to Australia to provide:

(a) "the report prepared by the accounting firm commissioned by the Australian government and used in devising the compensation arrangements to Howe; and

(b) in the schedule of the grant contract, the numbers relating to performance targets (these could be indicated in indexed form, or as a range), the headings for categories of capital expenditure and the numbers for capital expenditure (these could be indicated in indexed form, or as a range)."

6.14 On 14 January 1999, **Australia** submitted to the Panel the numbers relating to the performance targets, the headings for categories of capital expenditure and the numbers for capital expenditure, as well as unredacted versions of the letters from ALH to the Department of Industry, Science and Tourism in July 1997 and July 1998 reporting on Howe's actual performance against the interim performance targets for the periods 1 April-30 June 1997 and 1 July 1997-30 June 1998.

B. Establishment of the Panel

6.15 Australia asks the Panel to make an immediate ruling that the Panel was established inconsistently with the DSU and, therefore, the Panel should terminate these Panel proceedings. According to Australia, the DSU does not provide for the Panel to be established in the circumstances that prevailed. In particular, Australia argues that: the United States did not have the right to have a second panel established at the DSB meeting on 22 June 1998; the DSB did not have the right under the DSU to establish such a panel against the wishes of Australia and this was inconsistent with the DSU; accordingly, the Panel was not properly established; and consequently, the Panel should terminate its work immediately.

6.16 Australia notes that the United States asked the DSB to establish a panel on 9 January 1998 (WT/DS106/2), and that Australia did not oppose the right of the United States to have the DSB establish a panel, and this was done on 22 January 1998. That panel has never been composed, but it was established. That panel of the same title is in respect of the same matter, i.e. the claims that the "grants and loan" to Howe: "appear to violate the obligations of the government of Australia under Article 3 of the SCM Agreement … may constitute subsidies 'contingent, ..., in fact, upon export performance' within the meaning of Article 3.1(a) and footnote 4 of the SCM Agreement." These are the same in the first and second substantial paragraphs of WT/DS106/1 and the second substantial paragraph of WT/DS126/1. The matter in both WT/DS106/1 and WT/DS126/1 consisted of the same specific measures ("grants and loan") and the same claims about those measures. Accordingly, each of the requests was about the same matter to be eventually referred to the DSB. The resulting requests for establishment of a panel, WT/DS106/2 and WT/DS126/2, were again about exactly the same matter.

6.17 Australia states that, in WT/DS126/2, the United States also asked that its earlier request for a panel in WT/DS106/2 be withdrawn.[15] At the DSB meeting on 22 June 1998, the United States representative said that it had terminated that

[15] WT/DS126/2, 11 June 1998, last sentence.

panel.[16] The request for the establishment of a panel in WT/DS106/2 was not outstanding. The panel had been established on 22 January 1998 and, while it had not been composed, was still in existence. Either party could have had that panel composed at any time. The United States did not state any provision of the DSU under which it was seeking to terminate that panel or have it terminated by the DSB. The DSB did not terminate that Panel.[17] The Chair at the meeting of the DSB of 22 June 1998 said that the arguments regarding the establishment of the Panel could be raised before the Panel itself.[18]

6.18 According to Australia, there is no provision under the DSU that allows one party unilaterally to terminate a panel once it has been established. The DSU allows the process to be terminated by mutual agreement by way of Article 12.7 of the DSU. Article 12.12 of the DSU allows the complaining party to ask a panel to suspend its work. The panel is not obliged to do so, but if it does, then after the expiry of 12 months (arguably 6 months for cases under the expedited procedures of Article 4 of the SCM Agreement) the authority for establishment of the panel would lapse.[19] The complainant cannot demand the suspension, but it can seek it.

6.19 Australia asserts that if the complainant had the right under the DSU to terminate a panel unilaterally, then it would be clear from the text of the DSU that it had that right. However, the text of the DSU does not give it such a right. Indeed, it does not even have the right to require the suspension of the Panel's proceedings. One obvious reason for this is that while the terms of reference for the complaint and the timing of the complaint are very much in the hands of the complainant, some balance is given to the proceedings once the panel has been established. If the complainant could unilaterally terminate or suspend, and hence terminate a panel after the designated period, then it could, for example, do this if it did not like the Interim Report. That would allow it to avoid an adverse judgement and, if it desired, start again with a new panel virtually immediately. This sort of game-playing is not envisaged under the DSU. A Member has the right to a panel but it must then live with what it has sought and obtained from the DSB.

6.20 Accordingly, Australia contends, any attempt by the United States unilaterally to terminate the panel established pursuant to WT/DS106/2 was inconsistent with the DSU. A number of Members raised questions about the process at the DSB on 22 June 1998. Nonetheless, a panel was purportedly established on the same matter despite the objections of Australia, without the United States or any other participant providing any legal reasoning for having the rights of a Member overridden in this way. By way of clarification, Australia points out that

---

16 WT/DSB/M/46, 6 August 1998, para. 1 on p. 8 and the last paragraph on p. 9.

17 *Ibid.*, para. 5 on p. 9.

18 *Ibid.*, para. 2 on p. 10.

19 DSU, Article 12.12.

it is not arguing that it might not be possible to have a second, or any number of, panels established on the same matter by mutual consent of the parties. However, the issue here is what right a complainant has under the DSU to have more than one panel established on the same matter where there is no consensus. There was no consensus at the meeting when this Panel was established.[20] The process of negative consensus under the DSU is a radical change in the way issues are handled under the WTO, when compared to the GATT, and only applies to the strictly limited situations set out explicitly in the DSU.

6.21 With respect to the issue of whether the DSB must, or indeed has the authority to, terminate a panel at the request of the complainant, Australia sees nothing in the DSU to allow the DSB to terminate a panel, whether by consensus or no. Certainly any action where negative consensus applied would have to be explicit in the DSU: there is nothing in the DSU that provides for this. It is difficult to read even an implied authority to terminate a Panel even where consensus exists. Indeed, where there is consensus, the parties can terminate the panel proceedings by way of Article 12.7 of the DSU at any time where all parties to the dispute wish to do so. All that is required is agreement, which is required for a consensus decision by the DSB in any case.

6.22 With respect to the issue of whether a Member has the right to have a second panel established (in particular through a negative consensus decision) on the same matter, while the other panel is still in existence, Australia asserts that the DSU does not confer any such right. All that the DSU gives is the right to have one panel established on a matter provided that the correct procedures are followed. There is nothing to say that a Member can have any number of panels established on the same matter, which it can use at any time that it wishes.

6.23 Australia observes that the DSU has explicit provisions covering multiple complaints by more than one Member (Article 9 of the DSU) and the right of a third party to take a case of its own (Article 10.3 of the DSU), but that it does not provide for multiple panels by the same Member on the same matter. This was implicitly recognized by the United States when it sought in WT/DS126/2 and at the DSB meeting on 22 June 1998 unilaterally to terminate the existing panel (established pursuant to WT/DS106/2). Australia questions why, the United States sought to terminate the first panel in WT/DS126/2 at the DSB meeting on 22 June 1998 if it considered that it had the right to a second panel while the first one existed. On the one hand, if the United States had simply decided that it did not wish to pursue the panel established on 22 January 1998 (WT/DS106) and it considered that it could unilaterally terminate that Panel, why did it not do so before seeking consultations under WT/DS126/1 on 4 May 1998? Indeed, the United States never sought even to get Australia's agreement to terminate that Panel.

[20] Australia refers also to WT/DSB/M/46, 6 August 1998, para. 2 on p. 10.

6.24 According to Australia, the object and purpose of the DSU, including relevant special or additional rules and procedures such as Article 4 of the SCM Agreement, are to provide for the settlement of disputes on a matter. The DSU provides for the right to the automatic establishment of a panel to examine the matter subject to the required procedures having been met. The object and purpose of the text are to provide for panel examination. Once that has been provided for, there is no basis for the establishment of further panels to examine precisely the same matter while the existing panel still exists. Under Article 8.7 of the DSU and Article 4.12 of the SCM Agreement, the United States could at any time from 2 February 1998 have asked the Director-General to determine the composition of the panel by 9 February 1998 or any later date. This was 84 days before the United States sought further consultations under WT/DS126/1 and 133 days before it asked the DSB to establish a new panel on 22 June 1998.

6.25 Australia contends that the United States itself chose not to pursue the composition of the panel established on 22 January 1998, and that the United States cannot now use the fact that the panel had not been composed as the basis for seeking a new Panel. To give a Member the automatic right to have any number of panels on precisely the same matter, including under the expedited procedures of Article 4 of the SCM Agreement, is nowhere provided for under the DSU and so the establishment of a panel in such circumstances is inconsistent with the DSU.

6.26 Australia questions, in the alternative, what the situation would have been if the United States' action in seeking to terminate the panel on 22 June 1998 were indeed consistent with the DSU. While Australia considers that this was not the case, even if it were true, the United States would still not have had the right to the immediate establishment of a new panel. The right to a panel depends critically upon the correct procedures having been followed. Given the continuing existence of the panel established on 22 January 1998 (WT/DS106), the United States did not have the right under the DSU to start the procedures leading to the automatic establishment of a new panel. It is clear from Article 5.3 of the DSU that the purpose of the consultations is to reach a mutually satisfactory solution. Article 4.3 of the SCM Agreement says that "[t]he purpose of the consultations shall be to clarify the facts of the situation and to arrive at a mutually agreed solution." Where such consultations are about precisely the same matter for which a panel exists, it would be absurd to have separate consultations to seek a mutually satisfactory solution. That would not be consistent with the object and purpose of the text. Articles 11 and 12 of the DSU make it clear that it is envisaged that the panel process provides for obtaining a mutually satisfactory solution. Given that, it would be incoherent for the DSU to provide at the same time for a Member to have a new round of consultations under Article 4 of the DSU or Article 4 of the SCM Agreement in order to seek such a solution. Accordingly, the right to the consultation process under Article 4 of the DSU and Article 4 of the SCM Agreement does not exist while a panel on the same matter exists. Therefore, the United States would have been unable to satisfy the requirements under the DSU and Article 4 of the SCM Agreement necessary to obtain the right to have a panel established.

6.27 The **United States** asserts that the Panel should confirm that it was properly established and that it can and will consider the merits of the case presented to it by the United States. The DSU contains no bar to a second consultation request concerning the same measures. The DSU also contains no bar to the establishment of a second panel concerning the same measures. The Panel may not invent a bar to these proceedings where the negotiators of the DSU provided none; as provided in Article 3.2 of the DSU, panel recommendations and rulings "cannot add to or diminish the rights and obligations provided in the covered agreements."

6.28 The United States maintains that the facts detailed in its complaint have shown the following. The United States made a first request for consultations on this matter which did not include a statement of available evidence as required by Article 4.2 of the SCM Agreement. This request was legally inadequate to satisfy the requirements of Article 4.2. After realizing that this was the case, the United States then took the only action available to it to cure this essential defect; that is, the United States submitted a second request for consultations which identified the nature and extent of the available evidence establishing that the subsidies in question were prohibited export subsidies. The second consultation request was submitted because there is no procedure for amending a prior consultation request. With this second request, the United States commenced pursuit of a new dispute settlement complaint.

6.29 According to the United States, the Appellate Body recently endorsed that a complainant may pursue a second dispute settlement complaint on the same matter in *Guatemala - Antidumping Investigation Regarding Portland Cement from Mexico*[21] ("*Guatemala - Cement*"). In that case, the United States asserts, the Appellate Body found that the panel erred in considering the dispute because Mexico had failed to identify a specific anti-dumping measure in its panel request. In reversing the panel, the Appellate Body noted that nothing in its findings precluded Mexico from pursuing another procedurally proper dispute settlement complaint on the same matter. The United States observes that the panel considering the complaint by the European Community in *India - Patents*[22] has also addressed the issue of multiple dispute proceedings. In that dispute, India argued that the EC complaint should be concluded because that complaint could have been brought at the same time as the prior complaint by the United States on the same matter. The United States maintains that India argued, as Australia does here, for compulsory joinder of all claims in the first panel proceeding initiated. That panel rejected India's claim, as this Panel should reject

[21] WT/DS60/AB/R, adopted 25 November 1998.

[22] WT/DS79/R, adopted 21 October 1998.

Australia's. That panel noted that the rights of Member include "the freedom to determine whether and when to pursue a complaint under the DSU."[23]

6.30 The United States contends that, based upon *Guatemala - Cement*[24], Australia cannot dispute that the United States could have pursued another dispute settlement complaint on this matter if a panel had been composed based upon the first request for consultations and had later found that the proceedings should be terminated because the consultation request was inadequate. The Appellate Body made clear in *Guatemala - Cement* that no matter what the procedural defect may be in a Member's complaint, that Member does not thereby lose the right to bring a complaint. The Panel should reject any argument that the United States should lose any right to challenge the subsidies provided by Australia. Australia's objection to the convening of this Panel therefore only amounts to an objection to the sequence in which the same events would take place. The sequence argued by Australia - a ruling by the first panel, rejection of the United States' complaint and a new complaint -involves a considerable waste of time and resources of the WTO and of the parties.

6.31 In the view of the United States, the course of action taken by it did not in any way prejudice Australia. Furthermore, contrary to Australia's suggestion, this course of action does not invite game-playing. The United States is not suggesting that a complainant may unilaterally terminate panel proceedings at any time. In fact, this Panel need not address that question. The only issue before this Panel is whether a complainant may, before the panel has been composed, withdraw the panel request and request consultations on the same matter in order to pursue a new dispute settlement complaint. The United States asserts that the answer must be "yes". To find otherwise would lead to the absurd result that a complainant wishing to amend its consultation request after the establishment of the panel but before its composition must nonetheless proceed through the entire panel process, only to have to start over. To find otherwise would also force Members and a panel to proceed with a dispute that they know in advance will be fruitless.

6.32 The United States notes that Australia has also argued that the United States should have been forced to move forward with panel composition, rather than take action to cure the defects in its earlier consultation request and move forward anew. The United States notes that the panel examining the complaint of the European Community in *India - Patents*[25] has counselled that the rights of parties include the freedom to move forward with panel composition at whatever pace the parties desire. There have been a number of instances in the GATT/WTO in which parties have reached mutually satisfactory solutions dur-

[23] WT/DS79/R, para. 7.15, adopted 21 October 1998.

[24] WT/DS60/AB/R, adopted 25 November 1998.

[25] WT/DS79/R, adopted 21 October 1998.

ing the panel composition process. One recent example is the dispute brought by eight WTO Members, including both the United States and Australia, against agricultural subsidies of Hungary, in which a mutually satisfactory solution was negotiated during the panel composition process. Had the parties been forced to compose the panel, or lose their right to pursue the dispute, it is possible that there would have been no settlement in that dispute.

6.33 The United States further notes the Australian argument that the right to consultations under Article 4 of the DSU does not exist while a panel on the same matter exists; that the right to establishment of a panel under Article 6.2 is dependent on the proper procedural steps having been completed; and that Australia's objection at the DSB meeting of 22 June 1998 therefore had the effect of blocking the establishment of this Panel. The United States rejects all of these propositions. Nothing in the DSU limits the right of a Member to request consultations at any time. Indeed, the provisions of Article 4.1 of the SCM Agreement provide that consultations may be requested "*whenever* a Member has reason to believe that a prohibited subsidy is being granted or maintained by another Member." (emphasis supplied by the United States) Australia's argument would place the Panel in the position of rewriting the DSU to insert new rights and obligations not provided by the drafters. Moreover, Australia's argument would open the door to procedural blockage in a wide range of disputes.

6.34 The United States appreciates the points that Australia makes concerning the supposed danger of harassment. However, this Panel is not an appropriate forum to address these issues. An alternative forum exists to address these systemic concerns - the ongoing review of the DSU now taking place in the DSB. This Panel has the duty to make an objective assessment of the facts, and is required to base its findings on the language of the DSU. It cannot make a ruling divorced from the explicit language of the DSU to address a systemic concern.[26]

6.35 **Australia** points out that it did not object to the immediate establishment of the panel on 22 January 1998. However, Australia considers that it has an obligation to pursue the issue of the status of this Panel partly because of the real systemic implications. If panels were allowed to be established in this way, it would set an unfortunate precedent for the future. Australia deems that it has a right to an immediate ruling on this issue. It goes to the heart of fairness about whether the Panel should proceed or terminate the proceedings.

6.36 Australia maintains that negative consensus is an important step forward by the GATT/WTO system in guaranteeing that a Member can have a matter subject to examination by a panel, and guaranteeing that the outcome of the Panel (subject to the Appellate Body Report) will be adopted. It has proved itself to be a key to a more rigorous method of dispute settlement. However, Australia is strongly of the view that its use is strictly limited to those issues set out

[26] In this regard, the United States refers to *ibid.*, para. 7.23.

in the DSU. This goes to the heart of the legitimacy of the new dispute settlement system. It is fundamentally unfair not only to the other Member concerned but also to the Chair of the DSB, who as the real decision-maker under negative consensus, can be placed in an invidious position.

6.37 Australia states that at the DSB meeting of 22 June 1998, the Chair of the DSB said that Australia could raise this with the Panel.[27] That is what Australia has done. It is clear from the Minutes of that meeting that the Chair left this issue to be resolved in at least the first instance by the Panel, rather than letting it run to the Appellate Body. Australia argues that the claims and measures were the same in both WT/DS106/1 and WT/DS126/1, i.e. the same for both panels. Indeed, the United States admits as much when it refers to "the earlier panel request regarding the same subsidies".

6.38 According to Australia, the purpose of Article 6 of the DSU is to ensure that a Member can have a panel established to examine a matter, subject to the requirements of Article 4 of the DSU, and, in this case, Article 4 of the SCM Agreement. There is nothing to suggest that this provides for the use of negative consensus for the establishment of multiple panels by the same complainant against the same respondent. Australia is not discussing here whether or not two panels might be able to be established by mutual consent. Rather, Australia is focusing on the situation where consensus does not exist. Australia is arguing that the use of negative consensus must be jealously guarded. It must only be used in the narrow circumstances where it is explicitly provided for under the DSU.

6.39 Australia contends that the United States never asked Australia whether it was willing to have the panel under WT/DS106 abandoned and to allow the United States to start again. Australia was never asked whether it would agree to a new panel. Australia's systemic concern is that Australia was overridden at the DSB meeting on 22 June 1998 by the use of negative consensus when, in its view, the United States was not entitled as a right to a second panel. Regardless of Australia’s view, a number of Members had concerns about the legal basis of the approach of the United States. If the United States considered that it had the right to a panel, why then did it not explain why it had that right at the meeting.

6.40 In Australia's view, the text needs to be read in the context of its object and purpose. Where a Member has a complaint about a matter, i.e. a claim about a measure, it has the right to ask for consultations on that matter with the view to resolving it. If those consultations are unsuccessful, that Member has the right to have a panel established by the DSB to examine that matter. This right can be exercised through negative consensus. It then has the right to have the matter examined by the panel and either Member has the right to have the panel’s report (possibly modified by the Appellate Body) adopted.

---

[27] WT/DSB/M/46, 6 August 1998, p. 10.

6.41 Australia asserts that when a Member has a panel established on a matter, it has decided that the consultation process had been unsuccessful. Australia queries why it would then be entitled to another round of consultations under Article 4 of the DSU on the same matter. Clearly, while a panel is in existence there is no basis for calling for consultations under Article 4 of the DSU. There is no impediment to discussions while a panel is in existence. Indeed, Article 12.7 of the DSU clearly envisages the prospect of a mutually satisfactory solution right up to the time of the submission of the final report of the panel. This is consistent with Article 3.7 of the DSU that a mutually acceptable solution is the preferred outcome of the process. The United States had no need to invoke Article 4 of the DSU again on 4 May 1998 in order to hold consultations with Australia. Australia considers that the United States did not have the right under Article 4 of the DSU to invoke consultations on a matter for which a panel was still in existence.[28]

6.42 Australia observes that the United States could have asked the Director-General to compose the panel established on 22 January 1998 at any time that it wanted to from 2 February 1998. On 4 May 1998 if it wished to have a panel composed, it could have had one by 8 May 1998. Even on the basis of a 120 day period, the panel would have been concluded by 7 September 1998. Australia notes that the United States claimed at the DSB meeting to have the right unilaterally to terminate the panel established on 22 January 1998. The United States said: "we confirm that the United States has decided to terminate any action in pursuance of the DSB's decision following our request to establish a panel."[29] According to Australia, this was at odds with WT/DS126/2, where it said in the final paragraph that: "[t]he United States also asks that, at the next meeting of the Dispute Settlement Body, our earlier request for a panel, dated 9 January 1998, circulated as WT/DS106/2, regarding the same subsidies identified in the present request, be withdrawn." There was no outstanding request for a panel. The panel had been established nearly 5 months before.

6.43 Australia submits that it is unclear whether the United States considered that it wanted the DSB to terminate the first panel or whether it considered that it could do it unilaterally. Perhaps it thought both were true. What is clear, Australia continues, is that the United States thought that it needed to terminate the panel. Otherwise, it would not have sought to do so. The Chair of the DSB considered that the United States could not terminate the Panel unilaterally, since the minutes of that meeting of the DSB say: "The Chairman said that technically as from now two panels existed on this matter."[30] Clearly in the context of establishing this Panel, the Chair agreed implicitly that at least the first panel could not be terminated through negative consensus. There is, of course, nothing in the

---

[28] WT/DS126/3, 19 June 1998.

[29] WT/DSB/M/46, 6 August 1998, p. 9.

[30] WT/DSB/M/46, 6 August 1998, p. 9.

DSU that suggests that negative consensus applies to termination of panels. Indeed, Australia questions, why should there be? Negative consensus was introduced to ensure that a complainant could have its day in court and that neither party could block the adoption of a panel report. Negative consensus is to be used on only the rarest of occasions. There would have been no reason to have negative consensus to terminate a panel. The DSU already provides explicitly for termination by agreement between the parties under Article 12.7. In addition, there is nothing in the DSU that says that a panel, once established, has some lower status in terms of the respondent's rights before it is composed. To the contrary, both parties have the same rights, for example, to ask the Director-General to compose the panel.

6.44 In relation to the statement by the United States that there is no bar in the DSU against a second panel, Australia points out that this does not address the issue whether the United States had the right to use negative consensus for the establishment of this Panel. Australia believes that the examples provided by the United States are not relevant to this case. This is a situation where the consultations were with the same Member but under a different dispute proceeding.

6.45 With respect to the references by the United States to *Guatemala - Cement*[31], Australia agrees that Mexico's right to another panel in that dispute was endorsed by the Appellate Body. However, Australia points out, there are key differences in this case. The first is that the measure and hence, the matter in *Guatemala - Cement* was different from what was before that panel and what might be before a second panel. The other key difference was to do with the timing of Mexico's right to start again. Australia does not disagree with the right of a Member to a second panel. The difference of opinion between the United States and Australia is over when the right arises. *Guatemala - Cement* is now a completed panel. The January 1998 panel on automotive leather is not.

6.46 Responding to the United States' position that the sequence argued by Australia - a ruling by the first panel, rejection of the United States' complaint, and the filing of a new complaint - involves a waste of time and resources, Australia submits that the issue is that a complaining party has an obligation to meet the requirements of the DSU and the SCM Agreement in order to avoid wasting time. Australia does not accept that any Member who has *not* met those obligations can start again *during* a proceeding. The DSU does not provide for this. The discipline is on complaining parties to get it right at the time of request. Regarding the reference by the United States to the complaints by the European Community and the United States in *India - Patents*[32], Australia submits that the issue in this case is fundamentally different. The panels dealing with India's

[31] WT/DS60/AB/R, adopted 25 November 1998.

[32] WT/DS50/R, WT/DS50/AB/R, adopted 16 January 1998; WT/DS79/R, adopted 21 October 1998.

measures were requested by *different* Members and not, as in this case, by the *same* Member.

C. "Disclosure" Obligations under Article 4 of the SCM Agreement

6.47 **Australia** asks the Panel to rule that, in its request for consultations (WT/DS126/1), the United States failed to meet its disclosure obligations under Article 4 of the SCM Agreement and therefore, the Panel should terminate the proceedings, or rule immediately that the United States has not demonstrated its claims. Australia views this as an important systemic issue, going beyond the circumstances of this particular case.

6.48 Australia notes that Article 4.2 of the SCM Agreement requires that: "A request for consultations under paragraph 1 shall include *a statement of available evidence* with regard to the existence and nature of the subsidy in question." (emphasis supplied by Australia) According to Australia, the reference to "evidence with regard to the existence and nature of the subsidy" in Article 4.2 includes not only facts but also argumentation why such facts would lead the complainant to consider that the measure in question was in breach of Article 3 of the SCM Agreement. Australia cites the United States' request for consultations (WT/DS126/1)[33] and asserts that the United States' request says little more than that the United States has evidence without saying what it is. It made no attempt to set out what facts it would use to support its case. The United States exhibits were only received by the Australian Mission in Geneva on 16 November 1998.

6.49 According to Australia, the description of evidence given in WT/DS126/1 does not meet any reasonable standard of disclosure as called for in Article 4 of the SCM Agreement, and accordingly, WT/DS126/1 does not satisfy the requirements of Article 4.2 of the SCM Agreement. In Australia's view, the expedited procedures provided for under Article 4 of the SCM Agreement mean that, in a dispute under this Article, the complainant is limited by the evidence that it puts forward in the request for consultations. This is clear from Article 4.2 of the SCM Agreement on consultation and underlined by the draft

33 Australia cites the following paragraph from WT/DS126/1:

> "This evidence consists of numerous statements and representations made by the GOA, Howe and Howe's affiliated and/or parent companies that have appeared in the media, official GOA publications and GOA communications with the United States Government. This evidence also consists of financial statements of Howe and its affiliated and/or parent companies; documents relating to the markets for automotive leather and automobiles in Australia; and other relevant information and materials concerning Howe, GOA export subsidy programs and the Australian market for automotive leather and automobiles, including statements of experts on automotive leather and automobiles, and statements of members of the automotive leather and automobiles industries."

Rules of Procedures for the PGE.[34] Rule 9 of those draft procedures calls for simultaneous submissions. Under the WTO dispute settlement system, the obligation is on the complainant to make its case, i.e. "the burden of proof rests upon the party, whether complaining or defending, who asserts the affirmative of a particular claim or defence".[35] Accordingly, under expedited procedures such as those provided for in Article 4 of the SCM Agreement, it is necessary that the complainant set out all its facts and arguments prior to the establishment of the panel. Thus, Australia argues, the United States is limited to using that evidence and those arguments explicitly set out in WT/DS126/1.

6.50 Australia also points out that the timing of some of the exhibits raises serious systemic questions. The complainant is required to provide a statement of available evidence at the time of the request for consultations. An important systemic issue is how much of that evidence can be developed after the request for consultations, or after the establishment, or even composition, of the Panel, under Article 4 of the SCM Agreement, but not provided to the respondent until the time of the first written submission to the Panel. Some of the United States exhibits are dated well after the request for consultations in WT/DS126/1. For example, some are dated after the request for the establishment of the Panel, while some are even dated after the composition of the Panel. Other exhibits are not even dated and some are essentially without provenance.

6.51 In the view of Australia, apart from the requirements of Article 4 of the SCM Agreement, any expedited procedures make the receipt of new material virtually impossible to consider in a timely manner. This problem can be compounded when new material is in non-electronic form. This emphasizes that any exhibits should have been provided at the time consultations were requested, whereas not even a list of these exhibits was provided by the United States before they were delivered in conjunction with its first written submission to the Panel.

6.52 Australia asserts that the United States' first submission had some 315 pages of non-electronic exhibits, and that the paucity of information in WT/DS126/1 and the appearance of alleged facts and arguments not covered in WT/DS126/1 raise a serious systemic issue. The object and purpose of expedited procedures are to deal with a measure that is causing such injury that it needs to have a quick resolution under the DSU. The aim of abbreviated procedures is not to place respondents in a disadvantageous position or to allow extended manoeuvring by the complainant. This places the obligation on any Member having recourse to Article 4 of the SCM Agreement to provide the respondent with the facts and arguments in advance, indeed at the time of re-

---

[34] G/SCM/W/365/Rev.1, 24 June 1996.

[35] Appellate Body Report, *United States - Measure Affecting Imports of Woven Wool Shirts and Blouses from India ("United States-Shirts and Blouses")*, WT/DS33/AB/R, adopted 23 May 1997, DSR 1997:I, 323, at 335.

questing consultations. To allow a complainant to come forward with facts and arguments at the time of its first submission is inconsistent with Article 4 of the SCM Agreement. While, in this particular case, the time frame was extended by mutual agreement to beyond 90 days, the dispute remains under Article 4 of the SCM Agreement and such an extension does not affect the rights and obligations of the parties. Indeed, if the argument were to be made that this is some special case because of the extension of the time frame, the point would remain that the United States originally asked for consultations on this matter on 10 November 1997 and the communication referred to in WT/DS126/1 was dated 4 May 1998. If this was a genuine case for different procedures, then presumably the United States had made its case before then and could have provided Australia with the information at that time. Moreover, subsequently it was the United States that determined the precise date for its first submission through calling for the Director-General to compose the Panel. Presumably, it did that only after it had finalized its first submission, though at least two of its exhibits are dated later than that. While it would not have met the requirements of Article 4 of the SCM Agreement, the United States could have, even at that time, provided Australia with at least the facts that it intended to put forward.

6.53 The **United States** contends that the Panel should reject Australia's request. The plain language of Article 4.2 does not require that the consultation request include "argumentation". Nor does the rule require that a list of exhibits be included. Article 4.2 simply states that a statement of available evidence with regard to the existence and nature of the subsidy shall be included.

6.54 The United States submits that, as is now well-established, the provisions of the WTO Agreement must be interpreted in accordance with Article 31 of *the Vienna Convention on the Law of Treaties*[36] (the "*Vienna Convention*"), paragraph 1 of which provides: "A treaty shall be interpreted in good faith in accordance with the ordinary meaning to be given to the terms of the treaty in their context and in the light of its object and purpose." The ordinary meaning of the term "evidence" is as follows: "The available facts, circumstances, etc. supporting or otherwise a belief, proposition, etc., or indicating whether or not a thing is true or valid."[37]

6.55 According to the United States, Australia has confused the requirements of the consultation request with the parameters for the first submission by a complaining party. The Working Procedures in Appendix 3 of the DSU provide in paragraph 4 that: "Before the first substantive meeting of the panel with the parties, the parties to the dispute shall transmit to the panel written submissions in which they present *the facts of the case and their arguments.*" (emphasis sup-

[36] Done at Vienna, 23 May 1969, 1155 U.N.T.S. 221; 8 *International Legal Materials* 679 (1969).

[37] *The Concise Oxford Dictionary*, 8th ed., Clarendon Press, p. 405.

plied by the United States) There is no requirement in the DSU or the SCM Agreement that the complainant provide a statement of the facts and argument prior to the first submission. To impose such a requirement would render the first submission by the complainant pointless.

6.56 The United States maintains that the Panel must not lose sight of the facts that the provisions of Article 4.2 of the SCM Agreement relate to a request for consultations, not a panel request and not a panel submission. A request for consultations necessarily takes place before the consultations are held, at a time when the complaining party cannot be expected to know everything about the measure in question. Indeed, Article 4.3 of the SCM Agreement provides that one purpose of consultations is to "clarify the facts". The United States recalls that the panel in *United States - Imposition of Anti-Dumping Duties on Imports of Fresh and Chilled Atlantic Salmon from Norway* noted, "whereas the greatest degree of precision could be expected in the definition of specific claims in a panel request, the complaining Party could not be expected to define its specific claims with the same degree of precision at the time of its request for consultations." [38] If the evidentiary requirements of Article 4.2 are construed to require a complaining Member to know all about a subsidy at the time of the consultation request, this extreme burden will preclude recourse to Article 3 except by those Members with the largest resources for collection of information. According to the United States, this result was never intended by the drafters.

6.57 The United States argues that, even with regard to a panel request, the Appellate Body has found that it is sufficient "to list the provisions of the specific agreements alleged to have been violated without setting out detailed arguments as to which specific aspects of the measures at issue relate to which specific provisions of those agreements."[39] The Appellate Body has further noted that "there is a significant difference between the *claims* identified in the request for the establishment of a panel, which establish the panel's terms of reference under Article 7 of the DSU, and the *arguments* supporting those claims, which are set out and progressively clarified in the first written submissions, the rebuttal submissions and the first and second panel meetings with the parties."[40] *A fortiori*, there can be no requirement to present legal "arguments" in a consultation request that starts the process of inquiry and dispute resolution under the dispute settlement provisions of the WTO Agreement.

[38] ADP/87, adopted 27 April 1994, para. 334.

[39] Appellate Body Report, *European Communities - Regime for the Importation, Sale and Distribution of Bananas ("European Communities - Bananas")*, WT/DS27/AB/R, adopted 25 September 1997, para. 141.

[40] Appellate Body Report, *European Communities - Regime for the Importation, Sale and Distribution of Bananas ("European Communities - Bananas")*, WT/DS27/AB/R, adopted 25 September 1997, para. 141.

6.58 The United States asserts that a review of its consultation request in WT/DS126/1 shows that it included a detailed statement of the available evidence which supports the United States claim that the subsidies in question contravene Article 3 of the SCM Agreement and which meets the requirements of Article 4.2 of the SCM Agreement. The request for consultations in WT/DS126/1 specifically provided:

> "The United States bases this request for consultations on evidence indicating that the A$25 million loan and grants of up to A$30 million are in fact tied to Howe's actual or anticipated exportation or export earnings. In particular, this evidence indicates that:
>
> - the grants and loan provide benefits to Howe, a company with a troubled financial history that has received GOA export subsidies in the past and that has relied on these subsidies to expand the exportation of its products;
> - the grants and loan were provided to compensate Howe for the GOA's decision to excise automotive leather from two *de jure* export subsidy programme - the Textiles, Clothing and Footwear Import Credit Scheme (TCF) and the Export Facilitation Scheme for Automotive Products (EFS);
> - the grants and loan have the same purpose and effect as the TCF and EFS programme - that is, to allow Howe to continue to expand the exportation of its products;
> - the vast majority of Howe Leather's sales are exports, and this fact was well understood by the GOA when it agreed to provide the grants and loan to Howe;
> - the Australian market is unable to absorb Howe's current production of automotive leather and thus cannot absorb a significant increase in that production - leaving exports as the only way Howe can utilize its increased production capacity and meet the aggressive production requirements upon which the grants and/or loan are conditioned; and
> - the grants and loan provided to Howe, Australia's only exporter of automotive leather, differ from other subsidies given by the GOA and may well be unique.
>
> This evidence consists of numerous statements and representations made by the GOA, Howe and Howe's affiliated and/or parent companies that have appeared in the media, official GOA publications and GOA communications with

> the United States Government. This evidence also consists of financial statements of Howe and its affiliated and/or parent companies; documents relating to the markets for automotive leather and automobiles in Australia; and other relevant information and materials concerning Howe, GOA export subsidy programs and the Australian market for automotive leather and automobiles, including statements of experts on automotive leather and automobiles, and statements of members of the automotive leather and automobiles industries."

6.59 Referring to Australia's implication that, given the expedited timetable of this dispute, Australia has been put in a disadvantageous position because it did not receive the specific exhibits relied upon by the United States until the time of the United States' first submission, the United States points out that, first, the evidence in this case was extensively described in the consultation request. This provided ample notice to Australia of the facts and evidence upon which the United States based its belief that the subsidies in question violated Article 3 of the SCM Agreement. Furthermore, the vast majority, if not all, of the documents submitted with the United States' first submission fall within the description of the evidence provided in the consultation request, and the principal facts relied upon in the first submission parallel the facts stated in the consultation request. Given the description of the evidence and the statement of the facts included in the consultation request, it seems disingenuous for Australia to claim that it has been somehow blind-sided or surprised by the facts and argument in the United States' first submission. Indeed, the United States asserts, Australia is more familiar than the United States with the nature and extent of the subsidies in question as well as the specific statements by its own government, the media in Australia and Howe regarding the purpose of the replacement subsidies, the Australian automotive leather industry and the financial condition of Howe in particular.

6.60 The United States points out that Australia would prefer if the United States had been required to present its first submission at the time of the panel request, and that Australia has proposed exactly such a change in the rules in the current review of the DSU. However, the DSU and the SCM Agreement now provide only the requirements in Article 4.2 of the SCM Agreement and Articles 4.2 and 6.2 of the DSU, which the United States asserts that it has satisfied in this instance.

6.61 **Australia** reiterates that, under Article 4.2 of the SCM Agreement, the complainant is required to provide a "statement of available evidence". This is one of the conditions it must meet if it wants a panel established under the expedited time frames of Article 4 of the SCM Agreement. Australia asserts that the United States provided as a "statement of available evidence" in WT/DS126/1 a list of unspecified documents. It did not even provide citations of the documents it was referring to, let alone provide copies of those documents. Australia asks what use was that listing to Australia in assessing the case brought by the United States?

6.62 Australia submits that, at the time the complainant makes its request under Article 4.1 of the SCM Agreement, the ball is at its feet. It has total control over the paper work and over much of the timing of the process. If it follows the rules, then it can have a very quick outcome. However, it must follow the rules. In Australia's view, there is something essentially unfair and biased where the complainant can have expedited proceedings without the disclosure required under Article 4.2 of the SCM Agreement. If this practice were to be allowed, then a respondent could find itself in the future even making its first submission to the PGE on the basis of a statement that the complainant has evidence without specifying in any detail what it is.

6.63 In response to the statement of the United States on "disclosure" and on the meaning of "statement of available evidence", Australia states that the issue here is that under expedited procedures of the SCM Agreement, the respondent has to know what the evidence is in order to prepare its case. This is different from usual DSU requirements. The *quid pro quo* of expedited proceedings is that the complainant must show its hand of the time of the request for consultations. The purpose of expedited proceedings is not to disadvantage the respondent, but rather to obtain a quick outcome. According to Australia, Article 4.2 of the SCM Agreement is supposed to be a guarantee that information necessary for a respondent to defend itself is provided.

D. *Admissibility of Evidence*

6.64 **Australia** asserts that, in the alternative, if the Panel does not agree to its requests for an immediate ruling that the Panel proceedings should be terminated or that the United States has failed to establish its claims, the systemic issue of what evidence a panel (or the PGE) should accept still has to be resolved. If a statement in the request for consultations that amounts to little more in substance than "we have evidence" is regarded as sufficient to meet the disclosure requirements of Article 4 of the SCM Agreement, then that provision would be nullified. This could lead to legalizing a cat and mouse game between the complainant and the respondent, which would significantly alter the balance of rights under the SCM Agreement and, indeed, affect in a substantial way the balance of rights under the DSU. In Australia’s view, the purpose of expedited proceedings is not to disadvantage the respondent. Thus, as a systemic requirement, complainants have to follow clear disclosure requirements.

6.65 In this context, Australia asks the Panel to rule that, as a result of the failure of the United States to fulfil its "disclosure" obligations under Article 4 of the SCM Agreement, evidence submitted by the United States that was not provided in WT/DS126/1 should not be admissible in the proceedings before the Panel. In the alternative, Australia asks that the Panel rule that at least those facts and arguments not explicitly set out in WT/DS126/1 but which would have been available to the United States at the time it requested the consultations will be disregarded for the purposes of the proceedings of this Panel. In support of this, Australia notes that Article 4.2 of the SCM Agreement says: "[a] request for consultations under paragraph 1 shall include a statement of available evidence with regard to the existence and nature of the subsidy in question."

6.66 In addition, Australia alleges that the United States has referred to answers provided in the context of the consultations called for in WT/DS106/1 and urges the Panel to rule that any facts derived by the United States from those consultations, including Exhibit 2, and arguments by the United States based on them, are confidential to that process and not admissible before this Panel. According to Australia, this raises a different systemic issue. This was part of the consultative process that led to the establishment of a panel by the DSB on 22 January 1998. That is not the same panel as the current process. Under Article 4.6 of the DSU, such consultations are confidential to that panel process and so any material provided in that context is required to be treated as being confidential to that panel process. As a systemic matter, such evidence should not be admitted before this Panel without Australia's agreement (and there was no consultation on this), since it was provided under a separate, confidential procedure. As a systemic issue, if Members cannot have confidence that the confidentiality provisions of the DSU will be respected, then these procedures will be undermined.

6.67 The **United States** asserts that it has satisfied the requirements of Article 4.2 of the SCM Agreement, and so the Panel need not consider Australia's arguments. If the Panel finds it necessary to consider these arguments, the United States submits that it would be inconsistent with the DSU and the SCM Agreement to limit the Panel to consideration of only those facts explicitly set forth in the consultation request. Article 11 of the DSU directs a panel to "make an objective assessment of the matter before it, including an objective assessment of the facts of the case and the applicability of and conformity with the relevant covered agreements". The Panel's task of "objective assessment" under Article 11 is fundamentally incompatible with excluding from its examination relevant facts in the dispute before it. Australia argues that a supposed violation of Article 4.2 should be punished, but such a punishment is irrelevant and exceeds the authority given to the Panel under the DSU. If the consultation request in WT/DS126/1 has not satisfied the requirements of Article 4.2 of the SCM Agreement, the remedy would be for the complaining party to be required to start its case again.

6.68 According to the United States, no provision in the DSU or in the SCM Agreement provides a legal basis for the Panel to exclude facts simply because they were "available" at the time of consultations, but not explicitly stated in the consultation request. Article 4.2 of the SCM Agreement does not state that "all" available evidence must be included in a consultation request, or even that "the" available evidence must be included, thereby implying that the statement should be exhaustive. It simply requires that the complainant include "a statement of available evidence". Moreover, Australia does not suggest how the Panel should determine whether the evidence was "available" at the time of consultations. Just because a document may have been in existence at the time of consultations or a fact may have been ascertainable at that time, does not mean that the evidence was necessarily "available" to the complainant at that time. It would unduly prejudice a complainant if it could not continue its investigation and development of the facts after the request for consultations.

6.69 The United States submits that the Panel should reject the arguments raised by Australia on the issue of use in panel proceedings of material obtained during the consultations in WT/DS106/1. Article 4.6 of the DSU provides: "Consultations shall be confidential, and without prejudice to the rights of Members in *any* further proceedings" (emphasis supplied by the United States), without making any distinction whether the proceedings are in the same case or in other cases. There is no basis for distinguishing between the treatment of facts from consultations in a dispute used in a later phase of the same dispute, and the treatment of facts from consultations in one dispute used in another dispute. Indeed, the reference to "further proceedings" would seem to lead to the conclusion that if a panel excludes any evidence, it must start with evidence from earlier stages of the *same* dispute. Yet panels can base their conclusions on material from consultations, and have done so on many occasions. According to the United States, Article 4.6 cannot be interpreted so as to bar this widespread practice and frustrate the fact-finding ability of panels. Article 4.3 of the SCM Agreement provides that one purpose of consultations is to "clarify the facts". Yet there is no point in clarifying the facts if a complaining party cannot present the clarified facts to a panel. The logical implication of Australia's argument is that a complaining party should be required to present erroneous facts to the panel, even if the truth has been clarified in consultations.

6.70 The United States maintains that, in *India - Patents*, the Appellate Body recognized the widespread use in panel proceedings of facts from consultations:

> All parties engaged in dispute settlement under the DSU must be fully forthcoming from the very beginning both as to the claims involved in a dispute and as to the facts relating to those claims. Claims must be stated clearly. Facts must be disclosed freely. This must be so in consultations as well as in the more formal setting of panel proceedings. In fact, the demands of due process that are implicit in the DSU make this especially necessary during consultations. For the claims that are made and the facts that are established during consultations do much to shape the substance and the scope of subsequent panel proceedings.[41]

---

[41] WT/DS50/AB/R, adopted 16 January 1998 para. 94.

6.71 The United States points out that panels have also used material from other proceedings as a basis for their conclusions, for example, in *Argentina - Measures Affecting Imports of Textiles, Apparel, Footwear and Other Items.*[42] As seen from the arguments at paragraphs 3.136-3.140, 3.153 and 3.164 and following in that panel report, the United States presented evidence based on a document given by Argentina to the European Community during consultations with the European Community in a related, but different, matter - consultations which the United States had attended under Article 4.11 of the DSU. As paragraphs 6.48-6.50 of that panel report show, that panel relied on that evidence and those arguments as a basis for its factual and legal findings, and ruled that "the fact that the data was prepared by Argentina for other purposes is not relevant."[43] The Appellate Body later found: "We cannot find any error of law in the findings of the Panel based on the evidence submitted by the United States on average calculations ..."[44] - that is, the evidence from consultations between Argentina and the European Community.

6.72 In the view of the United States, the real meaning and relevance of Article 4.6 can be seen in the panel report in *United States - Restrictions on Imports of Cotton and Man-made Fibre Underwear*[45] ("*United States - Underwear*"). In that dispute, Costa Rica used information on settlement offers made by the United States to advance certain arguments to the panel. The United States recalls that the panel found that:

> In our view, the wording of Article 4.6 of the DSU makes it clear that offers made in the context of consultations are, in case a mutually agreed solution is not reached, of no legal consequence to the later stages of dispute settlement, as far as the rights of the parties to the dispute are concerned. Consequently, we will not base our findings on such information.[46]

The United States argues that Article 4.6 of the DSU does not provide a basis for panels to mete out sanctions and exclude relevant factual evidence. It simply calls for panels to disregard offers of settlement, and not to treat such offers as admissions of guilt.

6.73 **Australia** repeats that, pursuant to Article 4.6 of the DSU, the consultations under WT/DS106/1 are supposed to be confidential and without prejudice to the rights of any Member in further proceedings. As a systemic issue, in Australia's view, the United States has no right to use this information in the context of this Panel without obtaining leave from Australia. Of course, if the Panel rules

---

42 WT/DS56/R, adopted 22 April 1998.

43 *Ibid.*, para. 6.51.

44 WT/DS56/AB/R, adopted 22 April 1998, para. 61.

45 WT/DS24/R, adopted 25 February 1997.

46 *Ibid.*, para 7.27.

in favour of Australia on any of its other requests for preliminary rulings, then this issue becomes redundant.

VII. MAIN ARGUMENTS OF THE PARTIES

A. *Measures*

7.1 According to **Australia**, a key issue for any panel is what are the matters before it, in terms of claims and measures. Australia asserts that the United States documentation (WT/DS126/1 and WT/DS126/2) recognizes that there is more than one measure before the Panel. WT/DS126/1 says in its second substantial paragraph that: "these *measures* appear to violate the obligations of the [government of Australia]". (emphasis supplied by Australia) Similarly, WT/DS126/2 says in its second substantial paragraph that: "these *measures* are inconsistent" (emphasis supplied by Australia). In addition, throughout both documents, the United States consistently refers to "subsidies". Accordingly, Australia maintains, there are a number of different measures that the Panel will need to examine. Moreover, the Panel will need to examine these measures separately in respect of their consistency with Article 3.1(a) of the SCM Agreement.

7.2 Australia points out that the United States refers throughout WT/DS126/1 repeatedly to "grants" and to "the grants and loan". The only measures specifically referred to in WT/DS126/1 are: "a A$25 million loan, which was made on preferential and non-commercial terms, and grants of up to another A$30 million".[47] The United States goes on in the next sentence to refer to "*these measures* appear to violate ..." (emphasis supplied by Australia). In the third substantial paragraph of WT/DS126/1, the United States says that it: "bases this request for consultations on evidence indicating that the A$25 million loan and grants of up to A$30 million ... ." In five of the six tirets to this paragraph, the United States refers to "the grants and loan". The fourth substantial paragraph of WT/DS126/1 refers to "[t]his evidence". Australia argues that, in light of Article 4.2 of the SCM Agreement, since "evidence" is only referred to about "loan and grants" and "the grants and loan", these are the only measures covered by the claims of the United States.

7.3 Australia maintains that the "loan" is clearly the loan provided under the loan contract, and this leaves to be determined what is meant by "the grants". According to Australia, the United States has not proposed that the grant contract is a measure under the dispute. Instead, it asked for consultations about the actual payments, "the grants". There have been three payments made to date. Two were made in 1997 and one was made in July 1998, i.e. after not just the request for consultations but also after the establishment of the Panel. Australia

[47] WT/DS126/1, first sentence of the second paragraph.

contends that the term "grants" can only mean actual payments, since they have been distinguished from the actual grant contract, and that since the United States has referred to these payments severally, each of the grants before the Panel is a separate measure. This leaves the question of which payments under the grant contract are before the Panel.

7.4 Australia asserts that the second substantial paragraph of WT/DS126/1 says: "the [government of Australia] has provided subsidies to Howe that include ... grants of up to another A$30 million." The second tiret of the third substantial paragraph of WT/DS126/1 refers to "the grants and loan were provided". Similarly, the first substantial paragraph of WT/DS126/2 says: "the Government of Australia has provided subsidies ... [that] ... include grants ...." These references can only be to payments that had been made already. The only payments under the grant contract that had been made by the time of these documents, and indeed the date of the establishment of the Panel, were the first two payments in 1997 (of A$5 million and A$12.5 million). Accordingly, the only grants referred to by the United States as measures in its request for consultations, and for the establishment of a Panel, were these first two payments. Thus, these, together with the loan, are the only measures covered by the Panel's terms of reference.

7.5 Australia states that the United States' claims are that each of the individual payments covered by the terms of reference of the Panel falls under Article 3.1(a) of the SCM Agreement. The United States' claims deal with each of the payments under the grant contract that are before the Panel as one of the separate measures at issue. No other explanation is consistent with the text and the normal meaning of the terms "grant" and "grants". Australia asserts that, in the alternative, even if the Panel decided to consider payments made subsequent to WT/DS126/1, or even to the establishment of the Panel, it should consider each payment as a separate measure.

7.6 Again in the alternative, regardless of the view the Panel takes of the issue of what aspects of the grant contract are before it, Australia argues that the United States has correctly recognized that the loan is a quite separate measure from the grant contract or payments under the grant contract. The documentation consistently talks of "measures" rather than "measure" and the only consistent interpretation of that is that the Panel is to examine each of the measures separately. The Australian government entered into two separate, independent contracts with the company, the loan contract and the grant contract. These are legally different, unrelated instruments. The United States has not made any allegation to the contrary. Australia contends that the Panel will need to assess the status under Article 3.1(a) of the SCM Agreement of each of the measures before it (i.e. the loan and the first two payments under the grant contract) on its own merits (or if the Panel takes the view that the grant contract is a measure before it, then the loan contract and grant contract as separate measures). For the sake of argument, even if the Panel finds that one of the measures was not consistent, it could find that the others were consistent with Article 3.1(a) of the SCM Agreement.

7.7 According to Australia, the United States recognized that the grant contract was provided only to cover the period through to 2000. Indeed, it is a major theme to the United States' argument that the grant contract was a "replacement" for automotive leather being excised from the ICS and the EFS. The loan, on the other hand, was provided for 15 years regardless of the duration of the previous or any future domestic support arrangements that might be subsequently introduced covering automotive leather.

7.8 Australia submits that the terms of the loan contract and grant contract are different. The United States recognizes in its first submission in particular that there is no conditionality placed upon the loan other than the natural due diligence ones to ensure that the government gets its money back. Moreover, Australia points out, the two contracts are independent. Even if the company had received only the first payment under the grant contract, the loan would have continued. Thus, regardless of what happens to production, the loan will continue, so long as the company meets the interest and repayment conditions.

7.9 According to Australia, Articles 3.1(a) and 4 of the SCM Agreement are clear that Article 3.1(a) of the SCM Agreement is about individual subsidies, not about an aggregation of subsidies. When examining whether a subsidy falls under Article 3.1(a) of the SCM Agreement, it is necessary to look at each subsidy separately, measure by measure. There is no issue of aggregation such as can arise under Article 6.1(a) of the SCM Agreement. Australia points out that:

(a) the chapeau of Article 3.1 of the SCM Agreement refers to: "the following subsidies";

(b) footnote 4 of the SCM Agreement refers to "the granting of a subsidy" and "[t]he mere fact that a subsidy is granted";

(c) footnote 5 of the SCM Agreement refers to: "[m]easures referred to"; and

(d) Article 4 of the SCM Agreement continually refers to individual subsidy programmes, e.g.: "a prohibited subsidy" in paragraphs 1, 5 and 7; "the subsidy" in paragraphs 2, 3, and 7; and "the measure in question" in paragraph 5.

7.10 Accordingly, Australia argues, the Panel needs to consider the status of each measure quite separately under Article 3.1(a) and footnote 4 of the SCM Agreement. The fact that an enterprise receives more than one subsidy does not mean that the status of one measure under Article 3.1(a) of the SCM Agreement has any implication for other measures. Again, there are other provisions under the SCM Agreement where a Member can seek remedy if it considers that there is adverse effect from the aggregation of a number of subsidies, i.e. under Parts III and V of the SCM Agreement. However, this case is limited to Article 3.1(a) of Part II of the SCM Agreement. There is nothing in the text that suggests, and the United States has made no argument, that the existence of a measure in breach of a WTO obligation automatically determines the status under the WTO of any other measure benefiting the same enterprise. In particular, regardless of what finding the Panel makes about payments under the grant contract (or the grant contract itself), the United States has made no allegation that the loan is in any way contingent upon performance, let alone export performance.

7.11 The **United States** submits that, in its request for the establishment of the Panel (WT/DS126/2), the United States identified the specific measures at issue in this case: "a A$25 million preferential loan and grants of up to A$30 million." There are two contracts between the Australian government and Howe: a loan contract and a grant contract. The term "grants" includes any and all possible disbursements under the latter contract. That is why the measure is phrased in terms of "grants up to A$30 million." According to the United States, the measures that have been targeted in this case are therefore explicitly described in the panel request and Australia cannot claim that it did not have adequate notice in this case of the claims.

7.12 The United States argues that, contrary to Australia's assumption, the term "grants" does not serve to distinguish between actual payments and the grant contract. Rather, the term "grants" includes all possible disbursements, whether past or future, and otherwise serves to distinguish whether the funds were bestowed upon Howe pursuant to the loan contract or the grant contract. Nowhere in the request for consultations or the panel request is the term "grants" limited to actual payments. In the view of the United States, it is nonsensical to assume that the United States would pursue a dispute settlement complaint on only past payments made under a single contract and ignore any future payments that could be made under the same contract.

7.13 The United States contends that the Panel should reject Australia's argument that the only measures before the Panel are the A$25 million preferential loan and two payments made pursuant to the grant contract. In the view of the United States, Australia's arguments are not supported by any reasonable interpretation of the panel request. The measures at issue include the loan contract and the grant contract. Under Article 7.1 of the DSU, the terms of reference of this Panel are to examine "the matter refered to the DSB in WT/DS126/2." Pursuant to Article 6.2 of the DSU, in the request for the establishment of a panel in this case (WT/DS126/2), the United States identified the "specific measures at issue" as follows: "these subsidies include the provision by the Government of Australia to Howe of grants worth as much as A$30 million and a A$25 million loan on preferential and non-commercial terms." The United States underlines that the request states that the measures include (1) *the provision* by the government of grants worth as much as A$30 million; and (2) *a* loan. The ordinary meaning of the term "provision" is "the act or the instance of providing." [48] The act or instance of providing the grants in this case was the single grant contract. Thus, the measures at issue in this case, as explicitly described in the panel request, include the loan contract and the grant contract. The United States emphasizes that the grant contract includes the government's commitments to make payments and captures any and all possible disbursements under that contract.

7.14 Regarding the grant contract, **Australia** asserts that it has a right under the DSU to be informed by the complainant about the precise measure on which it is being challenged and the legal reason for it being considered to be a subsidy. Australia maintains that it would appear from the questioning to the United States by the Panel, that the Panel also is not clear about the issue. It is inappropriate that the United States should only be making the issue unequivocal at a late stage of the Panel proceedings.

7.15 According to Australia, this issue is relatively unimportant under Parts III and V of the SCM Agreement, since the issue there is one of whether there is subsidization or not, and if so, how to calculate it. Under Part II of the SCM Agreement, the issue can be more fundamental to the process. In this case, Australia states, the complainant is required to prove that the granting of the particular subsidy in question is in fact contingent upon export performance. The elements of proof can be different depending on the measure that is at issue. For example, the facts and argument required to demonstrate such proof regarding the grant contract would be different from the facts and argument regarding the first A$5 million payment.

7.16 With respect to the United States' assertion that "it is nonsensical to assume that the United States would pursue a dispute settlement complaint on only past payments", Australia states that this is not the issue. The issue is, rather, what were the measure or measures that the United States actually identified in its documentation. In this regard, Australia asserts that it is worth noting that the claims and measures are the same for the panels in both WT/DS106 and WT/DS126. However, the United States admitted that the request for consultations in WT/DS106/1 was inadequate in respect of Article 4.2 of the SCM Agreement. According to Australia, since that error in the United States' view was sufficient for it to force through the current Panel process, it would not be unreasonable to assume that there could well be other flaws in the documentation, (i.e. apart from the issue of disclosure under Article 4.2 of the SCM Agreement), including at least that the United States may not have requested what it wanted.

7.17 Australia disagrees with the reference by the United States to the request for the establishment of the Panel in WT/DS126/2. While the request for a panel may limit the scope of the Panel, it is not correct to argue that the request for the

[48] *The Concise Oxford Dictionary*, Clarendon Press, 8th ed., p. 962.

establishment of a panel can widen the scope. The original request for consultations (in this case WT/DS126/1) limits the scope. A panel cannot be established with a scope wider than that envisaged under the original request for consultations. In any case, in asking for "the establishment of a panel to examine the matter", paragraph 4 of WT/DS126/2 is referring to the matter covered by the consultations requested in WT/DS126/1 as set out in paragraph 3 of WT/DS126/2. Australia states that the act or instance of providing the grants is the provision of the tranches under the grant contract.

7.18 The **United States** argues, in the alternative, that if the Panel finds that one of the measures, i.e., the grant contract or the third payment thereunder, is not *explicitly* described in the panel request, the question becomes whether that measure is subsidiary, or so closely related, to a measure that is specifically identified, that the responding party can reasonably be found to have received adequate notice of the scope of the claims asserted by the complaining party. The United States refers to the following statement of the panel in *Japan - Measures Affecting Consumer Photographic Film and Paper* ("*Japan - Film*"):

> To fall within the terms of Article 6.2, it seems clear that a 'measure' not explicitly described in a panel request must have a clear relationship to a 'measure' that is specifically described therein, so that it can be said to be "included" in the specified 'measure.'[49]

7.19 According to the United States, in the instant case, there can be no question that the grant contract itself and all payments made pursuant to the grant contract are subsidiary or so closely related to the measure described in the panel request that Australia received adequate notice that the United States was challenging the grant contract, including any and all possible payments under that contract. It is self-evident that the grant contract and the payments actually disbursed pursuant to the contract, whether past or future at the time of the panel request, are subsidiary or closely related to the measure described as "the provision by the Government of Australia to Howe of grants worth as much as A$30 million." Thus, even if the Panel does not agree that the panel request *explicitly* describes the measures as the loan contract and the grant contract, it is clear that the measures as described can be said to have "included" the grant contract itself and all payments made thereunder.

7.20 The United States asserts that Australia devotes considerable time to arguing that the measures described in the *consultation* request limit the United States to challenging only the first two payments under the grant contract. Putting aside the fact that the language of the consultation request cannot be reasonably construed to impose such a limitation, it is the *panel request*, not the consultation request, that is relevant for determining the scope of the measures

[49] WT/DS44/R, adopted 31 March 1998, para 10.8.

before this Panel.[50] The panel request specifically identifies the measures at issue in this case to include the loan contract and the grant contract.

7.21 **Australia** disagrees with the interpretation made by the United States of paragraphs 10.8 and 10.9 of *Japan - Film*.[51] The issue in this current dispute is not about the inclusion of a subsidiary measure. Under the DSU, a claim must be specified, the specific measures at issue must be identified, and there must be a brief summary of the legal basis of the complaint sufficient to present the problem clearly. This has not been done for this dispute. Ultimately, it is up to the Panel to decide whether the United States' request in WT/DS126/1 was sufficient to provide the basis for a "curing" of its claims in subsequent submissions.

7.22 The **United States** submits that, in any event, contrary to Australia's assumption, the term "grants" as used in the consultation request does not serve to distinguish between actual payments and the grant contract. Indeed, the *Concise Oxford Dictionary* notes that the term "grant" means the "process of granting or the thing granted."[52] Thus, the only reasonable interpretation is that the term "grants" includes both the government's commitment to make payments and the payments themselves, including all possible disbursements, whether past or future. Nowhere in the consultation request, or the panel request for that matter, is the term "grants" limited to past payments.

7.23 In **Australia's** view, the "definition" given by the United States of "grant", i.e. "the process of granting or the thing granted", contains alternative meanings. In WT/DS126/1 the United States talks of "grants of up to A$30 million" (and in WT/DS126/2 of "grants worth as much as A$30 million"). The plural of "the process of granting" is "the processes of granting". Thus, on the basis of the first meaning the United States is apparently talking about "the processes of granting [of] up to A$30 million". Each of these *processes* must be in relation to an actual payment, since otherwise why not say "grant of up to A$30 million" if that is the meaning attributed by the United States to "grant"? This would suggest that the Panel should look at each of the payments separately. The same conclusion arises from using the second meaning "the thing granted". "Grants" then becomes "the things granted". Accordingly, "grants of up to A$30 million" becomes "the things granted of up to A$30 million."

7.24 Australia underlines that the identification of what the complainant considers to be the subsidy is critical to the argument of whether the granting of that subsidy meets the "in fact" standard of Footnote 4 of the SCM Agreement. This goes to the heart of what the measures are before the Panel and the alleged "existence and nature of the subsidy in question". Under Article 4.2 of the SCM

[50] WT/DS44/R, adopted 31 March 1998, para 10..9.
[51] WT/DS44/R, adopted 31 March 1998.
[52] *The Concise Oxford Dictionary*, Clarendon Press, 8th ed.

Agreement, these were supposed to be identified in the complainant's request for consultations.

7.25 In respect of the grant contract, Australia asserts that it remains unclear whether it is the grant contract that is the subsidy at issue or the individual payments under the grant contracts that are the subsidies at issue. This is central to what the United States must prove.

7.26 According to Australia, if it is the grant contract, then the issue is whether the granting of the grant contract was in fact tied to actual or anticipated exportation or export earnings. Of course, the two cases do overlap, since the way in which the actual grants are made go to the demonstration of the nature of the grant contract itself. The bases for the actual payments under the grant contract have necessarily to be looked at to see what was in fact agreed between the Australian government and the company. The record confirms conclusively that the payments were not tied to actual or anticipated exportation or export earnings. This, in turn, proves that the granting of the grant contract was not in fact tied to actual or anticipated exportation or export earnings. Australia reasons that, if, on the other hand, it is the individual grants under the grant contract, the granting of each of them must be considered separately. Trivially, the first tranche was only tied to the execution of the grant contract and to nothing else. Given the bases for the second and third tranches, there were clearly no ties to export performance.

B. Nature of the Evidence Presented

7.27 **Australia** has serious systemic concerns about the nature of those United States exhibits where the United States has chosen to use inter-governmental communications, without consultation with Australia. However, Australia recognizes that this is not an issue for the Panel except where the provenance has not been provided by the United States and the presentation may even be misleading.[53] On the other hand, it is important that the Panel address the issue of what cognizance it should give to media reports and other comments by private parties, including the company, in assessing governmental actions and decisions. Australia submits that the Panel should place little or no weight upon such exhibits, or at least take great care about assessing their probative value.

7.28 As an example of the risks of making misrepresentations of factual material, Australia points to a specific paragraph in the United States' submissions to the Panel.[54] In Australia's view, these numbers do not bear on the matter before

---

[53] Australia refers to a specific United States exhibit. See its arguments *infra.*, para. 7.196.

[54] This paragraph states:

> "These subsidies have led Howe to dramatically change its sales patterns. In the late 1980s, exports accounted for less than 10% of its total sales; by 1997, exports comprised 90 percent of Howe's sales. In addition, and as described in more detail below, the Australian

the Panel. However, the United States has chosen to compare unlike situations here. Until Howe was bought by ALH in 1994, it also produced furniture leather. A reorganization within the group of companies resulted in Howe dealing only with the group's automotive leather business. Before the reorganization, Howe used to export more than three-quarters of its automotive leather production. Given the growth in the global market for automotive leather both in Australia and in many other larger markets, it is not surprising that Howe's production has increased and that its sales to overseas markets have also increased. Australia states that business confidential information it provided to the Panel regarding Howe's sales figures over the period 1995/96 to 1997/98 showed that exports of automotive leather represented a significantly lower share of Howe's total sales in this period than suggested by media and other reports cited by the United States.

7.29 The **United States** asserts that it is worth noting that although Australia questions the probative value of media articles, it has not specifically disputed any of the information the United States has obtained from those articles.

7.30 The United States argues that Australia fails to counter any of the United States' factual evidence (such as Howe's current or anticipated exports or the small size of the Australian automotive leather market) with facts that would undermine their credibility. In fact, Australia does not even deny their truthfulness. Instead, Australia questions the probative value of relying upon newspaper and other media articles. However, it is entirely appropriate to rely on media articles in the absence of other inconsistent information. In fact, the evidence before the panel in *Indonesia - Certain Measures Affecting the Automobile Industry*[55] included information from newspaper articles. Although Australia argues that the statements by Australian government officials which appear in the press should be considered in their proper domestic political context, Australia does not offer any evidence rebutting the statements quoted from the media releases and articles.

7.31 The United States asserts that the Panel should note the variety and volume of sources relied upon by the United States in this case. The United States has not just cited one isolated newspaper article; it has offered a range of articles from well-respected newspapers to industry magazines. They all have the same theme: Australia provided replacement subsidies to Howe to support its export drive. Furthermore, the information obtained from the media articles was consistent with other sources presented, including press releases from the Australian government.

---

government's current replacement package for Howe is designed to subsidize the modernization and expansion of Howe's production capacity, so that it can more effectively compete in international markets and continue its rapid export-led growth."

[55] WT/DS54/R, WT/DS55/R, WT/DS59/R, WT/DS64/R, adopted 23 July 1998, para. 4.107.

7.32 **Australia** does not accept this characterization of its position by the United States. The fact that Australia has not commented on each of the media articles and other such exhibits does not mean that it accepts the conclusions that the United States has drawn from them. In particular, Australia does not accept that these media reports, with selective quotes and journalistic commentary, represent any sort of evidence of the rationale for Australian government decisions on trade and industry policy issues.

7.33 Australia assumes that the media reports are accurate citations.[56] But all that they represent are interpretations by the media. In Australia, as in most, if not all, countries, being internationally competitive and a successful exporter is seen as being admirable. Comments attributed to ministers and officials need to be taken in their proper domestic political context, where terms are not being used with the same meaning and precision as in the context of the WTO. It is commonplace for comments to focus on success in selling in foreign markets. However, that is not the same as saying that industry arrangements favour exports, or that in this case the comments represent evidence that the recognized purpose of the measures in question were to favour exports, or are in any way "in fact tied" to export performance.

7.34 Australia states that where quotations are cited they are necessarily selective (as are often the United States excerpts) and were, no doubt, given in quite different contexts. The ubiquitous "former senior official" is often quoted in the media without any level of authority (or current knowledge). It would hardly be a productive exercise, and of no value to the Panel, for Australia to try to track down the journalists and people interviewed and try to obtain from them what they had in mind at the time and what they thought their comments would mean in terms of footnote 4 of the SCM Agreement. Many of those interviewed presumably would be protected by journalistic confidence. If such exhibits are to be considered at all, they would need to be treated with great caution, since by their very nature they do not represent the views of government and are hardly in the realm of facts. The Panel's obligation under Article 11 of the DSU is to "make an objective assessment of the matter before it, including an objective assessment of the facts...." In Australia's view, relying on, and drawing factual conclusions from, such sources in any way would not be consistent with this obligation.

7.35 Against this background, Australia raises specific comment on some of the United States exhibits. For example, the United States purports to quote the Australian Deputy Prime Minister, Tim Fischer, as saying: "by dint of effort, we [the Australian government] have ensured that Howe Leather has been able to continue its export activity over the last 18 months." This quote is from a news-

[56] Although Australia also refers to its arguments *infra*, para. 7.196.

paper article of 29 September 1997 included in the United States exhibits.[57] There are a couple points that are worth making. First, the references to "export activity" and "the last 18 months" are for the period from the launching of the section 301 case in the United States and refer to preserving the right of Howe to sell to its United States customers, where clearly the petitioners did not want the original equipment manufacturers (OEM) market for automotive leather to be contested by non-US firms. This was about maintaining market access to the world's largest market for automotive leather in the face of the dispute with the United States, not about export subsidization. Secondly, the purported quotation goes on to say that this was done "while honouring all of our WTO commitments." The quote in the article also said that the new arrangements "fully complied with all the elements of the agreement reached with the US last year." If the United States chooses to introduce selective quotations as somehow representing "evidence" of the "recognized purpose" of the Australian government, it should choose such quotations more carefully, as read in full they leave no doubt that the government had no intent of introducing prohibited export subsidy arrangements.

7.36 The United States points out that the 18-month period referred to by Trade Minister Fischer included the six month period from April to September 1997. This was after the replacement package became operative.

7.37 Similarly, **Australia** continues, there is the media release by the Australian Minister for Industry, Science and Tourism, John Moore, of 27 December 1996[58] where Mr. Moore says that: "The package safeguards the jobs of around 500 employees and will ensure that Howe and Co. can continue to invest and grow as planned." This again underlines that the government's focus was not on some sort of circumvention arrangement in respect of export subsidies, but the much more immediate domestic task of maintaining jobs in disadvantaged regional areas, through WTO-consistent means.

7.38 In the same vein, Australia continues, Howe and its parent company did not make public comments in the context of the WTO Agreement. Presumably, when they commented in annual reports, they simply sought to inform their shareholders about their current commercial prospects, as they are required to do by domestic law. However, again this has no bearing on issues concerning footnote 4 of the SCM Agreement, and the legal issues involved in this case. The views of companies on trade policy or related legal issues that they would often find arcane are not relevant to the consistency, or otherwise, of government measures.

---

[57] "Fischer vows to fight US trade challenge", *The Australian*, September 29, 1997, United States Exhibit 45.

[58] Commonwealth Government safeguards Howe jobs", Media Release, December 27, 1996, United States Exhibit 2.

7.39 As one final example, Australia considers the quote that 'Howe's then Managing Director stated that he had been "assured" that Howe "would be compensated with an alternative arrangement that would help it continue to expand exports"'.[59] This needs to be put in context. This is a company that had been affected by a section 301 case in one of its major markets. The Managing Director was hardly going to send the wrong signal to potential customers. In the reality of the market-place, he had to confirm that the company was in business for the long haul in the United States market. The article implies that he did not know the details of the arrangements between Australia and the United States and clearly he did not know what the new arrangements would be. Indeed, how could he since they had not been designed, much less finalized, at that time. The sense of the article is that the Managing Director also recognized the need for any such assistance to be "within the WTO rules".[60] These are not the comments of someone being told that a covert scheme would be crafted. But rather it is a story about a firm that the government has said it would not abandon as a result of cutting automotive leather out of two entitlement schemes. That would be the plain reading interpretation of that article. As Australia has already stated, press articles are not government policy documents and are not always accurate in terms of facts, representation of individuals' statements and the spin given to a story by the author. Nevertheless, Australia asserts, the full context of the quotes clearly illustrates that WTO-consistency was an essential parameter for any new assistance arrangements for the company.

C. *Article 1 of the SCM Agreement*

1. *"Financial Contribution"*

7.40 The **United States** notes that, before addressing whether the measures in question constitute subsidies "contingent ... in fact upon export performance" within the meaning of Article 3.1(a) of the SCM Agreement, the Panel must first consider whether the measures fall within the definition of "subsidy" under Article 1 of the SCM Agreement.

7.41 The United States alleges that the assistance bestowed on Howe by the Australian government constitutes subsidies under Article 1 of the SCM Agreement. The Australian government directly transferred two significant sums of money to Howe, one in the form of a grant and the other in the form of a preferential loan. The United States observes that Article 1.1(a)(1)(i) of the SCM Agreement expressly states that both "grants" and "loans" qualify as "financial

---

[59] "Melbourne firm could lose in U.S. subsidies deal", *The Age*, November 25, 1996, p. 1, United States Exhibit 15.

[60] *Ibid.* Australia cites the following phrase: "He said that he did not know what else the US companies would have to complain about if an alternative arrangement was found that was within WTO rules."

contributions" by a government. Accordingly, the United States contends, the Australian government cannot dispute that the A$30 million grant and the A$25 million preferential loan provided to Howe constitute financial contributions within the meaning of the SCM Agreement. "

7.42 **Australia** submits that the loan is a subsidy under Part I of the SCM Agreement, without prejudice to issues such as calculation and its status under other parts of the SCM Agreement. Australia also states that the payments under the grant contract are subsidies within the meaning of the SCM Agreement. However, Australia submits that the United States has not demonstrated that the grant contract is a subsidy, even though, on at least due process grounds, it should have been required to do so in its first written submission to the Panel. Australia underlines that it agrees with the United States that the '"grants" ... qualify as "financial contributions" by a government'. However, the United States then jumps to "the grant" conferring a benefit, which could be a reference to the grant contract, or could possibly be a reference to each of the individual grants referred to in the previous paragraph. Even assuming for the sake of argument that the reference is to the grant contract, the United States did not demonstrate the nature of the "financial contribution", as required for defining a subsidy.

7.43 The **United States** notes Australia's assertion that the United States has not demonstrated that the grant contract itself is a subsidy. This is a dubious distinction. The grant contract is not a separate measure from the payments made pursuant to the contract. The grant measure at issue in this case is the Australian government's commitment to make grant payments to Howe, which subsumes the disbursements themselves. A legally enforceable promise by the government to provide funds constitutes an asset that Howe may rely upon in its business planning. As such it is a "financial contribution" that confers a "benefit" within the meaning of Article 1 of the SCM Agreement.

7.44 Furthermore, the United States asserts, if a party had to wait until the subsidy is paid out to challenge it, such a requirement would have the effect of eviscerating the SCM Agreement's disciplines for prohibited subsidies.

2. *"Benefit"*

7.45 The **United States** notes that to qualify as a "subsidy" within Article 1 of the SCM Agreement, the financial contribution must have conferred a "benefit". With respect to the grant, the benefit is self-evident: Howe has been given government money that it need not repay. The Australian government has provided Howe with a free source of capital that can be used to improve its productivity, decrease its labour and material costs, improve the quality of its automotive leather, lower its prices and generally enhance its competitiveness. Based upon an allocation of the benefits received, the total benefits conferred on Howe in 1998 were A$31,977,692.71.[61]

7.46 While the United States observes that a loan obviously differs from a grant in that it eventually must be repaid with interest, the United States asserts that there are several indications that the A$25 million loan at issue also conferred a "benefit" upon Howe. These include:

(a) The Five Year Holiday on Principal and Interest Payments Confers a "Benefit"

7.47 The United States contends that, under the terms of the loan, Howe is not required to pay principal or interest for the first five years, nor does interest accrue during this period. According to the United States, this is a valuable benefit to Howe. First, there is a substantial savings to Howe of the interest that it would have paid in the absence of the holiday. Using the interest costs that Howe's parent incurred for commercial borrowings as a benchmark, Howe saved approximately A$8,700,000 over the five-year period in interest payments.[62] Howe also received the additional benefit of being able to invest this money. For example, if Howe had invested the money in Australian government long-term bonds (a conservative illustration), Howe would have earned a total of A$8,625,000 over the five year period.[63] Accordingly, the total benefit to Howe conferred by the five year holiday on principal and interest payments based on a Australian government bond rate of 6.89% equals A$17,325,000.[64]

(b) The Loan Provided Howe with Credit Terms More Favorable Than Those Howe Could Have Obtained Commercially

7.48 The United States alleges that, in addition to supplying Howe with an interest-free loan for five years, the Australian government also provided Howe with credit terms more favorable than those it could have obtained commercially. The loan given to Howe reflects a preferential interest rate that, at the very least, the borrower would have to be creditworthy to receive. Yet, the United States argues, for a significant part of the past decade, Howe's financial condition has been precarious. In its fiscal year ending 30 June 1997, Howe's parent company, Australian Leather Upholstery Pty. Ltd., experienced a loss of A$6.9 million, which was attributable to Howe's poor financial performance.[65]

---

[61] United States Exhibit 50. See *infra*, para. 7.55 for a description of this Exhibit.

[62] United States Exhibit 51. See *infra*, para. 7.56 for a description of this Exhibit.

[63] United States Exhibit 51. See *infra*, para. 7.56 for a description of this Exhibit.

[64] *Ibid.*

[65] Australian Leather Holdings Limited, *Financial Statements*, June 30, 1997, pp. 20-21, United States Exhibit 26. According to the United States, the financial statements reveal that Howe is likely

Howe's parent also reported a A$2.6 million loss in the prior fiscal year, 1995/96.[66] These financial difficulties are also reflected in the public statements of Schaffer, the holding company for Howe's parent corporation. In its 1996 Annual Report, Schaffer reports that 1995-96 was a "difficult year for the automotive leather business" and that Howe's "poor manufacturing performance was a big disappointment" resulting "in a similarly substantial negative turnaround."[67] Such a track record was not unusual for Howe: in fiscal year 1993, it lost A$2.4 million[68] and in fiscal year 1989, it lost A$3.7 million.[69]

7.49 According to the United States, Howe's troubled financial history was well-known and widely acknowledged. For instance, the United States points out, a 1998 press report highlighted "the need for management changes to improve Howe's position and 'stop the red ink.'"[70] Similarly, another press article emphasized that Howe "would have dipped into losses in 1997 without the substantial contribution it accrued from trading in import credits."[71] Indeed, the Australian government has publicly acknowledged that depriving Howe of export assistance could sound the company's death knell. For instance, Minister John Moore characterized the replacement subsidies as "the minimum required (and confirmed by independent international auditors) for Howe to remain viable."[72]

7.50 In the view of the United States, these financial statements, press reports and government releases confirm that Howe was in deep financial trouble at the time of the loan. It thus appears unlikely that Howe would have been able to secure a 15-year loan amounting to approximately one-fourth of its total sales volume from any commercial lender and most certainly not on terms that even financially stable borrowers would find favorable. If Howe had been able to get a 15-year loan in its then-current state, the lender most likely would have required substantial collateral and would have charged an interest rate that was

the most important company within the Australia Leather Upholstery Pty. Ltd. group. Besides Howe, the group includes Howe & Co. (SA) (Pty.) Ltd. located in South Africa, Howe de Mexico SA de CV located in Mexico, and ALH Staff Superannuation Pty. Ltd. *Ibid.* at 20. The footnotes to this list indicated that the ALH Staff Superannuation Pty. Ltd. meets the definition of a small proprietary limited company as set out in the Corporations Law. *Ibid.* The financial statement also notes that the operations in South Africa and Mexico do not have a material effect on the accounts. *Ibid.* at 32. Thus, the United States asserts, the financial results identified for the Australian Leather Upholstery Pty. Ltd can reasonably be attributed to Howe's operations in Australia.

[66] *Ibid.*, pp 20-21.

[67] Schaffer Corporation, *Annual Report 1996*, pp. 2-3, United States Exhibit 34.

[68] Howe Leather, *1993 Annual Return*, March 29, 1994, p. 2, United States Exhibit 35.

[69] Howe Leather, *1990 Annual Return*, May 21, 1991, p. 5, United States Exhibit 36.

[70] "Australia: Leather Company's Hide Wearing Thin," *Australian*, February 2, 1998, United States Exhibit 37.

[71] "Sacred Cows vs. The Hide of Howe," *The Weekend Australian*, September 20-21, 1997, p. 52, United States Exhibit 22.

[72] United States Exhibit 18.

higher than the rate given to creditworthy companies. Yet, despite Howe's unprofitability, the Australian government not only gave Howe a loan, it provided preferential interest rates. The cut-rate financing is evident by comparing the interest charged Howe's holding company on its non-government loans and the rate the Australian government charged Howe in its new aid package. As of June 30, 1997, ALH reported A$31,373,000 in consolidated borrowings and A$3,647,000 in consolidated interest and other finance charges.[73] Based upon this information, the company's interest rate for its current borrowings was 11.62 per cent. In contrast, the A$25 million loan given to Howe was based on the government's long-term bond rate, which averaged 6.89 per cent for 1997, the year the loan was granted.[74] Adding two percentage points to this rate, as required by the terms of the loan, the interest on this loan would only be 8.89 per cent, or approximately three percentage points below the company's rate based upon its then-current borrowings. This results in saved interest payments, which clearly confer a benefit upon Howe.

(c) The Loan Is Not Adequately Secured

7.51 The United States alleges that a final indication of the beneficial nature of the A$25 million loan is the fact that it is not adequately secured. The loan appears to be secured by a second mortgage over the assets and undertakings of Howe's parent corporation, ALH.[75] However, the United States argues, a second mortgage of this nature would be inadequate for a commercial loan of this size and duration. For instance, Morgan Brooks Pty. Ltd. of Australia requires "[a] registered first mortgage over commercial, industrial, retail or residential investment real estate" for its commercial mortgages. In this instance, however, neither ALH nor Howe could have provided a lender with a first mortgage, since ALH's other borrowings - namely, its bank overdraft account, its commercial bills payable account, and a bank loan - appear to already have been encumbered by a first mortgage "over all the assets and undertakings" of ALH.[76] Accordingly, the United States submits, the fact that the government of Australia did not require Howe to pledge adequate security before extending the A$25 million loan constitutes yet another way in which the Australian government has conferred a "benefit" on Howe.

7.52 **Australia** submits that the loan is a subsidy under Part I of the SCM Agreement, without prejudice to issues such as calculation and its status under

---

73 Australian Leather Holdings Ltd, *June 30, 1997 Financial Statement*, December 5, 1997, pp. 7, 9, United States Exhibit 26.

74 United States Exhibit 53.

75 Australian Leather Holdings Ltd, *June 30, 1997 Financial Statement*, December 5, 1997, p. 24, United States Exhibit 26.

76 *Ibid.*, p. 23.

other parts of the SCM Agreement.[77] Australia also states that the payments under the grant contract are subsidies within the meaning of the SCM Agreement. It is up to the United States, rather than Australia, to demonstrate that the grant contract is a subsidy, and for Australia to respond to that. The United States appears not to have made such a demonstration, even though, on at least due process grounds, it should have been required to do so in its first written submission to the Panel.

7.53 While it is not relevant to the issue in Australia's view, Australia believes that it may be worthwhile commenting on the United States point about Howe being in financial trouble.[78] The evidentiary value of the facts put forward by the United States is highly questionable, but in any case they do not demonstrate this. There are many highly creditworthy companies that have short term and even long term losses. In Howe's case, an assessment of its creditworthy position would involve an analysis of Howe itself, its parent company and its ultimate controllers. It would involve an assessment of the creditworthiness of all of these entities. If this was a genuine concern of the United States at the time, why did it insist that the grant contract money be devoted largely to investment?

7.54 The **United States** observes that Australia confirmed that it does not dispute that the loan and the grant fall within the definition of "subsidy" in Article 1. In addition, Australia concedes that the loan was on concessional terms. With respect to Australia's assertion that the United States has not demonstrated that the grant contract itself is a subsidy, the United States maintains that the grant measure at issue in this case is the Australian government's commitment to make grant payments to Howe, which subsumes the disbursements themselves. A legally enforceable promise by the government to provide funds constitutes an asset that Howe may rely upon in its business planning. As such it is a "financial contribution" that confers a "benefit" within the meaning of Article 1 of the SCM Agreement.[79]

3. *Calculation and Allocation of the "Benefit"*

7.55 As noted in paragraphs 7.45-7.51 above, the **United States** made submissions relating to the calculation and allocation of benefits conferred upon Howe under the grant contract and the loan contract. With respect to the grant contract, the United States referred to its Exhibit 50. With respect to the loan contract, the United States referred to its Exhibit 51. A brief description of these exhibits follows. United States Exhibit 50 is a table entitled "Allocation of Benefits from Grants Received by Howe and Co. Pty. Ltd." It has four main columns. The first

---

[77] Australia disputed the calculation issues raised in this section. See the arguments of Australia *infra*, paras. 7.57-7.59 and 7.62-7.72.
[78] *Supra*, paras. 7.48-7.50.
[79] Also see arguments of the United States, *supra*, paras. 7.43-7.44.

lists the years 1997-2010, based upon an "estimated useful life of assets for Howe of 13 years". The second main column is headed "A$17,500,000 Grant Provided in 1997". The third main column is headed "A$12,500,000 Grant Provided in 1998". Both of the second and third columns are subdivided into two sub-columns: (i) "Unamortized Portion of Grant"; and (ii) "Interest Saved on Unamortized Portion". According to the United States, the latter is "calculated by multiplying unamortized amount of grant in given year by 11.6 per cent, which represents the interest rate Howe would have paid to finance the capital investment absent the grant. The interest rate was derived from information contained in the 1997 financial statement of Australian Leather Holdings, Ltd. (ALH), Howe's parent company. According to the statement, ALH's consolidated borrowings (A$31,373,000) divided by consolidated interest and other finance charges (A$3,647,000) yields an interest rate of 11.6 per cent for borrowings in 1997." The fourth main column of the table is headed "Total of Grants Provided". According to the United States, "Total benefits equal total unamortized portion of grant plus total interest saved on unamortized portion in given year (i.e., in 1999, benefits equal A$26,346,154 + A$3,056,154 = A$29,402,308)."

7.56 United States Exhibit 51 is a table entitled "Benefit to Howe Based Upon Repayment of $25 Million Loan After Five Years". It has four columns. The first column lists the years 1998-2002. The second column is entitled "Interest Saved". According to the United States, this refers to "Interest saved because of five-year interest holiday". The benefit is calculated as interest savings on remaining principal (outstanding principal x 11.6 per cent). The interest rate was derived from information contained in the 1997 financial statement of Australian Leather Holdings, Ltd. (ALH), Howe's parent company. According to the statement, "ALH's consolidated borrowings (A$31373,000) divided by consolidated interest and other finance charges (A$3,647,000) yields an interest rate of 11.6 per cent for borrowings in 1997." The third column in the table is entitled "Interest Earned". The United States explains that this refers to "Interest earned on A$25 million. Annual interest equals A$25 million x 6.9% (average GOA bond rate in annual 1997)." The fourth column is entitled "Total", and lists the totals of columns 2 and 3 for the years 1997-2002. It then adds all of these totals, resulting in a sum of A$17,325,000.

7.57 **Australia** points out that, with respect to the benefit conferred by the loan[80], the United States makes some sweeping assumptions about the way a subsidy might be calculated in the context of Part II of the SCM Agreement, regarding benefit to the recipient and allocation over time.[81] According to Australia, the issue of calculation and allocation of the measures is not before the

[80] See the arguments of the United States *supra*, paras. 7.45-7.51.

[81] Australia refers to *supra.*, paras. 7.46-7.51 and to United States Exhibit 51, which is described *supra*, para. 7.56.

Panel (that is, beyond the question of whether each of the measures before the Panel is indeed a subsidy). Accordingly, the Panel should not make any findings or suggestions on calculation and allocation issues.

7.58 While Australia maintains that calculation issues are not relevant to the Panel, Australia nevertheless asserts that the United States has grossly exaggerated the extent of subsidy provided by the loan, including the benefits in the first five years. This is not a case about United States countervailing duty methodology. For example, the United States[82] uses a method of determining the level of subsidy from a loan (which it describes as a conservative illustration), which assumes that the money is invested in government bonds. Clearly, in that case, the benefit to the company would be just the returns from the bonds.[83] No company would borrow at a high interest rate to invest at a lower one. It makes no economic sense to add the second and third columns in the table in United States Exhibit 51 to calculate the level of subsidy, since this is just double counting.

7.59 On the actual calculation of benefits under the grant contract, again as with the loan, this is not a case about United States countervailing duty methodology. Few, if any, other jurisdictions would, in an allocation scenario, add the total unamortized portion to the interest saved and call that the annual benefit. This leads to the calculated benefit from the potential maximum payments of A$30 million over 1996/97-1998/99 (July/June) as being A$31,977,692 in 1998 alone. The sum of the calculated annual benefits derived from the unamortized payments, excluding interest payments, comes to A$210 million in the table in United States Exhibit 50. This is seven times greater than the A$30 million cap on payments.

7.60 The **United States** notes that Australian government contends that the calculations "grossly exaggerate" and erroneously calculate the amount of benefit provided. Australia has misconstrued the United States' calculations for the benefits conferred by the grant and loan. With respect to the grant, the Australian government suggests that the United States is claiming that the total benefit provided for the A$30 million grant is A$210 million. That is not correct. The total "value" of the benefit to Howe *in 1998* was A$31,977,692. However, these benefits are *not* intended to be cumulative. The United States did not suggest that the annual benefit for each year would be added together to arrive at a "total benefit", as the Australian government suggests. Rather, these calculations represent the "value" of the benefit *in each particular year.* As the table in United States Exhibit 50 shows, the value of the benefit declines gradually over time.

---

[82] Australia refers to the United States argument in *supra*, para. 7.47, and to United States Exhibit 51, which is described *supra*, para. 7.56.

[83] Australia refers to the third column in the table in United States Exhibit 51. Australia states that this accepts solely for the sake of commenting on this calculation the use of the zero interest rate rather than allocating the 2% premium interest paid over the last ten years of the loan.

7.61 With respect to Australia's contention that the benefit conferred by the loan has been miscalculated, the United States submits that, again, Australia has misconstrued the benefit calculations. These calculations reflect the fact that Howe received a double benefit when it received a preferential loan with a five-year interest holiday. First, column two in United States Exhibit 51 represents the interest that Howe would have had to pay if Howe could have secured a commercial loan for A$25 million to finance its capital expenditures. Because Howe was not required to repay any interest for five years, it obviously received a benefit from this five-year holiday. The higher interest rate used in this column reflects the rate at which Howe would have had to borrow funds, based on the company's financial statement. The Australian government has provided no evidence to suggest that Howe's borrowing rate would be lower. In fact, its actual rate could have been considerably higher in light of its financial difficulties. The third column reflects the interest that Howe could have earned on A$25 million if it invested this money. If, as Australia suggests, Howe's investment yielded a higher return than the government bond rate, then the benefit to the company was even larger. In other words, the United States' use of the bond rate was a conservative estimate of Howe's return. Combining these two columns does not "double count" the same benefit because Howe was in fact receiving a double benefit. First, unlike a regular commercial loan, Howe is not required to pay back any interest for the first five years, as it would have had to do if it had borrowed money at a commercial rate. Thus, it is receiving the benefit of a five-year interest-free period. The benefit from the interest-free period is reflected in the second column. Moreover, Howe was given the money to use, and thus received a benefit from this receipt of funds. The benefit received from having access to these funds is reflected in the third column. Thus, the United States properly cumulated these two benefits to derive the full measure of the benefit from the loan for the first five years of the loan.

7.62 **Australia** continues to disagree with the United States calculations in United States Exhibits 50 and 51 even for countervail or other purposes. The United States clearly misunderstood the points that Australia made. The fact that Australia makes these comments should not be taken to imply that Australia accepts any aspect of the United States' approach in respect of the grant or loan contracts.

7.63 In respect of the grant contract, Australia observes that the United States confirms that the last column of its Exhibit 50 is supposed to set out the computed benefit in each year of the total possible payments under the grant contract. It is unclear what the United States means when it says that "these benefits are *not* intended to be cumulative." Benefits of allocation of subsidies must be in some sense cumulative, subject to present value considerations, otherwise the concept is meaningless. Australia contends that the figures of A$19,530,000 and A$31,977,692 for the benefits in 1997 and 1998, respectively, far exceed the total potential payments. However, Australia does agree with the implication of the first two rows that the potential payments have been totally expensed in the periods for which they would be received.

7.64 In respect of the loan contract, Australia asserts that the concept of benefit is based on the idea that enterprises borrow money to do something with it. The benefit for countervail purposes of a government loan is based on the difference between what the government charges and the comparable commercial rate (alternatively the borrowing cost of the government for a cost to government calculation). The benefit from the subsidy has nothing to do with what the enterprise does with the money so long as it is free to do what it wants with it. An enterprise that borrows commercially has exactly the same capacity as an enterprise benefiting from a government loan to use borrowed money to generate income.

7.65 Australia submits that the calculations in United States Exhibits 50 and 51 and the related arguments, while irrelevant to the current case, were wrong. According to Australia, the United States has not disputed this. Nor has it explained the disconnect between its approach to the allocation of the grants over time and its claim that they are tied to export performance. The specific period of the grant contract is to mid-2000 - no longer. The payments under the grant contract were based on reports for the period to mid-1998. If they were tied to export performance, then they became exhausted after the time period for those exports. Alternatively, under the logic of the United States' case about replacement measures, subsidies should be allocated across the period for the schemes they are supposedly replacing, i.e. through to mid-2000 or at most end-2000. Although irrelevant to this case, the allocation across lengthy periods on the basis of investment underlines that the United States in reality does not see any linkage between the measures and export performance.

7.66 In addition, Australia asserts that the United States' position on the issues of calculation and allocation inherently contradicts aspects of its argument on the issue of "contingent ... in fact" under Article 3.1(a) of the SCM Agreement. In the case of the loan, the United States first looks at the value of the loan over the period to 2002 and also at the rest of the loan period when referring to more favourable credit terms.[84] The United States has argued that the measure is a replacement for a programmes that ran until 2000 (30 June 2000 for ICS and 31 December 2000 for EFS) and that this in some way taints the replacement measures. It is arguing here about the benefits this measure allegedly provides the company over a fifteen year period, with even the first five years extending beyond 2000. An export subsidy must be tied, attached in some way, ("in law or in fact") to exports. Exports in turn must have, or be going, to occur in some particular period for the discipline to have any meaning. Australia argues that the

[84] Australia refers to *supra*, para 7.47 and to United States Exhibit 51, which is described *supra*, para. 7.56.

United States has not produced any facts that demonstrate that the loan should be considered to fall under Article 3.1(a) of the SCM Agreement. Its argument seems to be based solely on an association between the loan contract and the grant contract.

7.67 Australia also notes that the United States has allocated payments under the grant contract across the period to 2009 for the first two payments (i.e. those measures before the Panel) and 2010 for the total potential payment in 1998/99.[85] As in the case of the loan, this gives rise to inconsistencies in the United States' arguments. The facts presented by the United States state that the performance targets, investment and sales, are limited to the period to 2000, i.e. the grant contract only covers the period to 2000. Indeed, the United States' arguments about the grant contract's relationship with ICS and EFS turn on it being for the same period as the company would have attracted entitlements under those plans, i.e. mid-2000 and end-2000, respectively. However, United States Exhibit 50 seeks to allocate the first two payments and the residual potential payment over a thirteen-year investment period to 2010. The United States has not even made an allegation, let alone produced any facts, that there is any connection made by the Australian government to any form of performance after 30 June 2000. By allocating the entire A$30 million over an investment period, the United States appears to be arguing that none of the money paid out should be attributed to sales. On that basis, presumably no weight should be put on any of its arguments regarding linkages between payments and sales requirements.

7.68 Australia maintains that the United States is seeking to have it both ways through making an allocation across time as if for countervailing or possibly consideration of investment subsidies for the purposes of Article 6.1(a) of the SCM Agreement. Whatever relationship the second and third grant payments bore to any sales, those sales would have essentially gone. The United States argues that the grant contract is a substitute for ICS and EFS, over the remainder of their duration, but they both terminate in 2000, not in 2010. According to Australia, the reality is that the United States is focusing on a serious prejudice case, not a case under Article 3.1(a) of the SCM Agreement.

7.69 Australia asserts that the "in fact" condition in Article 3.1(a) of the SCM Agreement is there to deal with circumvention cases where a government provides money contingent on export performance but does so in a manner other than through legislation or legal contract. It is not there as a trade effects test, which would have to be assessed on a case-by-case basis. The United States has not produced or alleged that the contract involves circumvention. Rather, it relies on economic tests and arguments.

[85] Australia refers to *supra*, para. 7.45, and to United States Exhibit 50, which is described *supra*, para. 7.55.

7.70 Australia asserts that the work under Annex IV of the SCM Agreement to elaborate calculation issues for Article 6.1(a) of the SCM Agreement involves a merger of the cultures of the multilateral remedy and countervail. A number of Members have some problems with aspects of this. However, regardless of the merits of that work on allocation, there is nothing under Article 3.1(a) of the SCM Agreement that would allow such an allocation across time for the purposes of this rule. Article 3.1(a) is about actual exports. If a Member provided export subsidies, for the sake of example, assume that these were straightforward export subsidies contingent in law upon the export of 100 widgets. The measure would no longer be in place once those 100 widgets had been exported. The condition would no longer have any force. It would be absurd to suggest that somehow future activities of a company were tainted because past performance had been subsidized. This is not an issue for Part II of the SCM Agreement. It may be an issue for Part III, i.e. serious prejudice, but that would depend on the circumstances.

7.71 Australia argues that the United States, by presenting the measures as being allocated across time, is accepting that there is no linkage between the granting of the measures and export performance. Thus, the United States is implicitly accepting that the measures do not meet the "in fact" standard of Article 3.1(a) of the SCM Agreement and are consistent with that Article.

7.72 Of course, Australia continues, in many instances, there may be no remedy at all for a past measure, certainly not under Part II of the SCM Agreement. This is in keeping with GATT/WTO practice. It is important that there not be some confusion between the retrospectivity of serious prejudice cases and countervailing duty action, and normal rules under the WTO. If a tariff is found to be in breach of a binding, then the remedy is to bring it into conformity. It is not to go back and find all the importers of record who may have paid too much over whatever period the tariff was in force. In Australia's view, the job of the dispute settlement system is to obtain consistency, not retrospective compensation or penalty.

7.73 The **United States** asserts that it provided the subsidy calculations to demonstrate, as a preliminary matter, that the grant and loan did confer a benefit upon Howe. However, the Australian government has misinterpreted the United States' argument with respect to the calculation of the benefit. Australia suggests that the method used by the United States to value the benefit is inconsistent with the United States' position that these benefits were tied to exports. The method used to calculate the value of the benefit is not directly related to the question of whether a subsidy is, or is not, an export subsidy. The calculation methodology and the legal and factual criteria for "in fact" subsidies are not interchangeable. Rather, the calculation methodology simply reflects the common sense inference that a benefit received from a grant or a preferential loan will extend well beyond the precise moment that the grant or loan is given. Thus, Howe continues to benefit now from the past receipt of the replacement subsidies.

7.74 The United States submits that, in addition to demonstrating that a benefit was conferred, the benefit calculations are useful for determining an appropriate prospective remedy should the United States prevail in this case. Article 4.7 of the SCM Agreement provides that "[i]f the measure in question is found to be a prohibited subsidy, the panel shall recommend that the subsidizing Member withdraw the subsidy without delay." Although the subsidies in this case are non-recurring, the United States asserts that, given the substantial size of the subsidies involved, it is appropriate to allocate the amount of the subsidies over time in order to fashion an appropriate prospective remedy. This is because the subsidies continues to exist - and therefore may be "withdrawn" - for as long as they continue to benefit the recipient.

7.75 **Australia** submits that the United States did not ask the Panel to reach a finding on remedy beyond Article 4.7 of the SCM Agreement. Australia requests the Panel not to make a recommendation or suggestion on remedy consistent with Article 19.2 of the DSU. Were the Panel to find that some measure was inconsistent with Article 3.1(a) of the SCM Agreement, the way in which Australia chose to bring itself into compliance, if it were necessary to take any action at all, would depend on the actual findings of the Panel. Australia's obligations would be to bring itself into consistency regarding the nature of any outstanding measures.

7.76 The point Australia has made is that the argument that the benefit of the subsidies should be allocated across time means that the complainant would have to demonstrate that the tie to exports stretches across the same time period. By arguing about allocation across time, the United States has created an inconsistency in its approach. On the one hand, it implies that there is a tie to exports over a lengthy period. On the other hand, it argued about exports over 1997-2000 under the grant contract.

D. Article 3.1(a) of the SCM Agreement

1. Text of Article 3.1(a)

7.77 Article 3.1(a) of the SCM Agreement states:

> 3.1 Except as provided in the Agreement on Agriculture, the following subsidies, within the meaning of Article 1, shall be prohibited:
>
> (a) subsidies contingent, in law or in fact[4], whether solely or as one of several other conditions, upon export performance, including those illustrated in Annex I[5];

[4]This standard is met when the facts demonstrate that the granting of a subsidy, without having been made legally contingent upon export performance, is in fact tied to actual or anticipated exportation or export

earnings. The mere fact that a subsidy is granted to enterprises which export shall not for that reason alone be considered to be an export subsidy within the meaning of this provision.

[5]Measures referred to in Annex I as not constituting export subsidies shall not be prohibited under this or any other provision of this Agreement.

2. *Principles of Treaty Interpretation*

7.78 The **United States** recalls that Article 3.2 of the DSU provides that the covered agreements shall be interpreted in accordance with "customary rules of interpretation of public international law", and that the *Vienna Convention* sets forth the customary rules of treaty interpretation.[86] Accordingly, the rights and obligations of the parties under the SCM Agreement must be interpreted in accordance with the *Vienna Convention.* Article 31 of the *Vienna Convention* provides that "a treaty shall be interpreted in good faith in accordance with the ordinary meaning to be given to the terms of the treaty in their context and in light of its object and purpose." According to Article 32, recourse to supplementary means of interpretation including preparatory work, *inter alia*, may be had "in order to confirm the meaning resulting from the application of Article 31."

3. *Interpretation of the Phrase "Contingent in Law or in Fact upon Export Performance"*

(a) Application of the Customary Rules of Interpretation of Public International law

7.79 The **United States** notes that, in this case, the ordinary meaning of the text of Article 3.1 of the SCM Agreement prohibits the replacement subsidy package provided to Howe by the Australian government. Article 3.1(a) of the SCM Agreement prohibits "subsidies contingent in law *or in fact*, whether solely or as one of several other conditions, upon export performance." (emphasis supplied by the United States). Thus, the prohibition in Article 3.1(a) extends not only to subsidies *expressly* based on export performance (*de jure* export subsidies), but also to subsidies that are *in fact* based upon export performance (*de facto* export subsidies). The term "subsidy" is defined in Article 1 of the SCM Agreement as a "financial contribution" by a government, such as a loan or a grant, that confers a "benefit." The ordinary meaning of the term "benefit" is

---

[86] The United States asserts that the basic rules of treaty interpretation have been repeatedly relied on by the Appellate Body and WTO panels in interpreting the WTO Agreements, and refers to, e.g., *United States - Standards for Reformulated and Conventional Gasoline* ("*United States - Gasoline*"), WT/DS2/AB/R, 29 April 1996, DSR 1996:I, 3, at 16 ("[Article 31] forms part of the 'customary rules of interpretation of public international law' which the Appellate Body has been directed, by Article 3(2) of the DSU, to apply in seeking to clarify the provisions of the GATT 1994 and the other 'covered agreements'").

captured by its dictionary definition: a benefit is "a favourable or helpful factor or circumstance; advantage, profit."[87]

7.80 According to the United States, the dimensions and purpose of the prohibition on *de facto* export subsidies are illuminated by the drafting history of this provision. The Agreement on Interpretation and Application of Articles VI, XVI and XXIII of the GATT (the "Tokyo Round Subsidies Agreement") provided generally in Article 9 that "Signatories shall not grant export subsidies on products other than certain primary products", and this prohibition included all export subsidies - both *de jure* and *de facto.* During the Uruguay Round negotiations in Negotiating Group 10 on subsidies and countervailing measures, the European Community proposed that the application of the prohibition to *de facto* export subsidies be clarified:

> The prohibition of export subsidies in Article 9 of the Subsidies Code should be reformulated in order to define clearly its scope. This prohibition must apply to all export subsidies, that is, all government interventions which confer, through a charge on the public account (in the form of direct financial outlays or revenue foregone, such as tax relief and debt forgiveness), a benefit on a firm or an industry contingent upon export performance.
>
> In addition, since experience has shown that government practices may be easily manipulated or modified in order to avoid this prohibition, it is apparent that a prohibition only of those subsidies which are *de jure* (that is, expressly) made contingent upon export performance is open to circumvention.
>
> The prohibition, in the present discipline also applies to subsidies *de facto* contingent upon export. This, however, makes it necessary to provide for clearer guidance in identifying *de facto* export subsidies ... *De facto* export subsidies are those where facts which were known - or should clearly have been known - to the government when granting the subsidy demonstrate that the subsidy, without having been made expressly contingent upon export performance, was indeed intended to increase exports.[88]

7.81 The United States submits that footnote 4 in the text of Article 3.1 of the SCM Agreement clarifies that the "in fact" standard "is met when the facts demonstrate that the granting of the subsidy, without having been made legally con-

[87] *The Concise Oxford Dictionary*, 8th ed., p. 102.

[88] MTN.GNG/NG10/W/31, 27 November 1989, *Elements of the Negotiating Framework - Submission by the European Community*.

tingent upon export performance, is in fact tied to actual or anticipated exportation or export earnings." While the note also cautions against finding a *de facto* subsidy on "the mere fact that a subsidy is accorded to enterprises which export", this admonition is premised on finding an export subsidy based on "that reason alone", that is, where the fact that the recipients happen to export is the *only* factor indicating that a subsidy is a *de facto* export subsidy.

7.82 In addition, the United States contends, the Uruguay Round negotiations expanded the scope of a prohibited subsidy. Rather than requiring that export performance be the "only" or the "most important" element, Article 3.1(a) provides that export performance may be *either* the sole contingency for the subsidy *or* merely "one of several other conditions". The export requirement therefore does not need to carry preponderant weight in the approval of benefits to qualify as an export subsidy. Rather, an export subsidy will exist when actual or anticipated exportation is merely one of several potential criteria influencing the bestowal of benefits. This expansion of the definition in the SCM Agreement recognizes the serious and harmful consequences flowing from export subsidies. Thus, even in circumstances where export performance is only one of several criteria for award of the subsidy, a finding that the subsidy is a prohibited subsidy would be warranted and, indeed, compelled. Moreover, by explicitly including a footnote emphasizing that subsidies are prohibited without having been made expressly contingent upon export performance, the SCM Agreement recognizes that Members may well attempt to mask the export-orientation of particular benefits by claiming that they are bestowed without explicit contingencies. Yet, if the totality of the circumstances reveals that these benefits are designed to promote exports, then such benefits fall within the broad definition of Article 3.1(a).

7.83 **Australia** submits that the Panel is being asked to address a number of issues that have far-reaching implications for the interpretation of Article 3.1(a) of the SCM Agreement. Australia asserts that the Panel is being asked by the United States to widen the application of the "in fact" condition in Article 3.1(a) of the SCM Agreement to include the nature of any prior measure and to interpret it as a trade effects test on the basis of a subjective, case-by-case assessment of the level of exports by an enterprise. This movement away from the hard rules-based approach of Article 3 of the SCM Agreement was rejected by Australia.

7.84 Australia contends that the issue whether the subsidies are contingent "in fact" upon export performance has to be analyzed in the context of footnote 4 to Article 3.1(a) of the SCM Agreement, which defines, and thereby limits the scope of, "in fact". Australia asserts that the onus is on the United States to demonstrate that the conditions are met. *Inter alia*, the United States has to: (a) present the relevant "facts" to the Panel; and (b) prove that these facts demonstrate that the granting of the subsidy is in fact tied to actual or anticipated exportation or export earnings. This is not a question of analyzing the incidence of a subsidy as distributed between domestic and export sales. This is a matter of proving that the act of granting the subsidy is tied to export sales. According to Australia, the United States does not do that.

7.85 Australia argues that this means that the required proof is not one of economic inference but rather that the actual or anticipated exportation or export earnings are actually tied to the granting of the subsidy. The second sentence in footnote 4 means that it is not sufficient to look at a company's exports to demonstrate the "in fact" standard. Rather, the complainant must produce facts that show the granting is actually tied to export performance. The fact that an enterprise has a high level of exports, or the fact that its exports are increasing, do not demonstrate that the standard of footnote 4 has been met. The wording of the text is to distinguish between the situation where something is set out explicitly in legislation or regulation and where there is some non-legislative, administrative arrangement whereby the granting of the subsidy is actually tied to export performance. Australia states that neither is true in this case.

7.86 Australia asserts that the rules are more rigorous for export than domestic subsidies because export subsidies allow companies to sell more cheaply on export markets while benefiting from higher domestic prices. Hence, the original bi-level price test in Article XVI:4 of GATT 1947. This was obviously too simple to prevent circumvention and the rules were elaborated leading to the Illustrative List annexed to the Tokyo Round Subsidies Agreement. Again, these were all measures that targeted, that favoured, exports. There was never any suggestion that some high level of exports test would apply.

7.87 According to Australia, the SCM Agreement maintains the Illustrative List (with some changes and interpretations in Annexes II and III) and the concept of "export performance". For a subsidy to fall under Article 3.1(a) of the SCM Agreement, whether in law or in fact, its granting must be conditioned on "export performance". This is not about it being an exporting firm or being export ready. It is about favouring concrete, tangible exports.

7.88 Australia maintains that the SCM Agreement is permissive of subsidies that do not fall under Article 3.1. Such subsidies are not prohibited by the SCM Agreement. For example, traditional subsidies paid on the basis of production are clearly permitted under the SCM Agreement. This is reflected in the structure of the SCM Agreement, where Part II of the SCM Agreement does not apply to such subsidies, but instead Part III of the SCM Agreement provides for multilateral remedies for such measures where adverse effect can be demonstrated. Where adverse effects are alleged to be caused by subsidies in the sense of Article 5 of the SCM Agreement, a Member has a multilateral remedy under Article 7 of the SCM Agreement. In particular, for a case of serious prejudice, Article 6.3 of the SCM Agreement sets out criteria for the establishment of a case of serious prejudice. This is the basis for pursuing allegations of adverse effect for subsidies whose granting is not explicitly tied to export performance.

7.89 According to Australia, the essential difference is between a hard rules-based test and a trade effects test. Article 3.1(a) of the SCM Agreement sets out rules for a breach of the SCM Agreement and they are to be treated as strict criteria and not an effects-based set of tests. They call for facts to be established, rather than for a Panel to look at trade outcomes. Australia submits that the United States' position turns on the argument that some undefined level of exports by an enterprise is indicative of its status under Article 3.1(a) of the SCM Agreement.

7.90 Australia argues that the United States' approach, if accepted, would lead to results at clear variance with the object and purpose of the SCM Agreement, and indeed could lead to absurdities. In the case of an enterprise that exports, what would be the outcome if a panel were to judge that a high level of exports in itself met the "in fact" test of Article 3.1(a) of the SCM Agreement? No number, no bright line has been established under the SCM Agreement. How would a Member know whether a measure was to fall under Article 3.1(a) of the SCM Agreement? Would the threshold be 50%, 75%, or 90%? Would an increase in exports by a recipient potentially make a measure inconsistent after the decision to grant? In the view of Australia, it would be inappropriate for panels to make case by case judgments on these sorts of issues when it came to questions of violation of a rule such as Article 3.1(a) of the SCM Agreement. Provisions on rules need to provide clear guidance to Members without introducing a large element of subjectivity, which would be the case if the level of exports or other such concepts were to be introduced into any assessment under Article 3.1(a) of the SCM Agreement.

7.91 Australia asserts that, depending on the circumstances, a Member that considers that it is being adversely affected in some way by such a subsidy has a number of remedies open to it, including multilateral remedies under Article 7 of the SCM Agreement and Article 26 of the DSU, or countervailing duty provisions. Thus, under the SCM Agreement itself there are already remedies to be pursued in Parts III and V, rather than Part II. Australia notes that Article 27.4 (including footnote 55) of the SCM Agreement clearly envisages that the level of export subsidies can be quantified. This would be inconsistent with an approach that said that only a panel can determine what falls under the "in fact" provision of Article 3.1(a) of the SCM Agreement on a subjective, case-by-case basis. This would be further complicated if the performance of an enterprise could somehow change the status of a measure, which could arise under a level of exports approach.

7.92 As a further example, Australia notes that some unquantified level of exports test would cause a potential conflict with the purpose and operation of Article 13(c) of the Agreement on Agriculture ("Due Restraint"). The obligations on export subsidies under the Agreement Agriculture are quantitative and so need to be clear cut. If the definition of "export subsidy" under the Agreement on Agriculture includes measures meeting such an "in fact" test, then it would be virtually impossible for many Members to conform with quantitative disciplines of the Agreement on Agriculture. On the other hand if the definition of "export subsidy" under the Agreement on Agriculture does not include measures meeting such an "in fact" test, then they would not be given cover by the Due Restraint article and so be subject to the disciplines of the SCM Agreement. This is clearly not what was envisaged when the agreements were negotiated.

7.93 Australia asserts that the United States seeks to reinterpret the meaning of "in law or in fact" and footnote 4 in Article 3.1(a). The concepts of "*de jure*" and "*de facto*" do not appear in the SCM Agreement, or indeed in the Tokyo Round Subsidies Agreement. The assertion by the United States that Article 9 of the Tokyo Round Subsidies Agreement "included all export subsidies - both *de jure* and *de facto*" is simply an assertion and without any actual, concrete meaning. Article 9 of the Tokyo Round Subsidies Agreement did prohibit export subsidies, but this was not defined beyond the Illustrative List. There was no such division between *de jure* and *de facto* or any definition of what *de facto* might mean. Australia is not aware of any panel decision on this issue under the Tokyo Round Subsidies Agreement. If it had been the accepted jurisprudence that the notion extended to the much wider scope being argued here by the United States, it is surprising that it was never utilized by the United States or other signatories. In any case, the actual situation under the Tokyo Round Subsidies Agreement is irrelevant to the current case, which is under the WTO Agreement. This is not even a successor agreement.

7.94 Australia contends that the current SCM Agreement does not refer to "*de jure*" and "*de facto*" but to "in law" and "in fact" and the latter is defined and limited through footnote 4. While some broader definition might or might not have been in the mind of the European Community when it submitted MTN.GNG/NG/W/31 of 27 November 1989, the final text only emerged much later from the negotiations. Australia notes that a plain reading of the relevant section in the EC paper shows that it was concerned that the Tokyo Round Subsidies Agreement already covered subsidies "*de facto* contingent upon export" and that: "[t]his, however, makes it necessary to provide for clearer guidance in identifying *de facto* export subsidies, in order to *avoid undue extensions* of the category of export subsidies." (emphasis supplied by Australia) Australia suggests that this could be read as the European Community seeking to limit the scope of any new agreement in this area. The third paragraph of the same section makes it clear that the European Community is looking at a situation where: "*subsidies aim at distorting trade by favouring exports*. A mere reference to the *effect* if [sic] a subsidy on exports, as observed *ex post facto*, would be inconsistent with this rationale. If it cannot be shown that, on the basis of the facts which the government knew - or should clearly have known - when granting the subsidy, the intention of the government was in fact to favour exports, and therefore it cannot be said that the subsidy aims, *de jure* or *de facto*, at distorting trade, this subsidy should not be prohibited; it should rather be subject to remedial action if and when it produces demonstrable negative effects on trade."

7.95 Australia points out that, at that stage of the Uruguay Round negotiations, there were a number of proposals concerning the ambit of the provision in question. The United States, in MTN.GNG/NG10/W/29 of 22 November 1989, argued for the prohibition of: "[a]ny subsidies to a firm and/or firms [footnote omitted] predominantly engaged in export trade, *i.e.* whose exports exceed [X] per cent of total sales."[89] That was not accepted. Indeed, Australia submits, the argument of the United States before the Panel appears to be an attempt to achieve what it sought unsuccessfully in the Uruguay Round.

7.96 Australia notes that, in MTN.GNG/NG10/W/29, the United States did not call such subsidies export subsidies, but rather distinguished them from export subsidies by calling them "trade-related subsidies", but nonetheless prohibited. As with Article 3.1(b) of the SCM Agreement, such subsidies would have been prohibited but were not "export subsidies".

7.97 Australia states that, in MTN.GNG/NG10/W/38, this concept was listed as one of the reasons for the presumption of serious prejudice (Article 6.1(c)) with a footnote to the effect that it might appear instead under the prohibition article (then Article 1) with a different threshold percentage. This was a provision additional to, and separate from, the "in law or in fact" rule on export subsidies It was included under the deeming of serious prejudice provision (Article 6.1) in the Chair's consultation draft for MTN.GNG/NG10/W/38/Rev.2 with a square bracketed figure of 95% but without the footnote referencing the prohibition article (Article 3). Australia, at least, was opposed to the provision and presumably many other participants shared this view, because it was dropped completely from the actual version of MTN.GNG/NG10/W/38/Rev.2, which emerged from the consultations.

7.98 Australia asserts that this goes to demonstrate that Uruguay Round participants were not prepared to accept that a high level of exports should lead to a deeming of serious prejudice let alone prohibition. In addition, the draft provisions on prohibition for a high level of exports would have been separate from the "in fact or in law", which was already in the draft. Thus, the drafters of the text saw the high level of exports, while potentially creating a prohibited category under the agreement, as a category separate from the export subsidy (in law or in fact) category. Moreover, even the United States did not consider during the Uruguay Round that a high level of exports would satisfy an "in fact" test, since it did not characterize such situations as export subsidies but instead part of a separate category of trade-related subsidies.

7.99 According to Australia, this goes to underline that countries have always been careful not to confuse the categories for which disciplines are being negotiated, and not to overreach themselves on what it was sensible to seek disciplines from a practical point of view. The disciplines on export subsidies are in respect of subsidies that discriminate, that target, that favour, exports against domestic sales. Any other construction would lead to a potentially unworkable discipline

[89] See section I.1.b of MTN.GNG/NG10/W/29, 22 November 1989: *Elements of the Framework for Negotiations - Submission by the United States.*

and lead to uncertainty about its application by governments. That sort of uncertainty is what the new DSU is supposed to reduce because an automatic system without a high degree of certainty in its future application would undermine its legitimacy.

7.100 In the context of the negotiating history, Australia states, MTN.GNG/NG10/23[90] dated 7 November 1990 was circulated by the Chairperson of Negotiating Group 10 prior to the Ministerial meeting at Heysel in December 1990. The footnote to "in fact" (then numbered Footnote 3) read in its entirety[91]:

> This standard is met when*ever* the facts demonstrate that the granting of a subsidy, without having been made legally contingent upon export performance, is in *practice* tied to actual or anticipated exportation or export earnings. (emphasis supplied by Australia)

7.101 Thus, Australia states, the unagreed text that the Chairperson sent to Heysel in December 1990 had two very different aspects to that which is in the SCM Agreement, that is: (a) what the facts had to demonstrate was the standard of "in practice" rather than the much higher standard of "in fact"; and (b) the important, limiting qualifier of the second sentence had not been added. For Australia, the change in the drafting makes it clear that some participants were not prepared to accept a nebulous "in practice" standard. The current text appeared in the Draft Final Act, MTN.TNC/W/FA, of 20 December 1991, except that the change from "whenever" to "when", came later from the Legal Drafting Group.

7.102 Australia submits that the "in fact" standard in Article 3.1(a) of the SCM Agreement is not some undefined *de facto* standard. The "in fact" standard is defined in footnote 4. In order to establish that that standard is met, footnote 4 must be satisfied. This sets a high threshold for the complainant. The construction that the United States puts on Article 3.1(a) and footnote 4 of the SCM Agreement is not borne out by the drafting. The text of Article 3.1(a) says: "subsidies contingent, ... in fact, whether solely or as one of several other conditions, upon export performance ...[footnote 4 omitted]". In order to prove that any particular measure before the Panel satisfies this, the United States must prove that the measure is a subsidy contingent in fact, whether solely or as one of several other conditions, upon export performance, where the "in fact" standard is defined in footnote 4 of the SCM Agreement. The text is clear that "contingent in fact" is a condition that must be proven to exist.

7.103 Australia observes that the United States seeks to argue that: "the mere fact that a subsidy is accorded [*sic*] to enterprises which export" means "the fact that the recipients happen to export is the *only* factor indicating that a subsidy is

---

90 Australia states that this was originally circulated as MTN.GNG.NG10/W/38/Rev.3.

91 Australia noted that this formulation was first presented in MTN.GNG/NG10/W/38/Rev.2.

a *de facto* export subsidy."[92] According to Australia, this misrepresents the limitation inherent in the second sentence of footnote 4 of the SCM Agreement. This sentence means that the complainant cannot just look to an enterprise's exports as the grounds for proving the standard in the first sentence. Of course, it can be assumed that a case would only arise where there was exportation. Accordingly, the interpretation that the United States seeks to put on the limitation inherent in the second sentence of footnote 4 of the SCM Agreement would trivialize it. This additional sentence underlines that the level of exports by an enterprise cannot be the basis for proof of "in fact tied", i.e. the extent of exportation by the enterprise is not relevant for the required demonstration. Rather, the complainant must show that the granting of the subsidy is in fact tied in its application to export performance and so favours export over domestic sales.

7.104 Australia notes that the United States argues that: "[r]ather, an export subsidy will exist when actual or anticipated exportation is merely one of several *potential criteria influencing* the bestowal of benefits."[93] (emphasis supplied by Australia) Australia asserts that this is not what the text says, which is that the granting of the subsidy has to be in fact tied to actual or anticipated exportation or export earnings. This not only confuses what the United States might have wanted out of the Uruguay Round and what is in the SCM Agreement, but even seems to go well beyond it. The idea that "potential criteria" might determine whether a measure was in breach of a treaty obligation would make a nonsense of a binding treaty. Australia queries: Who would decide what are "potential criteria"? Presumably, either the complainant or the panel. There is no way in advance that a Member could decide what might be regarded as "potential criteria" by others when seeking to formulate its commercial policy in keeping with its treaty obligations. The recognition by a government that an enterprise exports and that internationally competitive industries are desirable does not somehow convert a subsidy that does not favour exports into a prohibited measure.

7.105 According to Australia, a logical conclusion of the United States' argument is that if a government gives an enterprise a subsidy in the knowledge that it exports, and does not expressly say that exportation is a bad thing, then the subsidy is prohibited. The government of virtually every Member provides subsidies that knowingly go to some enterprises that export and these governments are normally on the record that they consider exports a good thing, and indeed are on the record praising successful export industries. To suggest that suddenly all those measures fall within the scope of Article 3.1(a) of the SCM Agreement would be to radically upset the balance of obligations under the WTO Agreement and risk making the SCM Agreement, in particular, completely unworkable.

[92] See *supra*, para. 7.81.
[93] See *supra*, para. 7.82.

7.106 Australia maintains that the United States again seeks to widen the obvious meaning of the text through its argument that, by explicitly including a footnote emphasizing that subsidies are prohibited without having been made expressly contingent on export performance, the SCM Agreement recognizes that Members may well attempt to mask the export-orientation of particular benefits by claiming they are bestowed without explicit contingencies. This is not a rule about "expressly contingent" or "explicit contingencies". The "in law" standard is about the requirement of export performance being just that, in law, e.g. in legislation. The "in fact" standard is about "in fact tied" by some means such as an administrative instrument. Indeed, in both cases, the tie must be explicit, either in law or in fact. With respect to the United States' request that the Panel make a determination on the basis of the "facts and circumstances", Australia asserts that the findings by the Panel on each measure before it will need to be made on "the facts", not the "circumstances", and whether "the facts" demonstrate unequivocally that the standard in footnote 4 of the SCM Agreement is met.

7.107 Australia submits that, in accordance with the principles of treaty interpretation, the Panel needs to look at the wording in the treaty in its own context. The final text of the SCM Agreement is part of the balance of rights and obligations under the WTO. This includes the strict limitation under footnote 4 of the SCM Agreement to the scope of "in fact". Negotiating countries did not sign on to, and would not have signed on to, the sort of open ended interpretation that the United States is now seeking to read into the text. This provision must also be read in the context of Parts III and V of the SCM Agreement, where there is provision for multilateral and unilateral remedy from adverse effects allegedly being caused by subsidies. Quite apart from this case, a widening of the scope of the meaning of "in fact" would have a potentially far-reaching impact on the balance of Members' rights and obligations under the WTO.

7.108 Australia contends that the United States' arguments in this case regarding several measures in respect of a single enterprise can tend to obscure the substantial issues being dealt with. Rules regarding prohibition must relate to the type of measure involved, rather than leaving discretion to a panel to decide on the situation. Without that clarity, it would not be possible for Members to have any surety that they are complying with their treaty obligations. This is quite different from a trade effects test where there is no breach of treaty obligation but rather a subsequent obligation to remove the non-violation nullification or impairment (including serious prejudice under the SCM Agreement), if demonstrated.

7.109 In Australia's view, if there were to be some undefined concept such as a high level of exports or the possibility that an enterprise would increase its level of exports, which would render a measure prohibited according to a Panel ruling, then the treaty would be unworkable and Members would be able to challenge measures capriciously. Moreover, if an adverse interpretation were to rely upon there being only one enterprise in an industry, then this would be biased against smaller Members and would even potentially open the door to a future finding that the receipt by a sole domestic seller (which also exported) of any subsidy would be a prohibited measure. Australia states that this would clearly not be the object and purpose of the discipline under Article 3.1(a) of the SCM Agreement.

7.110 On the other hand, Australia asserts, consider the case where there were, say, two enterprises in an industry, one of which was domestically-oriented and one of which was export-oriented. The creation of a rule that meant that a subsidy programme was a prohibited measure when received by one company, but not when received by the other, would be a substantial move away from a sensible rules-based discipline. It would be a bias against smaller Members and would upset the balance of rights and obligations negotiated under the WTO. It would make the day-to-day provision of advice to governments on complying with their treaty obligations almost impossible to do with any certainty. At the end of the day, this would be a degeneration into the situation of a large Member being able to threaten a dispute with any smaller Member that did not fully comply with its demands, since there would no longer be a framework of objective rules against which Members could act to obtain the safe haven of compliance.

7.111 Australia submits that once the Rubicon has been crossed of using a subjective level of exports test as being the determinant for "in fact", the logical consequences become increasingly difficult to reconcile with a sensible regime. As one example, Australia considers the situation of any non-specific subsidy programme, i.e. non-specific in the sense of Articles 2.1, 2, and 4 of the SCM Agreement. Invariably, that subsidy will be being received by some enterprise that exports much of its product and indeed may even be wholly devoted to exports of some product. Australia queries whether that would mean that that measure is, in the hands of that enterprise, a prohibited measure under Article 3.1(a) of the SCM Agreement and so specific under Article 2.3 of the SCM Agreement? Would this then mean that the entire programme suddenly becomes specific? Australia maintains that these types of consequences would make the Agreement incoherent and potentially unworkable. Australia points out that, to put this in perspective, this is not an issue such as countervail, where there is a degree of discretion placed in the hands of the investigating authorities (at least in the first instance) to take decisions on such matters as the status of a measure. This case is dealing with the issue of the conditions under which the granting or maintenance of a measure is inconsistent with treaty obligations.

7.112 Australia stresses that the concepts of "in law" and "in fact" should not be confused with *de jure* and *de facto*, especially *de facto*. The text of the SCM Agreement could always have simply said "*de jure* or *de facto*" and left those terms undefined. Indeed, the United States said that these were in the Tokyo Round Subsidies Agreement implicitly.

7.113 Australia notes that what the text actually does is to introduce a new term, "in fact", and then it goes on to define it. While people will often use the expression "in fact" as being simply the translation of "*de facto*", this is not the case here. Thus, the use of expressions such as de jure and de facto in this context has the potential for semantic confusion. The expression "in fact" in Article 3.1(a) of the SCM Agreement is a special term defined in the agreement through Article 3.1(a), including, in particular, footnote 4. The application of the term is restricted through that definition.

7.114 Australia maintains that a key to the interpretation of "in law or in fact" is to ensure certainty to governments, to avoid harassment and the possibility of being at some stage found to be in breach of Article 3.1(a) of the SCM Agreement. The problems here would be compounded by any views about allocation of measures across time into the future, which would be impossible to bring into conformity ex post facto. Industries and governments would have great difficulty in living with that sort of uncertainty, which would undermine the legitimacy of the WTO with domestic constituents.

7.115 The **United States** argues that the inclusion of an "in fact" standard in Article 3.1(a) of the SCM Agreement inherently requires the Panel to conduct a case-by-case analysis of the relevant facts to determine whether the subsidy in question contravenes Article 3 of the SCM Agreement. However, that does not mean that the Panel must engage in an abstract or hypothetical analysis of when the standard in Article 3.1 may be satisfied. The Panel need only decide based upon the totality of facts before it whether the subsidies in question are "in fact tied to actual or anticipated exportation or export earnings." The Panel should look to the assumptions underlying the government's decision to grant the subsidy in order to determine whether the "in fact" standard has been met. The drafters of this provision recognized that an "in fact" export subsidy would depend on the particular facts surrounding the grant of the assistance. As footnote 4 to Article 3.1(a) states, the "in fact" standard is met "when *the facts* demonstrate" that the granting of the aid is tied to actual or anticipated exportation or export earnings.

7.116 For the United States, it is clear that the Panel is expected to review all of the facts surrounding the granting of the subsidy, whatever those facts may be. The drafters of the Agreement could have listed exactly *which* facts or factors are to be considered - as they did in other places in the Agreement. However, no such limitation was provided in this instance. The Panel must therefore take into consideration all the information relevant to making an "objective assessment of the facts of the case and the applicability of and conformity with the relevant agreement" as required under Article 11 of the DSU.

7.117 The United States declares that a case-by-case approach is entirely consistent with the requirements of Article 11 of the DSU. Indeed, in this respect, the Panel can draw on the experience of other panels and the Appellate Body in interpreting and applying Article III of GATT 1994 in cases of *de facto* discrimination. In its Report in *Japan - Taxes on Alcoholic Beverages*

("*Japan - Alcoholic Beverages*"), the Appellate Body explicitly endorsed a case-by-case approach to such disputes:

> We agree with the practice under the GATT 1947 of determining whether imported and domestic products are "like" on a case-by-case basis....
>
> ... In applying the criteria cited in *Border Tax Adjustments* to the facts of any particular case, and in considering other criteria that may also be relevant in certain cases, panels can only apply their best judgement in determining whether in fact products are "like". This will always involve an unavoidable element of individual, discretionary judgement.[94]

7.118 The United States asserts that drawing the line between *de facto* discrimination and legitimate domestic tax measures or regulations is a task which, in a sense, mirrors the task this Panel faces - yet past panels have showed themselves equal to the task of gathering and evaluating facts, and coming to legal conclusions on the basis of their best judgement of those facts.

7.119 The United States submits that the Panel's inquiry concerning *de facto* export subsidies can also be analogized to past panels' examination of the issue of whether discriminatory taxation is protective in nature. As the Appellate Body stated in *Japan - Alcoholic Beverages:*

> ... we believe that an examination in any case of whether dissimilar taxation has been applied so as to afford protection requires a comprehensive and objective analysis of the structure and application of the measure in question on domestic as compared to imported products. We believe it is possible to examine objectively the underlying criteria used in a particular tax measure, its structure, and its overall application to ascertain whether it is applied in a way that affords protection to domestic products.
>
> Although it is true that the aim of a measure may not be easily ascertained, nevertheless its protective application can most often be discerned from the design, the architecture, and the revealing structure of a measure. The very magnitude of the dissimilar taxation in a particular case may be evidence of such a protective application, as the Panel rightly concluded in this case. Most often, there will be other factors to be considered as well. In conducting this inquiry, panels should give full consideration to all the

[94] WT/DS8/AB/R, WT/DS10/AB/R, WT/DS11/AB/R, adopted 1 November 1996, DSR 1996:I, 97, at 113.

> relevant facts and all the relevant circumstances in any given case.[95]

7.120 The United States submits that the Panel should determine whether *these* subsidies are in fact "tied to" export performance by examining the totality of facts and circumstances in this case. Whether a tie exists may be objectively discerned from the history, design, architecture and the structure of the subsidies, corroborated by public statements by government officials, statements by the industry benefiting from the subsidies, the level of the recipient's exports and other relevant evidence. As stated above, footnote 4 to Article 3 directs the Panel to examine the facts by stating that the "in fact" standard is met "when *the facts* demonstrate" that the granting of the aid is tied to actual or anticipated exportation or export earnings. The United States asserts that even Australia agrees that establishing a violation of Article 3 involves a "matter of proving that the act of granting the subsidy is tied to export sales."

7.121 The United States observes that this approach is also consistent with the European Community's suggestion during the Uruguay Round negotiations that the "in fact" standard is met where the "facts which were known - or should clearly have been known - to the government when granting the subsidy demonstrate that the subsidy, without having been made expressly contingent upon export performance, was indeed intended to increase exports."[96]

7.122 The United States asserts that Australia's view that the "in fact" standard is met only when the subsidy is *explicitly* tied to exportation or export earnings through some means such as an administrative arrangement should be rejected as it would merge the categories of subsidies "contingent in law" and subsidies "contingent in fact." To the United States, Australia's proposed interpretation would effectively write the "in fact" language out of the SCM Agreement thereby partially defeating the purpose of the prohibition in Article 3. The distinction between the "in law" and "in fact" standard is that "in law" subsidies are explicitly contingent and "in fact" subsidies are implicitly contingent. The United States posits that these standards are not defined, as Australia suggests, by whether the contingency appears in legislation versus some type of administrative instrument.

7.123 The United States also argues that Australia's position is not supported by the negotiating history of the provision. The negotiating history of this provision demonstrates that the distinction between an "in fact" and an "in law" export subsidy is that an "in fact" subsidy does not make the conferring of the benefit

---

[95] WT/DS8/AB/R, WT/DS10/AB/R, WT/DS11/AB/R, adopted 1 November 1996, DSR 1996:I, 97, at 120; the United States asserts that this passage was also cited with approval in Appellate Body Report, *Canada - Certain Measures Concerning Periodicals*, WT/DS31/AB/R, adopted 30 July 1997, DSR 1997:I, 449, at 474-475.

[96] MTN.GNG/NG10/W/31, 27 November 1989, *Elements of the Negotiating Framework - Submission by the European Community*, United States Exhibit 57.

expressly contingent on export performance, in any form. The "in fact" standard was included because the countries negotiating the WTO Agreement were concerned that limiting their prohibition to subsidies with *express* export contingencies would permit governments to escape the sanctions of Article 3.1(a) by merely omitting an explicit reference to export performance from the characterization of the benefit. As the European Community warned: "experience has shown that government practices may be easily manipulated or modified in order to avoid [a *de jure*] prohibition...."[97] A prohibition of subsidies "which are *de jure* (that is, expressly) made contingent upon export performance is open to circumvention."[98] As a result of these concerns, both "in law" export subsidies - where government aid is "expressly contingent" upon export performance - and "in fact" export subsidies - where the exportation requirement is not explicit - were included as prohibited subsidies.

7.124 Furthermore, the United States asserts, imposing the requirement that prohibited export subsidies are only those that are explicitly contingent upon exports would defeat the purpose of prohibiting "in fact" export subsidies. If express statements of export contingency were required for both "in law" and "in fact" subsidies, governments could easily circumvent the prohibition in Article 3 by merely deleting explicit references to the export-contingency requirement. This was just the kind of "manipulation" that the "in fact" provision was designed to prevent. Since export subsidies are considered so egregious by the SCM Agreement that they are prohibited (rather than merely actionable), it seems unlikely that negotiators would have allowed countries to avoid their obligations by clever draftsmanship. Australia's proposed interpretation should therefore be rejected because it is at odds with the history and purpose of the provision.

7.125 The United States maintains that because Australia argues that both "in law" and "in fact" subsidies must have express statements of export contingency, it is forced to find another difference between these two forms of prohibited subsidies. Australia therefore suggests that "in law" export subsidies are those created by legislation or regulations, whereas "in fact" export subsidies are those set forth in non-legislative administrative instruments. Australia proposes that an "in fact" export subsidy may only be found if (1) the document creating the government aid is in the form of an administrative instrument, and (2) that instrument contains an express statement that the aid is export-contingent. To the United States, it is obvious that Australia has designed this test so that the instruments bestowing the subsidies upon Howe would fall outside of the definition of a prohibited export subsidy. However, Australia's attempt to distinguish "in law" and

---

[97] MTN.GNG/NG10/W/31, 27 November 1989, *Elements of the Negotiating Framework - Submission by the European Community*, United States Exhibit 57.

[98] *Ibid.*

"in fact" subsidies based on *the type of document* announcing the government aid must fail.

7.126 The United States declares that Australia's theory does not have a rational basis. There is no difference *in effect* between a government provision included in a law, a regulation or a document issued by a duly authorized government official in the form of an administrative instrument or executive order. All are issued by a government entity or official with the necessary legal authority to require adherence to its terms. All have the force and effect of law and must be honoured by the nation's public entities and private citizens. The distinguishing feature of "in law" and "in fact" subsidies cannot therefore be the type of document creating the subsidy - but whether or not the granting of the benefit is expressly or in fact tied to export performance.

7.127 Finally, the United States maintains, contrary to Australia's argument, the United States is not suggesting an expansion of the definition of prohibited export subsidies through the creation of an "unidentified level of exports" test or "trade effects" test. Australia bases this claim on its view that the United States' case turns on the argument that some undefined level of exports by an enterprise is indicative of its status as a prohibited subsidy. Examining a recipient's level of exports does not transform an "in fact" export subsidy case into a "trade effects" case. The level of an enterprise's exports is just one factor to be considered in determining whether that enterprise received a prohibited export subsidy. Footnote 4 to Article 3 does not preclude consideration of the level of exports, it simply proscribes finding a prohibited export subsidy based *solely* upon the level of exports. In fact, the explicit reference to level of exports in Article 3 seems to indicate that the drafters specifically contemplated that the level of exports would be taken into account in determining whether an "in fact" subsidy exists.

7.128 According to the United States, there is a significant difference between examining whether a subsidy was tied to exportation at the time it was granted (as is necessary in an "in fact" subsidy case) and what happens after a subsidy is conferred (as is required in an actionable subsidy case). Actionable subsidy cases examine the adverse effects of a subsidy evidenced by injury to a Member's domestic industry, nullification or impairment of a Member's benefits, or serious prejudice to a Member's interests.[99] The definition of "serious prejudice" also looks to the consequences of a subsidy, such as whether subsidized goods displaced a member's goods in the subsidizing country or in a third country market, whether significant price undercutting occurred, or whether a subsidized primary product was able to increase its world market share.[100] Regardless of the particular standard, all of these inquiries examine the subsidy's effect *after* it has

[99] SCM Agreement, Article 5.

[100] SCM Agreement, Article 6.3.

been granted. They do not address the facts as they existed at the time of the granting of the subsidy.

7.129 The United States asserts that nothing in the arguments it has presented suggests that a subsidy would necessarily be considered an "export subsidy" simply because exports increased after a subsidy was granted. In this case, the Panel must consider the facts underlying the decision to grant the aid which existed at the time the government made the decision and whether that decision was tied to actual or anticipated exportation or export earnings. The United States has not suggested that, in this case or any future case, an increase in exports after a subsidy has been provided could retroactively alter the nature of the subsidy. The United States has, therefore, not used a "trade effects" test for an "in fact" export subsidies case. Instead, the U.S. government has presented evidence of Howe's export performance at the time the decision to grant the subsidies was made, and Howe's expected export performance as anticipated at that time. This evidence meets the standard for determining an "in fact" subsidy set forth in footnote 4 to Article 3.1(a) of the SCM Agreement, which, as explained above, permits the consideration of an enterprise's level of exports.

7.130 **Australia** states that Article 3.1(a) of the SCM Agreement only prohibits subsidies that are contingent upon export performance, i.e. that favour exports over domestic sales. Australia notes that the United States has continued to quote selectively from the EC Uruguay Round negotiating paper, MTN/GNG/NG10/W/31, and to omit EC comments that underline that the issue in that paper for both *de jure* and *de facto* export subsidies was in respect of subsidies that favour exports.

7.131 Australia also asserts that the United States mischaracterizes the points made by Australia regarding "in fact" in saying that it would effectively write the "in fact" language out of the SCM Agreement. The United States appears to consider that "in law" is synonymous with "expressly". Of course, Australia states, "in law" means that it would be set out expressly in a legal instrument. However, it is quite possible for the granting of a subsidy to be expressly contingent upon export performance through administrative actions without it being expressly set out in law. Australia asserts that the Panel needs to address the meaning of "in law" and "in fact" under the SCM Agreement and not how the United States might consider that *de jure* and *de facto* should be used outside the WTO context. Under the *Vienna Convention*, the Panel needs to look at the ordinary meaning given to the words "in law". If, under the treaty, this were supposed to mean "expressly", as the United States seemed to be proposing, then it would have said so.

7.132 In the view of Australia, the purpose of the "in fact" provision is to provide a way of dealing with the situation where the administration of a subsidy programme allows the disbursement of funds to favour exports, i.e. to provide subsidies to firms tied to export performance. Interpreting the provision in this way is not to write the "in fact" standard out of the SCM Agreement, as suggested by the United States. Instead, according to Australia, what it achieves is: (a) to make it consistent with the language of the agreement: (b) to make it consistent with the language in Article 11 of the DSU by which panel cases have to be assessed; and (c) to make it consistent with a workable and balanced view of the object and purpose of Article 3.1(a) of the SCM Agreement. To allow a violation case to be won on weak inferential grounds would be at odds with a rules-based system. An "in fact" case may often be difficult to prove. However, the SCM Agreement provides fast, effective means of relief from adverse effect on a multilateral and unilateral level through Parts III and V. In the absence of a case under Parts III or V, it is highly questionable that a weak case, missing the facts to demonstrate that the granting of the measure was in fact tied to export performance, should be able to be addressed through Part II of the SCM Agreement.

7.133 Australia suggests that it may be useful to consider just a couple of possible examples of where the "in fact" provision would apply, i.e. where the administration of a subsidy programme allows the disbursement of subsidies to favour exports. Any number of hypothetical constructions of this sort can be created, for example:

(a) the administrators of a scheme have the authority to determine the amount of subsidy being provided to an individual firm and do so on the basis of exports rather than some other criteria such as investment or production; or

(b) the administrators of a scheme have the authority to discriminate amongst firms in the same industry by not paying the subsidy unless concrete export targets are met.

7.134 Australia submits that the term "in law" needs to be taken as meaning just that: in law. The text of Article 3.1(a) of the SCM Agreement makes the distinction between "in law" and "in fact". If the intent was to make the distinction between explicit and implicit, i.e. between expressly and some trade effects test, as seems to be being suggested by the United States, the text would have said so. For example, it could have read: "subsidies contingent, explicitly or implicitly, upon export performance" with a similar footnote as footnote 4 on "implicitly". However, that is not the text. The distinction is between "in law" and "in fact" where, in both cases, there must be an actual tie with export performance.

7.135 According to Australia, WTO rules on violation are not supposed to be about subjective judgments by panels on trade effects or mind-reading what ministers may have been thinking two years ago. Article 3.1(a) and footnote 4 of the SCM Agreement are about a panel reaching the conclusion, demonstrated through an objective assessment of facts, that the granting of a subsidy is contingent upon export performance, even though it may not be required in law.

7.136 Australia submits that, in a trivial sense, every panel must undertake a case-by-case examination and analysis of the dispute before it. However, the issue here is whether the outcome is to be an arbitrary one that could well vary from panel to panel, or whether there is to be the normal consistency and certainty required of a rules-based system with respect for a Member's sovereignty to be allowed to adopt measures that are not explicitly inconsistent with the WTO Agreement. The important principle at stake here is the necessity under a rules-based system for governments acting in good faith to be able to determine WTO consistency of proposals in advance of their implementation, and in the absence of a dispute and a panel decision. Unless a government can know in advance what its obligations are, it would be placed in a situation that would only risk bringing the rules into disrepute. Indeed, Article 3.2 of the DSU sets out that: "[t]he dispute settlement system of the WTO is a central element in providing *security and predictability* to the multilateral trading system." (emphasis supplied by Australia)

7.137 Australia reasserts that Article 3.1(a) of the SCM Agreement uses the phrases of "in law" and "in fact" with "in fact" limited through footnote 4 of the SCM Agreement. There is nothing in the ordinary meaning of the phrases or in the drafting history to suggest that these expressions should not be taken as meaning other than through either a legislative instrument or, alternatively, through administrative action of some sort. Indeed, the text requires a complainant to prove that "the facts demonstrate ... is in fact tied". This is not a call for arbitrary judgement, but rather expresses the necessity for the complainant to prove its case that the granting of the subsidy is actually tied to exportation or export earnings.

7.138 According to Australia, the SCM Agreement does not list which facts are to be considered because the issue is one of demonstration of an actual tie and so what needed to be listed was what the granting of the subsidy was to be "tied to", i.e. "actual or anticipated exportation or export earnings". These are the points that had to be listed and listed exhaustively. The text does not talk of some high proportion of benefits going to exports or the incidence of the subsidy in relation to exports. It could have, and the United States argued in the Uruguay Round negotiations that it should, but it did not. Instead, the final text requires a factual demonstration, i.e. an objective demonstration that the granting of the subsidy be tied to exportation or export earnings.

7.139 Australia takes note of the United States' citation from the Appellate Body Report in *Japan - Alcoholic Beverages* that "the examination requires a comprehensive and objective analysis" and that "it is possible to examine objectively the underlying criteria ... to ascertain whether it is applied in a way that affords protection to domestic products."[101] Australia states that this is an objective assessment of the impact of the tax measure. The first sentence of the sec-

[101] WT/DS8/AB/R, WT/DS10/AB/R, WT/DS11/AB/R, adopted 1 November 1996, DSR 1996:I, 97, at 120.

ond paragraph of the United States' citation from the Appellate Body Report[102] underlines that it is the actual measure and not some subjective assessment of the aim of the measure that is at issue. Moreover, Australia asserts, in that case, the Appellate Body goes on to emphasize that "[t]he dissimilar taxation must be more than *de minimis*."[103] This is quite different from this current dispute, which is not about affording protection in excess of *de minimis* levels, but rather whether the standard of Footnote 4 of the SCM Agreement is satisfied. A government can be expected to understand the impact of different taxation arrangements on products. However, it cannot be expected to foresee what view a panel might have on the incidence of a domestic subsidy.

7.140 Australia observes that the United States goes on to say that the Panel should, among other things, focus on "the design, architecture and the structure of the subsidies", picking up the phrase used by the Appellate Body in *Japan - Alcoholic Beverages*.[104] Read in context, the Appellate Body did not mean by "design" the "process of designing", since that would go back to fathoming the aim of the government concerned. The "design, architecture and the structure of the subsidies" can only refer to the legal structure of the subsidy arrangements and their administration, rather than the issue of intent or prior measures. Australia agrees that the Panel needs to look at the contracts, what they actually say, and how they were administered.

7.141 Australia alleges that the United States mischaracterizes the Australian position in respect of the difference between "in law" and "in fact". They are not the same. Australia considers that for the "in law" standard to be met it has to be just that - the contingency on export performance must be set out in law. This is clear from footnote 4 of the SCM Agreement, which refers to "legally contingent". By contrast, "in fact" would arise through explicit administrative action rather than being set out in law. The complainant has the obligation to prove that this is being done. The way in which a complainant would demonstrate that there is such administrative action will depend on the particular case.

7.142 Australia argues that it is clear from the United States' argument that it misunderstands the point being made by Australia by interpreting the Australian position to mean that an "in fact" export subsidy may only be found if (1) the document creating the government aid is in the form of an administrative instrument, and (2) that instrument contains an express statement that the aid is export-contingent. Australia did not say that there had to be a document creating the government aid and is not sure what the United States means when its says the

---

[102] WT/DS8/AB/R, WT/DS10/AB/R, WT/DS11/AB/R, adopted 1 November 1996, DSR 1996:I, 97, at 120. This sentence reads: "Although it is true that the aim of a measure may not be easily ascertained, nevertheless its protective application can most often be discerned from the design, the architecture, and the revealing structure of a measure."

[103] *Ibid.*, DSR 1996:I, 97, at 122, final paragraph.

[104] WT/DS8/AB/R, WT/DS10/AB/R, WT/DS11/AB/R, adopted 1 November 1996.

"document ... is in the form of an administrative instrument." There may be a language problem here. Moreover, Australia certainly did not say that "that instrument" [whatever it might mean] "contains an express statement ... ."

7.143 Australia contends that the distribution of any subsidy will have a legal basis and have to be administered to some degree, even if it is only to check the paper work and write out the cheques. For the "in law" standard to be met, the granting of the subsidy has to be "legally contingent" upon export performance. By contrast, the "in fact" standard is met when that distribution is still contingent upon export performance but when it is done administratively without it being legally contingent. For example, the administrative instrument might be Ministerial discretion in giving money to companies on the basis of their export earnings in the previous period. Conceptually, there are many ways in which this could be done. However, the payments must be actually tied to exportation or export earnings, either future or past, and this tie must be direct and not the result of some theoretical apportionment by the complainant between domestic and export sales because the company concerned exports.

7.144 Australia insists that it did not say that the complainant needs to find a piece of paper with an explicit tie in it, since that would be too high a threshold and defeat the purpose of preventing circumvention. However, the complainant must prove that the administration of the granting of the subsidy involved has some form of explicit tie.

7.145 With respect to the United States' argument that it proffered evidence of Howe's high level of exports to show what the Australian government considered *at the time* the aid was given, Australia argues that the United States clarifies that its legal argument relates only to what might have been considered as future export trends at the time the contracts were executed. Australia thus assumes that "*at the time* the aid was given" means the time of execution of the contracts rather than the actual time the decisions were taken to make payments after the first payment under the grant contract. The United States appears to be unconcerned here with what happens afterwards. To Australia, this appears to still mean that the United States' argument is no more than a level of exports test as the key criterion, rather than a demonstration that the granting of the subsidy is actually tied to exportation or export earnings. If actual export performance subsequent to the establishment of a programme is irrelevant, including to future payments, then there is no tie. The United States is not even arguing about the actual impact on exports let alone the legal issue of whether the granting is tied to export performance.

7.146 Australia maintains that the United States is saying that it is not making a case about what actually happens to exports subsequent to the execution of the contracts. This would mean that if the Panel considered that the issue was not the granting of the grant contract, but rather the granting of the grants under the grant contract, then the United States would consider that its arguments would not apply.

7.147 Regarding the United States comments that there is a significant difference between examining whether a subsidy was tied to exportation at the time it was granted and what happens after a subsidy is conferred, Australia states that the issue of prohibition under Article 3.1(a) of the SCM Agreement must be strictly construed. There is multilateral remedy for adverse effect under Part III of the SCM Agreement, including adverse effect caused by exports. The SCM Agreement makes provision for remedy under both Parts III and V where exports are causing adverse effect, in particular where there is an increase in exports that causes serious prejudice. In such circumstances, especially where Article 6.1(a) of the SCM Agreement applies, increased exports would usually make a case of serious prejudice difficult to rebut. A principle of interpretation is that:

> [o]ne of the corollaries of the "general rule of interpretation" in the *Vienna Convention* is that interpretation must give meaning and effect to all the terms of the treaty. An interpreter is not free to adopt a reading that would result in reducing whole clauses or paragraphs of a treaty to redundancy or inutility.[105]

Australia submits that the "in fact" test in Article 3.1(a) of the SCM Agreement is not there to deal with all cases where exports are causing injury. Rather it is there to deal with the situation of "in law or in fact" as Australia has described it. Members have Part III of the SCM Agreement to seek multilateral remedy in other cases.

(b) Operational Considerations

7.148 **Australia** adds that, apart from the issue of maintaining the balance of rights and obligations about what was negotiated in the Uruguay Round, a key issue here is to ensure that the interpretation of the disciplines under Article 3.1(a) is workable. This is not a situation where WTO rules are being implemented through domestic legislation, such as for countervailing. In that case, domestic law- makers and the courts will converge to a practical arrangement, which is in conformity with WTO obligations. The obligations of officials are domestic: to implement the domestic law subject to judicial review. The situation is quite different where officials have to give advice to their government, and ministers have to make decisions on that advice, about conformity of proposed new programmes with WTO rules. Of course, countervailing duty legislation has to go through this once, i.e. when changes are put in place, but not on a day-to-day basis when being implemented domestically. However, with industry

[105] Appellate Body Report, *United States -Gasoline*, WT/DS2/AB/R, adopted 20 May 1996, DSR 1996:I, 3, at 21.

policies in goods, services and intellectual property, officials have to give advice every day on the WTO-consistency of new policy proposals.

7.149 Australia underlines that it is critical that officials be able to give advice on clear-cut rules. Australia can accept that, in early stages, there may be some differences in view over rules, without being absolutely certain that that envelope for manoeuvre will be maintained after a dispute. But that is quite different from a situation where some form of *de facto* test would make it virtually impossible to give clear advice.

7.150 Australia states that it is a long-standing integral part of the GATT, and now the WTO, that there is always a small risk of a non-violation case. Australia states that government officials give advice on this where required, for example on subsidies in respect of bindings. However, that does not involve a treaty commitment. Ministers have to know whether an action would breach a treaty. They can accept that there might be complaints of the non-violation type, but that is absolutely different from a case of violation of a treaty commitment. If this dispute led to an outcome where a Member's government can never be certain about whether it is consistent with its WTO obligations, except by not having a policy at all, that will serve to bring the system into disrepute. Governments will not accept an edict that subsidies or some other policy instrument are going to be somehow banned by the back door. Indeed, one potential outcome is that governments will take less care rather than more.

7.151 Australia asserts that the structure of the SCM Agreement was to give greater certainty to governments in the provision of subsidies. The aim of defining a subsidy was to give greater certainty about what sort of measures might be subject to multilateral action and to countervailing duty action. The aim of the "red/amber/green" distinction was also to give safe harbour for green subsidies and to provide a more effective remedy for adverse effects case. In reality, there was little change to the categories of prohibited subsidies. Subsidies falling under Article 3.1(b) of the SCM Agreement were already covered (apart from GATT exceptions) by Article III of GATT (or indeed also under the WTO by paragraph 1 of the Annex to the Agreement on Trade-Related Investment Measures). Any interpretation that pushed back the boundaries of Article 3.1(a) of the SCM Agreement would lead to governments and industry being once again placed in the situation of great uncertainty about future action under the WTO.

7.152 Australia states that governments and industry can accept rules that apply to all Members provided that they know the ground rules, and provided that the status of proposed measures is clear. Members would all have difficulties dealing with a situation where no one would know until there was a WTO challenge. The situation would become absurd if, in addition, the success or otherwise of a challenge depended on economic developments or newspaper articles. The problems would be further compounded if the rules were seen to be different for small and large Members in their application. It would be a retrograde step for the WTO if Members with large domestic markets and numerous firms were implicitly subject to different rules than smaller Members with smaller domestic markets, and possibly single sellers, but a reliance on other markets for growth due to economic factors such as returns to scale.

7.153 Australia underlines that the Panel needs to bear in mind that whatever comes out of this Panel must result in an operational and workable system for governments acting in good faith if the WTO subsidies regime is not to be brought into disrepute. A government knows well when it provides greater protection for individual products such as in the GATT 1994 Article III:2 case cited by the United States. However, by contrast, it could not know in advance what view a panel would take if the grounds put forward by the United States were to be adopted by the Panel and the Appellate Body.

7.154 Similarly, Australia continues, if a government was paying money on the basis of export performance through administrative action, it would know that that was the case and it would know that it was in breach of its WTO obligations. The situation would be clear to the government concerned. However, by contrast, the United States' position is that even if a government knows that its decisions have absolutely nothing to do with exports, it might still be found to be in breach of its WTO obligations. A government would be faced with the situation where if a company, or some of the companies in an industry, are export-oriented or even just export, a panel might find that its WTO obligations had been inadvertently breached. That is not a viable situation, and underlines that the United States' approach to treaty interpretation would lead to absurd results.

7.155 Australia states that, in a rules-based system, officials must be able to give clear advice to governments whether proposals are consistent or inconsistent with WTO obligations, i.e. whether treaty obligations would be breached. This cannot be done on the basis that, for example, some firms in an industry depend on exports for their viability. In any small country many industries export and, regardless of the proportion of their product that they export, depend on other markets for achieving profitability and some economies of scale. The United States' position is that potentially a subsidy to a firm that does not export at all, and has no intention of exporting, can be a prohibited export subsidy under Article 3.1(a) of the SCM Agreement. This sort of scenario underlines that the United States' logic can lead to any number of absurd situations.

7.156 Australia reiterates that a rules-based system must provide clear guidance to governments about the nature of their WTO obligations. Governments can accept that where market developments lead to allegations of adverse effects by other Members, then there may be non-violation cases brought, including cases under Part III of the SCM Agreement, or alternatively exports can be subject to countervailing duty action. There is nothing new about that. What governments would find hard to accept is a situation where they would have no guidance and where they would breach treaty obligations quite inadvertently without prior warning.

7.157 Australia submits that the United States' position on the "in fact" standard would provide no guidance to Members about what might constitute a prohibited subsidy. It would provide *carte blanche* for trying to close markets through Part II of the SCM Agreement. Where a Member is suffering adverse effects it has other remedies, including countervailing action, which is subject to detailed rules. Indeed, virtually any case where subsidized imports are such as to cause material injury in an importing Member's market would provide sufficient evidence to be an "in fact" export subsidy in the eyes of the United States. This would serve to make much of Part III of the SCM Agreement redundant, inconsistent with the normal rules of treaty interpretation.

7.158 In addition, Australia continues, the way in which the United States has pursued the issue of the ICS and EFS gives rise to concerns about due process. These schemes do not apply to automotive leather. The view of the United States that the nature of a prior scheme affects the legal nature of a subsequent scheme has no basis. It would make the task of governments ensuring compliance with their international obligations all that much more difficult and conceptually could result in the absurd situation where two Members could have exactly the same scheme but their legal nature would be different because of differences in their prior arrangements. This just highlights the unreasonable basis of the position of the United States. For the Panel to reach some conclusion about the legal status of a measure that no longer exists and has never been subject to a dispute panel under the GATT system or the WTO, would be inconsistent with the central principle that Members' measures are presumed to be in conformity unless successfully challenged under the appropriate dispute settlement procedures.

7.159 The **United States** responds that it is the nature of legal rules that they are drafted in general terms and cannot be expected to provide bright-line tests for specifically resolving al hypothetical scenarios. That is why there are rules of treaty interpretation to help resolve interpretative issues and dispute settlement panels to apply general legal rules to particular factual situations. The drafters of the SCM Agreement chose to include an "in fact" standard, which by its nature requires a fact-based, case-by-case approach in its application. If the "in fact" provision of Article 3.1(a) is to fulfill the purpose for which it was intended - to prevent circumvention in fact of the prohibition in law against export subsidies - a case-by-case approach is necessary. If the drafters had regarded a case-by-case approach as undermining the stability of the WTO system, they obviously would not have included an "in fact" standard in the prohibition.

7.160 The United States maintains that some uncertainty is inevitable in a case-by-case approach. This uncertainty is diminished to a certain extent as the application of this provision is clarified by panel decisions. In conducting a case-by-case analysis, a panel must use its best judgment in objectively assessing the facts of the case. Likewise, in attempting to conform its conduct to the requirements of the SCM Agreement, a Member must use its best judgment in deciding whether a subsidy would fall within the prohibition in Article 3. Furthermore, exactly the same line of argument could be made concerning determinations of *de facto* discrimination under Article III of GATT 1994. Yet, the Appellate Body has recognized that such an approach does not undermine the stability and predictability of the WTO system, particularly in light of the benefit of this approach, namely preventing the circumvention of the prohibition at issue.

4. *Application of Article 3.1(a) of the SCM Agreement in this Dispute*

(a) "Contingent, in Law ... upon Export Performance"

7.161 The **United States** submits that, because Howe was granted the new aid package as a specific replacement for the *de jure* subsidies of the ICS and EFS export schemes from which it was excluded pursuant to the November 1996 settlement, the new subsidies are also *de jure* export subsidies. In its first written submission to the Panel, the United States said that it had been unable to document fully that the new subsidies are legally contingent upon Howe's export performance because, despite previous requests, the Australian government had refused to provide the United States with copies of Howe's proposal to the Australian government (and other documents relating thereto) which generated the additional aid or the resulting agreement between the Australian government and Howe setting forth the terms of the benefits and the criteria for their receipt.[106]

7.162 The United States believes that the replacement subsidy package accorded to Howe by the Australian government is a prohibited export subsidy within the meaning of Article 3 of the SCM Agreement; for this reason it requested that the Panel ask Australia to produce certain documents which would demonstrate, *inter alia*, whether the package is *de jure* or *de facto* an export subsidy.

7.163 **Australia** submits that the United States has put forward no evidence that any of the measures is contingent "in law" upon export performance. Indeed, in Australia's view, the issue of "in law" is not before the Panel, since in WT/DS126/1, while "in law or in fact" is part of a quote in the second paragraph, the terms of reference depend on the third paragraph which only discusses the "in fact" case. Australia observes that the United States does raise the issue of "in law" (or rather it refers to "*de jure*" by which it presumably means "in law") in its first written submission to the Panel. However, it presents no evidence and its argument appears to be the same as for its "in fact" case, i.e. that the measures were put in place following the excision of automotive leather from

[106] These documents were provided to the Panel and the United States at the first substantive meeting of the Panel with the parties, subject to procedures adopted by the Panel governing the handling of business confidential information.

the ICS and EFS. This does not demonstrate the "in law" condition. Indeed, Australia asserts, it demonstrates that is not germane even to the demonstration of the "in fact" condition. Similarly, the United States chose not to avail itself of the proper procedures under the SCM Agreement (Article 25.8) to seek information and so it can hardly argue on the basis of the lack of information.

(b) "Contingent ... in Fact ... upon Export Performance"

(i) General

7.164 The **United States** asserts that, even if the grant and loan contracts presented by Australia do not demonstrate that the replacement package is a *de jure* export subsidy, the Panel should find that the prohibition on export subsidies applies in situations like the one presented here: where a subsidy exists; and where that subsidy is *de facto* contingent on export performance. The Panel should determine that the grants and loan provided to Howe by the Australian government constitute *de facto* export subsidies on the basis of the totality of the facts and circumstances in this case.

7.165 According to the United States, the new financial aid package was specifically designed to compensate Howe for the export subsidies it forfeited under the settlement agreement with the United States. In addition, the Australian government intended that the new package would support Howe's current and future exports. When it provided these subsidies, the Australian government was fully aware that Howe was first and foremost an exporter and that the Australian market for automotive leather goods was minimal in comparison to the existing and potential export market for these goods. The Australian government was aware that, by 1997, exports constituted 90 per cent of Howe's sales. There can be no doubt that Howe's increased production will be destined for exportation, since Australia's small automotive leather market cannot absorb Howe's current production, much less any increase in sales or production. Finally, the structure of the aid package itself reveals that the new subsidies are in fact tied to Howe's anticipated export earnings. In light of the totality of the circumstances surrounding the provision by the government of Australia of these replacement subsidies to Howe, the United States considers that Australia has unquestionably bestowed a prohibited export subsidy upon Howe.

7.166 **Australia** submits that there is a clear distinction between "law" and "fact" in ordinary language. The terms "in law" and "in fact" are clearly used to distinguish between the ways in which the granting of a subsidy is made contingent upon export performance. "In law" means just that, "legally contingent" as used in Footnote 4 of the SCM Agreement. "In fact" is where the implementation is such as to tie the granting of the subsidy to actual or anticipated exportation or earnings. In particular, this occurs where a scheme is administered in such a way as to favour exports without being legally contingent on export performance. The loan contract and the grant contract prove that in neither case was there any legal contingency. In addition, there was no legal contingency for the payments under the grant contract. The contracts also show that there was no way in which they could be administered to tie the granting of subsidies to actual or anticipated exportation or earnings. There is no way in which they could be administered to favour exports over domestic sales.

7.167 According to Australia, the loan and grant contracts are separate legal instruments. The loan contract and other measures need to be considered separately on their merits in respect of consistency with Article 3.1(a) of the SCM Agreement. Australia asserts that it has shown that the granting of the loan contract clearly had no linkage to export performance, and that this is evident from the loan contract itself. Australia states that it has shown that the loan contract does not meet the "in fact" standard of Article 3.1(a) of the SCM Agreement.

7.168 Australia observes that there is a difference of views over the terms of reference of the Panel in respect to the grant contract. If the Panel accepts that it is the conditions of the granting of the individual payments that is at issue, then the United States has not even sought to show that the "in fact" standard was met. In addition, only the granting of the first payment and the granting of the second payment are before the Panel. Assuming, in the alternative, that the Panel concludes that the issue before it is the granting of the grant contract, then the granting of the grant contract clearly has no linkage to export performance. Australia maintains that it has shown this and that this is, in any case, evident from the grant contract itself. The functioning of the grant contract is shown by the way in which the actual payments were made where the record[107] shows that there was no tie to export performance. Australia states that it has shown that the grant contract does not meet the "in fact" standard under Article 3.1(a) of the SCM Agreement.

7.169 Australia asserts that the issue of the nature of the ICS and the EFS as they applied to automotive leather is not before the Panel and should not be addressed by the Panel. In Australia's view, under the WTO Agreement, there is a presumption that measures taken by Members are in conformity unless successfully challenged under the appropriate dispute settlement procedures of the DSU and the appropriate covered agreements.

(ii) Prior Measures and the Designing of Alternative Assistance to Howe

7.170 The **United States** argues that the A$30 million grant and the A$25 million preferential loan were provided to Howe solely because automotive leather

[107] Australia refers in this regard to business confidential information it provided to the Panel. Also see *infra*, para. 7.298.

was removed from the ICS and EFS export schemes. Since these industry programmes were clearly export subsidies and since the new financial aid was expressly designed to replace these benefits, the new assistance qualifies as a prohibited export subsidy.

7.171 In the view of the United States, there can be little doubt that the ICS and EFS export schemes are *de jure* export subsidies. The explicit purpose of both the ICS and the EFS programmes is export promotion. In order to achieve this goal, subsidies available under these programmes were made legally contingent upon export performance. The greater the value of a company's exports, the greater the value of subsidies it was eligible to receive. Between 1992 and 1997, Howe received at least A$29 million under the ICS programme and more than A$5 million under the EFS programme. By making subsidies under these programmes legally contingent upon exportation, both the ICS and EFS programmes clearly fell within the Article 3.1(a) of the SCM Agreement, which prohibits "subsidies contingent, in law . . . upon export performance."

7.172 The United States described the ICS and EFS as follows[108]:

> "Enacted in 1988, the Textiles, Clothing and Footwear Development Authority Act established the Australian Textiles, Clothing and Footwear Development Authority, the stated object of which is "to promote the restructuring and revitalization of the [textile, clothing and footwear] industries so as to improve their efficiency and international competitiveness."[109] To this end, the functions of the Authority are, *inter alia*, to "encourage and facilitate the development of plans aimed at increasing the international competitiveness of [Australian textile, clothing and footwear] producers by providing financial assistance to them for that purpose" and to develop "measures calculated to . . . increase the exports of TCF products produced in Australia . . . ."[110]
>
> Pursuant to this mandate, in 1991, the Australian government announced the creation of the [ICS] program, to be in effect from July 1, 1991, through June 30, 2000.[111] Under the [ICS] program, exporters of eligible textile, clothing and footwear products can earn import credits that may be

[108] Note that notes 109 - 123 are as they appeared in the United States submission.

[109] TCF Development Authority Act 1998, Part II, §6(a), Exhibit 6.

[110] *Ibid.* at Part II, § 7.

[111] Australian Customs Service, *TCF Import Credit Scheme: Administrative Arrangements* (March 1995), paras. 1.1 and 1.2. Exhibit 7. The TCF Import Credit Scheme is administered by the Australian Customs Service on behalf of the TCF Development Authority. *Ibid.* at para. 1.1.

used to reduce the import duties payable on eligible textile, clothing and footwear items by an amount up to the value of the credits held.[112] However, exporters are not required to use their credits as offsets against import duties. These credits may be transferred from one holder to another in exchange for a cash payment.[113]

Under the ICS program, the level of import credits that may be earned is explicitly conditioned upon export performance. Specifically, the value of import credits that can be earned is calculated as the F.O.B. value of an eligible export sale, multiplied by the Australian value-added content of the export sale (expressed as a percentage of sales volume).[114] This total, in turn, is multiplied by a specified "Export Phasing Rate."[115] Between 1991 and 1997, the Export Phasing Rate stood at .30 (*i.e.*, 30% of the F.O.B. value of the Australian value-added content of eligible textile, clothing and footwear exports). The Export Phasing Rate was recently reduced to .20.[116] Expressed as a formula:

Import credit = Export sale (FOB A$) x Australian value-added expressed as a percentage of sales volume x Export phasing rate[117] ...

The Australian government designed the EFS program to encourage the export of passenger motor vehicles ("PMV") and PMV components from Australia.[118] In its current form

---

[112] Australian Customs Service, *TCF Import Credit Scheme: Administrative Arrangements* (March 1995), paras. 1.1 and 1.2. Exhibit 7. The TCF Import Credit Scheme is administered by the Australian Customs Service on behalf of the TCF Development Authority. *Ibid.* at para. 1.1.

[113] *Ibid.* at para. 8.3.

[114] *Ibid.* at para. 5.1. The Textiles, Clothing & Footwear Development Authority has established value added rates across a range of categories and sub-categories for textile, clothing and footwear products, set out in Table 3 of the *TCF Import Credit Scheme: Administrative Arrangements* (March 1995). *Ibid.*, para. 5.4.

[115] *Ibid.* at para. 5.1.

[116] TCF Development Authority Act 1998 at para. 6.9. Under the TCF, the Export Phasing Rate stood at 30% of the Australian value added of eligible textile, clothing and footwear exports from July 1, 1991 through June 30, 1996. It was subsequently phased down to 25%, and is scheduled to decrease to 20% on July 1, 1998 and 15% on July 1, 1999.

[117] *Ibid.* at 7 (Part 5.1).

[118] *See* Statement of Minister of Industry, Science & Technology John Moore, "Government Announcement on Automotive Industry Policy to the Year 2000," p. 40 (March 1991) (remarking that the Australian Government's new policies are designed to make "the Export Facilitation Scheme

> since 1991,[119] the EFS program allows Australian manufacturers to earn A$1 of export credit for every dollar of eligible exports of covered automotive items.[120] The value of exports eligible to earn exports credits is equal to the Australian value-added content of eligible exports, calculated as the F.O.B. sales price less the value of any imported components and raw materials.[121]
>
> Export credits earned under this program can be used to obtain rebates on the duties payable on eligible imports of automotive vehicles and automotive components,[122] or may be sold for cash to any importer of eligible goods who may similarly seek such rebates.[123] The amount of import duty that can be rebated under this program is determined by a tariff reduction schedule that varies depending on the year in which the export credit is used. From a high of 37.5% of the tariff rate for export credits used in 1991, the schedule slowly scales back the amount of rebatable duty to 15% in the year 2000, the last scheduled year of the program.[124] For instance, in 1996 a company could receive a rebate equal to 25% of the export credit earned. Thus, if an exporter received A$1,000,000 of export credits, he or his transferee could obtain a rebate of $250,000 for import duties paid during that year."

7.173 The United States maintains that even Australia's Industry Commission recognized that the programmes are inconsistent with the Australia's WTO obligations:

> The Commission finds the [automotive] export facilitation scheme has been valuable to the industry. It has served its main purpose of introducing Australian products to world markets and will expire in 2000. The Commission will not recommend its continuation because its strategic value has

more flexible and rewarding to those firms prepared to make the investments needed to considerably expand their exports."), Exhibit 12.

[119] *See Ibid.* (discussing how the EFS program replaced and built upon previous assistance programs provided by the GOA to the Australian automotive sector).

[120] Australian Dept. Of Industry, Science & Technology, *Report on the State of the Automotive Industry 1994*, (June 1995), para. C:1.3.2, Exhibit 13.

[121] *Ibid.* at para. C:1.3. As expressed in C:1.3.6: F.O.B. selling price less imported components equals F.O.B. Australian content. F.O.B. Australian content less raw materials equals value-added.

[122] *Ibid.* at para. C:3.1.1 and C:3.2.

[123] *Ibid.* at para. C:2.1.4.

[124] Australian Dept. Of Industry, Science & Technology, *Report on the State of the Automotive Industry 1994*, (June 1995), at para.C:3.1.2 and C:3.1.3.

> been undermined by its vulnerability to challenge under the rules of the World Trade Organization.[125]

7.174 The United States observes that a similar assessment was made about the ICS programme:

> Recent actions by the US have highlighted the vulnerability of the [ICS] Scheme to challenge under the World Trade Organization (WTO) rules...[126]

7.175 The United States notes that one senior Australian government official even went so far as to state that "[t]here is no doubt the [ICS and EFS] schemes are illegal under the WTO."[127]

7.176 The United States recalls that, on 25 November 1996, the United States reached an agreement with the Australian government that removed automotive leather from eligibility under these two programmes. After the settlement, the Australian government could no longer provide Howe subsidies through the ICS and EFS programmes. However, the Australian government clearly wanted to continue to underwrite Howe's export drive. As a result, at the same time that it was negotiating the November 1996 settlement with the United States, the Australian government was also considering replacement measures for the very subsidies it was pledging to eliminate.

7.177 The United States argues that, anticipating its exclusion from the ICS and EFS programmes, Howe embarked on an extensive lobbying campaign to persuade the Australian government that its export prospects - which it forecast to be A$600 million through 2000 - were jeopardized without a substitute form of assistance. The United States cites a report in *The Weekend Australian*:

> Coincidentally, the company's lobbying effort climaxed on the day Air Force One with Clinton and his entourage on board touched down in Sydney.

---

[125] Industry Commission, Rep. No. 58, *The Automotive Industry: The Report* 351, May 26, 1997, United States Exhibit 39.

[126] Industry Commission, Rep. No. 59, *The Textile, Clothing and Footwear Industries: Report* 293, September 9, 1997, United States Exhibit 40.

[127] "Government may have to dismantle help schemes," *The Australian Financial Review*, October 3, 1996, United States Exhibit 4. According to the United States, the Australian media also recognized the "prohibited" nature of these programmes' subsidies. For instance, *The Australian Financial Review* ("US threat to car, ICS industries") noted on June 20, 1996 that "it had been known for some time that the export facilitation arrangements which operate under the TCF and car plans would not survive a WTO challenge." United States Exhibit 42. This same article also quoted a former senior official in Australia's Department of Foreign Affairs and Trade as stating, in regard to a possible U.S. challenge, that "[i]n simple terms, they [the ICS and EFS programs] are in trouble." The United States also refers to "A firm hand on reform," *The Australian Financial Review*, October 3, 1996 (editorial) ("All indications are that the schemes are indeed illegal and will be declared so in the WTO"), United States Exhibit 43.

> On the same day, [Howe's Managing Director] Heysen and a colleague flew to Canberra for a round of meetings with senior ministers and bureaucrats, beginning with officials of the Department of Industry, Science and Tourism.
>
> A meeting followed with staff from the offices of [DIST Minister John] Moore and the Prime Minister attended by then DIST secretary Greg Taylor.
>
> Then, to ensure all bases were covered, the opposition rooms were visited. Heysen met Simon Crean and Martin Ferguson, Industry and employment spokesmen respectively, and later in the day had an audience with [Deputy Prime Minister] Fischer.[128]

7.178 According to the United States, these lobbying efforts were amply rewarded. Even before the final agreement was reached with the United States, Howe's Managing Director, Chris Heysen, remarked that he had been "assured' that Howe "would be compensated with an alternative arrangement that would help it continue to expand exports."[129] Similarly, the *Sydney Morning Herald* reported that "it is understood that Howe Leather will be given a multi-million dollar payment for being excluded from the Import Credit Scheme [ICS] and the Export Facilitation Scheme [EFS]."[130]

7.179 In the view of the United States, that is precisely what happened. Just one month after agreeing with the United States to excise automotive leather from the ICS and EFS programmes, the Australian government formally announced that "[t]he Government has provided the package to Howe and Co. following the decision to excise automotive leather from the Import Credit and Export Facilitation Schemes from 1 April 1997, as part of the settlement of a recent trade dispute involving the United States."[131] Thus, with planned coincidence, the new aid package - characterized by the Australian government as "alternative assistance" - was provided to Howe just as automotive leather was being excised from two programmes that had the explicit purpose of export promotion.

7.180 The United States asserts that, against this backdrop, the link between the replacement package and Howe's export performance is quite obvious. The fact that the replacement package compensated Howe for its exclusion from receipt of ICS and EFS subsidies, as well as the sequence of events surrounding the

[128] "Sacred Cows vs The Hide of Howe," *The Weekend Australian*, Sept. 20-21, 1997, at 54, col. 6, United States Exhibit 22.

[129] "Melbourne firm could lose in US subsidies deal," *The Age*, November 25, 1996, at 1, United States Exhibit 15.

[130] "Backdown on Howe Subsidy," *The Sydney Morning Herald*, November 25, 1996, United States Exhibit 17.

[131] United States Exhibit 18.

announcement of the replacement package, indicate that the replacement package is no more than a thinly disguised attempt by the Australian government to continue to support Howe's export growth by modifying only the form, but not the substance, of its export subsidies.

7.181 **Australia** submits that the nature of prior measures is irrelevant to the establishment of the facts about the legal status of existing measures. These measures no longer apply to automotive leather and so are not relevant to the current Panel proceedings. The United States appears to be seeking to establish that the legal status of a previous measure determines in some way the legal status of a subsequent measure.[132] There is no basis for this in a rules-based regime such as the WTO. The status of each of the measures before the Panel needs to be judged on its merits. The United States is proposing a trade outcome or trade effects test. This may be appropriate in some cases of non-violation, but it is not appropriate under Part II of the SCM Agreement, where the issue is whether one or more of the measures before the Panel fall under Article 3.1(a) of the SCM Agreement. If the United States wanted to pursue the issue on the basis of trade effects, then it should have sought remedy under Part III of the SCM Agreement, i.e., under Article 7 rather than Article 4.

7.182 Australia argues that to accept that the legal status or nature of a previous measure in some way determines the status of an existing measure under the WTO, would be to inject a level of uncertainty and subjectivity into the WTO that would be quite inappropriate for a rules-based treaty. This would mean, amongst other things, that if there were two cases, one where an enterprise had been in receipt of, say, a subsidy and another enterprise had not been, a new measure could be prohibited when given to the first enterprise but not when given to the other. This would make a farce of a rules-based system. Article 3.1(a) of the SCM Agreement deals with a situation of law or fact where the type of the measure must determine its status.

7.183 According to Australia, the company concerned does not receive benefits under these programmes (ICS and EFS), since automotive leather was removed from their scope on 1 April 1997, and the United States recognizes this. The claim of the United States is limited to the measures before the Panel. The United States has not made a claim in respect of these programmes and that matter is not before this Panel. Rather, the United States has made an assertion about their status. It did not even provide any argumentation in WT/DS126/1 for that assertion.

[132] In the course of the Panel proceedings, the United States acknowledged that a prohibited export subsidy could be replaced by another form of assistance that is not tied to export performance and a Member could thus bring itself into conformity with the SCM Agreement. However, it maintains that Australia has not done so in this case.

7.184 Australia states that the United States has made a claim that the measures provided to Howe are inconsistent with Article 3.1(a) and so Article 3.2 of the SCM Agreement. This is not an issue of a trade effects test, but a matter regarding WTO rules. The United States has to establish that the conditions of footnote 4 of Article 3.1(a) are met. This is not a matter of whether or not when one measure is replaced by another there should be a markedly different production or trade outcome.

7.185 For the sake of argument, Australia asks the Panel to assume that a Member has a measure that has been found by a Panel to be inconsistent with the WTO Agreement. Its obligations are to remove the inconsistency. It does not have any obligation to ensure a particular trade outcome to satisfy the complainant. That is a political problem for the complainant, not the respondent. In the case of a subsidy, nothing in the WTO Agreement asserts that a subsidy inconsistent with Article 3.1(a) of the SCM Agreement cannot be replaced by a subsidy consistent with the SCM Agreement, or that any new subsidy or other measure must have a particular trade impact. This is in contrast to non-violation cases, including cases under Article 7 of the SCM Agreement, where the impact of an aggregation of measures may need to be dealt with.

7.186 Australia declares that Article 3.1(a) and footnote 4 of the SCM Agreement do not talk about replacement measures, but require that the United States establish certain facts. These must be facts in relation to the actual measures before the Panel and not the relationship to programmes which are no longer in effect for the product and company in question.

7.187 In the alternative, Australia continues, if the Panel decides to look at the trade impact of previous measures, it would still be unnecessary and outside of the Panel's terms of reference for it to make any finding on what the status of ICS and EFS were under the SCM Agreement when they applied to automotive leather. These programmes do not apply to the product and company in question and so are not before the Panel. It would be inappropriate and an abuse of process to allow the Panel proceedings to be used to reach findings on programmes that are not before the Panel as measures and on which no claims are being made. For the Panel to reach any views on the nature of these programmes as they apply to any products other than automotive leather would also be outside its terms of reference.

7.188 According to Australia, any argument based on previous measures and their trade effect for a particular company when compared to that of an existing measure has no place in the WTO rules environment. The idea that somehow a government would have to disrupt a firm's commercial linkages in order to ensure WTO compliance has no basis under the WTO Agreement and is not consistent with the WTO's focus on rules. Indeed, it might even be inconsistent with Article XI of GATT 1994 or the prohibition on grey area measures under Article 11 of the Agreement on Safeguards.

7.189 Nevertheless, since the United States has put forward, as exhibits, information provided under confidential, inter-governmental consultations, Australia states that it is worthwhile setting the record straight about the process leading to the current arrangements. The United States government was never in any doubt, and accepted, that there would be new assistance arrangements for Howe following the excision of automotive leather from ICS and EFS. Indeed, there were a large number of bilateral discussions on this issue between the Australian and United States Governments both before and after the public announcement of the proposed arrangements in late December 1996.

7.190 Indeed, Australia states, it was at the repeated request of the United States that Howe was obliged by the Australian government to devote such a major proportion of payments under the grant contract to investment, with the United States even objecting to having research and development counted against payments under the grant contract. One side effect of this was the new production premises at Thomastown and Rosedale. It was the United States that demanded this investment be made where it could well have asked for the money to be paid as a simple bounty on production.

7.191 At the same time, Australia continues, the United States wanted assurances that serious prejudice would not be caused by the new arrangements. According to Australia, the United States said that it would judge the new arrangements on that basis. To comply with this, Australia sought to ensure that the impact on the United States was minimized through limiting the level of per unit subsidy on sales. Australia understood that the United States government wanted Australia to ensure that the 5 per cent level in Article 6.1(a) of the SCM Agreement was not exceeded. The issue was how to meet the twin objectives of putting the money into investment, which basically meant paying the money at an early stage (unlike a traditional bounty, which could have been paid after production), and of keeping the level of subsidy below 5 per cent. The approach adopted was to cap the aggregate of payments under the grant contract at A$30 million to limit the overall level of *ad valorem* subsidization of sales over the period to mid-2000 while imposing investment targets, and of course the normal due diligence considerations associated with checking on the continued viability of the company before payments were made.

7.192 According to Australia, the intent was to meet the twin requests from the United States. This was the actual basis of the nature of the grant contract (and loan). The payments were not tied to exports. Indeed the first payment was simply made following the signing of the grant contract. Subsequent payments were related to best endeavours by the company on investment levels and sales. According to Australia, the United States recognizes this. This emphasis by the United States on the link to investment, while correct, underlines that the payments were not linked to export performance. If even investment subsidies were to be taken as measures falling under Article 3.1(a) of the SCM Agreement, then it is difficult to see what limitations would exist to such an open ended interpretation of "in fact" in Article 3.1(a) of the SCM Agreement.

7.193 The ultimate dispute with the United States, as Australia understands it, is in reality about the size of the subsidies, about the aggregation of the subsidization provided. In retrospect, it turned out that the discussions between Australian and United States officials had not resulted in a meeting of minds on this issue of size. On the other hand, the United States never came forward with any claims of serious prejudice to the United States industry, which Australia had undertaken to address if it arose. Moreover, the level of aggregate subsidization is irrelevant for the purposes of Article 3.1(a) of the SCM Agreement. If the United States had a problem with that, it could have taken the matter up under, for example, Part III of the SCM Agreement.

7.194 Australia submits that the "facts" adduced by the United States in the form of newspaper articles and Ministerial statements have to be taken in their political context. In any event, it would be difficult to accept that such articles, sometimes involving stories without attribution, should be considered to provide acceptable evidence. The company involved is competitive and innovative. It is not surprising in a small trading nation that comments on successful companies include references to export markets. That, however, does not mean that there was an attempt to circumvent Australia's WTO obligations and the United States has not produced any facts to show this.

7.195 Australia contends that the United States has tried to make much of some comment in the press. This hardly passes as proof. Indeed, the use by the United States of newspaper stories to demonstrate facts is questionable in the extreme. Newspaper comment in Australia cannot be taken as an accurate record of, or even to reflect, the views of government. It would be highly inappropriate for a Panel to take newspaper comment as the basis for determining that a Member was in breach of its treaty commitments.

7.196 In this regard, Australia comments on one United States exhibit by way of example. This purports to be a Media Release by the Minister for Industry, Science and Tourism on 27 December 1996, together with an attachment. The first page is a copy of a Media Release, which was provided to the United States in its Exhibit 2. According to Australia, this exhibit shows that the government was concerned about jobs, not about exports. The second page of this exhibit, which is portrayed as being part of the Media Release, was not that at all. It was a set of confidential talking points for discussions between the Australian Embassy and the United States government (USTR). What they demonstrate is no more than that the loan contract and grant contract were designed with the objectives of the United States government in mind and in consultation (though not ultimately agreement) with the United States, and not in isolation by Australia.

7.197 In Australia's view, when the United States seeks to argue that the company was in some way obliged to export to obtain the maximum amount of money it is unclear what it is suggesting. The SCM Agreement does not prohibit bounty, i.e. payments per unit of production by enterprises, or subsidies on investment by enterprises. Any enterprise receiving bounty or subsidies linked to investment would get more for more production or investment. What the United States is noting is that in this case there is a cap, a maximum of A$30 million, on what the company could receive in total regardless of how much it sold. There is no basis for arguing that to limit subsidization in this way should suddenly make a measure prohibited. The United States has not argued that the allocation of the limited quantum of money available in any way favours exports. Thus, there is no basis for this argument by the United States that any of the payments (or the grant contract) falls under Article 3.1(a) of the SCM Agreement.

7.198 The **United States** repeats that the grant and loan contracts at issue in this case were specifically and explicitly designed to compensate Howe for the prohibited export subsidies that it would have received under the ICS and EFS. The fact that the ICS and EFS programmes were *export* subsidies is highly relevant in determining the nature of the grant and loan contracts. Despite Australia's demand that each measure be judged on its own merits, the replacement subsidies that Howe received were not provided in a vacuum. The Australian government itself linked the ICS and EFS programmes with the grant/loan package by proudly announcing that "[t]he Government has provided the [grant and loan] package to Howe and Co. following the decision to excise automotive leather from the Import Credit and Export Facilitation Schemes."[133] Since footnote 4 to Article 3.1(a) directs the Panel to examine all "facts demonstrat[ing] that the granting of a subsidy ... is in fact tied to actual or anticipated exportation or export earnings," the Panel is obligated to consider these facts.[134]

7.199 Accordingly, the United States urges the Panel to consider the nature of the ICS and EFS programmes in determining whether the replacement subsidies constitute "in fact" export subsidies. The United States is not seeking a remedy with regard to these programmes (i.e., is not asking that the Panel request Australia to bring them into compliance with its obligations under the SCM Agreement). However, as the United States considers that the new subsidies are expressly linked to the old programmes, the nature of the prior programmes provides useful and important information in evaluating the nature of the subsequent measures.

7.200 The United States argues that, beginning in 1991, and continuing through April 1997, the Australian government gave Howe a series of overt, *de jure* export subsidies through the ICS and EFS. The United States avers that it has demonstrated that the explicit purpose of both the ICS and EFS programmes is export promotion. Under these programmes, Howe received import credits based on the domestic value-added content of its exports. Receipt of these import credits was directly contingent upon export performance. The more Howe ex-

[133] United States Exhibit 18.

[134] The United States also referred to certain business confidential information in making this argument.

ported, the more benefits it received and so the ICS and EFS programmes are plainly inconsistent with Article 3 of the SCM Agreement. According to the United States, when the new package is considered in this context, the link between it and Howe's export performance is obvious. The fact that the replacement package was specifically designed to compensate Howe for its exclusion from receipt of ICS and EFS export subsidies indicates that the replacement package is no more than a thinly disguised attempt by the Australian government to continue to promote exportation by Howe by modifying only the form, but not the substance, of its export subsidies.

7.201 The United States declares that Australia does not dispute and, indeed, cannot dispute that the ICS and EFS programmes are prohibited export subsidies. Rather, Australia contends that the Panel may not consider the nature of these programmes in determining whether the alternative assistance provided to Howe were export subsidies. However, the United States is not asking the Panel to find that Australia must withdraw the ICS and EFS programmes because they are prohibited export subsidies. Rather, the United States is simply asking that the Panel consider the nature of these prior measures in determining whether the replacement subsidies are in fact tied to export performance. The fact that the new subsidies were explicitly designed to compensate Howe for its exclusion from these two programmes means that the prior measures were factors in Australia's decision to grant Howe the new subsidies. This renders the nature of those measures highly relevant to the Panel's determination in this case regarding the nature of the current measures.

7.202 The United States submits, in the alternative, that even if the Panel were to decide not to consider the nature of the ICS and EFS programmes, the other evidence presented by the United States - which Australia did not in any way refute - leads to the inevitable conclusion that the grant and the preferential loan were tied to actual as well as anticipated exports and export earnings within the meaning of footnote 4 to Article 3.1(a). That evidence includes, among other supporting facts: the Australian government's statements at time of the new subsidies; the Australian government's knowledge at the time it conferred these benefits that Howe's exports constituted 90 per cent of its sales and the company had aggressive export plans; the grant and loan required Howe to increase its production even though the Australian leather market is too small to absorb any increased sales; and the benefits were provided only to Howe, which exports virtually all of its production, and not to any leather manufacturer that supplies the domestic market.

7.203 With respect to Australia's suggestion that the United States has somehow waived its claim that the new subsidies are prohibited export subsidies because it was consulted during the period that Australia was designing the replacement package, the United States asserts that, although it was consulted, it never agreed that a new subsidy package would necessarily comply with the requirements of Article 3 of the SCM Agreement. Australia, in fact, acknowledges this. The fact that the United States was consulted cannot change the nature of the replacement subsidies.

7.204 The United States adds that the consultations during the time that the replacement measures were being designed were in the context of settlement negotiations which ultimately proved unsuccessful. There was no agreement or endorsement by the United States with regard to the various settlement proposals.

7.205 In any event, the United States continues, statements or offers made during the course of settlement discussion in this case are of no legal consequence to this proceedings. Article 4.6 of the DSU provides that: "Consultations shall be confidential, and without prejudice to the rights of Members in any further proceedings." The question of whether statements made during settlement negotiations are relevant was address in the panel report in *United States - Underwear.*[135] In that dispute, Costa Rica improperly used information on settlement offers made by the United States to advance certain arguments to the panel. That panel found:

> In our view, the wording of Article 4.6 of the DSU makes it clear that *offers made in the context of consultations* are, in case a mutually agreed solution is not reached, of no legal consequence to the later stages of dispute settlement, as far as the rights of the parties to the dispute are concerned. Consequently, we will not base our findings on such information.[136] (emphasis supplied by the United States)

7.206 The United States insists that Article 4.6 of the DSU calls for panels to disregard offers of settlement, and not to treat such offers as a waiver or admission. Accordingly, this Panel should disregard all references by Australia to any purported statements made by the United States in the context of efforts to settle this case.

7.207 Australia emphasizes that the proposition by the United States that somehow the status or nature of a prior measure can determine the WTO status of a new measure, (or in this case measures) has no basis in the WTO and is without legal argument from the United States. GATT contracting parties, and now WTO Members, bring themselves into conformity with new rules, or after having lost disputes, by imposing new, consistent measures. There is nothing to suggest that losing a dispute means that suddenly a Member has less rights than before in maintaining a WTO-consistent regime. The idea of a penal regime where a Member was on parole in some sense after losing a case has no legal basis. It would be up to the United States to make a case. The United States has lost a number of disputes in the WTO, and in none of them has it said that that

[135] WT/DS24/R, adopted 25 February 1997.

[136] WT/DS24/R, adopted 25 February 1997, para. 7.27.

means it has to remove all measures bearing any relationship to the inconsistent ones. Nor has it said that its replacement measures were potentially inconsistent because they were measures aimed at replacing those found to be inconsistent. There is nothing in the WTO Agreement that suggests that existing measures can only be replaced with no policy at all. Australia makes the following additional points by way of rebuttal:

(a) EFS and ICS do not apply to automotive leather.

(b) Automotive leather was excised from EFS and ICS from 1 April 1997, before the request for consultations for this Panel.

(c) The nature and WTO status of EFS and ICS for automotive leather prior to 1 April 1997 are beyond the Panel's terms of reference.

(d) The nature and WTO status of EFS and ICS for products other than automotive leather are beyond the Panel's terms of reference.

(e) No GATT or WTO panel has found against EFS or ICS.

(f) Indeed, no GATT contracting party, no signatory to the Tokyo Round Subsidies Agreement, and no WTO Member has taken Australia to a Panel on EFS and ICS.

(g) In the absence of a panel report finding against these schemes, it would be highly inappropriate for this Panel to go outside its terms of reference to examine measures that are not before the Panel and indeed do not even apply to automotive leather. If the United States wants a ruling on the WTO status of the two schemes, then it is always open to it to take such a Panel. It is not for this Panel to do the United States work outside the Panel's terms of reference.

7.208 Australia observes that arguments about the EFS and ICS form the major part of the United States' case, and that it is the United States' allegations over these schemes that represent the United States' evidence that the new assistance also qualifies as a prohibited export subsidy. According to Australia, the concentration on the EFS and ICS, in circumstances where the United States has not sought to have its allegations about these schemes addressed by a panel under the DSU, is one more example of the United States seeking to override proper procedures in this Panel process. For the United States to be allowed to conduct these fishing expeditions would be another diminution of the legitimacy of the nature of WTO dispute settlement where panels have been tightly constrained in what they look at and on what they make findings.

7.209 Australia recalls that Article 11 of the DSU requires that the "panel should make an objective assessment of the matter before it, including an objective assessment of the facts of the case...." The Panel needs to limit itself to the facts in relation to subsidies provided to producers and exporters of automotive leather that are covered in its terms of reference. These do not include EFS and

ICS. Australia fails to understand the logic behind the United States' assertions. Members are permitted to change their industry settings with the obligation being that the new measures comply with their obligations. There is nothing in the WTO that suggests that existing measures can only be replaced with no policy at all. Australia avers that clearly, the new arrangements were part of the outcome from the bilateral settlement between Australia and the United States that also led to the excision of automotive leather from the EFS and ICS. Australia acknowledges that it is unlikely that the grant contract and the loan contract would have been provided in a circumstance other than the removal of automotive leather from the EFS and ICS. However, it is too simplistic to argue that that was the sole reason for providing them. In particular, they were provided because of the government's concern about regional job retention in the absence of any support for the company in the shorter term. To Australia, the argument by the United States that "since the EFS and ICS were clearly export subsidies and since the new financial aid was expressly designed to replace these benefits, the new assistance qualifies as a prohibited export subsidy" is a simple fallacy along the lines of: if a man has A and replaces it with B, then B is A.

7.210 In response to the assertion by the United States that the "benefits were provided only to Howe"[137], Australia states that since only one firm was involved, the arrangements were necessarily for only one firm. This is to state the obvious. It does not, however, have any significance in relation to the legal status of the measures involved.

7.211 Australia points out that the argument of the United States would make it very difficult for a Member to ever bring itself into conformity without simply removing all subsidization. For example, if a Member provided export subsidies in law and it wished to bring itself into conformity, under normal logic it could simply remove the provision that favoured exports over domestic sales and not discriminate. The United States would, in those circumstances, seem to start from the position that the new scheme was prohibited because of the nature of the previous arrangements. On the other hand, had that new arrangement been introduced in a case where there had been no subsidization, it would be consistent. This severance between the nature of a measure and its status is inconsistent with the rules-based regime of the WTO governing violation of treaty commitments.

7.212 Relying on business confidential information, the United States argues that there was clearly a link - which had been recognized by the Australian government - between the elimination of automotive leather from eligibility under the ICS and EFS and the granting of new assistance to Howe.

7.213 Furthermore, **Australia** argues, the disciplines on export subsidies are in respect of certain types of measures. This is not a matter of how much money is

---

[137] See *supra*, para.7.202.

provided by way of subsidy. Where a measure is replaced by another, all that matters is whether the new measure is consistent. Whether the level of subsidy is lower or higher is irrelevant.

7.214 Australia submits that, while the United States said that it was not proposing a trade effects test, it is proposing that the Panel in reality base its findings on the following: (a) the nature and status of prior measures; and (b) the level of exports of Howe of automotive leather.

7.215 According to Australia, the United States exhibits purporting to show what was in Australian Ministers' minds at the time the new assistance arrangements were designed do not demonstrate that what they had in mind was an export subsidy. Indeed, to the contrary, if the covert scenario originally implied by the United States had any semblance of truth in it, and if Ministers thought that there was any linkage with exports in the way suggested, it would not be credible that they would make any statements about exports at all. Australia provided business confidential information to the Panel concerning 1997-1998 audited sales data which, it asserts, underlines the lack of probative value of evidence submitted by the United States regarding, for example, Howe's high export levels.

7.216 In Australia's view, it is not credible that the United States and Australia would have been discussing a settlement that the United States considered to have been WTO-inconsistent. Discussions between the United States and Australia always envisaged that it was possible to provide WTO-consistent subsidies to Howe, but it was recognized that there was a risk of adverse effect, in particular, serious prejudice. The United States has not denied this. But its arguments about prior measures and the high level of exports of automotive leather by Howe were just as true then as now. Australia is not saying that the United States has given Australia a "waiver" in regard to the new assistance arrangements. Australia would agree that in the circumstances, the United States should not have brought this case, but Australia is not arguing here that the United States is estopped from doing so. However, the fact that the United States was involved in discussions with Australia over the details of the assistance package, until at least July 1997, demonstrates that the United States basic problem was about either the size of the loan and grants or some other aspect of the specific arrangements. Australia believes it is the former. If this is the case, then instead of taking and doing the work for a serious prejudice case, the United States is seeking to push out the boundaries of the SCM Agreement to obtain an export level test under Part II of the SCM Agreement. At the same time, the United States also appears to be attempting to push out the boundary of the DSU to obtain a prior measure test, which would have general application.

7.217 Australia asserts that, in respect of the specific arrangements, nothing could be more anodyne than the loan, with the United States making no substantial argument on its status. Similarly, once the trade effects test is taken away, the allegations about the grant contract and the payments under it also collapse.

7.218 Australia observes that the United States argues that although the United States was indeed consulted about the new subsidies, the United States never agreed that a new package would necessarily comply with the requirements of the Article 3 of the SCM Agreement. As the United States recognizes, Australia never said that the United States accepted any particular assistance arrangements. However, the United States clearly accepted that some arrangements would be acceptable, i.e. including being WTO consistent. Otherwise, it would have been being duplicitous during discussions where it sought and obtained in particular the devotion of much of the money provided under the grant contract to investment. Now, of course, the United States seeks to draw adverse inferences from the allocation of money to investment.

7.219 The **United States** responds that throughout Australia's submission and in response to written questions of the Panel, Australia states that the United States "understood and accepted" that an alternative assistance arrangement would be provided to producers of automotive leather. Although the United States notes that statements or offers made during the course of settlement discussions in a case are of no legal consequence to the proceeding[138] the United States asserts that it is necessary to correct this misstatement. According to the United States, it never "accepted" that alternative assistance would be provided to Howe. Australia never sought permission or acceptance from the United States to provide this assistance. Rather, Australia simply informed the United States that further assistance would be supplied. Although the United States was consulted in order to avoid further dispute settlement proceedings; as Australia acknowledges, the United States asserts that it never "agreed to or endorsed the assistance arrangement eventually implemented."

7.220 **Australia** states that the bilateral discussions between Australia and the United States, of course, did not reach the point of the United States signing off on the WTO status of the new assistance arrangements. Australia was prepared to engage in a lengthy consultative process to try and reach a mutually satisfactory solution to this issue. However, Australia contends, it should be noted that the pace of this case, and the long delays involved in it, were determined by the United States and throughout this period commercial uncertainty has hung over Howe. Nevertheless, the lengthy process of bilateral consultations also underlines the commitment of the Australian government to implement WTO-consistent arrangements. It demonstrates that the intent of the government was not to implement an export subsidy arrangement but, quite the contrary, to implement measures that would be not only completely WTO-consistent but also not cause adverse effects to the United States, while recognizing that the United

[138] The United States refers in this regard to Article 4.6 of the DSU and to Panel Report, *United States - Underwear*, WT/DS24/R, adopted 25 February 1997, para. 7.27.

States could always bring a case of serious prejudice to Australia and then, if necessary, to the WTO.

7.221 Australia recalls that there were a large number of bilateral discussions between the Australian and United States government both before and after the public announcement of the new assistance arrangements in late December 1996. These consultations included exchanges between officials from the Australian Embassy in Washington and USTR officials as well as direct contact between policy officers in Canberra involved in the development of the new assistance arrangements and officials in USTR.

7.222 According to Australia, in discussions prior to the 27 December 1996 announcement of the new assistance arrangements, USTR officials were advised of the broad framework proposed for the alternative assistance arrangements, including the fact that the arrangements would contain a one-off up-front grant payment. Australia asserts that the United States was concerned over the size of the alternative arrangements (originally A$80 million was proposed) and the likely impact the arrangements would have on the United States industry. This reflected the nature of the bilateral settlement. USTR officials made it clear immediately following the bilateral settlement between Ambassador Barshefsky and Mr. Fischer that they would judge the WTO-consistency or otherwise of the new scheme on whether it caused problems or serious prejudice to the United States industry. In response to the concerns expressed by the United States over the level of the arrangements, the amount originally proposed was reduced markedly and the loan element introduced.

7.223 Australia observes that, in the pre-announcement discussions on the alternative assistance arrangements, the United States also expressed particular concern over the proposed "up-front" payment and suggested that the arrangements may be more acceptable if the size of this up-front payment could be reduced and that the remainder could be paid conditionally (based mainly on investment activity) over the next couple of years or paid as a production warrant over the period 1 April 1997 to 31 December 2000. It was this broad payment structure that emerged in relation to the grant contract.

7.224 Australia notes that, after the 27 December 1996 announcement of the assistance arrangements, the bulk of the discussion between Australia and the United States was about how to adjust the arrangements to address the concerns of US industry. As a result of these discussions, a number of changes were made to the details of the arrangements. The adjustments were made continually until the grant and loan contracts were signed on 9 March 1997. Moreover, further discussions, at both Ministerial and senior officials levels, continued between Australia and the United States concerning the provisions on investment and other details of the assistance arrangements of concern to the United States until July 1997.

7.225 Australia underlines that the consultations on the new assistance arrangements were extensive. They were, of course, without prejudice to either

Australia's or the United States' WTO rights, but they do reflect that at least throughout this period the United States accepted that alternative assistance arrangements, consistent with Article 3.1(a) of the SCM Agreement, could be provided to Howe. Australia acknowledges that, despite these efforts, no final agreement could be reached with the United States government which met the concerns of the United States companies that initiated this complaint. Australia has not claimed that the United States ever agreed to or endorsed the assistance arrangements eventually implemented.

7.226 According to Australia, the panel report cited by the United States, *United States - Underwear*[139], is not applicable to this case. The *United States - Underwear* case was in the context of consultations under the DSU leading to the establishment of that particular panel and the allegedly compromising offer by the respondent. This case is the opposite, where Australia, in good faith, discussed with the United States what the new arrangements might be and how Australia might modify them to meet concerns of the United States.

7.227 Australia asserts that the record shows that the two governments were involved in discussions about the new support arrangements, where the prime issue was the extent of support. In Australia's mind there is and was no question about the acceptance by the United States that subsidies would be provided. There was no agreement on the new arrangements, but the discussions that took place on how the subsidies should be delivered, in particular the United States requests that the bulk of the money under the grant contract be on capital expenditure, had only one reasonable interpretation, i.e. that the United States accepted that subsidies were to be provided in one form or another.

7.228 Australia contends that the issue between the two countries was one of serious prejudice. If there had been any suggestion that the United States considered that there might potentially be a breach of Article 3.1(a) of the SCM Agreement, or indeed any other provision of the WTO, then the Australian government would have addressed it. Instead, there was the opposite scenario of the United States only raising the "in fact" provision of Article 3.1(a) of the SCM Agreement six months after binding legal domestic arrangements had been entered into by the Australian government and after the loan had been provided and the first two tranches of the grant contract paid out.

7.229 In Australia's view, the record shows that Australia was concerned to ensure WTO-consistency and, in particular, to ensure that there was no linkage with exports. Any government that was intent on doing something underhanded would have handled the issue quite differently. The reported comments on exports would, to the extent that they are accurate, simply demonstrate that the Australian government did not have anything in mind about linkages with export performance. This is also borne out by the nature of the grant contract and the

139 WT/DS24/R, adopted 25 February 1997.

basis on which actual payments were made under it. Clearly, there was no tie to export performance.

(iii) Intent

7.230 The **United States** submits that the Australian government intended the replacement package to support Howe's current and future exports.

7.231 The United States contends that the fact that the replacement package is meant to compensate Howe for its exclusion from the ICS and EFS export programmes is strong evidence that the true purpose of the replacement package - like the subsidy programmes that preceded it - is export promotion. Any doubts as to this fact are resolved by the numerous statements by Australian government and Howe officials that confirm that the replacement package is in fact tied to Howe's actual or anticipated exportation or export earnings. For instance, Australian Trade Minister Tim Fischer made it clear that the purpose of the replacement package is continued export promotion, in stating:

> by dint of effort we [the Australian government] have ensured that Howe Leather has been able to continue its export activity over the last 18 months.[140]

7.232 Similarly, Australia's Minister for Industry, Science and Tourism, John Moore, announced during negotiation of the replacement package that:

> We are working constructively with Howe Leather to ensure that they receive fair compensation. I am determined that this strongly performing export company should not be unfairly disadvantaged by the agreement reached at Manila.[141]

7.233 According to the United States, the Australian government was aware that, at the time the new subsidies were granted in 1997, exports constituted 90 per cent of Howe's sales. The fact that exports play the overwhelmingly dominant role in Howe's overall sales mix is not coincidental. As part of a nearly decade-long effort, the Australian government has financed Howe's transformation into a world-class exporter of automotive leather. As the Australian government has itself admitted, since at least 1991, Howe has received in excess of A$30 million worth of subsidies through two export-contingent subsidy programmes: the ICS and EFS. Because these subsidies were so lucrative, Howe was able to dramatically increase its exports. From less then 10 per cent of its

[140] "Fischer vows to fight US trade challenge," *The Australian*, September 29, 1997, United States Exhibit 45.

[141] Statement of Minister for Industry, Science & Tourism John Moore, "Resolution Removes Uncertainty for Industry," Nov. 25, 1996, United States Exhibit 16.

total sales in 1988, exports increased to 90 per cent of Howe's total sales for the nine months through March 1997.[142]

7.234 The United States alleges that, because the value of prior subsidies was legally tied to the value of Howe's exports, the Australian government necessarily had detailed information concerning Howe's export sales and their exponential increase throughout the 1990s. Beyond simply being aware of Howe's general level of exports, however, the Australian government was also aware that of the relative importance of exports in Howe's overall sales mix. For instance, even before the replacement package was announced, opposition employment spokesman Martin Ferguson is reported to have boasted that "[t]he company was a shining light with 90 per cent of Howe's production being for exports . . . ."[143]

7.235 In addition to being aware of Howe's past and current export performance, the Australian government was also aware of Howe's aggressive export plans. In Howe's November 1996 proposal to the Australian government seeking new subsidies, Howe reportedly predicted that its annual sales would roughly double - to $214 million - by 2000, "with the lion's share of the growth coming from exports."[144] In fact, not only was the Australian government aware of Howe's export ambitions, but it actually designed the replacement package to further facilitate and encourage Howe's ambitious export goals.

7.236 According to the United States, the fact that the replacement package is being provided to promote Howe's exports was also recognized, and welcomed, by Howe itself. During negotiation of the replacement package in late 1996, Howe's Managing Director, Chris Heysen, stated that he had been "assured" that Howe "would be compensated with an alternative arrangement that would help it continue to expand exports."[145] Similarly, in a 1997 interview with *World Leather Magazine*, Mr. Heysen noted that "[w]e have been strongly supported by the Australian Government and we are very confident now that our investment and export growth can continue as planned."[146]

7.237 And, the United States alleges, Howe has begun to achieve its export goals. In June 1998, Howe secured new orders totalling $300 million from major

---

[142] "Major Headache for the Howard Government," *A$ Adding Value*, July 5, 1996 ("Howe's exports have risen from less than ten percent of sales in 1988, to nearly ninety percent of sales."), United States Exhibit 5; "Howe Leather Wins Wheels Award," *World Leather*, February/March 1997 ("The company has increased its exports from 7% to 90% of sales over the last eight years . . . . "), United States Exhibit 4.

[143] "Trade Showdown," *Herald Sun*, November 20, 1996, United States Exhibit 30.

[144] "Sacred Cows vs The Hide of Howe," *The Weekend Australian*, September 20-21, 1997, United States Exhibit 22.

[145] "Melbourne firm could lose in US subsidy deal," *The Age*, November 25, 1996, at 1, United States Exhibit 15.

[146] "Howe Leather wins wheels award," *World Leather*, February/March 1997, United States Exhibit 4.

U.S. automobile companies.[147] There is no question that Howe's ability to secure these orders was directly attributable to the replacement subsidy package. The chairman of Howe's ultimate parent company, Schaffer Corp. Ltd., proudly declared that its new $300 million contracts "have been aided by the Commonwealth Government's support package to Howe in which over $30 million has been expended on the establishment of two world class operations for the manufacture of leather" at Rosedale and Thomastown.[148] Present at the opening of Howe's new state-of-the-art processing plant in Thomastown, the Australian Minister for Industry, Science & Tourism John Moore attributed Howe's success in "cracking" the U.S. car market to the government's "industry policy," which is based on innovation, investment and exports.[149]

7.238 The United States argues that, significantly, the replacement subsidies were not offered to other Australian tanners who supply leather for domestic consumption. The subsidies were therefore not meant simply to stimulate the production of leather for sale to Australian customers. Nor were they provided to other tanners who were eligible for export credits under the ICS and EFS export subsidy schemes since they had no need of further export aid. Rather, the financial package was only made available to the sole leather tanner who was denied access to the government's export schemes and whose exports account for virtually all of its production.

7.239 **Australia** asserts that the United States' arguments are of the nature of trying to establish intent by way of press comment.[150] In this connection, panels are not supposed to be mind readers about what governments, or individual ministers, might or might not have had in mind at the time of making decisions. As any official will know, the factors that influence decision-makers are many faceted. They usually relate to things such as jobs and employment, as in this case. Of course, such decisions may often have implications for imports and exports. There is nothing surprising about that from an economics point of view. However, to arrive at a conclusion, as does the United States, that this should mean that a measure is inconsistent with a treaty obligation is a large leap into the dark.

---

[147] J. Schaffer, Chairman & Managing Director, Schaffer Corp. Ltd., "Howe Leather Announces $300M in New US Contracts," June 18, 1998, United States Exhibit 47.

[148] J. Schaffer, Chairman & Managing Director, Schaffer Corp. Ltd., "Howe Leather Announces $300M in New US Contracts," June 18, 1998, United States Exhibit 47.. See also "Australia: Melbourne Firm in Push to Lift Exports by 15%" Australian Business Intelligence Daily Commercial News (Abstracts), June 15, 1998 (new government-funded high-technology tanning facility in Rosedale was "part of [Howe's] efforts to lift its exports above A$100 million a year"), United States Exhibit 48.

[149] Media Release, Statement of John Moore, Minister of Industry, Science & Tourism, "Australian Company Cracks US Car market With $300M Deal," June 18, 1998, United States Exhibit 49.

[150] See also Australia's arguments in this regard *supra* paras. 7.35, 7.194 and 7.195. With respect to the assertions of the United States, *supra*, para.7.238, see also Australia's arguments *supra*, para.7.210.

7.240 According to Australia, an assessment of the imputed objectives of governments is not the basis on which a rules-based system such as the WTO is supposed to operate. Rules about violation are not supposed to be based on guesses at the objectives of governments. They need to be based on facts and soundly based arguments. In Australia's view, neither of these is present in the case presented by the United States.

7.241 The **United States** insists that, in addition to the fact that the new subsidies were explicitly designed to replace the forfeited *de jure* export subsidies, there is strong evidence that the Australian government intended the replacement subsidies to support Howe's current and future exports. There are numerous statements by both Howe and the Australian government which confirm that the replacement package is, in fact, tied to Howe's actual or anticipated exportation or export earnings.

7.242 Furthermore, the United States argues, when providing the new assistance package to Howe, the government of Australia knew that the vast majority of Howe's operations were export-oriented and that additional subsidies would serve to increase Howe's exports. This is clear from Howe's long-standing participation in the ICS and EFS programmes, the information that Howe was obligated to provide to the government in order to obtain benefits under those programmes and information Australia relied upon in crafting the terms of the assistance package. Australian government officials have acknowledged that Howe's business is essentially an exporting business, and the Australian media has acclaimed Howe as an Australian exporting success story. Thus, according to the United States, there can be no doubt that the Australian government knew at the time it agreed to the assistance package that benefits conferred would finance the continuation of Howe's exports. The fact that the replacement package was provided to promote Howe's exports was also recognized and welcomed by Howe itself.

7.243 Australia argues that the facts of the situation are straightforward. In its view, automotive leather was removed from two entitlement programmes at the request of the United States. However, for the Australian government, politically and socially, there was a requirement to provide some new arrangements for Howe. Australia questions whether anyone would seriously think that Australia would intentionally engage in a dispute with the United States in order just to export more automotive leather. Australia notes that it had hoped that, with the new arrangements, the matter would have been resolved. Australia asserts that it is the legal structure and administration of the subsidy arrangements that should be assessed, rather than the issue of intent or the nature of any prior measures. Australia submits that the Panel should look at the contracts, to evaluate what they actually say and how they are administered. Referring to business confidential information it provided to the Panel, Australia argues that the payments under the grant contract were not based on Howe's export performance.

(iv) Conditions of the Assistance and the Size of the Domestic Market

Factors Including Level of Exports

7.244 The **United States** submits that the conditions of the replacement package and the limited size of the domestic market demonstrate that it is in fact tied to Howe's export earnings. According to the United States, to ensure that Howe would use these funds to increase its exports, the Australian government conditioned the grant on Howe dramatically increasing its sales, which, given the size of the domestic market, in turn meant dramatically increasing its exports. Howe had no choice but to continue to expand its exports in order to obtain the full benefits offered. The Australian government also conditioned receipt of the grant money upon Howe undertaking A$22.8 million in approved capital investment before the year 2000. In fact, according to the United States, Howe's ultimate parent, Schaffer Corp., Ltd. has admitted that the conditions of the subsidy were tied to future exports. In its half yearly report, Schaffer stated that the A$30 million grant was "based on projected exports and paid on performance criteria ... " and stated that the loan was given "to assist with the capital programme."

7.245 The United States observes that the terms of the grant provide that Howe will receive grant monies equal to 5 per cent of its estimated sales from April 1997 through December 2000, with a cap of A$30 million. Thus, in order for Howe to receive the full A$30 million grant for which it is eligible, it must generate A$600 million in sales over the life of the replacement programme. This means that Howe must dramatically increase its annual sales. In 1996/97, Howe's sales totaled approximately A$114.4 million.[151] Accordingly, Howe must increase its annual sales by an average of A$45.6 million a year qualify for the entire A$30 million grant.[152] Given that Howe tanned approximately 10,000 hides per week during the 1996/97 fiscal year, it would need to tan approximately 4,000 additional hides per week for it to achieve such a sales goal.[153]

[151] The United States calculated the A$114.4 figure by annualizing Howe production based on its sales for the first three-quarters of the year (A$85.8 million). The United States refers to Memorandum from Embassy of Australia to the Office of the United States Trade Representative, May 7, 1997, United States Exhibit 11.

[152] The United States asserts that, if Howe's sales were to remain at their 1996/97 levels, Howe would generate A$429 million in sales over the life of the grant program, entitling it to A$21.5 million in grant assistance. Howe would need to generate an extra A$171 million over the 3 3/4 year life of the grant program (bringing its total sales over the period to A$600 million total) for it to earn the full A$30 million; an average annual increase of A$45.6 million (A$171 / 3 3/4 years).

[153] According to the United States, given that Howe would need to increase its sales by A$45.6 million a year to qualify for the entire amount of the grant (assuming A$114 million in annual sales), Howe would have to also increase weekly production of 10,000 hides by 40 per cent or an additional 4000 hides per week to reach that sales goal.

7.246 According to the United States, the Australian government also conditioned receipt of the grant upon Howe undertaking A$22.8 million in approved capital investment before the year 2000. Howe fulfilled this requirement by constructing a new state-of-the-art finishing plant and a new processing facility.[154] Howe now has a production capacity of approximately 22,000 hides per week; almost double its 1996 capacity of 11,500 hides per week.[155]

7.247 However, the United States maintains, the, Australian leather market is now - and will remain in the future - too small to absorb Howe's increased production. At the time the replacement package was provided in 1997, the total weekly demand for automotive leather in Australia was approximately 1,400 hides per week.[156] This figure is unlikely to grow significantly in the near future. The Federation of Automotive Products Manufacturers projects that annual automobile production in Australia will increase by 15 per cent between 1997 and 2000.[157] Assuming a corresponding (15 per cent) increase in the demand for automotive leather, by 2000 the Australian market for automotive leather will require approximately 1,600 hides per week.[158] Needless to say, the United States asserts, the 200 additional hides that the Australian automotive leather market will demand by 2000 is far less than the 4,000 additional hides per week that Howe must sell in order for it to earn the full A$30 million grant, or the 22,000 hides per week that Howe is now capable of producing. The United States believes that the information it presents is sufficient to raise a presumption that the alleged facts are correct. Because Australia has not presented any evidence refuting this affirmative showing, the Panel should accept the evidence presented by the United States as reasonable estimates of the current and future demand in Australia for automobiles and automotive leather.

7.248 In response to questioning by the **Panel** about whether Australia agreed with the estimates submitted by the United States concerning the projected production of motor vehicles in Australia and the projected demand for cattle hides through 2000, **Australia** responded that it considered "that the question is not relevant to the issues before the Panel, since projected demand figures are quite unrelated to the issue of whether any of the measures is contingent upon export performance." Australia also considers that the Federation of Automotive Products Manufacturers projections are conservative. According to Australia, the

---

[154] J. Schaffer, Chairman & Managing Director, Schaffer Corp. Ltd., "Howe Leather Announces $300M in New US Contracts," June 18, 1998, United States Exhibit 47.

[155] Howe Leather, Dec. 1994, United States Exhibit 31; "Picking Winners," *Business Review 1997*, Oct. 13, 1997, United States Exhibit 32.

[156] Affidavit of Robert F. White, Senior Vice President, Eagle Ottawa Leather Company, United States Exhibit 27.

[157] Federation of Automotive Products Manufacturers, *Vehicle Production Forecasts*, March 1998, United States Exhibit 28.

[158] Affidavit of Robert F. White, Senior Vice President, Eagle Ottawa Leather Company, United States Exhibit 27.

medium-term outlook for the automobile market in Australia is buoyed by strong economic conditions but is also currently subject to another of other factors, including prevailing economic conditions in Asian markets, which potentially affect both exports and imports to Australia, as well as the transitional arrangements for the introduction of a goods and services tax. The current outlook is for stronger growth in domestically produced vehicles than was the outlook when the Federation of Automotive Products Manufacturers conducted its survey. However, Australia did not have "any other or more up-to-date public forecasts to provide to the Panel." Furthermore, Australia states that the evidence submitted by the United States relating to the projected demand in cattle hides rests "on several contestable assertions and assumptions." According to Australia, the current proportion of new vehicles ordered and/or sold containing leather seating and interior trimming could well be in excess of the 10 per cent penetration first estimated by the United States, and could perhaps even exceed the 15 per cent level later canvassed. Given that leather interiors as an option have grown from negligible levels over the past decade, there is scope for such growth to continue into the foreseeable future. Similarly, Australia asserts, there is scope for growth in the after-market for automotive leather, which is not well developed when compared with the United States market. However, Australia did not provide the Panel with any forecasts based on these different assumptions.

7.249 The **United States** notes that, although Australia states that the projected demand for automobiles in Australia as calculated by the Federation of Automotive Products Manufacturers is conservative, Australia states that it "does not have any more up to date public forecasts to provide to the Panel." According to the United States, the factual information concerning the projected demand for automobiles in Australia presented by the United States is therefore unrebutted.

7.250 Similarly, the United States observes that, although Australia questions the figures supplied with regard to the projected demand for automotive leather in Australia, it does not provide any alternative figures. The United States notes that a panel must accept a fact submitted to establish a *prima facie* case that is based upon evidence (1) which is sufficient to raise a presumption that the alleged fact or claim is correct; and (2) that has not been sufficiently rebutted by the opposing party.[159] In this case, the United States argues that the affidavit and the quotes from the Australian Federation of Automotive Product Manufacturers are sufficient to raise a presumption that the alleged facts are correct and because Australia has not presented any evidence to refute the United States' affirmative showing, the Panel must accept the evidence presented by the United States estimating the future demand in Australia for automobiles and automotive leather.

[159] The United States refers to *Japan - Measures Affecting Agricultural Products* ("*Japan - Agricultural Products*"), WT/DS76/R, circulated to Members on 27 October 1998, para. 7.10.

7.251 The United States submits that, given the large disparity between Howe's increased capacity and the domestic demand for its product, Howe's increased sales and production capacity will necessarily be targeted towards, and tied to, foreign markets. Even if the Australian market for automotive leather were to double between 1997 and 2000 (to almost 3,000 hides per week), this increased demand would take up less than 15 per cent of Howe's new production capacity. Clearly, the United States argues, for Howe to reach its sales goals and use its expanded capacity, it must increase its exports dramatically.

7.252 According to the United States, the anticipated increases in sales and production are consistent with promises Howe made in its bid for the replacement package. It has been reported that Howe "promis[ed] untold export riches ($600 million over the four years to the 2000)" to the Australian government in order to secure the new subsidies.[160] Specifically, Howe projected that its automotive leather sales would mushroom from $88.6 million in 1997 to $214 million by 2000, with the lion's share of the growth coming from exports.

7.253 **Australia** submits that the loan contract plainly has no possible connection with any sort of performance, let alone a tie to exports. Indeed, the United States has not even seriously tried to make a connection beyond questioning how the loan contract will be serviced. The loan contract itself provides the conditions under which the actual money was lent, including the assets of the parent company, ALH, being security for the loan and the terms under which payments are to be made by the parent company and Howe. Virtually all companies have loans as a matter of normal business practice, loans which have to be serviced and turned over as part of the normal cash flow of a company's operations. There is nothing particularly different about this loan. The loan contract was made on 9 March 1997. While it does extend to 1 February 2012, the government has no call on the money so long as the company makes repayments according to schedule. The level of sales is irrelevant so long as the company pays the government any monies owing, and the United States has not made any allegations or produced any facts to the contrary. How much the company produces and to whom it sells is irrelevant. The money is simply not recoverable except according to the loan contract, i.e. the repayments of principal and interest owing. There is no connection with sales, let alone exports, under the contractual relations between the company and the government.

7.254 With respect to the grant contract, Australia maintains that only the first two payments under the grant contract are measures before the Panel. These were both made by July 1997. The monies are not recoverable regardless of the actual level of sales by the company and so cannot be considered to be in some way in fact tied to exports. According to Australia, there is no way in which they

[160] "Sacred Cows vs. The Hide of Howe," *The Weekend Australian*, Sept. 20-21, 1997, p. 52, United States Exhibit 22.

could be linked in even the most tenuous way to future exports, let alone satisfy the stringent requirements for the "in fact" condition in Article 3.1(a) of the SCM Agreement. The first payment of A$5 million was made following the signing of the grant contract. This was an automatic payment. It was not tied to anything, let alone export performance. The second payment of A$12.5 million (the other measure before the Panel) was the maximum allowed. It was made on the basis that the company had satisfied its investment and sales targets on a best endeavours basis. There is no way that the company could have obtained more money regardless of how much it invested or sold.

7.255 In Australia's view, subsequent payments are not measures before the Panel. However, the maximum amount under the grant contract has been all but paid out, with the company exceeding its investment targets. The third payment was made on the basis of an assessment in July 1998 that the company had on balance performed satisfactorily on a best endeavours basis in respect of a combination of investment and production in 1997/98, as well as normal due diligence considerations such as whether the company was functioning properly. The government cannot take back that money provided that the company continues in business. The money has been paid out lawfully. The company could expand or reduce sales and the status of the payments under the grant contract would be unchanged. The money is gone and there is no connection with future sales, including sales for export.

7.256 The **United States** underlines that the terms of the assistance package and the limited size of the Australian market for automotive leather make clear that the subsidies are in fact tied to Howe's export performance. The fact that Australia thus far has paid out the maximum amounts in grants allowed under the assistance package - coupled with the fact that Howe's business is almost exclusively dedicated to exporting - indicate that Australia, in effect, has provided Howe with substantial financial benefits based on its export performance.

7.257 In respect of Australia's claim that the grants in the assistance package are calculated based on Howe's total production, not on exports, and therefore are not tied to export performance, the United States asserts that, given the large disparity between Howe's increased capacity and the domestic demand for its product, its increased production capacity resulting from the assistance package will necessarily be targeted towards, and tied to, foreign markets.

7.258 In respect of Australia's argument that the loan had no conditions for disbursement and therefore is not tied in any way to exports, the United States asserts that, first, although the loan contract is a separate measure, it is inextricably linked to the grant contract. Both these measures, which were announced at the same time, were provided to Howe to compensate for its exclusion from the export subsidies under the ICS and EFS programmes. In addition, the United States points out, Australia states with regard to the loan that "the level of sales is irrelevant so long as the company pays the government any monies owing…." The Australian government has stated publicly that the new subsidies were the minimum amount necessary to ensure the viability of the company and that "any amount less than provided by the assistance package would in all likelihood have seen the company fold." In the view of the United States, given the fact the company has no choice but to increase its exports in order to increase its sales given the limited size of the domestic market, the fact that the company exports over 90 per cent of its production, and the acknowledgement by the Australian government that the company's survival depended upon the new subsidies, the viability of the loan is necessarily contingent upon Howe's export earnings. If Howe does not export, the Australian government will not be repaid. Consequently, the loan is "in fact tied to Howe's actual or anticipated exportation or export earnings" as provided in Article 3.1 of the SCM Agreement.

7.259 According to the United States, it is also significant that the replacement subsidies provided to Howe have not been provided to other Australian producers of automotive leather for the Australian market. This reinforces the notion that the replacement package is not part of a general domestic subsidy programme intended to benefit the leather industry, but instead is more narrowly focused on a unique Australian business that overwhelmingly exports its products.

7.260 **Australia** responds by stating that it is unclear what is meant by the statement of the United States that the loan contract is "inextricably linked to" the grant contract, given that the time periods and conditions are quite different. Moreover, this does not explain how under Article 3.1(a) of the SCM Agreement, there is any justification for looking at a number of measures simultaneously to determine their WTO status. For a violation case, each measure before the Panel needs to be looked at separately, and the United States has not sought to rebut that through argument. Australia maintains that the loan is a separate measure that needs to be assessed separately in its own right.

7.261 With respect to the loan, Australia submits that there is no basis for the United States' assertions that 'if Howe does not export, the Australian government will not be repaid and that, consequently, the loan is "in fact tied to Howe's actual or anticipated exportation or *export earnings.*"', and no argument is presented by the United States to support them. In fact, there is no commercial or legal basis on which the loan contract could be interpreted in this way. The loan is to ALH and Howe. The loan is secured by ALH. The servicing of the loan contract will not commence before 2003. Precisely how the borrowers finally acquit the loan is a matter solely for the borrowers themselves, and there is nothing to support a claim that the loan can only be serviced through income generated from export sales, in particular export sales of automotive leather. The ability of ALH to repay does not rely solely on the domestic or export markets for automotive leather. These are currently important elements of the Group's operations, but it is impossible to say what the markets or the product mix will be when the major repayments are due. The loan contract determines the interest rate payable and the schedule for repayments of principal. It does not prescribe how ALH will fund the repayments or from where it will source these funds.

There is no tie to sales or export performance or to the product or products concerned.

7.262 Australia asserts that the continued commercial viability of the ALH Group, as with all firms, depends on sales in all markets and not just export markets. In Howe's case specifically the company has two main facilities: the tannery at Rosedale; and the finishing plant at Thomastown. The tannery produces wet blue hides and crust leather. These can go to many types of leather, both on domestic and export markets. While at the moment the production of Rosedale is going in the main to Thomastown, technically there is nothing fixed about this. In the longer term if the market changed, hides could go for other than automotive leather at Thomastown. Similarly, while some of the finishing and cutting machinery is adapted to the production of automotive leather, this is by no means fixed. The works can, and currently do, produce leather other than automotive leather. If the market for automotive leather changed, then the output from both Rosedale and Thomastown would change. This is the way all businesses work and adapt. Australia observes that the loan contract does not prevent Howe from producing and selling other products. It is impossible to say what the nature of the fashion and global market for automotive leather and other leathers will be by the end of the loan contract's repayment period. Certainly, there is nothing to suggest that it has to be paid back through production, let alone exports, of automotive leather.

7.263 Australia asserts that, regarding the first two payments under the grant contract (the only ones that Australia considers are before the Panel), the first payment was simply A$5 million, while the second payment was capped at A$12.5 million and this was paid in full. The first payment was made in March 1997 following the completion of the grant contract in March 1997. This was simply a flat payment and not subject to any assessment of investment or sales. It was not contingent on the company doing anything and so could not be linked in any way to export performance. The second payment was made in July 1997 against investment as well as sales. The maximum amount was paid of A$12.5 million because the government assessed that the company had used its best endeavours regarding investment and production in 1996/97. There was no way in which more could have been paid regardless of the actual amount of investment or sales. Australia argues that further payments are not before the Panel. However, the third payment was again made on the basis of an assessment in July 1998 that the company had on balance performed satisfactorily on a best endeavours basis in respect of a combination of investment and production in 1997/98, as well as normal due diligence considerations such as whether the company was functioning properly. Australia asserts that business confidential information it provided to the Panel supports its position that the payments to Howe under the grant contract were not based on Howe's export performance.

7.264 The **United States** considers that Australia's arguments regarding the "automatic" nature of the first grant payment and the fact that it preceded performance under the grant contract is flawed for two reasons. First, this payment, like the other payments, was made pursuant to the single grant contract which is tied to Howe's export performance. The facts in this case - including the prior "in law" automotive and textile export subsidies, Howe's exceptional export performance, the small size of the Australian market, the statements by high level Australian government officials and Howe - prove that the grant contract, which subsumes the grant payments, was provided in anticipation of exportation and export earnings. Furthermore, it is immaterial that this initial payment was automatically made prior to Howe's performance under the grant contract. Footnote 4 encompasses subsidies "tied to ... *anticipated* exportation or export earnings" (emphasis supplied by the United States); thus, exportation can follow the granting of the benefit. To be actionable as a prohibited subsidy, the facts need only demonstrate that, like in this case, the subsidy was provided because of foreseeable or probable export conduct.

7.265 Further, the United States contends, Australia asserts that the second and third grant payments are not "in fact" export subsidies because the grant contract does not require Howe actually to achieve any sales targets; instead, Howe only has to use its "best endeavours" to do so. The strict prohibition against export subsidies cannot, however, be so easily circumvented. Clearly, Australia conferred these payments in the expectation that Howe would attempt substantially to increase its exports. That Australia would provide grant payments even if Howe did not fulfill its ambitious promises only underscores the extent of Australia's commitment to this export-oriented company. In other words, regardless of whether it actually met its performance commitments, Howe would receive additional grant payments because any increased production would - given the small size of the Australian automotive market - necessarily be shipped abroad.

7.266 With respect to the grant contract, **Australia** asserts that Article 3.1(a) and footnote 4 of the SCM Agreement are about a panel reaching the conclusion demonstrated through an objective assessment of facts that the granting of a subsidy is contingent upon export performance, even though it may not be required in law. This contrasts sharply with the situation under the grant contract, where the official responsible for administering the Australian government's obligations under the contract is required *in law* to consider total sales and so does not discriminate between domestic and export sales. Indeed, Australia states, the United States has not even made an allegation that the administration of the grant contract, i.e. the actual disbursement of the grants, is in any way contingent on export performance.

7.267 Australia notes that the United States seems to consider that providing assistance to only one producer of automotive leather in Australia is significant. The fact is that Howe is the automotive leather industry in Australia. There is nothing in the WTO Agreement that says that Members cannot provide assistance to such firms, and the United States has not made any legal argument about this. This is a natural occurrence in a small country. Similarly, Australia points out, the United States seems to consider that it is significant that this company is the only firm to be benefiting from the arrangement. Again the history of this is clear, i.e. the arrangements cover just automotive leather with Howe being the only significant producer in Australia.

7.268 The **United States** repeats that the terms of the assistance package and the limited size of the Australian market for automotive leather make clear that subsidies are in fact tied to Howe's export performance. The Australian government conditioned receipt of the grant monies upon Howe dramatically increasing its sales and meeting certain capital investment requirements.

7.269 **Australia** responds that the United States has not demonstrated its assertion that the Australian government conditioned receipt of the grant money upon Howe dramatically increasing its sales. Indeed, the record shows that Howe simply received the first payment ($A5 million) on execution of the grant contract. The second payment of $A12.5 million was on the basis of the next three months, which was hardly time for a dramatic increase in exports. The third payment was on the basis of 1997/98, and again the record shows that this was not on the basis of increased sales of automotive leather. Australia bases these assertions on business confidential information it provided to the Panel.

7.270 Australia states that, in referring to "conditioned receipt of the grant money", the United States again appears to have moved from its position that the issue is the information available at the time of granting the grant contract to the issue of the basis for granting the individual payments. Otherwise it must be saying that the Australian Government did not care what the actual outcomes would be - if so, the standard of footnote 4 of the SCM Agreement can hardly have been met.

7.271 In addition, Australia submits, "conditioned receipt" is an interesting phrase. "Conditioned" means "subjected to conditions or limitations.[161] Thus, this phrase can only refer to the granting of the payments after the first payment and not to anything else. Clearly, the granting of the loan contract, the money under the loan contract, and the grant contract were not subject to any requirements. Moreover, the first payment under the grant contract was not subject to any conditions. In addition, the record shows that there was no such "conditioned receipt" related to exports. The United States asserts that the capital expenditure implies an enormous increase in production. The capital expenditure was on a new finishing plant and on a tannery. A tannery does not increase Howe's capacity to produce automotive leather. It aims to improve Howe's efficiency as an integrated operation. However, Howe sourced hides from other companies before the plant was established and still does. Some semi-processed hides are even imported. The capacity for producing automotive leather depends on the finishing plant. This was a replacement for an old plant. It was not an additional plant. Its purpose was to increase efficiency not to increase capacity. The efficiency dividend has had the effect of increasing practical capacity by

[161] *Shorter Oxford English Dictionary*, third ed.

about a quarter, but capacity does not reflect production levels. In the real world, plants rarely run at anything like the full theoretical capacity for extended periods of time. Indeed, a maximum weekly capacity figure cannot be directly translated into annual figures. The United States has simply taken an old press figure on production levels, derived a capacity figure, and come to the conclusion that production has doubled.[162]

7.272 The **United States** contends that, at the time the Australian government agreed to provide the assistance package, the Australian domestic automobile market could not absorb all of Howe's production, let alone any increased production. To the United States, the fact that Australia thus far has paid out the maximum amounts in grants allowed under the assistance package - coupled with the fact that Howe's business is almost exclusively dedicated to exporting - strongly indicates that Australia provided Howe with substantial financial benefits based on its export performance.

7.273 **Australia** responds that these arguments do not demonstrate that the granting of a subsidy was contingent upon export performance. Indeed, the record shows quite the contrary. The grants paid to Howe were not based on Howe's export performance. The final sentence of the United States' arguments in the previous paragraph - "[t]he fact that Australia has thus far paid out the maximum amounts in grants ..." - underscores that the United States is moving between its two stools of whether it is talking about the payments or the grant contract.

7.274 The **United States** insists that, because of the large disparity between Howe's increased capacity and the domestic demand for its product, Howe's increased production capacity resulting from the assistance package will necessarily be targeted towards, and tied to, foreign markets. The Australian government realized that Howe could not meet its "sales target" - that is, its expanded "export" goals - unless it substantially expanded its capacity. Thus, the capital investment made by Howe was needed before it could achieve the anticipated export levels. Simply saying that this money was tied to production and spent on Howe's investments is therefore not sufficient to break the link between the export-nature of these substantial benefits.

7.275 **Australia** responds that, clearly, if a firm exports, then in a trivial sense, some of its sales go to foreign markets. However, this is not the same as being "tied to, foreign markets" as stated by the United States. The grant contract shows that that was not the case. On the issue of investment, Australia has informed the Panel, and the United States has not denied, that it was at the insistence of the United States that the company was obliged to implement an investment programme amounting to much of the A$30 million of the grant con-

[162] Australia disputes the United States argument on this point, referring for support to business confidential information that it provided to the Panel regarding Howe's sales.

tract. This was done to meet the wishes of the United States not with any idea of linkage to exports in mind.

7.276 The **United States** asserts that the fact that export promotion is merely one of several objectives for a programme does not mean that a programme is not an export subsidy. Article 3.1(a) of the SCM Agreement specifically notes that export subsidies are prohibited when the subsidies are contingent upon export "whether solely or as one of several other conditions." Clearly, the United States argues, other conditions may be imposed on the recipient, but so long as the benefit is tied to exports, an export subsidy still exists. Indeed, in many instances, a subsidy may have more than one objective. As Australia has admitted in this case, the subsidy programme was given for two reasons: (1) to allow Howe to increase its investment; and (2) to ensure that Howe would reach its "sales" (or export) targets.[163] Thus, nothing in the SCM Agreement indicates or suggests that subsidy programmes must only have a single goal of promoting exports. The express language of the Agreement makes this clear. Rather, if one component of the subsidy programme is that the aid is tied to actual or anticipated exports, then the programme is an export subsidy.

7.277 The United States repeats that, although the loan contract is a separate measure, it is inextricably linked to the grant contract. Both these measures, which were announced at the same time, were provided to Howe to compensate for its exclusion from the export subsidies under the ICS and EFS programmes.[164] Finally, the Australian government stated publicly that the total replacement package was the minimum amount necessary to ensure the viability of the company and that "any amount less than provided by the assistance package would in all likelihood have seen the company fold.'[165] Clearly, the Australian government considers that the loan and the grant were always part of a single benefit package given to Howe.

7.278 **Australia** notes that the United States recognizes that the loan contract is a separate measure and does not deny that the two contracts (i.e. grant and loan) are legally separate instruments. Under Article 3.1(a) of the SCM Agreement, a panel is required to look at each subsidy separately to determine whether it meets the standards set out in that article. There is no provision for cumulating subsidies as there is under Parts III and V of the SCM Agreement. The Panel's terms of reference are clear that the loan contract is a separate measure and so needs to be looked at separately on its own merits.

[163] The United States cites certain paragraphs of Australia's first written submission in this regard. Australia states that it did not say this and that the United States has misunderstood its arguments.

[164] The United States also referred to certain business confidential information in making this argument.

[165] United States Exhibit 18.

7.279 According to Australia, the language of the contracts is simply the standard legal terminology used in contracts by the Australian Department of Industry, Science and Resources (previously Industry, Science and Tourism) and does not represent any legal relationship between them that would result in a nexus under Article 3.1(a) of the SCM Agreement. To the extent that the United States argues on the basis that the two contracts replaced the application of the ICS and EFS to automotive leather, then it is not logical to consider the two contracts together. The loan contract runs until 2012. The grant contract runs until 2000 for auditing purposes but its payments are on the basis of the period to mid-1998. On the other hand, the ICS and EFS terminate in 2000. Following the termination of the ICS in mid-2000, automotive leather is to be covered by the new general textile, clothing and footwear industry arrangements.

7.280 According to the **United States**, it is also significant that the replacement subsidies were designed and structured specifically for Howe after an accounting firm was commissioned to study the issue[166] and that no similar subsidies have been provided to other Australian producers of automotive leather for the Australian market. This reinforces the notion that the replacement package is not part of a general domestic subsidy programme intended to benefit the leather industry, but instead is more narrowly focused on supporting a unique Australian business that overwhelmingly exports its products.

7.281 In response, **Australia** states that the arrangements were designed and structured to try to meet the requests of the United States government. The circumstances of why these applied to automotive leather alone are clear and there are no other substantial, dedicated producers of automotive leather in Australia. In particular, there are no other producers of automotive leather for the original equipment manufacturers (OEM) market.

7.282 The **United States** asserts that Australia's argument that the United States has failed to demonstrate an "in fact" export subsidy is without merit. The argument of the Australian government that the grant and the loan are not "tied" to exports because Howe would not be required to return either the grant or loan if the company ceased exporting is both factually and legally incorrect. First, Howe was principally an exporter when the initial funds were given and it continues to export in significant volumes. As the Australian government indicated, Howe met its "sales target" as established by the grant contract, and the second and third payment of the grant were in fact dependent on Howe having met these goals. Thus, any export goals the Australian government may have expected from Howe were being met.

7.283 **Australia** states that these comments must arise from a misunderstanding by the United States. The relevant paragraphs to which the United States refers are in respect of the loan contract. The loan contract has nothing about sales, let

[166] United States Exhibit 18.

alone exports. Moreover, there is nothing that says where the money has to come from to service the obligations of ALH (including Howe) under the loan contract. There is nothing that ties the servicing of the loan contract to automotive leather, let alone to exports of automotive leather. The other provisions cited by the United States are about the grant contract and are about the past rather than the future, i.e. about 1996/97 and 1997/98. These payments were not based on Howe meeting any "export goals". The success or otherwise of Howe in making sales of automotive leather in the future, including to overseas markets, is not relevant. If Howe is unable to sell more automotive leather, or indeed if sales happened even to fall, there would be no recovery of the monies. The future performance of the company is not an issue. In addition, the grant contract was about investment and sales by the company and not just sales of automotive leather, i.e. it was not limited to automotive leather. There is clearly no connection to future sales of automotive leather, let alone any aspect of the grant contract being contingent upon export performance.

7.284 The **United States** argues that whether the grant or loan is recoverable if the recipient ceases to export is not dispositive of whether the programme is an "export subsidy" in law or in fact. Rather, the dispositive question is whether, *at the time* the subsidies were granted, they were tied to the *actual or anticipated* exportation or export earnings. In this case, the answer to this question is manifestly "yes." These funds were not given to just *any* company with the potential to increase its investment and sales. The funds were given to a company who was well known for its aggressive export plans and its past performance of exporting 90 per cent of its sales. Moreover, these funds were given to compensate Howe for losing two "in law" export subsidies, with the publicly stated purpose of promoting exports, and were given to Howe to increase its capacity even though the Australian market could in no way absorb Howe's expanded capacity to produce automotive leather. The United States maintains that thus, the overwhelming evidence - evidence that was never rebutted by Australia - demonstrates that the grant and loan were tied to anticipated exports and that the Australian government's expectations in this respect were not disappointed.

7.285 **Australia** contends that the United States appears to be arguing here about the conditions of the granting of the loan contract and the conditions of the granting of the grant contract. The United States is arguing that the fact that an enterprise exports and is anticipated to continue to export is equivalent to the granting of a subsidy being *tied* to exports or the anticipation of exports. The two concepts are not the same, apart from this linkage being ruled out by footnote 4 of the SCM Agreement. The acceptance of such a linkage would mean that giving a subsidy to any enterprise that is dependent on export markets would be prohibited. Conceptually, a company might export less than 50% of its production and still be financially dependent on exports. Indeed, this would often be the case.

7.286 Australia submits that, in the case of the grant contract, the United States appears to be arguing that the conditions under which the actual payments were made is irrelevant. This can only mean that the United States is saying that it does not matter on what basis decisions were taken to pay the money to the company. As a result, the United States is falling back on a level of exports test. This is not the standard set out in footnote 4 of the SCM Agreement. It does not demonstrate the *tie* required to conclude that the granting of the grant contract was contingent upon export performance.

7.287 According to the **United States**, the Australian government's suggestion that subsidies can only be "tied" to exports if the monies are refundable if export goals are not met would effectively negate the explicit language of the SCM Agreement. Footnote 4 to Article 3.1(a) of the SCM Agreement states that an export subsidy in fact exists "when the facts demonstrate that the granting of a subsidy, without having been made legally contingent upon export performance, is in fact tied to actual or *anticipated* exportation or export earnings"(emphasis supplied by the United States). The ordinary meaning of the term "anticipate" is "expect, foresee, or regard as probable."[167] The ordinary meaning of the term is incompatible with Australia's argument that a subsidy would only be conferred upon actual exportation or lost if the recipient is unable to demonstrate that the goods were exported.

7.288 **Australia** responds that the standard of footnote 4 of the SCM Agreement requires that the *tie* to actual or anticipated exportation or export earnings must be demonstrated. Australia has not said that this meant that there had to be a requirement for monies to be repaid if anticipated exports were not achieved. Presumably, if there was a legal requirement in respect of anticipated exports, then the subsidy would be in law contingent on export performance. There are many ways in which this could be handled administratively. For example, the administration might want to see delivery contracts for exports before paying money out or might penalize a company by reducing future payments. This goes to the crux of what is meant by "in fact" in Article 3.1(a) of the SCM Agreement. This is supposed to be about administration of schemes whereby payments are contingent on export performance while not being legally contingent upon export performance. In this particular case, the legal nature of the contracts specify the terms under which the monies are paid out and so remove the scope for such administrative action.

7.289 In response to questioning from the Panel, Australia asserted that the phrase "anticipated exportation or export earnings" has to be read not only in the context of the full phrase "actual or anticipated exportation or export earnings", but also in the context of the whole of Article 3.1(a) and footnote 4 of the SCM Agreement. The phrases "actual exportation or export earnings" and "anticipated exportation or export earnings" relate to the timing of the payments contingent upon export performance. The two phrases cover concrete exports that have

[167] *The Concise Oxford Dictionary,* Clarendon Press, 8th ed.

been made or will be made, respectively. The distinction between exportation and earnings relates to product volumes and earnings to cover all variations. For Australia, this underlines that the discipline is in respect of real export performance, and not some more far-reaching rule based on level of exports as proposed by the United States.

7.290 The **United States** asserts that, in making its assertion that the benefits were not "tied" to exports, the Australian government has misinterpreted a portion of the United States' argument. Australia suggests that the United States is arguing that "the cap" on the grant of A$30 million subsidy makes the measure prohibited. The United States is not arguing that the cap on the amount of the grant somehow affected the nature of the subsidy. Rather, as the Australian government itself indicates, the continued payment of the grant was tied to the volume of "sales." Given that the overwhelming majority of these "sales" could only be exports because of the small domestic market for automotive leather, the Australian government's own admission reveals that in fact, the grant was "tied" to exports.

7.291 **Australia** counters that the statement on which the United States comments in the above paragraph simply pointed out the false logic in the United States' argument about the company needing to increase its sales to A$600 million in order to obtain the full A$30 million and so this cap apparently meant that it was an export subsidy. The hypothetical point was made that Article 3.1(a) of the SCM Agreement is not supposed to prohibit bounty payments (i.e. payments based on the amount of production or sales). Many bounty schemes are uncapped and the more that is produced, the more the monies paid out. That does not make them prohibited. It would be absurd to have the situation where a cap on the amount of money suddenly made a bounty prohibited, which seemed to be the logic of the United States' position. This particular case is not about a bounty and the company did not have to achieve the levels of sales being talked about by the United States.

7.292 The **United States** contends that the Australian government's attempt to distort the facts and arguments raised in this case and apply them to some potential future situation should not dissuade the Panel from carefully analyzing the facts in this case. Despite Australia's claim, there would be no bias against smaller WTO Members if the Panel rules in favour of the United States in this proceeding. This case does not turn on the fact that Australia only has one exporter of automotive leather. If 100 companies had been excluded from Australia's textile and automotive leather programmes; and if those companies had high export levels; and if each then received the same grant and preferential loan bestowed on Howe; and if high-level government officials stated that the replacement subsidies were being given to ensure the continuation of their exports; and if the Australian automotive leather market could not absorb additional production; then an "in fact" export subsidy would still have been conferred - even though 100 companies were involved. In other words, this case does not turn on the fact that only one exporter received this benefit. Rather, the relevant fact highlighted by the United States was that only the exporter of leather received this benefit, not other Australian leather tanners that were not exporting. If the Australian government was interested simply in expanding its leather industry in Australia, presumably it would have provided benefits to all leather tanners, not just the one exporter. Thus, the Australian government's attempt to apply the facts of this case to a situation involving smaller WTO Members is not valid. As this demonstrates, smaller WTO Members will not be disadvantaged by an affirmative finding in this proceeding.

7.293 **Australia** maintains that the small country issue is about the relative size of domestic markets and the economies of scale in manufacturing processes. In a small country such as Australia, there would be a limited range of manufactured products where there would be 100 companies producing that product let alone with each having a high level of exports. On the other hand, in a country the size of the United States, it might be more likely for there to be 100 manufacturers of a particular product line, though it would be limited by the nature of the industry. For example, the automotive leather industry is highly concentrated in the United States.

7.294 Australia states that the United States' argument about other leather companies not receiving the same arrangements is irrelevant, given the background to this case. Automotive leather will be part of the new general textile, footwear and clothing industry arrangements due to come into force on 1 July 2000.

7.295 The **United States** argues that Australia’s concern about the same subsidy being treated as a domestic and export subsidy is unwarranted. In determining the existence of an "in fact" export subsidy, a panel must consider all of the facts surrounding the provision of the aid. It should look at whether and to what extent an industry is currently engaged in exporting and whether the proposed aid is provided in order to encourage increased exports. The fact that some entities in an industry export while others do not is just one of many facts that the Panel should consider in making its decision. If, on the basis of all of the facts surrounding the granting of the aid, the Panel makes an affirmative decision, the aid will be treated as an "in fact" export subsidy - regardless of whether it is provided to an exporting or non-exporting entity. In other words, all recipients will be treated the same once the decision on the nature of the subsidy is rendered.

7.296 To **Australia**, the previous paragraph highlights the inconsistency of the United States' position with the SCM Agreement and underlines the risk of moving away from normal rules of treaty interpretation in examining the meaning of Article 3.1(a) of the SCM Agreement. The United States says that ‘the aid will be treated as an "in fact" export subsidy - regardless of whether it is provided to an exporting or non-exporting entity.’ Thus, the United States admits that the logic of its argument is that the provision of a subsidy to an enterprise that does not even export anything at all could be prohibited as an export subsidy. There is no way in which a normal reading of the text could reach the conclusion that the granting of a subsidy to a non-exporting enterprise is contingent upon export performance. That sort of conclusion would be inconsistent with Article 3.2 of the DSU that sets out that: "[t]he dispute settlement system of the WTO is a central element in providing *security and predictability* to the multilateral trading system." (emphasis supplied by Australia)

7.297 Australia submitted information to the Panel concerning the specific percentage of Howe's total sales attributed to exports in 1997/98. Australia designated this information as "business confidential". The **United States** questions the specific percentage of Howe's total sales attributed to exports in 1997/98 that were submitted to the Panel, and points out that Australia refuses to provide the sales figures for Howe and does not otherwise explain how the numbers presented were calculated or provide any supporting documentation. As a result, the Panel is left without any means for assessing the probative value of Australia's statement. Furthermore, Australia cannot pick and choose which confidential information the Panel should rely on. Unless Australia produces all of the information requested, the Panel should disregard any assertions based on confidential information strategically selected by Australia for presentation to the Panel. In any event, Australia's belated assertion regarding Howe's level of exports seems questionable given the evidence the United States has submitted. These sources[168] indicate that, in 1996, when Australia was developing the compensation package, Howe's exports accounted for 90 per cent of its sales. Australia has provided no evidence to refute that fact. Instead, Australia has provided unsubstantiated information regarding Howe's export levels for the year 1997/98, which began on 1 July 1997, months after the replacement package was provided. However, the relevant number is the level of exports at the time the government made the decision to grant the subsidies. In this case, the undisputed evidence shows that Howe exported over 90 per cent of its production at that time.

7.298 Australia provided, as business confidential information, a breakdown of sales and exports over the three years 1995/96, 1996/97 and 1997/98. Australia asserts that this information shows the trend of sales and underlines the basis on

[168] The United States refers to the following: "...and the Hide of One Australian Tanner", *Australian Financial Review*, November 18, 1996, p. 18 ("'In 1988, we exported 7 per cent of our production; now we are exporting 90 per cent worth over £80 million a year' says the firm's managing director, Chris Heysen), United States Exhibit 3; "Howe leather wins wheels award", *World Leather*, February/March 1997 ("The company [Howe] has increased its exports from 7% to 90% over the last eight years"), United States Exhibit 4; "Major Headache for the Howard Government" *A$ Adding Value*, July 5, 1996 ("Howe's exports have risen from less than 10 percent of sales in 1988, to nearly ninety percent of sales"), United States Exhibit 5; "Trade Showdown", *Herald Sun*, November 20, 1996 ("The company was a shining light with 90 percent of Howe's production being for exports"), United States Exhibit 30; "Picking Winners", *Business Review*, October 13, 1997 ("Howe Leather exports in 1996/97, up from $55 million to $80 million, represent 90 percent of turnover"), United States Exhibit 32.

which the payments were made. Australia asserts that this information shows that the percentage of Howe's total sales for exports were significantly lower than asserted by the United States and demonstrates that the sources of United States data and the type of procedures of imputation used by the United States are fundamentally unreliable. In Australia's view, it also demonstrates that the "best endeavours" clauses of the grant contract are not tied in any way to achieving specific sales, let alone export levels. For Australia, this data also underlines the misunderstanding by the United States of the nature of the sales figures under the grant contract - in particular, that they are not limited to automotive leather.

Factors Other than Level of Exports

7.299 **Australia** observes that the United States says that: footnote 4 to Article 3 of the SCM Agreement "does not preclude consideration of the level of exports, it simply proscribes finding a prohibited export subsidy based solely on *the level of exports*"[169] (emphasis supplied by Australia). Australia argues that this can only mean that the United States agrees that it has to produce facts other than Howe's level of exports to demonstrate that the granting of each of the measures before the Panel is in fact tied to export performance. However, Australia asserts, the United States has not produced such facts. Its argument (which Australia rejects) rests on information regarding quite different prior measures (EFS/ICS) and media reports about a company that exports. This underlines the problem behind interpreting this provision to allow some conceptual examination of the level of exports at all. The level of exports of a company or industry depend on a wide range of factors often specific to the industry or the country that have nothing to do with any particular commercial policy of the government. The availability of export markets and the most profitable product mix can also change quickly as a result of factors quite divorced from any particular governmental assistance measure. If the facts other than the level of exports are sufficient to demonstrate that the granting of a subsidy is in fact tied to export performance, then there is no need to look to the level of exports. If they are not sufficient, then the measure should be found to be in conformity.

7.300 In the view of Australia, a panel's job is not to make subjective judgements about the factors that may influence a company's decisions to export or its success as an exporter. Rather, a panel has to make objective rulings on the basis of facts as to whether the granting of a particular subsidy provided to a company is contingent upon that company's export performance. Footnote 4 of the SCM Agreement requires that the facts demonstrate that the granting of the subsidy is in fact tied to export performance. It does not call for the Panel to make a judgement about the weight of circumstantial evidence regarding the trade effects of a measure. Whether the granting of a subsidy is contingent upon export

[169] *Supra*, para. 7.127.

performance is not a function of the level of exports of a company but of the facts about the granting of the subsidy.

7.301 The **United States** maintains that, in this case, the level of Howe's exports is just one fact among many that, when considered together, demonstrate that the replacement subsidies, like the subsidies Howe enjoyed under the prior *de jure* export subsidy programmes, are prohibited export subsidies. In the view of the United States, its proffering of Howe's current high level of exports and its aggressive export plans goes to the heart of an "in fact" subsidy determination. The United States is not attempting to demonstrate the adverse "trade effects" of a subsidy that has already been granted, i.e., what happened *after* the assistance was bestowed. Rather, the United States proffered evidence of Howe's high level of exports to show what Australian government considered *at the time* the aid was given. Australia's knowledge of Howe's dependence upon exports and Howe's future plans at the time the aid was given is strong evidence that the assistance was tied to export performance within the meaning of footnote 4.

7.302 The United States submits that it has presented substantial evidence demonstrating that the "granting" of the subsidies at issue was in fact tied to Howe's actual or anticipated exportation of export earnings. The United States asserts that, in an effort to avoid the prohibition in Article 3 of the SCM Agreement and distract the Panel from the facts, Australia mischaracterizes the extent of the United States' evidence by focusing entirely on Howe's level of exports. The United States' case clearly does not hinge entirely on the fact that Howe was exporting 90 per cent of its sales at the time Australia conferred the grant and preferential loan. While this high level of exports is an important fact for the Panel's consideration, it was only one of many significant facts demonstrating that the aid was tied to Howe's actual or anticipated exportation or export earnings within the meaning of Article 3.1(a), footnote 4 of the SCM Agreement. Such facts included the following:

(a) The replacement package was specifically and explicitly designed to compensate Howe for its exclusion from two "in law" export subsidy programmes that had helped transform Howe into a major exporter;

(b) The Australian government knew of, and in fact created, Howe's reliance on exports;

(c) The recognized purpose of the replacement package by both the Australian government and Howe - like the "in law" export subsidy programmes that preceded it - was export promotion;

(d) Howe had aggressive export plans;

(e) Howe must significantly increase its sales to receive the full A$30 million grant for which it is eligible; however, the Australian leather market is too small to absorb Howe's current - much less, its increased - production;

(f) The only way that Howe could increase its sales and utilize the expanded production capacity that it has acquired as a result of the replacement package is to significantly increase its exports; and

(g) The replacement package was provided only to Howe, who exports virtually all of its production, and not to any leather manufacturer that supplies the domestic market

7.303 The United States argues that Australia fails to counter any of the United States' factual assertions with facts that would undermine their credibility and asserts that the Panel should note the variety and volume of sources relied upon by the United States in this case.[170]

7.304 The United States recalls that, as noted by the recent panel in *Japan - Agricultural Products*, a panel must accept a fact submitted to establish a *prima facie* case that is based on "evidence (1) which is sufficient to raise a presumption that the alleged fact or claim is correct and (2) that has not been sufficiently rebutted by the opposing party."[171] Once a *prima facie* case has been made, the burden of proof shifts to the responding party.[172] As the Appellate Body stated:

> ...it is a generally-accepted canon of evidence in civil law, common law and, in fact, most jurisdictions, that the burden of proof rests upon the party, whether complaining or defending, who asserts the affirmative of a particular claim or defense. If that party adduces evidence sufficient to raise a presumption that what is claimed is true, the burden then shifts to the other party, who will fail unless it adduces sufficient evidence to rebut the presumption.[173]

7.305 The United States submits that the evidence presented by it, none of which has been refuted by Australia on the merits, establishes a *prima facie* violation of Article 3 of the SCM Agreement. Accordingly, the burden has shifted to Australia to demonstrate that the replacement subsidies were not in fact tied to Howe's export performance. Australia has presented no evidence and has failed to rebut the United States' affirmative showing. Instead, Australia relies on the argument that the Australian government did not intend to violate the SCM Agreement and that, for various unsound reasons, the Panel should simply ignore almost all of the relevant facts in this case. Australia insists that the compensation package is WTO-consistent because Australia claims it is. In the view

---

[170] Also see the United States arguments in this regard, *supra*, paras. 7.30-7.31.

[171] WT/DS76/R, circulated to Members on 27 October 1998, para. 7.10.

[172] Panel Report, *EC Measures Concerning Meat and Meat Products (Hormones),* WT/DS26/R, WT/DS48/R, adopted 13 February 1998, para. 8.51.

[173] Panel Report, *Japan - Film*, WT/DS44/R, adopted 22 April 1998, para. 10.29, citing Appellate Body Report, *United States - Shirts and Blouses*, WT/DS33/AB/R, adopted 23 May 1997, DSR 1997:I, 323, at 335.

of the United States, a review of the relevant evidence demonstrates to the contrary.

E. Remedy

7.306 **Australia** submits that, in the event that the Panel finds that a measure was or is inconsistent with Article 3.1(a) of the SCM Agreement, it considers that the Panel should not make any suggestion on how the Australian government should bring itself into conformity with Article 3.1(a) of the SCM Agreement.

F. Time Period for Implementation

7.307 **Australia** asserts that, in the event that the Panel finds that a measure was, or is, inconsistent with Article 3.1(a) of the SCM Agreement, then the Panel would need to include in its recommendations the time period which Australia has to bring itself into conformity with Article 3.1(a).

7.308 According to Australia, the central problem is that Australia does not know whether the Panel will find that any measure was inconsistent, whether any measure is inconsistent, what measure might be involved, and critically why it might be considered to be inconsistent. In the absence of the Panel's views, it is impossible to make an informed submission in this regard.

7.309 Australia states that the drafting of this provision was done against the background that the PGE would have come to its conclusions and reported to the panel. The panel would then make a recommendation on the time period. This would have involved the parties making submissions on the basis of knowing the precise findings and reasoning that would appear in the panel's Report. That at least made some sense. The draft Rules of Procedure for the PGE[174] envisaged that it would report to a panel 46 days after it had been asked for assistance. This would allow the panel to address the issue in the context of submission from the parties.

7.310 Accordingly, Australia argues this Panel should give the parties, in particular Australia, the right to present arguments about what would be the appropriate time period once the Panel's views are known. The most appropriate time would be after the receipt of the Interim Report. Failing that, Australia submits that the Panel should provide for a period for implementation of 7.5 months.

---

[174] G/SCM/W/365/Rev.1, 24 June 1996, Rule 12.2.

VIII. INTERIM REVIEW

8.1 On 15 March 1999, Australia and the United States requested the Panel to review, in accordance with Article 15.2 of the DSU, precise aspects of the interim report issued to the parties on 8 March 1999. Neither party requested a meeting with the Panel.

8.2 Australia requested a clarifying change to footnote 1, paragraph 1 of the Report. The Panel made this change. Australia also questioned the accuracy of a sentence in paragraph 2.3 of the Panel Report concerning the calculation of the maximum amount of the payments under the grant contract. In light of Australia's comments, we revised the sentence in question to reflect Australia's initial explanation in this regard. In addition, Australia asserted that a phrase in paragraph 9.69 of the Panel Report could be misleading. In light of Australia's comments, we revised the phrase in question.

8.3 The United States requested that the Panel reconsider its finding that the loan was not a subsidy that was "contingent ... in fact...upon export performance" within the meaning of Article 3.1(a) of the SCM Agreement. The United States re-emphasized certain factors, including factors based upon confidential business information submitted to the Panel, which, in its view, lead to the conclusion that the loan is "in fact" contingent upon export performance. The Panel did not make any change to its Report in light of the United States comments.

8.4 In its letter of 8 March 1999 transmitting the interim report to the parties, the Panel had indicated that it was "willing to consider brief arguments with respect to the issue of the time period within which the measures found to be prohibited subsidies must be withdrawn under Article 4.7 of the Agreement on Subsidies and Countervailing Measures". Australia made no comments in this regard. The United States endorsed the Panel's recommendation that prohibited subsidies provided to Howe be withdrawn within 90 days.

IX. FINDINGS

9.1 This dispute concerns certain financial assistance provided by the government of Australia to Howe and Company Proprietary Ltd. ("Howe"), the only dedicated producer and exporter of automotive leather in Australia. Automotive leather is primarily used for seat coverings and other interior components of automobiles, such as head and armrests, centre consoles and door trim.

9.2 On 7 October 1996, the United States requested consultations with Australia concerning subsidies available to leather under the Australian Textiles, Clothing and Footwear Import Credit Scheme[175] (the "ICS") and any other sub-

[175] The ICS has been in effect from 1 July 1991, and remains in effect through 30 June 2000. Under this programme, exporters of eligible textile, clothing and footwear products can earn import

sidies to leather granted or maintained in Australia prohibited under Article 3 of the SCM Agreement.[176] Following consultations, the United States and Australia reached a settlement on 24 November 1996. This settlement was announced on 25 November 1996.[177] Under the terms of settlement, the government of Australia would remove automotive leather from eligibility for benefits under the ICS, as well as under the Export Facilitation Scheme for Automotive Products[178] (the "EFS"), by 1 April 1997. On 26 March 1997, Australian Customs Notice No. 97/29 excised automotive leather from the ICS and EFS, effective 1 April 1997.

9.3 At the time of the settlement, the government of Australia announced a commitment to provide financial assistance to Howe, to help maintain its commercial viability in light of the settlement between Australia and the United States, which resulted in the removal of automotive leather from eligibility under the ICS and EFS programmes.[179] The government of Australia entered into two separate agreements, a grant contract and a loan contract, with Howe and its parent company, Australian Leather Holdings, Limited ("ALH") in March 1997.

9.4 The grant contract provides for three payments totalling up to a maximum of A$30 million, an amount estimated to equal approximately 5 per cent of Howe's expected sales for the period 1 April 1997-31 December 2000. The first payment of A$5 million was to be paid upon conclusion of the contract. The second and third payments, of up to A$12.5 million each, were to be paid in July

---

credits that may be used to reduce the import duties payable on eligible textile, clothing and footwear items by an amount up to the value of the credits held. Exporters are not required to use their credits as offsets against import duties, but may transfer them to another holder in exchange for a cash payment. The value of import credits that can be earned is calculated as the F.O.B. value of an eligible export sale, multiplied by the Australian value-added content of the export sale. This total is multiplied by a specified "Export Phasing Rate". *TCF Import Credit Scheme: Administrative Arrangements* (March 1995), United States Exhibit 7. The ICS is managed by the Australian Customs Service on behalf of the Australian Textiles, Clothing and Footwear Authority.

176 WT/DS57/1, G/SCM/D7/1, 9 October 1996.

177 We note that this mutually agreed solution was not notified to the DSB and the relevant Committee, as is required by Article 3.6 of the DSU.

178 The EFS has existed in its current form since 1991, and remains in effect until 31 December 2000. The EFS allows Australian manufacturers to earn A$1 of export credit for every dollar of eligible exports of covered automotive items. The value of exports eligible to earn export credits is equal to the Australian value-added content of eligible exports, calculated as the F.O.B. sales price less the value of any imported components and raw materials. Export credits earned under this programme can be used to obtain rebates on the duties payable on eligible imports of automotive vehicles and automotive components or may be sold for cash to any importer of eligible goods who may similarly seek such rebates. The amount of import duty that can be rebated under this programme is determined by a tariff reduction schedule that varies depending on the year in which the export credit is used. Australian Department of Industry, Science &Technology, *Report on the State of the Automotive Industry 1994* (June 1995), United States Exhibit 13.

179 See Media Release from the Hon. John Moore, MP, Minister for Industry, Science and Tourism, 25 November 1996, United States Exhibit 16. See also United States Exhibit 18. Australia has indicated that automotive leather will be included in new general textile, industry and clothing arrangements due to come into force in Australia on 1 July 2000.

1997 and 1998 respectively, on the basis of Howe's performance against the targets set out in the contract. The performance targets consist of sales targets and capital expenditure targets. With regard to sales, an overall target for Howe's aggregate sales over the entire term of the contract is established, broken down into interim targets. With respect to capital expenditure, the contract established an aggregate target of A$22.8 million over the four-year period in question, to be spent on approved investments directly tied to the production of automotive leather, also broken down into interim targets. Howe was required, under the contract, to use "best endeavours" to meet these targets, and to provide the Australian government with reports indicating its sales and capital expenditures.

9.5 The loan contract provides for a fifteen-year loan of SA25 million by the government of Australia to Howe and its parent company, ALH. For the first five-year period of this loan, Howe/ALH is not required to pay principal or interest. After the expiration of this five-year period, interest on the loan is to be based on the rate for Australian Commonwealth Bonds with a ten-year maturity, plus two percentage points. The loan is secured by a second lien over the assets and undertakings of ALH.

9.6 On 10 November 1997, the United States requested consultations regarding allegedly prohibited subsidies provided to Australian producers and exporters of automotive leather, including subsidies provided to Howe.[180] Consultations held between the United States and Australia on 16 December 1997 failed to resolve the dispute. At its meeting of 22 January 1998, the DSB established a panel in accordance with Article 4.4 of the SCM Agreement and Article 6 of the DSU pursuant to the request made by the United States on 9 January 1998. That panel was never composed.

9.7 On 4 May 1998, the United States again requested consultations with Australia regarding allegedly prohibited subsidies provided to Howe, alleging that "the [Government of Australia] has provided subsidies to Howe that include a A$25 million loan, which was made on preferential and non-commercial terms, and grants of up to another A$30 million. The United States believes that these measures appear to violate the obligations of the [Government of Australia] under Article 3 of the SCM Agreement". [181] On 11 June 1998, the United States requested the immediate establishment of a panel, and this Panel was established on 22 June 1998, with standard terms of reference.

A. *Preliminary Issues and Requests for Preliminary Rulings*

9.8 The United States and Australia each made requests for preliminary rulings in their first submissions. Specifically, the United States asked the Panel to

[180] WT/DS106/1, G/SCM/D17/1, 17 November 1997.

[181] WT/DS126/1, G/SCM/D20/1, 8 May 1998.

order Australia to produce certain documents. Australia asked the Panel to terminate its work, based on the argument that its establishment was inconsistent with the DSU, or in the alternative, because the United States had failed to meet its disclosure obligations under Article 4 of the SCM Agreement. Assuming the Panel denied the request to terminate, Australia asked the Panel to limit the United States to certain information and arguments in the presentation of its case, based on the argument that the United States failed to meet its disclosure obligations under Article 4 of the SCM Agreement.

9.9 Because these requests involved issues which had important implications for the conduct, indeed, the continuation, of this panel proceeding, we ruled on them at the end of the first meeting with the parties, without detailing our analysis and conclusions.[182] The following sets forth the reasoning underlying our oral rulings of 10 December 1998.

1. *Australia's Request for Termination Based in the Existence of Multiple Panels Regarding the Same Matter*

9.10 Australia requests that this Panel terminate its work and, in effect, disestablish itself, on the grounds that the DSU does not permit the establishment of a panel when another panel between the same parties with respect to the same matter is in existence.

9.11 Australia's request addresses two different and not necessarily related questions. The first is whether the United States had a right or was entitled under the DSU to unilaterally terminate the first panel, and the second is whether this Panel was properly established. The answer to the first question does not, in our view, control the answer to the second. Even assuming that Australia is correct in asserting that a panel may not be unilaterally terminated by the complainant

---

[182] The Chairperson read the Panel's rulings of 10 December 1998, as follows:

> "With respect to the United States request that we ask Australia to produce certain documents, we note that Australia has already submitted redacted versions of the loan and grant contracts. In addition, among the questions from the Panel to the parties are certain requests for information and documents which we have concluded are relevant to our consideration of the issues in this dispute, and therefore have asked Australia to submit.
>
> With respect to Australia's various requests for preliminary rulings, we have carefully considered the arguments of the parties, including the statements made yesterday and the responses to questions put to Australia. We have decided to **deny** Australia's request that we terminate these proceedings. We have also decided to **deny** Australia's request that we order the United States to limit itself to the information set forth in the request for consultations underlying this dispute".

The specific information requested by the Panel, as well as the information provided by Australia in response, are identified in paras. 6.10-6.14 *supra*.

after it is established - an issue we need not and do not decide - we conclude that this Panel must complete its consideration of the matter referred to it.

9.12 The establishment of a panel is the task of the DSB. It is by no means clear that, once the DSB has established a panel, as it did in this case at its meeting of 22 June 1998, the panel so established has the authority to rule on the propriety of its own establishment. Nothing in our terms of reference expressly authorizes us to consider whether the DSB acted correctly in establishing this Panel. Further, the issues raised by Australia's request are of a systemic nature, concerning questions of policy regarding the operation of the WTO dispute settlement system and an evaluation of the actions taken by the DSB, and thus might be more appropriately taken up in other fora.

9.13 Assuming this Panel does have the authority to rule on the propriety of its own establishment, the DSU does not explicitly address the issue of multiple panels between the same parties regarding the same matter, and thus does not expressly prohibit the establishment of such multiple panels. The DSU does, on the other hand, set forth the conditions and procedures which, if complied with, give the complainant a right to have a panel established. Article 4 governs requests for consultations and Article 6 addresses requests for panel establishment. In a dispute such as this one, concerning allegedly prohibited subsidies, the special or additional procedures in Articles 4.2 through 4.12 of the Agreement on Subsidies and Countervailing Measures ("SCM Agreement") are also applicable. Article 4.2 of the SCM Agreement deals with requests for consultations and Article 4.4 deals with requests for panel establishment. In order for a panel to be established in respect of a complaint concerning an allegedly prohibited subsidy, a Member must respect the applicable procedures for consultations and panel establishment set out in these provisions of the DSU and the SCM Agreement. If these procedures are followed, the DSU does not impose any further constraints upon the establishment of a panel.

9.14 In our view, Australia is asking this Panel to read into the DSU an implicit prohibition on multiple panels between the same parties regarding the same matter that does not exist in the text of the DSU. Australia's arguments in support of its position arise out of policy considerations and address the object and purpose of the DSU. In light of the fundamental importance in the WTO dispute settlement system of the right to have a panel established to examine a matter, in the absence of a consensus not to do so, we do not consider it appropriate in this dispute to read such an implicit prohibition into the DSU. This is particularly true given that the policy concerns expressed by Australia are purely theoretical and do not arise in this case. Specifically, this is not a case where a complainant is actively pursuing two proceedings with respect to the same matter - the United States has made it very clear that it is not pursuing the first dispute. To the contrary, the United States has sought to terminate the first dispute, and it is Australia which has sought to prevent that result. Nor is this a case where a complainant has sought a second panel before a first panel has completed its work with respect to the same matter because it was dissatisfied with developments in the first panel. Although the first panel in this case was established, it was never composed and thus never began its work.

9.15 For the foregoing reasons, we deny Australia's request to terminate this Panel, and will continue our work in accordance with our terms of reference.

2. *Compliance with Article 4.2 of the SCM Agreement*

9.16 Australia also asks us to terminate this Panel, or in the alternative, to disregard during the course of this proceeding all facts and arguments not explicitly set out in the request for consultations (WT/DS126/1), based on its assertion that the United States request for consultations does not comply with the requirements of Article 4.2 of the SCM Agreement.

9.17 Article 4.2 of the SCM Agreement provides:

> "A request for consultations under paragraph 1 [of Article 4] shall include a statement of available evidence with regard to the existence and nature of the subsidy in question".

Focusing on the term "available evidence" in Article 4.2, Australia argues that the *quid pro quo* for the accelerated dispute settlement procedure available under Article 4 of the SCM Agreement is that the complainant must "show its hand" at the outset of the proceedings in order to guarantee that information necessary for the respondent to defend itself is provided. In Australia's view, Article 4.2 imposes an obligation on the complainant to disclose, in its request for consultations, not only facts, but also the argumentation why such facts lead the complainant to believe there is a violation of Article 3.1.

9.18 The ordinary meaning of the phrase "include a statement of available evidence" does not, on its face, require disclosure of arguments in the request for consultations. Nothing in the context or object and purpose of Article 4.2, discussed below, suggests a different conclusion.

9.19 Turning to the question of what is required as a "statement of available evidence", we note that Australia reads this to require disclosure of **all** facts and evidence on which the complaining Member will rely in the course of the dispute. Indeed, Australia asserts that any exhibits should have been provided at the time consultations were requested.[183] The ordinary meaning of the phrase "statement of available evidence" does not support Australia's position. The word "evidence" is defined as "available facts, circumstances, etc., supporting or otherwise a belief, proposition, etc.".[184] "Available" is defined as "at one's disposal", and "statement" is defined as "expression in words".[185] Thus, based on the ordinary meaning of the terms, Article 4.2 requires a complaining Member to

183 Australia's first submission at para. 41, *supra*, para. 6.51.

184 *Concise Oxford Dictionary*, ninth ed., 1995.

185 *Ibid.*

include in the request for consultations an expression in words of the facts at its disposal at the time it requests consultations in support of the conclusion that it has, in the words of Article 4.1, "reason to believe that a prohibited subsidy is being granted or maintained". This is, in our view, considerably less than Australia would have Article 4.2 require.

9.20 Moreover, nothing in the context or object and purpose of Article 4.2 suggests to us that the statement of available evidence must be as comprehensive as Australia would require. The mere fact that proceedings under Article 4 of the SCM Agreement are accelerated by comparison to dispute settlement proceedings under the DSU does not, in our view, require us to read into Article 4.2 a requirement that the complainant disclose all facts and arguments in its request for consultations. In dispute settlement proceedings conducted pursuant to a normal schedule, a complaining Member is not even required to include a statement of the facts and arguments in a request for establishment of a panel - which comes considerably later in the dispute settlement process, after a consultation request has been made and after the parties have consulted. The complaining party is required only to identify the claims concerning the matter at issue; the facts and arguments on which it relies to establish its case must be submitted only in the first and subsequent submissions of the party to a panel.[186] To the extent that the additional requirement of Article 4.2 can be linked to the expedited nature of the proceedings, the additional requirement of a statement of available evidence satisfies the need adequately to apprise the responding Member of the information upon which the complaining Member bases its request for consultations, and serves in addition to inform the resulting consultations.

9.21 Looking at the United States request for consultations, we note that the statement of available evidence sets forth both the nature of the evidence at the United States' disposal being relied upon, and summarizes the facts the United States derived from that evidence which support a reason to believe Australia was granting or maintaining a prohibited subsidy.[187] This statement of available evidence was adequate to apprise Australia of the information on which the United States was basing its request for consultations and to inform the resulting consultations. Accordingly, we conclude that the United States request for consultations in this case is in compliance with the requirements of Article 4.2 in that it contains a sufficient statement of available evidence.

---

[186] In *European Communities - Bananas*, WT/DS27/AB/R, adopted 25 September 1997, para. 141, the Appellate Body stated:

> ... there is a significant difference between the *claims* identified in the request for the establishment of a panel, which establish the panel's terms of reference under Article 7 of the DSU, and the *arguments* supporting those claims, which are set out and progressively clarified in the first written submissions, the rebuttal submissions and the first and second panel meetings with the parties.

[187] See WT/DS126/1, excerpted *supra*, para. 6.58.

9.22 Based on the foregoing, we deny Australia's request to terminate this proceeding[188], and we further deny Australia's request that we disregard any facts and arguments not explicitly set out in the request for consultations.

3. *Limitation on Evidence and Arguments*

9.23 Australia also appears to be asking us to rule that, even assuming the United States statement of available evidence complied with the requirements of Article 4.2, the United States is limited to relying on the facts and arguments explicitly set out in its request for consultations in presenting its case to the Panel.

9.24 Australia reads the requirement of Article 4.2, that a request for consultations "include a statement of available evidence", in conjunction with the expedited nature of the proceedings, as requiring a panel to limit the complaining Member to using the evidence and arguments set forth in the request for consultations, and asserts that to allow a complainant to come forward with additional facts and arguments in its first submission is inconsistent with Article 4 of the SCM Agreement.[189]

9.25 A panel is obligated by Article 11 of the DSU to conduct "an objective assessment of the matter before it". Any evidentiary rulings we make must, therefore, be consistent with this obligation. In our view, a decision to limit the facts and arguments that the United States may present during the course of this proceeding to those set forth in the request for consultations would make it difficult, if not impossible, for us to fulfill our obligation to conduct an "objective assessment" of the matter before us.

9.26 As discussed above, Article 4.2 does not require a complaining Member to disclose arguments in the request for consultations. Thus, there is no basis for limiting the scope of arguments in this proceeding.

9.27 Article 4.2 does contain a requirement, not present in the DSU, that a complainant include a "statement of available evidence" in its request for consultations. However, we do not consider that the scope of the evidence that a panel may consider is limited in any way by such a statement of available evidence. In this respect, we note Article 4.3 of the SCM Agreement, which explicitly states that one of the purposes of consultations "shall be to *clarify the facts of the situation...*". (emphasis added) This provision implies that additional facts or evidence will be developed during consultations. Moreover, the Appellate Body has recognized that consultations play a significant role in developing the

[188] We note that, having determined that the United States statement of available evidence is adequate, we need not and do not reach any conclusions as to what action would be appropriate if that statement were not adequate.

[189] Australia's first submission at para. 42, *supra*, para. 6.52.

facts in a dispute settlement proceeding. For example, in *India - Patents*[190], the Appellate Body observed that "the claims that are made *and the facts that are established during consultations* do much to shape the substance and the scope of subsequent panel proceedings". (emphasis added) This is consistent with the view that a central purpose of consultations in general, and of consultations under Article 4 of the SCM Agreement in particular, is to clarify and develop the facts of the situation.

9.28 Moreover, we note that panels have, under Article 13.2 of the DSU, a general right to seek information "from any relevant source". Indeed, it is a common feature of panel proceedings for panelists to question parties about the facts and arguments underlying their positions. There is nothing in Article 4 of the SCM Agreement to suggest that this right is somehow limited by the expedited nature of dispute settlement proceedings conducted under that provision. If Australia's position were correct, a panel might be constrained from seeking out relevant information from the party, in this case the United States, that was limited to reliance on the facts set forth in its request for consultations. Similarly, under Australia's view, the defending party might introduce information during the panel proceedings, which the complaining party, in this case the United States, would not be able to rebut, as it would be limited to reliance on the facts set forth in its request for consultations. We do not believe Article 4.2 requires this result.

9.29 Finally, as noted above, in the usual case, a complaining Member is not even required to include its facts and arguments in a request for establishment of a panel - which comes considerably later in the dispute settlement process than the consultation request. This implies that the scope of the facts and evidence that may be considered in a dispute settlement proceeding should not be limited to those set out in the request for consultations, merely because a proceeding under Article 4 of the SCM Agreement is conducted on an accelerated time schedule. Article 4.2 does require a complaining Member to include more information about its case in its request for consultations than is otherwise required under the DSU. This serves to provide a responding Member with a better understanding of the matter in dispute, and serves as the basis for consultations. Specifically, the statement of available evidence informs the responding Member of the facts at the disposal of the complaining Member at the time it requests consultations that support the complaining Member's conclusion that it has "reason to believe" that a prohibited subsidy is being granted or maintained by the responding Member. The statement of available evidence thus informs the beginning of the dispute settlement process - it does not limit the scope of evidence and argument for the entire proceeding that may ensue to only what is in the request for consultations.

---

190 Appellate Body Report, *India - Patents*, WT/DS50/AB/R, adopted 16 January 1998, para. 94.

9.30 We therefore deny Australia's request that we limit the evidence and arguments on which the United States may rely in this proceeding to those set forth in the request for consultations, WT/DS126/1.[191]

4. *Information Acquired in the Context of Consultations Held Pursuant to the First Request (WT/DS106/1) and Exhibit 2 to the United States First Submission*

9.31 Australia also requests that we rule that information acquired in the context of consultations held pursuant to the first request by the United States, in document WT/DS106/1, including Exhibit 2 to the United States first submission, is not admissible before this Panel. Australia argues that those consultations, and any facts derived by the United States from those consultations, including Exhibit 2, and arguments based on those facts, are confidential to that panel process, and should therefore not be permitted in this panel process without Australia's agreement.

9.32 As Australia rightly notes, Article 4.6 of the DSU provides that "Consultations shall be confidential, and without prejudice to the rights of any Member in any further proceedings". However, in our view, this does not mean that facts and information developed in the course of consultations held pursuant to one request cannot be used in a panel proceeding concerning, as it does in this case, the same dispute, between the same parties, conducted pursuant to another, different request.

9.33 We recall that Article 11 of the DSU obliges a panel to conduct "an objective assessment of the matter before it". As discussed earlier, any evidentiary rulings we make must be consistent with this obligation. The panel in *Korea - Taxes on Alcoholic Beverages* recently confirmed the right of a party to a WTO dispute to use information learned in consultations in panel proceedings. After noting the requirement of confidentiality in Article 4.6 of the DSU, which the panel viewed as "essential if the parties are to be free to engage in meaningful consultations", the panel continued:

> "However, it is our view that this confidentiality extends only as far as requiring the parties to the consultations not to disclose any information obtained in the consultations to any parties that were not involved in those consultations. We are mindful of the fact that the panel proceedings between the parties remain confidential, and parties do not thereby breach any confidentiality by disclosing in those

[191] In this regard we note that, as a matter of fact, almost all of the evidence presented by the United States as exhibits to its first submission falls within the scope of what is described in the request for consultations.

> proceedings information acquired during the consultations. Indeed, in our view, the very essence of consultations is to enable the parties [to] gather correct and relevant information, for purposes of assisting them in arriving at a mutually agreed solution, or failing which, to assist them in presenting accurate information to the panel. It would seriously hamper the dispute settlement process if the information acquired during consultations could not be subsequently used by any party in the ensuing proceedings".[192]

9.34 Given that, in this case, the parties and the dispute are the same, no panel was actually composed or considered the dispute in the first-requested proceeding, and there are no third parties involved in either proceeding who might have learned information in the course of consultations, we cannot see any reason to exclude the United States Exhibit 2 from our consideration, merely because it was developed in the course of the consultations held pursuant to the first request.[193] Australia has failed to specify what other, if any, facts might have been derived by the United States from the earlier consultations, and so there is no basis for us to exclude any such facts.

9.35 We therefore deny Australia's request that we rule that information acquired in the context of consultations held pursuant to the first request by the United States, in document WT/DS106/1, including Exhibit 2 to the United States first submission, is not admissible before this Panel.

B. Are the Measures before the Panel Export Subsidies within the Meaning of Article 3.1(a) of the SCM Agreement?

1. What are the Measures before the Panel?

9.36 Australia argues that the measures before us are the A$25 million preferential loan to Howe and the first two payments made to Howe pursuant to the grant contract. Thus, in Australia's view, neither the third payment to Howe, made in June 1998, nor the grant contract itself are "measures" encompassed by the request for establishment, and are consequently not before us. The United States, on the other hand, asserts that its request for establishment in this dispute explicitly identifies the measures before the Panel as being the loan contract and

192 WT/DS75/R, WT/DS84/R, WT/DS75/AB/R, WT/DS84/AB/R, adopted 17 February 1999, para. 10.23. The referenced aspect of the Panel's ruling was not at issue before the Appellate Body.

193 There is nothing to indicate that there would have been any different answers had the same questions been asked by the United States during consultations held pursuant to the second request. We note Australia's view that there were no consultations held pursuant to the second request, although there was a meeting between the parties. Presumably, this view is based on Australia's position that the second request for consultations, and the second request for establishment, like this Panel which flowed from those requests, were inconsistent with the DSU.

the grant contract, including any and all possible disbursements under the latter contract. In the alternative, citing *Japan - Film*[194], the United States asserts that if the Panel were to conclude that either the grant contract or the third payment thereunder was not explicitly described in the request for establishment, these were clearly included in the request for establishment, as subsidiary or closely related to the specifically identified measures.

9.37 Australia attempts to draw a distinction, in particular, between the grant contract and the three payments made thereunder.[195] The issue is significant because the final payment under the grant contract was not made until after the Panel was established, and thus, in Australia's view, falls outside the Panel's terms of reference and cannot be considered by the Panel. Australia maintains that the Panel will have to consider the consistency with the SCM Agreement of each of the grant payments, and of the loan, separately, and could find that one or more were consistent, and the other(s) were not.

9.38 In our view, the distinction that Australia invites us to draw between the grant contract and the grant payments is artificial as regards the determination of what measures are before the Panel. The document setting out the "matter" before the Panel, and therefore governing the Panel's terms of reference, is the United States' request for establishment of a panel. In this document, the United States states:

> "The Government of Australia has provided subsidies [to Howe]. The United States understands that these subsidies include the provision by the Government of Australia to Howe of grants worth as much as A$30 million and a A$25 million loan on preferential and non-commercial terms". [196]

9.39 The ordinary meaning of the term "provision" is "the act or an instance of providing".[197] The act or instance of providing the grant payments in this case was the grant contract, which established the conditions for the disbursement of the grant funds. Thus, the language of the request for establishment specifically includes the grant contract. Moreover, the ordinary meaning of the term "grant" means "the process of granting or a thing granted",[198] and therefore includes both the government's commitment to make payments (that is, the grant contract), and the grant payments themselves, including all possible disbursements, whether past or future.

---

[194] WT/DS44/R, adopted 22 April 1998.

[195] Australia makes no distinction between the loan contract and the disbursement of the loan funds, and thus seems to accept that loan contract is a "measure" that is before the Panel. See Australia's first submission at para. 58 ("the 'loan' [referred to in the United States' panel request] is clearly the loan provided under the Loan contract"). *Supra*, para. 7.3.

[196] WT/DS126/2, 11 June 1998.

[197] *Concise Oxford Dictionary*, ninth ed., 1995.

[198] *Concise Oxford Dictionary*, ninth ed., 1995.

9.40 Thus, we conclude that the specific words of the request for establishment, which sets the terms of reference for this panel, cover the loan contract (which encompasses the single disbursement of the loan funds), the grant contract, and the individual payments made under the latter contract.[199]

9.41 Apart from the specific language used in the panel request itself, other considerations also support our conclusion that the measures before the Panel are not limited to the specific payments made under the grant contract prior to the request for establishment of this Panel, but include the contract itself and any payments thereunder. The grant contract is the specific legal instrument that lays out the terms and conditions for the individual payments to be made thereunder, and which therefore governs and defines the nature of those payments. The grant contract commits the government of Australia to make certain payments to Howe, provided the conditions established in the contract are satisfied. In our view, we have before us all the necessary information to rule on all the payments provided for in the grant contract.

9.42 Based on the foregoing, we do not consider it necessary to draw the distinction that Australia proposes between the grant contract and the grant payments for the purpose of defining the measures that are before the Panel, and conclude that the measures before us are the loan contract, the grant contract and the individual payments under the latter contract.

2. *Are the Measures before the Panel "Subsidies" within the Meaning of Article 1 of the SCM Agreement?*

9.43 The parties are in agreement that the loan is a subsidy within the meaning of Article 1 of the SCM Agreement. The parties are also in agreement that each of the three payments under the grant contract is also a subsidy within the meaning of Article 1 of the SCM Agreement. However, the parties are not in agreement whether the grant contract itself is a subsidy within the meaning of Article 1 of the SCM Agreement. Therefore, we turn now to that question.

9.44 The United States argues that the grant contract is a "financial contribution" that confers a "benefit" and is, therefore, a subsidy under Article 1 of the SCM Agreement. The United States asserts that Howe has been given a benefit in the form of government funds that it need not repay. Australia, on the other hand, asserts that the United States has not demonstrated that the grant contract is a subsidy, although, as noted above, it acknowledges that the payments authorized by that contract are subsidies, *i.e.* "financial contributions" that confer a "benefit".

[199] In light of our decision, we did not consider, and draw no conclusions regarding, the United States argument regarding subsidiary or closely related measures.

9.45 This issue is closely linked to our discussion above concerning what are the "measures" that are before the Panel. Australia does not dispute that the grant payments are, themselves, subsidies. The terms and conditions for the disbursement of the payments are provided for in the grant contract. In our view, each payment can be evaluated individually to determine whether it is a prohibited export subsidy, but only by reference to the criteria for disbursement set out in the grant contract. Thus, we need not decide whether or not the grant contract is a subsidy in order to evaluate the individual payments. We have determined above that, based on the specific language of the request for establishment, the grant contract is a measure that is before us in this case. The evaluation of the consistency of challenged elements of the grant contract must take into account what actually occurs, particularly in a case where the allegation is that the subsidies are contingent in fact on export performance. Therefore, we need not determine whether the grant contract is itself a subsidy in order to determine whether the payments made pursuant to that contract, which Australia acknowledges are subsidies, are prohibited export subsidies.

3. Are the Subsidies in Question "Contingent, in Law or in Fact" on Export Performance, within the Meaning of Article 3.1(a) of the SCM Agreement?

9.46 Article 3.1 of the SCM Agreement provides:

> "3.1 Except as provided in the Agreement on Agriculture, the following subsidies, within the meaning of Article 1, shall be prohibited:
>
> (a) subsidies contingent, in law or in fact[4] whether solely or as one of several other conditions, upon export performance, including those illustrated in Annex I[...];
>
> ---
>
> [4]This standard is met when the facts demonstrate that the granting of a subsidy, without having been made legally contingent upon export performance, is in fact tied to actual or anticipated exportation or export earnings. The mere fact that a subsidy is granted to enterprises which export shall not for that reason alone be considered to be an export subsidy within the meaning of this provision".

Article 3.2 of the SCM Agreement reinforces this prohibition, providing:

> "3.2 A Member shall neither grant nor maintain subsidies referred to in paragraph 1".

(a) Contingent in Law

9.47 The United States argued, in its first written submission to the Panel, that, because Howe was granted the new aid package as a specific replacement for the *de jure* subsidies of the ICS and EFS export schemes, the new subsidies are also *de jure* export subsidies. However, the United States did not pursue this line of argument in subsequent submissions, after it had received copies of the grant and loan contracts. Australia asserts that the United States put forward no evidence that any of the measures is contingent "in law" upon export performance, and moreover that this issue is not properly before the Panel as there is no claim regarding the question of "contingent in law" in the request for establishment.

9.48 In our view, the Panel's terms of reference include the issue of whether the subsidies in question are contingent "in law" on export performance. The United States panel request cites both the "in law" and "in fact" aspects of Article 3.1(a) of the SCM Agreement, and the United States claim is that the subsidies are inconsistent with Article 3.1(a). How those subsidies are inconsistent, whether because they are contingent in law or in fact upon export performance, is an aspect of the arguments put forward by the United States in support of its claim.

9.49 However, as the United States has not pressed its arguments in this regard, we consider that it has abandoned them. We therefore do not reach any conclusions on this issue, and, turn now to the question whether the subsidies in question are contingent in fact upon export performance.

(b) Contingent in Fact

9.50 The United States argues that the measures are subsidies contingent in fact on Howe's export performance, as they are tied to actual or anticipated exportation or export earnings. The United States favours a broad approach to the "contingent ... in fact" standard in Article 3.1(a), and emphasizes that this standard must be approached on a case-by-case basis, taking into account the structure and design of the measure at stake and the specific facts involved. In the United States view, the distinction between the "in law" and "in fact" standard is that "in law" subsidies are explicitly contingent, and "in fact" subsidies are implicitly contingent, upon export performance. Moreover, footnote 4 of the SCM Agreement does not preclude consideration of the fact of exportation or the level of exports; it simply proscribes finding a prohibited export subsidy based *solely* upon the level of exports. In fact, the explicit reference to level of exports in Article 3, in the United States view, indicates that the drafters specifically contemplated that the level of exports would be taken into account in determining whether a "contingent in fact" export subsidy exists. The United States argues that a contingent-in-fact export subsidy will exist when actual or anticipated exportation is merely one of several potential criteria influencing the bestowal of benefits. Thus, if the totality of the circumstances reveal that these benefits are designed to promote exports, then such benefits fall within the broad definition of Article 3.1(a). The United States urges us to look to the assumptions underlying the government's decision to grant the subsidy in order to determine whether the "in fact" standard has been met.

9.51 Australia favours a narrow approach to the "contingent ... in fact" test in Article 3.1(a).[200] In Australia's view, the contingent in fact standard is defined and limited by footnote 4 of the SCM Agreement. The distinction between "contingent in law" and "contingent in fact" is intended to distinguish between the situation where something is set out explicitly in legislation or regulation ("in law") and where there is some non-legislative, administrative arrangement whereby the granting of the subsidy is actually tied to export performance ("in fact"). The purpose of the "in fact" provision is to provide a way of dealing with the situation where the administration of a subsidy programme allows the disbursement of funds to favour exports, *i.e.* to provide subsidies to firms tied to export performance. Australia urges us to reject a test based on some "undefined level of exports" for determining whether a subsidy is a prohibited export subsidy. The facts must demonstrate that the granting of the subsidy is in fact tied to actual or anticipated exportation or export earnings. In other words, "the complainant must show that the granting of the subsidy is in fact tied in its application to export performance and so favours export over domestic sales".[201] In this regard, Australia argues that WTO rules need to provide clear guidance to Members, and the United States position would leave Member unable to plan domestic support policies in a way that would avoid running afoul of the prohibitions of Article 3.1(a).

9.52 The United States asserts that a subsidy must be found to be "in fact" contingent when actual or anticipated exportation is merely one of several criteria influencing the bestowal of benefits.[202] Thus, the United States asserts that if the totality of the circumstances reveals that the subsidy in question is designed to promote exports, then that subsidy comes within the ambit of Article 3.1(a), and is prohibited.[203] Australia argues, on the other hand, that in order to demonstrate that the granting of the subsidy is in fact tied in its application to export performance, it must be determined that the grant (or maintenance) of the subsidy favours export over domestic sales.[204]

---

200 Referring to the United States references to "*de jure*" and *de facto*" prohibited subsidies, Australia asserts that the United States arguments are misdirected, contending that the SCM Agreement does not refer to "*de jure*" and "*de facto*" export subsidies, but to contingent "in law" and contingent "in fact" export subsidies. In our view, the United States uses the phrase "*de facto*" interchangeably with the phrase "in fact". We thus conclude that the United States arguments clearly relate to the prohibition set forth in Article 3.1(a), regardless of the occasional use of the phrase *de facto*.

201 Australia's first submission, para. 101, *supra*, para.7.103.

202 United States first submission, para. 37, *supra*, para. 7.82.

203 United States first submission, para. 38, *supra*, para. 7.82.

204 Australia's first submission, para. 101, *supra*, para. 7.103.

9.53 The essential difference between the parties relates to the nature and scope of the relationship or connection that must exist between a subsidy and export performance in order for the subsidy to be "in fact" contingent upon export performance and, thus, a prohibited export subsidy within the meaning of Article 3.1(a) of the SCM Agreement. The resolution of this issue hinges upon the interpretation and application of the term "contingent ... in fact ... upon export performance" in Article 3.1(a) of the SCM Agreement.

9.54 Pursuant to Article 3.2 of the DSU, we must interpret Article 3.1(a) of the SCM Agreement "in accordance with customary rules of interpretation of public international law". According to established WTO practice, these rules are found in Article 31 of the *Vienna Convention*. Paragraph 1 of this Article states:

> "A treaty shall be interpreted in good faith and in accordance with the ordinary meaning to be given to the terms of the treaty in their context and in the light of its object and purpose".

9.55 An inquiry into the meaning of the term "contingent ... in fact" in Article 3.1(a) of the SCM Agreement must, therefore, begin with an examination of the ordinary meaning of the word "contingent". The ordinary meaning of "contingent" is "dependent for its existence on something else", "conditional; dependent on, upon".[205] The text of Article 3.1(a) also includes footnote 4, which states that the standard of "in fact" contingency is met if the facts demonstrate that the subsidy is "in fact tied to actual or anticipated exportation or export earnings". The ordinary meaning of "tied to" is "restrain or constrain to or from an action; limit or restrict as to behaviour, location, conditions, etc.".[206] Both of the terms used - "contingent ... in fact" and "in fact tied to" - suggest an interpretation that requires a close connection between the grant or maintenance of a subsidy and export performance.

9.56 In our view, the concept of "contingent ... in fact ... upon export performance", and the language of footnote 4 of the SCM Agreement, require us to examine all of the facts that actually surround the granting or maintenance of the subsidy in question, including the terms and structure of the subsidy, and the circumstances under which it was granted or maintained. A determination whether a subsidy is in fact contingent upon export performance cannot, in our view, be limited to an examination of the terms of the legal instruments or the administrative arrangements providing for the granting or maintenance of the subsidy in question. Such a determination would leave wide open the possibility of evasion of the prohibition of Article 3.1(a), and render meaningless the distinction between "in fact" and "in law" contingency. Moreover, while the second sentence of footnote 4 makes clear that the mere fact that a subsidy is granted to

205 *The New Shorter Oxford English Dictionary*, Vol. 1, 1993.

206 *Ibid.*

enterprises which export cannot be the sole basis for concluding that a subsidy is "in fact" contingent upon export performance, it does not preclude the consideration of that fact in a panel's analysis. Nor does it preclude consideration of the level of a particular company's exports. This suggests to us that factors other than the specific legal or administrative arrangements governing the granting or maintenance of the subsidy in question must be considered in determining whether a subsidy is "in fact" contingent upon export performance.

9.57 Based on the explicit language of Article 3.1(a) and footnote 4 of the SCM Agreement, in our view the determination of whether a subsidy is "contingent ... in fact" upon export performance requires us to examine all the facts concerning the grant or maintenance of the challenged subsidy, including the nature of the subsidy, its structure and operation, and the circumstances in which it was provided. In this context, Article 11 of the DSU requires a panel to make an objective assessment of the facts of the case. Obviously, the facts to be considered will depend on the specific circumstances of the subsidy in question, and will vary from case to case. In our view, all facts surrounding the grant and/or maintenance of the subsidy in question may be taken into consideration in the analysis. However, taken together, the facts considered must demonstrate that the grant or maintenance of the subsidy is conditioned upon actual or anticipated exportation or export earnings. The outcome of this analysis will obviously turn on the specific facts relating to each subsidy examined.

(c) Analysis of the Facts

9.58 The United States asserts that the status of the loan contract, the grant contract, and the grant payments is inextricably linked, and that the factual circumstances demonstrate that each of them is a subsidy contingent in fact upon export performance. In the United States view, the following facts demonstrate that the subsidies in question are prohibited export subsidies: the Australian government was aware that Howe was exporting 90 per cent of its sales at the time the government of Australia entered into the grant and loan contracts; the replacement package was specifically and explicitly designed to compensate Howe for its exclusion from two "in law" export subsidy programmes (the ICS and EFS programmes) that had helped transform Howe into a major exporter; the recognized purpose of the replacement package by both the Australian government and Howe was export promotion; Howe had aggressive export plans; Howe must significantly increase its sales to receive the full A$30 million grant for which it is eligible; however, the Australian leather market is too small to absorb Howe's current - much less, its increased - production; the only way that Howe could increase its sales and utilize the expanded production capacity that it has acquired as a result of the subsidies in question is to significantly increase its exports; and the subsidies in question were provided only to Howe, which exports virtually all of its production, and not to any leather manufacturer that supplies the domestic market.

9.59 Australia emphasizes that the measures before the Panel are individual measures, and each must be individually considered in determining whether it is consistent with the requirements of the SCM Agreement. With regard to the facts relied on by the United States, Australia asserts that the nature of prior measures (the ICS and EFS programmes) is not relevant and, in any case, these measures are outside the Panel's terms of reference; an assessment of the imputed objectives of governments is not the basis on which a rules-based system such as the WTO is supposed to operate; and the structure of the loan and the grant demonstrate that they are not linked in any way to Howe's export performance. With respect to the loan, Australia argues that the level of Howe's production and sales is irrelevant so long as the company pays the Government any monies owing. Precisely how Howe and ALH finally repay the loan is a matter solely for the borrowers themselves. The loan contract determines the interest rate payable and the schedule for repayments of principal. It does not prescribe how Howe and ALH will fund the repayments or from where it will source these funds. Australia notes that the ability of Howe/ALH to repay does not rely solely on the domestic or export markets for automotive leather. These are currently important elements of Howe/ALH's operations, but it is impossible to say what the markets or the product mix will be when the major repayments are due.

9.60 With respect to the grant payments, Australia argues that only the first two payments made under the grant contract are before the Panel. Because these monies are not recoverable regardless of the actual level of sales by Howe, they cannot be considered to be in fact tied to exports. In Australia's view, they are not linked to future exports, let alone satisfying what it considers the stringent requirements for the "in fact" condition in Article 3.1(a). Australia asserts that, in any event, the first payment of A$5 million was an automatic payment made following the signing of the grant contract, and was not tied to anything, let alone export performance. The second payment of A$12.5 million was made on the basis that the company had satisfied its investment and sales targets on a best endeavours basis, as well as normal due diligence considerations. There is no way in which the company could have obtained more money regardless of how much it invested or sold. Assuming the Panel considers the third grant payment, Australia asserts that it was made on the basis of an assessment that the company had performed satisfactorily on a best endeavours basis in respect of a combination of investment and production in 1997/98, as well as normal due diligence considerations. Again, Australia states that the government cannot take back that money, provided that Howe continues in business. The company could expand or reduce sales and the status of the payments under the grant contract would be unchanged. The money is gone and there is no connection with future sales, including sales for export.

9.61 We agree with Australia that we must consider the challenged measures individually to determine their consistency with the SCM Agreement. Merely because all the challenged subsidies form part of a single "package" of assistance to Howe does not mean that all of them are perforce either prohibited export subsidies or not. In this regard, we note that, in our view, it is perfectly possible for a Member to construct a package of subsidies to aid domestic industry, of which some are consistent with the SCM Agreement, and others are not. It is, therefore, necessary that each subsidy be evaluated on its own terms in deciding whether it is consistent with the SCM Agreement.

(i) The Payments under the Grant Contract

9.62 The grant contract provides for three subsidy payments up to a maximum of A$30 million. The contract is between the government of Australia and Howe and its parent company, ALH. However, the terms of the grant contract are specifically directed at Howe, and more particularly at Howe's automotive leather operations. The contract provides for an aggregate sales performance target for the period 1 April 1997 - 31 December 2000, broken down into four interim sales targets.[207] The contract provides for the funds to be disbursed in three payments during the first two years of the contract term.[208] The first payment of A$5 million was made upon the signing of the contract between Howe/ALH and the Australian government. The second and third payments of up to A$12.5 million each were to be made on specific dates in 1997 and 1998 upon receipt of a report from Howe showing performance against the sales performance and investment targets for the years ending 30 June 1997 and 30 June 1998, respectively, satisfactory to the Department of Industry, Science and Tourism. Howe is obliged by the contract to use its "best endeavours" to satisfy the performance targets set forth in the contract.

9.63 Australia has acknowledged that it is unlikely that the grant contract would have been entered into in a circumstance other than the removal of automotive leather from the EFS and ICS programmes. In this regard, we note Australia's argument that it is "simplistic" to conclude that this was the sole reason for providing the challenged assistance to Howe, pointing to, *inter alia*, the government's concern for job retention in the region in the absence of support for the company. However, we recall that Article 3.1(a) recognizes that there may be multiple conditions for the grant or maintenance of a subsidy, and explicitly prohibits a subsidy if one of the conditions is that the subsidy is contingent in fact upon export performance. In taking into consideration the fact that the government of Australia was providing assistance to Howe directly following the removal of automotive leather from eligibility for benefits under the EFS and ICS programmes, we do not make any legal conclusions about those pro-

[207] Howe is obligated to submit reports of its performance against the interim performance targets for each of the periods ending 30 June 1997, 1998, 1999 and 2000, as well as final report in September 2000.

[208] With the exception of a small portion of the third payment held back pending final assessment that Howe has satisfied the requirements of the contract, the maximum amount provided for in the grant contract, A$30 million, has already been paid to Howe.

grammes. The ICS and EFS themselves are not measures that fall within our terms of reference, and we need not draw any conclusions about whether they are prohibited export subsidies under the provisions of Article 3 of the SCM Agreement.

9.64 Australia argues that the nature of the ICS and EFS programmes cannot be considered in analyzing the consistency with the SCM Agreement of the challenged subsidies, including the grant payments, asserting that it must be possible for a government to provide subsidies to domestic firms without such assistance being automatically deemed a prohibited export subsidy even assuming the programme those firms previously benefited from was a prohibited subsidy. WTO Members cannot be prevented from replacing purported prohibited export subsidies with other measures that are not prohibited, thereby bringing themselves into compliance with their multilateral obligations under the SCM Agreement. We agree that, even assuming the ICS and EFS were prohibited export subsidies (a question on which we draw no conclusions), this would not, *ipso facto*, mean that any subsequent subsidy granted to a company that had previously benefited from those programmes would be a prohibited export subsidy.

9.65 Nevertheless, in this case, based upon evidence concerning those programmes submitted by the United States, the facts of which are undisputed by Australia, we observe that both the ICS and EFS programmes give incentives to Australian companies to export certain products. Howe earned significant benefits from its exports of automotive leather pursuant to those programmes. Automotive leather was removed from eligibility under those programmes, and the government of Australia entered into the loan contract and the grant contract providing financial assistance at least in part to tide Howe over after it had lost eligibility for benefits related to automotive leather under these programmes.[209] Public reports at the time indicated that the amount of the assistance provided for was that deemed necessary to ensure that Howe continued in business.[210]

[209] Australia has stated that automotive leather will be among the products eligible under the new programme it is developing to replace the ICS and EFS programmes, anticipated to be put into effect in 2000.

[210] In this regard, we note that Australia argues that the statements of government officials reported in the press cannot be considered evidence of the intent of the Australian government in providing assistance to Howe. We are not drawing any specific conclusions concerning the intent of the Australian government - we recognize that there may have been a number of purposes, a variety of "intent", involved in the decision to assist Howe subsequent to the removal of automotive leather from eligibility under the ICS and EFS programmes. Nonetheless, we consider the reports, both press and company, submitted by the United States as relevant to our analysis of the facts and circumstances surrounding the design and grant of that assistance. Moreover, to the extent that Australia has not specifically challenged the truth of the facts (or statements by individuals) reported, we conclude that we may consider these articles, and make our own judgment as to their appropriate weight and probative value. A commentator on the International Court of Justice's consideration of evidence and proof of facts has stated:

9.66 At the time the grant contract was concluded, Howe exported a significant portion of its production, and the Australian government was aware of this. The parties dispute the level of Howe's exports in relation to domestic sales. However, it is undisputed that Howe's exports had increased significantly during the period it benefited from the ICS and EFS programmes, and that at the time automotive leather was removed from eligibility under those programmes, the overwhelming majority of Howe's sales were for export. The government of Australia was concerned that Howe remain in business, and determined to give it a financial assistance package in order to ensure that it did so.[211] In these circumstances, it is clear to us that continued exports, that is, anticipated exportation, was an important condition in the provision of that assistance. We note, as discussed above, that footnote 4 of the SCM Agreement does not preclude consideration of the fact that a company exports, or of the level of its exports, in a prohibited subsidy examination. Rather, it merely proscribes finding a prohibited export subsidy based *solely* upon the fact that a subsidy is granted to a company which exports. While the fact of exportation cannot be the sole determinative fact in the evaluation, in our view, it is clearly a relevant factor in this case, as is the level of exports.

9.67 Moreover, it is clear that the Australian market for automotive leather is too small to absorb Howe's production, much less any expanded production that might result from the financial benefits accruing from the grant payments, and the required capital investments, which were to be specifically for automotive leather operations.[212] Therefore, we conclude that, in order to expand its sales in a manner that would enable it to reach the sales performance targets (interim

---

> "It appears to be the case that press reports, when significant but not denied by the responsible state, or when reporting other events such as official statements by responsible officials and agencies of that state, are accepted; [footnote omitted] but when they are uncorroborated or do not otherwise contain material with an independent title of credibility and persuasiveness, the tendency of the Court is to discount them almost entirely".

Highet, *Evidence and Proof of Facts*, in Damrosch, *The International Court of Justice at a Crossroads*, 1987. Similarly, we take into account the circumstances in which the reported remarks were made, the source, and whether the information is corroborated elsewhere or contrary evidence is offered, in assessing the value of these exhibits as evidence.

[211] In this regard, we note that Australia commissioned a report from an independent accounting firm concerning Howe's business, apparently in an effort to determine the nature and amount of financial assistance necessary to maintain Howe's commercial viability. However, although requested, this report was unfortunately not provided to the Panel, which considered that it would provide useful information on the circumstances surrounding the design of the financial assistance package to Howe. See, in particular, *supra*, paras. 6.10(a)-6.11.

[212] In this regard, we note that while Australia did not agree with the United States estimates concerning the size of the domestic market for automotive leather, calling it conservative, Australia did not provide any contrary or different forecasts upon which we might rely. See *supra*, para. 7.248. In these circumstances, we conclude that Australia has entirely failed to rebut the United States assertion on a question of fact, and we accept the United States estimates.

targets and the aggregate target) set out in the grant contract, Howe would, of necessity, have to continue and probably increase exports. At the time the contract was entered into, the government of Australia was aware of this necessity, and thus anticipated continued and possibly increased exports by Howe. In our view, these facts effectively transform the sales performance targets into export performance targets. We thus consider that Howe's anticipated export performance was one of the conditions for the grant of the subsidies. Australia argues that this consideration would lead to a result that would penalize small economies, where firms are often dependent on exports in order to achieve rational economic levels of production. Nevertheless, in the specific circumstances of this case, we find this consideration compelling evidence of the close tie between anticipated exportation and the grant of the subsidies.

9.68 We note that confidential business information provided by Australia indicates that, in fact, the proportion of Howe's sales going to export has not increased. However, we must make our determination on the facts that existed at the time the contract establishing the conditions for the grant payments was entered into. Thus, the fact that the anticipated exports may not have come to pass in the volumes anticipated does not affect our conclusion. Moreover, we note that confidential business information provided by Australia strongly suggests to us that the expectation of continued and increasing exports was an element in the assessment of Howe's compliance with the terms of the grant contract.

9.69 Australia insists that the fact that the grant contract was provided only to Howe, which exports a large proportion of its production, and not to any leather manufacturer that supplies the domestic market is irrelevant, since Howe was the only company affected by the removal of automotive leather from eligibility under the ICS and EFS programmes. Australia has confirmed that Howe is the only dedicated producer and exporter of automotive leather in Australia.[213] Australia specifically stated, in response to the Panel's question, that aside from the grant and loan to Howe, Australia does not have any subsidy specific to the Australian leather industry.[214] In our view, the fact that the government of Australia provided the subsidies in question only to Howe, the only *exporter* of automotive leather, is relevant, and supports the conclusion that one of the conditions for the subsidy was anticipated exportation and/or export earnings.

9.70 Australia argues that, because the grant funds cannot be taken back by the government once the payments are made, and because a change in Howe's level of exports would not affect the disbursement of the funds, the grant payments are not "in fact" contingent upon export performance. However, as noted above, in our view the pertinent consideration is the facts at the time the conditions for the grant payments were established, and not possible subsequent developments.

213 Response by Australia to Question 13 of the Panel, 17 December 1998.

214 Response by Australia to Question 14 of the Panel, 17 December 1998.

9.71 All of the facts, weighed together, lead us to conclude that the three subsidy payments under the grant contract are in fact tied to Howe's actual or anticipated exportation or export earnings.[215] These payments are conditioned on Howe's agreement to satisfy, on the basis of best endeavours, the aggregate performance targets. The second and third grant payments are, in addition, explicitly conditioned on satisfaction, on a best endeavours basis, of interim sales performance targets. Given the export-dependent nature of Howe's business, and the size of the Australian market, these sales performance targets are, in our view, effectively, export performance targets. The sales performance targets set out in the grant contract, in conjunction with the other facts enumerated above, therefore lead us to the conclusion that the grant of the subsidies was conditioned on anticipated exportation.

9.72 We therefore conclude that the payments under the grant contract are subsidies "contingent ... in fact" on export performance in violation of Article 3.1(a) of the SCM Agreement.

(ii) The Loan Contract

9.73 The loan contract provides for a fifteen-year loan of $A25 million by the Government of Australia to Howe/ALH. For the first five-year period of this loan, Howe/ALH is not required to pay principal or interest. After the expiration of this five-year period, interest on the loan is to be based on the rate for Australian Commonwealth Bonds with a ten-year maturity, plus two percentage points. The loan is secured by a second lien over the assets and undertakings of ALH.

9.74 There is nothing in the loan contract that explicitly links the loan to Howe's production or sales, and therefore nothing in its terms, the design of the loan payment, or the repayment provisions that would tie the loan directly to export performance, or even sales performance. Australia argues that under the loan contract, the level of production and sales is irrelevant so long as the company pays the government any monies owing.[216] The United States responds that the "viability of the loan is necessarily contingent upon Howe's export earnings"[217] given that the Australian government has acknowledged that the financial assistance provided for in the loan and grant contracts is the minimum amount necessary to ensure the viability of Howe, and that Howe has no choice but to export in order to maintain its production and sales levels in order to re-

---

[215] We note that our conclusion matches the understanding of the recipient of the subsidy payments. In March 1997, Schaffer Corporation, the parent of Howe and ALH, reported that the Australian government had "finalised a compensation package" for Howe/ALH, consisting, *inter alia* of "A grant of [A]$30 million based on projected exports and paid on performance criteria". Schaffer Corporation Limited Half Yearly Results to December 1996, Exhibit 1 to United States first submission, at page 2.

[216] Australia's first submission, para. 133, *supra*, para. 7.253.

[217] United States second submission, para. 41, *supra*, para. 7.258.

main in business and pay off the loan. The United States asserts that, "[i]f Howe does not export, the Australian government will not be repaid".[218]

9.75 While it may be true that some of the money to repay the loan is likely to be generated through export sales, we agree with Australia that it is ultimately up to Howe and ALH to decide upon the source of funds that will be used to repay the loan. The source of funding will not necessarily be export sales, and there is nothing in the facts before us to suggest that it was expected at the time the loan was entered into that export sales would generate the funds to repay the loan. In our view, the mere fact that one possible source of funds to pay off the loan is potential export earnings is insufficient to conclude that the loan was contingent in fact upon anticipated exportation or export earnings. In this regard, we note that Howe is a subsidiary of ALH and that ALH has other businesses and produces other products from which it could generate the funds to repay the loan. We recognize that other facts are relevant to our consideration of the nature of the loan contract. Included among these is the significance of exports in Howe's business, and the fact that loan was part of the overall "assistance package" given to Howe, which Australia acknowledged would probably not have occurred if Howe had not been removed from eligibility under the ICS and EFS programmes. However, the loan is secured by a lien on the assets and undertakings of ALH, which is itself responsible for repayment of the loan, and not merely on the assets and undertakings of Howe. Moreover, there is nothing in the terms of the loan contract itself which suggests a specific link to actual or anticipated exportation or export earnings, as there is in the terms of the grant contract. These factors persuade us that there is not a sufficiently close tie between the loan and anticipated exportation or export earnings.

9.76 Therefore, we conclude that the loan contract is not "contingent ... in fact ... upon export performance" within the meaning of Article 3.1(a) of the SCM Agreement.

X. CONCLUSIONS AND RECOMMENDATION

10.1 In conclusion, we find that:

(a) The loan from the Australian government to Howe/ALH is not a subsidy which is contingent upon export performance within the meaning of Article 3.1(a) of the SCM Agreement;

(b) The payments under the grant contract are subsidies within the meaning of Article 1 of the SCM Agreement which are contingent upon export performance within the meaning of Article 3.1(a) of that Agreement.

---

[218] United States second submission, para. 41, *supra*, para. 7.258.

10.2 Pursuant to Article 3.8 of the DSU, the finding in paragraph 10.1(b) also constitutes a case of *prima facie* nullification or impairment of benefits accruing to the United States under the SCM Agreement, which Australia has not rebutted.

10.3 Accordingly, pursuant to Article 4.7 of the SCM Agreement, we recommend that Australia withdraw the subsidies identified in paragraph 10.1(b) above without delay.

10.4 Article 4.7 further provides that "the panel shall specify in its recommendation the time-period within which the measure [*i.e.*, the measure found to be a prohibited subsidy] must be withdrawn". This is one of the first cases involving export subsidies to have been brought before the WTO, and there is consequently no experience or prior practice as to what factors should be considered in establishing the time-period within which the measure must be withdrawn. Presumably, the nature of the measures and issues regarding implementation might be relevant.

10.5 Australia has argued that, since the "normal" period of time for implementation of panel decisions under the DSU is fifteen months, and time periods in export subsidy disputes are halved pursuant to Article 4.12, a period of seven and one-half months would be appropriate.

10.6 Even assuming Australia is correct in its consideration of fifteen months as the "normal" period of time for implementation of panel decisions, a question we do not reach, we do not agree that one-half of that period is appropriate in a dispute involving export subsidies. In the first place, Article 4.12 specifically provides that "except for time periods specifically prescribed in this Article" the time periods otherwise provided for in the DSU should be halved in export subsidy disputes. Article 4.7, which provides that the subsidy shall be withdrawn "without delay", and that the panel shall specify the time-period for withdrawal of the measure in its recommendation, in our view establishes that the time-period for withdrawal is "specifically prescribed in this Article", that is, in Article 4 of the SCM Agreement itself. Moreover, we do not, as a factual matter, believe that a period of seven and one-half months can reasonably be described as corresponding to the requirement that the measure must be withdrawn "without delay".

10.7 In light of the nature of the measures, we consider that a 90-day period would be appropriate for the withdrawal of the measures. We therefore recommend that the measures be withdrawn within 90 days.

EUROPEAN COMMUNITIES - MEASURES CONCERNING MEAT AND MEAT PRODUCTS (HORMONES)

ORIGINAL COMPLAINT BY THE UNITED STATES

RECOURSE TO ARBITRATION BY THE EUROPEAN COMMUNITIES UNDER ARTICLE 22.6 OF THE DSU

Decision by the Arbitrators
WT/DS26/ARB

Circulated to Members on 12 July 1999

TABLE OF CONTENTS

I. INTRODUCTION

1. On 17 May 1999, the United States ("US"), pursuant to Article 22.2 of the DSU, requested the Dispute Settlement Body ("DSB") to authorize the sus-

pension of the application to the European Communities ("EC") and its member States of tariff concessions covering trade in an amount of US$ 202 million per year.[1] In a letter dated 2 June 1999, the EC objected to the level of suspension proposed by the US and requested that the matter be referred to arbitration. In its submissions, the EC quantified the level of trade impairment caused by the hormone ban on US bovine meat and meat products at a maximum of US$ 53,301,675. The EC also asked that the arbitrators request the US to submit a list with proposed suspension of concessions equivalent to the level of nullification or impairment, once this level had been determined by the arbitrators.

2. At its meeting of 3 June 1999, the DSB - referring to both the US and the EC request - noted that, pursuant to Article 22.6 of the DSU, the matter shall be referred to arbitration. Article 22.6 provides as follows:

> "When the situation described in paragraph 2 occurs [if the Member concerned fails to bring the measure found to be inconsistent with a covered agreement into compliance therewith or otherwise comply with the recommendations and rulings within the reasonable period of time determined pursuant to paragraph 3 of Article 21], the DSB, upon request, shall grant authorization to suspend concessions or other obligations within 30 days of the expiry of the reasonable period of time unless the DSB decides by consensus to reject the request. *However, if the Member concerned objects to the level of suspension proposed ... the matter shall be referred to arbitration.* Such arbitration shall be carried out by the original panel, if members are available, or by an arbitrator appointed by the Director-General and shall be completed within 60 days after the date of expiry of the reasonable period of time. Concessions or other obligations shall not be suspended during the course of the arbitration".[2]

The arbitration was carried out by the original panel (hereafter referred to as "the arbitrators"), namely:

Chairman:	Mr. Thomas Cottier
Members:	Mr. Peter Palecka
	Mr. Jun Yokota

3. The jurisdiction of the arbitrators and the effect of this arbitration report is set out in Article 22.7 of the DSU:

> "*The arbitrator* acting pursuant to paragraph 6 shall not examine the nature of the concessions or other obligations to be suspended but *shall determine whether the level of such suspension is*

[1] WT/DS26/19.

[2] Footnote omitted and emphasis added.

> *equivalent to the level of nullification or impairment* ... The parties shall accept the arbitrator's decision as final and the parties concerned shall not seek a second arbitration. The DSB shall be informed promptly of the decision of the arbitrator and shall upon request, grant authorization to suspend concessions or other obligations where the request is consistent with the decision of the arbitrator, unless the DSB decides by consensus to reject the request".[3]

The substantive provision at issue here is contained in Article 22.4 of the DSU:

> "The level of the suspension of concessions or other obligations authorized by the DSB shall be equivalent to the level of the nullification or impairment".

4. In this case, the arbitrators are called upon to "determine whether the level of ... suspension [of tariff concessions, as proposed by the US] is *equivalent* to the level of nullification or impairment"[4] caused to the US by the EC ban on imports of hormone treated beef and beef products.

5. The organizational meeting at which time-table and working procedures were adopted, was held on 4 June. On 7 June we received a paper from the US explaining the methodology it applied in calculating the proposed level of suspension. First written submissions were received from both parties on 11 June. Rebuttals were filed on 18 June. A meeting with the parties was held on 22 June. On 25 June we received answers to a list of questions we had submitted to the parties.

6. The main arguments of the parties are summarized below when examining each of the claims before us.

II. PRELIMINARY ISSUES

A. *Third-Party Rights*

7. Following a request by Canada for third-party rights and after careful consideration of the parties' arguments made at the organizational meeting of 4 June 1999 and in their written submissions, the arbitrators ruled as follows:

> The US and Canada are allowed to attend both arbitration hearings, to make a statement at the end of each hearing and to receive a copy of the written submissions made in both proceedings.
>
> The above ruling was made on the following grounds.

---

[3] Footnote omitted and emphasis added.

[4] Article 22.7 of the DSU, emphasis added.

- DSU provisions on panel proceedings, referred to by analogy in the arbitrators' working procedures, give the arbitrators discretion to decide on procedural matters not regulated in the DSU (Article 12.1 of the DSU) in accordance with due process.[5] The DSU does not address the issue of third-party participation in Article 22 arbitration proceedings.
- US and Canadian rights may be affected in both arbitration proceedings:

  First, the estimates for high quality beef ("HQB") exports, foregone because of the hormone ban, are to be based on a tariff quota that allegedly needs to be shared between Canada and the US. A determination in one proceeding may thus be decisive for the determination in the other.

  Second, several methodologies are proposed to calculate lost export opportunities. Given the fact that the product scope (HQB and edible bovine offal ("EBO")) and relevant trade barriers (hormone ban and HQB tariff quota) are the same in both proceedings, both arbitration panels (composed of the same three individuals) may consider it necessary to adopt the same or very similar methodologies. This is all the more necessary because the arbitrators are called upon to arrive at a specific determination on the amount of nullification and impairment caused by the ban. They are therefore not limited, as in most panel proceedings, to ruling only on the consistency of the amounts proposed by the US and Canada with DSU provisions.[6] Due process thus requires that all three parties receive the opportunity to comment on the methodologies proposed by each of the parties.
- In contrast, the EC has not shown how third-party participation would prejudice its rights. No specific arguments were made demonstrating that third party participation would substantially impair the EC's interests or due process rights.

---

5 In this respect see footnote 138 in the Appellate Body Report on *EC - Measures Concerning Meat and Meat Products (Hormones)*, adopted on 13 February 1998, WT/DS26/AB/R, WT/DS48/AB/R: "[T]he DSU, and in particular its Appendix 3, leave panels a margin of discretion to deal, always in accordance with due process, with specific situations that may arise in a particular case and that are not explicitly regulated. Within this context, an appellant requesting the Appellate Body to reverse a panel's ruling on matters of procedure must demonstrate the prejudice generated by such legal ruling".

6 See paragraph 12.

B. *Burden of Proof and the Role of Arbitrators under Article 22 of the DSU*

8. Both parties made extensive submissions on the question of who bears the burden of proof in Article 22 arbitration procedures. Each party submitted that the burden of proof rests on the other party.

9. WTO Members, as sovereign entities, can be *presumed* to act in conformity with their WTO obligations. A party claiming that a Member has acted *inconsistently* with WTO rules bears the burden of proving that inconsistency. The act at issue here is the US proposal to suspend concessions. The WTO rule in question is Article 22.4 prescribing that the level of suspension be equivalent to the level of nullification and impairment. The EC challenges the conformity of the US proposal with the said WTO rule. It is thus for the EC to prove that the US proposal is inconsistent with Article 22.4. Following well-established WTO jurisprudence, this means that it is for the EC to submit arguments and evidence sufficient to establish a *prima facie* case or presumption that the level of suspension proposed by the US is *not* equivalent to the level of nullification and impairment caused by the EC hormone ban. Once the EC has done so, however, it is for the US to submit arguments and evidence sufficient to rebut that presumption. Should all arguments and evidence remain in equipoise, the EC, as the party bearing the original burden of proof, would lose.

10. The same rules apply where the existence of a specific *fact* is alleged; in this case, for example, where a party relies on a decrease of beef consumption in the EC or the use of edible beef offal as pet food. It is for the party alleging the fact to prove its existence.

11. The duty that rests on *all* parties to produce evidence and to collaborate in presenting evidence to the arbitrators - an issue to be distinguished from the question of who bears the burden of proof - is crucial in Article 22 arbitration proceedings. The EC is required to submit evidence showing that the proposal is *not* equivalent. However, at the same time and as soon as it can, the US is required to come forward with evidence explaining how it arrived at its proposal and showing why its proposal *is* equivalent to the trade impairment it has suffered. Some of the evidence - such as data on trade with third countries, export capabilities and affected exporters - may, indeed, be in the sole possession of the US, being the party that suffered the trade impairment. This explains why we requested the US to submit a so-called methodology paper.[7]

12. There is, however, a difference between our task here and the task given to a panel. In the event we decide that the US proposal is *not* WTO consistent, i.e. that the suggested amount is too high, we should not end our examination the way panels do, namely by requesting the DSB to recommend that the measure be

---

[7] See paragraph 5.

brought into conformity with WTO obligations. Following the approach of the arbitrators in the *Bananas* case - where the proposed amount of US$ 520 million was reduced to US$ 191.4 million - we would be called upon to go further. In pursuit of the basic DSU objectives of prompt and positive settlement of disputes[8], we would have to estimate the level of suspension we consider to be equivalent to the impairment suffered.[9] This is the essential task and responsibility conferred on the arbitrators in order to settle the dispute. In our view, such approach is implicitly called for in Article 22.7:

> "The parties shall accept the arbitrator's decision as final and the parties concerned shall not seek a second arbitration. The DSB shall be informed promptly of the decision of the arbitrator and shall upon request, grant authorization to suspend concessions or other obligations where the request is consistent with the decision of the arbitrator, unless the DSB decides by consensus to reject the request".

C. *Product Coverage of the US Proposal to Suspend Concessions*

13. The US proposal to suspend tariff concessions vis-à-vis the EC and its member States includes a list of products that covers trade in an amount significantly higher than the proposed US$ 202 million.[10] As stated in the request itself, the US intends to implement the suspension

> "by directing the U.S. Customs Service to impose duties in excess of bound rates on a list of products to be drawn from the list attached to this request. The trade value of the final list of products subject to increased duties will be equivalent, on an annual basis, to US$202 million".

The US has not yet determined the final list of EC products that will be subject to the suspension of tariff concessions. Answering questions by the arbitrators, the US stated that the degree of the suspension (i.e. the level of the tariff to be imposed) would be 100 per cent on each of the selected products.[11]

---

[8] See Articles 3.3 and 3.7.

[9] If this were not done, the Member requesting suspension would need to make new estimates and arguably submit a new proposal. This proposal could again meet objections and might be referred back to arbitration. To avoid this potentially endless loop, the arbitrators - in the event they find that the proposal is *not* equivalent to the trade impairment - have to come up with their own estimate, i.e. their own figure.

[10] According to US Exhibit 35, the proposed list of products covers trade in an amount of US$ 918.073 million (see also Annex II).

[11] US answer to arbitrators' questions 9 and 10.

1. The EC Request for a Definite List of Products

14. In its objection to the US proposal for suspension, as well as at the DSB meeting during which this case was referred to arbitration, the EC complained about the above outlined US approach. The EC asks us "to request the United States to submit a list with proposed suspension of concessions equivalent to the level of nullification or impairment, once this level has been determined by the arbitrator".[12] In other words, the EC requests the arbitrators to first decide on the amount of trade impairment, to then request a specific product list from the US and to finally determine whether both are "equivalent". The US objects to this EC request.[13]

15. The arbitrators are unable to follow the EC request. No support for this request can be found in the DSU.

16. The authorization given by the DSB under Article 22.6 of the DSU is an authorization "to suspend [the application to the Member concerned of] concessions or other obligations [under the covered agreements]".[14] In our view, the limitations linked to this DSB authorization are those set out in the proposal made by the requesting Member on the basis of which the authorization is granted. In the event tariff concessions are to be suspended, only products that appear on the product list attached to the request for suspension can be subject to suspension. This follows from the minimum requirements attached to a request to suspend concessions or other obligations. They are, in our view: (1) the request must set out a specific level of suspension, i.e. a level equivalent to the nullification and impairment caused by the WTO inconsistent measure, pursuant to Article 22.4[15]; and (2) the request must specify the agreement and sector(s) under which concessions or other obligations would be suspended, pursuant to Article 22.3.[16]

---

[12] WT/DS26/20.

[13] In contrast to this case, in the *Bananas* dispute the list of products attached to the US request for suspension corresponded, at least according to US calculations, to the US estimate of trade impairment of US$ 520 million. Once the arbitrators had lowered the level of trade impairment to US$ 191.4 million, the US submitted a new request to the DSB meeting. At that meeting the US received authorisation to suspend concessions equivalent to an amount of US$ 191.4 million. Subsequently, the US selected a number of products from the original list that, according to US calculations, were equivalent in value to the authorized US$ 191.4 million. The EC objected to the US approach of not providing a definite product list at the DSB meeting during which authorisation was granted. The US stated that there was nothing in the DSU to the effect that such a list should be attached to a request for authorization to suspend concessions (Minutes of the DSB meeting of 19 April 1999, WT/DSB/M/59).

[14] Article 22.6 of the DSU. Bracketed text added is from Article 22.2 of the DSU.

[15] In respect of the first requirement see further paragraph 21.

[16] The more precise a request for suspension is in terms of product coverage, type and degree of suspension, etc..., the better. Such precision can only be encouraged in pursuit of the DSU objectives of "providing security and predictability to the multilateral trading system" (Article 3.2) and seeking prompt and positive solutions to disputes (Articles 3.3 and 3.7). It would also be welcome in

17. Neither can support for the EC request be found in other provisions of Article 22. Instead, they prescribe the following: (1) the "DSB shall not authorize suspension of concessions or other obligations if a covered agreement prohibits such suspension" (Article 22.5); (2) "[c]oncessions or other obligations shall not be suspended during the course of the arbitration" (Article 22.6 *in fine*); and (3) the suspension "shall only be applied until such time as the measure found to be inconsistent with a covered agreement has been removed, or the Member that must implement recommendations or rulings provides a solution to the nullification or impairment of benefits, or a mutually satisfactory solution is reached" (Article 22.8).

18. In our view, the determination of other aspects related to the suspension remain the prerogative of the Member requesting the suspension. We note, in particular, that the Member in respect of whom concessions or other obligations would be suspended, can object to "*the level* of suspension proposed"[17] and that an arbitrator has to "determine whether *the level* of such suspension is equivalent to *the level* of nullification or impairment".[18] Arbitrators are explicitly prohibited from "examin[ing] *the nature* of the concessions or other obligations to be suspended"[19] (other than under Articles 22.3 and 22.5).

19. On these grounds, we cannot require that the US further specify the nature of the proposed suspension. As agreed by all parties involved in this dispute[20], in case a proposal for suspension were to target, for example, only biscuits with a 100 per cent tariff *ad valorem*, it would not be for the arbitrators to decide that, for example, cheese and not biscuits should be targeted; that a 150 per cent tariff should be imposed instead of a 100 per cent tariff; or that tariff increases should be levied on a product weight basis, not *ad valorem*. All of these are *qualitative* aspects of the proposed suspension touching upon the "nature" of concessions to be withdrawn. They fall outside the arbitrators' jurisdiction.

20. What we do have to determine, however, is whether the overall proposed level of suspension is *equivalent* to the level of nullification and impairment. This involves a *quantitative* - not a qualitative - assessment of the proposed suspension. As noted by the arbitrators in the *Bananas* case, "[i]t is impossible to ensure correspondence or identity between two levels if one of the two is not clearly defined".[21] Therefore, as a prerequisite for ensuring equivalence between the two levels, we have to be able to determine, not only the "level of the nullifi-

light of the statement in Article 3.10 that "all Members will engage in [DSU] procedures in good faith in an effort to resolve the dispute".

17 Article 22.6, emphasis added.

18 Article 22.7, emphasis added.

19 *Ibid.*

20 Answers to arbitrators' Question 1.

21 WT/DS/ARB, para. 4.2.

cation and impairment", but also the "level of the suspension of concessions or other obligations". To give effect to the obligation of equivalence in Article 22.4, the Member requesting suspension thus has to identify the level of suspension of concessions it proposes in a way that allows us to determine equivalence.

21. In this case the US has to - and did - identify the products that may be subject to suspension in a way that allowed us to attribute an annual trade value to each of these products when subject to the additional tariff proposed, namely a 100 per cent tariff (assuming this tariff is prohibitive). We have carried out that task in Section IV below. Once this is done, however, the US is free to pick products from that list - not outside the list - equalling a total trade value that does not exceed the amount of trade impairment we find. In our view, this obligation to sufficiently specify the level of suspension flows directly from the requirement of ensuring equivalence in Article 22.4, the substantive provision we have to enforce here. It is part of the first element under the minimum requirements we outlined above, namely to set out a specific level of suspension, i.e. a level equivalent to the nullification and impairment caused by the WTO inconsistent measure.

2. *The EC Objection to a "Carousel" Type of Suspension of Concessions*

22. The EC raised an additional objection in respect of the product coverage of the US proposal for suspension. Referring to statements made by the US Trade Representative, the EC submits that the US claims to be free to resort to a "carousel" type of suspension where the concessions and other obligations subject to suspension would change every now and then, in particular in terms of product coverage. The EC claims that in doing so the US would decide not only which concessions or other obligations would be suspended, but also unilaterally decide whether the level of such suspension of concessions or other obligations is in fact equivalent to the level of nullification and impairment determined by arbitration. Replying to our questions, the US submitted that "[a]lthough nothing in the DSU prevents future changes to the list [of products subject to suspension] ..., the United States has no current intent to make such changes".[22] We thus assume that the US - in good faith and based upon this unilateral promise - will not implement the suspension of concessions in a "carousel" manner. We therefore do not need to consider whether such an approach would require an adjustment in the way in which the effect of an authorized suspension is calculated.

23. As explained above[23], we do not have jurisdiction to set a definite list of products that can be subject to suspension. It is for the US to draw up that list. In our view, it has to do so within the bounds of the product list put before the

[22] US answer to arbitrators' Question 11.

[23] See paragraphs 18-19.

DSB. We also agree with the EC that once this list is made or once the US has defined a method of suspension, that list or method necessarily needs to cover trade in an amount not exceeding (i.e. equivalent to or less than) the nullification and impairment we find. This matter of equivalence is not one to be determined exclusively by the US.[24] The US has an obligation to ensure equivalence pursuant to Article 22.4 of the DSU.[25] In its reply to our questions, the US submitted that it "will scrupulously comply with the requirement that the level of suspension of concessions not exceed the level of nullification or impairment to be found by the Arbitrator".[26]

III. CALCULATION OF THE LEVEL OF NULLIFICATION AND IMPAIRMENT CAUSED BY THE EC HORMONE BAN

A. *Summary of the Parties' Basic Methodologies*

1. *United States*

24. The US submits that the EC hormone ban impairs US exports in two respects. First, because of the ban US high quality beef ("HQB") that has been treated with hormones, cannot be imported into the EC market. More particularly, US hormone-treated HQB does not qualify for importation under the 11,500 tonnes tariff quota for HQB granted by the EC.

25. Second, because of the ban US edible beef offal ("EBO") for human consumption that has been treated with hormones is not allowed for importation into the EC.[27] For such imports the EC does not apply a tariff quota.

26. The US adopted the following approach in respect of both HQB and EBO: (1) it examined relevant actual US exports during a recent period in which the EC was, in the US view, failing to comply with its WTO obligations; and (2) it estimated the relevant exports that would have existed during the same period if: (a) the EC were acting in compliance with its WTO obligations; (b) the long-term economic adjustments resulting from compliance were reflected; and (c) all other factors were held constant. The US refers to the estimate in (2) as "the counterfactual". Harm to US exports is estimated as the difference between the actual value of exports in (1) and the estimated value in the counterfactual (2).

27. In respect of the amount to be deducted as actual value of exports ("current exports") - entering the EC notwithstanding the hormone ban - the US sub-

---

[24] See paragraphs 20-21.

[25] See Section IV below.

[26] US answers to arbitrators' Questions 1, 2, 4, 9, 10 and 11, *Introduction*, p. 1.

[27] EBO treated with hormones is considered by the EC as unsuitable for human consumption. It cannot enter the EC market under the tariff headings summed up in footnote 44. However, such beef offal - treated with hormones - still enters the EC for use in pet food under other tariff headings, not subject to the ban.

mits that the existing level of US exports of beef and beef offal will not continue in the future due to the EC's decision of 30 April 1999. This decision implied a ban on *all* imports of US beef and beef products - including those that, according to the US, have *not* been treated with hormones - as of 15 June 1999.[28] It was taken by the EC following sampling and analyses for the detection of residues of hormones in fresh bovine meat and liver imported from the US that had shown the presence of xenobiotic growth promoting hormones.[29] On 15 June 1999, the EC suspended the imposition of a total ban until 15 December 1999. It did so in order to allow US establishments and authorities to make the necessary adaptations to ensure the absence of residues of xenobiotic growth promoting hormones. In the interim, however, the EC has instituted a procedure to test 100 per cent of all US beef and beef products shipments at the port of entry and to hold these products until test results are available ("100 per cent test and hold procedure"). Noting that the EC had not yet published the 15 June 1999 decision in the Official Journal, the US argued that even after the Commission Decision had been published and after US exports of non-treated beef and beef products would again be permitted, the 100 per cent test and hold procedure would continue to stop virtually all US exports of such products because of the delays and expenses involved.

28. For these reasons, the US requests that no amount be deducted for "current exports" in respect of either HQB or EBO.

29. With regard to HQB, the US calculation of lost exports is based on two figures: (a) the quantity of US exports, but for the ban, under the EC's market-access commitments; and (b) the average export price at which the exports would be sold. The US argues that it would have fully filled the tariff quota of 11,500 tonnes but for the EC import ban. It estimates the price of US HQB but for the ban at US$ 5,342 per tonne, a figure that it qualifies as a "conservative estimate". Following this methodology, the US estimates the level of nullification and impairment with regard to HQB at US$ 61.4 million.

30. In respect of EBO, the US calculation of lost US exports to the EC market involved a two-step process. In a first step - to calculate what US exports would have been but for the ban - the US estimated total beef offal production and, taking into account trade data, it calculated EC beef offal consumption (using the so-called "balance sheet approach"). The US used the eight-year period 1981-88 prior to the ban as a base period. It stressed that this approach significantly underestimates very favourable world-wide export trends in the period subsequent to the ban. In a second step, the US calculated additional trade benefits to US beef offal exports if market development investments had continued but for the import ban. As a result of these calculations, the US estimates the

---

[28] Commission Decision 1999/301/EC of 30 April 1999, US Exhibit 2.

[29] Growth promoting hormones not naturally occurring in cattle.

level of nullification and impairment with regard to EBO for human consumption at US$ 140 million.

2. *European Communities*

31. In respect of HQB, the EC submits that the US, together with Canada, can export HQB to the EC market as long as it complies with the conditions linked to the tariff quota. The approach followed by the EC is to compare the situation that existed before the introduction of the import ban with the current situation. The EC submits that possible short-term effects were eliminated by taking the average figures and data of the period 1986 to 1988 and 1996 to 1998. The value of US exports to the EC was obtained by converting ECU into US$ by applying the conversion rates as they were recorded during the years concerned. The level of nullification and impairment identified by the EC in respect of HQB using this approach is US$ 1,683,350.

32. In respect of EBO, the EC notes that edible offal is a by-product of meat production. It submits that consumer behavior in respect of offal follows the same pattern as that observed for meat. If consumption of meat declines, for example, because of a negative perception of the meat produced, a similar decline will take place in the consumption of offal. The EC refers to the constant drop in beef consumption within the EC in recent years, as well as to the BSE crisis, and argues that this decline is also reflected in a drop of consumption of bovine offal. The EC submits that only offal for human consumption is affected by the import ban. It adds that overall production of offal in the EC over the last 12 years increased significantly, while the consumption of offal decreased. As a result, the EC, originally a net importer of offal, became a net exporter.

33. The EC estimates US exports of EBO but for the ban, using the 1986-1988 average value as a base from which to deduct "current exports", defined as the 1996-98 average value of US exports of EBO to the EC. The EC further notes that EC imports of EBO were subject to a general downward trend irrespective of the origin of the products, warranting a downward adjustment in value of 25.47 per cent. It also submits that the prohibition of growth hormones only concerns the quantities of EBO actually used for human consumption, not those used for pet food. For these reasons, the EC makes an additional downward adjustment in quantities of 31.7 per cent. The EC accordingly estimates the level of nullification and impairment with regard to EBO for human consumption to be US$ 51,618,325.

B. *General Approach of the Arbitrators*

34. We carefully examined the claims, arguments and evidence submitted by the parties in light of the rules on burden of proof and the role of arbitrators under Article 22 of the DSU outlined above.[30]

35. Based upon the record before us, in particular evidence submitted by the EC demonstrating that the US assessments were not always appropriate, we consider that the EC established a *prima facie* case that the level of suspension proposed by the US is *not* equivalent to the level of nullification and impairment caused by the ban. In our view, the US failed to rebut this presumption. We were, therefore, not able to accept in full the estimates proposed by the US. We were not convinced either by all of the EC alternatives. We could, however, accept certain elements of both the US and the EC methodologies. As explained earlier[31], in such circumstances, the essential task and responsibility of the arbitrators is to make their own estimate, on the basis of all arguments and evidence submitted by the parties. In doing so, we follow the rules on burden of proof set out in paragraphs 9-11.

C. *Guidelines for the Calculation of Nullification and Impairment*

36. To determine whether the proposed level of suspension (US$ 202 million) is "equivalent" to the level of nullification and impairment caused by the hormone ban, we have, of course, to determine what this level of nullification and impairment is.

37. The US does so by estimating the value of foregone US exports arising from the EC's failure to comply with the recommendations and rulings of the DSB. The EC submits that the calculation of nullification and impairment can only be based on the situation in which the US would have found itself if the EC had withdrawn, or otherwise had brought into conformity, the inconsistent trade measure.

38. Upon careful consideration of the claims and arguments set forth by the parties, we consider that our starting-point is as follows: <u>what would annual prospective US exports of hormone-treated beef and beef products to the EC be *if the EC had withdrawn the ban on 13 May 1999*</u>? 13 May 1999 is the date of expiration of the reasonable period of time granted to the EC to implement the panel and Appellate Body reports. In accordance with DSU provisions, it was by 13 May 1999 that the EC had to bring its beef import regime into conformity with the SPS Agreement. We cannot assume that the EC from 1989 onwards, i.e. from the time it imposed the ban, was under a legal obligation to withdraw the ban. We note, in this respect, that the violations found were violations of the

[30] See Section II.B.

[31] See paragraph 12.

SPS Agreement, an agreement only in existence from 1 January 1995 onwards.[32] The EC does not contest that it has not brought the measure into conformity with its WTO obligations. Nor does it contest that the "counterfactual" we need to look at in these proceedings is a situation without the ban. The EC did not propose that we examine any other alternative that would meet its obligations under the SPS Agreement.

39. We are, furthermore, of the view that the effect of suspending concessions should not exceed that of the EC bringing the measure into conformity with WTO rules on 13 May 1999. This stems directly from the DSU itself. The DSU characterizes full and prompt implementation of DSB recommendations as the *first* objective and *preferred* solution. The suspension of concessions, in contrast, is only a temporary measure of last resort to be applied only until such time as full implementation or a mutually agreed solution is obtained.[33] To allow the effect of suspension of concessions to exceed that of bringing the measure into conformity with WTO rules would not be justifiable in view of DSU objectives.

40. We note further that we agree with the arbitrators in the *Bananas* case that

> "the authorization to suspend concessions or other obligations is a temporary measure pending full implementation by the Member concerned. ... this *temporary* nature indicates that it is the purpose of countermeasures to *induce compliance*. But this purpose does not mean that the DSB should grant authorization to suspend concessions beyond what is *equivalent* to the level of nullification or impairment. In our view, there is nothing in Article 22.1 of the DSU, let alone in paragraphs 4 and 7 of Article 22, that could be read as a justification for counter-measures of a *punitive* nature".[34]

41. The question we thus have to answer here is: what would annual prospective US exports of hormone-treated beef and beef products to the EC be if the EC had withdrawn the ban on 13 May 1999? An answer to this question, like any question about future events, can only be a reasoned estimate. It is necessarily based on certain assumptions. In making those estimates and assumptions, we need to guard against claims of lost opportunities where the causal link with the inconsistent hormone ban is less than apparent, i.e. where exports are allegedly foregone not because of the ban but due to other circumstances.[35]

---

[32] It might be argued that the ban also violated GATT 1947. However, no legal findings on this were ever made.

[33] See Articles 3.7, 21.1, 22.1 and 22.8 of the DSU.

[34] Op. cit., para. 6.3.

[35] In this respect, see the Decision by the Arbitrators in *EC - Regime for the Importation, Sale and Distribution of Bananas*, Recourse to Arbitration by the EC under Article 22.6 of the DSU (hereafter "the *Bananas* case"): "We are of the view that the benchmark for the calculation of nulli-

42. In this sense, our task of estimating nullification and impairment is very different from that of a panel examining the WTO conformity of certain measures. Once a panel has found a WTO inconsistency, it can *presume* - pursuant to Article 3.8 of the DSU - that the inconsistency has caused nullification and impairment. On that ground the panel can give redress to the winning party under Article XXIII of GATT 1994 or corresponding provisions in other WTO agreements. What normally counts for a panel is competitive opportunities and breaches of WTO rules[36], not actual trade flows. A panel does not normally need to further assess the nullification and impairment caused; it can presume its existence. We, in contrast, have to go one step further. We can take it for granted here that the hormone ban is WTO inconsistent. What we have to do is to estimate the nullification and impairment caused by it (and presumed to exist pursuant to Article 3.8 of the DSU). To do so in the present case, we have to focus on trade flows. We must estimate trade foregone due to the ban's continuing existence beyond 13 May 1999.

43. Both products referred to by the US - high quality beef and edible beef offal - once certified as *not* having been treated with hormones, do currently enter the EC market, with the ban in place. To assess the trade impairment caused by the hormone ban, we first estimate, for each product category, the *total* value of US beef or beef products - hormone treated or not - that would enter the EC annually if the ban would have been withdrawn on 13 May 1999. To estimate the nullification and impairment caused by the hormone ban we then deduct from that total value the current value of US exports of HQB and EBO, i.e. those that have *not* been treated with hormones. We assume that these "current exports", adjusted for other factors as explained below, are representative of the exports that will occur in the future with the ban in place. The end result provides us the estimated value of hormone treated HQB and EBO exports that would enter the EC but for the ban's continuing existence beyond 13 May 1999.

44. Our calculations are based on exports at the f.o.b. stage - excluding insurance and freight - an approach which all parties have used in their calculations. We use f.o.b. prices to ensure comparability with the customs valuation method of the suspension of concessions proposed by the US.

---

fication or impairment of US trade flows should be losses in US exports of goods to the European Communities and losses by US service suppliers in services supply in or to the European Communities. However, we are of the opinion that losses of US exports in goods or services *between the US and third countries* do not constitute nullification or impairment of even *indirect* benefits accruing to the US under the GATT or the GATS for which the European Communities could face suspension of concessions" (circulated on 6 April 1999, WT/DS/ARB, para. 6.12, italics in original).

[36] This includes so-called "non-violation nullification and impairment" claims under Article XXIII:1(b) of GATT 1994.

D. *The Value of "Current Exports"*

45. With reference to the EC Decision on test and hold, the US requests that no amount be deducted for "current exports".[37] The EC submits that the full amount of "current exports", i.e. annual average 1996-1998 exports, should be deducted. The test and hold effect on US exports has been alleged by the US. It is thus for the US to prove it.[38] According to US export certificates issued for May and June 1999, exports of US HQB to the EC declined by about 75 per cent compared to the same period in 1998. The decline in respect of EBO is on the order of 98 per cent.

46. It is difficult to assess the lasting trade impact of the recent EC measures. The available data relates to a short period of time. The sudden drop of EC imports from the US may be temporary but so should the suspension of concessions. If the parties reach an agreement on appropriate control and oversight, trade flows may normalize. Referring to the EC statement that "[t]he Commission does not plan to stop the existing imports of hormone-free bovine meat" and the US intention to meet current EC import requirements, we are hopeful that such agreement can be reached. In the meantime, we consider it reasonable to assume that the 100 per cent test and hold procedure will have a certain dampening effect on EC imports from the US.

47. We thus consider that 1996-1998 figures are not representative, *in casu*, overestimate, the exports that will actually occur in the future with the ban in place. On these grounds we decided to reduce current exports (annual 1996-1998 average) by 25 per cent in our estimates for both HQB and EBO.

E. *Nullification and Impairment in Respect of High Quality Beef*

1. *Volume of the Tariff Quota*

48. All parties, including Canada as a third party, agree that the EC market for HQB exports from the US *and* Canada - with or without the ban - is limited by a tariff quota of 11,500 tonnes at an in-quota tariff rate of 20 per cent *ad valorem*.[39] This quota is to be shared between the US and Canada. The out-of-quota rate is considered by all parties to be prohibitive.

49. In addition, the US considers that whatever the amount of Canadian imports under the tariff quota, that amount needs to be topped up with the US share under the tariff quota so that the US alone is allowed to export a total of 11,500

37 See paragraphs 28-29.

38 See paragraph 10.

39 The tariff classification for this category in respect of which the US alleges trade impairment is: HS 0201 (Meat of Bovine Animals, Fresh or Chilled), HS 0202 (Meat of Bovine Animals, Frozen), HS 0206 1095 (Edible Offal of Bovine Animals, Fresh or Chilled, Thick Skirt and Thin Skirt) and HS 0206 2991 (Edible Offal of Bovine Animals, Frozen, Thick Skirt and Thin Skirt).

tonnes. The US submits that it has this right to an annual amount of 11,500 tonnes as a consequence of bilateral US-EC and US-Austria agreements in this respect. For 10,000 tonnes of the 11,500 tonnes, the US refers, in particular, to an 1981 US-EC exchange of letters confirming that even if Canada would take a share of the quota, the US could still count on exporting the full amount of 10,000 tonnes.[40] In respect of the remaining 1,500 tonnes, the US refers to the fact that this volume was originally negotiated bilaterally between the US and Austria and was only later, as a consequence of Austria's accession to the EC, added to the 10,000 tonnes tariff quota opened by the EC in favour of the US and Canada.

50. We cannot agree that but for the ban, i.e., the situation we have to consider here, the US would be allowed to export a total of 11,500 tonnes irrespective of the amount exported by Canada. The autonomous quota rights claimed by the US - irrespective of their legal status and consistency with WTO rules - are not rights under any of the WTO agreements covered by the DSU. The rights thus alleged are derived from bilateral agreements that cannot be properly enforced on their own in WTO dispute settlement.[41] If the EC were to agree that it would grant these independent rights, i.e., that 11,500 tonnes of US HQB could be exported to the EC once the ban is lifted, we could be required to take this autonomous quota amount into account in our estimates as a matter of fact, provided that these rights are consistent with WTO rules. However, the EC contests that the US has such rights. Moreover, the legal validity and enforceability of such rights and bilateral agreements invoked by the US is questionable for the following reasons.

51. Both bilateral agreements were concluded *before* the relevant EC schedules that explicitly allocated the quota to both the US and Canada. Moreover, both bilateral agreements were negotiated in a GATT/WTO context where concessions are normally negotiated first on a bilateral level and then "multilateralized" through binding schedules. Once this is done, the bilateral agreement, as a result of which the concession is granted, is superseded by the multilateral schedule. Both the bilateral agreements and the relevant parts of the EC schedule deal with the same subject-matter. Considering the GATT/WTO specific circumstances of their conclusion, the bilateral agreements would appear to be incompatible with the multilateral EC schedule - a quota allocated to only one Member as opposed to a quota allocated to two Members. On these grounds we consider it appropriate to conclude that the EC schedule, in accordance with

---

[40] Letter dated 28 July 1981 by Mr. Villain, then Director-General of Agriculture at the EC Commission, to the US Agricultural Counsellor in Brussels, US Exhibit 19.

[41] In this respect see the Appellate Body Report on *EC - Measures Affecting the Importation of Certain Poultry Products*, adopted on 23 July 1998, WT/DS69/AB/R, paras. 77-85. Of course, even though the bilateral agreements themselves cannot be enforced through the DSU, the performance of these agreements could give rise to a valid claim under WTO rules.

Article 30 of the Vienna Convention on the Law of Treaties[42], has superseded and prevails over the bilateral agreements.

52. Recalling that, as outlined above in paragraph 10, the US - as the party that invoked the bilateral agreements - bears the burden of proving to the arbitrators that these bilateral agreements exist and are enforceable, we consider that the US has not met its burden. We cannot, therefore, take any autonomous quota rights into account when estimating US HQB exports to the EC but for the ban.

53. On these grounds, we consider that a ceiling of 11,500 tonnes is applicable in respect of the combined US *and* Canadian exports of HQB to the EC.

2. *Estimated Utilization of the 11,500 Tonnes Tariff Quota*

54. The US submits that the entire tariff quota would be filled but for the ban. The EC, referring to the fact that the tariff quota has never been filled in the past - not even before the ban - argues that the tariff quota would only be filled to the same extent as before the ban (1986-1988 average).

55. In this respect, we considered, in particular, the following elements: (1) the fact that the tariff quota represents only a negligible portion of total EC beef consumption; (2) the fact that all HQB tariff quotas allocated by the EC to other countries such as Argentina, Australia, Brazil, New Zealand and Uruguay have over the years been fully or almost fully utilized; and (3) the high production and export capacities of the US beef industry. On these grounds, we can reasonably expect that under the "counterfactual" the tariff quota would be 100 per cent filled.

3. *Estimated Tariff Quota Share of the US*

56. Given our conclusions above, we next have to estimate the US share in the 11,500 tonnes tariff quota.

57. Our approach here is based on the US' and Canada's past performance with respect to HQB exports as well as beef exports in general. We considered, in particular, the following elements. Firstly, the proportions of US and Canadian HQB exports in third country export markets, such as Japan, Korea, Switzerland and Taiwan. The US share of HQB exports has been above 94 per cent in these markets in the 1996-98 period, except in Taiwan where US exports averaged 90 per cent over the last three years. Secondly, the general proportions of US and Canadian beef exports. The US share of North American beef exports to the rest of the world was 96 per cent on average in 1996-98, although the US

[42] Article 30, entitled "Application of successive treaties relating to the same subject-matter", in its paragraph 3, states: "When all the parties to the earlier treaty are parties also to the later treaty but the earlier treaty is not terminated or suspended in operation under article 59, the earlier treaty applies only to the extent that its provisions are compatible with those of the later treaty".

share, including US-Canada trade, was approximately 70 per cent. Thirdly, the proportions of US and Canadian beef exports to the EC (a 94 per cent share for the US in 1998). Fourthly, changes in the relative proportions of US and Canadian exports. The general tendency in both the EC and third country markets in recent years has been an increase of Canada's share at the expense of the US.

58. Taking these elements into account, we consider a US share of 92 per cent a reasonable estimate.

4. *Estimated Prices under the Counterfactual*

59. In this respect, we consider the US suggestion of US$ 5,342 per tonne (f.o.b.) to be reasonable.

60. We note that this price is higher than current unit values of US beef entering the EC. A substantial share of current US exports are whole carcasses, not treated with hormones. We consider it reasonable to expect that without the hormone ban a considerable share of the tariff quota would be filled with high quality hormone-treated cuts to maximize the trade value of the tariff quota. If the ban were lifted, an increase in price could thus be reasonably expected.

61. Consequently, we calculate the total value of US HQB exports to the EC under the counterfactual to be US$ 56,518,360.

5. *Estimated Value of "Current Exports" to be Deducted*

62. As noted earlier[43], to estimate the nullification and impairment caused by the hormone ban we have to deduct from the total value of US exports under the counterfactual, the current value of US exports of non-hormone treated HQB.

63. The EC suggests that US exports in the 1996-1998 period are representative for exports that would occur in the future with the ban in place. The main US argument in this respect was dealt with in paragraphs 45-47. We decided to reduce current US exports by 25 per cent. In other words, we assumed that only 75 per cent of current exports would enter the market in the future due to the 100 per cent test and hold procedure recently imposed by the EC. As a base from which to deduct these 25 per cent we follow the EC suggestion and use the average annual 1996-1998 exports.

64. On this basis we calculate the value of current exports to be deducted from the estimated exports under the counterfactual to be US$ 23,853,584.

---

[43] See paragraph 43.

6. *Estimate of Nullification and Impairment in Respect of HQB*

65. Following our estimates developed above, we calculate the total amount of nullification and impairment caused by the hormone ban on US exports of HQB to be **US$ 32,664,776**.

F. *Nullification and Impairment in Respect of Edible Beef Offal*

1. *Estimated Volume of US EBO Exports under the "Counterfactual"*

66. Unlike the EC import market for HQB, US exports of EBO to the EC are subject to tariffs only, not to a tariff quota.[44] The tariff levied on imports of EBO - according to the US, 4 per cent *ad valorem* - is also much lower than the in-quota tariff for HQB (20 per cent *ad valorem*). Therefore, a different methodology to calculate trade impairment in respect of EBO is warranted. In respect of HQB, we could assume that imports but for the ban would be subject to a ceiling of 11,500 tonnes. In respect of EBO, one of the major tasks is to estimate potential exports of US EBO in the absence of the ban. The US and EC arguments in this respect are summarized above.[45]

67. We consider average US exports of EBO in 1986-1988 to be a representative starting-point for our calculations of total exports under the counterfactual, i.e. assuming the ban would have been lifted on 13 May 1999. However, it is clear to us that these pre-ban figures reflect a market situation that is quite different from the current market situation for EBO in the EC. We must therefore make certain adjustments.

68. We consider it reasonable to make a downward adjustment to the pre-ban exports to take account of the demonstrated decline in "apparent consumption" of EBO in the EC market since the imposition of the ban.[46] At the same time, we note that part of this decline in apparent consumption was caused by the hormone ban itself. Data for 1988 compared to 1989 - when the ban was first imposed - show a sharp drop in EBO imports. In order to take account of this decline related to the ban, we calculated the absolute *difference* between (i) the

[44] The tariff classification for this category in respect of which the US alleges trade impairment is: HS 020610 (Offal of Bovine Animals, Edible, Fresh or Chilled), HS 020621 (Tongue of Bovine Animals, Edible, Frozen), HS 020622 (Livers of Bovine Animals, Edible, Frozen), HS 020629 (Offal of Bovine Animals, Not Elsewhere Specified, Edible, Frozen, e.g., Hearts, Kidneys, Sweetbreads), but excluding HS 0206 1095 and 0206 2991, tariff items that are covered by the HQB tariff quota (see footnote 39 above).

[45] See Section III.A of this report.

[46] The consumption figures we used were calculated following the balance sheet approach, i.e. consumption equals production plus imports minus exports, assuming no change in stocks. This is referred to as the "apparent consumption".

trend import volumes for the years 1989-91 (estimated by way of an extrapolation of the actual import volumes for the period 1981-88) and (ii) the *actual* import volumes for the years 1989-91. The annual average of this *difference* was then added to actual imports in each of the years 1995-97. The apparent consumption of edible beef offal for 1995-97 was calculated on the basis of these adjusted import figures. As a result of this approach, we estimate the downward adjustment factor for apparent consumption to be 18.4 per cent. We assume that the volume of US exports to the EC but for the ban would have declined in proportion to the decline in apparent consumption.

69. On this basis, we estimate annual US exports of EBO in case the ban had been lifted on 13 May 1999 to be 53,503 tonnes.

2. *Estimated Price of US EBO Exports under the "Counterfactual"*

70. We consider the US suggestion of an export price of US$ 1,689 per tonne (f.o.b.) to be reasonable. This price is lower than the average 1996-1998 unit price of current US exports with the ban in place (US$ 2,420 per tonne). This is so because EBO prices would be expected to fall should the ban be lifted, as a result of an increased volume of imports. The EC uses a 1986-1988 average price of US$ 1684 per tonne, a price very similar to the US suggestion we use.

71. Consequently, we calculate the total value of US EBO exports to the EC under the counterfactual to be US$ 90,367,391.

3. *Estimated Value of "Current Exports" to be Deducted*

72. As noted earlier[47], to estimate the nullification and impairment caused by the hormone ban we have to deduct from the total value of exports under the counterfactual, the current value of US exports of EBO.

73. The EC suggests that US exports in the 1996-1998 period are representative for exports that would occur in the future with the ban in place. The main US argument in this respect was dealt with in paragraphs 45-47. We decided to reduce current US exports by 25 per cent. In other words, we assumed that only 75 per cent of current exports would enter the market in the future due to the 100 per cent test and hold procedure recently imposed by the EC. As a base from which to deduct these 25 per cent we follow the EC suggestion and use the average annual 1996-1998 exports.

74. On this basis we calculate the value of current exports to be deducted from the estimated exports under the counterfactual to be US$ 1,845,569.

[47] See paragraph 43.

4. *Adjustment Requested by the EC for US EBO Exports Used not for Human Consumption but in Pet Food*

75. All data provided by the parties in respect of EBO - on the basis of which both the estimated *total* value of US exports but for the ban and *current* US exports with the ban in place, were calculated - do not distinguish between EBO for human consumption and EBO for pet food. In contrast, the US claim of trade impairment caused by the ban only extends to EBO for human consumption, not that used for pet food. This is so because the hormone ban itself does not apply to - and therefore does not hamper trade in - EBO used for pet food. It is difficult to estimate how much of the EBO ends up in pet food since both categories of EBO are imported under the same tariff heading. The EC estimates the share of EBO imports from the US that is used in pet food at 31.7 per cent. The US agrees that 5 per cent of all EBO is used in pet food.[48] Neither party has provided documentary evidence in support of these figures. In particular, the EC - the party claiming that a deduction should be made because of EBO use in pet food - has not substantiated its allegation of 31.7 per cent. For these reasons, we made an adjustment of 5 per cent only.

5. *The US Claim in Respect of Exports that Would Have Resulted from Foregone Marketing Campaigns*

76. The US submits that additional US exports of EBO to the EC - worth US$ 20.1 million - would have been realized from US marketing and promotional efforts that would have taken place but for the hormone ban. These foregone expenditures, according to the US, a minimum average of US$ 1.189 million each year, would allegedly have continued after 1989 - the year the ban was imposed - under US government-funded marketing programmes of proven success.

77. We decided not to take these allegedly lost exports into account. As noted in paragraph 38, the estimate we have to make is based on what would have happened had the hormone ban been withdrawn on 13 May 1999. We cannot assume, under the "counterfactual", that the ban was never imposed and, therefore, that US marketing efforts would have continued after 1989 until now. Moreover, even assuming that US marketing efforts would have resumed had the ban been lifted on 13 May 1999, we consider the causal link between the hormone ban and the allegedly lost exports since 13 May 1999 to be too remote. Taking such lost exports into account would, in our view, be too speculative.[49]

[48] US first submission, footnote 37.

[49] See paragraph 41.

6. Estimate of Nullification and Impairment in Respect of EBO

78. Following our estimates developed above, we calculate the total amount of nullification and impairment caused by the hormone ban on US exports of EBO to be **US$ 84,095,731**.

G. Total Nullification and Impairment

79. As a result of both calculations developed above, we estimate the total nullification and impairment caused by the EC hormone ban on US exports of beef and beef products at **US$ 116.8 million**. The elements of this estimate are reproduced in Annex I to this report.

IV. ASSESSMENT OF THE PROPOSED LEVEL OF SUSPENSION OF CONCESSIONS

80. In reply to questions by the arbitrators, the US submitted for each product on the proposed suspension list the average import value of EC exports to the US over a three-year period (1996-1998). We consider the calculations thus provided to be reasonable. They are reproduced in Annex II to this report.

81. As noted in paragraph 21 above, the US is free to pick products from the proposed list as long as the total trade value is lower than or equivalent to the amount of nullification and impairment we have found, namely US$ 116.8 million. In this respect, we also refer to paragraph 22.

82. We received confirmation from the US that the actual level of suspension once implemented will be equivalent to the level of nullification and impairment we have found. All we can do at this stage is to encourage the US to stand by this confirmation and to abide by Article 22.4 of the DSU. In the event of a future dispute on this issue, we note that the EC could start normal - or arguably even expedited - DSU procedures challenging the consistency of the level of US suspension with Article 22.4.

V. AWARD OF THE ARBITRATORS

83. For the reasons set out above, the arbitrators determine that the level of nullification or impairment suffered by the United States in the matter *European Communities - Measures Concerning Meat and Meat Products (Hormones)* is **US$ 116.8 million** per year.

84. Accordingly, the arbitrators decide that the suspension by the United States of the application to the European Communities and its member States of tariff concessions and related obligations under GATT 1994 covering trade in a maximum amount of US$ 116.8 million per year would be consistent with Article 22.4 of the DSU.

ANNEX I

High quality beef: **US$ 32,664,776**

= [(11,500 * 1)	* 0.92	* 5,342]	-	(31,804,779	* 0.75)
TRQ TRQ fill	US share	price/t (f.o.b.)		current exports (f.o.b.)	25% reduction for "test & hold"

Edible beef offal: **US$ 84,095,731**

= [(65,568	* 0.816	* 1,689)	-	(2,460,759	* 0.75)]	* 0.95
av. 86-88 exports	18.4% adjustment for decline in consumption but for the ban	price/t (f.o.b.)		current exports (f.o.b.)	25% reduction for "test & hold"	5% reduction for pet food usage

Total: **High quality beef and Edible beef offal**

US$ 116.8 million

ANNEX II
List of products for suspension of concessions proposed by the US [50]

Tariff Item or Heading[51]	Description	Average import value (1996-98) '000 US$
0201	Meat of bovine animals, fresh or chilled	1,210
0202	Meat of bovine animals, frozen	317
0203	Meat of swine (pork), fresh, chilled or frozen	119,677
0206	Edible offal of bovine animals, swine, sheep, goats, horses etc., fresh, chilled or frozen	1,588
0207	Meat and edible offal of poultry (chickens, ducks, geese, turkeys and guineas), fresh, chilled or frozen	5
02101100	Hams, shoulders and cuts thereof with bone in, salted, in brine, dried or smoked	2,469
02101200	Bellies (streaky) and cuts thereof of swine, salted, in brine, dried or smoked	546
02102000	Meat of bovine animals, salted, in brine, dried or smoked	21
02109020	Meat and edible offal of chickens, ducks, geese, turkeys and guineas, salted, in brine, dried or smoked; flour and meal of these animals	5
02109040	Meat and edible offal nesoi, salted, in brine, dried or smoked; flour and meal, nesoi	1
04064020	Roquefort cheese in original loaves, not grated or powdered, not processed	3,780
04064040	Roquefort cheese, other than in original loaves, not grated or powdered, not processed	489
05040000	Guts, bladders and stomachs of animals (other than fish), whole and pieces thereof	28,209
06039000	Cut flowers and flower buds, suitable for bouquets or ornamental purposes, dried, dyed, bleached, impregnated or otherwise prepared	3,776
06049100	Foliage, branches and other parts of plants without flowers or flower buds, and grasses, suitable for bouquets or ornamental purposes, fresh	3,614
06049930	Foliage, branches, parts of plants without flowers or buds, and grasses, suitable for bouquets or ornamental purposes, dried or bleached	3,038

[50] See WT/DS26/19 and US answer to arbitrators' question 10.

[51] Note by the US: "The product descriptions supplied below for the items of the Harmonized Tariff Schedule of the United States ("HTS") are for the convenience of the reader and are not intended to delimit in any way the scope of the products that would be subject to increased duties".

Tariff Item or Heading[51]	Description	Average import value (1996-98) '000 US$
07020020	Tomatoes, fresh or chilled, entered during Mar.1 to July 14, or the period Sept.1 to Nov.14 in any year	38,926
07020040	Tomatoes, fresh or chilled, entered during July 15 to Aug.31 in any year	9,597
07020060	Tomatoes, fresh or chilled, entered from Nov. 15 thru the last day of Feb. of the following year	17,374
07031040	Onions, other than onion sets or pearl onions not over 16 mm in diameter, and shallots, fresh or chilled	5,505
07095200	Truffles, fresh or chilled	3,219
07129010	Dried carrots, whole, cut, sliced, broken or in powder, but not further prepared	3,010
07129074 and	Dried tomatoes, in powder	5,137[52]
07129078	Dried tomatoes, whole, cut, sliced or broken but not further prepared	
08024000	Chestnuts, fresh or dried, shelled or in shell	9,098
09042020	Paprika, dried or crushed or ground	10,252
10040000	Oats	36,477
11041200	Rolled or flaked grains of oats	513
11042200	Grains of oats, hulled, pearled, clipped, sliced, kibbled or otherwise worked, but not rolled or flaked	1,024
15059000	Fatty substances derived from wool grease (including lanolin)	4,853
1601	Sausages and similar products, of meat, meat offal or blood; food preparations based on these products	5,952
16021000	Homogenized preparations of meat, meat offal or blood, nesoi	2
16022020	Prepared or preserved liver of goose	1,072
16022040	Prepared or preserved liver of any animal other than of goose	347
16023100	Prepared or preserved meat or meat offal of turkeys, nesoi	4
16023200	Prepared or preserved meat or meat offal of chickens, nesoi	0
16023900	Prepared or preserved meat or meat offal of ducks, geese or guineas, nesoi	26
16024110	Prepared or preserved pork ham and cuts thereof, containing cereals or vegetables	0

52 By 1999, "Tomatoes, dried" (tariff heading 07129075) was sub-divided in the two current sub-headings (07129074 and 07129078). For the new two sub-headings no separate 1996-1998 import data is available. The figure in this table represents the average 1996-1998 import value of the former tariff heading 071129075.

Tariff Item or Heading[51]	Description	Average import value (1996-98) '000 US$
16024120	Pork hams and cuts thereof, not containing cereals or vegetables, boned and cooked and packed in airtight containers	56,437
16024190	Prepared or preserved pork hams and cuts thereof, not containing cereals or vegetables, nesoi	590
16024220	Pork shoulders and cuts thereof, boned and cooked and packed in airtight containers	27,101
16024240	Prepared or preserved pork shoulders and cuts thereof, other than boned and cooked and packed in airtight containers	57
16024910	Prepared or preserved pork offal, including mixtures	16
16024920	Pork other than ham and shoulder and cuts thereof, not containing cereals or vegetables, boned and cooked and packed in airtight containers	6,437
16024940	Prepared or preserved pork, not containing cereals or vegetables, nesoi	3,466
16024960	Prepared or preserved pork mixed with beef	4,222
16024990	Prepared or preserved pork, nesoi	219
16025005	Prepared or preserved offal of bovine animals	0
16025009	Prepared or preserved meat of bovine animals, cured or pickled, not containing cereals or vegetables	47
16025010	Corned beef in airtight containers	36
16025020	Prepared or preserved beef in airtight containers, other than corned beef, not containing cereals or vegetables	118
16025060	Prepared or preserved meat of bovine animals, not containing cereals or vegetables, nesoi	0
16025090	Prepared or preserved meat of bovine animals, containing cereals or vegetables	12
17041000	Chewing gum, not containing cocoa, whether or not sugar-coated	4,556
17049025	Sugar confectionary cough drops, not containing cocoa	56,577
18063100	Chocolate and other cocoa preparations, in blocks, slabs or bars, filled, not in bulk	17,853
19054000	Rusks, toasted bread and similar toasted products	9,800
20021000	Tomatoes, whole or in pieces, prepared or preserved otherwise than by vinegar or acetic acid	18,876
20029040 and	Tomatoes, in powder, prepared or preserved otherwise than by vinegar or acetic acid	11,290[53]

[53] By 1999 "Tomato paste" (tariff heading 20029000) was sub-divided in the two current sub-headings (20029040 and 20029080). Since the US provided 1996-98 import value data only for one

Tariff Item or Heading[51]	Description	Average import value (1996-98) '000 US$
20029080	Tomatoes (including paste and puree) prepared or preserved otherwise than by vinegar or acetic acid, nesoi	
20079905	Lingonberry and raspberry jams	3,063
20083042	Satsumas, prepared or preserved, in airtight containers, aggregate quantity n/o 40,000 metric tons/calendar yr	18,934
20083046	Satsumas, prepared or preserved, in airtight containers, aggregate quantity o/40,000 metric tons/calendar yr	5,163
20084000	Pears, otherwise prepared or preserved, nesoi	2,841
20087000	Peaches (excluding nectarines), otherwise prepared or preserved, nesoi	10,994
20096000	Grape juice (including grape must), concentrated or not concentrated	8,669
20098060	Juice of any other single fruit, nesoi, (including cherries and berries), concentrated or not concentrated	21,360
20099040	Mixtures of fruit juices, or mixtures of vegetable and fruit juices, concentrated or not concentrated	6,546
21013000	Roasted chicory and other roasted coffee substitutes and extracts, essences and concentrates thereof	3,935
21033040	Prepared mustard	5,462
121041000	Soups and broths and preparations therefor	5,748
22011000	Mineral waters and aerated waters, not containing added sugar or other sweetening matter nor flavoured	125,261
23099010	Mixed feed or mixed feed ingredients used in animal feeding	44,024
35061050	Products suitable for use as glues or adhesives, nesoi, not exceeding 1 kg, put up for retail sale	26,299
55041000	Artificial staple fibers, not carded, combed or otherwise processed for spinning, of viscose rayon	25,539
55101100	Yarn (other than sewing thread) containing 85% or more by weight of artificial staple fibers, singles, not put up for retail sale	30,462
85102000	Hair clippers, with self-contained electric motor	15,176
87112000	Motorcycles (incl. mopeds) and cycles, fitted w/recip. internal-combustion piston engine w/capacity o/50 but n/o 250 cc	7,914

of the two current sub-headings, notably sub-heading 20029080 (value: '000 US$ 1,687), the above represents the average import value 1996-98 for the former tariff heading 20029000. The amount of '000 US$ 918,073 provided by the US in Exhibit 35 includes the import value for sub-heading 20029080 in addition to the import value for the tariff heading 20029000.

Tariff Item or Heading[51]	**Description**	**Average import value (1996-98) '000 US$**
87113000	Motorcycles (incl. mopeds) and cycles, fitted w/recip. internal-combustion piston engine w/capacity o/250 but n/o 500 cc	10,152

EUROPEAN COMMUNITIES - MEASURES CONCERNING MEAT AND MEAT PRODUCTS (HORMONES)

ORIGINAL COMPLAINT BY CANADA

RECOURSE TO ARBITRATION BY THE EUROPEAN COMMUNITIES UNDER ARTICLE 22.6 OF THE DSU

Decision by the Arbitrators
WT/DS48/ARB

Circulated to Members on 12 July 1999

TABLE OF CONTENTS

I. INTRODUCTION

1. On 20 May 1999, Canada, pursuant to Article 22.2 of the DSU, requested the Dispute Settlement Body ("DSB") to authorize the suspension of the application to the European Communities ("EC") and its member States of tariff concessions covering trade in an amount of CDN$ 75 million per year.[1] In a letter dated 2 June 1999, the EC objected to the level of suspension proposed by Canada and requested that the matter be referred to arbitration. In its submissions, the EC quantified the level of trade impairment caused by the hormone ban on Canadian bovine meat and meat products at a maximum of CDN$ 3,537,769. The EC also asked that the arbitrators request Canada to submit a list with pro-

[1] WT/DS48/17.

posed suspension of concessions equivalent to the level of nullification or impairment, once this level had been determined by the arbitrators.

2. At its meeting of 3 June 1999, the DSB - referring to both the Canadian and the EC request -noted that, pursuant to Article 22.6 of the DSU, the matter shall be referred to arbitration. Article 22.6 provides as follows:

> "When the situation described in paragraph 2 occurs [if the Member concerned fails to bring the measure found to be inconsistent with a covered agreement into compliance therewith or otherwise comply with the recommendations and rulings within the reasonable period of time determined pursuant to paragraph 3 of Article 21], the DSB, upon request, shall grant authorization to suspend concessions or other obligations within 30 days of the expiry of the reasonable period of time unless the DSB decides by consensus to reject the request. *However, if the Member concerned objects to the level of suspension proposed ... the matter shall be referred to arbitration*. Such arbitration shall be carried out by the original panel, if members are available, or by an arbitrator appointed by the Director-General and shall be completed within 60 days after the date of expiry of the reasonable period of time. Concessions or other obligations shall not be suspended during the course of the arbitration".[2]

The arbitration was carried out by the original panel (hereafter referred to as "the arbitrators"), namely:

Chairman:	Mr. Thomas Cottier
Members:	Mr. Peter Palecka
	Mr. Jun Yokota

3. The jurisdiction of the arbitrators and the effect of this arbitration report is set out in Article 22.7 of the DSU:

> "*The arbitrator* acting pursuant to paragraph 6 shall not examine the nature of the concessions or other obligations to be suspended but *shall determine whether the level of such suspension is equivalent to the level of nullification or impairment* ... The parties shall accept the arbitrator's decision as final and the parties concerned shall not seek a second arbitration. The DSB shall be informed promptly of the decision of the arbitrator and shall upon request, grant authorization to suspend concessions or other obligations where the request is consistent with the decision of the ar-

[2] Footnote omitted and emphasis added.

> bitrator, unless the DSB decides by consensus to reject the request".[3]

The substantive provision at issue here is contained in Article 22.4 of the DSU:

> "The level of the suspension of concessions or other obligations authorized by the DSB shall be equivalent to the level of the nullification or impairment".

4. In this case, the arbitrators are called upon to "determine whether the level of ... suspension [of tariff concessions, as proposed by Canada] is *equivalent* to the level of nullification or impairment"[4] caused to Canada by the EC ban on imports of hormone treated beef and beef products.

5. The organizational meeting at which time-table and working procedures were adopted, was held on 4 June. On 7 June we received a paper from Canada explaining the methodology it applied in calculating the proposed level of suspension. First written submissions were received from both parties on 11 June. Rebuttals were filed on 18 June. A meeting with the parties was held on 22 June. On 25 June we received answers to a list of questions we had submitted to the parties.

6. The main arguments of the parties are summarized below when examining each of the claims before us.

II. PRELIMINARY ISSUES

A. *Third-Party Rights*

7. Following a request by the United States ("US") for third-party rights and after careful consideration of the parties' arguments made at the organizational meeting of 4 June 1999 and in their written submissions, the arbitrators ruled as follows:

> The US and Canada are allowed to attend both arbitration hearings, to make a statement at the end of each hearing and to receive a copy of the written submissions made in both proceedings.
>
> The above ruling was made on the following grounds.
>
> - DSU provisions on panel proceedings, referred to by analogy in the arbitrators' working procedures, give the arbitrators discretion to decide on procedural matters not regulated in the DSU (Article 12.1 of the DSU) in accordance with due proc-

[3] Footnote omitted and emphasis added.

[4] Article 22.7 of the DSU, emphasis added.

ess.[5] The DSU does not address the issue of third-party participation in Article 22 arbitration proceedings.

- US and Canadian rights may be affected in both arbitration proceedings:

  First, the estimates for high quality beef ("HQB") exports, foregone because of the hormone ban, are to be based on a tariff quota that allegedly needs to be shared between Canada and the US. A determination in one proceeding may thus be decisive for the determination in the other.

  Second, several methodologies are proposed to calculate lost export opportunities. Given the fact that the product scope (HQB and edible bovine offal ("EBO")) and relevant trade barriers (hormone ban and HQB tariff quota) are the same in both proceedings, both arbitration panels (composed of the same three individuals) may consider it necessary to adopt the same or very similar methodologies. This is all the more necessary because the arbitrators are called upon to arrive at a specific determination on the amount of nullification and impairment caused by the ban.[6] They are therefore not limited, as in most panel proceedings, to ruling only on the consistency of the amounts proposed by the US and Canada with DSU provisions. Due process thus requires that all three parties receive the opportunity to comment on the methodologies proposed by each of the parties.

- In contrast, the EC has not shown how third-party participation would prejudice its rights. No specific arguments were made demonstrating that third party participation would substantially impair the EC's interests or due process rights.

B. Burden of Proof and the Role of Arbitrators under Article 22 of the DSU

8. Both parties made extensive submissions on the question of who bears the burden of proof in Article 22 arbitration procedures. Each party submitted that the burden of proof rests on the other party.

---

[5] In this respect see footnote 138 in the Appellate Body Report on *EC - Measures Concerning Meat and Meat Products (Hormones)*, adopted on 13 February 1998, WT/DS26/15, WT/DS48/13: "[T]he DSU, and in particular its Appendix 3, leave panels a margin of discretion to deal, always in accordance with due process, with specific situations that may arise in a particular case and that are not explicitly regulated. Within this context, an appellant requesting the Appellate Body to reverse a panel's ruling on matters of procedure must demonstrate the prejudice generated by such legal ruling".

[6] See paragraph 12.

9. WTO Members, as sovereign entities, can be *presumed* to act in conformity with their WTO obligations. A party claiming that a Member has acted *inconsistently* with WTO rules bears the burden of proving that inconsistency. The act at issue here is the Canadian proposal to suspend concessions. The WTO rule in question is Article 22.4 prescribing that the level of suspension be equivalent to the level of nullification and impairment. The EC challenges the conformity of the Canadian proposal with the said WTO rule. It is thus for the EC to prove that the Canadian proposal is inconsistent with Article 22.4. Following well-established WTO jurisprudence, this means that it is for the EC to submit arguments and evidence sufficient to establish a *prima facie* case or presumption that the level of suspension proposed by Canada is *not* equivalent to the level of nullification and impairment caused by the EC hormone ban. Once the EC has done so, however, it is for the Canada to submit arguments and evidence sufficient to rebut that presumption. Should all arguments and evidence remain in equipoise, the EC, as the party bearing the original burden of proof, would lose.

10. The same rules apply where the existence of a specific *fact* is alleged; in this case, for example, where a party relies on a decrease of beef consumption in the EC or the use of edible bovine offal as pet food. It is for the party alleging the fact to prove its existence.

11. The duty that rests on *all* parties to produce evidence and to collaborate in presenting evidence to the arbitrators - an issue to be distinguished from the question of who bears the burden of proof - is crucial in Article 22 arbitration proceedings. The EC is required to submit evidence showing that the proposal is *not* equivalent. However, at the same time and as soon as it can, Canada is required to come forward with evidence explaining how it arrived at its proposal and showing why its proposal *is* equivalent to the trade impairment it has suffered. Some of the evidence - such as data on trade with third countries, export capabilities and affected exporters - may, indeed, be in the sole possession of Canada, being the party that suffered the trade impairment. This explains why we requested Canada to submit a so-called methodology paper.[7]

12. There is, however, a difference between our task here and the task given to a panel. In the event we decide that the Canadian proposal is *not* WTO consistent (i.e. the suggested amount is too high), we should not end our examination the way panels do, namely by requesting the DSB to recommend that the measure be brought into conformity with WTO obligations. Following the approach of the arbitrators in the *Bananas* case - where the proposed amount of US$ 520 million was reduced to US$ 191.4 million - we would be called upon to go further. In pursuit of the basic DSU objectives of prompt and positive set-

[7] See paragraph 5.

tlement of disputes[8], we would have to estimate the level of suspension we consider to be equivalent to the impairment suffered.[9] This is the essential task and responsibility conferred on the arbitrators in order to settle the dispute. In our view, such approach is implicitly called for in Article 22.7:

> "The parties shall accept the arbitrator's decision as final and the parties concerned shall not seek a second arbitration. The DSB shall be informed promptly of the decision of the arbitrator and shall upon request, grant authorization to suspend concessions or other obligations where the request is consistent with the decision of the arbitrator, unless the DSB decides by consensus to reject the request".

C. *Product Coverage of the Canadian Proposal to Suspend Concessions*

13. The Canadian proposal to suspend tariff concessions vis-à-vis the EC and its member States includes a list of products that covers trade in an amount significantly higher than the proposed CDN$ 75 million.[10] As stated in the request itself, the list of products attached to the request

> "is a proposed list of products on which concessions could be withdrawn, and on which public comment is now being received. This list is attached for ease of reference. The trade value of the final list of products subject to increased tariffs will be equivalent, on an annual basis, to Can$ 75 million".

Canada has not yet determined the final list of EC products that will be subject to the suspension of tariff concessions. Canada did determine the degree of the suspension (i.e. the level of the tariff to be imposed), namely a 100 per cent tariff on each of the selected products.

14. In its objection to the Canadian proposal for suspension, as well as at the DSB meeting during which this case was referred to arbitration, the EC complained about the above outlined approach taken by Canada. The EC asks us "to request Canada to submit a list with proposed suspension of concessions equivalent to the level of nullification or impairment, once this level has been

---

8 See Articles 3.3 and 3.7.

9 If this were not done, the Member requesting suspension would need to make new estimates and arguably submit a new proposal. This proposal could again meet objections and might be referred back to arbitration. To avoid this potentially endless loop, the arbitrators - in the event they find that the proposal is *not* equivalent to the trade impairment - have to come up with their own estimate, i.e. their own figure.

10 According to Canada's answers to the arbitrators questions, the proposed list of products covers trade in an amount of CDN$ 316,412,782.

determined by the arbitrator".[11] In other words, the EC requests the arbitrators to first decide on the amount of trade impairment, to then request a specific product list from Canada and to finally determine whether both are "equivalent". Canada objects to this EC request.[12]

15. The arbitrators are unable to follow the EC request. No support for this request can be found in the DSU.

16. The authorization given by the DSB under Article 22.6 of the DSU is an authorization "to suspend [the application to the Member concerned of] concessions or other obligations [under the covered agreements]".[13] In our view, the limitations linked to this DSB authorization are those set out in the proposal made by the requesting Member on the basis of which the authorization is granted. In the event tariff concessions are to be suspended, only products that appear on the product list attached to the request for suspension can be subject to suspension. This follows from the minimum requirements attached to a request to suspend concessions or other obligations. They are, in our view: (1) the request must set out a specific level of suspension, i.e. a level equivalent to the nullification and impairment caused by the WTO inconsistent measure, pursuant to Article 22.4[14]; and (2) the request must specify the agreement and sector(s) under which concessions or other obligations would be suspended, pursuant to Article 22.3.[15]

17. Neither can support for the EC request be found in other provisions of Article 22. Instead, they prescribe the following: (1) the "DSB shall not authorize suspension of concessions or other obligations if a covered agreement prohibits such suspension" (Article 22.5); (2) "[c]oncessions or other obligations shall not be suspended during the course of the arbitration" (Article 22.6 *in fine*); and (3) the

---

11 WT/DS48/17.

12 In contrast to this case, in the *Bananas* dispute the list of products attached to the US request for suspension corresponded, at least according to US calculations, to the US estimate of trade impairment of US$ 520 million. Once the arbitrators had lowered the level of trade impairment to US$ 191.4 million, the US submitted a new request to the DSB meeting. At that meeting the US received authorization to suspend concessions equivalent to an amount of US$ 191.4 million. Subsequently, the US selected a number of products from the original list that, according to US calculations, were equivalent in value to the authorized US$ 191.4 million. The EC objected to the US approach of not providing a definite product list at the DSB meeting during which authorization was granted. The US stated that there was nothing in the DSU to the effect that such a list should be attached to a request for authorization to suspend concessions (Minutes of the DSB meeting of 19 April 1999, WT/DSB/M/59).

13 Article 22.6 of the DSU. Bracketed text added is from Article 22.2 of the DSU.

14 In respect of the first requirement see further paragraph 21.

15 The more precise a request for suspension is in terms of product coverage, type and degree of suspension, etc..., the better. Such precision can only be encouraged in pursuit of the DSU objectives of "providing security and predictability to the multilateral trading system" (Article 3.2) and seeking prompt and positive solutions to disputes (Articles 3.3 and 3.7). It would also be welcome in light of the statement in Article 3.10 that "all Members will engage in [DSU] procedures in good faith in an effort to resolve the dispute".

suspension "shall only be applied until such time as the measure found to be inconsistent with a covered agreement has been removed, or the Member that must implement recommendations or rulings provides a solution to the nullification or impairment of benefits, or a mutually satisfactory solution is reached" (Article 22.8).

18. In our view, the determination of other aspects related to the suspension remain the prerogative of the Member requesting the suspension. We note, in particular, that the Member in respect of whom concessions or other obligations would be suspended, can object to "*the level* of suspension proposed"[16] and that an arbitrator has to "determine whether *the level* of such suspension is equivalent to *the level* of nullification or impairment".[17] Arbitrators are explicitly prohibited from "examin[ing] *the nature* of the concessions or other obligations to be suspended"[18] (other than under Articles 22.3 and 22.5).

19. On these grounds, we cannot require that Canada further specify the nature of the proposed suspension. As agreed by all parties involved in this dispute[19], in case a proposal for suspension were to target, for example, only biscuits with a 100 per cent tariff *ad valorem*, it would not be for the arbitrators to decide that, for example, cheese and not biscuits should be targeted; that a 150 per cent tariff should be imposed instead of a 100 per cent tariff; or that tariff increases should be levied on a product weight basis, not *ad valorem*. All of these are *qualitative* aspects of the proposed suspension touching upon the "nature" of concessions to be withdrawn. They fall outside the arbitrators' jurisdiction.

20. What we do have to determine, however, is whether the overall proposed level of suspension is *equivalent* to the level of nullification and impairment. This involves a *quantitative* - not a qualitative - assessment of the proposed suspension. As noted by the arbitrators in the *Bananas* case, "[i]t is impossible to ensure correspondence or identity between two levels if one of the two is not clearly defined".[20] Therefore, as a prerequisite for ensuring equivalence between the two levels, we have to be able to determine, not only the "level of the nullification and impairment", but also the "level of the suspension of concessions or other obligations". To give effect to the obligation of equivalence in Article 22.4, the Member requesting suspension thus has to identify the level of suspension of concessions it proposes in a way that allows us to determine equivalence.

21. In this case Canada has to - and did - identify the products that may be subject to suspension in a way that allowed us to attribute an annual trade value to each of these products when subject to the additional tariff proposed, namely a 100 per cent tariff (assuming this tariff is prohibitive). We have carried out that

16 Article 22.6, emphasis added.
17 Article 22.7, emphasis added.
18 Article 22.7, emphasis added.
19 Answers to arbitrators' Question 1.
20 WT/DS/ARB, para. 4.2.

task in Section IV below. Once this is done, however, Canada is free to pick products from that list - not outside the list - equalling a total trade value that does not exceed the amount of trade impairment we find. In our view, this obligation to sufficiently specify the level of suspension flows directly from the requirement of ensuring equivalence in Article 22.4, the substantive provision we have to enforce here. It is part of the first element under the minimum requirements we outlined above, namely to set out a specific level of suspension, i.e. a level equivalent to the nullification and impairment caused by the WTO inconsistent measure.

III. CALCULATION OF THE LEVEL OF NULLIFICATION AND IMPAIRMENT CAUSED BY THE EC HORMONE BAN

A. *Summary of the Parties' Basic Methodologies*

1. *Canada*

22. Canada submits that the EC hormone ban impairs Canadian exports in two respects. First, because of the ban Canadian high quality beef ("HQB") that has been treated with hormones, cannot be imported into the EC market. More particularly, Canadian hormone-treated HQB does not qualify for importation under the 11,500 tonnes tariff quota for HQB granted by the EC.

23. Second, because of the ban Canadian edible beef offal ("EBO") for human consumption that has been treated with hormones is not allowed for importation into the EC.[21] For such imports the EC does not apply a tariff quota.

24. In respect of HQB, Canada submits that EC regulations do not make a distinction between Canadian and US beef for purposes of administering the 11,500 tonnes tariff quota. Canada argues that for purposes of estimating trade impairment, both Canada and the US should be allocated 50 per cent of the undivided joint interest in the tariff quota, i.e. 5,750 tonnes each. In support of this, Canada refers to its considerable export capacity for meat of bovine animals. It further argues that since the pre-ban period (1981-88) the Canadian cattle and beef industry have undergone considerable transformation, illustrated by a substantial expansion of production and, in particular, by a dramatic export growth in recent years.

25. In calculating the value of its potential exports under the tariff quota, Canada used the average North American price in 1998 for choice ribeye roll and choice beef loin cuts of bovine animals, namely CDN$ 10,805 per tonne. To

---

[21] EBO treated with hormones is considered by the EC as unsuitable for human consumption. It cannot enter the EC market under the tariff headings summed up in footnote 32. However, such beef offal - treated with hormones - still enters the EC for use in pet food under other tariff headings, not subject to the ban.

arrive at the nullification and impairment caused by the hormone ban, Canada deducted the trade value of its 1998 exports of HQB. On this basis, Canada estimates the value of its expected trade of HQB to be CDN$ 62.1 million.

26. In order to calculate the trade impairment in respect of EBO, Canada's starting-point is to estimate trade flows of EBO between North America (i.e. Canada and the US), the EC and the rest of the world, in the absence of the ban. To do this, Canada utilizes the *Armington Framework Market Share Model.*[22] Canada submits that the basic assumption of the Armington Framework is that similar products are imperfect substitutes given that they can be differentiated by origin of production. According to Canada, trade models that make this assumption usually employ a two-step process to estimate the demand for the product examined. In a first step, the demand/expenditure of a group is determined irrespective of the source of origin. In a second step, this demand/expenditure is allocated among the identified suppliers based on the place of origin and/or the form of the product. The Armington model assumes that the allocation of demand/expenditure of one group is not dependent on any other group’s demand/expenditure. Therefore, one of the major assumptions of the Armington model is that the marginal rate of substitution between any two products of the same kind is independent of the consumption of other kinds of products. Thus, according to Canada, the two key features of this framework are that it allows for two-way trade between groups and it differentiates products based on source of production.

27. In order to calculate the potential export value Canada (1) uses 1988 data for the determination of the pre-ban situation regarding trade flows, market shares and prices; (2) uses 1997 as the most recent year because it is the last year for which a complete data set was available; (3) defines the EC, North America (i.e. Canada and the US) and the rest of the world as the three regions used in the analysis; and (4) assumes that edible bovine offal production is a function of the price of beef rather than the price of edible beef offal, as the latter was a by-product of beef production.

28. According to Canada's calculations, in the absence of the ban North American EBO exports to the EC would have been approximately 71,205 tonnes. Based on Canada's share in North America’s total EBO exports (including US-Canada trade) between 1996 and 1998, Canada estimates its share to be 10.8 per cent or 7,690 tonnes. This volume, multiplied by the EBO price derived from the Armington model, gives the value of potential Canadian EBO exports to the EC. To arrive at the nullification and impairment caused by the hormone ban, Canada deducted from the potential exports the value of its 1998 exports of

[22] Paul S. Armington, *A Theory of Demand for Products Distinguished by Place of Production* (IMF Staff Papers, Volume XVI, No. 1, March 1969), pp. 159-178, Annex B to Canada's first submission.

EBO to the EC. As a result, Canada estimates the level of nullification and impairment to be CDN $ 17.1 million.

2. *European Communities*

29. In respect of HQB, the EC submits that Canada, together with the US, can export HQB to the EC market as long as it complies with the conditions linked to the tariff quota. The approach followed by the EC is to compare the situation that existed before the introduction of the import ban with the current situation. The EC submits that possible short-term effects were eliminated by taking the average figures and data of the period 1986 to 1988 and 1996 to 1998. The value of Canadian exports to the EC was obtained by converting ECU into CDN$ by applying the conversion rates as they were recorded during the years concerned. The level of nullification and impairment identified by the EC in respect of HQB using this approach is zero given that the value of current Canadian exports of HQB to the EC is higher than that prior to the ban.

30. The EC further submits that in the period prior to the ban, Canada's share of the tariff quota never amounted to more than 3 per cent of the total in-quota quantity. The EC argues that Canadian export prices of HQB are significantly higher than US prices, rendering the Canadian product entirely non-competitive when compared to US beef. In addition, the EC submits that in the period from 1988 to 1998, Canadian beef producer prices increased, whereas EC beef producer prices dropped substantially, in particular following the reform of the common agricultural policy of the EC (as from 1992).

31. In respect of EBO, the EC notes that edible offal is a by-product of meat production. It submits that consumer behavior in respect of offal follows the same pattern as that observed for meat. If consumption of meat declines, for example, because of a negative perception of the meat produced, a similar decline will take place in the consumption of offal. The EC refers to the constant drop in beef consumption within the EC in recent years, as well as to the BSE crisis, and argues that this decline is also reflected in a drop of consumption of bovine offal. The EC submits that only offal for human consumption is affected by the import ban. It adds that overall production of offal in the EC over the last 12 years increased significantly, while the consumption of offal decreased. As a result, the EC, originally a net importer of offal, became into a net exporter.

32. The EC estimates Canadian exports of EBO but for the ban, using the 1986-1988 average value as a base from which to deduct "current exports", defined as the 1996-98 average value of Canadian exports of EBO to the EC. The EC further notes that EC imports of EBO were subject to a general downward trend irrespective of the origin of the products, warranting a downward adjustment in value of 25.47 per cent. It also submits that the prohibition of growth hormones only concerns the quantities of EBO actually used for human consumption, not those used for pet food. For these reasons, the EC makes an additional downward adjustment in quantities of 31.7 per cent. The EC accordingly

estimates the level of nullification and impairment with regard to EBO for human consumption to be CDN$ 3,537,769.

B. General Approach of the Arbitrators

33. We carefully examined the claims, arguments and evidence submitted by the parties in light of the rules on burden of proof and the role of arbitrators under Article 22 of the DSU outlined above.[23]

34. Based upon the record before us, in particular evidence submitted by the EC demonstrating that the Canadian assessments were not always appropriate, we consider that the EC established a *prima facie* case that the level of suspension proposed by Canada is *not* equivalent to the level of nullification and impairment caused by the ban. In our view, Canada failed to rebut this presumption. We were, therefore, not able to accept in full the estimates proposed by Canada. We were not convinced either by all of the EC alternatives. We could, however, accept certain elements of both the Canadian and the EC methodologies. As explained earlier[24], in such circumstances, the essential task and responsibility of the arbitrators is to make their own estimate, on the basis of all arguments and evidence submitted by the parties. In doing so, we follow the rules on burden of proof set out in paragraphs 9-11.

C. Guidelines for the Calculation of Nullification and Impairment

35. To determine whether the proposed level of suspension (CDN$ 75 million) is "equivalent" to the level of nullification and impairment caused by the hormone ban, we have, of course, to determine what this level of nullification and impairment is.

36. Canada states that it is expected to estimate the amount of trade that would be occurring in the absence of the EC ban. The EC submits that the calculation of nullification and impairment can only be based on the situation in which Canada would have found itself if the EC had withdrawn, or otherwise had brought into conformity, the inconsistent trade measure.

37. Upon careful consideration of the claims and arguments set forth by the parties, we consider that our starting-point is as follows: <u>what would annual prospective Canadian exports of hormone-treated beef and beef products to the EC be *if the EC had withdrawn the ban on 13 May 1999*</u>? 13 May 1999 is the date of expiration of the reasonable period of time granted to the EC to implement the panel and Appellate Body reports. In accordance with DSU provisions, it was by 13 May 1999 that the EC had to bring its beef import regime into con-

[23] See Section II.B.
[24] See paragraph 12.

formity with the SPS Agreement. We cannot assume that the EC from 1989 onwards, i.e. from the time it imposed the ban, was under a legal obligation to withdraw the ban. We note, in this respect, that the violations found were violations of the SPS Agreement, an agreement only in existence from 1 January 1995 onwards.[25] The EC does not contest that it has not brought the measure into conformity with its WTO obligations. Nor does it contest that the "counterfactual" we need to look at in these proceedings is a situation without the ban. The EC did not propose that we examine any other alternative that would meet its obligations under the SPS Agreement.

38. We are, furthermore, of the view that the effect of suspending concessions should not exceed that of the EC bringing the measure into conformity with WTO rules on 13 May 1999. This stems directly from the DSU itself. The DSU characterizes full and prompt implementation of DSB recommendations as the *first* objective and *preferred* solution. The suspension of concessions, in contrast, is only a temporary measure of last resort to be applied only until such time as full implementation or a mutually agreed solution is obtained.[26] To allow the effect of suspension of concessions to exceed that of bringing the measure into conformity with WTO rules would not be justifiable in view of DSU objectives.

39. We note further that we agree with the arbitrators in the *Bananas* case that

> "the authorization to suspend concessions or other obligations is a temporary measure pending full implementation by the Member concerned. ... this *temporary* nature indicates that it is the purpose of countermeasures to *induce compliance*. But this purpose does not mean that the DSB should grant authorization to suspend concessions beyond what is *equivalent* to the level of nullification or impairment. In our view, there is nothing in Article 22.1 of the DSU, let alone in paragraphs 4 and 7 of Article 22, that could be read as a justification for counter-measures of a *punitive* nature".[27]

40. The question we thus have to answer here is: what would annual prospective Canadian exports of hormone-treated beef and beef products to the EC be if the EC had withdrawn the ban on 13 May 1999? An answer to this question, like any question about future events, can only be a reasoned estimate. It is necessarily based on certain assumptions. In making those estimates and assumptions, we need to guard against claims of lost opportunities where the causal link with the inconsistent hormone ban is less than apparent, i.e. where

---

[25] It might be argued that the ban also violated GATT 1947. However, no legal findings on this were ever made.

[26] See Articles 3.7, 21.1, 22.1 and 22.8 of the DSU.

[27] Op. cit., para. 6.3.

exports are allegedly foregone not because of the ban but due to other circumstances.[28]

41. In this sense, our task of estimating nullification and impairment is very different from that of a panel examining the WTO conformity of certain measures. Once a panel has found a WTO inconsistency, it can *presume* - pursuant to Article 3.8 of the DSU - that the inconsistency has caused nullification and impairment. On that ground the panel can give redress to the winning party under Article XXIII of GATT 1994 or corresponding provisions in other WTO agreements. What normally counts for a panel is competitive opportunities and breaches of WTO rules[29], not actual trade flows. A panel does not normally need to further assess the nullification and impairment caused; it can presume its existence. We, in contrast, have to go one step further. We can take it for granted here that the hormone ban is WTO inconsistent. What we have to do is to estimate the nullification and impairment caused by it (and presumed to exist pursuant to Article 3.8 of the DSU). To do so in the present case, we have to focus on trade flows. We must estimate trade foregone due to the ban's continuing existence beyond 13 May 1999.

42. Both products referred to by Canada - high quality beef and edible beef offal - once certified as *not* having been treated with hormones, do currently enter the EC market, with the ban in place. To assess the trade impairment caused by the hormone ban, we first estimate, for each product category, the *total* value of Canadian beef or beef products - hormone treated or not - that would enter the EC annually if the ban would have been withdrawn on 13 May 1999. To estimate the nullification and impairment caused by the hormone ban we then deduct from that total value the current value of Canadian exports of HQB and EBO, i.e. those that have *not* been treated with hormones. We assume that these "current exports", adjusted for other factors as explained below, are representative of the exports that will occur in the future with the ban in place. The end result provides us the estimated value of hormone treated HQB and EBO exports that would enter the EC but for the ban's continuing existence beyond 13 May 1999.

---

[28] In this respect, see the Decision by the Arbitrators in *EC - Regime for the Importation, Sale and Distribution of Bananas*, Recourse to Arbitration by the EC under Article 22.6 of the DSU (hereafter "the *Bananas* case"): "We are of the view that the benchmark for the calculation of nullification or impairment of US trade flows should be losses in US exports of goods to the European Communities and losses by US service suppliers in services supply in or to the European Communities. However, we are of the opinion that losses of US exports in goods or services *between the US and third countries* do not constitute nullification or impairment of even *indirect* benefits accruing to the US under the GATT or the GATS for which the European Communities could face suspension of concessions" (circulated on 6 April 1999, WT/DS/ARB, para. 6.12, italics in original).

[29] This includes so-called "non-violation nullification and impairment" claims under Article XXIII:1(b) of GATT 1994.

43. Our calculations are based on exports at the f.o.b. stage - excluding insurance and freight - an approach which all parties have used in their calculations. We use f.o.b. prices to ensure comparability with the customs valuation method of suspension of concessions proposed by Canada.

D. *Nullification and Impairment in Respect of High Quality Beef*

1. *Volume of the Tariff Quota*

44. All parties, including the US as a third party, agree that the EC market for HQB exports from the US *and* Canada - with or without the ban - is limited by a tariff quota of 11,500 tonnes at an in-quota tariff rate of 20 per cent *ad valorem.*[30] This quota is to be shared between the US and Canada. The out-of-quota rate is considered by all parties to be prohibitive.

2. *Estimated Utilization of the 11,500 Tonnes Tariff Quota*

45. Canada submits that the entire tariff quota would be filled but for the ban. The EC, referring to the fact that the tariff quota has never been filled in the past - not even before the ban - argues that the tariff quota would only be filled to the same extent as before the ban (1986-1988 average).

46. In this respect, we considered, in particular, the following elements: (1) the fact that the tariff quota represents only a negligible portion of total EC beef consumption; (2) the fact that all HQB tariff quotas allocated by the EC to other countries such as Argentina, Australia, Brazil, New Zealand and Uruguay have over the years been fully or almost fully utilized; and (3) the high production and export capacities of the Canadian beef industry. On these grounds, we can reasonably expect that under the "counterfactual" the tariff quota would be 100 per cent filled.

3. *Estimated Tariff Quota Share of Canada*

47. Given our conclusions above, we next have to estimate the Canadian share in the 11,500 tonnes tariff quota.

48. Our approach here is based on Canada's and the US' past performance with respect to HQB exports as well as beef exports in general. We considered, in particular, the following elements. Firstly, the proportions of Canadian and US HQB exports in third country export markets, such as Japan, Korea, Switzerland and Taiwan. The Canadian share of HQB exports has been below 6 per

---

[30] The tariff classification for this category in respect of which Canada alleges trade impairment is: HS 0201 (Meat of Bovine Animals, Fresh or Chilled), HS 0202 (Meat of Bovine Animals, Frozen), HS 0206 1095 (Edible Offal of Bovine Animals, Fresh or Chilled, Thick Skirt and Thin Skirt) and HS 0206 2991 (Edible Offal of Bovine Animals, Frozen, Thick Skirt and Thin Skirt).

cent in these markets in the 1996-98 period, except in Taiwan where Canadian exports averaged 10 per cent over the last three years. Secondly, the general proportions of Canadian and US beef exports. Canada's share of North American beef exports to the rest of the world was 4per cent on average in 1996-98, although Canada's share, including Canada-US trade, was approximately 30 per cent. Thirdly, the proportions of Canadian and US beef exports to the EC (a 6 per cent share for Canada in 1998). Fourthly, changes in the relative proportions of Canadian and US exports. The general tendency in both the EC and third country markets in recent years has been an increase of Canada's share at the expense of the US.

49. Taking these elements into account, we consider a Canadian share of 8 per cent a reasonable estimate.

4. *Estimated Prices under the Counterfactual*

50. Canada suggests a price of CDN$ 10,805 per tonne which corresponds, according to Canada, to the 1998 average price for North American choice ribeye roll and choice beef loin cuts, both top quality beef cuts. Considering evidence submitted by the EC on current average prices obtained for Canadian beef and relevant price ratios before the ban, we are of the view that the suggested price is too high.

51. In this respect, we refer to the price suggested by the US, a third party in this dispute (US$ 5,342 per tonne). In response to questions from the arbitrators, Canada submits that in the absence of the ban one can expect that Canadian and US prices for HQB would be very similar as similar cuts would be shipped. We agree with Canada that it is reasonable to expect that without the hormone ban a considerable share of the tariff quota would be filled with high quality hormone-treated cuts fetching higher prices than current Canadian exports that include all types of cuts, of both high and low value. This would occur in order to maximize the value of exports entering the EC market under the tariff quota. We note, however, that average Canadian beef export prices in trade with the EC have been consistently higher than corresponding US prices. We thus use a higher price in our estimate than the price suggested by the US but lower than the price suggested by Canada.

52. On that basis, we consider a price of CDN$ 8,594 per tonne (f.o.b.) to be reasonable. Consequently, we calculate the total value of Canadian HQB exports to the EC under the counterfactual to be CDN$ 7,906,480.

5. Estimated Value of "Current Exports" to be Deducted

53. As noted earlier[31], to estimate the nullification and impairment caused by the hormone ban we have to deduct from the total value of Canadian exports under the counterfactual, the current value of Canadian exports of non-hormone treated HQB.

54. The EC suggests that Canadian exports in the 1996-1998 period are representative for exports that would occur in the future with the ban in place. Canada suggests deducting the 1998 value of its beef exports to the EC. We consider it more appropriate to deduct the 1996-1998 average actual Canadian exports to the EC, in light of the point made by the EC that short-term effects need to be eliminated.

55. On this basis we calculate the value of current exports to be deducted from the estimated exports under the counterfactual to be CDN$ 2,265,843.

6. Estimate of Nullification and Impairment in Respect of HQB

56. Following our estimates developed above, we calculate the total amount of nullification and impairment caused by the hormone ban on Canadian exports of HQB to be **CDN$ 5,640,637**.

E. Nullification and Impairment in Respect of Edible Beef Offal

1. Estimated Volume of Canadian EBO Exports under the "Counterfactual"

57. Unlike the EC import market for HQB, Canadian exports of EBO to the EC are subject to tariffs only, not to a tariff quota.[32] The tariff levied on imports of EBO - according to Canada, ranging from 2.3 per cent *ad valorem* to free - is also much lower than the in-quota tariff for HQB (20 per cent *ad valorem*). Therefore, a different methodology to calculate trade impairment in respect of EBO is warranted. In respect of HQB, we could assume that imports but for the ban would be subject to a ceiling of 11,500 tonnes. In respect of EBO, one of the major tasks is to estimate potential exports of Canadian EBO in the absence of

---

[31] See paragraph 43.

[32] The tariff classification for this category in respect of which Canada alleges trade impairment is: HS 020610 (Offal of Bovine Animals, Edible, Fresh or Chilled), HS 020621 (Tongue of Bovine Animals, Edible, Frozen), HS 020622 (Livers of Bovine Animals, Edible, Frozen), HS 020629 (Offal of Bovine Animals, Not Elsewhere Specified, Edible, Frozen, e.g., Hearts, Kidneys, Sweetbreads), but excluding HS 0206 1095 and 0206 2991, tariff items that are covered by the HQB tariff quota (see footnote 39 above).

the ban. Canada's and the EC arguments in this respect were summarized above.[33]

58. We consider average Canadian exports of EBO in 1986-1988 to be a representative starting-point for our calculations of total exports under the counterfactual, i.e. assuming the ban would have been lifted on 13 May 1999. However, it is clear to us that these pre-ban figures reflect a market situation that is quite different from the current market situation for EBO in the EC. We must therefore make certain adjustments.

59. We consider it reasonable to make a downward adjustment to the pre-ban exports to take account of the demonstrated decline in "apparent consumption" of EBO in the EC market since the imposition of the ban.[34] At the same time, we note that part of this decline in apparent consumption was caused by the hormone ban itself. Data for 1988 compared to 1989 - when the ban was first imposed - show a sharp drop in EBO imports. In order to take account of this decline related to the ban, we calculated the absolute *difference* between (i) the *trend* import volumes for the years 1989-91 (estimated by way of an extrapolation of the actual import volumes for the period 1981-88) and (ii) the *actual* import volumes for the years 1989-91. The annual average of this *difference* was then added to actual imports in each of the years 1995-97. The apparent consumption of edible beef offal for 1995-97 was calculated on the basis of these adjusted import figures. As a result of this approach, we estimate the downward adjustment factor for apparent consumption to be 18.4 per cent. We assume that the volume of Canadian exports to the EC but for the ban would have declined in proportion to the decline in apparent consumption.

60. On this basis, we estimate annual Canadian exports of EBO in case the ban had been lifted on 13 May 1999 to be 2,630 tonnes. We note that our estimate for the Canadian share in total North American EBO exports to the EC is lower than the share claimed by Canada. We recall, however, that our estimate (4.7 per cent) is considerably higher than the current Canadian share in North American EBO exports to the EC with the ban in place. From 1996-1998 Canada only exported 2 tonnes of EBO to the EC. For these reasons, we consider our estimate to be reasonable.

2. *Estimated Price of Canadian EBO Exports under the "Counterfactual"*

61. Canada suggests reference to a North American price of US$ 1,501 per tonne (f.o.b.). The US, third party in this dispute, refers to a higher price of US$

[33] See Section III.A of this report.

[34] The consumption figures we used were calculated following the balance sheet approach, i.e. consumption equals production plus imports minus exports, assuming no change in stocks. This is referred to as the "apparent consumption".

1,689 or CDN$ 2,381 per tonne (f.o.b.). The latter price is lower than the average 1996-1998 unit price of current US exports with the ban in place (US$ 2,420 per tonne).[35] This is so because EBO prices would be expected to fall should the ban be lifted, as a result of an increased volume of imports. The EC uses a 1986-1988 average price of CDN$ 2,301 per tonne, a price very similar to the US suggestion and higher than the Canadian suggestion. We consider the price suggested by the US to be reasonable.

62. Consequently, we calculate the total value of Canadian EBO exports to the EC under the counterfactual to be CDN$ 6,261,954.

3. *Estimated Value of "Current Exports" to be Deducted*

63. As noted earlier[36], to estimate the nullification and impairment caused by the hormone ban we have to deduct from the total value of exports under the counterfactual, the current value of Canadian exports of EBO.

64. Canada suggests deducting 1998 imports. We consider it more appropriate to deduct a 1996-1998 average of actual Canadian exports to the EC in light of the point made by the EC that short-term effects need to be eliminated.

65. On this basis we calculate that the value of current exports to be deducted from the estimated exports under the counterfactual to be CDN$ 2,151.

4. *Adjustment Requested by the EC for Canadian EBO Exports Used not for Human Consumption but in Pet Food*

66. All data provided by the parties in respect of EBO - on the basis of which both the estimated *total* value of Canadian exports but for the ban and *current* Canadian exports with the ban in place, were calculated - do not distinguish between EBO for human consumption and EBO for pet food. In contrast, Canada's claim of trade impairment caused by the ban only extends to EBO for human consumption, not that used for pet food. This is so because the hormone ban itself does not apply to - and therefore does not hamper trade in - EBO used for pet food. It is difficult to estimate how much of the EBO ends up in pet food since both categories of EBO are imported under the same tariff heading. The EC estimates the share of EBO imports from Canada that is used in pet food at 31.7 per cent. Canada agrees that 10 per cent of all EBO is used in pet food.[37] Neither party has provided documentary evidence in support of these figures. In particular, the EC - the party claiming that a deduction should be made because

[35] Since Canada only exported two tonnes of EBO to the EC in the 1996-1998 period we consider these US prices to be more relevant than current Canadian prices.

[36] See paragraph 43.

[37] Annex B, p. 2, to Canada's second submission.

of EBO use in pet food - has not substantiated its allegation of 31.7 per cent. For these reasons, we made an adjustment of 10per cent only.

5. *Estimate of Nullification and Impairment in Respect of EBO*

67. Following our estimates developed above, we calculate the total amount of nullification and impairment caused by the hormone ban on Canadian exports of EBO to be **CDN$ 5,633,823**.

F. *Total Nullification and Impairment*

68. As a result of both calculations developed above, we estimate the total nullification and impairment caused by the EC hormone ban on Canadian exports of beef and beef products at **CDN$ 11.3 million**. The elements of this estimate are reproduced in Annex I to this report.

IV. ASSESSMENT OF THE PROPOSED LEVEL OF SUSPENSION OF CONCESSIONS

69. In reply to questions by the arbitrators, Canada submitted for each product on the proposed suspension list the average import value of EC exports to Canada over a three-year period (1996-1998). We consider the calculations thus provided to be reasonable. They are reproduced in Annex II to this report.

70. As noted in paragraph 21 above, Canada is free to pick products from the proposed list as long as the total trade value is lower than or equivalent to the amount of nullification and impairment we have found, namely CDN$ 11.3 million.

71. We received confirmation from Canada that the actual level of suspension once implemented will be equivalent to the level of nullification and impairment we have found. All we can do at this stage is to encourage Canada to stand by this confirmation and to abide by Article 22.4 of the DSU. In the event of a future dispute on this issue, we note that the EC could start normal - or arguably even expedited - DSU procedures challenging the consistency of the level of the Canadian suspension with Article 22.4.

V. AWARD OF THE ARBITRATORS

72. For the reasons set out above, the arbitrators determine that the level of nullification or impairment suffered by Canada in the matter *European Communities - Measures Concerning Meat and Meat Products (Hormones)* is **CDN$ 11.3 million** per year.

73. Accordingly, the arbitrators decide that the suspension by Canada of the application to the European Communities and its member States of tariff concessions and related obligations under GATT 1994 covering trade in a maximum amount of CDN$ 11.3 million per year would be consistent with Article 22.4 of the DSU.

ANNEX I

High quality beef: **CDN$ 5,640,637**

= [(11,500 * 1)	* 0.08	* 8,594]	-	(2,265,843
TRQ TRQ fill	Can share	price/t (f.o.b.)		current exports (f.o.b.)

Edible beef offal: **CDN$ 5,633,823**

= [(3,223	* 0.816	* 2,381)	- 2,151]	* 0.90
av. 86-88 exports	18.4% adjustment for decline in consumption but for the ban	price/t (f.o.b.)	current exports (f.o.b.)	10% reduction for pet food usage

Total: **High quality beef and Edible beef offal**

CDN$ 11.3 million

ANNEX II
List of products for suspension of concessions proposed by Canada[38]

Tariff Item or Heading	Description	Average import value (1996-98) CDN$
0201	Meat of bovine animals, fresh or chilled	746
0202	Meat of bovine animals, frozen	44,396
0203	Meat of swine, fresh, chilled, frozen	24,942,418
0206.29	Bovine edible offal, frozen	129
0707.00.99	Cucumbers and gherkins, fresh or chilled	4,687,027
0709.60	Peppers of the genus Capsicum or Pimenta, fresh, chilled	14,233,362
1108.13	Potato starch	4,823,942
1109	Wheat gluten, whether or not dried	4,245,776
1602.20.90	Livers of any animal prepared or preserved, Other	235,579
1602.41	Hams and cuts thereof of swine prepared or preserved	476,300
1602.42	Shoulders and cuts thereof of swine prepared or preserved	1,398,558
1602.49	Swine meat & meat offal, excl. livers/incl. Mixtures, prepared or preserved	236,338
1602.50	Bovine meat and meat offal, excl. livers, prepared or preserved	425,675
1704.90.90	Sugar, confectionery, (incl. white chocolate), not containing cocoa	39,088,695
1806.90.90	Chocolates, and Chocolate confectionery, put up for retail sale	75,523,171
1905.20	Gingerbread and the like	5,301,767
1905.30	Sweet biscuits, waffles and wafers	54,180,233
2002.10	Tomatoes, whole or in pieces prepared or preserved o/t by vinegar or acetic acid	18,984,239
2007.99	Jams, fruit jellies, fruit or nut purée & paste, ckd prep. sugared, sweetened or not	7,488,896
2008.70	Peaches o/w prep. or preserved whether or not sugared, sweetened or not	9,213,227

[38] See WT/DS48/17 and Canada's answer to arbitrators' question 10.

Tariff Item or Heading	Description	Average import value (1996-98) CDN$
2104.10	Soups and broths and preparations thereof	2,797,645
2201.10	Mineral and aerated waters not containing sugar or sweetening matter nor flavoured	25,026,538
2208.50	Gin	12,435,709
2208.60	Vodka	10,622,416

BRAZIL - EXPORT FINANCING PROGRAMME FOR AIRCRAFT

Report of the Appellate Body

WT/DS46/AB/R

Adopted by the Dispute Settlement Body on 20 August 1999

Brazil, *Appellant/Appellee*	Present:
Canada, *Appellant/Appellee*	El-Naggar, Presiding Member
European Communities, *Third Participant*	Bacchus, Member
United States, *Third Participant*	Ehlermann, Member

TABLE OF CONTENTS

I. INTRODUCTION

1. Brazil and Canada appeal from certain issues of law and legal interpretation in the Panel Report, *Brazil - Export Financing Programme for Aircraft* (the "Panel Report").[1] The Panel was established to consider a complaint by Canada with respect to certain export subsidies granted under the Brazilian *Programa de Financiamento às Exportações* ("PROEX") on sales of aircraft to foreign purchasers of Empresa Brasileira de Aeronáutica S.A. ("Embraer"), a Brazilian manufacturer of regional aircraft.[2]

2. The Panel described certain factual aspects of PROEX at paragraphs 2.1 to 2.6 of the Panel Report. Below we provide a summary of these factual aspects, focusing on the details relating to interest rate equalization subsidies under PROEX to the regional aircraft industry.

3. PROEX is administered by the Comitê de Crédito as Exportações (the "Committee"), an inter-agency group within the Ministry of Finance in Brazil. Day-to-day operations of PROEX are conducted by the Bank of Brazil.[3] Under PROEX, the Government of Brazil provides interest rate equalization subsidies for sales by Brazilian exporters, including Embraer.

4. For sales of regional aircraft, PROEX interest rate equalization subsidies amount to 3.8 percentage points of the actual interest rate on any particular transaction.[4] The lending bank charges its normal interest rate for the transaction, and receives payment from two sources: the purchaser, and the Government of Brazil. Of the total interest rate payments, the Government of Brazil pays 3.8 percentage points, and the purchaser pays the rest. In this way, PROEX reduces the financing costs of the purchaser and, thus, reduces the overall cost to the purchaser of purchasing an Embraer aircraft.

5. The involvement of PROEX in aircraft financing transactions begins when the manufacturer - Embraer - requests approval for PROEX interest rate equalization subsidies before the conclusion of a formal contract with a buyer. If the Committee approves the request, it then issues a letter of commitment to the manufacturer, committing the Government of Brazil to PROEX support, provided that the buyer and the manufacturer conclude a contract for the transaction within a specified period of time, usually 90 days (subject to renewal), and in

---

[1] WT/DS46/R, 14 April 1999.

[2] The Panel noted that, in its submissions, Canada defines the regional aircraft market as consisting of commercial aircraft with 20-90 seats, whether turboprop or jet. Panel Report, footnote 188.

[3] *Ibid.*, para. 2.4.

[4] Panel Report, para. 2.3.

accordance with the terms and conditions set forth in the original request.[5] The letter of commitment usually provides that PROEX payments will be made in 30 equal and consecutive semi-annual instalments during a financing period of 15 years. The first instalment payment is typically due six months after the delivery date of each aircraft.[6]

6. PROEX interest rate equalization subsidies begin after the aircraft is exported and paid for by the purchaser. The payments are made in the form of bonds issued by PROEX to the financing institution. After each export transaction is confirmed, the Bank of Brazil applies to the National Treasury of Brazil for the issuance of bonds designated as National Treasury Note - Series I ("NTN-I") bonds. The National Treasury issues these bonds and transfers them to the Bank of Brazil, which in turn passes the bonds to the lending bank (or its agent bank). The lending bank can redeem the bonds on a semi-annual basis for the duration of the financing, or can sell them on the market at a discount immediately upon receipt.[7] NTN-I bonds are denominated in Brazilian currency, indexed to the dollar as of the date the bonds are issued. The bonds can only be redeemed in Brazil, and only in Brazilian currency.[8]

7. The Panel considered claims by Canada that PROEX is inconsistent with the prohibition on export subsidies under Article 3.1(a) of the *Agreement on Subsidies and Countervailing Measures* (the "*SCM Agreement*"). The Panel Report was circulated to the Members of the World Trade Organization (the "WTO") on 14 April 1999. The Panel reached the conclusion that PROEX interest rate equalization payments are subsidies within the meaning of Article 1 of the *SCM Agreement*, and are contingent upon export under Article 3.1(a) of that Agreement. In reaching this conclusion, the Panel found that the PROEX interest rate equalization payments were not "permitted" under the first paragraph of item (k) of the Illustrative List of Export Subsidies in Annex I of the *SCM Agreement* (the "Illustrative List"). The Panel also found that Brazil failed to comply with certain of the conditions of Article 27.4 of the *SCM Agreement*, and that, therefore, the prohibition in Article 3.1(a) of the *SCM Agreement* applied to Brazil.[9] Having found that PROEX payments are inconsistent with Article 3.1(a), the Panel recommended that Brazil withdraw the subsidies within 90 days pursuant to Article 4.7 of the *SCM Agreement*.[10]

---

5 Panel Report, para. 2.5.

6 Panel Report, para. 2.6; sample letter of commitment provided by Brazil.

7 *Ibid.*, para. 2.6.

8 *Ibid.*

9 Panel Report, para. 8.1. We note that for the purposes of determining whether there was an increase in "the level of … export subsidies" under Article 27.4, the Panel examined subsidies under PROEX, and also under BEFIEX, which provides tax relief to exporters. Panel Report, paras. 4.160 and 7.75.

10 *Ibid.*, paras. 8.2 and 8.5.

8. On 3 May 1999, Brazil notified the Dispute Settlement Body (the "DSB") of its intention to appeal certain issues of law covered in the Panel Report and legal interpretations developed by the Panel, pursuant to Article 4.8 of the *SCM Agreement* and paragraph 4 of Article 16 of the *Understanding on Rules and Procedures Governing the Settlement of Disputes* (the "DSU"), and filed a Notice of Appeal pursuant to Rules 20 and 31(1) of the *Working Procedures for Appellate Review* (the "*Working Procedures*"). On 13 May 1998, Brazil filed its appellant's submission.[11] On 18 May 1998, Canada filed its own appellant's submission.[12] On 28 May 1998, Brazil[13] and Canada[14] both filed appellee's submissions. On the same day, the European Communities and the United States filed third participant's submissions.[15]

9. As described more fully in Section III of this Report, by joint letter of 27 May 1999, Brazil and Canada requested that the Appellate Body apply, *mutatis mutandis*, the Procedures Governing Business Confidential Information adopted by the Panel in this case. A preliminary hearing on this issue was held on 10 June 1999, with this Division sitting jointly with the Division of the Appellate Body hearing the appeal in *Canada - Measures Affecting the Export of Civilian Aircraft* ("*Canada - Aircraft*"),[16] and a preliminary ruling was issued by this Division on 11 June 1999.

10. The oral hearing in the appeal was held on 17 June 1999. The participants and third participants presented oral arguments and responded to questions put to them by the Members of the Division hearing the appeal.

II. ARGUMENTS OF THE PARTICIPANTS AND THE THIRD PARTICIPANTS

A. *Claims of Error by Brazil - Appellant*

1. *Consultations*

11. As appellant, Brazil argues that certain measures about which the parties did not consult were not properly before the Panel. Specifically, Canada's July 1998 request for the establishment of a panel referred to certain Brazilian measures that were enacted in 1997 and 1998, long after consultations had concluded. Those measures are: Provisional Measure 1700/15, Provisional Measure 1629/13, Decree No. 2414 of 12/9/97, Resolution of the National Monetary Council No. 2490/98, Resolution of the National Monetary Council No.

---

11 Pursuant to Rule 21(1) of the *Working Procedures*.

12 Pursuant to Rule 23(1) of the *Working Procedures*.

13 Pursuant to Rule 23(3) of the *Working Procedures*.

14 Pursuant to Rule 22 of the *Working Procedures*.

15 Pursuant to Rule 24 of the *Working Procedures*.

16 WT/DS70/AB/R, circulated to WTO Members on 2 August 1999.

2452/97, Resolution of the National Monetary Council No. 2381/97, Resolution of the National Monetary Council No. 2380/97, MICT Order 28/98, MICT Order 23/98, MICT Order 7/98, MICT Order 121/97, MICT Order 83/97, MICT Order 53/97, MICT Order 34/97, and MICT Order 33/97.[17] As these measures did not exist at the time Canada's request for the establishment of the Panel was made, Brazil maintains that these measures were not properly before the Panel.

12. Brazil argues that the Panel erred in concluding that these 1997 and 1998 measures were properly before it. The Panel came to this conclusion because "the request for consultations related to the same general subject as the request for establishment of a panel, i.e., 'export subsidies under PROEX'"[18], and that "the consultations and request for establishment relate to what is fundamentally the same 'dispute', because they involve essentially the same practice, i.e., the payment of export subsidies under PROEX."[19]

13. In Brazil's view, the issue is whether particular measures that the parties themselves acknowledge were neither included in the consultation request nor the subject of consultations can, nevertheless, properly be before a panel. Article 4.7 of the DSU provides that a complainant may request the establishment of a panel only if "the consultations" fail to settle a dispute. A request for the establishment of a panel must include only measures that were either identified in the request for consultations or raised subsequently during the consultations. Brazil contends that both Article 6.2 of the DSU and Article 4.4 of the *SCM Agreement* provide a necessary and limiting connection between the subject matter of the panel request and the subject matter of the consultations.

2. *Are PROEX Interest Rate Equalization Payments Used "To Secure a Material Advantage in the Field of Export Credit Terms"?*

14. Brazil acknowledges that the PROEX interest equalization scheme is a subsidy under Article 1 of the *SCM Agreement* that is contingent upon export under Article 3.1(a) of that Agreement. Nonetheless, Brazil argues that PROEX interest equalization payments for aircraft are "permitted" by the terms of item (k) of the Illustrative List. Under the express terms of item (k), government payment in support of export credit constitutes a prohibited export subsidy only "in so far as they are used to secure a material advantage in the field of export credit terms". It follows, *a contrario*, that they do not constitute prohibited export subsidies if they are not used "to secure a material advantage in the field of export credit terms." Moreover, PROEX payments are not, in fact, used "to se-

---

[17] Panel Report, para. 4.1.

[18] Panel Report, para. 7.8.

[19] *Ibid.*, para. 7.11.

cure a material advantage in the field of export credit terms." Therefore, according to Brazil, PROEX payments are allowed under the *SCM Agreement*.

15. Brazil also argues that the justification for the PROEX subsidies are twofold. First, PROEX subsidies simply compensate for higher interest rates incurred on transactions involving Embraer that result from what it terms "Brazil risk". "Brazil risk" occurs because a Brazilian commercial entity cannot avoid bearing the additional cost of Brazil sovereign risk when it raises capital or finances a purchase or a sale. Brazil sovereign risk results from the perception in the market for debt securities as to the likelihood of repayment on schedule.[20] Brazil presented evidence to the Panel that PROEX payments are not "used to secure a material advantage" on *two types* of transactions: transactions in which the lender is a financial institution *inside* Brazil; and transactions in which the lender is *outside* Brazil. When the lender is inside Brazil, PROEX offsets the "Brazil risk" incurred by the *lender*. When the lender is outside Brazil, *Embraer itself* incurs "Brazil risk". According to Brazil, the Panel and the other participants ignored the distinction between these two types of transactions, and ignored the fact that Brazil offered separate arguments that these two types of transactions do not "secure a material advantage".

16. Brazil contends that, PROEX subsidies are intended to "match" the subsidies provided by the Government of Canada to Bombardier. Canada provides a wide range of subsidies for Canadian regional aircraft, and these subsidies reduce the price of the aircraft.

17. In support of its position, Brazil notes first that the verb "secure", which is found in the "material advantage" clause of item (k), has been defined to mean "succeed in obtaining or achieving; gain possession of" and "to procure". The verb "secure" (or "securing") is used no fewer than 14 times in WTO Agreements, and, that, in every instance the word "obtain" (or "obtaining") would be an accurate synonym. "Secure" is used in this sense in item (k) as well, referring to action by a Member to obtain, to gain possession of, or to procure a material advantage "in the field of export credit terms" for itself or its nationals, such as Embraer. Brazil maintains that the Panel's interpretation leads to an interpretation of item (k) that covers action by Brazil to "confer" or "bestow", by providing more favourable financing terms, a material advantage on the nationals of other Members who purchase from the Brazilian exporter.

18. Next, Brazil argues that the Panel's interpretation reduces the "material advantage" clause to "redundancy or inutility" by construing the clause to include within this prohibition nothing more than payments that improve "the terms that would otherwise have been be [sic] available to the purchaser with respect to the transaction in question."[21] The Panel's interpretation of the "mate-

---

[20] Panel Report, paras. 4.94-4.96.

[21] Panel Report, para. 7.37.

rial advantage" clause adds nothing to item (k) because all payments of costs incurred will improve the terms that would have been available in their absence.

19. Also, Brazil contends that the Panel's interpretation is inconsistent with the context of the "material advantage" clause. Footnote 5 of the *SCM Agreement* specifies that Annex I contains not only a list of prohibited exported subsidies, but also measures that do not constitute export subsidies, such as in items (b), (h), (i) and (k). Comparing the structure of item (j) and item (k), the two provisions share a similar structure in that they define practices that constitute prohibited export subsidies with language that limits the scope of the definition. In the case of item (j) regarding export credit guarantee or insurance programmes, the limiting language is "premium rates which are inadequate to cover the long-term operating costs and losses of the programmes." In the case of item (k) regarding export credit terms, the limiting language is "in so far as [government payments] are not used to secure a material advantage in the field of export credit terms." Thus, practices covered by the first paragraph of item (k) are prohibited only "in so far as they are used to secure a material advantage in the field of export credit terms." Otherwise, Brazil contends, they are, *a contrario*, permitted.

20. In addition, Brazil asserts that its interpretation is confirmed both by the preparatory work relating to the *SCM Agreement* and by the circumstances that led to the inclusion of the "material advantage" clause in item (k). The language that now comprises the first paragraph of item (k), without the "material advantage" clause, had its origins in rules adopted in 1958 by the Organization for European Economic Cooperation. The provision was included *verbatim* in a 1960 Report of a GATT Working Party on Subsidies. This report provided the basis for the Illustrative List of Export Subsidies in the *Agreement on Interpretation and Application of Articles VI, XVI and XXIII of the General Agreement on Tariffs and Trade* (the "*Tokyo Round SCM Code*"), which was concluded in 1979. The previous year, in 1978, just prior to the conclusion of the Tokyo Round, the Organization for Economic Cooperation and Development (the "OECD") concluded the *OECD Arrangement on Guidelines for Officially Supported Export Credits* (the "*OECD Arrangement*"). Because the *OECD Arrangement* expressly permitted the provision by governments of certain export credits, an exception was inserted by the Tokyo Round negotiators as the second paragraph of item (k) for practices that conform to the interest rate provisions of certain international undertakings on export credits - the "safe harbour" clause. Some time after deciding to include this OECD "safe harbour" clause, the GATT negotiators added the "material advantage" clause to the first paragraph of item (k). According to one of the negotiators at the time, the "material advantage" clause was intended to provide "a weak injury test in the event of a departure from the basic GATT [subsidy] standard." The "material advantage" clause was intended to restrict the definition of this type of export subsidy to instances where a "material advantage" has been "secured". If no "material advantage" is secured, no export subsidy exists. Thus, Brazil concludes that the Panel's inter-

pretation of the "material advantage" clause denies the words of that clause any meaningful effect and should therefore be reversed.

21. Finally, with respect to the availability of item (k) as an "affirmative defence", Brazil notes the Panel's concern that Brazil's interpretation could lead to "inconsistent results"[22], because a measure in the form of a payment could be found to be a prohibited export subsidy when challenged by one complainant yet found not to be a prohibited subsidy when challenged by a different complainant. Brazil responds that such "inconsistent" results are both anticipated and permitted by a number of covered agreements, including Part III and Part V of the *SCM Agreement*, as well as the *Agreement on Implementation of Article VI of the General Agreement on Tariffs and Trade 1994* and the *Agreement on Safeguards*.

3. *Has Brazil Increased the Level of its Export Subsidies?*

(a) Actual Expenditures or Budgeted Amounts

22. Brazil states that in determining whether Brazil has increased the level of subsidies in a manner inconsistent with Article 27.4 of the *SCM Agreement*, the criterion should be the budgeted amounts, not the level of expenditure. The Panel's conclusion on this issue was in error.

23. Brazil first notes that PROEX budgetary numbers are not simply estimates of amounts to be paid, but are actual appropriations that may be used by beneficiaries of the programme. The appropriate definition of the word "grant" in footnote 55 is "agree to, promise, undertake". The result of the budgetary appropriation is that Brazil agrees to, promises, and undertakes to make a specified amount of funds available in the next fiscal year to the private sector for export subsidies under PROEX. Brazil argues that its budgetary appropriations have been "granted", as used in the context of footnote 55, and are, therefore, the appropriate basis for determining the level of export subsidies.

24. In Brazil's view, the context provided by Article 25 of the *SCM Agreement* confirms that the budgeted amount of subsidies is the relevant criterion for calculating the increase in the level of export subsidies under Article 27.4. Article 25 provides that notifications shall contain the "subsidy per unit or, in cases where this is not possible, the total amount or the annual amount budgeted for that subsidy ... ." Because PROEX payments are not provided on a per unit or lump sum basis, Brazil, in accordance with Article 25.3(ii), notified PROEX on the basis of the annual amount budgeted. Nothing in Article 27 suggests, let alone supports, the notion that Members should use one basis for notifying the level of their subsidies under Article 25 of the *SCM Agreement* and another

[22] Panel Report, para. 7.27.

basis for determining whether the level of export subsidies has increased for purposes of Article 27.4.

(b) When are PROEX Subsidies "Granted"?

25. Brazil argues that a subsidy occurs within the meaning of Article 1 of the *SCM Agreement* when the Brazilian authorities issue a letter of commitment to the parties to a proposed transaction. The Panel's conclusion that the letter of commitment itself is not a subsidy, because it is neither a direct transfer of funds nor a potential direct transfer of funds under Article 1.1 of the *SCM Agreement*, was erroneous. Neither the text of the *SCM Agreement* nor logic supports the Panel's finding that in order to qualify as a "potential direct transfer of funds" within the meaning of Article 1.1(a)(1)(i) of the *SCM Agreement*, a measure must give rise to a benefit and thus confer a subsidy irrespective of whether any payment occurs. The ordinary meaning of "potential direct transfer of funds" includes a letter of commitment, and Brazil notes the Panel's statement that the word "potential" has been defined as "possible as opposed to actual" or "capable of coming into being." These definitions apply not only to loan guarantees expressly mentioned in Article 1.1(a)(i) of the *SCM Agreement*, but also to the PROEX letters of commitment. The letter of commitment makes PROEX support "possible" and "capable of coming into being", and therefore constitutes a "potential direct transfer of funds". The letter of commitment benefits Embraer by permitting it to offer its potential customers financing on terms more favourable than it would be able to offer otherwise. This benefit exists *regardless* of whether a formal contract is signed. In Brazil's view, Canada acknowledges this point in its assertion that Brazil has "intensified" subsidization by making long-term commitments in recent months.

26. Brazil also argues that the Panel's finding on this issue is contrary to its statement that "the object and purpose of the *SCM Agreement* ... is to reduce economic distortions caused by subsidies."[23] Although Brazil denies that PROEX subsidies cause economic distortions, any distortions that would be caused by such subsidies would occur at the time the letter of commitment was issued, for it is this commitment that determines whether the purchaser awards the contract to Embraer or to a competitor.

27. Finally, Brazil notes that, under domestic law, the Government of Brazil is "legally liable" for damages should it fail to provide a PROEX payment to which it is committed by virtue of a letter of commitment, when private parties have acted in good faith in reliance on this commitment. Thus, a ruling by the Appellate Body that PROEX subsidies that have already been committed must be withdrawn would force Brazil to violate its domestic legal obligations. An

[23] Panel Report, para. 7.66.

interpretation of the *SCM Agreement* that would require Members to breach their contractual financial commitments would be "unfortunate" from the perspective of both the international trading and financial systems.

4. *Recommendation of the Panel*

28. Brazil notes that Article 4.12 of the *SCM Agreement* provides that, when specific time periods are not provided by Article 4, "time-periods applicable under the DSU for the conduct of such disputes shall be half the time prescribed therein." Brazil disagrees with the Panel's conclusion that Brazil should withdraw its export subsidy within 90 days, instead of within the seven and one-half months that would be half the 15-month period set out in Article 21.3(c) of the DSU. Brazil does not contend that 90 days or some other period (including a longer period) might not be appropriate in a particular case. However, there must be good reason for such a conclusion. The Panel's "brief, cursory treatment of the question" provides "no reason whatsoever" for departing from the seven and one-half month "standard" provided by Article 4.12 of the *SCM Agreement* and Article 21.3(c) of the DSU.

B. *Arguments by Canada - Appellee*

1. *Consultations*

29. Canada agrees with the Panel's finding that "the consultations and request for establishment [of a panel] relate to what is fundamentally the same 'dispute', because they involve essentially the same practice, i.e., the payment of export subsidies under PROEX."[24] In this case, Canada's request for consultations, dated 18 June 1996, was made under Article 4 of the *SCM Agreement* and Article 4 of the DSU, in respect of "certain export subsidies granted under the Brazilian *Programa de Financiamento às Exportações* (PROEX) to foreign purchasers of Brazil's Embraer aircraft."[25] Canada's request for a panel, dated 10 July 1998, was in respect of "the payment of export subsidies through interest rate equalization and export financing programmes under PROEX."[26] The measures alleged by Brazil to have been improperly before the Panel as of 10 July 1998 constitute the legislative and regulatory basis for the granting of the PROEX subsidies. The specific instruments set out in its request for the establishment of a panel merely reflect amendments and replacements to the measures underlying PROEX. In Canada's view, the measures at issue form the continuing legislative and regulatory basis for PROEX subsidy payments, which were the

[24] Panel Report, para. 7.11.
[25] WT/DS46/1, G/SCM/D3/1, 21 June 1996.
[26] WT/DS46/5, 13 July 1998.

"matter" in the request for consultations and in the request for establishment of a panel.

2. *Are PROEX Interest Rate Equalization Payments Used "To Secure a Material Advantage in the Field of Export Credit Terms"?*

30. Canada notes Brazil's claim that whether export credit terms "secure a material advantage" should be based on the terms available in the "marketplace", which, according to Brazil, includes the terms available to all companies in the industry from private and public sources. Canada disagrees with this interpretation, and submits that "material advantage" refers to export credit terms that provide an advantage to a purchaser over the terms otherwise available in the private international financing market. The Panel followed this approach, and specifically rejected Brazil's argument, stating, *inter alia*, that such an approach could lead to a "race to the bottom" in which Members justified the provision of export subsidies on the grounds that other Members were providing them as well.

31. Canada contests Brazil's interpretation that PROEX payments are not "used to secure a material advantage" in the sense of item (k) because they are designed to offset Brazil's risk and Canada's level of subsidies. PROEX export subsidies are, in fact, "used to secure a material advantage", as they provide credit terms for the purchaser more favourable than those that could be obtained in the market. Where a government, financial institution, exporter or purchaser uses an export credit or a payment to gain an advantage or benefit for a beneficiary (i.e., purchasers of exported goods) relative to the international financing market, such practice "secure[s] a material advantage" under item (k) and is an export subsidy prohibited by Article 3.1.

32. Canada rejects Brazil's claim that the Panel's analysis reduces the "material advantage" clause to a nullity. The Panel's finding was that the "material advantage" clause is used to determine whether the subsidy puts the recipient in a better position than if the recipient had obtained financing without government support in the international financing market. Item (k) refers to a situation where a government lends funds at an interest rate that is below the rate it would pay for raising such funds or a similar situation where the government makes up for costs incurred by private lenders. The "material advantage" clause provides that such practice is an export subsidy only when the resulting terms are more favourable than those available in the international financial markets. Without the "material advantage" clause, simply lending below the cost of funds or paying the costs incurred by exporters or financial institutions in obtaining credits would be an export subsidy regardless of the financing terms that result. It is possible for a government to correct for high costs of country risks without providing terms that are more favourable than those available on the market. There-

fore, Canada concludes that the "material advantage" clause is not reduced to a nullity under the Panel's interpretation.

33. Canada states also that Brazil's reliance on the negotiating history is misplaced, because neither Canada nor the Panel has denied that the "material advantage" clause should be given meaning.

34. Canada rejects Brazil's interpretation that PROEX payments are permitted under item (k) on an *a contrario* basis. Such interpretation would convert the Illustrative List into an exhaustive list of prohibited export subsidies, which it is not. The use of the word "including" in Article 3 of the *SCM Agreement* clearly indicates that there are measures other than those listed in the Illustrative List that could be covered by Article 3. Thus, the use of *a contrario* inferences in the Illustrative List is inappropriate. According to Canada, Brazil's interpretation is not supported by footnote 5, which provides that "measures referred to in Annex I as not constituting export subsidies shall not be prohibited under this or any other provision of this Agreement."

35. Canada notes that there is nothing in the first paragraph of item (k) that indicates that measures not meeting the item (k) criteria are to be "permitted" under footnote 5. The Brazilian argument for an *a contrario* finding that certain measures are "permitted" under the Illustrative List should be rejected because, instead of a "list with numerous references to what is an export subsidy", the Annex becomes "a list with numerous references to what is not an export subsidy." Moreover, nothing in the text of the *SCM Agreement* supports the view of the United States that each item in the Illustrative List "sets forth the standard" for when a particular type of measure is a subsidy.

36. Finally, Canada addresses the question of whether PROEX results in a "payment" within the meaning of item (k). The first part of the first paragraph of item (k) refers to a situation where a government lends funds at an interest rate that is below the rate it would pay for raising such funds. The phrase "the costs incurred … in obtaining credits" in the second part of item (k) refers to a similar situation, but with private financing. PROEX subsidies have little to do with Embraer's cost of raising funds to provide financing. In fact, PROEX export subsidies are typically paid when sales are financed by non-Brazilian financial institutions. The higher cost of credit due to "Brazil risk" is not an issue. Thus, PROEX subsidies are not payments to cover the added costs incurred by exporters or Brazilian financial institutions in raising funds used for financing purchases. In Canada's view, they are simply cash grants made for the benefit of purchasers of Brazilian exported products, and do not constitute payments within the meaning of the first paragraph of item (k).

3. *Has Brazil Increased the Level of its Export Subsidies?*

(a) Actual Expenditures or Budgeted Amounts

37. In Canada's view, Article 27.4's prohibition that a developing country Member "shall not increase the level of its export subsidies" refers to the level of expenditures, not to the level of budgetary appropriations. In support of the Panel's finding that actual expenditures should be used for the purposes of this measurement, Canada argues first of all that the *SCM Agreement* as a whole, and Article 1 of that Agreement in particular, is phrased in terms of transfers of value, such as when payments are made. The text of footnote 55 refers to "the level of export subsidies *granted*". (emphasis added) It does not refer to the level of export subsidies "budgeted". Moreover, where disciplines have been imposed on subsidies elsewhere in the *WTO Agreement*, the disciplines are based on expenditure levels.

38. Canada then argues that interpreting "level of ... export subsidies" to mean expenditures is consistent with the object and purpose of the *SCM Agreement*, which is "to reduce the economic distortions caused by subsidies." Such distortions are caused by actual expenditures of export subsidies, not by budgeting or planning for subsidies.

39. Canada notes that certain "absurdities" result from Brazil's argument that the "level of its export subsidies" should be based on budgetary amounts. First, a developing country could have budgeted a large amount of export subsidies in 1994 without actually spending them, in order to expand its actual expenditures of export subsidies in later years. Second, it could create a situation where a developing country Member that does not *grant* export subsidies could lose the protection provided by Article 27 if it *budgets* for export subsidies at a level higher than its 1994 calendar year baseline. Conversely, a Member that maintains its budget at its previous level, but overspends on actual expenditures, would not be in breach of this condition.

40. With respect to Brazil's alternative definition of "grant" as "agree to, promise, undertake", Canada agrees with the Panel's finding that, in this context, this suggested definition is "inapposite".[27] Brazil's argument that it "grants" PROEX subsidies when they are appropriated in the budget is inconsistent with Brazil's argument on the timing of a subsidy, in which Brazil claims that the PROEX subsidy is granted by the letter of commitment and not by the issuance of the bonds. In addition, Brazil's argument is incorrect because a subsidy cannot be said to have been "granted" when neither a beneficiary nor an amount have been identified.

41. Finally, Canada maintains that Brazil's argument that its notification of subsidies under Article 25 is based on budgeted amounts is irrelevant. The pur-

[27] Panel Report, footnote 220.

pose of Article 25 is quite different from Article 27.4. Article 27.4 provides a limited and conditional exception to the prohibition on export subsidies if developing country Members place a ceiling on their overall expenditures on export subsidies, whereas Article 25 requires Members to report all subsidies. Moreover, under Article 25, budgeted amounts are to be used in such notifications only where it is not possible to notify on a per unit basis.

(b) When Are PROEX Subsidies "Granted"?

42. Canada argues that the Panel correctly found that the issuance of bonds, as opposed to the letter of commitment, is the point at which a subsidy occurs under PROEX. This issue is really about effective implementation of the *SCM Agreement*. If the PROEX subsidy is found to be granted when letters of commitment are issued, Brazil can "lock in" the conditional commitments it has made, as well as any it is continuing to make, with respect to the letters of commitment. That is, if it is the letter of commitment that results in a "grant", all existing letters of commitment, i.e., those that have already been issued, will be consistent with WTO rules.

43. Canada submits that Brazil's argument is not consistent with the ordinary meaning of "potential direct transfer of funds" in Article 1.1(a)(1)(i) in the light of its context and object and purpose. Looking at the context of the provision demonstrates that the Panel was correct that "potential direct transfer of funds" refers only to loan guarantees or to similar measures. Under Article 1.1 of the *SCM Agreement* a "financial contribution" can exist only if the measure in question is capable of conferring a "benefit". The example of a "potential direct transfer of funds" provided in Article 1.1 - loan guarantees - re-inforces this interpretation. Loan guarantees are capable of being paid out in the future in the event of default by the debtor, but they confer a benefit even if they are not. Thus, to be considered a "potential direct transfer of funds", a government practice must be capable of becoming a payment, and confer a "benefit", *even if no payment is made*.

44. Canada argues that the letter of commitment is incapable of conferring a "benefit" in and of itself. A commitment is entered into before a sale even occurs. It becomes "binding" only when certain conditions are met. No money is transferred unless there is an export delivery. Thus, the issuance of the letter of commitment itself does not confer a "benefit". The letter of commitment only anticipates possible future benefits if subsidies are actually granted. Until an actual delivery is made, and bonds are consequently issued, no "benefit" can be said to exist.

45. Canada maintains that additional context for this conclusion is provided by the absence of the word "potential" in any of the other examples of "financial contributions" provided in Article 1.1. This omission is evidence that the drafters did not intend that "potential direct transfer of funds" should cover every

promise to provide a "financial contribution" in the future. Rather, it should be restricted to the meaning elucidated by the example of loan guarantees.

46. Canada argues, furthermore, that if Brazil's argument is accepted, the result will simply be that Brazil will be in violation of its Article 3 obligations at an earlier date. Canada explains that it submitted evidence showing that if the letter of commitment were to be used as the point at which the subsidy occurs, Brazil would not have been in compliance, since 1996, with its obligation in Article 27.4 not to increase the level of its subsidies.

47. Canada notes Brazil's argument that any economic distortion occurs at the time the letter of commitment is issued. Canada responds by pointing out that, from the standpoint of *reducing* economic distortion, it is more effective to define the subsidy as the issuance of bonds. If the subsidy is defined as the issuance of a letter of commitment, then the result will be greater trade distortions, because the continued issuance of PROEX bonds under existing letters of commitment will result in many more subsidized aircraft being built in Brazil. In response to Brazil's argument that, under Brazilian law, it is legally liable for damages if it does not uphold a letter of commitment, Canada responds by stating that Members may not "contract out" of their WTO obligations.

48. In response to the European Communities' argument that subsidies should be deemed "granted" when a sales contract is signed, Canada responds that even after a contract is signed, bonds will not be issued if the aircraft is not delivered and exported.

4. *Recommendation of the Panel*

49. Canada notes Brazil's argument that the Panel's recommendation for the time period for withdrawal of the subsidy should be extended from 90 days to seven and one-half months.

50. In reply, Canada states that Article 4.7 of the *SCM Agreement* instructs panels, whenever subsidies are found to be prohibited, to require that such subsidies be withdrawn "without delay." Unlike Article 21.3(c) of the DSU, this requirement is not qualified in any way. The difference in the language between the two provisions makes clear that Article 21.3(c) of the DSU is not the benchmark for determining the period for withdrawing prohibited subsidies in this case.

51. Canada notes also that Article 4.12 of the *SCM Agreement* is only applicable with respect to time-limits for the purposes of the "conduct of ... disputes." However, Article 4.12 refers to only *disputes*, not to the period of *implementation*, which is fundamentally different from the periods for the conduct of disputes. Accordingly, Article 4.12 is of no value in interpreting withdrawal of subsidies "without delay", which is relevant only to implementation.

52. Canada argues that Article 7.9 of the *SCM Agreement* provides that countermeasures may be imposed if actionable subsidies are not withdrawn

within six months of the adoption of the panel or Appellate Body report. It is logical that where a subsidy is required to be withdrawn "without delay", the timeframe for withdrawal must be shorter than the six month period provided under Article 7.9 and in no circumstances should be longer than six months.

53. Canada asks the Appellate Body to recommend that PROEX export subsidies be withdrawn without delay as of the date of adoption of the Panel and Appellate Body Reports, because Brazil is continuing to grant new subsidies and maintain old subsidies, and is intensifying efforts to enter into long-term subsidization commitments before the end of the implementation period.

54. Finally, Canada recalls that its request for a three-month period for withdrawal was made in view of its analysis that "withdrawal" meant stopping the payments of bonds paid in semi-annual instalments. Canada notes that if Brazil does not need to effect a legislative or regulatory change to stop these payments, withdrawal could come even faster.

C. Claims of Error by Canada - Appellant

1. Burden of Proof under Article 27.4 of the SCM Agreement

55. Canada is appealing the issue of the proper allocation of the burden of proof under Article 27.4 of the *SCM Agreement* even though the finding did not affect the outcome of the case. Article 27.4 is an "exception" to Article 3, and therefore Brazil, as the party invoking the "exception", has the burden of proof. The Panel's conclusion that Article 27 is not an exception was based on the fact that Article 27 is phrased as "[t]he prohibition of [Article 3.1(a)] ... shall not apply to ... ." Article 27 should not be considered an element of a claim of violation of Article 3.1(a), as opposed to an affirmative defense or exception, simply because the words "exception" or "exemption" were not explicitly used in Article 27. Rather, like Article XX of the GATT 1994, Article 27.2 contains an exception to the obligations of Article 3.1(a). Therefore, the burden of proof is on the party invoking Article 27. Although the words "exception" or "exemption" are not explicitly used in Article 27, Canada asserts that it should be regarded as an affirmative defence, not an element in a claim of violation of Article 3.1(a).

2. Has Brazil Increased the Level of its Export Subsidies?

(a) Constant or Nominal Dollars

56. Canada argues that the Panel's finding that it is appropriate in this case to use constant dollars in order to provide a more meaningful assessment of whether Brazil has increased the level of its export subsidies is "unreasoned" and does not respect the text, context and the object and purpose of the *SCM Agreement*.

57. Canada submits that there is no explicit provision for conversion of the level of export subsidies to a constant value either in Article 27.4 or in footnote 55. Moreover, paragraph 5 of Annex IV of the *SCM Agreement* specifically provides for inflation adjustment. Thus, the fact that the drafters did not provide for inflation adjustment in Article 27 gives rise to the "commonplace inference" that they did not intend for inflation to be taken into account in this provision. Indeed, there is no guidance in the Agreement on how indexation should be accomplished if it were to be used.

58. In the alternative, Canada argues that the one provision in the *SCM Agreement* where indexation is used - paragraph 5 of Annex IV - only applies if the amounts would be significantly affected by inflation. Canada notes that a large part of Brazil's trade takes place in U.S. dollars, that PROEX bonds are indexed to U.S. dollars, and that the PROEX budget and expenditures are notified to the WTO in U.S. dollars. Given that Brazil expressed its export subsidies in the currency of a non-inflationary economy, and, therefore, inflation could not have had a significant effect, in Canada's view, there is no basis for the Panel's conclusion that constant dollars provide a more "meaningful assessment" as to whether Brazil has increased the level of its export subsidies.

3. *Conditional Appeal: "Maintaining" Subsidies under Article 3.2 of the* SCM Agreement

59. In its appellant's submission, Canada argues that if the Appellate Body reverses the Panel's finding that subsidies are "granted" at the time bonds are issued, not when the letter of commitment is issued, the Appellate Body should then complete the legal analysis, relying on the factual record before the Panel. To this end, the Appellate Body should find that subsequent issuance of PROEX bonds upon the delivery of the subject aircraft is inconsistent with Brazil's obligation not to "maintain" prohibited export subsidies under Article 3.2 of the Agreement.

60. Canada notes the overall importance of this issue by quoting the Panel's statement that if there were no prospective discipline for the provision of subsidies, "the SCM Agreement's prohibitions could not be invoked until a particular prohibited subsidy had actually been paid." [28] If the Appellate Body does not give proper meaning to the word "maintain" in Article 3.2, the *SCM Agreement* will be rendered ineffective because Brazil will be free to provide prohibited export subsidies for many years after the deadline for implementation of the report, as long as the letter of commitment was provided before the report was adopted. For the same reason, the eight-year phase out period in Article 27.4 will be extended indefinitely.

[28] Panel Report, footnote 187.

61. Canada notes that the plain meaning of "maintain" is "go on with, continue, persevere in; preserve or retain; cause to continue". The issuance of the PROEX bonds causes the PROEX subsidy to continue to exist, and consequently preserves that subsidy, and, therefore, "maintains" a prohibited subsidy within the meaning of Article 3.2 of the *SCM Agreement*. In the context of Article 27, this interpretation would lead to the commitment to issue PROEX bonds extending past the end of the eight-year phase out period, and, therefore, "maintain" a prohibited export subsidy beyond the phase out deadline.

D. Arguments by Brazil - Appellee

1. Burden of Proof under Article 27.4 of the SCM Agreement

62. In Brazil's view, the Panel correctly disagreed with Canada's argument that the temporary exemption provided for developing countries in Article 27.2 is the legal equivalent of the permanent exception from *GATT 1994* obligations for all Members provided by Article XX of *GATT 1994*.

63. Brazil argues that Article 27, entitled "Special and Differential Treatment of Developing Country Members", is in no way subordinate to Article 3 or any other article of the *SCM Agreement*, nor is it to be narrowly interpreted in favor of any other provision. Rather, Article 27 is a transitional arrangement with its own terms. In Brazil's view, the temporary legitimacy of developing country Member's export subsidies is presumed unless it is proven that a particular Member is not in compliance with its obligations under Article 27.

64. In Brazil's view, if Article 27 is read in the order in which its terms are set out, the meaning is clear. Article 27.2 begins: "Article 3 shall not apply". For Article 3 to apply, the burden of proof must reside with the complainant to demonstrate that the conditions of Article 27 are not met, and Article 3 therefore does apply. Otherwise, Article 3 always would apply, subject only to the ability of a developing country Member to bear the burden of proof under Article 27. The fact that non-application depends upon compliance with Article 27.4 does not alter the ordinary meaning of "shall not apply". A *seriatim* reading of Article 27 first establishes that Article 3 does not apply, and only then reaches the "subject to compliance" clause in Article 27.2(b).

65. Brazil further argues that both the context and the object and purpose of Article 27 support the Panel's conclusion. The context is provided by the title, "Special and Differential Treatment of Developing Country Members". This title is indicative of the nature of the provision, and expresses a concern for the well-being of developing country Members. Thus, a high degree of liberality in interpretation of this provision is required. Similarly, the object and purpose is stated in the first paragraph of Article 27, which reads: "Members recognize that subsidies may play an important role in economic development programmes of developing country Members." According to Brazil, Canada's arguments placing

the burden of proof under Article 27 on developing country Members ignore the context and the object and purpose.

66. Brazil notes two final points. First, placing the burden of proof on a complaining party would *not* mean that potential complainants would be frustrated by a lack of information. Information of this nature is available in the panel proceedings and through Article 25 subsidy notifications. In this case, Brazil has provided information through both avenues. Second, Article 27.7 of the *SCM Agreement* provides that a Member adversely affected by export subsidies has an additional avenue for a complaint under the provisions of Article 7 of that Agreement.

2. *Has Brazil Increased the Level of its Export Subsidies?*

(a) Constant or Nominal Dollars

67. Brazil notes that Canada appeals the Panel's decision to use constant dollars to measure the level of increase in export subsidies, on two grounds: 1) the Panel confined its conclusion to "this case"; and 2) use of a constant measure of value is contrary to the ordinary meaning of the phrase "level of ... export subsidies".

68. In Brazil's view, the Panel's confining of its conclusion to the facts of this case is a proper, prudent exercise of judicial economy. The Panel had to decide only this case, not another case, and there is nothing irreversible in the Panel's approach.

69. Brazil notes Canada's argument that because Article 27.4 does not explicitly require the use of constant value, panels are prohibited from using that measure. Brazil draws the opposite conclusion from the terms of Article 27.4: since Article 27.4 does not prohibit the use of constant value, nothing in the *SCM Agreement* precludes the Panel's conclusion.

70. Brazil argues further that the use of a constant measure is required if the special rules for developing countries in Article 27 are to be given genuine meaning. The Appellate Body may take "judicial notice" that currencies tend to depreciate over time because of inflationary pressures, and these pressures are greatest in developing countries. A failure to adjust the level of export subsidies for inflation would effectively repeal the Article 27 "exemption". Brazil explains that the fact that Brazil reported its subsidies in dollars means that the inflation rate was smaller than it otherwise would have been, but inflation was present nevertheless, and the Panel properly allowed for it.

3. *Conditional Appeal: "Maintaining" Subsidies under Article 3.2 of the SCM Agreement*

71. Brazil notes Canada's argument that if the Appellate Body reverses the Panel and finds that the subsidy occurs at the point the letter of commitment is

issued, then it should make an additional finding that the issuance of the NTN-I bonds constitutes "maintaining" a subsidy under Article 3.2. Brazil agrees with Canada that "maintain" is defined as "go on with, continue, persevere in; preserve or retain; cause to continue". However, what must not be "maintained" under the *SCM Agreement* are "subsidies," a term Brazil claims that Canada defines in the *Canada - Aircraft* appellate proceeding as the equivalent of "subsidy programme". Thus, it is simply the subsidy programme itself, in this case PROEX, which must not be "maintained".

72. Brazil first notes that the word "maintain" logically applies only to subsidies granted prior to the effective date of the WTO, 1 January 1995. If subsidies were granted before that date, they would be consistent with the requirements of Article 3.2 of the *SCM Agreement* if that paragraph did not prohibit the maintenance of such subsidies.

73. Brazil argues that, in this case, the "subsidy" occurs when the letter of commitment is issued. The subsequent issuance of the bonds is no more the maintenance of a subsidy than is the subsequent payment received by redeeming the bonds over the life of the financing. The only way the PROEX subsidy would be "maintained" is if Brazil did not withdraw the subsidy element of the programme in the event of adoption of a report finding PROEX to be inconsistent with Brazil's WTO obligations. By contrast, it would not be "maintaining" the PROEX subsidy if it eliminated PROEX and simply continued to honour contractual obligations made before the elimination of the programme.

74. Brazil refers to Canada's argument that this interpretation allows Members to "contract out" of their obligations. In response, Brazil contends that, to the extent that this is true, it is true of virtually any subsidy that is subsequently determined to be inconsistent with WTO obligations. For example, a finding that a low-interest loan is a subsidy would not require the borrower to agree to less favourable terms. It simply requires that no new low-interest loans be granted.

75. Brazil notes that subsidy programmes often utilize payments made over a long period. Indeed, Canada's most recent subsidy notification under Article 25 demonstrates that it has made payments under certain programmes after the termination of the programme. In Brazil's view, the honouring of prior subsidy commitments cannot constitute "maintaining" export subsidies under Article 3.2 of the *SCM Agreement*.

E. Arguments by Third Participants

1. European Communities

(a) "Material Advantage" Clause of Item (k) of the Illustrative List of Export Subsidies

76. The European Communities disagrees with the Panel's interpretation of the "material advantage" clause in item (k) of the Illustrative List. In the Euro-

pean Communities' view, this clause allows Members to "match" the export credits granted by other Members, even if the rates provided are less than commercial rates. The second paragraph of item (k) explicitly permits certain export credit practices under conditions which conform to the *OECD Arrangement*. The *OECD Arrangement* authorizes participants to apply interest rates lower than the designated minimum interest rate, the Commercial Interest Reference Rate (the "CIRR"), in order to "match" the rates applied by other participants or by non-participants in the Arrangement. The level at which the minimum interest rates, as well as the "matching" mechanism, are set, demonstrates that the purpose of the *OECD Arrangement* is to ensure that export credits do not distort competition, rather than to ensure that export credits are always offered at "commercial rates". The European Communities believes that the second paragraph of item (k) provides context for the "material advantage" clause in the first paragraph of item (k), and that this clause in the first paragraph serves the same purpose as the second paragraph.

77. The European Communities then argues that footnote 5 to Article 3.1(a) of the *SCM Agreement* does not include *a contrario* inferences. On the contrary, footnote 5 requires an "affirmative statement" in the Illustrative List to the effect that a measure does not constitute an export subsidy. The second paragraph of item (k) provides an example of such an "affirmative statement"; this paragraph describes the type of measure to which footnote 5 refers as "not constituting export subsidies". By contrast, the language of the "material advantage" clause in the first paragraph of item (k) does not constitute such an "affirmative statement". The "material advantage" clause simply defines the scope of the prohibition in the first paragraph of item (k). Therefore, the European Communities concludes that the "material advantage" clause is not an example of the type of measure to which footnote 5 refers.

78. The European Communities disagrees with the United States position that the Panel made an "alternative finding" related to the "material advantage" clause. What the United States calls a "finding" is in reality merely an "interpretation". The difficulty arises because the Panel has treated Brazil's argument for an exception under item (k) as an affirmative defence. In fact, item (k) is in the nature of a prohibition. Thus, according to the European Communities, the Panel's decision to place the burden of proof on Brazil was in error.

(b) Has Brazil Increased the Level of its Export Subsidies?

(i) Actual Expenditures or Budgeted Amounts

79. The European Communities agrees with the Panel's finding that actual expenditures should be used to determine whether there is an increase in the "level of ... export subsidies" under Article 27.4. Footnote 55 of the

SCM Agreement indicates that the relevant "level of … export subsidies" is that of the subsidies "granted". Authorization given by the budgetary authority of a Member to the executive to spend funds does not create any rights for the potential beneficiaries of the fund. Therefore, in the European Communities' view, the PROEX payments may not be deemed "granted" until the sales contracts are concluded.

(ii) When are PROEX Subsidies "Granted"

80. According to the European Communities, PROEX payments should be deemed "granted" when a definitive purchase contract (i.e., not a simple option contract) is signed by Embraer and the foreign purchaser. The European Communities agrees with the Panel that the issuance of a letter of commitment is not sufficient to consider that the subsidy has been "granted", since the obligation to issue the bonds is conditional upon the conclusion of a sales contract. Each of the parties is free to sign or not to sign the contract after the letter of commitment has been issued, and in at least some cases letters of commitment are issued with respect to option contracts. The benefit to Embraer occurs upon concluding a sales contract.

81. The European Communities maintains that if the PROEX payments are deemed "granted" by the Appellate Body when the aircraft is physically exported, all bond issues will be prohibited in the future by virtue of the Appellate Body ruling. As a result, bonds may not be issued even under those existing sale contracts for which export has not yet occurred. This would be "extremely disruptive" of the rights of private parties under sales contracts that have already been concluded and are legally enforceable. Furthermore, any harm caused by the subsidy occurs at the moment when the sales contract is signed.

82. The European Communities notes that the United States made a similar argument in *Australia - Subsidies Provided to Producers and Exporters of Automotive Leather*[29], where the United States claimed that a contract between the Government of Australia and a private party to provide a grant constituted a "subsidy" within the meaning of Article 1 of the *SCM Agreement*.

(c) Recommendation of the Panel

83. The European Communities does not express any views on whether the 90-day period for withdrawal of PROEX subsidies set by the Panel is appropriate, particularly given the Panel's failure to advance specific reasoning for its conclusion. However, the European Communities considers that Brazil's rationale for applying a seven and one-half month period is incorrect. A period of seven and one-half months could under no circumstances qualify as implemen-

[29] Adopted 16 June 1999, WT/DS126/R, para. 7.43.

tation "without delay." Moreover, the use of the 15 month period referred to in Article 21.3(c) is inappropriate as a guideline.

84. The European Communities notes that Article 4.12 only applies with respect to time-periods for the "conduct of ... disputes". The implementation of a panel report, however, is not part of the "conduct" of a dispute.

85. The European Communities attaches great importance to the principle in Article 3.2 of the DSU that no retroactive remedies may be imposed.

(d) Conditional Appeal: "Maintaining" Subsidies Under Article 3.2 of the *SCM Agreement*

86. With respect to Canada's argument that the continued issuance of bonds violates the prohibitions in Article 3.2 on "maintaining" export subsidies, the European Communities notes briefly that Canada's position is incompatible with the principle that the DSB's rulings and recommendations are not retroactive. If Canada's argument were accepted, it would require Members to recover subsidies that have already been "granted". The obligation not to "maintain" prohibited subsidies is intended to address the situation where a Member grants prohibited subsidies within the framework of a specific programme. Article 3.2 simply requires that this programme not be "maintained", that is, it must be abolished.

2. *United States*

(a) Burden of Proof Under Article 27.4 of the *SCM Agreement*

87. The United States notes that it agrees with the arguments made by Canada that the burden of proof under Article 27 is on the developing country Member to show that it is in compliance with the provisions of Article 27.4.

(b) Are PROEX Interest Rate Equalization Payments Used "To Secure a Material Advantage in the Field of Export Credit Terms"?

88. The United States notes two separate findings by the Panel on the "material advantage" clause in item (k) of the Illustrative List. First, the Panel found that an item (k) payment is "used to secure a material advantage" where the payment makes available export credit on terms more favourable than otherwise available in the marketplace. Second, the Panel made an alternative finding based on the assumption that Brazil was correct in its assertion that the "material advantage" clause required an examination of export credit terms available with respect to competing products exported from other Members. In this alternative finding, the Panel found that the field of export credit terms is limited to interest rates, grace periods, transaction costs, maturities and the like, and does not en-

compass the price at which the product is sold.[30] The United States argues that the Panel's first finding was incorrect as a matter of law, but that the Panel's alternative finding was correct and should be upheld by the Appellate Body.

89. According to the United States, the Panel's first finding reads the "material advantage" clause out of item (k). The United States states that, under this first finding by the Panel, any payment by a government of costs incurred by exporters or financial institutions in obtaining credits necessarily results in "terms which are more favourable than would otherwise be available" in the marketplace, and, therefore, any advantage becomes a "material advantage".

90. In addition, the United States argues, by adopting an interpretation that renders the "material advantage" clause meaningless, the Panel's first finding ignores the fact that, in addition to listing practices that *do* constitute prohibited export subsidies, the Illustrative List also lists some practices that do *not* constitute prohibited export subsidies. The intent of the drafters in using the term "illustrative" was to signify that not all types of potential export subsidy practices are addressed by the Illustrative List. However, where an item of the Illustrative List does address a particular type of practice, that item sets forth the standard for determining whether that practice is, or is not, a prohibited export subsidy. Thus, when item (k) provides that export credits constitute prohibited export subsidies "in so far as they are used to secure a material advantage in the field of export credit terms", item (k), by necessary implication, also provides, *a contrario*, that export credits do not constitute prohibited export subsidies if they are not "used to secure a material advantage in the field of export credit terms".

91. The United States argues that the Panel's alternative finding was correct. According to the United States, a Member would not "secure a material advantage" if it merely "matched" export credits offered by another Member. Here, however, a different set of facts occurred. Here, the Panel properly rejected Brazil's argument for a comparison of Brazil's export credit terms to Canada's non-export credit subsidies, by limiting the "field of export credit terms" to "items directly related to export credits, such as interest rates, grace periods, transaction costs, maturities and the like." [31]

92. The United States concludes that because Brazil does not appear to have demonstrated, or even claimed, that PROEX financing is intended to match "export credit terms" under the standard adopted by the Panel in its alternative finding, the Appellate Body should uphold the Panel's alternative finding.

[30] Panel Report, para. 7.28.
[31] Panel Report, para. 7.28.

(c) Has Brazil Increased the Level of its Export Subsidies?

(i) Actual Expenditures or Budgeted Amounts

93. The United States notes that Brazil's appeal focuses on "dueling dictionary definitions" of the verb "to grant", arguing that the term also means "[a]gree to, promise, undertake". Brazil argues that because budgeted amounts are appropriate for Article 25, they are therefore appropriate for Article 27 as well.

94. In the view of the United States, Article 25 establishes exactly the opposite. Clause (ii) contemplates three methods of measuring subsidies. Budgeted subsidies is the third method listed in Article 25, and that method is only to be used in cases where the other two methods are not possible. The preferred method, subsidy per unit, contemplates the use of actual subsidies, which leads to a reasonable inference that the use of actual expenditures is the normal rule for purposes of the *SCM Agreement.*

(ii) Constant or Nominal Dollars

95. The United States agrees with Canada that the use of constant dollars was not the appropriate means of determining whether Brazil had increased the "level of its subsidies" under Article 27.4 - with one exception. The United States disagrees with Canada's reliance on the reference to inflation adjustments in paragraph 5 of Article IV of the *SCM Agreement* as evidence that the drafters intended to preclude the consideration of inflation in all other instances. The fact that the drafters of the *SCM Agreement* referenced an inflation adjustment in Annex IV does not necessarily mean that they intended to preclude a consideration of inflation for all other purposes. A more likely explanation is that the drafters did not consider the issue in other contexts.

96. The United States raises a concern that the application of an all-purpose, undefined inflation adjustment for purposes of assessing a Member's compliance with its commitments would add a considerable element of uncertainty to the rights and obligations of Members, because a Member's compliance or non-compliance could depend entirely upon the particular deflator chosen by a dispute settlement panel. As a result, the proper interpretation of Article 27.4 is that the level of export subsidies should be assessed in nominal, rather than constant, terms.

(d) Recommendation of the Panel

97. The United States disagrees with Brazil that the requirement in Article 4.12 that the time periods in the DSU be halved applies in the context of withdrawal of subsidies. Under Brazil's argument, the time period for withdrawal of the subsidy should be seven and one-half months, or one half the 15 months pro-

vided in Article 21.3(c). The United States agrees with the Panel's rejection of the Brazilian argument, for two reasons. First, Article 4.12 applies "except for time-periods specifically prescribed in [Article 4]". However, a time period for implementation *is* specifically prescribed in Article 4.7, namely, the time-period to be specified by the panel. Second, under the DSU, there is no set time period for implementation that can be halved under Article 4.12. The 15 months referred to in Article 21.3(c) is "only a guideline", and is only relevant if immediate compliance is impracticable.

(e) Conditional Appeal: "Maintaining" Subsidies Under Article 3.2 of the *SCM Agreement*

98. The United States agrees with Canada that if the Appellate Body finds that the letter of commitment is the point at which the subsidy occurs, it should also find that the issuance of PROEX bonds pursuant to existing letters of commitment is inconsistent with the prohibition in Article 3.2 that Members shall not "maintain" export subsidies. The United States then offers the following additional observations.

99. The United States disagrees with what it considers Brazil's "implicit" position that a subsidy comes into, and goes out of, existence simultaneously at the moment of its granting. It is well-accepted that the timing and duration of a subsidy are two different things, and that a subsidy can have a duration that extends over a period of years. When a subsidy is properly allocated over a period of several years, the withdrawal of that portion of the subsidy allocated to future time periods would not constitute a retroactive remedy. Rather, it would constitute prospective implementation based on a recognition of the distinction between the measure conferring a subsidy and the subsidy itself.

100. The United States rejects the argument of Brazil that issuance of new bonds under existing letters of commitment cannot be stopped because it would be disruptive to private parties. Virtually all WTO dispute settlement rulings will cause disruption to private parties. The United States refers to the Award of the Arbitrator in *Indonesia - Certain Measures Affecting the Automobile Industry* ("*Indonesia - Automobiles*"),[32] which notes that some degree of adjustment by the domestic industry occurs in response to every ruling.

101. The United States further notes that the European Communities, which supported Brazil's argument on this point at the Panel stage, took a "contradictory" position in the panel report in *Indonesia - Automobiles*.[33] In that case, the

[32] Award of the Arbitrator, WT/DS54/15, WT/DS55/14, WT/DS59/13, WT/DS64/12, 7 December 1998, para. 23.

[33] Adopted 23 July 1998, WT/DS54/R, WT/DS55/R, WT/DS59/R, WT/DS64/R, paras. 5.276-5.278.

European Communities argued that the "withdrawal" of a subsidy could entail the recovery by the subsidizing government of previously bestowed subsidies.

102. The United States contends that Canada's argument that Brazil must not pay out additional prohibited subsidies in the form of PROEX bonds is correct, and is consistent with the *SCM Agreement* and the DSU. Otherwise, dispute settlement would be largely useless as a tool for addressing distortive subsidies. Regardless of whether the letter of commitment or the issuance of a bond constitutes the PROEX subsidy, the appropriate outcome is that Brazil must refrain from issuing new bonds and withdraw the subsidy.

III. PRELIMINARY PROCEDURAL MATTER AND RULING

A. *Procedures Governing Business Confidential Information*

103. By joint letter of 27 May 1999, Brazil and Canada requested that we apply, *mutatis mutandis*, the Procedures Governing Business Confidential Information adopted by the Panel in this case (the "BCI Procedures"). In their request, they also asked that certain of the BCI Procedures be applied to the third participants in this appeal; in particular, that the third participants designate authorized representatives who would be required to file declarations of non-disclosure with the Presiding Member of this Division before being allowed to view any information designated as "business confidential" or to attend portions of the oral hearing when such information may be discussed.

104. By letter of 31 May 1999, we invited the participants to file legal memoranda in support of their request, and offered each an opportunity to respond to the legal memorandum submitted by the other. The third participants were also given an opportunity to file legal memoranda. Brazil and Canada submitted legal memoranda on 2 June 1999. On 4 June 1999, the third participants, the European Communities and the United States, also filed legal memoranda. On the same date, Brazil and Canada each filed a written response to the memorandum previously submitted by the other on 2 June 1999. A preliminary hearing on this issue was held on 10 June 1999, with this Division sitting jointly with the Division of the Appellate Body hearing the appeal in *Canada - Aircraft*.[34]

1. *Arguments of Participants and Third Participants*

(a) Canada

105. Canada considers that Article 18.2 of the DSU does not provide adequate procedural protection for confidential proprietary business information of the type that is before the Appellate Body in this case. This information is not in the

[34] *Supra*, footnote 16.

public domain and would be of significant commercial interest, particularly to competitors of the enterprises that it concerns.

106. Canada observes that, in the absence of procedures to protect business confidential information at the appellate review stage, Brazil made references in its other appellant's submission and in its appellee's submission to business confidential information that Canada had submitted to the Panel under the BCI Procedures. The information submitted by Brazil was not, therefore, subject to any procedures to protect its confidentiality. Canada also argues that the Appellate Body should adopt procedures to ensure that the questions it poses at the oral hearing can be given a complete response, where necessary by reference to business confidential information included in the panel record.

107. In adopting procedures for protecting business confidential information, Canada submits that the Appellate Body must balance two competing interests, both rooted in fairness and due process, and neither having a claim to better protection than the other. First, both the Appellate Body and the participants must be given reasonable access to the information that was introduced into evidence before the Panel. Second, however, additional procedural safeguards are necessary to provide private business interests with adequate protection for their proprietary business information when Canada or Brazil deems it necessary to refer to such evidence in support of its case. Canada, therefore, requests that, pursuant to Rule 16(1) of the *Working Procedures*, the Appellate Body adopt, *mutatis mutandis*, the Panel's BCI procedures and the "Declaration of Non-Disclosure" set out in Annexes I and II of the Panel Report.

(b) Brazil

108. Brazil states that it agreed to join in Canada's request that the Appellate Body adopt procedures for protecting business confidential information as a good faith attempt to accommodate Canada's concerns on confidentiality. Brazil notes two qualifications to its acceptance in principle of the BCI Procedures by the Appellate Body. First, the procedures should not unduly restrict the access of authorized persons to the information. Second, the procedures must be limited to business proprietary information of private parties who are not subject to the confidentiality obligations of the DSU.

109. Brazil recalls that in its submissions to the Appellate Body, it cited certain information that Canada had designated before the Panel as business confidential information. Brazil does not consider that this particular information is, in any sense, business confidential information entitled to special protection.

110. Brazil emphasizes that, in including certain information Canada had designated as "business confidential" before the Panel, in its submissions to the Appellate Body, and in serving those submissions on Canada and on the third participants in this appeal, it did not act inconsistently with either the letter or the spirit of the DSU. Brazil notes that Rule 18(2) of the *Working Procedures* required it to serve its written submissions on Canada as well as the third partici-

pants, and Brazil states that it "has no reason to doubt" that the third participants will comply with their obligations under Article VII:1 of the *Rules of Conduct for the Understanding on Rules and Procedures Governing the Settlement of Disputes* (the "*Rules of Conduct*"). Brazil maintains as well that the confidentiality provisions of Article 18.2 of the DSU also apply to the third participants.

(c) European Communities

111. The European Communities considers that the BCI Procedures are based on the administrative protective order system used in countervailing duty procedures before the administrative authorities of certain Members of the WTO. This system cannot simply be transplanted into the WTO.

112. The European Communities contends that the proposed procedures for protecting business confidential information are inconsistent with the DSU in two ways. First, the proposed procedures deprive Members of rights contained in the DSU. They are inconsistent with Article 18.1 of the DSU, which forbids *ex parte* communications with a panel or the Appellate Body. In the case of the Appellate Body, the prohibition against *ex parte* communications also extends to third participants under Rule 19(1) of the *Working Procedures*. Such procedures would deny a party to a dispute access to business confidential information if that party could not accept the procedures for protecting business confidential information developed by the panel or the Appellate Body Division. The proposed procedures for protecting business confidential information are also inconsistent with Rule 18(2) of the *Working Procedures*, which requires "every document" filed by a participant or a third participant to be served on the other participants and third participants.

113. Second, the proposed procedures would impose new obligations on Members and create new rights for Members, contrary to Article 3.2 of the DSU. Such additional procedures would restrict access to certain documents to defined places, thereby restricting a party's ability to consider them. They would require the receiving party to permit the providing party to inspect the safe in its Mission where the information is to be stored. The European Communities argues that this is "tantamount to a waiver of the immunity enjoyed by those premises under international law". In addition, the procedures would require officials of the European Communities to sign undertakings incompatible with the "conduct of their duties".

114. The European Communities submits that Articles 14 and 18.2 of the DSU regulate the question of confidentiality in dispute settlement proceedings. If information is designated as confidential by a party to a dispute, Article 18.2 requires the other parties to take all necessary precautions according to their own administrative traditions and structures. The "bad faith" of other Members cannot be presumed. The proper place to resolve problems posed by the treatment of confidential information is in the current review of the DSU by WTO Members.

(d) United States

115. The United States argues that the need for additional procedures for protecting business confidential information is *extremely important*, "because it goes to the viability of WTO dispute settlement as a vehicle for preserving the rights and obligations of Members". In the view of the United States, "basic considerations of due process, as well as the need to preserve rights and obligations of Members, require the Appellate Body to apply such procedures". As a consequence, the United States has no objection to the joint request made by Brazil and Canada.

116. The United States makes three general arguments in support of the use of additional procedures for protecting business confidential information in WTO dispute settlement proceedings. First, the United States argues that nothing in the DSU precludes panels or the Appellate Body from adopting additional procedures for protecting business confidential information. On the contrary, Article 12.1 of the DSU explicitly allows panels to deviate from the working procedures set out in Appendix 3 of the DSU. The United States believes that the Appellate Body has authority comparable to that of panels to adopt such procedures as a result of Article 17.9 of the DSU and Article 16(1) of the *Working Procedures*.

117. Second, the United States argues that the application of procedures for protecting business confidential information promotes important objectives because Members' rights and obligations under the covered agreements can only be preserved if due process is accorded to both the complaining party and the responding party. The United States maintains that the demands of due process are not satisfied, however, if the absence of such procedures precludes a Member from properly making its case.

118. Third, the United States maintains, contrary to the position taken by the European Communities, that a Member's national laws do not provide a basis for depriving another Member of its rights under the *WTO Agreement*. Thus, the United States asserts, the claim by the European Communities that its officials would be unable, under their staff regulations, to accept the undertakings proposed "should not be allowed".

2. *Ruling and Reasons*

119. In our preliminary ruling of 11 June 1999, we concluded that it is not necessary, under all the circumstances of this case, to adopt *additional* procedures to protect business confidential information in these appellate proceedings. Our ruling was as follows:

> Pursuant to Article 17.9 of the *Understanding on Rules and Procedures Governing the Settlement of Disputes* (the "DSU"), the Appellate Body has the authority to draw up its own Working Procedures. Under Rule 16.1 of

our *Working Procedures for Appellate Review*, a Division of the Appellate Body may adopt additional procedures for the orderly conduct of a particular appeal, provided that any such additional procedures are not inconsistent with the DSU, the other covered agreements and the *Working Procedures for Appellate Review*. We have concluded, however, that it is not necessary, under all the circumstances of this case, to adopt *additional* procedures to protect "business confidential information" during these appellate proceedings.

We note that, with respect to "business confidential information" submitted to the Panel that remains currently in the possession of the participants, Article XII of the Panel Procedures Governing Business Confidential Information required the parties, "[a]t the conclusion of the Panel", to "return any printed or binary-encoded Business Confidential information in their possession to the party that submitted such Business Confidential (sic)" and to "destroy all tapes and transcripts of the Panel hearings that contain Business Confidential information, unless the parties mutually agree otherwise." It thus appears that each participant has an obligation, under the Panel Procedures, to return any Business Confidential information submitted by the other participant. The WTO Secretariat, assisting the Panel, was required, by the Panel Procedures, to "transmit any printed or binary-encoded Business Confidential information, plus all tapes and transcripts of the panel hearings that contain Business Confidential Information, to the Appellate Body as part of the record of the Panel proceedings." That information will be kept in a secure, locked cabinet in the Appellate Body Secretariat.

We also note that *all* Members are obliged, by the provisions of the DSU, to treat these proceedings of the Appellate Body, including written submissions and other documents filed by the participants and the third participants, as confidential. We are confident that the participants and the third participants in this appeal will *fully respect* their obligations under the DSU, recognizing that a Member's obligation to maintain the confidentiality of these proceedings extends also to the individuals whom that Member selects to act as its representatives, counsel and consultants.

> Accordingly, we decline the request of Brazil and Canada. The reasons for this ruling will be set out more fully in the Appellate Body Report in this appeal.

120. We have no further reasons to add to the first two paragraphs of our ruling above. The following is an elaboration of the reasons in the third paragraph of our ruling. Our ruling applies only to the request for *additional* procedures to protect "business confidential information" in these appellate proceedings, and it, therefore, has no effect on the BCI Procedures adopted by the Panel. Neither the Panel's decision to adopt BCI Procedures, nor the content of those Procedures, has been appealed.

121. With respect to appellate proceedings, in particular, the provisions of the DSU impose an obligation of confidentiality which applies to WTO Members generally as well as to Appellate Body Members and staff. In this respect, Article 17.10 of the DSU states, without qualification, that "[t]he *proceedings* of the Appellate Body *shall be confidential.*" (emphasis added) The word "proceeding" has been defined as follows:

> In a general sense, the form and manner of conducting juridical business before a court or judicial officer. Regular and orderly progress in form of law, *including all possible steps in an action from its commencement to the execution of judgment.*[35] (emphasis added)

More broadly, the word "proceedings" has been defined as "the business transacted by a court".[36] In its ordinary meaning, we take "proceedings" to include, in an appellate proceeding, any written submissions, legal memoranda, written responses to questions, and oral statements by the participants and the third participants; the conduct of the oral hearing before the Appellate Body, including any transcripts or tapes of that hearing; and the deliberations, the exchange of views and internal workings of the Appellate Body.

122. Article 18.2 of the DSU also contains rules protecting the confidentiality of written submissions and information submitted to the Appellate Body:

> *Written submissions to the panel or the Appellate Body shall be treated as confidential*, but shall be made available to the parties to the dispute. Nothing in this Understanding shall preclude a party to a dispute from disclosing statements of its own positions to the public. *Members shall treat as confidential information submitted by another Member to the panel or the Appellate Body* which that Member has designated as confidential. A party to a dis-

35 *Black's Law Dictionary*, (West Publishing Co., 1990), p. 1204.

36 *The New Shorter Oxford English Dictionary*, (Clarendon Press, 1993), Vol. II, at 2364.

> pute shall also, upon request of a Member, provide a non-confidential summary of the information contained in its written submissions that could be disclosed to the public. (emphasis added)

123. In our view, the provisions of Articles 17.10 and 18.2 apply to all Members of the WTO, and oblige them to maintain the confidentiality of any submissions or information submitted, or received, in an Appellate Body proceeding. Moreover, those provisions oblige Members to ensure that such confidentiality is fully respected by any person that a Member selects to act as its representative, counsel or consultant. In this respect, we note, with approval, the following statement made by the panel in *Indonesia - Automobiles*:

> We would like to emphasize that *all members of parties' delegations - whether or not they are government employees - are present as representatives of their governments, and as such are subject to the provisions of the DSU and of the standard working procedures, including Articles 18.1 and 18.2 of the DSU and paragraphs 2 and 3 of those procedures.* In particular, parties are required to treat as confidential all submissions to the Panel and all information so designated by other Members; and, in addition, the Panel meets in closed session. Accordingly, *we expect that all delegations will fully respect those obligations and will treat these proceedings with the utmost circumspection and discretion.*[37] (emphasis added)

124. Finally, we wish to recall that Members of the Appellate Body and its staff are covered by Article VII:1 of the *Rules of Conduct*,[38] which provides:

> Each covered person *shall at all times maintain the confidentiality of dispute settlement deliberations and proceedings together with any information identified by a party as confidential.* (emphasis added)

125. For these reasons, we do not consider that it is necessary, under all the circumstances of this case, to adopt *additional* procedures for the protection of business confidential information in these appellate proceedings. We, therefore, decline the request of Brazil and Canada.

---

[37] *Supra*, footnote 33.

[38] The *Rules of Conduct* have been directly incorporated into the *Working Procedures* (see Rule 8 of those *Working Procedures*).

IV. ISSUES RAISED IN THIS APPEAL

126. The following issues are raised in this appeal:

(a) whether the Panel erred in finding that certain regulatory instruments specified in the request for the establishment of a panel, but not discussed in the consultations, were properly before the Panel;

(b) whether the Panel erred in finding that in a dispute involving a claim of violation of Article 3.1(a) of the *SCM Agreement* by a developing country Member, the complaining party has the burden of proving that the developing country Member in question has not acted in conformity with the provisions of Article 27.4 of that Agreement;

(c) whether the Panel erred in interpreting and applying the phrase "shall not increase the level of its export subsidies" under Article 27.4 of the *SCM Agreement*, in particular, in finding that:

i) the "proper point of reference" for the purpose of determining whether a Member has increased the level of its export subsidies is actual expenditures, rather than budgeted amounts;

ii) the export subsidies for regional aircraft under PROEX should be considered to be "granted" when the NTN-I bonds are issued, rather than when the letter of commitment is issued; and

iii) it is appropriate in this case to use constant dollars, rather than nominal dollars, in assessing whether Brazil has increased the level of its export subsidies;

(d) whether the Panel erred in finding that Brazil had failed to demonstrate that the export subsidies for regional aircraft under PROEX are not "used to secure a material advantage in the field of export credit terms" under item (k) of the Illustrative List;

(e) whether the Panel erred in recommending that Brazil withdraw its subsidies within 90 days; and

(f) if we find that the export subsidies for regional aircraft under PROEX are "granted" at the time of issuance of a letter of commitment, whether the subsequent issuance of NTN-I bonds is consistent with Brazil's obligation not to "maintain" prohibited export subsidies under Article 3.2 of the *SCM Agreement*.

V. CONSULTATIONS

127. Brazil argues on appeal that certain regulatory instruments relating to PROEX were not properly before the Panel because those instruments came into

effect in 1997 and 1998 - after consultations were held between Canada and Brazil.[39] Canada maintains that these instruments were properly before the Panel because Canada's request for consultations[40], dated 18 June 1996, and its request for the establishment of a panel[41], dated 10 July 1998, referred to the same "matter", that is, to "PROEX and prohibited subsidies granted thereunder."[42] Furthermore, according to Canada, "the programme has remained unchanged *in its essence*."[43]

128. On this preliminary objection by Brazil, the Panel made the following ruling:

> Applying this analysis to the case at hand, we recall that Brazil and Canada consulted "regarding certain export subsidies granted under the Brazilian *Programa de Financiamento ás Exportações* (PROEX) to foreign purchasers of Brazil's EMBRAER aircraft", and that the request for establishment of a panel relates to "export subsidies under PROEX". We consider that the consultations and request for establishment relate to what is fundamentally the same "dispute", because they involve essentially the same practice, i.e., the payment of export subsidies under PROEX. Under these circumstances, and notwithstanding the fact that both the authorizing legal instrument and certain other legal instruments relating to the administration of the PROEX interest equalization regime changed or were only introduced subsequent to the last consultations, we cannot say that Canada has failed to comply with the requirements of Article 4.7 of the DSU.[44]

129. In its request for consultations of 18 June 1996, Canada described the specific measures at issue as "certain export subsidies granted under the Brazilian *Programa de Financiamento às Exportações* (PROEX) to foreign purchasers of Brazil's Embraer aircraft".[45] In its request for the establishment of a panel, Canada identified the specific measures at issue as follows:

> On 18 June 1996, the Government of Canada requested consultations with the Government of Brazil concerning certain export subsidies granted under the *Programa de*

39 Brazil's appellant's submission, paras. 4-18.
40 WT/DS46/1, G/SCM/D3/1, 21 June 1996.
41 WT/DS46/5, 13 July 1998.
42 Canada's appellee's submission, para. 30.
43 *Ibid*.
44 Panel Report, para. 7.11.
45 WT/DS46/1, G/SCM/D3/1, 21 June 1996.

> *Financiamento às Exportações* (PROEX) to foreign purchasers of Brazil's Embraer aircraft.
>
> ...
>
> The Brazilian measures in question *include* Provisional Measure 1700-15 replacing Provisional Measure 1629-13 and Law 8187 establishing PROEX; Law no. 8249/91; Decree no. 2414 of December 8, 1997; Resolutions of the National Monetary Council nos. 2490/98, 2452/97; 2381/97, 2380/97, 2224/95; Circular DIRIN 5; Resolution No. 50 of the Federal Senate of June 13, 1993; MICT Orders 28/98, 23/98, 7/98, 121/97, 83/97, 53/97, 34/97, 33/97 and MF/MICT Order 314/95; and Central Bank Circular no. 2601. *These measures provide for the payment of export subsidies through interest rate equalization and export financing programmes under PROEX.*[46] (emphasis added)

130. We note that Brazil and Canada consulted about "certain export subsidies granted under the Brazilian *Programa de Financiamento às Exportações* (PROEX) to foreign purchasers of Brazil's Embraer aircraft"[47], and that the request for the establishment of a panel also relates to "the payment of export subsidies through interest rate equalization and export financing programmes under PROEX."[48] We have been advised by Brazil that the regulatory instruments that came into effect in 1997 and 1998, after the consultations had taken place, and that relate to the administration of PROEX, did not change the essence of that regime.[49]

131. In our view, Articles 4 and 6 of the DSU, as well as paragraphs 1 to 4 of Article 4 of the *SCM Agreement*, set forth a process by which a complaining party must request consultations, and consultations must be held, before a matter may be referred to the DSB for the establishment of a panel. Under Article 4.3 of the *SCM Agreement*, moreover, the purpose of consultations is "to clarify the facts of the situation and to arrive at a mutually agreed solution."

132. We do not believe, however, that Articles 4 and 6 of the DSU, or paragraphs 1 to 4 of Article 4 of the *SCM Agreement*, require a *precise and exact identity* between the specific measures that were the subject of consultations and the specific measures identified in the request for the establishment of a panel.

---

46 WT/DS46/5, 13 July 1998.

47 WT/DS46/1, G/SCM/D3/1, 21 June 1996.

48 WT/DS46/5, 13 July 1998.

49 Answer by Brazil to questions at the oral hearing, 17 June 1999. These specific measures are listed in paragraph 11, *supra*.

As stated by the Panel, "[o]ne purpose of consultations, as set forth in Article 4.3 of the SCM Agreement, is to 'clarify the facts of the situation', and it can be expected that information obtained during the course of consultations may enable the complainant to focus the scope of the matter with respect to which it seeks establishment of a panel."[50] We are confident that the specific measures at issue in this case are the Brazilian export subsidies for regional aircraft under PROEX. Consultations were held by the parties on these subsidies, and it is these same subsidies that were referred to the DSB for the establishment of a panel. We emphasize that the regulatory instruments that came into effect in 1997 and 1998 did not change the essence of the export subsidies for regional aircraft under PROEX.

133. For these reasons, we conclude that the export subsidies for regional aircraft under PROEX, including the regulatory instruments that came into effect after consultations were held between Canada and Brazil, were properly before the Panel.

VI. BURDEN OF PROOF UNDER ARTICLE 27.4 OF THE *SCM AGREEMENT*

134. Canada appeals the Panel's finding that, in a case involving a claim of violation of Article 3.1(a) against a developing country Member, the complaining party has the burden of demonstrating that the developing country Member in question has not complied with at least one of the elements of Article 27.4.

135. The Panel found as follows:

> Where, as here, it is agreed that the Member in question is a developing country Member within the meaning of Article 27.2(b), it is for the Member alleging a violation of Article 3.1(a) of the SCM Agreement to demonstrate that the substantive obligation in that provision - the prohibition on export subsidies - applies to the developing country Member complained against. That is, it is for the complaining Member to demonstrate that the developing country Member in question is not in compliance with at least one of the elements laid out in Article 27.4.[51]

136. Canada asserts that Article 27.4 is in the nature of a conditional exception or an affirmative defence for a developing country Member, and that, therefore, the burden of proof rests with the respondent developing country Member - in this case, Brazil.[52] Brazil, on the other hand, maintains that Article 27 is a tran-

[50] Panel Report, para. 7.9.

[51] Panel Report, para. 7.57.

[52] Canada's appellant's submission, paras. 15-21.

sitional provision that contains a set of special and differential rights and obligations for developing country Members, and that, therefore, the complaining party - here, Canada - has the burden of proving that the developing country Member is not in compliance with Article 27.4.[53]

137. In *United States - Measures Affecting Imports of Woven Wool Shirts and Blouses from India*, we stated that "the burden of proof rests upon the party ... who asserts the *affirmative of a particular claim or defence*."[54] (emphasis added) There, we also noted that "Articles XX and XI:(2)(c)(i) are limited exceptions from obligations under certain other provisions of the GATT 1994, not positive rules establishing obligations in themselves. They are in the nature of affirmative defences."[55] We have also stated previously that the simple characterization of a provision of an agreement as an "exception" to a specific obligation does not, in itself, determine which party has the burden of proof. In *EC Measures Concerning Meat and Meat Products* (*Hormones*), we stated:

> The general rule in a dispute settlement proceeding requiring a complaining party to establish a *prima facie* case of inconsistency with a provision of the *SPS Agreement* before the burden of showing consistency with that provision is taken on by the defending party, is *not* avoided by simply describing that same provision as an "exception".[56]

138. Article 3.1(a) of the *SCM Agreement*, states, in relevant part:

> 3.1 ... the following subsidies, within the meaning of Article 1, shall be prohibited:
>
> (a) subsidies contingent, in law or in fact, whether solely or as one of several other conditions, upon export performance, including those illustrated in Annex I;
>
> ...

Article 27.2(b) of the *SCM Agreement* provides as follows:

> 27.2 The prohibition of paragraph 1(a) of Article 3 *shall not apply* to:
>
> ...
>
> (b) other developing country Members for a period of eight years from the date of entry into force of the WTO Agreement, *subject to*

[53] Brazil's appellee's submission, paras. 2-12.

[54] Adopted 23 May 1997, WT/DS33/AB/R, DSR 1997:I, 323, at 335.

[55] Adopted 23 May 1997, WT/DS33/AB/R, DSR 1997:I, 323, at 337.

[56] Adopted 13 February 1998, WT/DS26/AB/R, WT/DS48/AB/R, para. 104.

> *compliance with the provisions in paragraph 4.*
>
> (emphasis added)

Article 27.4 of the *SCM Agreement* reads, in relevant part:

> 27.4 Any developing country Member referred to in paragraph 2(b) shall phase out its export subsidies within the eight-year period, preferably in a progressive manner. However, a developing country Member shall not increase the level of its export subsidies[55], and shall eliminate them within a period shorter than that provided for in this paragraph when the use of such export subsidies is inconsistent with its development needs.
>
> [55]For a developing country Member not granting export subsidies as of the date of entry into force of the WTO Agreement, this paragraph shall apply on the basis of the level of export subsidies granted in 1986.

139. The ordinary meaning of the text of Article 27.2(b) is clear. For a period of eight years after the date of entry into force of the *WTO Agreement*, the prohibition on export subsidies in paragraph 1(a) of Article 3 of the *SCM Agreement does not apply* to developing country Members described in Article 27.2(b) - as long as they comply with the provisions of Article 27.4. With respect to the *application* of the prohibition of export subsidies in Article 3.1(a) of the *SCM Agreement*, paragraphs 2 and 4 of Article 27 contain a carefully negotiated balance of rights and obligations for developing country Members. During the transitional period from 1 January 1995 to 1 January 2003, certain developing country Members are *entitled* to the *non-application* of Article 3.1(a), *provided* that they comply with the specific obligations set forth in Article 27.4. Put another way, when a developing country Member complies with the conditions in Article 27.4, a claim of violation of Article 3.1(a) cannot be entertained during the transitional period, because the export subsidy prohibition in Article 3 simply *does not apply* to that developing country Member.

140. The title of Article 27 is "Special and Differential Treatment of Developing Country Members". Paragraph 1 of that Article provides that "Members recognize that subsidies may play an important role in economic development programmes of developing country Members." Both from its title and from its terms, it is clear that Article 27 is intended to provide special and differential treatment for developing country Members, under certain specified conditions. In our view, too, paragraph 4 of Article 27 provides certain obligations that developing country Members must fulfill if they are to benefit from this special and differential treatment during the transitional period. On reading paragraphs 2(b) and 4 of Article 27 together, it is clear that the conditions set forth in paragraph 4 are *positive obligations* for developing country Members, *not* affirma-

tive defences. If a developing country Member complies with the obligations in Article 27.4, the prohibition on export subsidies in Article 3.1(a) simply does not apply. However, if that developing country Member does *not* comply with those obligations, Article 3.1(a) *does* apply.

141. For these reasons, we agree with the Panel that the burden is on the complaining party (*in casu* Canada) to demonstrate that the developing country Member (*in casu* Brazil) is not in compliance with at least one of the elements set forth in Article 27.4. If such non-compliance is demonstrated, then, and only then, does the prohibition of Article 3.1(a) *apply* to that developing country Member.

VII. HAS BRAZIL INCREASED THE LEVEL OF ITS EXPORT SUBSIDIES?

142. Our ruling on the issue of the burden of proof under Article 27.4 has implications not only for determining which party has the burden of proof in demonstrating whether the conditions of Article 27.4 are met, but also for determining whether or not Article 3.1(a) *applies* to the developing country Member in question. In this case, the Panel, having determined correctly that the complaining party had the burden of proof in demonstrating whether the developing country Member had complied with Article 27.4, then failed to apply the logic of its own reasoning in examining Canada's claim that Brazil had acted inconsistently with its obligations under Article 3.1(a).

143. The Panel commenced its legal reasoning by considering whether the interest rate equalization payments for regional aircraft under PROEX constitute "subsidies" within the meaning of Article 1 of the *SCM Agreement* which are "contingent ... upon export performance" within the meaning of Article 3.1(a) of that Agreement.[57] As Brazil had not disputed these two issues, the Panel concluded that the payments under PROEX relating to exports of Brazilian regional aircraft are subsidies contingent upon export performance.[58] The Panel then went on to examine an "affirmative defence" put forward by Brazil, that is, whether PROEX support for the regional aircraft industry, even if it did constitute an "export subsidy", was nevertheless "permitted" by item (k) of the Illustrative List.[59] Given the Panel's correct analysis of the relationship between Articles 27 and 3.1(a) in its reasoning on the burden of proof[60], we find it odd that the Panel then went on to examine, in the following order: first, whether the conditions of Article 3.1(a) of the *SCM Agreement* had been met; next, a con-

57 Panel Report, paras. 7.12-7.13.

58 *Ibid.*, para. 7.14.

59 *Ibid.*, paras. 7.15-7.37.

60 Panel Report, paras. 7.49 and 7.56-7.57.

tention by Brazil of an "affirmative defence" to a claim of violation of Article 3.1(a), based on item (k) of the Illustrative List; and, only then, whether Brazil had complied with the conditions of Article 27.4 so as to determine whether the prohibition of export subsidies in Article 3.1(a) even *applied* to Brazil in this case. The Panel should not have considered Brazil's "affirmative defence" based on item (k) of the Illustrative List *before* determining whether Article 3.1(a) even applied to Brazil.

144. Our interpretation of the relationship between Article 27 and Article 3.1(a) of the *SCM Agreement* leads us, in this appeal, to examine, first, the issues appealed relating to whether Brazil has increased the level of its export subsidies contrary to the provisions of Article 27.4. Only if we determine that Brazil has not complied with the conditions of Article 27.4, and thereby find that the provisions of Article 3.1(a) do in fact *apply* to Brazil, will we need to examine Brazil's appeal of the Panel's findings relating to its alleged "affirmative defence" under item (k) of the Illustrative List.

145. The Panel made a number of findings in its analysis of whether Brazil has increased "the level of its export subsidies" under Article 27.4 of the *SCM Agreement*. Brazil appeals two of these findings, and Canada appeals one. Brazil appeals the Panel's finding that actual expenditures, rather than budgeted amounts, is the "proper point of reference" for determining whether Brazil has increased the level of its export subsidies.[61] Brazil also appeals the Panel's finding that PROEX subsidies for regional aircraft are "granted" when the NTN-I bonds are issued, not when the letter of commitment is issued. Canada appeals the Panel's conclusion that it is appropriate, in this case, to use constant dollars, rather than nominal dollars, in assessing whether Brazil has increased the level of its export subsidies.

A. *Actual Expenditures or Budgeted Amounts*

146. Brazil argues that the Panel erred in using actual expenditures, rather than budgetary appropriations, in determining whether Brazil had increased the level of its export subsidies.[62] Canada argues that the Panel was correct in examining actual expenditures, rather than budgetary appropriations.[63]

147. The Panel found that "the level of a Member's export subsidies in its ordinary meaning refers to the level of subsidies *actually provided*, not the level of subsidies which a Member planned or authorized its government to provide through its budgetary process."[64] (emphasis added) The Panel said this view was confirmed by footnote 55 to the *SCM Agreement*, which provides that, "[f]or a

[61] Panel Report, para. 7.65.
[62] Brazil's appellant's submission, paras. 19-25.
[63] Canada's appellee's submission, paras. 48-62.
[64] Panel Report, para. 7.65.

developing country Member not *granting* export subsidies as of the date of entry into force of the *WTO Agreement*, this paragraph shall apply on the basis of the level of export subsidies *granted* in 1986." (emphasis added) The Panel noted that "[t]he verb 'grant' has been defined to mean, *inter alia*, 'to bestow by a formal act' and 'give, bestow, confer'." [65]

148. We agree with the Panel's reasoning on this issue. To us, the word "granted" used in this context means "something actually provided". Thus, to determine the amount of export subsidies "granted" in a particular year, we believe that the actual amounts *provided* by a government, and not just those *authorized* or *appropriated* in its budget for that year, is the proper measure. A government does not always spend the entire amount appropriated in its annual budget for a designated purpose. Therefore, in this case, to determine the level of export subsidies for the purposes of Article 27.4, we believe that the proper reference is to actual expenditures by a government, and not to budgetary appropriations.

149. In coming to this conclusion, we are not persuaded by Brazil's argument relating to the notification provisions of Article 25 of the *SCM Agreement*. We note that Article 25 has a fundamentally different purpose from Article 27 of the *SCM Agreement*. Whereas Article 25 aims to promote transparency by requiring Members to notify their subsidies, without prejudging the legal status of those subsidies[66], Article 27 imposes positive obligations on developing country Members with respect to export subsidies. In interpreting the phrase "the level of its export subsidies" in Article 27.4, we believe the most appropriate context is footnote 55, which is, it will be recalled, a footnote to that very phrase in Article 27.4. Because of its different purpose, Article 25 is considerably less useful as context in interpreting the phrase "the level of its export subsidies" in Article 27.4. Moreover, the provisions of Article 25 do not contradict the conclusion we draw from footnote 55. In particular, in paragraph 3 of Article 25, Members are required to ensure that their notifications contain, *inter alia*, the following information:

> ...
>
> (ii) *subsidy per unit or, in cases where this is not possible*, the *total amount* or the *annual amount budgeted* for that subsidy ... (emphasis added)

We note that the *preferred* notification method is on the basis of subsidy per unit. It is only in cases where it is not possible to provide information on that basis that the total amount, or the annual amount budgeted for that subsidy, may

---

65 Panel Report, para. 7.65.

66 Article 25.7 of the *SCM Agreement* states that "notification of a measure does not prejudge either its legal status under GATT 1994 and this Agreement, the effects under this Agreement, or the nature of the measure itself."

be reported. For transparency purposes, we can understand why Members would want to know what subsidies other Members have planned or projected. Yet this consideration is different from the objective of determining whether a developing country Member has increased "the level of its export subsidies" under Article 27.4.

150. Accordingly, we uphold the finding of the Panel that the "proper point of reference" in determining whether a Member has increased the level of its export subsidies under Article 27.4 is actual expenditures, rather than budgeted amounts or appropriations.[67]

B. *When are PROEX Subsidies "Granted"?*

151. One of the legal issues the Panel considered in determining whether Brazil had increased the level of its export subsidies was "the question of when PROEX payments should be considered to have been 'granted' for the purposes of calculating the level of Brazil's export subsidies in terms of expenditures." [68] In examining this issue, the Panel considered two questions: *what is the form* of "financial contribution" made by PROEX, within the meaning of Article 1.1(a)(1) of the *SCM Agreement*? And, *when* does the "subsidy" that is created, in part, by that "financial contribution", "exist" within the meaning of Article 1.1? Brazil argued, before the Panel, that the form of financial contribution involved in this dispute is a "potential direct transfer of funds", within the meaning of Article 1.1(a)(1)(i), which "exists" at the time a letter of commitment is issued.[69] Canada argued, before the Panel, that PROEX subsidies for regional aircraft involve a "direct transfer of funds", within the meaning of Article 1.1(a)(1)(i), which "exists" either when payments are made pursuant to an NTN-I bond or, in the alternative, when NTN-I bonds are issued to an agent bank.[70]

152. In analyzing the form of "financial contribution" made by export subsidies for regional aircraft under PROEX, the Panel said, *inter alia*:

> We believe that a "potential direct transfer of funds" exists only where the action in question gives rise to a benefit and thus confers a subsidy irrespective of whether any payment occurs.[71]
>
> ...

[67] Panel Report, para. 7.65.
[68] Panel Report, para. 7.67.
[69] *Ibid.*, paras. 4.20 and 7.67.
[70] *Ibid.*, paras. 4.22 and 7.67.
[71] *Ibid.*, para. 7.68.

> ... In this case, however, it clearly is not the alleged "potential direct transfer of funds", i.e., the letter of commitment, that confers the benefit. Rather, the benefit in the PROEX interest rate equalization scheme derives from the fact that a payment, i.e., a direct transfer of funds, has been or will be made.[72]

153. The Panel then posed the question of *when* Brazil can be considered to "grant" PROEX payments. The Panel gave the following answer:

> As noted above, the verb "grant" has been defined to mean, *inter alia*, "to bestow by formal act" and "give, bestow, confer". Arguably, therefore PROEX payments may be "granted" where the unconditional legal right of the beneficiary to receive the payments has arisen, even if the payments themselves have not yet occurred. It is clear to us, however, that PROEX payments have not yet been "granted" at the time a letter of commitment is issued. We note that the issuance of a letter of commitment, even if legally binding on the Government of Brazil in the event certain conditions are fulfilled, provides no assurance that PROEX payments will actually be made. To the contrary, at the time the letter of commitment is issued no export sales contract has been signed, and the letter of commitment expires if a contract that conforms to the request for approval is not negotiated and signed within 90 days. ... Rather, the right to receive the PROEX payments only arises after the conditions relating to receipt of PROEX payments, and specifically the condition that the product in question actually be exported, has been fulfilled.[73]

154. In our view, the Panel reached the correct conclusion. However, it did so on the basis of faulty reasoning. The issue in this case is when the subsidies for regional aircraft under PROEX should be considered to have been "granted" *for the purposes of calculating the level of Brazil's export subsidies under Article 27.4 of the SCM Agreement*. The issue is *not* whether or when there is a "financial contribution", or whether or when the "subsidy" "exists", within the meaning of Article 1.1 of that Agreement.

155. The Panel noted, early in its findings, that Brazil did not dispute the assertion by Canada that PROEX support for the regional aircraft industry constitutes an export subsidy.[74] On this, the Panel stated:

---

[72] Panel Report, para. 7.70.

[73] Panel Report, para. 7.71.

[74] *Ibid.*, para. 7.12.

> As noted above, the parties agree that PROEX payments are subsidies within the meaning of Article 1 of the SCM Agreement which are contingent upon exportation within the meaning of Article 3.1(a) of the Agreement, and we agree with them.[75]

156. Thus, the issue before the Panel under the heading "Has Brazil increased the level of its export subsidies?" [76] was simply this: given that the export subsidies in this case were already deemed to "exist", when were they "granted"? At issue was the interpretation and application of Article 27.4, *not* of Article 1. It is pursuant to the provisions of Article 27.4 that Brazil is obliged not to increase "the level of its export subsidies". And, to ascertain the meaning of this phrase, it is necessary to look, again, at footnote 55, which is affixed to Article 27.4 and which speaks of "the level of export subsidies *granted*" (emphasis added) by a developing country Member. Consequently, for the purposes of Article 27.4, we see the issue of the *existence* of a subsidy and the issue of the point at which that subsidy is *granted* as two legally distinct issues. Only one of those issues is raised here and, therefore, must be addressed. That issue is: when is this subsidy, which admittedly exists, actually *granted*?

157. In our view, the Panel did not have to determine whether the export subsidies for regional aircraft under PROEX constituted a "direct transfer of funds" or a "potential direct transfer of funds", within the meaning of Article 1.1(a)(i), in order to determine when the subsidies are "granted" for the purposes of Article 27.4. Moreover, the Panel compounded its error in finding that the "financial contribution" in the case of PROEX subsidies is *not* a "potential direct transfer of funds" by reasoning that a letter of commitment does not confer a "benefit".[77] In this way, in its interpretation of Article 1.1(a)(i), the Panel imported the notion of a "benefit" into the definition of a "financial contribution". This was a mistake. We see the issues - and the respective definitions - of a "financial contribution" and a "benefit" as two separate legal elements in Article 1.1 of the *SCM Agreement*, which *together* determine whether a subsidy *exists*, and not whether it is *granted* for the purpose of calculating the level of a developing country Member's export subsidies under Article 27.4 of that Agreement.

158. In addressing the correct legal question under Article 27.4, our answer is that export subsidies for regional aircraft under PROEX are "granted" when the NTN-I bonds are issued. We agree with the Panel that "PROEX payments may be 'granted' where the unconditional legal right of the beneficiary to receive the payments has arisen, even if the payments themselves have not yet occurred." [78] We also agree with the Panel that the export subsidies for regional aircraft under

---

[75] Panel Report, para. 7.13.

[76] *Ibid.*, see title above paragraph 7.58 and following.

[77] Panel Report, para. 7.70.

[78] Panel Report, para. 7.71.

PROEX have not yet been "granted" when the letter of commitment is issued, because, at that point, the export sales contract has not yet been concluded and the export shipments have not yet occurred.[79] For the purposes of Article 27.4, we conclude that the export subsidies for regional aircraft under PROEX are "granted" when all the legal conditions have been fulfilled that entitle the beneficiary to receive the subsidies. We share the Panel's view that such an unconditional legal right exists when the NTN-I bonds are issued.[80]

159. For these reasons, we uphold the Panel's conclusion that the export subsidies for regional aircraft under PROEX are "granted", for the purposes of Article 27.4 of the *SCM Agreement*, when the NTN-I bonds are issued, and not when the letter of commitment is issued. However, we wish to emphasize the modifications we have made in the Panel's legal reasoning. We wish to underscore especially that we find that it was not relevant, for the purpose of calculating the level of Brazil's export subsidies under Article 27.4, for the Panel to decide whether the "financial contribution" for PROEX subsidies involved a "direct transfer of funds" or a "potential direct transfer of funds" under Article 1.1 of the *SCM Agreement.*

C. Constant or Nominal Dollars

160. On appeal, Canada argues that the Panel's statement that it was "appropriate in this case" to use constant dollars, rather than nominal dollars, to assess whether Brazil had increased the level of its export subsidies is "unreasoned" and "does not respect the text, context and the object and purpose of the SCM Agreement."[81] Canada maintains that there is no explicit provision for the conversion of the level of export subsidies to a constant value either in Article 27.4 or in footnote 55 of the *SCM Agreement.* With respect to the context of the *SCM Agreement*, Canada asserts that, where the negotiators intended to provide adjustments for inflation, they did so, but that such indexation is not so provided in Article 27.[82] In reply, Brazil argues that the Panel was correct in its conclusion based on the facts of this case. Brazil contends that the use of a constant value is required if the special rules for developing country Members in Article 27 are to be given genuine meaning.[83]

161. On this issue, the Panel said the following:

> In our view, however, *it is appropriate in this case* to use constant dollars, as that will provide a more meaningful assessment as to whether Brazil has increased the level of its

---

79 Panel Report, para. 7.71.
80 *Ibid.*, para. 7.72.
81 Canada's appellant's submission, para. 24.
82 *Ibid.*, paras. 28-30.
83 Brazil's appellee's submission, paras. 17-18.

> export subsidies. We note that, in this case, *the conclusion with respect to this issue would be the same whether constant or nominal dollars are used.*[84]
>
> (emphasis added)
>
> ...

The Panel concluded:

> Applying the foregoing criteria to these *undisputed data*, we conclude that Brazil had by 1997 increased the level of its export subsidies above that prevailing in 1994, *whether the data are expressed in nominal or in constant dollars.* The increase for 1998 was even more substantial than that for 1997, reflecting as it does data for only the first ten months of the year.[85] (emphasis added)

162. We note that the Panel did *not* make a legal finding that the level of a developing country Member's export subsidies must be measured, in every case, using a constant value. The Panel simply made a pragmatic observation that using constant dollars is appropriate *in this case*. The Panel also noted that, in this case, "the conclusion with respect to this issue *would be the same* whether constant or nominal dollars are used." [86] (emphasis added) In examining the data before it relating to Brazilian export subsidies under PROEX and BEFIEX, the Panel examined data denominated *both* in current US dollars and in 1994 constant US dollars.[87] The conclusion of the Panel was "that Brazil had by 1997 increased the level of its export subsidies above that prevailing in 1994, *whether the data are expressed in nominal or in constant dollars*." [88] (emphasis added)

163. As the Panel relied on data denominated *both* in current dollars and in constant dollars, we see no reason to overturn this conclusion of the Panel. Moreover, in our view, to take no account of inflation in assessing the level of export subsidies granted by a developing country Member would render the special and differential treatment provisions of Article 27 meaningless. For these reasons, we uphold the conclusion of the Panel in paragraph 7.75 of the Panel Report.

164. And, for all these reasons, we uphold the overall conclusion of the Panel, in paragraph 7.76 of the Panel Report, that "Brazil has 'increased the level of its export subsidies' within the meaning of Article 27.4 of the SCM Agreement." And, thus, we find that Article 3.1(a) applies to Brazil in this case, because Brazil has not complied with the provisions of Article 27.4.

---

84 Panel Report, para. 7.73.

85 Panel Report, para. 7.75.

86 *Ibid.*, para. 7.73.

87 *Ibid.*, para. 7.75, Table 9.

88 *Ibid.*, para. 7.75.

VIII. ARE PROEX INTEREST RATE EQUALIZATION PAYMENTS USED "TO SECURE A MATERIAL ADVANTAGE IN THE FIELD OF EXPORT CREDIT TERMS"?

165. Having determined that Brazil has not complied with the provisions of Article 27.4, we conclude that the prohibition of Article 3.1(a) applies to Brazil in this case. We must therefore examine Brazil's appeal of the finding of the Panel relating to Brazil's alleged "affirmative defence" under item (k) of the Illustrative List.

166. Brazil appeals the Panel's conclusion that Brazil failed to demonstrate that PROEX payments are not "used to secure a material advantage in the field of export credit terms", and the Panel's consequent rejection of Brazil's "affirmative defence" based on item (k) of the Illustrative List.[89] Brazil argues that the Panel erred in its interpretation of the phrase "used to secure a material advantage in the field of export credit terms", both with respect to the ordinary meaning of the word "secure"[90] and by determining "advantage" with respect to "the terms that would have been available in the absence of the payment".[91] Also, Brazil contends that the Panel misconstrued the context of the "material advantage" clause, in particular, in its assessment of the origins of item (k) in the *Tokyo Round SCM Code*.[92]

167. In Canada's view, the Panel did not err in its interpretation of the "material advantage" clause in item (k), either with respect to its analysis of the ordinary meaning or the context of that clause.[93] Thus, Canada argues that the Panel properly rejected Brazil's alleged "affirmative defence" based on item (k).

168. Item (k) of the Illustrative List provides as follows:

> (k) The grant by governments (or special institutions controlled by and/or acting under the authority of governments) of export credits at rates below those which they actually have to pay for the funds so employed (or would have to pay if they borrowed on international capital markets in order to obtain funds of the same maturity and other credit terms and denominated in the same currency as the export

---

89 Brazil's appellant's submission, paras. 47-52. From Brazil's responses to questioning during the oral hearing, we understand Brazil's underlying argument to be the following: PROEX subsidies are not "used to secure a material advantage" in the sense of item (k) because they are designed only to offset "Brazil risk" and to "match" the subsidies given by the Government of Canada to Bombardier - the competitor of Embraer in the regional aircraft industry.

90 Brazil's appellant's submission, paras. 53-57.

91 *Ibid.*, paras. 58-60.

92 *Ibid.*, paras. 61-66.

93 Canada's appellee's submission, paras. 144-158.

> credit), or the payment by them of all or part of the costs incurred by exporters or financial institutions in obtaining credits, *in so far as they are used to secure a material advantage in the field of export credit terms.*
>
> Provided, however, that if a Member is a party to an international undertaking on official export credits to which at least twelve original Members to this Agreement are parties as of 1 January 1979 (or a successor undertaking which has been adopted by those original Members), or if in practice a Member applies the interest rates provisions of the relevant undertaking, an export credit practice which is in conformity with those provisions shall not be considered an export subsidy prohibited by this Agreement.
>
> (emphasis added)

169. Before the Panel, Brazil contended that, although PROEX payments are export subsidies, they are nevertheless "permitted" by item (k) of the Illustrative List.[94] The Panel noted that to rule in favour of Brazil on this issue, it would need to find for Brazil on all of the following three points: first, that PROEX payments are "the payment by [governments] of all or part of the costs incurred by exporters or financial institutions in obtaining credits"; second, that PROEX payments are not "used to secure a material advantage in the field of export credit terms"; and, third, that a "payment" within the meaning of item (k) which is not "used to secure a material advantage in the field of export credit terms" is "permitted" by the *SCM Agreement* even though it is a subsidy which is contingent upon export performance within the meaning of Article 3.1(a) of that Agreement. The Panel also noted that Brazil had explicitly acknowledged that the "material advantage" clause in item (k) constitutes an "affirmative defence", and, therefore, that the burden of establishing that "defence" was on Brazil.[95]

170. The Panel concluded as follows:

> In conclusion, we consider that an item (k) payment is "used to secure a material advantage" where the payment has resulted in the availability of export credit on terms which are more favourable than the terms that would otherwise have been be [sic] available to the purchaser with respect to the transaction in question. Even if we were to assume, as argued by Brazil, that PROEX payments are the

[94] Panel Report, para. 7.15.

[95] *Ibid.*, para. 7.17.

> "payment by [a government] of all or part of the costs incurred by exporters or financial institutions in obtaining credits", and that such payments can be deemed to be "permitted" by item (k) where they are not "used to secure a material advantage in the field of export credit terms" - issues we need not here decide - Brazil has failed to demonstrate the PROEX payments are not "used to secure a material advantage in the field of export credit terms". Accordingly, we reject Brazil's affirmative defense based on item (k) of the Illustrative List.[96]

171. In coming to this conclusion, the Panel first interpreted the phrase "used to secure a material advantage in the field of export credit terms", and then applied its interpretation to the facts relating to export subsidies for regional aircraft under PROEX. In its reasoning on this issue, the Panel made four, not entirely consistent, statements of its interpretation.[97]

172. In examining the ordinary meaning of the phrase "used to secure a material advantage in the field of export credit terms" in item (k), the Panel noted that the word "advantage" has been defined as "a more favorable or improved position" and as a "superior position".[98] The Panel also concurred with Brazil that "advantage" involves the concept of comparison. The Panel went on to say, however, that:

> ... nothing in the text of the first paragraph of item (k) indicates that the examination of material advantage involves a comparison *with the export credit terms available with respect to competing products from other Members*. To the contrary, we consider that, in its ordinary meaning, a payment is "used to secure a material advantage in the field of export credit terms" where the payment is used to secure export credit terms that are <u>materially more favorable than the terms that would have been available in the absence of the payment</u>. Accordingly, we consider that an item (k) payment is "used to secure a material advantage" where the payment has resulted in the availability of export credit on terms which are <u>more favourable than the terms that would otherwise be available in the marketplace to the purchaser with respect to the transaction in question</u>.[99]
>
> (italics in the original, underlining added)

[96] Panel Report, para. 7.37.

[97] Panel Report, paras. 7.23, 7.33 and 7.37.

[98] *Ibid.*, para. 7.23.

[99] *Ibid.*

173. The Panel then considered the context of the "material advantage" clause generally in the *SCM Agreement*, and stated that, "the general approach of the SCM Agreement to determining whether a measure is a subsidy and thus subject to discipline is whether the measure confers a 'benefit' within the meaning of Article 1." [100] The Panel also discussed its view of the object and purpose of the *SCM Agreement*, which it stated "is to impose multilateral disciplines on subsidies which distort international trade." [101] The Panel reasoned that Brazil's approach of allowing a Member to "match" the export subsidies granted by another Member "would entail a race to the bottom, as each WTO Member sought to justify the provision of export subsidies on the grounds that other Members were doing the same." [102]

174. Then, before examining the facts, the Panel again stated its interpretation of the "material advantage" clause in item (k), this time, as follows:

> For the reasons discussed above, we consider that an item (k) payment is "used to secure a material advantage" and is thus a prohibited export subsidy where the payment has resulted in the availability of export credit on terms which are *more favourable than the terms that would otherwise be available in the marketplace to the purchaser with respect to the transaction in question.*[103] (emphasis added)

175. Finally, in its concluding paragraph, the Panel repeated its interpretation of the "material advantage" clause of item (k) as follows:

> In conclusion, we consider that an item (k) payment is "used to secure a material advantage" where the payment has resulted in the availability of export credit on terms which are *more favourable than the terms that would otherwise have been be* [*sic*] *available to the purchaser with respect to the transaction in question.*[104] (emphasis added)

176. We note that, in its very first statement of its interpretation of the "material advantage" clause, the Panel characterized "material advantage" as "*materially* more favorable than the terms that would have been available in the absence of the payment." [105] (emphasis added) However, we observe also that, in its subsequent statements, the Panel interpreted "material advantage" as simply "more favourable than the terms that would otherwise be available in the mar-

---

[100] Panel Report, para. 7.24.
[101] *Ibid*., para. 7.26.
[102] Panel Report, para. 7.26.
[103] *Ibid*., para. 7.33.
[104] *Ibid*., para. 7.37.
[105] *Ibid*., para. 7.23 (second to last sentence).

ketplace to the purchaser with respect to the transaction in question."[106] (emphasis added) In the latter interpretation, the Panel omitted the word "material".

177. As always, we examine the terms of the provision at issue, in this case, the "material advantage" clause of item (k). We look first to the ordinary meaning of the language used. We agree with the Panel's statement that the ordinary meaning of the word "advantage" is "a more favorable or improved position" or a "superior position". However, we note that item (k) does not refer simply to "advantage". The word "advantage" is qualified by the adjective "material". As mentioned before, in its ultimate interpretation of the phrase "used to secure a material advantage" which the Panel finally adopted and applied to the export subsidies for regional aircraft under PROEX, the Panel read the word "material" out of item (k). This, we consider to be an error.

178. We also note that in two of its interpretive statements[107], the Panel used the "marketplace" as the benchmark for comparing the subsidies on sales of regional aircraft under PROEX. However, in two other statements[108], the Panel made no reference to the "marketplace" as the basis for comparison. In one of those two statements, it referred, instead, more generally, to "the terms that would have been available in the absence of the payment." For the purposes of our analysis, we will assume that the Panel meant to use the "marketplace" as the benchmark for determining whether the PROEX subsidies were "used to secure a material advantage".

179. We note that the Panel adopted an interpretation of the "material advantage" clause in item (k) of the Illustrative List that is, in effect, the same as the interpretation of the term "benefit" in Article 1.1(b) of the *SCM Agreement* adopted by the panel in *Canada - Aircraft*.[109] If the "material advantage" clause in item (k) is to have *any* meaning, it must mean something different from "benefit" in Article 1.1(b). It will be recalled that for any payment to be a "subsidy" within the meaning of Article 1.1, that payment must consist of both a "financial contribution" and a "benefit". The first paragraph of item (k) describes a type of subsidy that is deemed to be a prohibited export subsidy. Obviously, when a payment by a government constitutes a "financial contribution" and confers a "benefit", it is, a "subsidy" under Article 1.1. Thus, the phrase in item (k), "in so far as they are used to secure a material advantage", would have no meaning if it were simply to be equated with the term "benefit" in the definition of "subsidy". As a matter of treaty interpretation, this cannot be so.[110] Therefore,

---

[106] Panel Report, paras. 7.23 (last sentence), 7.33 and 7.37.

[107] Panel Report, paras. 7.23 (last sentence) and 7.33.

[108] *Ibid.*, paras. 7.23 (second to last sentence) and 7.37.

[109] WT/DS70/R, circulated to WTO Members on 14 April 1999, paras. 9.112 and 9.120 (as upheld by the Appellate Body, *supra*, footnote 16, paras. 154-162).

[110] As we stated in our report in *United States - Standards for Reformulated and Conventional Gasoline* ("*United States - Gasoline*"), "[a]n interpreter is not free to adopt a reading that would

we consider it an error to interpret the "material advantage" clause in item (k) of the Illustrative List as meaning the same as the term "benefit" in Article 1.1(b) of the *SCM Agreement*.

180. We note that there are two paragraphs in item (k), and that the "material advantage" clause appears in the first paragraph. Furthermore, the second paragraph is a proviso to the first paragraph. The second paragraph applies when a Member is "a party to an international undertaking on official export credits" which satisfies the conditions of the proviso, or when a Member "applies the interest rates provisions of the relevant undertaking". In such circumstances, an "export credit practice" which is in conformity with the provisions of "an international undertaking on official export credits" shall not be considered an export subsidy prohibited by the *SCM Agreement*. The *OECD Arrangement* is an "international undertaking on official export credits" that satisfies the requirements of the proviso in the second paragraph in item (k). However, Brazil did not invoke the proviso in the second paragraph of item (k) in its defence. Brazil argued before the Panel that it "has concluded that conformity to the OECD provisions is too expensive." [111]

181. Thus, this case falls under the first paragraph, and not under the proviso of the second paragraph, of item (k) of the Illustrative List. Consequently, the issue here is whether the export subsidies for regional aircraft under PROEX "are used to secure" for Brazil "a material advantage in the field of export credit terms". Nevertheless, we see the second paragraph of item (k) as useful context for interpreting the "material advantage" clause in the text of the first paragraph. The *OECD Arrangement* establishes minimum interest rate guidelines for export credits supported by its participants ("officially-supported export credits"). Article 15 of the Arrangement defines the minimum interest rates applicable to officially-supported export credits as the Commercial Interest Reference Rates ("CIRRs"). Article 16 provides a methodology by which a CIRR, for the currency of each participant, may be determined for this purpose. We believe that the *OECD Arrangement* can be appropriately viewed as one example of an international undertaking providing a specific market benchmark by which to assess whether payments by governments, coming within the provisions of item (k), are "used to secure a material advantage in the field of export credit terms". Therefore, in our view, the appropriate comparison to be made in determining whether a payment is "used to secure a material advantage", within the meaning of item (k), is between the actual interest rate applicable in a particular export

result in reducing whole clauses or paragraphs of a treaty to redundancy or inutility." Adopted 20 May 1996, WT/DS2/AB/R, DSR 1996:I, 3, at 21. This statement is quoted with approval in *Japan - Taxes on Alcoholic Beverages*, adopted 1 November 1996, WT/DS8/AB/R, WT/DS10/AB/R, WT/DS11/AB/R, DSR 1996:I, 97, at 106.

[111] Oral Statement of Brazil at First Meeting of the Panel, para. 22. See also Oral Statement of Brazil at Second Meeting of the Panel, paras. 54 and 56.

sales transaction after deduction of the government payment (the "*net* interest rate") and the relevant CIRR.

182. It should be noted that the commercial interest rate with respect to a loan in any given currency varies according to the length of maturity as well as the creditworthiness of the borrower. Thus, a potential borrower is not faced with a single commercial interest rate, but rather with a range of rates. Under the *OECD Arrangement*, a CIRR is the *minimum* commercial rate available in that range for a particular currency. In any given case, whether or not a government payment is used to secure a "*material* advantage", as opposed to an "advantage" that is not "material", may well depend on where the *net* interest rate applicable to the particular transaction at issue in that case stands in relation to the range of commercial rates available. The fact that a particular *net* interest rate is below the relevant CIRR is a positive indication that the government payment in that case has been "used to secure a material advantage in the field of export credit terms".

183. Brazil has conceded that it has the burden of proving an alleged "affirmative defence" under item (k). In light of our analysis, it was for Brazil to establish a *prima facie* case that the export subsidies for regional aircraft under PROEX do not result in net interest rates below the relevant CIRR. We note, however, that Brazil did not provide *any information* to the Panel on this point. We also note that Brazil declined to provide this information, even when specifically requested to do so by the Panel.[112] Because Brazil provided *no information* on the net interest rates paid by purchasers of Embraer aircraft in actual export sales transactions, we have no basis on which to compare the net interest rates resulting from the interest rate equalization payments made under PROEX with the relevant CIRR.

184. Accordingly, we find that Brazil has failed to meet its burden of proving that export subsidies for regional aircraft under PROEX are not "used to secure a material advantage in the field of export credit terms" within the meaning of item (k) of the Illustrative List.

185. We are aware that the *OECD Arrangement* allows a government to "match", under certain conditions, officially-supported export credit terms provided by another government. In a particular case, this could result in net interest rates below the relevant CIRR. We are persuaded that "matching" in the sense of the *OECD Arrangement* is not applicable in this case. Before the Panel, Brazil argued for an interpretation of the clause "in the field of export credit terms" that would include as an "export credit term" the price at which a product is sold, and maintained that, therefore, Brazil was entitled to "offset" *all the subsidies* provided to Bombardier by the Government of Canada. The Panel rejected Brazil's

[112] Reply of Brazil to the Panel's Questions for the Parties, 23 December 1998, Brazil's response to Question 34, pp. 7-8.

argument, finding instead that "[w]e see nothing in the ordinary meaning of the phrase to suggest that 'the field of export credit terms' generally encompasses the price at which a product is sold."[113] We note that this finding was *not* appealed by either Brazil or Canada. Even if we were to assume that the "matching" provisions of the *OECD Arrangement* apply in this case (an argument Brazil did not make), those provisions clearly do not allow a comparison to be made between the net interest rates applied as a consequence of subsidies granted by a particular Member and the total amount of subsidies provided by another Member. We also note that under PROEX, the interest rate equalization subsidies for regional aircraft are provided at an "across-the-board" rate of 3.8 per cent for *all* export sales transactions.[114] That rate is fixed, and does not vary depending on the total amount of subsidies provided by another Member to its regional aircraft manufacturers. Thus, we cannot accept Brazil's argument that the export subsidies for regional aircraft under PROEX should be "permitted" because they "match" the total subsidies provided to Bombardier by the Government of Canada.

186. For all these reasons, we do not agree with the Panel's interpretation of the phrase "used to secure a material advantage in the field of export credit terms" in item (k) of the Illustrative List. We do, however, agree with the Panel's conclusion that "Brazil has failed to demonstrate the PROEX payments are not 'used to secure a material advantage in the field of export credit terms'."[115] We, therefore, uphold the Panel's rejection of the "affirmative defence" claimed by Brazil on the basis of item (k) of the Illustrative List.

187. In so doing, we do not rule on whether the export subsidies for regional aircraft under PROEX are "the payment by [governments] of all or part of the costs incurred by exporters or financial institutions in obtaining credits". Nor do we opine on whether a "payment" within the meaning of item (k) which is not "used to secure a material advantage within the field of export credit terms" is, *a contrario*, "permitted" by the *SCM Agreement*, even though it is a subsidy which is contingent upon export performance within the meaning of Article 3.1(a) of that Agreement. The Panel did not rule on these issues, and the lack of Panel findings on these issues was not appealed.

IX. RECOMMENDATION OF THE PANEL

188. Brazil appeals the Panel's recommendation that Brazil shall withdraw the export subsidies for regional aircraft under PROEX within 90 days, stating that

[113] Panel Report, para. 7.28.
[114] Panel Report, para. 2.3.
[115] Panel Report, para. 7.37.

"the Panel's conclusion that 90 days is the proper time-period is in error."[116] Brazil argues that although Article 4.7 of the *SCM Agreement* directs a panel to specify the time-period within which a prohibited subsidy must be withdrawn, that provision does not specify a particular time-period. Brazil argues also that under Article 4.12 of the *SCM Agreement*, "except for time-periods specifically prescribed in ... Article [4], time-periods applicable under the DSU for the conduct of such disputes shall be half the time prescribed therein." Brazil maintains that Article 21.3(c) of the DSU provides that the time-period allowed for implementation of DSB rulings and recommendations "normally should not exceed 15 months, unless there are 'particular circumstances' justifying a longer or shorter period."[117] Therefore, Brazil maintains that the Panel should have concluded that Brazil must withdraw its export subsidies within half of fifteen months, that is, within seven and one-half months, rather than within 90 days.[118]

189. Article 4.7 of the *SCM Agreement* provides:

> If the measure in question is found to be a prohibited subsidy, the Panel *shall recommend* that the subsidizing Member *withdraw* the subsidy *without delay*. In this regard, the Panel *shall specify* in its recommendation the time period within which the measure must be withdrawn. (emphasis added)

190. In this case, the Panel, in examining the language of Article 4.7 of the *SCM Agreement*, considered that it was *required* to make the recommendation provided for in that Article, and, therefore, recommended that Brazil withdraw its subsidies "without delay".[119] The Panel also determined that the requirement that Brazil withdraw its subsidies "without delay" meant that, in the circumstances of this case, Brazil shall withdraw its subsidies within 90 days.[120]

191. We note that Article 4.7 of the *SCM Agreement* is listed in Appendix 2 to the DSU as a "special or additional rule or procedure" on dispute settlement. We note also that Article 4.7 contains several elements which are different from the provisions of Articles 19 and 21 of the DSU with respect to recommendations by a panel and implementation of rulings and recommendations of the DSB. For example, Article 19 of the DSU requires a panel to recommend that the Member concerned bring its measure "into conformity" with the covered agreements. In contrast, Article 4.7 of the *SCM Agreement* requires a panel to recommend that the subsidizing Member *withdraw* the subsidy. In addition, paragraph 1 of Article 21 of the DSU requires "prompt compliance with recommendations or rulings of the DSB", and paragraph 3 of that Article allows an

[116] Brazil's appellant's submission, para. 82.
[117] Brazil's appellant's submission, para. 80.
[118] Brazil's appellant's submission, para. 82.
[119] Panel Report, para. 8.4.
[120] *Ibid.*, para. 8.5.

implementing Member "a reasonable period of time" to implement the recommendations or rulings of the DSB, where it is impracticable to comply immediately. In contrast, Article 4.7 of the *SCM Agreement* requires a panel to recommend that a subsidy be withdrawn "without delay".

192. With respect to implementation of the recommendations or rulings of the DSB in a dispute brought under Article 4 of the *SCM Agreement*, there is a significant difference between the relevant rules and procedures of the DSU and the special or additional rules and procedures set forth in Article 4.7 of the *SCM Agreement*. Therefore, the provisions of Article 21.3 of the DSU are not relevant in determining the period of time for implementation of a finding of inconsistency with the prohibited subsidies provisions of Part II of the *SCM Agreement*. Furthermore, we do not agree with Brazil that Article 4.12 of the *SCM Agreement* is applicable in this situation. In our view, the Panel was correct in its reasoning and conclusion on this issue. Article 4.7 of the *SCM Agreement*, which is applicable to this case, stipulates a time-period. It states that a subsidy must be withdrawn "without delay". That is the recommendation the Panel made.

193. Finally, we note that although Canada requested that we recommend that Brazil withdraw the export subsidies on regional aircraft under PROEX as of the date of adoption of the Appellate Body and Panel Reports[121], Canada did not formally appeal this issue. Canada's request was made in its appellee's submission, and was not included in its appellant's submission. We therefore decline this request by Canada.[122]

194. Based on our analysis above, we see no reason to disturb the Panel's recommendation that, in this case, "without delay" means 90 days and, therefore, Brazil must withdraw the export subsidies for regional aircraft under PROEX within 90 days.

X. CONDITIONAL APPEAL: "MAINTAINING" SUBSIDIES UNDER ARTICLE 3.2 OF THE *SCM AGREEMENT*

195. Canada makes a conditional appeal. Canada requests that, if we accept Brazil's argument and reverse the finding of the Panel that the export subsidies for regional aircraft under PROEX are "granted" at the time of issuance of the NTN-I bonds for the purposes of Article 27.4 of the *SCM Agreement*, then we should also reverse the Panel's decision not to make a finding on whether Brazil had acted inconsistently with its obligations not to "maintain" export subsidies

[121] Canada's appellee's submission, para. 169.

[122] In *United States - Gasoline*, we similarly declined to address claims of appeal made by Brazil and Venezuela in their appellees' submissions, finding that the issues were not properly appealed in accordance with the *Working Procedures*. *Supra*, footnote 110, at 11.

under Article 3.2 of that Agreement.[123] As we have not accepted Brazil's argument and have, therefore, not reversed the finding of the Panel on when the export subsidies for regional aircraft under PROEX are "granted", it is not necessary for us to consider this conditional appeal by Canada.

XI. FINDINGS AND CONCLUSIONS

196. For the reasons set out in this Report, the Appellate Body:

(a) upholds the ruling of the Panel that certain regulatory instruments specified in the request for the establishment of a panel, but not discussed in the consultations, were measures properly before the Panel;

(b) upholds the finding of the Panel that, in a dispute involving a claim of violation of Article 3.1(a) of the *SCM Agreement* by a developing country Member, the complaining party has the burden of proving that the developing country Member in question has not acted in compliance with the provisions of Article 27.4 of that Agreement;

(c) upholds the appealed findings of the Panel relating to the Panel's determination that Brazil had failed to comply with its obligations under Article 27.4 of the *SCM Agreement* to "not increase the level of its export subsidies", and, in particular, upholds the following findings of the Panel:

(i) that the "proper point of reference" for the purpose of determining whether a Member has increased the level of its export subsidies is actual expenditures, rather than budgeted amounts;

(ii) that for the purposes of Article 27.4, the export subsidies for regional aircraft under PROEX should be considered to be "granted" when the NTN-I bonds are issued, rather than when the letter of commitment is issued; and

(iii) that it is appropriate in this case to use constant dollars, rather than nominal dollars, in assessing whether Brazil has increased the level of its export subsidies; and,

therefore, upholds the overall conclusions of the Panel that Brazil has not complied with the provisions of Article 27.4 of the *SCM Agreement*, with the result that the export subsidy prohibition in Article 3.1(a) applies to Brazil;

---

[123] Canada's appellant's submission, paras. 47-57.

(d) reverses and modifies the interpretation by the Panel of the phrase "used to secure a material advantage in the field of export credit terms" in item (k) of the Illustrative List; but upholds the conclusion of the Panel that Brazil failed to demonstrate that the export subsidies for regional aircraft under PROEX are not "used to secure a material advantage in the field of export credit terms" within the meaning of item (k); and, therefore, upholds the Panel's rejection of the "affirmative defence" claimed by Brazil on the basis of item (k) of the Illustrative List;

(e) upholds the recommendation of the Panel that Brazil shall withdraw the export subsidies for regional aircraft under PROEX within 90 days; and

(f) in light of the finding in (c)(ii) above, makes no finding on the conditional appeal by Canada on whether the issuance of the NTN-I bonds is consistent with Brazil's obligation not to "maintain" prohibited export subsidies under Article 3.2 of the *SCM Agreement*.

197. The Appellate Body recommends that the DSB request Brazil to bring its measures found in this Report, and in the Panel Report as modified by this Report, to be inconsistent with its obligations under the *SCM Agreement* into conformity with the provisions of that Agreement. In this respect, we recall that we uphold the recommendation of the Panel that Brazil shall withdraw the export subsidies for regional aircraft under PROEX within 90 days.

BRAZIL - EXPORT FINANCING PROGRAMME FOR AIRCRAFT

Report of the Panel

WT/DS46/R

Adopted by the Dispute Settlement Body on 20 August 1999 as modified by the Appellate Body Report

TABLE OF CONTENTS

I. INTRODUCTION

1.1 On 18 June 1996, Canada requested consultations with Brazil under Article 4 of the Agreement on Subsidies and Countervailing Measures ("SCM Agreement") and Article 4 of the Understanding on Rules and Procedures Governing the Settlement of Disputes ("DSU"), regarding "certain export subsidies granted under the Brazilian Programa de Financiamento as Exportações ("PROEX") to foreign purchasers of Brazil's EMBRAER aircraft."[1]

1.2 Canada and Brazil held consultations on 22 and 25 July 1996 in Geneva, but failed to reach a mutually satisfactory solution. On 16 September 1996, Canada requested the establishment of a panel under Articles 4 and 30 of the SCM Agreement and Articles 4 and 6 of the DSU.[2] In a communication dated 23 September 1996 and addressed to the Dispute Settlement Body ("DSB"), Brazil reserved its rights to invoke Article 27 of the SCM Agreement before any panel that was established to examine the matter at issue, and requested that the terms of reference proposed by Canada explicitly recognize Brazil's right to do so.

1.3 On 3 October 1996, Canada again requested the establishment of a panel.[3] That request was subsequently withdrawn to allow the parties to seek a mutually satisfactory solution to the problem.

1.4 On 10 July 1998, Canada again requested the establishment of a panel under Article 4 of the SCM Agreement.

1.5 At its meeting on 23 July 1998, the Dispute Settlement Body ("DSB") established a Panel in accordance with Article 4 of the SCM Agreement with the following standard terms of reference:

> "To examine, in the light of the relevant provisions of the SCM Agreement, the matter referred to the DSB by Canada in document WT/DS46/5 and to make such findings as will assist the DSB in making

---

[1] *See* Canada's request for consultations, WT/DS46/1.

[2] WT/DS46/5; 13 July 1998.

[3] WT/DS46/4; 4 October 1996.

the recommendations or in giving the rulings provided for in that agreement."[4]

1.6 The European Communities ("EC") and the United States ("US") reserved their rights to participate in the panel proceedings as third parties.[5]

1.7 On 16 October 1998, Canada requested the Director-General of the WTO to determine the composition of the Panel, pursuant to Article 8.7 of the DSU. On 22 October 1998, the Director-General composed the Panel as follows:

Chairman:	Mr. Dariusz Rosati
Members:	Professor Akio Shimizu
	Mr. Kajit Sukhum

1.8 The Panel met with the parties on 23/24 November 1998 and 14 December 1998. It met with the third parties on 24 November 1998.

1.9 The Panel submitted its interim report to the parties on 17 February 1999. On 25 February 1999 both parties submitted written requests for the Panel to review precise aspects of the interim report, and on 3 March 1999 each party submitted written comments regarding the other's request. Neither party requested a further meeting with the Panel. The Panel submitted its final report to the parties on 12 March 1999.

1.10 Given the nature of the dispute, and with the agreement of the parties, special procedures were created by the Panel for handling business confidential information. The special procedures are found in Annex 1 to this report. Under paragraph VII:2 of these procedures, "[t]he Panel shall not disclose Business Confidential Information in its interim and final reports, but may make statements of conclusion drawn from such information." Thus, where Business Confidential Information had been submitted by a party in support of a claim, it is mentioned in the report, but details of such information are not disclosed.

II. FACTUAL ASPECTS

2.1 This dispute concerns payments under the interest rate equalization component of the Programa de Financiamento as Exportações ("PROEX"), the export financing support programme of Brazil, on exports of Brazilian regional aircraft. PROEX was created by the Government of Brazil on 1 June 1991 by Law No. 8187/91 and is currently being maintained by provisional measures issued by the Brazilian government on a monthly basis.[6] PROEX provides ex-

[4] WT/DS46/7; 28 October 1998.

[5] WT/DS46/6; 19 August 1998.

[6] As of the date of the request for the establishment of a panel, the relevant legal instrument was Provisional Measure 1700/15 of 30 June 1998. It replaced Provisional Measure 1629-13 of 12

port credits to Brazilian exporters either through direct financing or interest rate equalization payments.[7]

2.2 With direct financing, Brazil lends a portion of the funds required for the transaction. With interest equalization, underlying legal instruments provide that the "National Treasury grant[s] to the financing party an equalization payment to cover, at most, the difference between the interest charges contracted with the buyer and the cost to the financing party of raising the required funds."[8]

2.3 The financing terms for which interest rate equalization payments are made are set by Ministerial Decrees. The terms, determined by the product to be exported, vary normally from one year to ten years. In the case of regional aircraft, however, this term has been extended to 15 years. The length of the financing term, in turn, determines the spread to be equalized: the payment ranges from 2 percentage points per annum, up to 3.8 percentage points per annum for a term of nine years or more.[9] The spread is fixed and does not vary depending on the lender's actual cost of funds.[10]

2.4 PROEX is administered by the Comitê de Crédito as Exportações ("Committee"), a 13-agency group, with the Ministry of Finance serving as its executive. Day-to-day operations of PROEX are conducted by the Banco do Brasil. For applications for financing transactions not exceeding US$5 million, whose terms otherwise fall within PROEX guidelines, Banco do Brasil has pre-approved authority to provide PROEX support without requesting the approval of the Committee. All other applications are referred to the Committee, which has the authority to waive some of the published PROEX guidelines. In the case of regional jet aircraft, the most frequent waiver has been to extend the length of the financing term from ten to fifteen years.

2.5 PROEX involvement in aircraft financing transactions begins when the manufacturer requests a letter of approval from the Committee prior to conclusion of a formal agreement with the buyer. This request sets forth the terms and conditions of the proposed transaction. If the Committee approves, it issues a letter of commitment to the manufacturer. This letter commits PROEX to providing support as specified for the transaction provided that the contract is entered into according to the terms and conditions contained in the request for approval, and provided that it is entered into within a specified period of time, usu-

---

February 1998, which had replaced the basic law establishing PROEX, Law No. 8.187 of 1 June 1991, as amended by Resolution 2380 of 25 April 1997.

[7] Law No. 8.187, 1 June1991 (Exhibit Bra-3), replaced by Provisional Measure No. 1629, 12 February 1998 (Exhibit Bra-4).

[8] *See*, for example, Resolution 2380/97 of 25 April 1997.

[9] *See* Central Bank of Brazil Circular Letter number 2.601 dated 29 November 1995. Prior to that date, the spread to be equalised for financing for a term of nine years or more was 3.5 percentage points.

[10] *Evaluation of the Brazilian Export Program* ("Finan Report") p. 2.7.

ally 90 days. If a contract is not entered into within the specified time, the commitment contained in the letter of approval expires.

2.6 PROEX interest equalization payments, pursuant to the commitment, begin after the aircraft is exported and paid for by the purchaser. PROEX payments are made to the lending financial institution in the form of non-interest bearing National Treasury Bonds (Notas do Tesouro Nacional - Série I) referred to as NTN-I bonds. These are denominated in Brazilian Reais indexed to the United States dollar. The bonds are issued by the Brazilian National Treasury to its agent bank, Banco do Brasil, which then passes them on to the lending banks financing the transaction. The bonds are issued in the name of the lending bank which can decide to redeem them on a semi-annual basis for the duration of the financing or discount them for a lump sum in the market. PROEX resembles a series of zero coupon bonds which mature at six months intervals over the course of the financing period. The bonds can only be redeemed in Brazil and only in Brazilian currency at the exchange rate prevailing at the time of payment. If the lending bank is outside of Brazil, it may appoint a Brazilian bank as its agent to receive the semi-annual payments on its behalf.

III. FINDINGS AND RECOMMENDATIONS REQUESTED BY THE PARTIES

A. *Findings of Fact*

3.1 **Canada** requests the Panel to make the following findings of fact:

(a) That PROEX interest equalization payments are made in the form of instalments or lump sums.

(b) That PROEX interest equalization payments have been made in respect of the following transactions: (a) *Brasilia 120 model* (Skywest, Great Lakes Airlines; Rio Sul and other unspecified transactions); (b) *ERJ-145 model* (American Eagle; British Regional; Portugalia; Regional; Rio Sul; Siv Am; Wexford; Continental Express ("COEX"); Trans States; Luxair; City Airlines; and other unspecified transactions).

(c) That the level of PROEX and BEFIEX expenditures has increased since 1 January 1995 and, as a result, the level of Brazilian export subsidies has increased since that date.

(d) That PROEX and BEFIEX, and therefore Brazilian export subsidies, are not being phased out by 31 December 2002.

B. *Findings of Law*

3.2 **Canada** requests the Panel to make the following findings of law:

(a) That, as admitted by Brazil, PROEX interest equalization payments are export subsidies within the meaning of Article 3 of the SCM Agreement.

(b) That, more specifically, but without foregoing the generality of the previous finding, PROEX interest equalization payments made in respect of the following transactions are prohibited export subsidies: (a) *Brasilia 120 model* (Skywest, Great Lakes Airlines; Rio Sul and other unspecified transactions); (b) *ERJ-145 model* (American Eagle; British Regional; Portugalia; Regional; Rio Sul; Siv Am; Wexford; Continental Express ("COEX"); Trans States; Luxair; City Airlines; and other unspecified transactions).

(c) That the first paragraph of Item (k) of Annex 1 of the SCM Agreement does not provide an exception to Article 3.

(d) That, even if the first paragraph of Item (k) does provide, through an a contrario inference such an exception, PROEX interest equalization payments are not payments within the meaning of Item (k), or do provide a material advantage in the field of export credit terms, and as such do not fall within the exception.

(e) That Brazil does not meet the conditions set out in Article 27.4 and that, as a result, it does not benefit from the eight year grace period from the general prohibition on export subsidies in Article 3, provided for developing countries under Article 27.2(b).

C. Recommendations

3.3 In its first written submission to the Panel, **Canada** requested the Panel to make the following recommendations:

(a) "Brazil shall not grant new subsidies under PROEX, including subsidies promised or committed, but not yet granted, on regional aircraft not yet delivered";

(b) "Brazil shall no longer maintain existing subsidies under PROEX and must terminate such subsidies no later than three months after the adoption of the Report of the Panel by the DSB"; and

(c) "Brazil shall withdraw without delay PROEX subsidies granted pursuant to transactions entered into following the composition of the Panel on October 22, 1998."

In its second oral submission to the Panel, **Canada** further requested the Panel to make the following recommendations:

(d) That, if the Panel finds that PROEX interest equalization export subsidies are granted on an instalment basis at the time of the periodic payment of the subsidies, the Panel recommend that such payments be terminated no later than 3 months after the date of the adoption of the Panel's Report by the Dispute Settlement Body, in respect of aircraft that have already been delivered or in respect of any aircraft delivered after that date.

(e) That, if the Panel finds that PROEX subsidies are granted at the time of the delivery of the aircraft, the Panel recommend that no such subsidies be granted in respect of any aircraft delivered after the date of the adoption of the Panel's Report by the DSB.

(f) That the Panel recommend that any PROEX interest equalization export subsidies paid or granted in respect of any new orders of aircraft between the date of the composition of the Panel on October 22, 1998 and the date that the Panel Report is adopted by the DSB be withdrawn as prohibited export subsidies intended to circumvent the Panel's recommendations.

3.4 **Brazil** requests the Panel to find that "PROEX is not inconsistent with Brazil's obligations under Article 3 of the Agreement on Subsidies and Countervailing Measures."

IV. MAIN ARGUMENTS OF THE PARTIES

A. *Preliminary Objection*

4.1 **Brazil** raises a preliminary objection to the Panel's consideration of certain measures listed in Canada's request for the establishment of a Panel on the ground that the parties never consulted about these measures. The measures with regard to which Brazil raises this objection are Provisional Measures 1700/15 and 1629/13; Decree No. 2414 of 12/9/97; Resolutions of the National Monetary Council Nos. 2490/98, 2452/97, 2381/97 and 2380/97; and MICT Orders 28/98, 23/98, 7/98, 121/97, 83/97, 53/97, 34/97 and 33/97.

4.2 Brazil submits that the parties consulted in Geneva on 22 and 25 July 1996 and on 4 November 1996, and in Brasilia on 21-22 November 1996. However, since each of the identified measures was either enacted or implemented after consultations were held, they could not have been the subject of consultations. Brazil further argues that although the parties met in Rio de Janeiro on 8-9 June 1998 and in Washington D.C. on 25-26 June 1998, they did not consult on the identified measures. In any case, Provisional Measure 1700/15 was enacted on 30 June 1998 and, as such, post-dated even the Washington meeting.

4.3 Brazil argues that it is the absolute right of every Member to consult about a challenged measure before being required to defend it before a Panel. Measures which were not consulted upon by the parties could not properly be within the terms of reference of the Panel and as such should not be examined by the Panel. If Members were to have the right to ask for the establishment of a panel without having consulted about the measures, it would undermine the importance of consultations in the WTO dispute settlement mechanism and undermine the practical significance of Article 4 of the DSU.

4.4 In response to a question from the panel,[11] Brazil stated that its preliminary objection is grounded in both the provisions of the DSU and the SCM Agreement. Brazil submitted that in *Japan - Measures Affecting Agricultural Products*[12], the parties disagreed as to whether consultations occurred regarding the measure at issue. Japan argued that they had not consulted, while the United States asserted that the parties in fact had consulted with regard to the measure.[13]

4.5 Brazil argues that this dispute is very different. Brazil submits that in this dispute both Brazil and Canada agree that consultations did not encompass the measures in issue. The assertion to the contrary in the request for the establishment of a panel was an obvious and admitted error. Consequently, unlike *Japan - Agricultural Products*, there is no question that consultations regarding these measures did not take place.[14]

4.6 Brazil asserts that in *Japan - Agricultural Products*, as well as in E*uropean Communities -Bananas*[15], which is cited in that decision, the Panel was faced with an inability to resolve a factual disagreement between the parties. Brazil submits that those Panels had no way of determining what, in fact, had taken place at consultations. In these circumstances, both Panels reasonably relied upon the text of the request for the establishment of a panel which was incorporated in the terms of reference.[16] This Panel is not faced with the need to resolve a factual dispute between the Parties concerning the subject matter of consultations. It is faced, however, with the responsibility, stated by the Appellate Body in *Bananas*, "to examine the request for the establishment of the panel very carefully to ensure its compliance with both the letter and the spirit of Article 6.2 of the DSU."[17]

4.7 Brazil submits that pursuant to Article 30 of the SCM Agreement, Article 6.2 of the DSU is applicable to the request for the establishment of a panel in this proceeding. Article 6.2 of the DSU specifies that panel requests shall indicate whether consultations were held and identify the specific measures at issue. Both the letter and the spirit of Article 6.2 of the DSU require that consultations with regard to the specific measures at issue must have taken place in order for a

---

[11] Brazil's Response to Questions From the Panel, No. 3.

[12] *Japan - Measures Affecting Agricultural Products*, WT/DS76/R, para. 8.4., circulated to Members on 27 October 1998. Japan notified its intention to appeal on 24 November 1998.

[13] *Ibid.*

[14] *Ibid.*

[15] *European Communities - Regime for the Importation, Sale and Distribution of Bananas*; WT/DS27/AB/R; as modified by the Appellate Body report was adopted by the DSB on 25 September 1997.

[16] *Supra* note 13.

[17] *Supra* note 16, WT/DS27/AB/R, para. 142.

measure to be properly within the terms of reference.[18] Brazil further submits that Article 4 of the DSU requires that parties consult regarding a matter *before* resorting to a panel. Article 4.4 of the DSU provides that if a Member does not respond within a specific period of time "after the date of receipt of the request, *then* the Member that requested the holding of consultations may proceed directly to request the establishment of a panel." (emphasis in original.) Likewise, Article 4.7 provides that "*If the consultations fail to settle a dispute* ... the complaining party may request the establishment of a panel." (emphasis in original). Finally, Article 6.2 requires that when requesting the establishment of a panel the complaining party must "indicate whether consultations were held."[19]

4.8 **Canada**, which notes that the subject of its challenge was "export subsidies paid under PROEX...on all exported Brazilian regional aircraft, in whatever amount and regardless of the specific legislative instrument that underlies the programme," accepts that the specific legislative instruments which Brazil wants to exclude from consideration by the Panel were not consulted about by the parties. In its response to a question from the Panel whether it would regard its meetings with Brazil in Rio de Janeiro and Washington D. C. in the first half of 1998 as consultations within the meaning of Article 4 of the DSU, Canada stated that it "agrees with Brazil that the meetings...were not consultations within the meaning of Article 4.4 of the DSU. The specific legislative instruments listed in Canada's request for a Panel were not discussed during these negotiations, as these negotiations were aimed at bringing the subsidies themselves under some form of discipline."

4.9 Canada urges the Panel, however, to reject Brazil's argument that the contested measures are not properly within its terms of reference on two main grounds.

4.10 First, **Canada** argues that Brazil's request has no basis in the DSU, the SCM Agreement or WTO practice. The "matter" referred to in its request for the establishment of a panel in accordance with Article 4.4 of the SCM Agreement was "the payment of export subsidies...under PROEX," and this is the "same prohibited subsidy" on which the parties had consulted. The legislative changes enacted in the period between the two requests did not fundamentally change the character of the "prohibited subsidy" subject to the consultations.

4.11 Canada notes that the measures listed in Brazil's preliminary objection are the specific legislative and regulatory instruments underlying the prohibited subsidies with respect to which Canada requested consultations. These specific measures were identified in Canada's request for establishment of a panel in accordance with Article 4.4 of the SCM Agreement and Article 6.2 of the DSU. In Canada's view, the question at issue is the nature and strength of the connection

---

18 *Supra* note 14.

19 *Supra* note 14.

that must exist between the "prohibited subsidy" in SCM Agreement Article 4.1 with respect to which consultations have been requested, and the "matter" in the request for a Panel, as set out in SCM Agreement Article 4.4. Canada asserts that the appropriate test to be applied in determining whether the "matter" in the request for a Panel had been subject to consultations is not whether the request for consultations and the request for a Panel are in all respects identical.

4.12 Canada gives two reasons in support of this proposition. It relies on the statement of the Appellate Body in *India - Patents* that "the claims that are made and the facts that are established during consultations do much to shape the substance and the scope of subsequent Panel proceedings."[20] Canada submits that this observation is equally valid in respect of the facts that are established, and the measures identified, in the period between the request for consultations and the request for a panel.

4.13 Canada's second reason for its proposition is that a request for a Panel must meet the criteria set out in Article 6.2 of the DSU. Thus, whereas it is necessary to list the "specific measures" at issue under Article 6.2 of the DSU, it is not necessary to do so in a request for consultations. Canada acknowledges that Article 4.4 of the DSU is not a licence for a fishing expedition, as a request for a panel cannot be on a matter on which no consultations have taken place. There must be a connection between the two requests. The matter subject to the request for a panel must be rationally connected to the prohibited subsidy subject to the consultations and flow directly from it. Canada reiterated that the matter in its request for a panel is the same as the prohibited subsidy on which consultations were requested. The specific measures identified in the request for a panel in accordance with Article 6.2 of the DSU are rationally and directly connected to the prohibited subsidy on which consultations were requested.

4.14 Canada also argues that the Brazilian challenge, which seems to be based on Article 4 of the DSU, ignores the provisions of Article 4 of the SCM Agreement, which is also cited in its request for consultations. As Article 4 of the SCM Agreement contains special rules applicable to disputes concerning the grant of subsidies and countervailing measures, it should be read together with the relevant provisions of the DSU, as mandated by Article 1.2 of the DSU. The requirements for a request for consultations are found in Article 4.2 of the SCM Agreement, which relevantly provides that "[a] request for consultations...shall include a statement of available evidence with regard to the existence and nature of the subsidy in question," and Article 4.4 of the DSU, which relevantly provides that "[a]ny request for consultations shall be submitted in writing and shall give the reasons for the request, including identification of the measures at issue and an indication of the legal basis of the complaint." Canada submits that the

[20] *India - Patent Protection for Pharmaceutical and Agricultural Chemical Products*, WT/DS50/AB/R, para 94, report of the Appellate Body adopted 16 January 1998.

objectives of consultations as set out in Article 4.3 of the SCM Agreement and in Article 4.5 of the DSU are virtually the same. Under both Articles, the stated purpose is to enable the parties to clarify the facts of the situation and to arrive at a mutually agreed solution. If consultations should fail to settle the dispute, parties have a right under both Article 4.4 of the SCM Agreement and Article 6.1 of the DSU to request the establishment of a panel. Canada submits that there are no conflicts between the relevant provisions of the SCM Agreement and the DSU and that they should be interpreted together in a manner that preserves the comprehensive, integrated nature of the WTO dispute settlement system.[21]

4.15 Canada submits that the facts of this case are different from those in *Argentina - Textiles and Apparel.*[22] There, the matter in dispute was specific duties on footwear that had, by the time the matter came before the Panel, been revoked and replaced by safeguard measures. The complainant, the United States, argued that Argentina was likely to reintroduce the tariffs, and so the Panel should examine the revoked tariffs. Relying on GATT and WTO jurisprudence, the Panel refused to examine a measure that had been revoked even before the Panel was established and its terms of reference had been set. In the present case, the matter at issue has not been revoked or replaced. It is still in force and the legislative and regulatory instruments underlying the PROEX programme are being re-enacted in the form of provisional decrees and ministerial orders on a periodic basis.

4.16 **Canada** submits that the interpreter of a treaty must avoid an interpretation that would lead to an unreasonable or absurd result. Given that PROEX is now governed by a Presidential Decree that must be renewed every month, Brazil's argument, if it were to prevail, would bar examination by the WTO of PROEX altogether, as every request for consultations would be in respect of a specific measure that would have been superseded by another measure at the time that a Panel would be established, meaning that no WTO panel would be able to examine PROEX in its current form at any given time. If Brazil's argument were to prevail, in every case subject to dispute settlement, a responding party would be able to frustrate the WTO dispute settlement system through the simple device of periodic re-enactments of impugned measures. Such an outcome would be manifestly inconsistent with "predictability and security," the central objectives of the WTO dispute settlement system. Brazil's argument would turn the system into a procedural nullity.

---

[21] *Guatemala - Anti-Dumping Investigation Regarding Portland Cement from Mexico*, WT/DS60/AB/R, paras 64-67, report of the Appellate Body adopted on 25 November 1998.

[22] *Argentina - Measures Affecting Imports of Footwear, Textiles, Apparel and Other Items*, WT/DS56/R; report of the Panel adopted on 22 April 1998.

B. *Whether PROEX Payments Are Subsidies Within the Meaning of Article 1 of the SCM Agreement that are Contingent upon Export Performance Within the Meaning of Article 3.1 (a) of that Agreement*

4.17 **Canada** submits that PROEX payments are grants by the Government of Brazil to purchasers of exported Brazilian regional aircraft. These payments reduce the purchaser's net interest rate - sometimes by as much as half of the interest rates available in the market - over the term of a financed transaction. Alternatively, the bonds which are issued by the Brazilian government for such payments may be discounted in the market for a lump sum to be received by the purchaser in the form of a discount on the price of the aircraft. Either way, these payments lower the cost of exported Brazilian regional aircraft for the purchaser. As such, this financial contribution by the Government of Brazil confers a benefit and constitutes a "subsidy" within the meaning of Article 1.1 of the SCM Agreement. Canada further submits that since PROEX subsidies are paid only on the exportation of products from Brazil, they are "contingent on export performance" and therefore prohibited under Article 3.1 of the SCM Agreement.

4.18 **Brazil** concedes that "PROEX interest equalization payments for aircraft constitute an export subsidy." It reaffirms this view in its answer to a question from the Panel by stating that "Brazil has not denied that PROEX interest equalization payments for aircraft fulfil the definition of a subsidy within the meaning of Article 3.1(a). Brazil argues, however, that PROEX is exempt from the prohibition of Article 3.1(a) by virtue of Article 27 and, totally apart from Article 27, by virtue of item (k) of the Illustrative List."

1. *Whether there is a Financial Contribution by the Brazilian Government*

4.19 **Canada** argues that PROEX payments are a direct transfer of funds by the Brazilian government and as such constitute a financial contribution within the meaning of Article 1.1(a)(1)(i) of the SCM Agreement. Canada argues, in the alternative, that if the Panel should find that the issuance of treasury bonds and payment by the Government of Brazil on the redemption of such bonds is not a "direct transfer of funds" within the meaning of Article 1.1(a)(1)(i) of the SCM Agreement, PROEX payments should be regarded as an indirect financial contribution by a government through a funding mechanism or a private body entrusted or directed, in the sense of Article 1.1(a)(1)(iv) of the SCM Agreement, to transfer payments made by the Government of Brazil upon the redemption of treasury bonds issued under PROEX to the ultimate beneficiaries.

4.20 **Brazil** does not contest that actual PROEX payments constitute a financial contribution by the Brazilian government. In response to a question from the Panel as to whether the "issuance, or commitment to issue, NTN-I bonds represented a "potential direct transfer of funds or liabilities" within the meaning of

Article 1.1(a)(i) of the SCM Agreement," Brazil stated that in its view the issuance of a PROEX commitment letter constitutes a "potential direct transfer of funds." Brazil further maintains that since PROEX assistance begins with the letter of approval, the Brazilian Government could be said to grant a subsidy within the meaning of Article 1 of the SCM Agreement at the point when it "issues or enters into a commitment to issue bonds in support of an export transaction."[23] In this respect, Brazil agrees with the arguments advanced by the European Communities as a third party in this dispute.[24]

2. *Time at which the Financial Contribution is Made*

4.21 **Canada** submits that the point at which a subsidy is determined to exist can have a crucial impact not only on the total "level of subsidies," but also on whether Brazil is meeting its obligations under Article 27 of the SCM Agreement. In this respect, Canada appears to be addressing the arguments presented by the European Communities as a third party in this dispute, as adopted by Brazil.[25]

4.22 Canada argues that the Brazilian government makes a financial contribution at the point when the bonds are redeemed or, in the alternative, at the point when the bonds are issued upon the delivery of the aircraft. It disagrees with the European Communities and Brazil that the Brazilian government makes a financial contribution when "it issues, or enters into a commitment to issue, bonds in support of an export transaction."

4.23 Canada argues that simply entering into a commitment to pay a subsidy at some point in the future cannot constitute a financial contribution within the meaning of Article 1.1(a)(1)(i) of the SCM Agreement, although it agrees with the European Communities that it is necessary to view each grant within the context of the broader commitment under which it is made. That is, each periodic payment under PROEX should be viewed in the context of the commitment in accordance with which such payment is made. An acontextual examination of specific payments under a scheme could make determining the existence of a subsidy impossible.

4.24 Canada, however, maintains that entering into a commitment when no money has changed hands could not, in itself, be considered a "financial contribution" or a subsidy. This is because commitments, even those by governments, may not always be kept. Canada introduced evidence, which according to it, demonstrated that some airline companies which dealt with EMBRAER, the Brazilian manufacturer of regional aircraft, were of the same view and assumed

---

23 Brazil's Second Written Submission, para. 46 and Brazil's Response to Questions From the Panel, No.32.

24 *See*, the third party submission of the European Communities, para. 5.5 of this report.

25 *See*, the third party submission of the European Communities, para. 5.4 of this report.

that it was possible that the Brazilian government may not honour its commitments.

4.25 **Brazil** contests the arguments of Canada regarding when a subsidy is granted. In its submissions, Brazil explained the operation of PROEX with regard to interest equalization payments. In an oral statement before the panel, it also summarized that an application is made and, if the application is in order, that the Banco de Brasil, as agent for PROEX, makes a legally binding commitment. Brazil stated that it would be liable for damages if it did not honour its commitment.[26] Brazil also submitted as an exhibit a legal opinion from a Brazilian legal scholar supporting its position.[27]

4.26 Brazil argued that this commitment is to provide specified PROEX benefits if the transaction is concluded, within a specified time, in accordance with the terms contained in the application. The most important parts of this commitment concern the number of airplanes covered and the price. Both ultimately may be lower than listed in the application, but neither can be greater. When this commitment is issued, Brazil becomes legally obligated to furnish PROEX benefits, and the private parties are free to act in reliance on this commitment. Production is scheduled. Parts and components are purchased. Crew training begins. Both the manufacturer and the airline incur a variety of expenses associated with the production, acquisition, and use of a new aircraft. When actual export occurs, PROEX is paid in the form of NTN-I's, generally 30 non-interest bearing bonds redeemable over the next 15 years. The entire face amount of the 30 bonds is charged to the budget for the year of export.[28]

4.27 Specifically, Brazil argued that the steps taken by the manufacturer include commitments and investments regarding the acquisition of raw materials, supplies and equipment necessary for the production of the aircraft. This involves contractual obligations between the manufacturer and suppliers of such major components as engines, avionics, and landing gear. It may involve increases in the workforce. Positions are scheduled in the workline so that the contracted aircraft may be delivered on time. Finally, the aircraft is manufactured and exported to the purchaser. At the point of export the bonds are issued. At that stage, the manufacturer has incurred all of the expenses involved in producing aircraft ready to be flown.[29]

4.28 Brazil argued that the steps taken by purchasers are not as extensive as those taken by the manufacturer, but they are significant and involve the commitment of resources. These steps include investments regarding the preparation for the start of operations with the new aircraft, including crew training and es-

---

26 Brazil's Second Oral Statement, para. 71.

27 *See* para. 4.33 of this report.

28 Brazil's Second Oral Statement, para. 72.

29 Brazil's Response to Questions From the Panel, No. 31.

tablishment of a maintenance infrastructure along the points where the aircraft will be flown. Typically schedules are arranged, and promotional expenses incurred. In addition, purchasers are responsible for complying with numerous regulatory requirements of the jurisdictions in which the aircraft will be flown, a process begun before the arrival of the aircraft.[30]

4.29 In these circumstances, Brazil submits that it is clear that the granting of the subsidy occurs at the point at which Brazil makes a legally binding commitment to provide PROEX payments, a commitment on which private actors can and do rely.

4.30 In responding to a question from the Panel asking Brazil to clarify the nature of a "firm order,"[31] Brazil explained that a firm order is a binding contract, imposing rights and obligations on both the buyer and the seller. It represents a commitment by the buyer to purchase an agreed number of aircraft, in accordance with and under the terms and conditions of a binding, legal purchase agreement, and an obligation on the seller to produce and deliver the aircraft to a buyer.

4.31 Brazil further submits that there are no circumstances under which a purchaser (or a seller) may cancel a firm order by its unilateral action. Of course, as with any contract, either party would be excused from performance if the other failed to comply with its obligations under the purchase agreement. For example, a purchaser could cancel a firm order if the manufacturer failed to provide the financing support required by the purchase agreement. In addition, aircraft purchase agreements typically permit the purchaser to cancel a firm order if excusable delays in delivery amount to 300 days or longer, or if non-excusable delays amount to 90 days or longer. The purchase agreement would specify reasons for delay that would be considered excusable. In addition, purchasers typically may cancel firm orders upon the accidental damage or destruction of the aircraft before its acceptance by the purchaser. Brazil submits it is not common for a purchaser of a civil aircraft to cancel a firm order.

4.32 Brazil states that in the event of cancellation of a firm order, a purchaser would be liable for damages under the law of the jurisdiction specified in the purchase agreement. In addition, the purchaser normally would lose all amounts previously paid to the manufacturer. Alternatively, depending upon the terms of the purchase agreement, the purchaser would be liable for liquidated damages.

4.33 Brazil states that a firm order differs from an option only in that the purchaser is not obligated to buy, but if the purchaser elects to do so, the manufacturer is obligated to sell. Thus, an option is equivalent to a "call" acquired by the purchaser. In confidential business information submitted in response to a question from the panel, Brazil provided a letter of commitment that showed that the

---

30 Brazil's Response to Questions From the Panel, No. 31.

31 Brazil's Response to Questions From the Panel, No. 29.

Brazilian Government makes no distinction between firm orders and options when granting letters of commitment. [32]As such, Brazil disagrees with Canada as to the legal consequences of a letter of commitment. It is of the view that upon the fulfilment of the conditions specified by the Banco do Brasil, the letter becomes irrevocable, in the sense that if the Brazilian government should default, it could be sued for damages in the Brazilian courts. The view of Brazil is confirmed in an opinion prepared by Professor Luiz Olavo Baptisa, who in response to a question[33] from the Panel regarding the legal consequences of a "letter of commitment" stated that :

> "[W]ithin the validity period of the Letters of Commitment and provided there are no pending debts from the exporter [EMBRAER] to the Government of Brazil, it is illegal and not viable the cancellation or the revoking of the interest rate equalization concessions made for the referred to transactions. To accept the cancellation or the revoking of the Letters of Commitment unilaterally done by the administration, other than being clearly illegal, would cause doubts and uncertainties to business and legal relationships and it would also allow the exporter to go to the Courts against the Government of Brazil for indemnification purposes. Therefore it is irrelevant the issue related to the timing of issuance of the NTN-1, [sic], for the issuance of such bonds is nothing else than the materialization of an obligation created upon the issuance of the Letters of Commitment."

4.34 **Canada** submits that the commitment to issue a bond is simply the mechanism by which the Government of Brazil entrusts private entities to make the payment, in periodic instalments or in lump sum, of the subsidies in question to the purchasers of exported Brazilian regional aircraft, in the sense of Article 1.1(a)(iv) of the SCM Agreement. In this sense, the date of the commitment says little about the actual payment of the subsidies that would take place under Article 1.1(a)(iv).

4.35 Canada contends that the European Communities and Brazilian position on the timing of a subsidy is not applicable, at least in the circumstances of this case. On the facts of this case, Canada argues that the phrase "potential direct transfer of funds or liabilities" is irrelevant. In the context of the SCM Agreement, the phrase "potential direct transfer of funds or liabilities" encompasses government practices such as loan guarantees and agricultural crop insurance, but does not include conditional promises or commitments to grant subsidies at

---

32 Brazil's Response to Questions From the Panel, No. 31 (Exhibit Bra-15).

33 The question from the Panel was as follows: "Please explain in what sense the 'letter of commitment' represents a binding legal commitment by Brazil. In particular, would the government of Brazil be legally entitled to revoke the letter of commitment before such time as the bonds are issued. If not, please indicate the precise legal instrument and relevant language establishing the legal obligation of Brazil?"

some point in the future. The distinction relates to the legal enforceability of a "potential" transfer such as a loan guarantee, as opposed to the contingent nature of a promise or a "commitment" to grant subsidies at some point in the future if certain purchases are made. For example, financial institutions as a matter of course list [loan] guarantees or other contingent liabilities such as insurance commitments as "liabilities." This is not the same as promises or commitments to consider and to give subsidies if purchases are made. The promise to pay subsidies upon future purchase is simply too remote to fit within the terms of "potential direct transfer of funds."

4.36 Canada argues that since PROEX subsidies are not expensed in the Brazilian budget until after the aircraft is delivered, it cannot be argued that, at the time of the order of the aircraft (firm, conditional or optional), the promise to pay a subsidy if an order is exercised amounts to a "potential transfer of funds." The consequences of a failure on the part of EMBRAER to provide financing that was a condition of an order would simply be that the buyer would be relieved of its obligation to purchase the aircraft. Canada further argues that the situation becomes more complicated in the case of option contracts for future deliveries negotiated in a sales agreement. An "option" may be agreed to in recognition of a "commitment" to pay subsidies in the event an option to purchase is exercised by a purchaser. However, such an option may not be exercised. Any "commitment" in respect of such options is not a subsidy unless the option is exercised - that is, a sale takes place - and until the aircraft is delivered - that is, until it becomes necessary for the purchaser to pay for the aircraft and therefore benefit from the subsidies promised. In such instances, the issuance of the Brazilian bonds occurs only after the financing party declares that the goods have been shipped and the exchange contracts have been settled for the total value of the export.

4.37 Canada submits that a "financial contribution" may be found to exist under the PROEX interest equalization scheme at one of only two points, namely (i) where a payment is made pursuant to a NTN-I bond that becomes due; or (ii) where NTN-I bonds are issued to the agent bank at the point of delivery of the aircraft and the cost to government is effectively (though not actually) incurred through expensing in the budget. In the case of the former, the two elements of "subsidy" - a net charge to the treasury and an advantage above and beyond the market are coterminous at the point of each instalment of PROEX subsidies. In the case of the latter, it may be argued that that is also the point at which the terms of a promised subsidy are finally crystallized.

4.38 Canada, however, submits that if the Panel were to decide that a financial contribution is made by the Brazilian government at the point of the issuance of a letter of commitment, then this characterization would significantly increase the level of annual expenditure of export subsidies for the purposes of the second condition of Article 27.4, that is, the requirement not to increase such subsidies. Canada provided calculations based on evidence put forward by Brazil to show that if Brazil is correct in its argument that the issuance of the letter of commitment constitutes the grant of a subsidy, then Brazil has clearly not been in compliance since 1996 with the condition not to increase the level of its export subsidies.

4.39 With respect to the legal opinion submitted by Brazil, Canada submitted that the question of whether domestic legal consequences flow from breaking a commitment to pay export subsidies is not relevant for this Panel. The issue before the Panel is Brazil's obligation, in international law, not to grant and not to maintain export subsidies that are illegal under Article 3 of the SCM Agreement.

3. *Whether PROEX Payments Confer a Benefit*

4.40 **Canada** argues that the ordinary meaning of "benefit" in context and with a view to the object and purpose of the SCM Agreement accords well with the dictionary definition of the term: a benefit is an advantage.[34] A financial contribution that is not repayable - in other words, a grant - bestows an advantage. Such a contribution, when made by a government, directly or indirectly, amounts to a subsidy. According to the terms of the law under which PROEX payments are made, they are never to be repaid by the beneficiary. As such they amount to outright grants. This alone, in Canada's view, demonstrates the benefit conferred by PROEX.

4.41 Canada argues that since EMBRAER entered into the regional jet market with the certification of the EMB-145 model (now ERJ-145) in 1996, followed by the launch of the 37-seat ERJ-135 in 1997, it has captured over half of the regional aircraft market, and has announced plans to increase its production of regional jets to 12 a month, enough to satisfy, on its own, the demand for regional jet aircraft in this market segment for the foreseeable future. Canada argues that it is PROEX payments which have enabled EMBRAER to become a dominant player in the regional jet aircraft industry and increased its market share. According to Canada, EMBRAER has acknowledged in various documents and communications the benefit conferred by PROEX including in the following news release dated 18 May 1998: "EMBRAER receives up to 3.8 per cent equalization interest rate support from the Brazilian government to help offset high domestic interest rates carried for financing Brazilian exports to foreign buyers."

4.42 Canada argues that the above statement of EMBRAER, while technically correct, is also misleading in one important respect. PROEX payments to foreign

---

[34] Canada relies on *The Concise Oxford Dictionary of Current English*, J.B. Sykes, Ed. (Oxford: Clarendon Press, 1982) at 83; Nolan, Joseph R. and J. M. Nolan-Haley, *Black's Law Dictionary*, (St. Paul: West Publishing Co., 6th ed; 1990) at p158. Canada notes that the French version of the SCM Agreement notes "*si un avantage est ainsi conféré.*" "*Avantage*" translates into "advantage"; Atkins, Beryl T., et. al., *Robert Collins Dictionnaire Nouvelle Édition* (London: Collins, 1987) at p. 56.

purchasers of Brazilian civil aircraft reduce the rate of interest payable by purchasers of regional aircraft by 3.8 percentage points below the rate freely negotiated in the international market by such purchasers. These payments have nothing to do with "high domestic interest rates." Indeed, from at least as early as 1994, PROEX payments have been available where "foreign banks and credit institutions" have financed Brazilian exports.[35]

4.43 Canada maintains that, contrary to the assertions of EMBRAER and the Government of Brazil about "leveling the playing field," these payments reduce the interest rate paid by purchasers of Brazilian aircraft to (often non-Brazilian) financiers to levels considerably lower than those that may be obtained in the international financing market. Canada introduced evidence in which airlines such as Comair, Skywest and ASA have acknowledged that Brazilian export subsidies brought down their financing costs by about 1.8 to 3.5 percentage points below market-based costs of financing. PROEX payments thus generally reduce by about half the actual interest paid by such purchasers. As such, they serve as an important part of EMBRAER's success in the market. Canada referred to a number of industry reports that, according to it, supported its argument that PROEX payments conferred a benefit. One industry report dated 10 August 1998 observed that:

> "Of the regional aircraft manufacturers, EMBRAER has the distinct benefit of having the most developed financing programme, sponsored by the Brazilian government, called PROEX. The PROEX programme is underwritten by the government in Brazil to enhance trade in its aircraft and nearly 1,500 other items and products from Brazil. It promised commercial airlines savings of up to $3.5 million per aircraft. It also allows for a *subsidized interest rate* that is 3.8 percentage points less than the market rate, along with a 15-year term…As mentioned, *the primary advantage EMBRAER has over its competitors is its PROEX financing programme*." [36](emphasis in original)

4.44 Canada also adduced as evidence an investors' circular on EMBRAER issued on 26 August 1998, that noted the following:

> "Dependence on Government Financing: EMBRAER's ERJ-145's most significant orders with American Eagle (for 42 firm orders and 25 options) and Continental (for 25 firm orders and 175 options) were made possible through the use of government financing - the BNDES-Exim and PROEX programmes, designed to assist the country's exporters by extending financing for up to 15 years *at interest rates below what the*

---

35 Canada notes that Resolution 2380, which sets out the criteria governing PROEX, specifically states that, "[t]he right to interest equalization is not interrupted, excluded or transferred if the notes relating to the export credit are negotiated abroad."

36 "Regional Jets: Making Props Passe", Industry Report, Warburg Dillion Read, 10 August 1998, at 17-18.

company would obtain on its own...[W]e estimate that the bulk of the company's orders to date have been dependent ...[sic] on the Brazilian government's willingness (and ability) to finance the sales."[37] (emphasis in original)

Canada concludes by asserting that PROEX payments amount to outright grants whether received in a stream of payments or in a lump sum. There is no obligation to repay any portion of PROEX payments received. These payments reduce the cost of exported Brazilian aircraft to the purchaser, and therefore confer a "benefit" for the purpose of Article 1.1.

4.45 As noted above,[38] **Brazil** does not contest that actual PROEX payments confer a benefit within the meaning of Article 1.1(a)(2) of the SCM Agreement. Brazil adopts, however, the argument of the European Communities that a subsidy is granted within the meaning of Article 1 of the SCM Agreement by the Brazilian government at the point when it "issues or enters into a commitment to issue bonds in support of an export transaction."

4.46 Further, Brazil disputes Canada's claim that "PROEX export subsidies are made for the benefit of foreign purchasers that, for the most part, borrow funds from non-Brazilian institutions on the basis of their own credit risk."[39] Brazil noted, in response to a question from the Panel, that there were only four transactions involving the EMB-120 entered into since 1 January 1995 and that in each the lender was inside of Brazil; in none of the transactions was the lender outside Brazil. Of the 11 transactions involving the ERJ-145, seven involved lenders inside of Brazil, while only four involved lenders outside Brazil.[40]

4.47 Brazil also submitted that Brazil risk has a dramatic and severe impact on all financial terms and transactions involving Brazil, including export credit terms.[41] Brazil accepts that when the lender is outside of Brazil that Brazil risk does not apply to that lender, but argues that Brazil risk continues to apply to Brazilian exporters as well as Brazilian financial institutions when the lender is outside of Brazil and is reflected in their higher costs.[42] Brazil submitted that EMBRAER itself bears Brazil risk and that the costs it incurs in obtaining credits for its customers outside of Brazil, from lenders outside of Brazil, reflect Brazil risk.[43]

4.48 Finally, Brazil disputes Canada's reference that Brazilian subsidies brought down the financing costs of specific airlines below market-based costs

[37] Bear Stearns *Buy Recommendation* for Empresa Brazileira deAeronáutica S.A. EMBRAER, 26 August 1998 at 7. *See* Canadian Documentary Annex tab 32.

[38] *See* para. 4.20 of this report.

[39] Brazil's Second Written Submission, para. 49.

[40] *Ibid.* at paras. 49 - 56.

[41] *See* paras. 4.94 - 4.101 of this report.

[42] *See* para. 4.81 of this report.

[43] Brazil's Second Written Submission, para. 53; *see* Section 2.2.

of financing. Brazil stated that it does not make PROEX payments to airlines. PROEX interest equalization payments are made only to financial institutions.[44] Brazil noted that PROEX was preceded by FINEX, which was ended in 1991. FINEX involved what was essentially an open-ended commitment from the Government of Brazil to equalize the spread for Brazil risk. The Brazilian government determined that FINEX, which incurred bad debts totalling over US$3.5 billion by 1991, was too expensive, and decided in 1991 to replace FINEX with PROEX, the terms of which are more limited. Existing FINEX commitments were honoured after the programme's termination.[45] Regarding the transaction involving Sky West, Brazil states it has no first-hand information concerning the statements made by this airline concerning direct payment of subsidies to it from Brazil. If Sky West in fact is receiving such payments, Brazil presumes they are from transactions involving FINEX. In any event, Brazil makes no PROEX payments to airlines themselves.[46] Brazil does not acknowledge that any sales of Brazilian manufactured regional aircraft supported by PROEX interest rate equalization were "made at an interest rate below that of the CIRR rate (taking into account interest rate equalization)."

4. *Whether PROEX Payments are Contingent upon Export Performance*

4.49 **Canada** argues that a subsidy is "contingent ... upon export performance" when it is conditional on or tied to exports; that is, where it is available only on condition that goods are exported. Since PROEX subsidies are paid only on the exportation of products from Brazil, they are "contingent on export performance" within the meaning of Article 3.1(a) of the SCM Agreement.

4.50 Canada maintains that regulations supporting PROEX make it clear that it is contingent upon the exports of goods or services. The Provisional Measure continuing the operation of PROEX does so only with respect to "operations to finance the export of domestic goods or services." Under Article 6 of Monetary Council Resolution No. 2380/97, national treasury bonds for the payment of PROEX subsidies will be issued "only after the financing party or its legal representative declares to the Banco do Brasil that … the goods have been shipped." According to Article 5(2) of Order 33/97, which identifies the goods eligible for PROEX subsidies, "[g]oods shall be eligible for interest equalization only if their [Registration of Export form] has been completed." Indeed, Brazil noted in its official response to questions posed by Canada and other WTO Members at

44 Brazil's Second Written Submission, paras. 49-56.

45 *Ibid.*

46 *See* para. 4.110.

the Committee on Subsidies and Countervailing Measures that, "[PROEX] provides financing for Brazilian exports and not for sales in the domestic market."[47]

4.51 **Brazil** does not contest that PROEX payments are contingent upon export performance. It, however, contends that they are not prohibited as claimed by Canada.

C. Whether PROEX Payments are Permitted Subsidies under Item (k) of the Illustrative List of Export Subsidies

4.52 **Brazil** argues that although the promise of PROEX payments is a subsidy that is contingent upon export performance, it is not prohibited by virtue of item (k) of the Illustrative List of Export Subsidies, which includes within the definition of prohibited subsidies "the payment by [governments] of all or part of the costs incurred by exporters or financial institutions in obtaining credits, in so far as they are used to secure a material advantage in the field of export credit terms." Brazil asserts that the "converse of this statement is that such payments are *permitted* in so far as they are not used to secure a material advantage in the field of export credit terms" (italics in original). Brazil submits that since PROEX payments are not used to secure a material advantage in the field of export credit terms, they are permitted by the Illustrative List of Export Subsidies. Brazil submits that even if it were determined that PROEX is used to secure an advantage in the field of export credits, that alone would not be enough to determine that PROEX is prohibited. It would also be necessary to determine that the advantage is *material*.[48] **Canada** disagrees with Brazil on its interpretation of item (k) of the Illustrative List of Export Subsidies. It submits that the approach adopted by Brazil is not permissible under the SCM Agreement and that, in any event, PROEX payments are used to secure a material advantage in the field of export credit terms. As such, they are not permitted under item (k) of the Illustrative List, even if it were applicable in this instance.

1. Whether Item (k) of the Illustrative List of Export Subsidies May Be Used a Contrario

4.53 **Brazil** argues that the interpretation advanced by it is in accordance with Article 31 of the Vienna Convention on the Law of Treaties, which provides that a treaty "shall be interpreted in good faith in accordance with the ordinary meaning to be given to the terms of the treaty in their context and in the light of its object and purpose." Brazil submits that the ordinary meaning of the words "in so far as they are used to secure a material advantage in the field of export credit terms" make clear that when governments grant credits below the cost of

47 *See* WTO Document G/SCM/Q2/BRA/8, 25 August 1998, at p. 3.
48 Brazil's First Oral Statement, para. 47.

funds or when they pay part or all of the costs incurred by financial institutions or exporters in obtaining funds, in so far as these activities are used to secure a material advantage, they are prohibited. A necessary corollary is that when these activities are not so used, they are not prohibited.

4.54 In response to a question from the Panel, Brazil stated that the "material advantage" clause of item (k) constituted an affirmative defence and that it was up to the party seeking to rely on it to demonstrate that its measures are not being used to secure a material advantage in the field of export credit terms. Brazil argues that since PROEX payments are not used to secure a material advantage in the field of export credit terms, it has discharged this burden.

4.55 **Canada** argues that Brazil's characterization of the first paragraph of item (k) as an exception is incorrect. It contends that contrary to the specific direction of the DSU, as amplified and repeated in WTO jurisprudence by the Appellate Body, Brazil does not "follow all of the steps of applying the 'customary rules of interpretation of public international law.'" Canada submits the basic rule is that "[a] treaty interpreter must begin with, and focus upon, the text of the particular provision to be interpreted." [49] Canada submits that the applicable provisions are footnote 5 and item (k). Footnote 5 provides that "[m]easures referred to in Annex I as not constituting export subsidies shall not be prohibited under this or any other provision of this Agreement." Canada argues that Brazil does not articulate the legal basis for its interpretation of the first paragraph of item (k) as providing an exception within the meaning of footnote 5. Brazil simply quotes the first paragraph of item (k) of Annex I and casually notes the a contrario implication that a measure that does not fit squarely within the terms of item (k) is therefore not prohibited. Its legal analysis fails, however, to consider footnote 5.

4.56 Canada asserts that the ordinary meaning of the phrase "measures referred to" in footnote 5 does not encompass an a contrario inference, as Brazil seems to argue. Brazil's interpretation is inconsistent with the direct references in Annex I to measures "not constituting export subsidies."

4.57 Canada argues that there are four exceptions that fit within the meaning of footnote 5. First, the last paragraph of footnote 59 states, in respect of item (e), that "Paragraph (e) is not intended to limit a Member from taking measures to avoid the double taxation of foreign sourced income earned by its enterprises or the enterprises of another Member." This language ("is not intended to limit ...") is similar in structure to GATT Article XX ("nothing in this Agreement shall be construed to prevent the adoption ... of measures ..."). Accordingly, the last paragraph of item (e) provides that the identified measures are not export subsidies and are, therefore, not prohibited under Article 3. The second excep-

[49] *United States - Import Prohibition of Certain Shrimp and Shrimps products*, WT/DS58/AB/R, para. 114, report of the Appellate Body adopted on 6 November 1998.

tion is to be found in item (h) of the Illustrative List, which states "provided, however, that prior-stage cumulative indirect taxes may be exempted, remitted or deferred on exported products even when not exempted, remitted or deferred on like products when sold for domestic consumption, if the prior-stage cumulative indirect taxes are levied on inputs that are consumed in the production of the exported product (making normal allowance for waste)." Canada submits that the second subordinate clause of item (h) carves out an *exception* from the scope of the opening clause of item (h) and that it is this type of exception which is contemplated by footnote 5. The third exception, according to Canada, is to be found in the second subordinate clause of the first sentence of item (i), which contains similar language ("provided, however ...") used in item (h). Canada further submits that the fourth and last exception in the Illustrative List is to be found in the second paragraph of item (k) and not in the last paragraph as contended by Brazil.

4.58 Canada submits that a measure that meets the criteria of item (k) is *ipso facto* an export subsidy and therefore prohibited. In respect of such a measure, it is not necessary for a complainant to establish that the export credit in question is a "subsidy" within the meaning of Article 1, or that it is "contingent on export performance." Rather, a complainant may simply demonstrate that a government export credit is granted below its cost of funds so as to "secure a material advantage in the field of export credits"; such an export credit would be prohibited. It does not follow, however, that where a measure does not fit squarely within the first paragraph of item (k), it is, by virtue of that fact alone, not prohibited.

4.59 Canada argues that if the Brazilian argument were accepted, it would turn the Illustrative List into an exhaustive list of export subsidies, as a subsidy which does not meet the exact criteria of an item in Annex I would not be prohibited. Such an outcome would not accord with the ordinary meaning of the terms of the Illustrative List, is not supported by the negotiating history of the Illustrative List, and would lead to a manifestly absurd or unreasonable result.

4.60 Canada submits that Annex I, by its very terms, is an illustrative list of export subsidies. Nothing in Article 3 indicates that the Illustrative List is exhaustive of the universe of export subsidies. Indeed, the use of the word "including" in Article 3 clearly indicates that there are measures or activities other than those listed in the Illustrative List that could be caught by that Article; that is, there could be subsidies that do not meet the exact definitions set out in Annex I that would, nevertheless, be prohibited under Article 3.

4.61 Canada argues that the negotiating history of the Illustrative List confirms its view. The origins of the Illustrative List can be found in a proposal submitted by the Government of France to the Working Party established to bring into force the provisions of Article XVI:4 of the GATT 1947.[50] Canada submits that the Working Party considered and adopted a list of measures that were generally to be considered as subsidies in the sense of Article XVI:4. It agreed, however, that "this list should not be considered exhaustive or to limit in any way the generality of the provisions of paragraph 4 of Article XVI."[51] Canada argues that for the purposes of Article XVI:4, if a practice fell within the examples set out in the Illustrative List, it would be considered an export subsidy. If it did not, however, it did not mean that it was not an export subsidy; rather, an independent analysis under Article XVI or, subsequently, under the Tokyo Round Subsidies Code had to be undertaken to determine whether the practice was an export subsidy.

4.62 Canada contends that the first paragraph of item (k) is no different. According to this paragraph, the payment by a government "of all or part of the costs incurred by exporters or financial institutions in obtaining credits" is clearly prohibited by Article 3 where the payment is "used to secure a material advantage in the field of export credit terms." If, however, such payment does not fit item (k) squarely - if Brazil can show that no "material advantage" was bestowed - a complaining party can still establish that the payment is a subsidy, that it is contingent on export performance, and that it is therefore prohibited under Article 3.

4.63 Canada insists that Brazil's approach, if it were to hold, would produce a manifestly absurd result. The absurdity of the Brazilian argument is highlighted by the following example: item (a) provides that "[t]he provision by governments of direct subsidies to a firm or an industry contingent upon export performance [shall be prohibited]." If Brazil's interpretation prevails, the a contrario operation of item (a) would exclude indirect export subsidies, subsidies provided through non-governmental agents, and subsidies granted to natural persons from the scope of Article 3. That is to say, Annex I would contradict, implicitly and explicitly, the very terms of Article 3.

4.64 **Brazil** considers that the interpretation of item (k) advanced by Canada and the European Communities would render the words of item (k) meaningless and conflict with the view expressed by the Appellate Body in the *Gasoline* case: "One of the corollaries of the 'general rule of interpretation' in the *Vienna Convention* is that interpretation must give meaning and effect to all the terms of a treaty. An interpreter is not free to adopt a reading that would result in reducing whole clauses or paragraphs to redundancy or inutility."[52] A reading that did not accept these words of limitation in their ordinary meaning would reduce

[50] *Report of the Working Party on Subsidies*, Contracting Parties, Seventeenth Session, November 1960, L/1381 at pp. 4-7.
[51] *Ibid.*
[52] *United States - Standards for Reformulated and Conventional Gasoline*, WT/DS2/AB/R, DSR 1996:I, 3, at 21, report of the Appellate Body adopted 20 May 1996.

them to total inutility. The interpretation of Canada and the European Communities ignores the ordinary meaning of the words and is "the equivalent of eliminating the clause entirely and placing a full stop after the word "credits" in the next to last line of the first paragraph of item (k)." Such an interpretation, in its view, is contrary to the customary rules of interpretation of public international law as enunciated by the Appellate Body in the *United States - Gasoline* case.

4.65 Brazil submits that the "material advantage" clause of item (k) does not mean that *any* measure that does not confer a material advantage would not be prohibited. It means only that measures that otherwise would be prohibited by item (k) would not be prohibited. Specifically, the first paragraph of item (k) refers to two practices and two practices only: first, it refers to the grant by governments of export credits at rates below those which they actually have to pay for funds, and second, it refers to the payment by governments of all or part of the costs incurred by exporters or financial institutions in obtaining credits. Both of these practices are prohibited by the first sentence of item (k) "in so far as *they* are used to secure a material advantage in the field of export credit terms." In other words, the "material advantage" clause of item (k) refers to and limits only the two practices specified earlier in the same paragraph. Brazil argues that the "material advantage" clause does not "exempt from the prohibition of Article 3 any and all practices of whatever kind that happen not to confer a material advantage." It submits that Canada's view that it is only the second paragraph (the OECD safe-haven clause) which provides an exception to the prohibition of the first paragraph is implausible, as such a reading of the item completely ignores the specific treaty language that is the "material advantage" clause. Canada's interpretation of the item would be no different if a full stop, or a period, appeared after the word "credits" in the second to last line of item (k), with all of the remaining words deleted. As a result, Brazil argues that Canada's interpretation is not consistent with the customary rules of interpretation of public international law, as codified in the *Vienna Convention on the Law of Treaties*, is not consistent with the holding of the Appellate Body in the *Gasoline* case and other cases, and does violence to the bargain reached between developed and developing countries in the Uruguay Round.[53]

4.66 Brazil argues that the "safe haven" of the second paragraph of item (k) does not negate or derogate from the plain meaning of the text of the first paragraph. The ordinary meaning of the text of the second paragraph is that a Member may engage in one of the activities specified in the first paragraph, even if in doing so it gains a material advantage, provided it is in conformity with the OECD Guidelines referred to in the second paragraph. In essence, there are three tiers to item (k). The first tier specifies the practices that constitute prohibited export subsidies. The second tier adds the "material advantage" clause, the ordi-

[53] Brazil's Second Oral Statement, paras. 51-53.

nary meaning of which is that it qualifies the prohibition of the first tier. The third tier is the second paragraph which adds another limitation on the first two tiers, by providing that a practice in conformity with the relevant provisions of the OECD Guidelines shall be permitted regardless of whether it is used to confer a material advantage.

4.67 Brazil submits that to the extent that the "material advantage" clause defines an area of government activity and provides that it is permitted, it does indeed derogate from Article 3.1(a). There is nothing alarming about this. Footnote 5 provides that, "[m]easures referred to in Annex I as not constituting export subsidies shall not be prohibited under this or any other provision of this Agreement." The "material advantage" clause is one of those measures. There are others. For example, item (i) specifies that the remission or drawback of import charges will constitute an export subsidy prohibited by Article 3.1(a) if it is "in excess of those levied on imported inputs that are consumed in the production of the exported product." The converse of necessity is true: the remission or drawback of import charges *not* in excess of those levied on imported inputs that are consumed in the production of the exported product is not prohibited. No other reading of the text of the "in excess" clause of item (i) makes sense.

4.68 Addressing the argument of Canada that its interpretation of item (k) would turn the illustrative list of export subsidies into an exhaustive list and produce absurdities such as the one claimed in paragraph 4.47 above, Brazil argues that Canada is mistaken and has misconstrued its interpretation of item (k). Brazil submits that the limiting language in item (a), which is the counterpart to the "material advantage" language of item (k) is not "direct." It is "contingent upon export performance." The "provision by governments of direct subsidies to a firm or an industry" is a subsidy, but it is not prohibited subsidy *unless* it is "contingent upon export performance" (italics in original).[54]

4.69 Brazil also referred to the duty drawback provisions of item (i) of Annex I. Brazil argues that item (i), as Canada has noted, contains a "provided, however" clause which defines activity that is not an export subsidy. However, item (i) has more. In its very first sentence it defines the prohibited drawback payments as those "*in excess* of those levied on imported products that are consumed in the production of the exported product." Drawback payments *not* in excess of those levied on imported products consumed in the production of an exported product are *not* prohibited.[55]

4.70 Brazil also argues that item (h), as Canada notes, also contains a "provided, however" clause, but it too contains more in its first sentence. This sentence specifies that the exemption, remission or deferral of prior-stage cumulative indirect taxes on exported products that are "in excess of the exemption,

[54] Brazil's Second Oral Statement, paras. 42-44.

[55] Brazil's Second Oral Statement, at paras. 47-49 and 54-56.

remission or deferral of like prior-stage cumulative indirect taxes" sold for domestic consumption constitutes a prohibited subsidy. Brazil submits that the only logical reading of this language is that exemption, remission or deferral for exports that is *not* in excess of those imposed for domestic consumption is *not* prohibited.[56] (emphasis in original)

4.71 Brazil submits that the "material advantage" clause of the first paragraph of item (k) serves the same function as these provisions and that it defines and limits the prior portion of the sentence.[57]

2. *Whether PROEX Payments are Payments within the Meaning of Item (k) of the Illustrative List*

4.72 **Canada** submits that although PROEX subsidies are related to export credits, they do not constitute a "payment" by [governments] of all or part of the costs incurred by exporters or financial institutions in obtaining credits" within the meaning of the second clause of the first paragraph of item (k), given their nature as periodic cash grants to the purchasers of civil aircraft.

4.73 Canada submits that its interpretation of the first paragraph of item (k) is as follows. The first part of item (k) refers to a situation where a government lends funds at an interest rate that is below the rate it would pay for raising such funds. The phrase "the costs incurred … in obtaining credits" in the second part of item (k) refers to a similar situation, but with private financing. That is, where an exporter or a financial institution obtains credits at rates higher than the rates at which it would lend to a purchaser and incurs a cost as a result, and a government pays for all or part of this difference.

4.74 Canada submits that its interpretation is consistent with the response given by the Counsel for Brazil to a question from the Panel. He stated that PROEX payments were not made to cover the development costs of EMBRAER aircraft. He also stated that these export subsidies were not paid to cover EMBRAER's higher cost of funds, but rather they covered the costs incurred when EMBRAER raised the funds necessary to finance the sales of its aircraft. Canada argues that, implicit in this, is Brazil's interpretation of the phrase "payment by [governments] of all or part of the costs incurred by exporters or financial institutions in obtaining credits" in item (k): the costs incurred by - in this case - the exporter, EMBRAER, in raising funds to finance the purchase of its product.

4.75 Canada submits that PROEX subsidies have little to do with EMBRAER's cost of raising funds to provide financing. Rather, PROEX export subsidies are in practice paid when non-Brazilian purchasers finance their pur-

56 Brazil's Second Oral Statement, at paras. 47-49 and 54-56.

57 *Ibid.*

chases through non-Brazilian lenders. Canada gives the example of Mesa Airlines, an American regional airline and a purchaser of EMBRAER aircraft.[58] Mesa financed its purchase through CoreStates Bank, a US bank. EMBRAER did not provide the financing in that transaction, but the transaction received PROEX support. The PROEX subsidy in that case was, therefore, not a "payment" of the costs incurred by the exporter, EMBRAER within the meaning of item (k) of the Illustrative List. PROEX export subsidies are not payments to cover the costs incurred by exporters or Brazilian financial institutions in raising funds used for financing purchases. They are simply cash grants made for the benefit of purchasers of Brazilian exported products. They do not, therefore, fall within the first paragraph of item (k).

4.76 **Brazil** submits that PROEX export subsidies constitute a payment by the Government of Brazil of all or part of the costs incurred by EMBRAER or financial institutions in obtaining credits within the meaning of item (k) of the Illustrative List. With respect to Canada's argument that PROEX payments do not relate to costs incurred by *Brazilian* financial institutions in obtaining credits, Brazil argues that the relevant language of item (k) refers to "financial institutions," not to "Brazilian financial institutions" or financial institutions of any nationality. At any rate, contrary to the assertions of Canada, in most of the transactions concluded by EMBRAER, "the lender was a Brazilian lender inside Brazil, not a financial institution outside Brazil."

4.77 With respect to Canada's argument that PROEX subsidies has little to do with *EMBRAER's* cost of raising funds, and in response to a question from the Panel,[59] Brazil stated that it is undisputed that in international transactions involving the sale of aircraft, it is the exporter who has to provide or arrange for financing. The financial package offered by the exporter is second only to the characteristics of the aircraft in making the sale. Brazil asserts that the Canadian manufacturer of regional civil aircraft, Bombardier, has, or is in the process of establishing its own subsidiary that will provide or arrange for financing to its

---

[58] Canada also gives the examples of three other airlines, namely Comair, Skywest and Trans State Airlines. In the case of the first two airlines, Canada argues that PROEX payments "simply reduced the rate of interest paid, to one significantly below that prevailing in the international market. Canada claims that PROEX export subsidies were not, in those cases, "payments" made to defray "costs incurred" by the exporter, EMBRAER, within the meaning of item (k)." In the case of the last transaction, a term issued by the financing bank, Bank of America, Canada claims that "offered to arrange the payment of PROEX export subsidies, either in lump sum or in instalments over the life of the proposed financing. The offer of payment of the PROEX subsidies was not conditional on EMBRAER providing the financing. Nor was it conditional on a Brazilian financial institution providing the financing."

[59] The question from the Panel was as follows: "Please explain fully your view that PROEX payments are payments of 'costs incurred by exporters or financial institutions in obtaining credits': In what sense does EMBRAER or a financial institution, whether Brazilian or other, "obtain" credits? Could it not rather be said in this case that financial institutions 'provide' credits which are 'obtained' by the purchaser?"

customers. EMBRAER does not have such a subsidiary, but is not relieved from the necessity of putting together a financing package for its customers that is competitive with what Bombardier offers. In doing so, it incurs costs, such as those documented by Dr. Finan with regard to the Continental Express transaction. In this situation, EMBRAER may be viewed as "obtaining" funds with which to provide a financial package, or "obtaining" an acceptable package from other sources for the benefit of its customers.[60]

4.78 In its response to a question from the Panel whether there was a difference between the "cost of credit" and "the cost of obtaining credits,"[61] Brazil stated that in the context of item (k), there is no meaningful distinction between the cost of credit and the cost of obtaining credit. To "obtain," according to Webster's Third International Dictionary, is "to gain or attain possession." A synonym is "get." When one "gets" a loan one "obtains" it. That the cost of this action may be spread out over the life of the loan does not change the fact that it is a cost of obtaining the loan in the first instance. The "risk spread" added to the basic interest rate is certainly a cost to "obtain" the credit. This cost varies from borrower to borrower depending on their respective creditworthiness. The "cost of credit" is the basic cost charged for borrowers with the best credit ratings. A Brazilian company or financial institution carries the "risk spread" of Brazil on top of its own credit rating. This is a cost to "obtain" the credit, which would not be granted unless the borrower agreed to pay for it, on top of the basic "cost of credit," over the life of the loan. Other borrowers with better credit ratings - or that do not carry a high country "risk spread" - would not have to pay for these costs. Therefore the "risk spread" could not be interpreted as part of the "cost of credit," since it is applied in a differentiated manner.

3. *Whether PROEX Payments are Used to Secure a Material Advantage in the Field of Export Credit Terms*

4.79 **Brazil** contends that although PROEX payments confer a benefit within the meaning of Article 1 of the SCM Agreement, "they are not used to secure a material advantage in the field of export credit terms." Brazil notes that the term "material advantage" is not defined in the Agreement, and argues that the words should be given their ordinary meaning. Brazil relies on the Webster's Third New International Dictionary of the English Language, which defines "material" as "being of real importance or great consequence." "Advantage" is defined as "a more favorable or improved condition." Thus, any more favourable or improved condition secured by the Brazilian aircraft exporter or financial institu-

60 "Brazil Risk" is explained in detail in paras. 4.94 - 4.101.

61 The question from the panel was phrased as follows: "In what sense can interest rate payments be seen as costs of 'obtaining' credits as opposed to costs of carrying them? Is there a distinction between the 'cost of credit' and the 'cost of *obtaining* credits'?"

tions as a result of PROEX must be of real importance or of great consequence, before they would be prohibited under the SCM Agreement.

4.80 Brazil argues that the concept of material advantage includes comparison - advantage *vis-à-vis* someone or something. Two points of comparison are relevant to the determination in this dispute of whether PROEX is used by Brazil to secure a material advantage in the field of export credit terms: (i) Brazil risk and (ii) Canada's subsidies to Bombardier. On either measure alone, PROEX provides no material advantage. To demonstrate that PROEX subsidies do not secure a material advantage "in the field of export credit terms", Brazil introduced as evidence a report prepared by Dr. Finan ("Finan Report").

(a) Summary of the Evidence Presented by Dr. Finan

4.81 The Finan Report states that this dispute involves a unique set of facts and circumstances that must be acknowledged in order to correctly evaluate material advantage in the field of export credits, particularly as it relates to regional aircraft exports.[62] First, the dispute is between a developed country and a developing country both of which maintain export subsidy programmes that benefit regional aircraft exports. Second, the dispute concerns the export of capital goods, which have a different set of financing requirements relative to non-capital goods or agricultural products. Financing is of a longer term (15 years or longer) and is based on "buyer credits." Third, the dispute concerns the only two manufacturers of 50-seat regional jet aircraft in the world. Bombardier was the first to manufacturer this type of aircraft. Canada defined the terms for export credits that Brazil was required to match. It concludes that Brazil cannot match Canada's terms in kind.[63]

4.82 The Finan Report identifies the major elements of export credit terms as (1) the export price of the aircraft, (2) the term of financing, and (3) interest rates, including factors that determine the interest rate.

4.83 In evaluating material advantage, the Finan Report evaluated two types of Canadian subsidies, direct and indirect, that benefited Canada's export credit terms.[64] The Finan Report assesses whether there is a material advantage given to Brazil through the export credits of the PROEX programme. To do so, the Finan Report compares PROEX benefits to the aircraft buyer with the benefits provided to the aircraft buyer by all of Canada's subsidy programmes that directly or indirectly affect export credit terms.[65]

---

62 Finan Report, pp. 1.1 - 1.3.
63 *Ibid.* at p. 3.20.
64 *Ibid.* at p. 1.8.
65 Finan Report, at pp. 1.8 - 1.9.

4.84 The Finan Report submits that evaluating material advantage requires evaluating one country's set of export credit terms relative to another country's set of export credit terms by applying a consistent methodology appropriate under the facts and circumstances. The Finan Report further states that determining the present value of total subsidy benefits is the most reliable way to determine material advantage in this dispute, with the present value of PROEX benefits compared to the reduction in the present value of financing costs resulting from all of Canada's export supports.[66] The Finan Report argues that Bombardier, its suppliers, and its customers have been and are subsidized by the Government of Canada and the Provinces of Ontario and Québec through a variety of programmes; Bombardier was the first to enter the regional jet market, and therefore Canada was able to define any and all export credit terms. The Finan Report claims that Brazil was forced to match Canada's terms in order to be competitive; and many regional aircraft buyers have weak credit ratings, and thus rely heavily on the export credit packages offered by official export credit agencies.[67] The Finan Report submits that, because of Brazil's weak credit rating and sovereign risk element, Brazil is unable to match Canada's export credit terms in kind.[68]

4.85 The second part of the Finan Report discusses the PROEX programme, evaluates why it is necessary in Brazil's situation, and details Brazil risk. The Finan Report concludes that a Brazilian commercial entity cannot avoid bearing the additional cost of Brazil sovereign risk when it raises financial capital or finances a purchase or a sale.[69]

4.86 The third part of the Finan Report evaluates the effect of PROEX on the Brazilian regional aircraft market and concludes that PROEX does not provide Brazil with a material advantage in the field of export credit terms for exports of regional aircraft. Based on data provided by EMBRAER, the Brazilian aircraft manufacturer, the Finan Report details the firm orders for all manufacturers of the 50-seat regional jet, both before and after PROEX came into effect (there are only two manufacturers of the 50-seat regional jet: Bombardier of Canada and EMBRAER of Brazil). The Finan Report concludes that even after PROEX began to be applied to exports of regional aircraft, Bombardier's CRJ still captured 57 per cent of the firm orders.[70]

4.87 The Finan Report also attempted to quantify the Canadian export subsidies received by Bombardier or its suppliers, although it notes at page 3.23 that benefits presented in the report "constitute only a sample, or subset, of the total benefits conveyed to Bombardier by the Government of Canada and the provin-

66 Finan Report, at pp. 1.9 - 1.17.

67 *Ibid.* at p. 1.11.

68 *Ibid.* at p. 1.13.

69 *Ibid.* at pp. 2.1 - 2.4.

70 *Ibid.* at pp. 3.1 - 3.2; the table is found at p. 3.2.

cial governments of Ontario and Québec" because of a lack of transparency in Canada's programmes.[71] According to the Finan Report, Canada's total direct and indirect benefits provided to Bombardier ranged between US$1,883 thousand to US$2,446 thousand.

4.88 The Finan Report states that based on the Canadian supports, the total present value for reduced financing costs per CRJ (Bombardier's 50 seat jet aircraft) to be delivered in 1998 ranges from US$4.4 million to US$6.0 million. Again, Brazil argues these figures are only a subset of the actual figures, which may be much higher.[72] Hence, the Finan Report concluded that EMBRAER through the PROEX programme did not achieve a material advantage in export credit terms relative to Bombardier.[73]

4.89 The Finan Report provided six appendices to support its presentation, consisting of market return benchmarks, Bombardier regional aircraft deliveries, EMBRAER's cost of capital analysis, EMBRAER-Brazil specific risk, calculation of present value of Canadian subsidies, and a description of the method applied to determine material advantage.

4.90 **Brazil** argues that given the language of the SCM Agreement, together with the unique set of facts and circumstances surrounding this dispute, there are three methods of determining that PROEX provides no material advantage: (1) if the lender is situated in Brazil, because there is Brazil risk in the cost of funds for Brazilian lending institutions; (2) if the lender is outside Brazil, because EMBRAER bears increased costs associated with obtaining financing for its exports due to Brazil risk; and (3) independent of the location of the lender, i.e., even if the lender is outside Brazil, Canada's subsidies to Bombardier are greater than the assistance provided by PROEX.[74]

4.91 Relying on Dr. Finan's presentation at the Second Panel Meeting, Brazil states that there are four categories of transactions involving EMBRAER aircraft purchases: (1) purchaser is located inside Brazil and financed by a Brazilian bank; (2) purchaser is located inside Brazil and financed by a non-Brazilian bank; (3) purchaser is located outside Brazil and financed by a Brazilian bank; and (4) purchaser is located outside Brazil and financed by a non-Brazil based financing source.[75] Brazil argues that all deals financed by a bank in Brazil contain Brazil risk (i.e., situations 1 and 3).[76] Brazil also argued that there are no purchasers inside Brazil financed by a non-Brazilian bank that benefit from

[71] Finan Report, at p. 3.9.
[72] *Ibid.* at p. 3.23.
[73] *Ibid.* at pp. 3.22, 3.25; the table is found at p. 3.25 of the Finan Report.
[74] Oral Presentation of Dr. William F. Finan at Second Panel Meeting, p. 3.
[75] Oral Presentation of Dr. William F. Finan at Second Panel Meeting (Graphic Presented to the Panel).
[76] Brazil's Response to Questions From the Panel, No. 12.

PROEX (i.e., situation 2).[77] Brazil also argues that deals outside of Brazil contain Brazil risk (i.e., situation 4).[78] Brazil contends the first two categories of transactions are not at issue in this dispute (i.e., situations 1 and 2). According to Brazil, with respect to the latter two categories of transactions (i.e. situations 3 and 4), deals financed by a bank in Brazil and deals financed outside Brazil both contain Brazil risk-related costs. In such deals, the Brazil risk-related costs are an amount greater than PROEX's assistance. According to Brazil, when compared to the subsidies given to Bombardier, clearly PROEX also provides no material advantage. [79] Therefore, when the two are considered together, it is clear that it is Canada's programmes, not Brazil's, that secure a material advantage in the field of export credit terms.

4.92 **Canada** submits that PROEX payments are used to secure a material advantage in the field of export credit terms. In Canada's view, a material advantage is "secured when a government provides export credit at rates that are lower than those prevailing in the international financing market. A material advantage is secured, in addition, when payments by governments to exporters or financial institutions result in interest rates that are lower than those prevailing in the international market." Canada submits in that connection that the relevant rates to be considered in the international market are the London Inter Bank Offer Rate (LIBOR) or the United States (US) Treasuries rate plus a spread that reflects the credit risk of the transaction.[80]

4.93 Canada confirms its view that the appropriate benchmark is either LIBOR or US Treasury rates in its response to the following question from the Panel: "Should material advantage be assessed by reference to (a) whether the export

77 Brazil's Response to Questions From the Panel, No. 12.

78 *Ibid.*; Dr. Finan's Oral Statement at the Second Meeting of the Panel (statement contains confidential business information).

79 *Supra* note 77.

80 In a floating rate transaction, the lender sets an interest rate that will be moved up or down in relation to general movements in interest rates in the wider economy. In the floating-rate aircraft financing transactions, the benchmark used (to reflect the "general movements in interest rates") is the three-month or the six-month LIBOR. LIBOR is the rate of interest at which banks offer to lend money to one another in the "wholesale" money markets in the City of London. Although LIBOR figures are available for the major currencies, the US dollar tends to be the currency of choice in international financing activities related to aircraft. They tend to quote interest rates they would charge as "basis points (or bps) above LIBOR." These "basis points above LIBOR" are what is known as the "spread" charged by a lender - the additional charge that reflects the credit risk of the transaction. This credit risk is based on the credit quality of the borrower and incorporates other criteria determined by the lender to be relevant to the transaction, such as the value of any asset being financed, any security interests in the assets of the borrower, or any third-party guarantees. If three-month LIBOR were (for example) six per cent, a bank may choose to lend to a purchaser at (for example) seven and a quarter per cent, or 125 basis points (bps) above three-month LIBOR. In fixed-rate transactions, the borrower's interest payments are set at the outset of the transaction and are not subject to variation in the underlying interest rate. In aircraft financing transactions (which are mostly US dollar-denominated) the benchmark used is US Treasury.

credit terms with respect to a given transaction are improved by virtue of the government payment or (b) whether the export credit terms available to a purchaser for a given transaction benefiting from a payment are better than the terms that would have been available to that purchaser with respect to transactions involving competing products?":

> "[N]either (a) nor (b) is appropriate for assessing material advantage. With respect to (a), "the government payment" in question could be applied in combination with an officially supported export credit. In this sense, the question would not be whether any export credit terms for a given transaction have been improved, but whether the final export credit terms are in line with terms and conditions available in the international financing market. Under (b), the point of reference would continue to be the export credit terms available to a competing product in line with the international financing market and clearly not subsidized credit terms for other products. To measure export credit terms as against subsidized credit terms would be unworkable: an export credit could be found to be an export subsidy if measured against one competing product, but not so against another. It is Canada's position that material advantage should be assessed with respect to the international financing market. The international financing market is defined by the benchmarks that have been discussed by Canada (LIBOR or US Treasuries plus a spread that reflects the credit risk of transaction)."

(b) "Brazil Risk"

4.94 **Brazil** submits that in financial markets, the debt securities of all governments bear a "sovereign risk" premium. This risk premium reflects the views of participants in those markets as to the likelihood of repayment on schedule. Generally the debt securities of the United States bear no risk premium, and, as a result, the sovereign risk of the securities of other governments may be measured as the amount of additional interest markets demand for those securities compared to the securities of the United States. For developed countries, such as Canada, this premium is extremely low or non-existent. For developing countries, such as Brazil, this premium can be quite high. The risk premium is normally referred to in terms of "basis points," with 100 basis points equalling one per cent. As described in detail in the Finan Report,[81] which has been tendered in evidence by Brazil, the risk premium for securities issued by the Government of Brazil in recent years has varied between a high of 1,300 basis points in the first quarter of 1995 and a low of 400 basis points in the third quarter of 1997. However, by the third quarter of 1998, Brazilian sovereign risk rose again to over 1,000 basis points, an increase in the spread for Brazil risk of 6 percentage

[81] The credibility of the Finan Report has been contested by Canada; *see* paras. 4.122 and 4.139.

points or 600 basis points due to the Asian debt crisis and the Russian debt default and generally the volatility in the financial markets.

4.95 Brazil further notes that during the same period, Canada's spread remained virtually unchanged. The reality with which Brazil and other developing countries must live is that with globalized financial markets, when others catch a cold, they may catch pneumonia. The risk markets assign to both Brazilian and Canadian debt is reflected in the ratings they receive from financial services. According to Standard & Poor's, the rating on Brazil's foreign currency denominated debt is BB-, while the rating on Canada's is AA+. What this means in real terms is that in the third quarter of 1998 the yield on the Brazilian 10-year C-Bond was 15.75 per cent, while the yield on the Canadian 10-year bond was 5.25 per cent, or 10.5 percentage points lower. Those 10.5 percentage points represent the difference between Brazil risk and Canada risk.

4.96 Brazil submits that the "Brazil risk" has a dramatic and severe impact on all financial terms and transactions involving Brazil, including export credit terms. The adverse impact in the area of export credit terms is particularly severe in the regional aircraft industry, where market custom, established by developed countries long before Brazil became a factor, is that the manufacturer supports the financing of its aircraft. Brazil submits that one consequence of Brazil risk is that EMBRAER cannot compete in providing manufacturer's supports that match in-kind Bombardier's.[82] Brazil submits that aircraft trade is conducted in US dollars, which means that direct financing must be made available in US dollars. The OECD rate for US dollars is in the vicinity of 6 per cent. The OECD Agreement permits members to provide financing at the OECD rate for US dollars regardless of a member's cost of acquiring dollars. While item (k) of the Illustrative List essentially extends this permission to all WTO Members regardless of whether they are members of the OECD, for Brazil and other developing countries, the cost of acquiring dollars is very high because of the compensation demanded by lenders for "Brazil risk [or developing country risk]."

4.97 First, Brazil argued at the first meeting of the Panel[83] that paragraph (k) makes clear that the developed country Members of the WTO that are also Members of the Organization for Economic Cooperation and Development - the OECD - have taken care of themselves. It does so by providing that an export credit practice which is in conformity with the interest rates provisions of "an international undertaking on official export credits to which at least twelve original Members to this Agreement are parties as of 1 January 1979" shall not be considered to be a prohibited export subsidy. This is a reference to the so-called OECD Agreement or Guidelines.

82 Finan Report, p. 3.20.
83 Brazil's First Oral Statement, para. 21.

4.98 Brazil argued that developing countries did not bargain for the OECD "alternative" in the Uruguay Round. They are not members of the OECD. They have no voice in the OECD. Developing countries bargained for the temporary exemption of Article 27, and for the "material advantage" language of item (k) precisely because, when Article 27's protection expires, they needed something they could afford in view of the fact that the developed countries had their own self-designed exemption, which is presently in the second paragraph of item (k).

4.99 Brazil asserts that while it could take advantage of the OECD provisions in paragraph (k) of Annex I by borrowing US dollars for approximately 16 per cent and lending them for approximately 6 per cent, absorbing a 10 per cent loss in the process, this is hardly a viable alternative from a fiscal viewpoint. PROEX is more affordable to Brazil.[84] Brazil further submits that apart from the high cost of borrowing dollars, the OECD exemption would not have helped it to counteract the incentives provided by Canada to Bombardier, especially considering that under the OECD Guidelines, the maximum term for aircraft financing permitted to OECD members is 10 years, yet Canada established the practice in the regional aircraft industry of granting 15 year financing to Bombardier.[85] Brazil further notes that "developing countries did not bargain for the OECD "alternative" during the Uruguay Round…[T]hey bargained for the temporary exemption of Article 27, and for the "material advantage" language of item (k) precisely because, when Article 27's protection expires, they need something they could afford in view of the fact that the developed countries had their own self-designed exemption which is presently in the second paragraph of item (k)." In response to a direct question from the panel,[86] to support its position that developed country Members bargained for the "material advantage" language of item (k), Brazil submitted a July 7, 1990 proposal made during the Uruguay Round

[84] In this respect, the Panel posed the following question to the parties: "Brazil argues in its first oral statement (paras. 22-25) that developing country Members may not in practice act in accordance with the OECD Arrangement because it is too expensive for developing countries to raise dollars at a high rate of interest reflecting sovereign risk and then lend those dollars at Arrangement interest rates. The Arrangement, however, applies to "official support" whether given by means of "direct credits/financing, refinancing, *interest rate support*, guarantee or insurance" (emphasis added). In the case of interest rate support, the supporting government presumably need not either provide the principal amount itself or guarantee its repayment. Accordingly, how is Brazil's argument relevant in the context of "interest rate support"? Brazil's response was as follows: "[The] argument was made in the context of the first sentence of the first paragraph of item (k). With regard to interest rate support, Brazil would note that David J. Blair, in *Trade Negotiations in the OECD*…states at page 42: "There are a number of ways in which governments can give support to export financing. Official support may include insurance against commercial and political risk, guarantees of repayment, and insurance against cost-inflation and foreign exchange risk. Governments may also give financial support in the form of direct credits, refinancing and the *subsidisation of interest rates*…Brazil…[reiterates] that, in practice all financing with lenders inside Brazil has been done at LIBOR-plus or the CIRR rate" (emphasis in original).

[85] *See* para. 4.137.

[86] Brazil's Response to Questions From the Panel, No. 42.

by a developed country to delete the 'material advantage' language of item (k). Brazil and other developing countries opposed this initiative. The proposal was rejected and the language remained in item (k).[87]

4.100 Brazil submits that no private institution in any country can expect to borrow at rates below those made available to its government. The risk premium markets assign to private borrowers includes the sovereign risk of their governments in addition to their own enterprise-specific risk. Thus, any Brazilian exporter or financial institution attempting to obtain funds for export credits is handicapped from the start with a 10.5 per cent or 1,050 basis point risk premium compared to a Canadian counterpart, or a counterpart in other developed countries. Relying on the Finan report, Brazil asserts that to support the financing of EMBRAER aircraft, EMBRAER and Brazilian financial institutions must pay a premium of 1,000 basis points or more above what Bombardier and Canadian financial institutions must pay. PROEX offsets only 380 basis points of this premium. Brazil deduces that "[a]t current rates, approximately 670 basis points (1,050-380) [is] left for the private sector to absorb. Thus, in these circumstances, when the lender is inside Brazil, PROEX provides no material advantage and thus is not a prohibited export subsidy. Moreover, in the transactions when the lender was inside Brazil, the actual interest rate was always above LIBOR or the OECD rate in practice."

4.101 Further, according to Brazil, when the lender is a non-Brazilian financial institution outside of Brazil, it may be true that Brazil risk does not apply to that lender's cost of funds. But Brazil risk continues to apply to EMBRAER, and paragraph (k) of Annex I permits equalization payments that reflect the costs incurred by exporters such as EMBRAER as well as by financial institutions.[88] To establish how "Brazil risk" is present even in a transaction when the lender is outside of Brazil, Brazil submitted detailed, confidential business information to the Panel and its expert, Dr. Finan, gave a detailed presentation to the Panel.[89]

4.102 **Canada** challenges the accuracy of Dr. Finan's presentations[90] and submits that the argument by Brazil that PROEX subsidies are necessary to counter alleged developed country market advantages is baseless and unwarranted on the facts. Canada further submits that "even assuming that the "Brazil risk" argument is relevant, the argument must fail... If the [true] purpose of PROEX export subsidies were to reduce the "Brazil risk," they would be paid to the Brazilian lender that incurs the higher costs of borrowing, as indeed item (k) pro-

---

87 *See* para. 4.98 of this report.

88 Brazil's First Oral Statement, para. 38; Brazil's Second Written Submission, para. 52. Brazil argues that EMBRAER itself bears Brazil risk, and therefore that the costs it incurs in obtaining credits for its customers outside of Brazil, from lenders outside of Brazil, reflect Brazil risk. Brazil's Second Written Submission, para. 53. *See also* para. 4.47.

89 *See* para. 4.117.

90 *See* paras. 4.122 and 4.139.

vides. Such payments would be made to a purchaser only in the unlikely circumstance that it has borrowed at a higher interest rate than that prevailing in the international market. Any such subsidy would directly reflect and offset such risk premium."

4.103 Canada "challenges vigorously" Brazil's assertion that it does not "seriously challenge" its argument that "when the lender is inside of Brazil, PROEX provides no material advantage and thus is not a prohibited export subsidy." Canada also denies that it accepts that "when the lender was inside Brazil, the actual interest rate was always above LIBOR or the OECD rate in practice." Canada submits that when assessing material advantage, "the question is not whether the lender faces a "Brazil risk" (or any other special cost) compared to other potential lenders. Rather, it is whether as a result of the PROEX export subsidy - whatever the motivation - the borrower obtains terms that are better than those available in the international financing market." Canada further submits that "in most, if not all, instances where financing is done in Brazil, it is done through...[Brazil's National Bank for Economic and Social Development] (BNDES). And when BNDES lends money to airlines, it does so at international commercial rates. Therefore, PROEX export subsidies, when applied to financing offered by BNDES, bring down the already commercial interest rate to one that is significantly below the international market." Canada provided evidence which, it submitted, offered proof that PROEX payments reduced the interest rate levels to be paid by a number of airlines significantly below "both LIBOR plus a credit risk premium and the OECD rates."[91]

4.104 Canada submits that BNDES financing removes "Brazil risk" entirely. By doing so, it enhances the value of the PROEX export subsidy to the recipient. This is done in two steps. First, by lending at LIBOR-plus or the OECD rates, BNDES neutralizes the financing question - that is, a purchaser does not have to look around for financing in the market. Indeed, the interest rates offered by BNDES-Exim, the new name for Brazil export financing programme, are set out in its web pages. It states that interest rates on its financing are equal to LIBOR plus 1 or 2 per cent, plus a risk premium. Canada noted in particular news reports indicating that BNDES financing had been announced for two transactions worth $3.2 billion in purchases by American Airlines. The amount financed by BNDES in one of the two transactions, $2.2 billion, was over five times the total

[91] In particular, Canada noted that where Brazil has provided financing - for example, in the cases of Skywest and British Regional - the "post-equalisation" rate of interest offered by Brazil has been significantly below the OECD Consensus benchmark. Indeed, the effective interest rates offered by Brazil have been lower than the applicable yield on US Treasuries, themselves benchmarks for the OECD rate. Canada argued that the evidence it had adduced had not been contradicted or even questioned by Brazil. Further, the PROEX subsidy for aircraft is fixed at 3.8 per cent, regardless of the interest rate in the financing. To be operable in a manner consistent with the Consensus, the PROEX programme would have to provide for the adjustment of the subsidy in each transaction, so that it would compensate only for any excess in the financing rate over the OECD Consensus rate.

amount of financing by the Export Development Corporation of Canada for Canadian regional jet delivered since 1995. Canada pointed out that American Airlines was not a small regional airline that was unable to obtain financing and that needed help from BNDES. The credit rating of AMR was, indeed, better than that of Brazil.

4.105 Canada further argues that BNDES financing completely undermines Brazil's argument that the "safe haven" of paragraph two of Item (k) is "of little or no practical value to developing countries." Brazil's export credit practices under BNDES - that is, excluding PROEX export subsidies - operate on precisely the same principles as those set out in this "safe haven" that Brazil alleges is of no use or value to developing countries because of the high cost of acquiring dollars. Canada states that if BNDES and PROEX simply reduced the interest rate offered to an airline to one that is above LIBOR or OECD rates, it would not have initiated the case against Brazil. BNDES lent to prospective purchasers at these international rates after which PROEX export subsidies were granted. In effect, Canada argues, PROEX has nothing to do with "Brazil risk."

4.106 Canada further submits that the second way in which BNDES absorbs "Brazil risk" is this: "By being the lender, BNDES absorbs the Brazil risk in the PROEX bonds - that is, the risk that PROEX export subsidies would not be paid. Given the tendency of some lending institutions to discount the bonds for a lump sum because of Brazil risk, by being the lender, Brazil absorbs this risk as well. Airlines no longer have to advise their shareholders that there is a risk that subsidies would not be paid. As long as they are the ones owing money to Brazil - at subsidized rates, of course - there is no risk that the subsidies would not be paid."

4.107 Canada submits that the evidence it has adduced in this case proves that "PROEX export subsidies are made for the benefit of foreign purchasers that, for the most part, borrow funds from non-Brazilian institutions on the basis of their own credit risk." Canada submits that this fact has not been disputed by Brazil, as its largest customer, Continental Airlines, financed its initial purchase of 25 ERJ-145s from a lender outside of Brazil at rates that in no way reflected a Brazil risk premium. Canada asserts that the Brazilian argument that non-Brazilian purchasers of Brazilian goods suffer from financing costs solely on the basis of the Brazilian origin of the goods is without foundation. It "strains credulity to argue that non-Brazilian purchasers who obtain financing on their own credit, sometimes backed by guarantees offered by non-Brazilian suppliers, and often in non-Brazilian financing markets are somehow affected by a "Brazil risk"." Canada further submits that "financing offerings on the market for EMBRAER products have received ratings higher than that of Brazil's, based, as EMBRAER has noted, "not only on the liquidity of Continental Express [the purchasing airline] but also on the evaluation of EMBRAER and of the ERJ-145 aircraft." Canada also submits that a recent poll of financiers, lessors and airlines by the reputable industry journal *Airfinance Journal* noted a higher ranking for the ERJ-145 among investors than the Canadian Regional Jet. EMBRAER products were also considered to be easier to finance than those of British Aerospace and ATR, both European manufacturers of long standing." Canada also notes that EMBRAER is supported by developed country suppliers in the production and development of its aircraft.

4.108 Canada argues that contrary to Brazil's assertions, PROEX export subsidies do indeed "secure a material advantage." This fact has been acknowledged by EMBRAER and Brazilian government officials and a number of airlines, which have publicly stated that they were influenced in their decision to purchase EMBRAER aircraft because of the financial incentive provided by PROEX. One such airline, according to Canada, is the American regional airline Comair, which "noted a 2 to 2.5 percentage point difference between commercial rates it pays on its purchase of Canadair Regional Jets and subsidized interest rates paid on the purchase of Brazilian regional aircraft." Other airlines include Skywest, also another American regional airline, which has acknowledged that "the rate of interest on long-term debt subject to Brazilian export subsidies was 4.0 per cent. At the same time, the unsubsidized rate of interest points other long-term debts ranged from 6.36 to 8.5 per cent - a difference of 2.36 to 4.5 percentage points in interest rates."

4.109 **Brazil** disputes Canada's claim that "the average rate of interest paid by Skywest was only *4 per cent.*" It submits that Canada mischaracterizes the information on the record. Canada's information does not contain any evidence regarding the final financing of the Sky West sale. It contains no evidence of PROEX benefits of any kind, whether interest equalization or direct financing, having been made available. Brazil recalled that in its earlier submission and in the Finan Report, that PROEX direct financing has never been used for aircraft. In addition, Brazil referred to the full-length English translations of PROEX measures, specifically Law No. 8187, which established PROEX, and Provisional Measures 1629-13 and 1700-15, which replaced Law No. 8187, that it submitted to the Panel. For all three measures, Article 1 governs direct financing and Article 2 governs interest equalization. But Article 2 says that interest equalization is only available for operations "not included" (Law No. 8187) or "not covered" (Provisional Measures) by the direct financing scheme. As a result, Brazil argues that Article 2 of these measures precludes the possibility of both PROEX direct financing and interest equalization being made available in the same transaction. Brazil also disputes Canada's claim that Brazil provides both BNDES financing at roughly OECD rates, and then uses PROEX to bring the rate several points below both LIBOR and OECD rates. First, Brazil argues, Canada provides no evidence to support this contention, other than the statement of Sky West that "subsidy payments through the export support programme of the Federative Republic of Brazil" reduced the annual average interest rate on its long term debt to approximately 4.0 per cent. Brazil stated categorically that it does not make PROEX payments to Sky West or any other airline. Brazil argued that PROEX payments are made only to financial institutions. Brazil submitted that this does not mean that the Sky West statement necessarily is inaccurate, however; it simply means that, if accurate, it is not relevant to this dispute.[92]

4.110 Brazil recalled that PROEX was preceded by FINEX.[93] Brazil has no first-hand information concerning the statements made in the Sky West report concerning direct payment of subsidies to Sky West from Brazil. If Sky West in fact is receiving such payments, Brazil presumes they are from transactions involving FINEX.[94]

4.111 With regard to BNDES, Brazil states BNDES is a bank, which operates on normal banking principles, and is not within the terms of reference of this dispute.[95]

4.112 Brazil argues in paragraph 51 of its Second Written Submission, when the lender was inside Brazil, the actual interest rate was always above LIBOR or the OECD rate in practice.[96] According to Brazil, the term "in practice" refers to the fact that the Brazil sovereign risk premium, calculated as the spread over the US 10-year Treasury Bond, has never been fully compensated by the maximum allowable spread equalized under PROEX. Figures 2.3 and 2.4 of the Finan Report clearly demonstrate this fact, according to Brazil. Therefore, private lenders inside Brazil would not be able to fully offset their cost of capital, since they cannot obtain capital at costs lower than the Brazilian government. "In practice," Brazilian authorities supervise the relationship between the risk spread and the equalization margins provided by PROEX, to ensure that PROEX payments do not overcompensate the risk spread. Brazil argues that Canada never disputed this rationale during the proceedings of the Panel.[97]

4.113 Brazil argues that Canada's mistake is in assuming that PROEX equalization payments are made to the manufacturer or to the buyer of the aircraft, who would get subsidies on top of international commercial rates. But all payments from the PROEX equalization programme are made to the financing institution, including BNDES, so that it may offset part of the costs it incurs in obtaining the funds that will be lent at internationally competitive rates.[98] Further, Brazil does not acknowledge that any sales of EMBRAER regional aircraft supported by PROEX interest rate equalization were "made at an interest rate below that of the CIRR rate (taking into account interest rate equalization)," as Canada alleges.[99] Brazil argues that when aircraft purchasers are financed by Brazilian banks as the lender, PROEX only offsets the Brazil risk in the cost of funds for

92 Brazil's Comments on Additional Information Submitted by Canada, paras. 3-12.

93 *See* para. 4.48 of this report.

94 *Supra* note 93 at para. 14.

95 *Ibid.* at para. 16.

96 Brazil's Response to Questions From the Panel, No. 34, subpart 1.

97 *Ibid.*

98 *Ibid.*

99 Brazil's Response to Questions From the Panel, No. 34, subpart 2.

the Brazilian banks. When the aircraft is purchased under a lease structure and a non-Brazilian lender provides the debt, the relevant measure for the purpose of determining material advantage is EMBRAER's costs related to the obtaining of the credits. As illustrated by Dr. Finan's confidential business information presentation at the Second Panel meeting, these Brazil risk-related transaction costs exceed the PROEX equalization payment. Also, when the lender is outside of Brazil, totally apart from Brazil risk, Brazil argues that EMBRAER is adversely affected by the subsidies provided by Canada to its exporter (without regard to whether or not those subsidies are consistent with Canada's WTO obligations).[100]

4.114 Brazil alleges that Canada has misinterpreted its submissions regarding the purpose of PROEX and the way the programme is administered. Brazil argues that it has never claimed "market failure" as the justification for PROEX. PROEX, it submits, is justified by the objective facts of the market, as has been demonstrated in the Finan report and elaborated on during the Panel meetings. Figure 2.3 of the Finan Report depicted Brazil risk as measured by the spread between Brazilian and US bonds. In the aircraft sector itself, there is no market "failure" as such; rather, it is appropriate to allege market "fixing" by Canada. In 1996, EMBRAER brought its ERJ-145 into a market that, for the previous four years, had been the exclusive domain of Canada's Bombardier. The characteristics of this market were set by numerous Canadian measures - the benefits conferred by Canada's Export Development Corporation and the Canada Account; the development and production subsidies made by Technology Partnerships Canada and its predecessor programmes; the measures implemented by Ontario and Québec. The 15 or more year financing term was but one characteristic of this market. "Market failure" is not the term for this set of circumstances; "market rigging" is more appropriate. Brazil could not match the Canadian benefits dollar for dollar. No developing country could. PROEX was simply an effort to level somewhat the tilted playing field. Brazil notes, and it was uncontested by Canada, that Mr. Ian Gillespie, President of Canada's Export Development Corporation, told a committee of Canada's Parliament that, "The goal for Canada is to make sure that we have a competitive advantage for Canadian exporters, not just a level playing field." [101]

4.115 Brazil argues that Canada is wrong in its view that it is not the sovereign risk of Brazil that is important, but the sovereign risk of the country in which the aircraft is operated. Brazil submits that while the sovereign risk of the country of operation may be relevant to a lender, it is a totally different risk from the sovereign risk that raises the costs of funds in the country of export. Thus, while "Brazil risk" may not be applicable when the lender is outside of Brazil, it would

[100] Brazil's Response to Questions From the Panel, No. 34, subpart 2; *see* para. 4.117.
[101] Brazil's First Oral Statement, para. 41.

still continue to apply to EMBRAER. PROEX offsets part of the added cost in obtaining credits that financial institutions and exporters experience as a result of Brazil risk, not the risk of the country of operation.

4.116 Brazil submits that the Canadian argument that rates charged to foreign purchasers of Brazilian products do not reflect "Brazil risk" is wrong and misunderstands the nature of "Brazil risk" and how PROEX operates to level the playing field. It further submits that Canada misunderstood the COEX transaction, which it has referred to many times. Brazil stated that the COEX transaction was unique not only because it involved a non-Brazilian lender and a non-Brazilian customer, but also because it was the first transaction and is the largest transaction, to date. To establish how "Brazil risk" is present even in a transaction when the lender is outside of Brazil, Brazil submitted detailed, confidential business information to the Panel and its expert, Dr. Finan, gave a detailed presentation to the Panel, subject to its working procedures. The Panel and Canada had an opportunity to submit questions regarding the presentation.[102]

4.117 In his statement to the Panel during the second meeting with the Parties, Dr. Finan documented the additional costs to EMBRAER due to "Brazil risk" of obtaining credits in a transaction where both the aircraft purchaser and the financing sources were located outside Brazil. He specifically provided documentation concerning the facts and circumstances of the COEX transaction. Since the details of the transactions were business confidential, Brazil provided its information to the Panel in the following business confidential submissions: (1) "Oral Statement of Dr. William F. Finan on Behalf of Brazil," a written submission to the Panel provided at the second panel meeting; (2) "Evaluating Brazil Risk in the Continental Express Transaction," an oral submission and copies of graphics provided to the Panel at the second panel meeting; and (3) "Supplemental Submission of the Government of Brazil Response to the Panel's Request for Sources of Information for Dr. William F. Finan's Presentation 'Evaluating Brazil Risk in the Continental Express Transaction" submitted 21 December 1998. Brazil also provided business confidential information in follow-up questions from both Canada and the Panel regarding the COEX presentation.

4.118 Dr. Finan reported that on 4 July 1996, COEX entered into an agreement that covered the purchase of up to 200 ERJ-145's. The price of each aircraft, net of the PROEX benefit, is financed via a mix of equity and debt, with 20 per cent equity provided by third party providers and 80 per cent provided by debt in the form of Enhanced Equipment Trust Certificates ("EETC's"). But because EMBRAER is a developing country-based aircraft manufacturer, Brazil submits that providers of equity to the COEX leveraged lease arrangement would not

[102] The information that Brazil submitted to the Panel regarding the COEX transaction contained confidential business information, so pursuant to the Rules of Procedure which were adopted by the Panel, not all the relevant information was disclosed; *see* para. 4.117 of this report.

accept EMBRAER's guarantee of the residual value of the aircraft (an RVG), which is critical to competitively financing an aircraft. Brazil also submits that EMBRAER could not obtain equity financing on its own and that the reason for the equity holder's refusal to accept an RVG from EMBRAER was "Brazil risk".

4.119 Dr. Finan argued that EMBRAER company risk was not the reason equity holders refused to accept EMBRAER's RVG. Dr. Finan submitted that the Standard and Poor's ("S&P's") ratings of EETC's also support this conclusion. Dr. Finan noted that S&P grants the highest rated class of certificates, an A+ rating, classifying the certificates are of investment grade quality. Dr. Finan argued that although holders of EETC's bear risks that include both aircraft and manufacturer risks, the EMBRAER-related company-related risks are not considered to be sufficiently significant to preclude S&P from assigning an investment grade rating to the highest rated tranche of COEX EETC's. As a result, Dr. Finan concluded that neither EMBRAER company risk nor risk associated with EMBRAER aircraft design and operating performance is the basis for the equity providers' refusal to accept an EMBRAER RVG.

4.120 Dr. Finan concluded that because of "Brazil risk," "EMBRAER was required to enter into a complex, expensive-to-maintain financing structure that brought in a third party...These added costs were well in excess of the typical transaction costs associated with setting up and maintaining a leveraged lease financing structure for an aircraft." The "Brazil-related costs in the COEX deal [arose] from: (i) added transaction costs borne by EMBRAER in having to support an unusually complex financing structure that reduced Brazil risk exposure for the equity holders, (2) special payments to the third party to obtain the 20 per cent equity financing, and (3) a special escrow account."

4.121 Brazil further submits that, contrary to Canadian assertions, most of the transactions involved a lender inside Brazil.[103]

4.122 **Canada** contests the evidence presented by Dr. Finan in connection with the COEX transaction on three grounds. First, it argues that the cost "allegedly incurred by EMBRAER was not reflected in a higher price to COEX that was then reduced with the aid of subsidies. Rather, PROEX export subsidies provided a discount to COEX on an already discounted price...resulting in a final cost to COEX [which was substantially lower than the original contract price]." Second, Canada points out that "[T]he nature of the costs incurred by EMBRAER in arranging financing for the COEX deal do not result from "Brazil risk": they are costs that are normally incurred by manufacturers in putting together financing packages in similar situations. Finally, Canada argues that "the methodology [followed] in assessing the value of the costs allegedly incurred by EMBRAER is seriously flawed" and notes that it is not in any way clear why the

[103] *See* para. 4.46 of this report.

compensation allegedly made necessary by "Brazil risk" should not be limited to the actual expense rather than the opportunity cost.

4. *Interpretation of the Phrase "in the Field of Export Credit Terms" in Item (k)*

4.123 **Brazil** argues that PROEX subsidies do not secure a material advantage "in the field of export credit terms", because under the terms of item (k) of the Illustrative List, PROEX subsidies should be compared with the "numerous Canadian subsidies that translate into export credit terms." Brazil submits that the phrase "field of export credit terms" should encompass these subsidies which are provided by the Canadian government to Bombardier, its competitor in the regional civil aircraft market.

4.124 **Brazil** refers to the First Written Submission of Canada to the Panel and endorses the statement made by it that, in the regional aircraft industry, the phrase "field of export credit terms" *includes* transaction costs and interest costs. Brazil argues, however, that the phrase encompasses far more than that. It submits that Canada has admitted that the phrase encompasses "financing terms for export transactions," which is broader than the narrower scope of transaction and interest costs argument adopted by Canada later in the dispute. Brazil noted[104] that in Canada's first written submission to the Panel, Canada stated at paragraph 22 that aircraft are capital assets and "few carriers have the financial capacity to make outright purchases of such capital assets." Canada goes on to explain, at paragraph 23, that anything that affects the financing cost of an aircraft should be considered an export credit in the regional aircraft market. Brazil noted that Canada stated that:

> [a]cquisition costs, especially financing programmes, are the largest non-operating performance related selling point a manufacturer uses in marketing its aircraft. Indeed, aircraft selection is often driven by the lowest monthly financing cost, as regional airlines are motivated to purchase aircraft on the basis of profitability of given routes: the lower the financing cost, the greater the number of routes that become profitable. The financing structure of a transaction is therefore one of the most important elements in determining whether a particular aircraft would be profitable for an airline.

Brazil noted its agreement with these statements.[105]

4.125 Brazil argues that it is necessary for EMBRAER to offer a competitive financial package to its customers as a direct result of the practices adopted by

[104] Brazil's First Oral Statement, paras. 42-45; Brazil's Response Questions From the Panel, No. 9.
[105] Brazil's First Oral Statement, paras. 42-45.

Canada and the OECD Members who are active in the commercial aircraft industry. Brazil submits that they have adopted the practice of offering subsidized financing to the airline customers of their aircraft manufacturers.[106] Brazil argues that Canada tilts the playing field in its favor by influencing financing for aircraft. Brazil submits that aircraft financing cost is composed of three essential elements: the rate of interest, the duration of the loan, and the aircraft price. All three affect the crucial monthly cost of the airplane to the airline. Governments may lower this payment by measures that affect any of these three broad elements. Brazil claims that Canada's programmes affect all of these in a way that tilts the playing field in its favor.[107] In Brazil's view, Canada's position in its first written submission confirms the understanding that both Canada and Brazil agreed that, in the field of regional aircraft, the "field of export credit terms" encompasses far more than transaction and interest costs. Brazil submits that Canada's claim that, as applied to regional aircraft, the phrase "field of export credit terms" does not encompass all of the factors that affect the crucial monthly aircraft payment, including price, is inconsistent with the position it took in its first submission. It is also inconsistent with its attack on PROEX itself, for Brazil argues that PROEX is an "export credit term" as that phrase is used in the SCM Agreement.[108] Brazil argues that the practice of governments of paying all or part of the costs incurred by exporters or financial institutions in obtaining credits is within the "export credit terms" portion of Annex I of the Agreement - item (k). PROEX represents such a practice by Brazil.[109] Further, Brazil submitted to the Panel a study prepared by the accounting firm of Ernst & Young that was given to Brazil by Canada in the course of previous negotiations regarding a possible bilateral agreement. According to Brazil, Canada was of the view that the Ernst & Young study was an authoritative analysis of the financial impact PROEX and represented it to Brazil as such. The Ernst & Young study is discussed in the Finan Report and analyzes PROEX in terms of its price impact on the aircraft, noting that the benefit will vary from one transaction to another since the aircraft price, financing terms, percentage of equalization and interest rate may vary.[110] Brazil submits that the point Ernst & Young made, and the point with which Brazil agrees, is that in the regional aircraft industry, any factor that affects monthly cost affects financing. In essence, in order to establish the typical aircraft financing conditions it is necessary to include the aircraft price.[111] An analysis that ignores this fact invites Members to "fine-tune" their programmes so that they comply with the provisions of the Agreement narrowly-construed, not in their context, and not in light of the Agreement's object and

[106] Brazil's Second Written Submission, para. 54.
[107] Brazil's First Oral Statement, para. 46.
[108] Brazil's Second Written Submission, para. 39.
[109] *Ibid.* at para. 40.
[110] *Ibid.* at para. 41.
[111] Response to Questions From the Panel, No. 9.

purpose.[112] Brazil agrees both with Canada's view and with Ernst and Young's view that, in so far as regional aircraft are concerned, anything that affects the crucial monthly cost of the airplane to the airline is an export credit term. As explained at pages 1.4 to 1.6 of the Finan Report, and detailed in Table 1.1 at page 1.7 of the report, Brazil again argued that the crucial monthly financing cost of the airplane is composed of three essential elements: the rate of interest, the duration of the loan, and the price. In Brazil's view, all are properly export credit terms for regional aircraft since all refer to the financing terms for export transactions for this particular market.[113]

4.126 In response to a question from the panel,[114] Brazil submits that the Parties appear to agree that, in so far as regional aircraft are concerned, the particular market characteristics that prevail necessitates a broad definition of "export credit terms." The two most important characteristics are that aircraft are (1) a capital good and (2) the exporter is expected to provide a financing package to the buyer. Under the facts and circumstances present in this dispute, Brazil argued that price must be included as an element of export credit terms since only by including it can a comparison be made of the benefit the aircraft purchaser receives from Canada's numerous subsidy programmes that affect buyer's credits versus the benefit received from Brazil's single PROEX programme.[115]

4.127 **Canada** does not agree with the definition of the phrase "in the field of export credit terms" put forward by the Brazilian government. Canada submits that when the phrase is interpreted using principles of treaty interpretation in customary international law, it would become clear that it refers to interest rates and other transaction costs in an export financing transaction. The phrase does not, therefore, have the all-encompassing interpretation given to it by Brazil.

4.128 Canada submits that in applying the principles of the Vienna Convention, the first step is to determine the ordinary meaning of a provision. The phrase "export credit terms " means "the financing terms for export transactions." Financing terms, in turn, refer to transaction costs (fees, etc.) and interest costs associated with financing a transaction. The context of the phrase supports this ordinary meaning. The first paragraph of item (k) is concerned with the grant by governments of export credits "at rates below those which they actually have to pay for the funds so employed" and the payment of all or part of the costs of obtaining funds incurred by exporters or financial institutions. The second paragraph refers to Members' applying the interest rate provisions of the relevant undertaking, which is the OECD consensus. The context of the phrase "export

[112] *Supra* note 109 at para. 42.

[113] *Supra* note 112.

[114] The Panel's question 9 asked Brazil to: "Please provide further explanation why, in the view of Brazil, 'the field of export credits' relates to all subsidies provided by a Member, and is not limited to terms directly related to export credits themselves."

[115] *Supra* note 112.

credit terms" does not, therefore, support Brazil's assertion that the phrase "should include either the "price" of the aircraft or alleged subsidies for comparative purposes. The phrase refers to "interest rates and other costs specifically related to export financing transactions."

4.129 Canada further submits that the phrase refers to an objective standard against which "material advantage" should be measured, rather than "a case-driven and indeterminate standard." In the context of item (k), it is clear that the phrase "field of export credit terms" "simply means...the international market for financing." Brazil's argument that comparison should be made with Canadian government subsidies to Bombardier is incorrect and ignores the ordinary meaning of the relevant words. The relevant dictionary definitions of "field" are "all the competitors in a race or all except those specified" or "an area of operation or activity." Field, therefore, does not mean one player out of many. Field of export credit terms does not refer to the activities of one country alone. It does not mean "numerous...subsidies" of one country with respect to one company alone.

4.130 Canada argues that in context, the word "field" refers to an "area" of a certain practice, or "all" participants who engage in that practice. The practice is "export credit terms," or export financing. In business terms, this reference to a general practice would be called "the market." The appropriate benchmark therefore is the interest rates and other transaction costs offered in the international financing market. The phrase "export credit terms" refers to interest rates and other transaction costs related to export financing. It does not include research and development contributions. Neither does it include the privatization of state-owned enterprises, nor numerous other subsidies, as contended by Brazil and certainly not the price of the goods being financed.

(a) Canada's Alleged Subsidies to Bombardier

4.131 **Brazil** argues that the determination of whether PROEX is used to secure a material advantage in the field of export credit terms for regional aircraft should be made by comparing the total package of benefits offered by Canada. This is because, Brazil argues in its First Written Submission,[116] producers of aircraft sell more than aircraft; they also "sell" financing. The total financing package affects the total cost of the aircraft. This is crucial to the customers, the airlines, which look essentially to the total monthly cost to finance an aircraft for a given route. From this perspective, Brazil submits that every element that affects that monthly payment is significant.[117]

[116] Brazil's First Written Submission, para. 6.7.
[117] *See* paras. 4.124 - 4.126.

4.132 Brazil refers to its interpretation of the phrase "in the field of export credit terms" and states that such a comparison would reveal that it is Canadian subsidies to Bombardier which secure a material advantage in the field of export credit terms. Brazil submits in its First Written Submission[118] that Canada is determined to feed "the seemingly endless appetite of Canadian exporters for financial support."[119] Canada has the stated goal of moving from sixth to fourth internationally in aerospace ahead of Germany and Japan.[120] As documented by the Finan Report, Brazil argues that Canada has granted an array of subsidies to its regional aircraft producer, Bombardier, in an effort to succeed.[121] This array of subsidies, which Brazil argues far exceeds anything Brazil or other developing countries could afford, is a reality which Brazil submits translates into advantageous export credit terms for Canada's aircraft manufacturer, and with which Brazil must contend if its producer is to have any chance in the market. Brazil argues in its First Written Submission that it is unable to match Canada's subsidies in kind. Developing countries, with their limited resources, Brazil submits, are in no position to meet the subsidy offerings of developed countries.[122]

4.133 Brazil submits that it is not requesting the Panel to make any ruling regarding the consistency or inconsistency of Canada's subsidies with its obligations under the SCM Agreement. What is relevant to the issue before this Panel is the very existence of Canada's subsidies, not their consistency with the Agreement. As argued by Brazil in its First Written Submission,[123] this is because these subsidies have a direct bearing on the question of whether PROEX provides a material advantage in the field of export credit terms regardless of whether they are in conformity with Canada's obligations. For example, one Member may provide support which conforms to the interest rates provisions of the Arrangement on Guidelines for Officially Supported Export Credits of the OECD, which is referenced by Annex I(k) of the SCM Agreement - "an international undertaking on official export credits to which at least twelve original Members to this Agreement are parties as of 1 January 1979." Another Member may provide support in a different form. To determine whether the latter provides a material advantage, it is necessary to examine the former, regardless of the former's conformity to the terms of the SCM Agreement.

4.134 The magnitude of Canada's subsidies, and the extent to which it is willing to open its treasury to achieve the goal of surpassing Germany and Japan in

118 Brazil's First Written Submission, para. 4.10.

119 Export Development Corporation, 1995 *Chairman and President's Message*, p. 4 (Exhibit Bra-5).

120 Industry Canada, News Release, December 17, 1996 (Exhibit Bra-6). *See also* TPC Annual Report 1996-1997, p.5 (Exhibit Bra-7).

121 Finan Report, Part 3.

122 Brazil's First Written Submission, para. 6.9.

123 *Ibid.* at para. 4.11.

aerospace, can be appreciated by the remarks of M. Henri Souquieres, Vice President of the Export Development Corporation, Canada's export credit agency. As documented in the Finan Report, M. Souquieres stated in 1996 that the EDC alone funded more than 25 per cent of Canada's total aerospace development in the previous three years, with the transportation sector taking more than $1.7 billion in 1995. He states that support for Bombardier's 50-seat Canadair regional jet accounted for 62 per cent of this Can$1.7 billion total, or Can$1.0 billion, or US$770 million. This 1995 support works out to US$18.3 million per regional jet delivered in 1995. This is virtually 100 per cent of the List price of the airplane. To be sure, 1995 was the year before EMBRAER's 1996 entry into the market, but support of this magnitude given to Bombardier in 1995 certainly contributed significantly to the market conditions in which EMBRAER had to compete in 1996 and thereafter.

4.135 Brazil submits that among the subsidies given to the regional aircraft industry in Canada by the Government of Canada and two of its provinces, Québec and Ontario include the following: (i) Export Development Corporation equity investments, loan guarantees, insurance, and direct financing; (ii) Canada Account, a special fund for projects that do not meet even the relaxed criteria for EDC support; (iii) Technology Partnerships Canada support for the development costs of Bombardier's regional aircraft; (iv) Technology Partnerships Canada support for Bombardier's suppliers; (v) Ontario Aerospace Corporation dealings with Bombardier on less than commercial terms; and (vi) Programs of the Government of Québec. Brazil noted as an illustration of Canada's programmes that Bombardier is now producing a 70 seat regional jet, with the aid of a Technology Partnerships Canada "investment" of $87 million. In its written submission Brazil has explained why this "investment" is little more than an outright gift.[124] Brazil reported that EMBRAER has considered producing a 70 seat aircraft, but has not yet been able to do so. Brazil notes that EMBRAER has cited development costs as the obstacle to producing the larger airplane and has opted, instead, for a 35 seat aircraft, which permits it to use much of the technology from the 50-seat ERJ-145.[125] Brazil acknowledges that whether EMBRAER would have produced a 70-seat regional jet had it received an $87-million "investment" from the Government of Brazil is uncertain. But Brazil argues that there is no question that such a contribution would have made an enormous difference. If EMBRAER eventually launches such an airplane, its price will have to reflect 100 per cent of the development costs. There is no "Technology Partnerships Brazil" to pick up the product development bill and throw millions of dollars EMBRAER's way.[126] The price of the Bombardier jet, in contrast, will not have to reflect 100 per cent of its development costs. At a minimum it will not have to

[124] Brazil's First Oral Statement, para. 54.

[125] *Ibid.* at para. 55.

[126] Brazil's First Oral Statement,para. 56.

repay the $87 million "investment" from Technology Partnerships Canada.[127] As a consequence, all other things being equal, Brazil submits that the selling price of a Bombardier aircraft that benefits from the $87 million subsidy will be lower than the selling price of an EMBRAER aircraft that does not benefit from such a subsidy. This lower selling price immediately translates into the financing structure of a transaction and is, as Brazil notes Canada says at paragraph 23 of its first written submission, "one of the most important elements in determining whether a particular aircraft would be profitable for an airline." Brazil argues that all of Canada's programmes contribute to lowering the monthly financing cost of regional aircraft.[128]

4.136 Brazil submits that the cost of Canadian subsidies is beyond the reach of Brazil or any developing country. Because of the general lack of transparency of Canada's programmes, it was difficult to estimate the contribution from all of them. For those where subsidies could be calculated, however, the aggregate benefits ranged from US$1.883 billion to US$2.446 billion.[129] This undoubtedly is a conservative figure given M. Souquieres' report of Can$1.0 billion of support from one agency - EDC - in one year - 1995 - alone.[130]

4.137 Brazil refers to its "Brazilian risk" argument and states that in the case of loan guarantees, the credit rating of the country guaranteeing the loan is very important as it would affect the terms of the loan granted by the lender. Brazil submits, in paragraph 6.10 of its First Written Submission, that the Finan Report makes clear why developing countries, such as Brazil, are unable to match the subsidy programmes of developed countries in kind.[131] In the case of loan guarantees, for example, Brazil argues it is clearly a matter of country risk. It notes in that connection that "[a] guarantee on a loan to a financially risky regional airline guaranteed by Canada offers the lender the security of Canada's sovereign risk; the same loan guaranteed by Brazil offers a sovereign risk that today is more than 1,000 basis points or 10 percentage points above Canada's." Brazil submits that in evaluating the question of material advantage, it is essential for the Panel to be mindful of the difficulties developing countries inescapably face in this area. Brazil also argues that, without question, Bombardier enjoys a decided advantage over EMBRAER in having better access to financial capital on more favorable terms. This is simply a manifestation of Canada's advantage as a developed country, in having a stronger capital market that does not bear a significant spread for sovereign (or country) risk. Relative to Brazil, and any other developing country, better access to cheaper financial capital simply gets factored into the overall advantage of Canada as a location for aerospace manufac-

[127] Brazil's First Oral Statement, para. 57.
[128] *Ibid.* at para. 58.
[129] Finan Report, p. 3.8.
[130] Finan Report, at p. 1.1.
[131] *Ibid.* at pp. 1.12-1.14.

turing. The relevant issue for the dispute at hand is that the Brazil risk premium precludes the Government of Brazil from providing certain types of export credits to aircraft purchasers.[132]

4.138 **Canada** disputes the assertion of Brazil that PROEX is the only Brazilian programme from which EMBRAER benefits. It states that EMBRAER has been the beneficiary of many different types of support since its privatization in 1994. On its own publicly accessible website, EMBRAER acknowledges that: "As a Brazilian corporation which manufactures and exports capital goods, EMBRAER has the support of ...FINAMEX, FINAME, BNDES and PROEX" managed by "Banco do Brasil S.A." These Brazilian Government agencies play a very important role in boosting our exports." In the light of all these subsidy programmes, Canada submits that Brazil's repeated assertions about its inability to finance EMBRAER's sales are difficult to believe. In 1997, EMBRAER publicly stated in an Offering Circular aimed at attracting investors that it expected to export ERJ-145 totalling US$3.3 billion with support from PROEX. It also stated that "[t]he Brazilian government has also been an important source of export financing for...[its] customers." Canada notes that the first instalment of this support was in 1997 when BNDES advanced a US$1 billion loan to American Airlines to finance the sale of 42 ERJ-145s.

4.139 Canada notes that the credibility of the Finan Report is compromised by methodological errors and unsubstantiated allegations. In particular, it does not distinguish between alleged benefits that have already been received and those that hypothetically may be received in the future, the timeframes for evaluating alleged subsidies appear to have been chosen arbitrarily and the report purports to show that the subsidy value of a repayable loan or contribution is greater than the subsidy value of a grant of the same amount. Canada also notes that according to Brazil's calculations, $3.4 to $4.7 million of Canada's alleged subsidies of $4.4 to $6 million come from the Export Development Corporation (EDC). The difficulty with the analysis is that in many of the transactions involving competition between Bombardier and EMBRAER, the EDC was not even involved in offering financing because of the impeccable credit rating of those airlines including Luxair, British Regional Airlines and British Midlands. Canada submits that according to the calculation in the Finan Report then "all other alleged subsidies in Canada's alleged "vast array" amounted to only $1 million to $1.4 million, as compared with the $2.45 million of subsidies paid by Brazil through PROEX. Thus, even under the standard proposed by Brazil, PROEX secures a material advantage in the field of export credit terms.

4.140 Canada argues that PROEX subsidies are paid also when Bombardier is not involved in competition with EMBRAER for a contract. Thus, Brazil's argument that it provides subsidies to match the subsidies that Bombardier re-

[132] Finan Report, at p. 3.20.

ceives from the Canadian government is without merit. Canada submits that the competition between Fairchild Dornier and EMBRAER is interesting, as it demonstrates that Brazil provides PROEX subsidies, even in cases where its competitor has not even been accused of benefiting from subsidies.

4.141 Canada contends the Brazilian argument that EMBRAER suffers from market disadvantages vis-à-vis Bombardier because EMBRAER is a developing country manufacturer of regional jet aircraft is patently false. EMBRAER, it submits, is a well-established regional aircraft manufacturer, having sold commercial aircraft around the world for over two decades. EMBRAER is, in fact, larger than the United States - German aircraft manufacturer Fairchild Dornier, one of its developed country competitors. EMBRAER has survived when Saab and Fokker, two major developed country turboprop manufacturers, have failed. If EMBRAER were facing difficulties, it would not have announced its intention to increase production to 12 regional jets a month, enough to satisfy the worldwide total demand in the regional aircraft market in the coming years.

4.142 Canada submits that EMBRAER's receives extensive support from its developed country suppliers and as such it cannot claim to be an isolated developing country manufacturer. Canada relies on the following observation in a study prepared in 1997 by the investment bankers Deutsche Morgan Grenfell:

> "Under EMBRAER's risk-sharing package for the EMB-145, the company is effectively financed by its suppliers: under the terms of the agreement, the company only pays suppliers for components for the aircraft after delivery to the client and the payment for the aircraft are received."

Canada further submits that more than one third (US$130 million) of the costs of development of the ERJ-145 (US$350 million) were borne by these "partner-suppliers." EMBRAER's suppliers also provide guarantees to improve the financing terms offered to EMBRAER's customers. Brazil's assertion about EMBRAER is not, therefore, correct.

4.143 Canada argues that market disadvantages between private sector competitors is not a justifiable ground for export subsidization. Carried to its logical conclusion, Brazil's interpretation of item (k) of the Illustrative List would permit WTO Members - including developed countries - to provide subsidies to compensate for their own perceived market disadvantages.

4.144 **Brazil** disputes that PROEX subsidies provide US$2.45 million. As documented in the Finan Report, Brazil used the number for comparison purposes only against the US$4.4 million to $6.0 million conservative estimate it prepared regarding Canadian subsidies. The US$2.45 million figure stated in the

Ernst & Young Report had been previously presented to Brazil as authoritative of Canada's view regarding PROEX.[133]

4.145 Brazil disputes Canada's implication that PROEX is made available even when Bombardier is not involved. Canada cites Fairchild-Dornier, a German-US manufacturer of regional aircraft.[134] Brazil stated that when Canada refers to Fairchild-Dornier's "small size and uncertain credit," the Panel should understand that Fairchild-Dornier is a division of the giant US conglomerate, Fairchild Aerospace. It has already launched a new family of jet liners, including a 70 seat jet, to be followed by 50 and 90 seat versions. Brazil notes that EMBRAER, for lack of funds, had to back away from the 70 seat market, and concentrate on the 35 seat market as an alternative to the 50 seat jet.[135] Second, Canada offers the statements of officials of Fairchild-Dornier as proof that PROEX secures a material advantage in the 35 seat segment of the market. These statements allegedly reflect what airline customers claim EMBRAER was saying to them - the customers. Brazil argues that this information constitutes double, if not triple, hearsay. Brazil notes that an airline buyer, negotiating with two manufacturers, has an incentive to tell each of the manufacturers that its offer is not as good as the other. The potential for exaggeration, if not fabrication, in such a situation is obvious. But regardless of the veracity of the statements of the officials of Fairchild-Dornier, the fact is that they do not speak for Brazil and PROEX and, for that matter, neither do the officials of EMBRAER. Brazil is not responsible for what an EMBRAER salesman may tell an airline. Much less is it responsible for what an airline may tell another company that EMBRAER may or may not have said. Brazil is responsible for what it does, and that is simply to offset part of the cost of obtaining funds, incurred by financial institutions and exporters, in a manner that does not secure a material advantage in the field of export credit terms.[136]

4.146 In addition, Brazil argues that Brazil risk continues to apply to EMBRAER when the lender is a non-Brazilian financial institution, even though Brazil risk does not apply to the lender's cost of funds. In response to a question from the panel,[137] Brazil notes that the statement does not refer to the higher cost of capital raised by EMBRAER for use in development and production of civil aircraft, for example. Brazil acknowledges that EMBRAER faces higher capital costs than its developed country competitors and that paragraph (k) does not permit subsidies to offset such costs. However, Brazil argues that paragraph (k) does permit subsidies to offset "all or part of the costs incurred by exporters or

---

[133] *See* para. 4.125.

[134] Brazil's Second Oral Statement, para. 63.

[135] Brazil's Second Oral Statement, para. 64.

[136] Brazil's Second Oral Statement, paras. 65-67.

[137] Brazil's Response to Questions From the Panel, No. 11.

financial institutions in obtaining credits." Since this is the function of PROEX, Brazil argues that PROEX is consistent with the SCM Agreement.[138]

D. Arguments under Article 27 of the SCM Agreement

4.147 **Brazil** argues that even if PROEX payments are found to be prohibited export subsidies, Article 27 permits developing countries such as Brazil to maintain export subsidies for a period of eight years from the date of entry into force of the WTO Agreement. Brazil submits that the only obligation it has to satisfy is that it has not increased the level of its export subsidies since 1991, the year PROEX was enacted and implemented. It introduced evidence which, according to it, demonstrated that it has not increased the level of its export subsidies and, as such, was entitled to have recourse to Article 27. **Canada** does not contest that Brazil is a developing country entitled to invoke Article 27 as an affirmative defence. It argues, however, that since Article 27 is an exception to Article 3, Brazil has to adduce evidence to prove that it has complied with the conditions set out by Article 27.4. It argues that contrary to Brazil's assertion that it has to satisfy only one requirement, there are two other conditions it has to satisfy, namely (i) that it must *phase out* its export subsidies within eight years after the entry into force of the WTO Agreement, that is by 31 December 2002; (ii) that it must phase out its export subsidies in a shorter period than eight years, if the use of such export subsidies are inconsistent with its development needs. Canada argues that Brazil has not complied with the conditions set forth in Article 27.4 and, as such, it cannot escape the prohibition against export subsidies in Article 3.1(a) of the SCM Agreement.

1. Whether Article 27 is Lex Specialis to Article 3 of the SCM Agreement

4.148 **Brazil** submits that Article 27 is *lex specialis* to Article 3 in that it provides special rules with regard to the export subsidy programmes of developing countries. Consequently, as to developing countries, it displaces Article 3, which is *lex generalis*. Brazil further submits that because Article 27 is *lex specialis* to Article 3, developing countries are not expected to comply with the provisions of the latter: As far as export subsidies are concerned, Article 27 provides the sole standard applicable to developing countries. Brazil further argues that since Canada has not alleged a breach of Article 27, its complaint must be rejected by the Panel, as Brazil cannot be held to be in breach of Article 3.

4.149 **Canada** disagrees with Brazil that Article 27 is *lex specialis* to Article 3. It argues that *lex specialis* is invoked where a choice has to be made as between conflicting treaty obligations. The value of this maxim is questionable even in

[138] Brazil's Response to Questions From the Panel, No. 11.

the context of treaties in conflict; its elevation to a *principle of interpretation* in respect of articles within the same treaty should be viewed with scepticism. Canada submits that at issue is the relationship between general provisions in a treaty and provisions for special application, or exceptions to such general provisions. As there is no conflict between Articles 3 and 27, in the sense that adherence to one will lead to a violation of the other, this maxim is entirely inapplicable in this case. Canada recalls that Article 27.2 of the SCM Agreement provides, in relevant part:

> The prohibition of paragraph 1(a) of Article 3 shall not apply to: ... (b) other developing country Members for a period of eight years from the date of entry into force of the WTO Agreement, subject to compliance with the provisions in paragraph 4.

Canada submits that by the very terms of Article 27.2, Article 3 shall not apply to Brazil for a period of eight years from the date of entry into force of the WTO Agreement, subject to compliance with the provisions in paragraph 4. By necessary implication, and contrary to Brazil's interpretation, if Brazil does not comply with Article 27.4, then Article 3 shall apply to Brazil. Thus, it is certainly possible for developing countries, such as Brazil, "to act in a manner inconsistent with Article 3." Canada asserts that any other interpretation would be contrary to the principle of effectiveness, as endorsed and applied by the Appellate Body in the *United States - Gasoline* case:

> One of the corollaries of the 'general rule of interpretation' in the Vienna Convention is that interpretation must give meaning and effect to all terms of the treaty. An interpreter is not free to adopt a reading that would result in reducing whole clauses or paragraphs of a treaty to redundancy or inutility.[139]

Canada argues that Brazil's interpretation, if it were accepted, would give no meaning to the phrase "subject to compliance with the provisions in paragraph 4." Such an interpretation is not tenable.

4.150 Canada further submits that Brazil's letter sent to the Chairman of the DSB, dated 23 September 1996, demonstrates that it agreed that it had to *invoke* Article 27 in response to Canada's challenge. It states "Brazil reserves its rights to invoke Article 27 of the Agreement on SCM before any Panel established to examine the matter at issue, and requests that the terms of reference proposed by Canada explicitly recognize Brazil's right to do so." Canada asserts that it was under no obligation to include Article 27 in its request for a Panel and that it recognizes Brazil's right, as an "other developing country" under Article 27.2(b), to invoke Article 27 as a positive defence. However, as Brazil has not

[139] *United States - Standards for Reformulated and Conventional Gasoline*, W/DS2/AB/R, report of the Appellate Body adopted on May 20, 1997, DSR 1996:I, 3, at 21.

shown that it meets the conditions contained in Article 27.4, PROEX does not benefit from the exception contained in Article 27.

2. *Which Party Bears the Burden of Proof*

4.151 **Canada** argues that Article 27 is an exception to the application of Article 3 of the SCM Agreement. This is because Article 27.2 does not contain a substantive obligation that is capable of violation. The only consequence of inconsistency with Article 27.2 (that is, non-compliance with the conditions set out in Article 27.4) is that the exemption from Article 3 contained in Article 27.2 would not apply. This is the sense in which Article 27.2 is an exception, the burden of establishing which rests with the party invoking it, rather a substantive obligation that must be proven by the complaining party. Irrespective of how Article 27 is characterized, the burden of proof does not shift to the complaining Party. This is because it is Article 3.1(a) which sets out the general prohibition on export subsidies. Where a complainant alleges that a WTO Member is providing subsidies that are inconsistent with Article 3, it has the burden of establishing its claim. If it does so, then the responding party has the burden of establishing that the claim of the complainant is unfounded. This is a negative defence. Alternatively, a responding party may argue that it benefits from the provisions of another Article or Agreement or, indeed, principle of international law, that could supersede the claim already established. This is an affirmative defence, and the party advancing such a claim has the burden of establishing it. Whether this is called an exception or a special regime is immaterial to the underlying issue: an affirmative defence that has the potential of trumping the claim of a complainant, when that complainant has met its burden of presenting a *prima facie* case, must be established by the Party advancing that defence.

4.152 Canada submits that the weight of the burden, of course, varies from case to case, and from provision to provision. For example, developing countries that are identified in Annex VII to the SCM Agreement may dispose of their burden simply by referring to the Annex. This is manifestly not the case with respect to "other" developing countries. Canada agrees that the affirmative defence of Article 27 may be invoked as a matter of legal right. At the same time, developing countries that expect to benefit from the grace period must establish that they meet the conditions set out in that Article. This is no different from saying that any Member that wishes to take advantage of its legal right to enact measures that would fall under GATT Article XX would have to meet the criteria in the introductory paragraph of GATT Article XX. Accordingly, if Brazil claims that Article 27 applies to it, Brazil must establish that it falls properly within its terms. That is, it must establish that it is a developing country Member and that it is using the eight-year period to phase out its prohibited subsidies; that it is not using this period to increase its level of subsidies; and that it is phasing them out earlier if the subsidies no longer serve its development needs. Brazil, as the party advancing the affirmative defence, has the burden of proving that it has met the conditions set out in Article 27, in particular Article 27.4, to be able to benefit from such an exception. It has not done so.

4.153 **Brazil** disagrees with Canada that it has the burden of proof in this case. It argues that if Canada's interpretation of Article 27 were to be accepted, it would reverse the bargain which was struck during the Uruguay Round. [140] It submits that Article 27 is not an exception to Article 3. Like other provisions dealing with special and differential treatment for developing countries and economies in transition, it is co-equal with all other Articles of the WTO Agreement. It is in no way subordinate to Article 3 or any other Article of the SCM Agreement. Brazil further submits that Article 27 is a transitional arrangement that, by its own terms, will terminate eight years after entry into force of the WTO Agreement.

4.154 In response to a question from the panel,[141] Brazil argues that the crucial question is which party bears the burden of proof. As the Appellate Body recognized in *United States - Measure Affecting Imports of Woven Wool Shirts and Blouses*[142] international tribunals have generally and consistently accepted and applied the rule that the party who asserts a fact is responsible for providing proof. Brazil submits that since Canada claims that Brazil is not entitled to the protection of Article 27.2, it is Canada's burden to show, pursuant to Article 27.4, that Brazil has increased the level of its export subsidies. Brazil argues that

---

[140] In this respect, the Panel posed the following question to Brazil: "Brazil argues in its second oral statement that '[d]eveloping country Members bargained for the temporary exemption of Article 27, *and for the 'material advantage' language of item (k)* precisely because, when Article 27's protection expires, they needed something they could afford in view of the fact that the developed countries had their self-designed exemption, which is presently in the second paragraph of item (k).' (Emphasis added). Taking into account that the 'material advantage' clause of item (k) was imported unchanged from the Tokyo Round Subsidies Code, can Brazil adduce any support for this assertion?" Brazil responded as follows: "It is true that the 'material advantage' clause was in the Tokyo Round Code. However, during the Uruguay Round a proposal was made by a developed country to delete the language. Brazil and other developing countries opposed this initiative. Attached as Exhibit Bra-19 is a copy of a 7/7/90 proposed change to the Illustrative List. The proposal was rejected and the language remained in item (k)." **Canada** points out that there is no mention of "developing country" in item (k), if indeed this were something developing countries for. In any event, as Canada has observed, given the explicit wording of item (k) - which does not restrict its application to developing countries - if Brazil's interpretation for item (k) were accepted, it would simply encourage competitive export subsidisation, by developed and developing countries alike. Such a proposition is hardly to be welcomed by developing countries that would have to compete with legal export subsidies paid by developed countries. As well, nothing in the document adduced by Brazil identifies the proposal to remove the last clause of item (k) as one advanced by a developed country; nothing in the document suggests that the opposition to the proposal was based on development status; nothing indicates that the failure to remove this clause was something that developing countries bargained for. Brazil's interpretation thus places as much strain on the negotiating history as it does on the plain text, read in context, of item (k), and must therefore be rejected.

[141] Brazil's Response to Questions From the Panel, No. 16.

[142] *United States - Measures Affecting Imports of Woven Wool Shirts and Blouses from India*, WT/DS33/AB/R, report of the Appellate Body adopted on 23 May 1997.

Canada's attempt to impose the burden of proof on Brazil is an attempt to negate the temporary special and differential treatment provisions for which Brazil and other developing countries specifically negotiated during the Uruguay Round.

4.155 Brazil disputes Canada's argument, presented at paragraphs 70 and 71 of its first written submission, that Brazil must show that its "exercise of the right under the limited and conditional exception set out in Article 27 does not 'devalue or 'negate' the rights of other WTO Members under Article 3." Brazil notes that the language used by Canada comes from the Appellate Body Report in *United States - Import Prohibition of Certain Shrimp and Shrimp Products.*[143] It construes Article XX of GATT 1994, which lists "*General Exceptions*" to that agreement. But Brazil argues that Article 27 of the SCM Agreement is very different. It is not a "general exception" but a temporary *exemption* that was bargained for in the Uruguay Round. It does not "devalue" or "negate" rights of other WTO Members, but simply delays the imposition of certain new obligations on developing countries. The fact that developing countries are exempt from the requirements of Article 3.1(a) for a period of eight years does not mean that Members must endure adverse effects from developing country exports for eight years. Brazil notes that if those subsidies are causing adverse effects, Members have a remedy in Article 7.[144]

4.156 In this regard, citing paragraph 7 of Canada's First Written Submission, Brazil notes that Canada's stated purpose in bringing this dispute was because of the alleged "damage caused by PROEX subsidies." Brazil argues that if this is indeed the case, then by the terms of Article 27.7, Canada may pursue the remedies set out in Article 7 of the Subsidies Agreement. Brazil believes that the reason Canada both complains about the alleged negative impact of PROEX on its regional aircraft industry and fails to pursue an Article 7 remedy is that Canada knows it cannot show the required negative impact.[145]

4.157 Brazil submits that the clearly stated object and purpose of Article 27 is to provide special and differential treatment to developing country Members. Its context is made clear from its first paragraph which states without qualification that, "Members recognize that subsidies may play an important role in economic development programmes of developing country Members." The Article consists of carefully negotiated language that reflects a carefully drawn balance of rights and obligations of Members. Its text states explicitly and unequivocally that "the prohibition of paragraph 1(a) of Article 3 shall not apply" to developing countries, subject to specified conditions. It is the burden of Canada, as the complaining party, to establish that Brazil has not complied with these conditions.

---

143 *Supra* note 49.

144 Brazil's Response to Questions From the Panel, No. 22.

145 Brazil's Response to Questions From the Panel, No. 22.

4.158 Brazil acknowledges that it does have a responsibility under Article 27, but that responsibility is not the burden of establishing the applicability of Article 27. Brazil's sole responsibility under Article 27 is the duty imposed on all Members by public international law under the "rule of collaboration," recognized by the Panel in *Argentina - Measures Affecting Imports of Footwear, Textiles, Apparel and Other Items.*[146] That is the duty to make available to the Panel and the parties relevant information in its sole possession. Brazil claims to have satisfied this obligation by making available data to enable an assessment to be carried out to determine whether it has met the condition imposed by Article 27.4. Brazil asserts that the duty to collaborate in the production of relevant information is not the same as the burden of establishing the non-applicability of article 27. That is the responsibility of Canada, and that is a responsibility that Canada has not met. Canada has not even alleged that Brazil has acted contrary to the requirements of Article 27, let alone produced positive evidence in that regard.

3. Arguments Relating to Article 27.4 of the SCM Agreement

4.159 **Canada** states that it agrees that Brazil is a developing country within the meaning of Article 27.2(b), but does not agree that Brazil has met the remaining conditions imposed by Article 27.4. **Brazil** argues that it has met all the conditions imposed by Article 27.4, and it is up to Canada to prove the contrary.

(a) Whether Brazil Has Increased its Level of Export Subsidies

4.160 **Brazil** submits that when PROEX began in 1991, it took over the existing liabilities and responsibilities of an earlier programme, FINEX, which was terminated. In addition, at that time, Brazil maintained an export subsidy programme called BEFIEX ,which provided tax relief for exporters. Table 1 sets forth the PROEX budget for each year since its 1991 inception through 1998, as well as the amount of taxes relieved under BEFIEX from the same year, 1991, through 1997. As could be seen from the Table, both PROEX and BEFIEX individually are below their 1991 levels, as is their combined total. Accordingly, Brazil argues that it has not increased the level of its export subsidies since 1991.

[146] *Supra* note 22.

TABLE 1

Level of Brazil's Export Subsidies (Figures in US$ millions)

Year	PROEX Budget	BEFIEX - Taxes Relieved	PROEX & BEFIEX
1991	1,594.22	445.9	2,040.12
1992	627.20	298.0	925.20
1993	1,440.39	199.2	1,639.59
1994	981.38	218.8	1,200.18
1995	1,069.79	146.0	1,215.79
1996	495.08	102.3	597.38
1997	834.43	59.2	893.63
1998	1,263.01		

Source: Brazilian Government

4.161 **Canada** disagrees with Brazil that it has not increased the level of its export subsidies. Canada notes that Brazil's budget allocation for export subsidies in 1998 exceed the 1994 level, and that the PROEX budget that the Government has requested from the Brazilian Congress for 1999 would bring Brazil's budget allocation to a level that is 10 per cent greater than the 1994 benchmark. Canada challenges the selection of 1991 as the benchmark year, and argues that expenditures as opposed to budgetary amounts should be calculated in order to determine whether Brazil has complied with its obligations under Article 27. Relying on Tables 2 and 3 below, Canada claims that Brazil has increased total expenditures by 40 per cent since 1994. This increase was based on a comparison of 1994 figures with figures for the first nine months of 1998. Comparing the first ten months January - October 1998 with the full twelve months of 1994, the increase in Brazil's expenditures on export subsidies is now 53 per cent as seen from Table 2. Canada subsequently revised this figure to 60 per cent based on PROEX expenditure figures provided by Brazil in its Second Written Submission to the Panel for the January - October 1998 period ($538 million rather than $520 million as shown in Table 2).

TABLE 2

PROEX and BEFIEX Expenditures US$ millions			
Year	**PROEX**	**BEFIEX**	**TOTAL**
1994	121	219	340
1995	124	146	270
1996	184	102	286
1997	353	59	412
1998 (Jan-Oct)	520	0	520

Source: PROEX: 1994-1997: Banco do Brasil; Estado do Sao Paulo

Canada argues that if expenditures in November and December are equivalent to average monthly expenditures in the first ten months of this year, expenditures on export subsidies in 1998 will be over 80 per cent higher than in 1994. This increase in expenditure is fully consistent with the stated objectives of the Government of Brazil as articulated by President Fernando Henrique Cardoso during the third anniversary of the "Real Plan":

> "Among [the measures aimed at reducing the "Brazil cost"] are: a) an extensive reformulation of the Export Financing Program (... PROEX), expanding the List of eligible products and extending financing to the production phase to make it more attractive and effective. Whereas the government paid out US$82 million and US$115 million in 1995 and 1996, respectively, expenditures of no less than US$1 billion are anticipated for 1997."

4.162 Canada submits that while expenditures have not yet reached the level of US$1 billion forecast by the President, PROEX expenditures solely for the purpose of supporting EMBRAER aircraft already scheduled to be delivered in 1999 will total $400 million as demonstrated in Table 3 below.

TABLE 3

Proex Expenditures to Support Embraer Sales (Million US$)

Year	Total Export Subsidies	PROEX to Support EMBRAER Sales	Percentage of Total Export Subsidies
1996	286	31	11%
1997	412	122	30%
1998 (9 Months)	472	219	46%
1998 (Forecast)	624	282	45%
1999 (Forecast)	?	399	?

Source: Total Export Subsidies : 1996-1998 Jan-Sept : Banco do Brasil

Canada argues that these increases in expenditures under PROEX have not been accidental. On the contrary, they are the result of concerted expansions in the scope of the programme. The changes to PROEX since the entry into force of the SCM Agreement include: the increase of the coverage of interest equalization from 85 to 100 per cent of the value of the export; lengthening of the PROEX term for aircraft from 10 to 15 years; the expansion of the list of eligible products by over 30 per cent; the introduction of lump sum payments of equalization; the extension of interest equalization to financing for the production of exports and, most recently, the elimination of restrictions on the use of PROEX financing and equalization in the same transaction. These very expansions support Canada's later submission that Brazil has taken no steps to *phase out* PROEX, as it is required to do under Article 27(4).

4.163 **Brazil** does not contest the accuracy of the data submitted by Canada from 1994 through the third quarter of 1998. Brazil argues that since 1991 is the year PROEX was established, it must be the proper starting benchmark for this comparison.[147]

4.164 Brazil submits that Canada chose to ignore the data from 1991 through 1993 and, as a result, provided the Panel with a distorted picture of Brazil's expenditures regarding export subsidies since PROEX's inception. Brazil refers the Panel to Exhibit Bra-10 which, according to it, provides the complete series of expenditure data from 1991 through 1997, and preliminary data for the period from January through October 1998.[148]

[147] Brazil's Response to Questions From the Panel, No. 19.
[148] Brazil's Response to Questions From the Panel, No. 19.

TABLE 4

Complete Series of PROEX Expenditure Data from 1991 through 1997, and Preliminary Data for the period January through October 1998

PROEX and BEFIEX Expenditures US$ millions			
Year	**PROEX**	**BEFIEX**	**TOTAL**
1991	342	459	788
1992	215	298	513
1993	197	199	396
1994	121	219	340
1995	124	146	270
1996	184	102	287
1997	353	59	413
1998(Jan-Oct)	538		538

Source: Exhibit Bra-10

Similarly, for comparison and at the request of the Panel,[149] Brazil submitted a chart showing expenditures from 1991 through partial 1998 in constant 1991 dollars (Table 4 is not in constant 1991 dollars).[150] In addition, Brazil also submitted the information from 1985 through partial 1998 in constant 1991 US dollars.[151]

[149] Brazil's Response to Questions From the Panel, No. 44.

[150] Exhibit Bra-20 (see Table 5).

[151] Brazil's Response to Questions From the Panel, No. 45; Exhibit Bra-21.

TABLE 5

PROEX Expenditures from 1985 through 1997, and Preliminary Data for 1998 in Constant 1991 U.S. Dollars

PROEX and BEFIEX Expenditures 1991 US$ millions			
Year	**PROEX**	**BEFIEX**	**TOTAL**
1985	1,609	427	2,036
1986	1,298	602	1,900
1987	1,200	506	1,706
1988	1,154	544	1,698
1989	866	461	1,327
1990	489	533	1,022
1991	342	446	788
1992	209	290	499
1993	187	189	376
1994	112	203	315
1995	112	132	244
1996	164	91	255
1997	308	52	360
1998(Jan-Oct)	465		465

Source: Exhibit Bra-21, Exhibit Bra-20.

4.165 Further, Brazil maintains that it has not increased the level of its export subsidies and corrected two errors in Table 1. First, Brazil states that it omitted to indicate that the PROEX value for 1998 was calculated using the average exchange rate for the period January through September. The values of previous years were calculated with the average exchange rate for the entire year. This means that the 1998 PROEX budget indicated in Table 1 is "inflated," since it does not take into account the devaluation of the Real against the US dollar in the last quarter of 1998. Second, Brazil did not adjust the US dollar amount to which Brazilian currency had been converted to make the comparison in constant 1991 dollars. Brazil argues that it is absolutely necessary when measuring the level of export subsidies over an eight-year period to use a constant point of comparison. Thus adjusted, Brazil introduced evidence which showed that the current level of export subsidies is even further below the 1991 benchmark.

TABLE 6

Brazil's Export Subsidies in Constant 1991 U.S. Dollars

PROEX and BEFIEX (Budget-1991) US$ millions			
Year	**PROEX**	**BEFIEX**	**TOTAL**
1991	1,594	446	2,040
1992	610	290	900
1993	1,366	189	1,555
1994	909	203	1,111
1995	968	132	1,101
1996	440	91	531
1997	728	52	780
1998(Jan-Oct)	1,092		1,092

Source: Exhibit Bra-11

4.166 Brazil, continuing to dispute Canada's assertion that the appropriate benchmark was 1994, further submitted data, which according to it, established that even if 1994 was used, Brazil's level of export subsidies in subsequent years, when measured against 1994 in constant dollars, had not increased.

TABLE 7

Brazil's Export Subsidies in Constant 1994 U.S. Dollars

PROEX and BEFIEX (Budget-1994) US$ millions			
Year	**PROEX**	**BEFIEX**	**TOTAL**
1994	981	219	1,200
1995	1,046	143	1,188
1996	475	98	573
1997	786	56	842
1998(Jan-Oct)	1,179		1,179

Source: Exhibit Bra-12

4.167 **Canada** disagrees with Brazil that Article 27 mandates the use of constant dollars. It argues that there is no provision in Article 27 for conversion of the level of export subsidies into constant dollars and that if the drafters of Article 27 had intended the benchmark to be adjusted for inflation, they would have specifically provided for it. That is what they did in Annex IV of the SCM Agreement. Canada further argues that it is immaterial whether constant or current dollars is used, as in both cases, the level of Brazilian export subsidies increased since the entry into force of the WTO Agreement, as demonstrated in Table 8 below.

TABLE 8

Brazilian Export Subsidies (PROEX AND BEFIEX) Measured in Constant and Current Dollars from 1994

	Total Expenditures (current US$)	**Total Expenditures (1994 constant US$)**
1994	339.6	340
1995	269.5	263
1996	286.7	275
1997	412.5	389
1998**	537.8	502

Source: Brazil exhibit 20

(i) Which Year is the Appropriate Benchmark Year

4.168 **Canada** submits that the figures submitted by Brazil to demonstrate that its level of export subsidies have not increased are not relevant, as the selection of 1991 as the benchmark year is erroneous. Canada argues that the relevant base year for determining whether there has been an increase in the level of export subsidies under Article 27.4 is 1994, as the condition in Article 27.4 became effective on 1 January 1995. Thus, to benefit from the Article 27 exception, developing countries may not increase their level of export subsidies as of 1 January 1995. Any increase in the level of export subsidies prevailing as of the date of entry into force of the WTO Agreement would mean that the developing country in question would lose the exemption provided in Article 27.

4.169 Canada submits that its interpretation is supported by footnote 55 to Article 27.4, which makes it clear that the benchmark period is one calendar year. Footnote 55 provides that "[f]or a developing country Member not granting export subsidies as of the date of entry into force of the WTO Agreement, this paragraph shall apply on the basis of the level of export subsidies granted in 1986." Canada submits that since Brazil was granting export subsidies on the date of entry into force of the WTO Agreement, the exception in footnote 55 does not apply and that the appropriate benchmark period for determining whether there has been an increase in the level of export subsidies is the calendar year immediately preceding 1 January 1995, i.e.,1994.

4.170 **Brazil** argues that given the peculiar circumstances of this case, 1991 is the appropriate benchmark, especially considering that it is the year in which PROEX was first enacted. The benchmark for other cases may be different, depending upon the circumstances of those cases. Brazil asserts that Canada's proposal to use 1994 as the benchmark could have a widely diverse impact, depending upon the particular circumstances of a developing country in 1994. Should the Panel adopt Canada's suggestion, given the volatile nature of developing country economies, the benefits for which they negotiated in Article 27 might not be available to them, depending upon circumstances beyond their control.

4.171 Brazil submits that if the Panel does not choose to utilize a benchmark year reasonably tailored to the case before it, the Panel should consider utilizing a weighted average of the three or four years prior to the entry into force of the WTO Agreement as the benchmark. This methodology, argues Brazil, would help reduce the distortion of the impact of a single year on the volatile economies of developing countries. Brazil notes, in that connection, that the PROEX budget in the period 1991-1998 experienced an average year-to-year swing of 43 per cent in US dollars. Brazil believes that other developing countries are likely to present similar patterns.

4.172 **Canada** argues that there is nothing in the text of Article 27.4, nor indeed the context of Article 27 in the SCM Agreement as a whole, which supports Brazil's interpretation. Canada submits that designating as the benchmark the year that a programme begins is inconsistent with the language of Article 27.4. If Brazil's interpretation were to be accepted, it would mean designating a different benchmark year for each export subsidy programme that makes up a developing country Member's overall export subsidies, with the exception of agricultural subsidies. Such a situation will be inconsistent with the plain language of footnote 55 of the SCM Agreement, which designates 1986 as the single benchmark year for a developing country Member's overall export subsidies where that Member does not grant export subsidies as of the date of entry into force of the WTO Agreement.

4.173 Canada submits that it is clear from the text of the SCM Agreement that 1994 is the benchmark year for Article 27.4. Given that the SCM Agreement became effective on 1 January 1995, the condition regarding increase of export subsidies became effective as of that time. The level of export subsidies at that time must be the level in 1994. This interpretation is confirmed by Footnote 55, which provides the reference to export subsidies granted as of the date of entry into force of the WTO Agreement, as well as reference to a calendar year.

4.174 Canada submits that Brazil's interpretation would produce absurd results. It is not unusual for a subsidy programme to initially be administered at a low level, with an increase over time. This would be the case particularly with respect to developing country Members that initiated subsidy programmes years ago and had increased these budgets significantly by 1994. Brazil's interpretation would seriously prejudice the export subsidy programmes of such developing country Members. Canada further submits that Brazil's argument that Canada's interpretation is too rigid and would "impose a benchmark on developing countries over which they have no control" is without merit. Canada asserts that the opposite is true, as the negotiation of the WTO Agreement was completed at the end of 1993. Members planning to invoke Article 27 knew that their phase out obligations under Article 27.4 would apply as of January 1, 1995. In any case, the argument that Members have no control over the 1994 benchmark makes no sense in relation to an obligation freely entered into by states.

4.175 Canada also disagrees with Brazil that the Panel should consider using a weighted average of the three or four years prior to the entry into force of the WTO Agreement. It notes that such an interpretation is completely without support in the text and context of the SCM Agreement. Where the WTO Agreements specify that averaging over a period of years should be used, it is done so expressly as in Article 6.3(d) of the SCM Agreement, Article 5.1(b) and Annex 2 of the Agreement on Agriculture and paragraph 6(a) of the Understanding on the Interpretation of Article XXVIII of the General Agreement on Tariffs and Trade 1994. Furthermore, Brazil's interpretation is inconsistent with the use of a single year as a benchmark in footnote 55 of the SCM Agreement. Brazil's alternate interpretation would apply a different standard to developing country Members falling within footnote 55 and other developing country Members. The former would be subject to a calendar year benchmark, while the latter would be subject to a multi-year weighted average. Canada submits that its interpretation avoids this inconsistency by applying the same standard in both instances - the level of export subsidies granted over a calendar year.

ii) What are the Relevant Indicators for Determining Whether a Member Has Increased the Level of its Export Subsidies

4.176 The parties are agreed that, in determining whether a Member has increased its level of export subsidies under Article 27.4 of the SCM Agreement, regard should be had to the overall level of subsidization, not the level of export subsidies for some given product, however defined. They disagree, however, whether agricultural subsidies should be included in the calculation. **Canada** is of the view that the phrase "level of export subsidies" in Article 27.4 excludes agricultural subsidies that conform to Part V of the Agreement on Agriculture in accordance with Article 13(c) of that Agreement. It claims that this interpretation of the phrase is consistent with the context of Article 27, as agricultural export subsidies are subject to special rules and separate reduction commitments in the Agreement on Agriculture. This is confirmed in the reference at the beginning of Article 3 of the SCM Agreement: "Except as provided in the Agreement on Agriculture." Article 27 provides an exception to Article 3, and not to the Agreement on Agriculture. Accordingly, the phase out requirement in Article 27.4 must also apply "[e]xcept as provided in the Agreement on Agriculture." Such an interpretation is also consistent with Article 13(c) of the Agreement on Agriculture, which exempts from the prohibition in Article 3, agricultural export subsidies that conform fully with Part V of the Agreement on Agriculture. Given that such subsidies are already exempted from the application of Article 3, they should not be included in the calculation of subsidies for the sole purpose of determining whether *another* exception would be available.

4.177 **Brazil** disagrees with Canada that agricultural subsidies should not be included in the calculation of the level of export subsidies. In its response to a question[152] from the Panel as to whether it agreed with the interpretation proposed by Canada, it stated that "Article 27 makes no distinction between subsidies granted to agricultural or industrialized products. The calculation of the level of export subsidies should include all export subsidies being granted as of the date of entry into force of the WTO agreement." Brazil stated, however, that neither PROEX nor BEFIEX are agricultural subsidies, nor are they granted for the benefit of agricultural products. BEFIEX benefited industrial firms that imported inputs or capital goods and exported industrialized goods, while PROEX benefited Brazilian capital and consumer goods as well as services.[153]

(iii) Whether "Level of Export Subsidies" Refers to Expenditure or to Budgetary Appropriations

4.178 **Canada** argues that the phrase "level of export subsidies" appearing in Article 27.4 refers to expenditures, not budgetary appropriations, as claimed by Brazil. Canada submits that when viewed in isolation, the ordinary meaning of "level" could encompass either expenditures or budgeted amounts. However, viewed in its context within the SCM Agreement and the other WTO agreements, "level of export subsidies" can only be interpreted to refer to expenditures.

4.179 Three contextual aspects of the SCM Agreement and other WTO agreements support this interpretation. First, starting from the definition of subsidies in Article 1, the SCM Agreement as a whole is phrased in terms of transfers of value, such as when payments are made, and not the amount that a Member has budgeted for subsidies - that is, the amount that a Member intends or expects to transfer. For example: (a) Article 1.1(a)(1) refers to a "financial contribution" by a government, and not to the budgeting of a financial contribution; (b) Article 1.1(a)(1)(i)-(iv) refers to "direct transfers of funds," foregone revenue, the provision of goods and services, and payments to a funding mechanism rather than budgeting for such activities; (c) Article 3.2 provides that Members shall not grant nor maintain export subsidies, but does not constrain them from budgeting for such subsidies; (d) the dispute settlement mechanism in Article 4 can be in-

152 The question posed by the Panel was as follows: "...Does Brazil agree that agricultural subsidies should not be included in performing the calculation of the level of export subsidies...?"

153 Brazil referred to WTO Doc. G/SCM/Q2/BRA/8.

voked when a Member has reason to believe that a prohibited subsidy is being "granted or maintained," not just when such subsidies are budgeted or planned; and (e) the notification provisions in Article 25 state that the primary basis for notifying subsidies is on an expenditure basis - only where this is not possible, should such notification be done on a budgetary basis. This indicates that where budgeted amounts were intended, they were specifically provided for.

4.180 Canada argues that the text of footnote 55 to the SCM Agreement defines the base year for determining whether certain developing country Members have increased the level of their export subsidies in terms of "the level of export subsidies granted in 1986." Footnote 55 does not refer to the level of export subsidies "budgeted." Third, where disciplines have been imposed elsewhere in the WTO agreements on levels of subsidies, the disciplines are based on expenditure levels. The Agreement on Agriculture establishes base levels for domestic and export subsidies on an expenditure basis. Where that Agreement refers to "budgetary outlays," the term is understood to mean government expenditures, not budgeted amounts.

4.181 Canada argues that interpreting the phrase "level of export subsidies" to mean expenditure levels is also consistent with the object and purpose of the SCM Agreement: to reduce the economic distortions caused by subsidies. Economic distortions are caused by actual expenditure of export subsidies, not by budgeting or planning for such subsidies. Brazil's interpretation would imply that a developing country Member could have budgeted a large amount of export subsidies in 1994 without having to expend them, only to expand its actual expenditure of export subsidies.

4.182 Second, Canada also argues that the Brazilian interpretation would create an absurdity. It could create a situation where a developing country Member that does not grant any export subsidies could lose the protection provided by Article 27 if it budgets for export subsidies at a level higher than its 1994 calendar year baseline. Conversely, a Member that maintains its budget at its previous level, but overspends on actual expenditures, would not be in breach of this condition.

4.183 **Brazil** disagrees with Canada that its interpretation is supported by the text of the SCM Agreement. It argues that the approach adopted by Canada in arriving at that judgment ignores the teaching of the Appellate Body in *United States - Import Prohibition of Certain Shrimp and Shrimp Products*: "A treaty interpreter must begin with, and focus upon, the text of the particular provision to be interpreted. It is in the words constituting that provision, read in their context, that the object and purpose of the states parties to the treaty must first be sought."[154] Brazil alleges that Canada disregarded this teaching of the Appellate

[154] *United States - Import Prohibition of Certain Shrimp and Shrimps products*, WT/DS58/AB/R, para 114, report of the Appellate Body adopted on 6 November 1998.

Body as it looked at "other articles of the SCM Agreement, Articles 1, 3, 4, 25, and even to another Agreement - the Agreement on Agriculture.

4.184 Brazil submits that Canada does not accurately reflect what those other Articles specify. For example, Canada claims that "the notification provisions of Article 25 state that the primary basis for notifying subsidies is on an expenditure basis - only where this is not possible," Canada continues, "should such notification be done on a budgetary basis." But Brazil argues that the notification provisions of Article 25 state nothing of the kind. The relevant provision is Article 25.3 (ii) which provides:

"Members shall ensure that their notifications contain the following information:

***

(ii) subsidy per unit or, in cases where this is not possible, the total amount or the annual amount budgeted for that subsidy (indicating, if possible, the average subsidy per unit in the previous year);"

4.185 Brazil submits that whereas the word "expenditure" does not even appear in the article, the word "budgeted" clearly does appear and clearly is a proper basis. Brazil argues that it is clear that this provision states a preference for reporting on a per unit basis. But for a subsidy like PROEX, this is not possible. It does not operate on a per unit basis. Therefore, "the total annual amount budgeted for that subsidy" quite properly was the basis for Brazil's notification to the Subsidies Committee, and is the appropriate benchmark for measuring the level of subsidies for this reason as well as for the reasons given by Brazil. Brazil argues that the budgeted amount includes the total value of all commitments contracted for or anticipated in the coming year. Thus, to take a simple example: If a commitment has been made to provide PROEX benefits for a single airplane to be exported in the coming year, and if the total amount of payments on that single airplane over 15 years is $3 million, the entire $3 million is included in the budget for the coming year.

4.186 Brazil submits that budgeted amounts, rather than expenditures, are the proper basis of comparison because they are the responsibility of the Member governments of the WTO. The degree to which a government's budgeted amount may be utilized in any given year is determined not by the government, but by the private sector. Under Canada's approach, a Member could increase its budgeted amounts and meet the requirements of Article 27.4 if, for whatever reason, private sector utilization declined. Conversely, a government progressively phasing out its subsidies would not be in compliance if the private sector utilized a sufficiently larger share of a smaller budget. The Canadian approach puts the responsibility for establishing the level of export subsidies on the private sector, not on Member governments. Apart from the amounts they budget, however, governments have no control over expenditures. An approach that would result in the determination being made on the basis of private action rather than government decision should not be utilized.

4.187 Brazil claims that the Canadian argument that budgets may be overspent and therefore are not a reliable measurement of the level of export subsidies misunderstands the Portuguese term "dotação orçamentária" which has, somewhat loosely, been translated as "budget." This term does not mean budget in the sense of a statement of probable or estimated expenditures that may or may not be accurate. In context it corresponds to "budgetary appropriation." PROEX budget numbers are actually the "dotação orçamentária" for the programme. They refer to the specific amount of funds reserved for payment to the beneficiaries of the programme. Payments may not be made when the funds of the "dotação orçamentária" are depleted. Consequently, there is no possibility of overpayment of the budgeted amount - more accurately the budgetary appropriation - as suggested by Canada.

4.188 Brazil submits that Canada's interpretation of footnote 55 does not give a complete picture. While Canada points out the absence of the word "budgeted" in the footnote, it does not mention the absence of the word "expenditure" or "paid" or any other term that would signify an actual expenditure. The negotiators certainly could have used such a term if that was what they meant. That in fact is what they did in the Agreement on Agriculture where the term used is "budgetary outlay." The ordinary meaning of the verb "grant" appearing in footnote 55 is "to agree, consent" or "to promise, undertake (which means 'to give formal promise or pledge')." This is, in fact, what the Portuguese term "dotação orçamentária" signifies: a formal, legally binding promise - not an estimate - to the Brazilian exporter or financial institution to provide the funds earmarked for PROEX in the budget, on a first-come first-served basis, until the appropriated resources are depleted.

4.189 Brazil submits that while it agrees with Canada that the use of expenditure levels is consistent with the object and purpose of the Subsidies Agreement, which is to "reduce the economic distortions caused by subsidies," it is also of the view that budgetary appropriation levels are also consistent with this particular objective of the Agreement. Brazil further submits that the Canadian argument that its interpretation would produce absurd results is without merit. Brazil argues that if a developing country Member were to budget a large amount of export subsidies in 1994 without having to expend them, only to expand its actual expenditure of export subsidies, such an approach would raise serious issues under Article 18 of the Vienna Convention on the Law of Treaties, which obliges states to refrain from acts which would defeat the object and purpose of a treaty prior to its entry into force. Second, to the extent that Members could take such action consistently with Article 18 of the Vienna Convention, this only reinforces Brazil's argument that the Panel should not select one particular year to serve as the benchmark. Third, the historic data demonstrates that Brazil did not artificially expand the 1994 budget numbers, which are lower than those of previous years.[155] Fourth, Canada has presented no evidence that would justify its suggestion that other developing country Members may have acted contrary to their obligations under Article 18 of the Vienna Convention and, in the absence of such evidence, the Panel should not assume that they have.

4.190 Brazil argues that if it is true that developing country Members have the burden of proof and that 1994 is the appropriate benchmark, as argued by Canada, then Article 27 would have been completely unavailable to developing countries in 1995, if the level of export subsidies were measured on an expenditure basis. It would have been impossible for the developing country to prove that the 1995 level was below the benchmark level. For example, suppose a complaint had been brought at a point in 1995 when only first quarter expenditure statistics were available. Suppose that for all of the benchmark year (or the average of several years) expenditures were 100 while first quarter benchmark expenditures were 25. Assuming that the comparison should be on a quarter to quarter basis (which is not at all clear from the text) what would be the result if first quarter 1995 expenditures were 30? The fact that the first quarter 1995 subsidies were ahead of the same period in the benchmark period would not necessarily mean that the pattern would hold for the full year. It could well be that the total would be substantially less than the benchmark's hypothetical 100, but how could the developing country prove it? Indeed, at no time during 1995 could a developing country prove the total level of 1995 expenditures, since not all of those expenditures would yet have occurred. Consequently, during 1995, on Canada's theory, Article 27 would have been unavailable to developing countries. For that matter, if the burden of proof is on the complaining party, as Brazil argues, the use of expenditures would mean a developed country also would have been unable to bring a prohibited subsidies case in 1995. No Member could prove what 1995 expenditures would be during 1995 itself.

4.191 Brazil submits that the Canadian suggestion could not be a proper basis for interpreting the provisions of Article 27.4. Whatever the appropriate benchmark, there is nothing in the text, the context, or the object and purpose of Article 27 to support the proposition that one benchmark would be used in 1995 and another in subsequent years.

4.192 Brazil argues that use of expenditures as the measure of the level, particularly when combined with Canada's insistence that it is the developing country that bears the burden of proof under Article 27, would have resulted in Article 27's being a complete nullity in the first year of the WTO's existence, 1995. If a developing country had been the subject of a prohibited subsidy complaint in 1995, it could not have proved during that year that the expended

[155] See Table 4 (Exhibit Bra-10) and Table 5 (Exhibit Bra-21).

amount had *not* increased on an annual basis compared to 1994. It could not have done so until the entire year was over because, even though at any given point in the year the expenditures might have been below those of the prior year, it would have been impossible to prove that they could not have exceeded 1994 before the end of 1995. Developing countries effectively would have lost one of the eight years of exemption for which they had bargained.[156]

4.193 Brazil argues that an interpretation that would have rendered Article 27 inoperative for the first year of its existence is not a reasonable interpretation. It contradicts the words of the Appellate Body in the appeal of a case that, itself, began in 1995: *United States - Standards for Reformulated and Conventional Gasoline*. In this case, the Appellate Body stated that an interpretation of the terms of a treaty "must give meaning and *effect* to all the terms of a treaty"[157] (emphasis in original). Canada's interpretation would not have given *effect* to Article 27 during 1995 (emphasis in original).

4.194 Brazil argues that the fact that this problem ended with the end of 1995 does not rescue Canada's flawed interpretation today. There is nothing in Article 27 that would support the view that one method for calculating the level of export subsidies was to apply in 1995 and another method in the subsequent seven years. A method that would not work in 1995 may not, therefore, be used in subsequent years. Canada's method of 1994 as the benchmark and the developing country with the burden of proof would not have worked in 1995, and therefore may not be used in subsequent years. Further, Brazil submits that Canada's claim that Brazil has increased the level of its export subsidies is contradicted by Tables 1,[158] 6[159] and 7,[160] which show that since entry into force of the Uruguay Round Agreements - whether 1991 or 1994 is the proper base year - Brazil has not increased the level of its export subsidies.

4.195 **Canada** argues that the Brazilian argument that its interpretation would place control in the hands of the private sector is unmeritorious. It states that it finds it odd that any government expenditure could be said to be controlled by the private sector. Canada submits that while the utilization of PROEX by Brazilian exporters might have been below what the Brazilian Government would have liked at the time of the entry into force of the SCM Agreement, this cannot excuse Brazil from its WTO obligations. Brazil's interpretation, if allowed, would enable it to actually increase the distortions to trade resulting from its export subsidies, as long as those subsidies are below a level that was budgeted

---

[156] Brazil's Second Written Submission, para. 11.

[157] *United States - Standards for Reformulated and Conventional Gasoline*, WT/DS2/AB/R, DSR 1996:I, 3, at 21, report of the Appellate Body adopted on 20 May 1996.

[158] Exhibit Bra-8.

[159] Exhibit Bra-11.

[160] Exhibit Bra-12.

but never, in fact, achieved. This would clearly be at odds with the object and purpose of the SCM Agreement.

4.196 Canada disagrees with Brazil that its interpretation would have effectively resulted in developing country Members losing one year of their grace period, i.e., 1995. It submits that the opposite is more likely to be true: it would have been easy for a responding party, at any point in 1995, to demonstrate that its expenditures were below those of the entirety of 1994, as long as it was not radically increasing its level of export subsidies. In effect, the conditions of Article 27 by their very nature require a certain length of time for an accurate and persuasive interpretation of the facts. Canada submits that this is one of the reasons that Canada waited several years before bringing this challenge, as there is now enough data to show conclusively that Brazil has not met the conditions of Article 27.

4.197 Canada contests Brazil's argument that Canada had misinterpreted Article 25. While Canada's argument may have been interpreted as meaning that the word "expenditure" appears in Article 25.3, which is obviously not the case, it is equally obvious that the term "subsidy" in Article 25 must refer to expenditures since, where budgeted amounts are provided for, the word "budgeted" is specifically used in opposition to the general word "subsidy", which can only be taken as meaning expenditures.

4.198 Canada dismisses the Brazilian claim that its budget numbers are not just estimates but authorized expenditures. It would appear that the budget numbers state "total autorizado." Yet in its submissions, Brazil explains how its expenditure statistics, which contain the same figures put forward by Canada, meet the standards of the International Monetary Fund, since they reflect the full face amount on the PROEX bonds issued each year. This, according to Canada, confirms the irrelevance of the budget numbers and the appropriateness of using the expenditure figures, which reflect the value of the PROEX bonds emitted in that year.

4.199 Canada concludes that it is clear from the foregoing that Brazil has not complied with the requirement set out in Article 27.4 that a developing country Member must not increase the level of its export subsidies. While Canada accepts Brazil's definition of its export subsidies including the two programmes PROEX and BEFIEX, it does not accept the submission of Brazil that it has not increased the level of its export subsidies since the entry into force of the WTO Agreement. Brazil's assertion is contradicted by tables 2 and 3 which show that since the entry into force of the WTO Agreement, Brazil has increased the level of its export subsidies.

(b) Arguments Relating to the Requirement to "Phase Out" Export Subsidies Within Eight Years

4.200 **Canada** submits that Article 27.4 of the SCM Agreement, which provides, in relevant part, that "[a]ny developing country Member referred to in paragraph 2(b) shall phase out its export subsidies within the eight-year period, preferably in a progressive manner" should be interpreted in the light of customary rules of international law. Canada submits that the *Concise Oxford Dictionary of the English Language* defines the verb "phase out" as "to bring gradually ... out of use." The adverb "gradually" is further defined as taking place "by degrees, slowly progressive, not rapid, steep, or abrupt."

4.201 The principal interpretative challenge, according to Canada, is how to reconcile the fact that Article 27 expressly indicates only a *preference* for a "progressive" phase-out, while the term "phase-out" itself and its context within Article 27.4 can be read to mean a gradual, or a slowly progressive termination of the scheme over eight years. Canada notes that "progressive" is defined, in reference to tax rates for example, as indicating an "increasing rate." Thus, the internal construction of paragraph 4 indicates that to comply with the "phase-out" requirement, a developing country Member would have to prove that: (a) it is bringing its export subsidies out of use in a staged manner; and (b) it does not intend to bring its subsidies to a "rapid, steep, or abrupt" end before the end of the eight-year period. Canada adds that a developing country Member should, but is not required to, reduce its export subsidies at an increasing rate. It also asserts that a developing country Member must terminate its export subsidies at the end of the phase-out period. "Terminate," in the context of Articles 27 and 3, means to cease granting or maintaining export subsidies. The maintenance of PROEX subsidies beyond the phase out period through the continuation of PROEX export subsidies by the Government of Brazil is inconsistent with this requirement.[161]

---

161 In this respect, the Panel posed the following question to Canada: [Given the possibility] that the SCM Committee may extend the eight-year period during which a developing country Member may provide export subsidies, [how could it] be determined in advance for what period a developing country Member will be allowed to provide export subsidies, how could a panel conclude in advance of the end of the period that the Member had not complied with its obligation to eliminate its export subsidies by the end of that period? In its response, Canada stated that "… The condition to 'phase out' is not modified by the possibility of an extension. The condition to 'phase-out' has both substance and legal effect regardless of the possibility that the SCM Committee might extend the grace period. This is so for two reasons. First, the condition to 'phase out' is qualified by the imperative 'shall.' If a developing country Member wishes to benefit from the grace period in Article 27, it 'shall' phase out its export subsidies in the interim. In other words, developing countries are given an additional eight years in which they may distort the international economy through export subsidies, but only on condition that they reduce the distortions so caused by phasing out such trade distorting subsidies over the grace period. Second, a developing country Member that wishes to benefit from an extension of the grace period must enter into consultations with the SCM

4.202 Canada argues that the context of the phase-out requirement, and the object and purpose of the SCM Agreement in general, and Article 27 in particular, support this reading of the term. Canada observes that the SCM Agreement is the most comprehensive set of disciplines on subsidies and countervailing measures ever achieved in multilateral trade negotiations. For that reason, the Article 27 exception should not be read in isolation, either from the other disciplines of the SCM Agreement, or from the historical background from which it emerged. The recognition in Article 27.1 that "subsidies may play an important role in economic and development programmes of developing country Members," should be viewed as part of a broader package of disciplines aimed at controlling the economically distorting impact of specific subsidies. Among such subsidies, export subsidies have the most egregious impact on the international economy. Therefore, the transition period provided for certain developing countries in Articles 27.2(b) and 27.4 should be interpreted and applied as precisely that: a period in which such Members may make the adjustments necessary, in a staged manner, to bring their export subsidies within the ambit of control of Articles 3 and 4.

4.203 Canada submits that the negotiating history of and background to Article 27 provide further support for the above interpretation and analysis. Article 27 is a strengthened version of Article 14 of the Subsidies Code.[162] The Subsidies Code exempted developing country signatories from the commitment in Article 9 not to grant export subsidies. The principal obligation of developing country signatories was set out in Article 14(5):

> "A developing country signatory should endeavour to enter into a commitment to reduce or eliminate export subsidies when the use of such export subsidies is inconsistent with its competitive and development needs."

4.204 Canada further submits that the evolution of this provision into the much more stringent obligations set out in the SCM Agreement can be traced through early checklists prepared by the GATT Secretariat for the Negotiating Group on Subsidies and Countervailing Measures of the Uruguay Round. Among the points for negotiation was the following:

Committee at least a year in advance of the termination date. That is, as soon as a Member 'deems it necessary' to apply export subsidies beyond the eight year period, it must first enter into consultations with the Committee. That Member cannot simply prejudge the Committee's decision by making commitments to pay subsidies beyond the grace period and thereby causing tremendous market disruption. And a developing country Member has to justify to the SCM Committee that the subsidy in question should continue. The extension is not, therefore, unilaterally determined, is by no means certain and as such does not modify the imperative to 'phase out' export subsidies to benefit from the eight-year grace period."

[162] Agreement on Interpretation and Application of Article VI, XVI and XXIII of the General Agreement of Tariffs and Trade, (the Subsidies Code), The Texts of the Tokyo Round Agreements, (Geneva: General Agreement on Tariffs and Trade, 1986), at page 51.

> "The right of developing countries to grant export subsidies should not be subject to any special conditions or limitations. Export subsidies granted by developing countries should not be subject to countervailing duties or countermeasures if the country concerned agrees to phase out these export subsidies within an agreed time framework."[163]

Canada asserts that in the end, the SCM Agreement provided much stronger disciplines than both the Subsidies Code and the early negotiating objectives of some signatories. The export subsidies of developing country Members other than those set out in Annex VII are subject to strict limitations and conditions. The Subsidies Code's exhortation to phase out export subsidies that were not consistent with the development needs of a developing country signatory has been supplanted by an obligation to phase out those export subsidies within two years for products in which export competitiveness has been reached. All other export subsidies of such developing country Members must be phased out within an eight-year transition period.[164] In keeping with this evolution, and given the clear wording of Article 27.4, Brazil, according to Canada, must prove that it is in the process of bringing out of use, in a staged manner, its export subsidies.

4.205 Canada submits that, on its face, PROEX does not meet these conditions. The expansions to the PROEX programme confirm that Brazil has taken no steps, and intends to take no steps, to phase out the programme. PROEX does not have a termination date and no programme of phased reductions is in place for PROEX subsidies. Moreover, the financing period provided for in the scheme (10 to 15 years) put PROEX subsidies for aircraft outside the eight-year transition period. Most significant, carriers such as American Airlines have firm orders or options to be delivered well after 1 January 2003 on which they expect to be paid PROEX export subsidies. Thus, the Government of Brazil has already committed to paying export subsidies outside the grace period. Canada asserts that the PROEX export subsidy does not meet the phase out condition provided for in Article 27.4, and as such cannot benefit from the exemptions provided for in Articles 27.2 and 27.7. All such export subsidies are prohibited by Article 3.1(a) and must be terminated immediately in accordance with Article 4.7.

---

[163] GATT Documents MTN.GNG/NG10/W/9, 7 September 1987, at page 23; and MTN.GNG/NG10/W/9/Rev.1, 22 October 1987; and TN.GNG/NG10/ W/9/Rev.2, 2 December 1987. The Secretariat noted that the checklist was based on written submissions circulated in other GATT documents. In addition, the Secretariat states that: "[a]n attempt has been made to include also issues raised in oral statements at the three first meetings of the Group. In accordance with its purpose, the checklist contains only issues proposed for negotiations and not comments of a general nature or comments made on other participants' proposals."

[164] "An Analysis of the Proposed Uruguay Round Agreement, with Particular Emphasis on Aspects of Interest to Developing Economies," GATT Secretariat, MTN.TNC/W/122,) MTN.GNG/W/30, 29 November 1993, at page 58 .

4.206 **Brazil** disagrees with Canada that it has the burden of establishing its eligibility for the "phase out" clause, or any other clause, in Article 27. Brazil submits that if Canada believes that it is not entitled to the exemption for which it and other developing countries in the Uruguay Round bargained, it is up to Canada to prove it.

4.207 Brazil submits that putting aside the issue of burden of proof, it is clear that the "phase out" requirement in Article 27.4 is not a "phase down" requirement, which is what Canada implies. Article 27.4 specifies that a developing country Member "shall phase out its export subsidies within the eight-year period, preferably in a progressive manner." The ordinary meaning of the words "in a progressive manner" is that there should be a downward trend over the eight years. Yet Article 27.4 states that this should occur "preferably." It is not mandatory. Thus, a developing country that fails to phase out its export subsidies "progressively" does not lose entitlement to Article 27's benefits. Canada attempts to read into this language a requirement to phase export subsidies out of use "in a staged manner," somehow contrasting this "progressive" phase out with the "real" phase out, which would be rapid, steep, or abrupt. There is absolutely no support in the text of Article 27 or any other part of the Agreement for such a requirement.

4.208 Brazil asserts that Canada's argument that PROEX payments over the financing period are inconsistent with the clause, as some of those payments will occur after the eight-year exemption period has ended, is without any merit. Brazil notes that PROEX subsidies are granted in connection with the export sale of the aircraft. They are disbursed every six months for the period of the financing of the aircraft, which, in most cases, is 15 years. These payments are made to the holders of the NTN-I's, which are a form of bond. As each NTN-I becomes due, it is retired. The PROEX subsidy itself is granted when the commitment is made. The entire subsidy is paid when the aircraft is exported. Brazil submits that it includes the full face amount (*i.e.*, undiscounted) in its budget for the year in which the delivery is made, not over the financing period of approximately 15 years. This is in accordance with the standards of the International Monetary Fund which require that the full amount of the subsidy be included in the budget for the year in which it is made available. Thus, to count the later disbursement of funds in accordance with the PROEX commitment as a subsidy would be to double count the subsidy.[165]

4.209 **Canada** asserts that Brazil has misunderstood its submission. It asserts that "phase out" should not be equated with "phase down." "Phase down" simply means "reduce gradually." "Phase out" means "bring gradually out of use." In other words, the term "phase out" includes the idea of "phase down," but also the idea to eliminate at some point. Canada also takes issue with Brazil's use of

[165] Brazil's Second Written Submission, para. 20.

the Article 27.4 phrase "preferably in a progressive manner" to infer that while there should be a downward trend, this is not mandatory. The word "progressive" means that the phase out should preferably be carried out at an increasing rate. That is to say, the higher the level of subsidies, the higher the rate of reduction - much like progressive taxation.

(i) Arguments Relating to the Issue of Inconsistency with Developing Country Member's Development Needs

4.210 **Canada** submits that the third condition of Article 27 is that export subsidies shall be phased out in a period shorter than eight years if they are inconsistent with a country's development needs. It argues that this provision is not a self-judging provision and should be applied on the basis of objective standards. Canada suggests that one such standard is the domestic content rules of PROEX established by Brazil.

4.211 Canada argues that domestic content rules are typically incorporated into export financing and export support programmes with the objective of ensuring that a government's expenditure of foreign exchange is focussed on supporting domestic rather than foreign production. Under the terms of the PROEX regulations, exports with a domestic content ratio of 60 per cent or more are eligible for interest equalization payments on 100 per cent of their value. For goods with a domestic content index of less than 60 per cent, the percentage eligible for interest equalization is reduced according to a formula. For example, for the ERJ-145, which has a domestic content index of approximately 15 per cent, the formula dictates that only 55 per cent of the value of the aircraft should be eligible for interest equalization. However, PROEX interest equalization is paid on 100 per cent of the value of the aircraft because of a waiver granted to EMBRAER. Canada also submits that there are provisions for foreign-produced spare parts to be included in the "export" package and these spare parts can make up 30 per cent of the value of the export package. Thus, export subsidy payments can be paid on spare parts with zero Brazilian content.

4.212 **Brazil** disagrees with Canada that in order for it to avail itself of the provisions of Article 27, it has to establish that PROEX is consistent with its development needs. Brazil argues that Article 27 *presumes* that the development needs of developing countries require subsidies, as is made plain by the first paragraph of Article 27, which provides that "Members recognize that subsidies may play an important role in economic development programmes of developing country Members." Brazil submits that under Canada's theory, a Member may challenge any developing country's export subsidies at any time, and the developing country has the immediate burden of proving that they are consistent with its development needs. A developed country, Canada argues, could ask for consultations tomorrow on every developing country Member's export subsidies and begin a process of requiring every developing country to prove that those subsidies are consistent with its development needs. And it could do so a month later, and a month after that in a never-ending process of harassment.

4.213 Brazil argues that such a situation would effectively do away with Article 27. At the very least, it would reverse the bargain of the Uruguay Round. By explicitly recognizing the legitimacy of export subsidies for developing countries, Article 27.1 effectively presumes that subsidies are consistent with a developing country's development needs. Article 27.4, in turn, provides that such subsidies shall be eliminated in less than eight years "when the use of such subsidies is inconsistent with" a Member's development needs. That language clearly means that the burden is on the party challenging a developing country's subsidies to prove that the situation envisioned by Article 27.1 has changed by adducing evidence that the subsides in question are inconsistent with a Member's development needs. Brazil submits that any other interpretation would undo the bargain of the Uruguay Round and ignore the holding of the Appellate Body in *United States - Shirts and Blouses*, which makes clear that the burden is on Canada, the challenger to this presumption.[166]

4.214 Brazil argues further that if there is any doubt concerning Brazil's development needs, the following will demonstrate the extent of the needs of Brazil: (a) Brazil experienced a US$30 billion drain on its foreign currency reserve in a matter of days due to factors completely outside Brazil and entirely unrelated to the health of Brazil's economy; (b) Brazil is still suffering the brunt of the international financial crises, and prospects for the near future are uncertain; (c) UNCTAD reports that in 1997 the current account deficit was $33.5 billion, down from a $6 billion surplus four years earlier; (d) the trade deficit in 1997 was nearly $20 billion, contrasted with a $12 billion surplus five years earlier; (e) in the second quarter of 1998 domestic interest rates for borrowers were 92.2 per cent per year; (f) in 1997 the public deficit was 4.3 per cent of GDP; there was a surplus only three years earlier; and (g) unemployment is at the highest level of all the years covered in the UNCTAD report, 1989 through the first half of 1998.

4.215 Brazil argues that the domestic content ratio argument of Canada is without any merit. Noting Article 2 of TRIMs, Brazil notes a certain irony in the accusation, as traditionally there has been the accusation in the GATT that the content requirements of developing countries were too high and burdensome. In any event, there is no domestic content requirement in Article 27, and Canada's attempt to insert one is totally without justification.

4.216 **Canada** disagrees with Brazil that it wants to insert a domestic content requirement into Article 27. Its argument is that PROEX contains domestic content requirements, placed there for reasons related to development needs, and

---

[166] *United States - Measure Affecting Imports of Woven Wool Shirts and Blouses from India*, WT/DS33/AB/R, report of the Appellate Body adopted on 23 May 1997.

that these requirements are not being fulfilled in the case of aircraft exports. According to Canada, Brazil has not contested this point. Canada submits that the recital of the economic problems facing Brazil as a result of the global financial crises does not establish that PROEX is consistent with its development needs. Brazil should have explained how PROEX helps Brazil overcome these problems or, more generally, contributes to meeting Brazil's development needs, for example by contributing to its foreign exchange earnings.

4.217 In respect of Canada's submission that Brazil should have explained how PROEX helps it to overcome the problems identified in paragraph 4.133 above, and in response to a question[167] from the Panel, **Brazil** stated that:

> "The importance of exports - and PROEX therefore - is not limited to the correction of current account imbalances or to supply additional economic stimulus or job positions, although it is certainly necessary for these purposes. The achievement of a competitive level of exports is an integral part of the major goal of increasing the productivity and "tradability" of the Brazilian economy as a whole. The idea is to do away with the structural and conceptual distortions that resulted from decades of the protectionist "import substitution model." The external market should be viewed not as an occasional alternative to the internal market in times of slow economic growth, but as part of medium and long term strategic planning. The exposure to external markets must be increased and PROEX plays a crucial role in this regard. In an article about the stabilization and opening of the Brazilian economy, economist Antonio Correa de Lacerda underlines the importance of full integration with the world markets and identifies four basic hurdles for the exporting sector: (a) extremely high interest rates (average overnight interest rates are around 30 per cent) and difficult access to internationally competitive financing; (b) a burdensome tributary system; (c) a complex bureaucratic structure; and (d) a significant structural "Brazil cost"...PROEX helps overcome the first of the hurdles listed by Correa de Lacerda and is a crucial factor in the strategy [of the government]...to consolidate the transformation of Brazil into an open and stable economy."

[167] The question posed by the Panel was as follows: "In its second submission..., Brazil indicated that in its view Article 27 presumes that the development needs of developing country Member require subsidies, but states that it is ready to provide the Panel with support for the position that PROEX is consistent with Brazil's development needs if the Panel so requests. In paragraph 16 of its oral statement to the second meeting of the Panel, Brazil identified development difficulties facing it but did not explicitly explain the link between PROEX interest rate equalisation and those development difficulties. Could Brazil please elaborate?"

4.218 **Canada** submits that Brazil's explanation amounts to nothing more than a statement that the PROEX export subsidy is necessary to increase exports. This cannot be considered to be a sufficient explanation of why an export subsidy is not inconsistent with Brazil's development needs. Any export subsidy, properly administered, should increase exports. Brazil's explanation in no way rebuts Canada's comment that PROEX, as applied in civil aircraft sector, is inconsistent with Brazil's own view of its development needs as indicated in the very same programme through its domestic content requirements.

E. Arguments Relating to the Panel's Recommendations

4.219 **Canada** argues that as PROEX payments constitute prohibited subsidies within the meaning of the SCM Agreement, Brazil must neither grant nor maintain such payments as stipulated in Article 3.1 of the SCM Agreement. Brazil must not: (i) enter into new arrangements by which PROEX would be paid; (ii) begin paying subsidies promised or committed, such as those in respect of aircraft that have yet to be delivered, including on the conversion of options to firm orders; and (iii) continue to pay PROEX subsidies.

4.220 In addition to the recommendations sought by Canada under Paragraphs 3.1 - 3.3 of this report, Canada further submits that Article 4.7 of the SCM Agreement sets out the specific remedy available to it, as well as the grant of authority to the Panel with respect to the application of Article 3.2. It argues that the Panel may recommend the withdrawal of subsidies already granted where the circumstances of the case and the distortions caused by the subsidies in question warrant such a remedy. In this light, Canada submits that in respect of transactions entered into by EMBRAER and subsidies granted by Brazil in the period between the composition of the Panel and the adoption of the Report of the Panel, the Panel should make a specific recommendation, for the following reason. In a report issued on August 10, 1998, the investment bankers Bear Stearns gave the following advice to prospective customers of EMBRAER aircraft:

> "Finally, cognizant that a WTO decision is eminent [*sic*] and may result in the ending of an attractive subsidy, any remaining potential customers who were considering a future purchase may decide to anticipate orders with EMBRAER over the 12 months before the ruling is handed down."

4.221 Canada submits that the particular circumstances of the regional aircraft market require that the Panel fashion a specific remedy in respect of subsidies granted to induce sales in anticipation of an adverse ruling by the Panel, as termination of PROEX subsidies after the adoption of the Panel report would not, in such circumstances, redress the harm that would be caused by such subsidies. Accordingly, Canada urges the Panel to recommend the withdrawal of subsidies granted pursuant to transactions entered into in the period following the composition of the Panel on October 22, 1998.

4.222 Canada submits that "without delay" in respect of new subsidy arrangements must mean as of the date of adoption of the Report of the Panel by the

DSB. Canada further submits that "without delay" in respect of existing subsidies or subsidies already granted means as soon as practicable to terminate the arrangements and, in any event, no later than ninety days after the adoption of the Report of the Panel by the DSB.

4.223 **Brazil** submits that Canada's request for a detailed, specific remedy goes beyond the powers of the Panel to grant even if the Panel were to agree with Canada on the merits of this dispute. Brazil asserts that Article 4.7 of the Subsidies Agreement specifies that, "If the measure in question is found to be a prohibited subsidy, the Panel shall recommend that the subsidizing Member withdraw the subsidy without delay." The Panel is authorized to do no more. Specifically, the means by which any withdrawal is accomplished is for the Member concerned to determine. Accordingly, the Panel should reject Canada's request for a specific remedy.

4.224 Responding to the arguments of Brazil and the third parties in this dispute that its request for specific recommendations go beyond the mandate of the Panel, **Canada** made the following two points: First, that at no point had it asked the Panel to "dictate the means by which a subsidy is to be withdrawn." Canada did note that the obligation in Article 3.2 was simple: a Member shall not grant, and shall not maintain, prohibited subsidies. Where such subsidies were found to exist under a programme, Article 3.2 prohibits the granting of new subsidies and the maintenance of existing ones. Canada asked the Panel to recommend that Brazil abide by its explicit obligation in Article 3.2 of the SCM Agreement.

4.225 Second, Canada agrees that it is seeking recommendations from the Panel that are different from recommendations previously made by panels under GATT and WTO practice. Canada submits, however, that the present dispute is very different from any other dispute settlement procedure conducted to date under the GATT or the WTO Agreement. Canada argued that its position was supported by two considerations. First, the SCM Agreement as a whole and the dispute settlement procedure in Article 4 are novel and unique in the WTO. Second, and more to the point, Article 4.7 - the grant of authority to the Panel to make recommendations - is also new and unique. It is, indeed, a "special or additional" procedure in the sense of Article 1.2 of the DSU. For this reason, previous GATT and WTO practice is of limited value as guidance in interpreting the remedy provisions of Article 4 - except perhaps to draw the *a contrario* conclusion that Article 4.7 should *not* be interpreted to mean the same thing as Article 19 of the DSU. Article 4.7 provides the Panel with the authority to recommend the *withdrawal* of a *subsidy*, and not simply, as Article 19 provides, to bring a subsidy *programme into conformity* with the SCM Agreement. As the authority of the Panel is significantly different from the authority reflected in the "overwhelming preponderance" of practice prior to the entry into force of the WTO Agreement, the Panel may exercise this novel authority in a way that would be different from prevailing GATT and WTO practice (emphasis in original).

V. ARGUMENTS PRESENTED BY THIRD PARTIES

A. *European Communities*

5.1 The European Communities submits that although Brazil has stated that it does not contest the existence of a subsidy in this case, nor indeed that it is contingent upon export performance, it will nonetheless be essential for the Panel to precisely define the subsidy at issue. The European Communities asserts that this has implications for the analysis under Article 27.4 of the SCM Agreement and, if Brazil's measure should be considered contrary to Brazil's WTO obligations, for the action which will be required of Brazil to implement the Panel's recommendations. The European Communities further note that the approach taken by the Panel in this case will be an important precedent for the interpretation of Article 1 of the SCM Agreement in future cases.

5.2 The European Communities refer to Article 1 of the SCM Agreement which defines a subsidy as being a financial contribution by a government and which confers a benefit. The European Communities observes that payments by Brazil to effect interest rate equalization are made by means of zero-coupon bonds maturing on interest payment dates and being worth 3.8 per cent of the capital outstanding. Canada, the European Communities submit, analyses the payments under these bonds as "financial contributions" of the kinds mentioned in subparagraph (i) or alternatively (iv) of Article 1.1(a)(1) of the SCM Agreement. The European Communities argue that Canada's analysis is incomplete, as it overlooks certain important considerations.

5.3 The European Communities submits that Canada does not identify the beneficiary of the subsidy in its legal analysis. The European Communities argues that the direct recipient of these payments will not necessarily be the purchaser - it will be the holder of the bonds on maturity, as it appears that the purchaser may "elect to pay instead a more commercial rate of interest to obtain a lump-sum reduction in the purchase price through the sale of the bonds in the market."

5.4 The European Communities submits that although Canada characterizes PROEX payments as "outright grants whether received in a stream of payments or in a lump sum," it does not draw the consequences of these alternative "payments" for the case at hand. The European Communities submits that it is important to do so, as an analysis which considers that PROEX confers a series of subsidies in the form of payments over 15 years will result in different contributions to the total "levels of export subsides" in each year compared with an analysis which treats PROEX as an outright subsidy in the form of a lump sum payment. It will therefore affect Brazil's compliance with its obligations under Article 27.4 of the SCM Agreement to phase out its export subsidies and not increase their level. The two alternative analyses also have different consequences in the event of a Panel recommendation to Brazil to "withdraw" the measure and the subsidy under Article 4.7 of the SCM Agreement.

5.5 The European Communities submits that the key to clarifying this issue lies in carefully considering the notion of "financial contribution" in Article 1.1 of the SCM Agreement. While in Canada's analysis, this is assumed to mean "payments," the European Communities submits that Article 1.1(a) of the SCM Agreement deliberately permits a much broader interpretation. For example a "financial contribution" under Article 1.1(a)(1)(i) of the SCM Agreement may be not only a "transfer of funds" but also a "potential direct transfer of funds or liabilities." Also, the other items in the List make clear that payments need not be immediate but may be simply committed. The European Communities argues that given the facts of the case, the Brazilian government makes a financial contribution when it issues, or enters into a commitment to issue, bonds in support of an export transaction. The facts of this case show that the issue of these bonds has an immediately realizable value which supports the export sale. This is also the point in time when the ultimate and intended beneficiary, the Brazilian exporter, obtains its benefit by concluding an export sale, on the basis of the existence of a financial incentive without which the sale may not have taken place.

5.6 The European Communities considers that this interpretation is supported by a consideration of the context of Article 1 of the SCM Agreement, its object and purpose as well as general principles of law. The European Communities submit that the relevant elements of context and legal principles which the European Communities submit should guide the Panel are as follows:

- Article 4.7 of the SCM Agreement provides that a finding by the Panel that PROEX is a prohibited subsidy would require it to recommend "that the subsidy be withdrawn without delay" and to specify in its recommendation "the time period in which the measure must be withdrawn."
- One purpose of the dispute settlement system is to provide "security and predictability to the multilateral trading system" (Article 3.2 DSU). The same provision also provides that "recommendations and rulings of the DSB shall not add to or diminish rights and obligations provided for in the covered agreements." A corollary of this for the European Communities is that the dispute settlement system cannot produce retroactive effects. Nothing in the SCM Agreement demonstrates a contrary intention.
- The WTO Agreements, like international law in general, lay down rights and obligations for the states and international organizations which are its Members. They do not create rights and obligations for private parties.
- It is a general principle of law that legitimate expectations should be protected.

5.7 The European Communities asserts that these elements of context and legal principles support its interpretation of Article 1.1 of the SCM Agreement.

An interpretation of the SCM Agreement which would consider the *payments* under the bonds to constitute subsidies (rather than the fact of entering into a legal obligation to make such payments in support of an export sale) could also have as its result that a scheme could never be considered a subsidy until actual payments are made; this interpretation would unjustifiably limit the scope of Article 1 of the SCM Agreement (which specifically refers to "potential transfers of funds"). Moreover, such an approach would entail that, in case the Panel makes a finding against PROEX, Brazil would be required to withdraw the subsidy and therefore all subsidies not yet granted, i.e., payments could no longer be made under Brazilian government bonds or that a purchaser of EMBRAER aircraft would have to pay a higher price than that resulting from the contract. This would be extremely disruptive of the rights of private parties, purchasers, suppliers and banks. In addition, since in this case the payments are "tied" to specific contracts and made to a person other than the ultimate or intended beneficiary of the subsidy, such an interpretation could not contribute to removing the harm of any prohibited subsidy. It is therefore to be avoided in such a context.

5.8 The European Communities submits that a recommendation of the Panel to withdraw the subsidy based on the assumption that each payment made under a PROEX contract constituted a separate financial contribution would probably be impossible to implement. It would inevitably lead to countermeasures under Article 4.10 of the SCM Agreement.

5.9 The European Communities considers that this interpretation is particularly appropriate in the present case of an alleged prohibited subsidy in the aircraft sector in order to ensure a remedy consistent with the intention of the SCM Agreement and the general principles of international law. The remedy may not, of course, be the same in, for instance, countervailing duty cases, where there is a requirement to establish the existence of a quantifiable amount of subsidy. The European Communities submits that the issue of when the financial contribution is made and the benefit granted should not be confused with the issue of the appropriate timing and level of duties in a countervailing duty investigation; there, the investigating authorities aim to "capture" the benefit of the subsidy for the purpose of "offsetting" it through the imposition of countervailing duties and may therefore take into consideration the actual flow of cash as a reasonable basis for quantifying the benefit in any given investigation period.

5.10 The European Communities submits, based on the above analysis, that a financial contribution is made, and a benefit is conferred, when a binding commitment of PROEX support for an export-contingent sales contract is concluded. The European Communities is aware of the practice of concluding option contracts for the purchase of aircraft. These are of many different kinds and the application of the above principles to them will depend on their precise terms.

5.11 The European Communities submits that if it is considered that a financial contribution is made, and a benefit is conferred, when a binding commitment of PROEX support for an export-contingent sales contract is concluded, then it would not be feasible to require Brazil to "withdraw the subsidy" for contracts already concluded by EMBRAER with PROEX support, as demanded by Canada. There is no basis in the Dispute Settlement Understanding or the SCM Agreement for the Panel to make a recommendation retroactive to 22 October 1998.

5.12 The European Communities confirms its view that the Brazilian government grants a subsidy when it "issues or enters into a commitment to issue bonds in support of an export transaction" in its response to the following question from the Panel: "The European Union argues that under Article 1 of the SCM Agreement, the Brazilian government grants a subsidy when it 'issues or enters into a commitment to issue bonds in support of an export transaction' as opposed to when the payments are actually made. Would such a finding limit the impact of a panel recommendation, as only future commitments with the support of PROEX would be affected? Would the view of the European Union be affected if a disproportionate number of contracts were concluded between the date of establishment of the panel and when the panel/Appellate Body report is adopted?"

> "PROEX payments, [which] are made to the lending financial institution in the form of non-interest bearing National Treasury Bonds, ... may either be redeemed on a semi-annual basis for the duration of the financing period or may be sold on the market and the proceeds paid to the purchaser as a lump sum. This clearly demonstrates that the subsidy is granted at the moment the PROEX commitment is made by Brazil in connection with the binding purchase contract for an aircraft to which it is tied; the subsequent "use" of the subsidy is left to the discretion of the purchaser...As a result in these specific circumstances (contract-specific subsidies), a Panel recommendation cannot affect subsidies already granted without disrupting the rights of private parties, purchasers, suppliers and banks...[A] Panel recommendation in this case can only relate to definitive PROEX commitments made after the adoption of a Report by the Dispute Settlement Body. Accordingly, it will not apply to PROEX commitments made on aircraft sales contracts which are binding before the report is adopted...The European Communities realizes that this position means that, if the Panel finds the PROEX subsidies to be prohibited, this will mean that there is no "remedy" against certain past subsidies. However, this is an unavoidable consequence of the present rules and must be accepted. Canada's potential remedy in the present case can only be to have the PROEX scheme modified or terminated for the future...The absence of remedy for past and consummated violations is a well-known feature of the GATT/WTO system. First, it is inherent in the principle that DSB rulings do not have retroactive effect. Second, it is established and accepted that it can lead in some cases to there being no remedy at all for the complaining party. [The decision]...of the Panel in

> *Norway - Procurement of Toll Collection Equipment for the City of Trondheim*[168],... [a case under the Agreement on Government Procurement] is still. pertinent...[There the Panel] did not consider it appropriate for it to recommend that Norway negotiate a mutually satisfactory solution with the United States that took into account the lost opportunities of the United States companies in the procurement or that, in the event that such a negotiation did not yield a mutually satisfactory result, the Committee be prepared to authorize the United States to withdraw benefits under the Agreement from Norway with respect to opportunities to bid of equal value to the Trondheim contract."

5.13 The European Communities disagrees with Brazil's *a contrario* interpretation of the item (k) of the Illustrative List. If this interpretation were to be accepted, it could change Annex I of the SCM Agreement from an illustrative to an exhaustive list of export subsidies. The European Communities submits that there is a clear contrast between the first and second paragraphs of item (k) of the Illustrative List. The first paragraph, the only one on which Brazil relies, declares to be an export subsidy certain measures "in so far as they are used to secure a material advantage in the field of export credit terms." This defines the scope of the prohibition; it does not derogate from Article 3.1(a). The second paragraph provides that export credit practices within certain defined limits "shall not be considered an export subsidy prohibited by this Agreement." The second paragraph is covered by footnote 5; the first paragraph is not.

5.14 The European Communities submits that the OECD Guidelines on Officially Supported Export Credits clearly satisfy the requirements of paragraph 2 of item (k) of Annex I of the SCM Agreement. All export credit activities which conform to the OECD Guidelines, are not prohibited under Article 3.1 or any other provision of the SCM Agreement. Thus, for purposes of the SCM Agreement, paragraph 2 of item (k) of the SCM Agreement creates a "safe haven" for Member export credit practices which conform to the OECD Guidelines. The European Communities submits that the OECD guidelines place important restrictions on the ability of member countries to subsidize. Measures which effectively reduce rates below those of the Arrangement, fall outside the "safe haven" and are subject to the full rigours of the SCM Agreement. If they constitute a subsidy and are export contingent, they are prohibited.

5.15 In response to a question[169] from the Panel concerning the scope of item (k) of the Illustrative List of Export Subsidies, the European Communities

---

[168] *See*, GPR/DS.2/R, adopted on 13 May 1992, paras. 4.21, 4.24 and 4.26.

[169] The question posed by the Panel was as follows: "It could be argued that the phrase "in the field of export credits" as used in item (k) of the Annex I of the SCM Agreement is limited to the interest rates and other transaction costs. Assuming for the sake of argument that this view is correct, what would be the appropriate benchmark for a comparison? Specifically, should the export credit terms of a transaction supported by PROEX interest rate equalization be compared to the export credit

reiterated its view that Brazil's interpretation of item (k) of the Illustrative List was unjustified and not supported by the text of the SCM Agreement:

> "[T]he first paragraph of Annex I(k) to the...[SCM Agreement should be seen] to be defining an *illustrative* prohibition (i.e., *not* exhaustively defining the scope of Article 3.1 (a) in this sector) and that the second paragraph by contrast contained an exception, not only from the first paragraph but from the whole...[SCM Agreement] (the OECD "safe haven")...Since the first paragraph contains an *illustrative prohibition*, it does not much matter whether the term "in the field of export credits" is limited to interest rates and transaction costs. The same prohibition would apply, if not under this paragraph, then under Article 3.1(a), to other elements of a transaction than interest rates and transaction costs that have the same effect as a subsidy (in other words, bringing the effective rate below the applicable Arrangement rate)...Of the two benchmarks proposed by the question, the first would lead to the whole of the PROEX being considered contrary to the first paragraph of item (k) since PROEX operates to reduce the commercial interest rate available to the transaction by 3.8 per cent. The second benchmark would lead to PROEX being contrary to that paragraph only when the commercial interest rate available to the transaction exceeds the OECD Arrangement by less than 3.8 per cent...The [European Communities] considers that the context of this paragraph (and in particular the second paragraph of item (k) which even more clearly reflects the intention that export credits should not distort competition) pleads in favour of the material advantage being assessed by comparison with the generally available or OECD arrangement rate."

5.16 The European Communities submits that while it recognizes that subsidies may be important in the economic development of developing countries and does not wish to impose any new obligations on developing countries in this respect, Article 27.4 of the SCM Agreement should not be interpreted to exempt developing countries unconditionally from the disciplines of Article 3.1 of the SCM Agreement. Article 27.4 imposes a number of conditions which should be respected. These are that export subsidies shall be (a) phased out during this period, preferably in a progressive manner; (b) they should not be increased and (c) be eliminated earlier if the use of such export subsidies is inconsistent with the country's development needs. Since Article 27.4 is a conditional exception to a basic prohibition of the SCM Agreement,

---

terms that would be available to that purchaser of EMBRAER aircraft on the market for the purchase of those aircraft if the PROEX interest rate equalization were not available for the transaction, or should it relate to the export credit terms available (including through official financing at OECD consensus rates by a Participant to the OECD Arrangement) to the purchaser if it purchased a competing aircraft".

these conditions should be strictly adhered to if a developing country Member were to avail itself of the exemption provided by the Article.

5.17 With respect to the relationship between Articles 3 and 27 of the SCM Agreement, the European Communities in a response to questions from the Panel stated:

> "[There seems] to be no basis to consider that Article 27 is *lex specialis* to Article 3.1(a), as this term is normally understood. A *lex specialis* would contain a complete set of rules. Article 27 does not. It contains certain exceptions or derogations and the conditions for their application. The rules which apply where the conditions are not met, are not found in Article 27, but in other provisions of the Agreement...If the Panel were to agree with Brazil that Article 27 is *lex specialis*, the burden of proof would be borne by Canada. If, on the other hand, Article 27 is considered to be an exception, it would be for Brazil, as the party invoking the exception, to prove that the conditions of paragraph 4 are fulfilled. Since Article 27.4 is a conditional exception to a basic prohibition of the [SCM Agreement], these conditions should be strictly adhered to...[T]his conclusion is confirmed by the corresponding procedural exemption contained in Article 27.7. This is made subject to the same conditions as the substantive exception...Indeed, since the Parties agreed to the applicability of Article 4 of the [SCM Agreement], they have implicitly assumed that Article 27...is not *lex specialis*. Otherwise Brazil would presumably have objected to the application of the procedure in Article 4 of the [SCM Agreement], at least until such time as Canada had demonstrated that the conditions of paragraphs 2 to 5 of Article 27 were not fulfilled."

B. United States

5.18 The **United States** submits that Brazil's claim that it could provide export subsidies to counter non-export credit subsidies offered by another Member has no basis in WTO law, neither is it supported by a standard *Vienna Convention* analysis. The United States claims that Brazil's approach is incorrect, and, perhaps recognizing the weakness of its position, Brazil does not even argue that its approach is supported by such an analysis. The ordinary meaning of the phrase "to secure a material advantage in the field of export credit terms" does not support Brazil's position. The phrase refers to the "field of export credit terms" and not to the "field of subsidies in general." Moreover, the United States is not aware of anything in the context or object and purpose of the SCM Agreement that would warrant departing from the ordinary meaning of the phrase in question.

5.19 In a response to a question[170] from the Panel regarding which benchmark should be used to determine whether PROEX secures material advantage in the field of export credit terms, the United States stated that:

> "Within the context of the OECD Arrangement on Guidelines for Officially Supported Export Credits (the Arrangement), the provision of export credit terms outside the boundaries of the Arrangement is considered to imbalance the playing field (thereby generating the possibility of material advantage) and, therefore, to be subject to compensatory actions (e.g., matching). Hence, in the context of this question, the relevant reference point for comparison in evaluating the possible existence of material advantage are the terms available through the Arrangement (e.g., CIRR levels and repayment limits).

5.20 The United States submits that the following specific recommendations requested by Canada go far beyond the mandate of the Panel:

- Brazil shall not grant new subsidies under PROEX, including subsidies promised or committed, but not yet granted, on regional aircraft not yet delivered;
- Brazil shall no longer maintain existing subsidies under PROEX and must terminate such subsidies no later than three months after the adoption of the Report of the Panel by the DSB; and
- Brazil shall withdraw without delay PROEX subsidies granted pursuant to transactions entered into following the composition of the Panel on October 22, 1998.

The United States argues not only are they inconsistent with the express terms of Article 4.7 of the SCM Agreement, but also the Understanding on Rules and Procedures Governing the Settlement of Disputes ("DSU"), and established GATT 1947 and WTO practice. Consequently, should the Panel agree with Canada on the merits, it should reject the requested remedies. The Panel should, instead, make a general recommendation that Brazil withdraw its PROEX subsidies without delay, and leave it to Brazil, in the first instance, to determine how such a withdrawal can best be accomplished. The United States notes, however, that under Article 4.7 of the SCM Agreement, the Panel also must specify the time period within which the subsidies must be withdrawn.

5.21 The United States argues that the specific recommendations[171] requested by Canada go far beyond the types of recommendations made by the overwhelming preponderance of prior GATT 1947 and WTO Panels. In virtually

[170] The same question was posed to the European Communities; *ibid.*

[171] By "specific" recommendation, the United States means a recommendation that requires a party to take a particular, specific action in order to cure a WTO-inconsistency found by a Panel.

every case in which a Panel has found a measure to be inconsistent with a GATT obligation, Panels have issued the general recommendation that the country "bring its measures . . . into conformity with GATT."[172] This well-established practice is codified in Article 19.1 of the DSU, which provides: "Where a Panel or the Appellate Body concludes that a measure is inconsistent with a covered agreement, it shall recommend that the Member concerned bring the measure into conformity with that agreement." Indeed, in the first case to work its way through the new dispute settlement system, the recommendations of both the Panel and the Appellate Body carefully adhered to Article 19.1.[173] Moreover, in the first WTO dispute to focus on the propriety of specific recommendations, the Panel found that Article 19.1 precluded such recommendations. In rejecting a request by Mexico for specific recommendations, the Panel in the *Guatemala - Cement* case stated:

> "In our view, this language clearly establishes a distinction between the **recommendation** of a Panel, and the **means** by which that recommendation is to be implemented. The former is governed by Article 19.1, and is limited to a particular form. The latter may be suggested by a Panel, but the choice of means is decided, in the first instance, by the Member concerned. Of course, it is possible that the prevailing Member in the dispute may not be satisfied with the Member's implementation. The DSU recognizes this possibility, and provides for recourse to the dispute settlement procedures to resolve any such disagreements.[174] (emphasis in original)

5.22 The United States argues that the requirement that Panels make general recommendations reflects the purpose and role of dispute settlement in the WTO, and before it the GATT 1947. Article 3.4 of the DSU provides that "[r]ecommendations and rulings made by the DSB shall be aimed at achieving a satisfactory settlement of the matter," and Article 3.7 provides that "[a] solution mutually acceptable to the parties to a dispute . . . is clearly to be preferred." To this end, Article 11 of the DSU directs Panels to "consult regularly with the par-

---

[172] See, for example, *Canada - Measures Affecting Exports of Unprocessed Herring and Salmon*, L/6268, adopted 22 March 1988, BISD 35S/98, 115, para. 5.1. The United States noted that the number of panel reports in which panels have made recommendations using similar language is well in excess of 100.

[173] In its report on *United States - Standards for Reformulated and Conventional Gasoline*, adopted 20 May 1996, WT/DS2/AB/R, the Appellate Body recommended "that the Dispute Settlement Body request the United States to bring the baseline establishment rules contained in Part 80 of Title 40 of the Code of Federal Regulations into conformity with its obligations under the General Agreement." The Panel in that case issued a virtually identical recommendation. WT/DS2/R, para 8.2, adopted 20 May 1996.

[174] *Guatemala - Anti-Dumping Investigation Regarding Portland Cement from Mexico,* WT/DS60/R, report of the Panel circulated on 19 June 1998, para. 8.3, reversed on other grounds, WT/DS60/AB/R, report of the Appellate Body adopted on 25 November 1998.

ties to the dispute and give them adequate opportunity to develop a mutually satisfactory solution." Ideally, a mutually agreed solution will be achieved before a Panel issues its report. However, if this does not occur, a general Panel recommendation that directs a party to conform with its obligations still leaves parties with the necessary room to cooperate in arriving at a mutually agreed solution. Indeed, a Member generally has many options available to it to bring a measure into conformity with its WTO obligations. A Panel cannot and should not prejudge by its recommendation the solution to be arrived at by the parties to the dispute after the DSB adopts the Panel's report.

5.23 The United States further notes that the requirement that panels issue general recommendations comports with the nature of a Panel's expertise, which lies in the interpretation of covered agreements. Panels generally lack expertise in the domestic law of a defending party.[175] Thus, while it is appropriate for a Panel to determine in a particular case that a Member's legislation was applied in a manner inconsistent with that country's obligations under a WTO agreement, it is not appropriate for a Panel to dictate which of the available options a party must take to bring its actions into conformity with its international obligations. The compliance process under the DSU makes the precise manner of implementation a matter to be determined in the first instance by the Member concerned, subject to limited rights to compensation or retaliation by parties that have successfully invoked the dispute settlement procedures. In Article 19 of the DSU, the drafters precluded a Panel from prejudging the outcome of this process in their recommendations.

5.24 The United States observes that the preceding analysis is not affected by the existence of Article 4.7 of the SCM Agreement, a provision which, pursuant to Article 1.2 and Appendix 2 of the DSU, is a special or additional rule and procedure. While Article 4.7 prescribes a recommendation (withdrawal of the subsidy) that is different from the recommendation prescribed in Article 19.1 of the DSU (bring the measure into conformity), there is nothing in the text, context, or object and purpose of Article 4.7 indicating that Panels have greater freedom in a prohibited subsidies dispute to dictate the means by which a subsidy is to be withdrawn. Indeed, the text of Article 4.7 suggests exactly the opposite. In Article 4.7, the drafters expressly granted Panels the authority to recommend the *timing* of withdrawal, but did not confer a similar express grant of authority on Panels to recommend the *means* of withdrawal. This suggests that the drafters consciously refrained from granting Panels the authority to recommend, in the first instance, the means of withdrawal.

[175] See Article 8.3 of the DSU, which provides that citizens of Members whose governments are parties to a dispute normally shall not serve on a Panel concerned with that dispute, absent agreement by the parties.

5.25 The United States submits that in the first subsidies case to work its way through the WTO dispute settlement system, the Panel declined to make a specific recommendation. In the *Indonesia - Autos* case, the United States and the European Communities alleged that subsidies provided by Indonesia caused serious prejudice to their respective interests.[176] Article 7.8 of the SCM Agreement, which is a special or additional rule and procedure under Article 1.2 and Appendix 2 of the DSU, essentially provides that where a complainant proves its case of serious prejudice, the subsidizing Member "shall take appropriate steps to remove the adverse effects or shall withdraw the subsidy." In *Indonesia - Autos*, the Panel found that the European Communities had proved its serious prejudice case, but declined to specify the means by which Indonesia had to eliminate the adverse effects or withdraw the subsidies.[177]

5.26 The United States submits that the issue as to when the Brazilian government grants a subsidy is not that "important" in this particular case. In a response to a question[178] posed by the Panel, it stated that:

> "The United States does not...contest [the argument of the European Communities regarding] the timing of this particular subsidy...[It] does not believe, [however], that the timing of the subsidy in this case is an important issue. Here, the United States simply notes that there is a difference between the "timing" and the "duration" of a subsidy. The timing of a subsidy deals with the question of how long a subsidy lasts, and would seem to be the more relevant issue for purposes of the instant dispute...[T]he United States does disagree with the [European Communities] regarding the conclusions to be drawn from this fact. More specifically, the United States does not believe that there is anything in the SCM Agreement in particular, or in public international law in general, that would preclude repayment of a subsidy by the recipient as one means of withdrawing a subsidy within the meaning of Article 4.7 of the SCM Agreement. The point made by the United States in its third-party submission was that it is not for the Panel to specify the means by which a subsidy is to be withdrawn. The United States agrees with the proposition that remedies in the WTO dispute settlement system are not retroactive. However, in the case of a subsidy that is properly allocated over several years (as appears to be the case with respect to PROEX subsidies in question), the withdrawal of that portion of the subsidy allocated to future time periods would not constitute a retroactive remedy or retroactive implementation. Instead, it would constitute prospective implementation based on a recognition of the distinction between the measure conferring

[176] *Indonesia - Certain Measures Affecting the Automobile Industry*,WT/DS54/R, report of the Panel adopted 23 July 1998, paras. 3.3(e) and 3.4(h).

[177] *Ibid.*, paras. 15.3-15.4.

[178] The same question was posed to the European Communities: *see*, para. 5.12 of this report.

a subsidy and the subsidy itself. In this regard, the...[European Communities] focuses on the timing of the subsidy, but ignores the duration of the subsidy. While a subsidy comes into existence at a particular point in time, the benefit of the subsidy can extend over a period of years, depending on the nature of the subsidy in question...[T]he argument that repayment (or a cessation of future payments on PROEX government bonds) would be disruptive to private parties proves too much. The United States submits that it is the rare case in which the behaviour of private parties is *not* disrupted when WTO dispute settlement results in a recommendation and ruling that a Member withdraw a measure on which private parties have come to rely or on which they have based their plans. Moreover, it is difficult to see how anyone, whether in the private or governmental sector, could have legitimate expectations regarding subsidies found to be prohibited by the WTO. The United States also sees no merit to the [European Communities] distinction between the remedy available in a WTO dispute and the remedy available in a countervailing duty case, and notes that the EU does not cite anything in the text of the SCM Agreement to support this distinction. Both types of cases provide a means for offsetting the artificial benefit bestowed on recipients of a subsidy. In a countervailing duty case, this takes the form of an offsetting duty (or an undertaking which, *inter alia*, may require the elimination of the subsidy). In a WTO dispute, the remedy may take the form of a withdrawal of the subsidy (and, thus, the benefit inherent in the subsidy)."

5.27 The United States further maintains that the interpretation of the European Communities would "eviscerate the utility of WTO dispute settlement as a vehicle for addressing trade distortive subsidies. As an example, assume that Country X provides a $1 billion grant to Company Y. The purpose of the grant is to allow Company Y to construct a facility that will produce widgets for export. A WTO panel finds that the grant is a prohibited subsidy, but at the time when the DSB adopts the panel report, Country X already has disbursed the $1 billion to Company Y and Company Y already has contracted for construction of the facility... as the United States understands the position of the [European Communities], the best remedy that could come from this case is that Country X could not provide another subsidy to Company Y. However, widgets produced by Company Y would continue to be subsidized by virtue of the $1 billion grant."

5.28 The United States submits that such a result would be absurd, which could neither be justified "by the terms of the SCM Agreement, the DSU, or public international law...[It] would render the increased disciplines of the SCM Agreement meaningless. Instead, the appropriate outcome would be a withdrawal of that portion of the $1 billion grant allocated to future time-period. How such a withdrawal would occur would depend on the domestic law of Country X. If a withdrawal was not permissible under the domestic law, then compensation or countermeasures would be appropriate".

5.29 In a response to a question from the Panel as to whether it agreed with the Brazilian argument that "because Article 27 is *lex specialis* to Article 3 of the SCM Agreement, Article 3 does not apply to developing countries. Therefore, it is not possible for developing countries to act in a manner inconsistent with Article 3", the United States stated that:

> "As a general matter, the United States does not see any basis for the above-quoted argument...Article 27.2(b), by its very terms, excuses a developing country Member, such as Brazil, from the prohibition in Article 3.1(a) *only if* it complies with Article 27.4. The United States disagrees with the proposition that the general legal principle of *lex specialis* (assuming it applies to this dispute at all), could override the plain text of a treaty."

Relying on the ruling of the Appellate Body in *United States - Measure Affecting Imports of Woven Wool Shirts and Blouses from India*[179], the United States was of the view that since "the relevant provisions of Article 27...[operated] as affirmative defences against the prohibition in Article 3.1(a), the initial burden of proof was on Brazil.

VI. INTERIM REVIEW

6.1 On 25 February 1999 both parties submitted written requests for the Panel to review precise aspects of the interim report, and on 3 March 1999 each party submitted written comments regarding the other's request. Neither party requested a further meeting with the Panel.

6.2 Canada notes that, in paragraph 7.18 and in footnotes 194 and 195 of the interim report (footnotes 197 and 198 of this report) , we considered but failed to make findings on two legal issues related to Brazil's affirmative defense based on the first paragraph of item (k) of the Illustrative List of Export Subsidies. In Canada's view, the principle of judicial economy does not properly apply to these issues, and the Panel should have resolved them. Canada states that, as the Appellate Body observed in *Australia - Salmon*[180], the aim of dispute settlement, according to Article 3.7 of the DSU, is to "secure a positive solution to the dispute." Accordingly,

> "A Panel has to address those claims on which a finding is necessary in order to enable the DSB to make sufficiently precise rec-

[179] *Supra*, footnote 142.

[180] *Australia - Measures Affecting the Importation of Salmon*, WT/DS18/AB/R, Report of the Appellate Body adopted on 6 November 1998.

> ommendations and rulings so as to allow for prompt compliance by a Member with those recommendations and rulings...."[181]

6.3 Canada contends that Brazil has argued that the first paragraph of item (k) is an exception that provides cover for PROEX payments. As it stands, the Interim Report concludes that PROEX, an admitted export subsidy, is applied in such a way that it would not benefit from the "material advantage" clause of this item. The import of the Panel's findings is that Brazil could not bring PROEX payments into compliance by, for example, simply adjusting the *rate* of subsidization and then arguing that these payments no longer "secure a material advantage". Canada considers that the Panel should give this point greater precision by finding that the first paragraph of item (k) cannot be used as an exception at all, and that in any event, PROEX payments are not "payments" within the meaning of item (k).

6.4 In paragraph 7.18 of our interim report, we found that Brazil's "material advantage" defense under the first paragraph of item (k) could succeed only if Brazil prevailed on three legal issues. We concluded that PROEX payments were "used to secure a material advantage in the field of export credit terms", and declined to reach the other two legal issues presented with respect to that defense. In considering Canada's argument that we should address the remaining legal issues, we note that, in *Australia - Salmon*, the Appellate Body addressed the circumstances under which a panel might or might not address certain *claims* raised by a complainant. In this case, however, the question is whether we should have reached all legal *issues* related to a particular claim. In any event, Canada has not convinced us that, in this case, deciding the remaining legal issues would provide any further guidance with respect to compliance with the recommendations and rulings of the DSB. Thus, recalling that the purpose of the dispute settlement process is to "secure a positive solution to the dispute", and because in our view issues of legal interpretation are best addressed in concrete cases where they are necessary to resolve the case at hand, we decline to take up Canada's invitation to resolve the two legal issues in question.

6.5 Brazil argues that the appropriate time-period to withdraw the subsidy noted in paragraph 8.5 of the Report should be seven and one-half months. In Brazil's view, since Article 4.7 of the SCM Agreement does not specify a specific time-period, the time-period set forth in Article 21.3(c) of the DSU should be halved pursuant to Article 4.12 of the SCM Agreement. Brazil further contends that no evidence has been presented in this case to justify departing from the seven and one-half month guideline. Brazil further notes that PROEX was created by the Brazilian Congress, and that any changes therefore must also be enacted by Congress. It is therefore impracticable for Brazil to comply with the

[181] *Australia - Measures Affecting the Importation of Salmon*, WT/DS18/AB/R, Report of the Appellate Body adopted on 6 November 1998, para. 223.

Panel's recommendation within 90 days. Finally, Brazil noted that the world financial crisis had had a significant and detrimental effect on Brazil. Brazil noted that, in *Indonesia - Autos*, the arbitrator allocated Indonesia an additional period of six months over and above the time required for the completion of its domestic rule-making process pursuant to Article 21.2 of the DSU.[182]

6.6 Canada responds that, at issue in this dispute is not the PROEX programme *as such*, but the way that programme is *applied* to the export sales of regional aircraft. Brazil can comply with the recommendation of the Panel simply by stopping the payment of such subsidies on exported regional aircraft delivered after the date of adoption of the Panel Report. Because neither the annulled PROEX legislation nor the monthly Presidential decrees that currently maintain the programme are mandatory, there is no legal requirement for Congressional action before the payment of PROEX export subsidies - that is, the issuance of NTN-1 bonds - on the delivery of exported aircraft is stopped. Canada further argues that Article 4.12 applies only to the "conduct of such disputes", not to implementation, and that the "reasonable period of time" standard set forth in Article 21.3(c) is not the benchmark of "without delay" for the purposes of Article 4.7 of the SCM Agreement. Finally, Canada argues that it is not apparent how Brazil's mention of its status as a developing country Member or mention of its current financial crisis in any way affects the period of time for compliance with the Panel's recommendation.

6.7 We decline Brazil's request to modify the time-period set forth in paragraph 8.5. Assuming that the time-period set forth in Article 21.3(c) of the DSU, as halved pursuant to Article 4.12 of the SCM Agreement, is applicable to disputes under Article 4 of the SCM Agreement - an issue we do not decide - Article 21.3(c) of the DSU merely states that the "reasonable period of time" to implement panel or Appellate Body recommendations "should not exceed" 15 months. In this case, and reading that provision in conjunction with the requirement of Article 4.7 that the subsidy be withdrawn "without delay", we do not consider that a seven and one-half month time-period would be appropriate. We note that, while PROEX was created by legislation, it is currently maintained in force through Provisional Measures issued by the Brazilian government on a monthly basis. In any event, we recall Canada's view that implementation does not in the first instance require the modification of the PROEX interest rate equalization scheme itself, but merely a cessation in the issuance of new bonds upon exportation of Brazilian regional aircraft. Nor do we consider that, in the particular circumstances of this case, Article 21.2 of the DSU would warrant stretching the ordinary meaning of the phrase "without delay" to provide for an

---

[182] *Indonesia - Certain Measures Affecting the Automobile Industry*, Award of the Arbitrator, WT/DS64/15, WT/DS55/14, WT/DS59/13, WT/DS64/12, para. 24.

implementation period of seven and one-half months. Accordingly, we have not modified the time-period specified for withdrawal of the measure.

6.8 Canada states that it is implicit in our findings and conclusions that all of the conditions of Article 27 have to be met before a developing country Member may benefit from Article 27, and asks that we state this explicitly. We have modified paragraphs 7.57 and 8.1(c) in response to Canada's request. We have also clarified our findings through modifications to paragraphs 8.1(a), 8.1(b) and footnote 198. Finally, we have made other minor modifications of a typographical nature, including those in paragraphs 7.13, 7.30, 7.34, 7.53, 7.56, 7.68, 7.71, 7.72, 7.73, 7.75 and footnotes 198, 200, 215, 220, 231, and 241.

VII. FINDINGS

A. *The Measures at Issue*

7.1 In its request for establishment of a panel (WT/DS46/5), Canada asks that the Panel "consider and find that export subsidies under PROEX are inconsistent with Article 3 of the SCM Agreement." In its first submission to the Panel, Canada clarifies that "[a]t issue in this dispute is whether the *Programa de Financiamento ás Exportações* (PROEX) . . . confers export subsidies on sales of Brazilian regional aircraft that are prohibited under Article 3 of the . . . SCM Agreement"[183], and asks the Panel to find that "payments made under the 'Interest Equalization' component of PROEX on exported Brazilian regional aircraft" constitute prohibited subsidies.[184] In its second submission, Canada states that "the 'matter' subject to its request for a Panel was PROEX and the export subsidies paid under that programme to civil aircraft. This was the same 'prohibited subsidy' on which Canada had requested consultations."[185] A few paragraphs later, Canada states that "it is Canada's submission that export subsidies paid under PROEX, the Brazilian export subsidy programme, on all exported Brazilian regional aircraft, in whatever amount and regardless of the specific legislative instrument that underlies the programme, are prohibited by Article 3 and must be withdrawn. It is this practice that is the subject of Canada's challenge."[186]

7.2 We note that there is a certain lack of clarity regarding the precise measures being challenged by Canada. We do not understand Canada to be alleging

[183] Canada first submission, paragraph 1.

[184] Canada first submission, paragraph 2. Although Canada's request for establishment of a panel also identifies "export financing under PROEX", i.e., PROEX direct export financing, Canada states that it "does not challenge PROEX Financing in this dispute." Canada first submission, paragraph 30.

[185] Canada second submission, paragraph 19.

[186] Canada second submission, paragraph 23.

that the interest rate equalization component of the PROEX programme *per se* is the prohibited measure, because Canada does not seek a finding or recommendation with respect to the programme itself.[187] In fact, it limits itself to challenging PROEX payments relating to the particular sector of regional aircraft.[188] On the other hand, neither is Canada restricting its challenge to a particular specified payment or payments already made pursuant to the interest rate equalization component of PROEX. To the contrary, although Canada identifies specific transactions with respect to which it considers that PROEX payments have been or will be made, Canada is arguing that all PROEX payments, to the extent they relate to exported Brazilian regional aircraft, *including payments to be made in the future pursuant to the PROEX interest rate equalization scheme,* are prohibited subsidies. Thus, we understand Canada to be challenging not only specific payments, but more generally the practice involving PROEX payments relating to exported Brazilian regional aircraft (which we will hereafter refer to as "PROEX payments"). In order to analyze this contention, we are required to go beyond an examination of individual PROEX payments that have been identified and look more generally at the nature and operation of the PROEX interest rate equalization scheme which governs the payment of the alleged export subsidies.[189]

7.3 Because Canada is challenging not only specific PROEX payments relating to regional aircraft, but more generally the practice of providing PROEX payments, we do not and could not have before us a comprehensive list of the transactions supported by PROEX interest rate equalization which are challenged by Canada. We note however that Brazil has provided a list of post 1

---

[187] Because we understand that Canada has not challenged the PROEX programme *per se*, we need not address the issue whether the PROEX programme may be subject to challenge under Article 4 of the SCM Agreement. We note however that in our view the effective operation of the SCM Agreement requires that a party be able in some manner to obtain prospective discipline on the provision of subsidies in cases where it can be established in advance, based upon the legal framework governing the provision of those subsidies, that they would be inconsistent with Article 3 of the SCM Agreement. Otherwise, the SCM Agreement's prohibitions could not be invoked until a particular prohibited subsidy had actually been paid. This would be tantamount to the proverbial closing of the barn door after the cows have gone.

[188] In its request for findings, Canada sometimes refers to "civil aircraft" and at other times refers to "regional aircraft". Judging from the totality of Canada's submissions, however, we conclude that Canada is challenging PROEX interest rate equalization payments only with respect to regional aircraft. Canada defines the regional aircraft market as consisting of commercial aircraft with 20-90 seats, whether turboprop or jet. On the basis of the evidence before us, it appears that three EMBRAER aircraft -the ERJ-145, the ERJ-135 and the EMB-120 - fall within this definition.

[189] As discussed in the following section of these findings, there are a wide range of legislative and regulatory instruments which collectively govern the operation of the PROEX programme. As these provisions have changed over time, certain aspects of the operation of PROEX interest rate equalization have also changed. In assessing the consistency of PROEX payments with the SCM Agreement, we will examine the operation of the regime up to and as of the date of the request for establishment of a panel by Canada.

January 1995 transactions supported by PROEX interest rate equalization relating to two Brazilian regional aircraft, the EMB-120 and the ERJ-145, and Canada has requested that we make specific findings regarding PROEX payments relating to these transactions. The transactions relating to the EMB-120 involve Great Lakes Airlines, Rio Sul, Skywest and "others", while those relating to the ERJ-145 involve American Eagle, British Regional, City Airlines, Continental Express, Luxair, Portugalia, Regional, Rio Sul, Siv Am, Trans States, Wexford and "other". Thus, the payments subject to challenge in this dispute include, but are not limited to, PROEX payments made or to be made with respect to the transactions identified above.

B. Preliminary Objection by Brazil

7.4 Canada's request for establishment of a panel (WT/DS46/5) contains a list of provisional measures, laws, decrees and other legal instruments which govern the operation of the PROEX programme. Brazil objects to the Panel's consideration of certain of these "measures" on the grounds that they were enacted or implemented subsequent to the last consultations between the parties and, as a result, were not and could not have been the subject of consultations. Brazil contends that Article 6.2 of the DSU requires that consultations with respect to the specific measures at issue must have taken place in order for a measure to be within a panel's terms of reference. Brazil further argues that Article 4 of the DSU requires that parties consult regarding a matter before resorting to a panel with respect to that matter.

7.5 Canada acknowledges that the legal instruments in question did not exist at the time consultations were held and thus were not themselves the subject of consultations. It contends, however, that the "matter" referred to in Canada's request for establishment of a panel - the payment of export subsidies under PROEX - was the same prohibited subsidy with respect to which the parties held consultations, in the sense that that matter is directly connected to the prohibited subsidy subject to the consultations and flows directly from it. Canada further notes that the Provisional Measure underlying PROEX must be renewed every month, and that Brazil's argument, if accepted, would bar examination of PROEX by a WTO dispute settlement panel altogether.

7.6 The objections raised by Brazil present us with an issue regarding the relationship between the matter before a panel as defined by its terms of reference and the matter consulted upon. Specifically, we must consider whether and to what extent a panel is limited in its consideration of the matter identified in its terms of reference by the scope of the matter with respect to which consultations were held. In considering this question in this dispute, we must apply not only the relevant provisions of the DSU, but also the special or additional dispute settlement provisions found in Article 4.2 through 4.12 of the SCM Agreement, keeping in mind the injunction of Article 1.2 of the DSU that, "[t]o the extent there is a difference between the rules and procedures of the [DSU] and the special or additional rules and procedures set forth in Appendix 2, the special or additional rules and procedures in Appendix 2 shall prevail."

7.7 In examining this issue, we first recall that our terms of reference are the standard terms of reference provided for in Article 7.1 of the DSU. Under those terms of reference, we are required to examine the "matter referred to the DSB" by Canada in its request for establishment (WT/DS46/5). As the Appellate Body explained in *Guatemala - Anti-Dumping Investigation Regarding Portland Cement from Mexico*[190] "the '*matter* referred to the DSB', therefore, consists of two elements: the specific *measures* at issue and the *legal basis of the complaint* (or the *claims*)"(emphasis in original). The Appellate Body derived the meaning of the term "matter" in Article 7 of the DSU from Article 6.2 of the DSU, which requires that a request for establishment of a panel "identify the specific measures at issue and provide a brief summary of the legal basis of the complaint...." In this case, the measures alleged by Canada in its request for establishment of a panel to be inconsistent with the SCM Agreement are "export subsidies under PROEX." Thus, although Canada in its request for establishment of a panel identifies a list of legal instruments which it refers to as "measures", Canada is not, in our view, alleging that each of these legal instruments separately represents a measure inconsistent with Article 3 of the SCM Agreement. Rather, the legal instruments identified by Canada taken collectively represent a list of legal instruments relating to the payment of the alleged export subsidies under the PROEX scheme.

7.8 Turning next to Canada's request for consultations, we note that Article 4.4 of the DSU requires that a request for consultations "give the reasons for the request, including identification of the measures at issue and an indication of the legal basis for the complaint." Article 4.2 of the SCM Agreement requires a statement of available evidence with regard to "the existence and nature of the subsidy in question" and Article 4.3 of the SCM Agreement requires the Member "granting or maintaining the subsidy in question" to enter into consultations as quickly a possible. In this case, Canada requested consultations "regarding certain export subsidies granted under the Brazilian *Programa de Financiamento ás Exportações* (PROEX) to foreign purchasers of Brazil's EMBRAER aircraft." Thus, it is clear to us that the request for consultations related to the same general subject as the request for establishment of a panel, i.e., "export subsidies under PROEX". The request for consultations does not, however, identify the particular legal instruments which Brazil contends that we should not consider, nor could it have, because those particular legal instruments did not exist at the time the request for consultations was made. In fact, it is clear that the PROEX regime (and thus potentially the attributes of the PROEX payments under it) has changed over time, and that between the date the last con-

[190] Adopted 25 November 1998, WT/DS60/AB/R, para. 72.

sultations were held and the date that establishment of a panel was requested, some such changes occurred.

7.9 We recall that our terms of reference are based upon Canada's request for establishment of a panel, and not upon Canada's request for consultations. These terms of reference were established by the DSB pursuant to Article 7.1 of the DSU and establish the parameters for our work.[191] Nothing in the text of the DSU or Article 4 of the SCM Agreement provides that the scope of a panel's work is governed by the scope of prior consultations. Nor do we consider that we should seek to somehow imply such a requirement into the WTO Agreement. One purpose of consultations, as set forth in Article 4.3 of the SCM Agreement, is to "clarify the facts of the situation",[192] and it can be expected that information obtained during the course of consultations may enable the complainant to focus the scope of the matter with respect to which it seeks establishment of a panel. Thus, to limit the scope of the panel proceedings to the identical matter with respect to which consultations were held could undermine the effectiveness of the panel process.

7.10 We do not believe, however, that the question of consultations is completely outside our consideration. A party is not entitled to request establishment of a panel unless consultations have been held. Specifically, Article 4.7 of the DSU provides that a complaining party may request establishment of a panel only if "consultations fail to settle a dispute". Similarly, Article 4.4 of the SCM Agreement allows a "matter" to be referred to the DSB for establishment of a panel only if consultations have failed to lead to a mutually agreed solution. Given that Article 6.1 of the DSU and Article 4.4 of the SCM Agreement essentially require the DSB to establish a panel automatically upon request of a party, a panel cannot rely upon the DSB to ascertain that requisite consultations have been held and to establish a panel only in those cases.[193] Accordingly, we consider that a panel may consider whether consultations have been held with re-

---

[191] *See, e.g., India - Patent Protection for Pharmaceutical and Agricultural Chemical Products*, adopted 16 January 1998, WT/DS50/AB/R, para. 92 ("The jurisdiction of a panel is established by that Panel's terms of reference, which are governed by Article 7 of the DSU.").

[192] As the Appellate Body has noted, "the claims that are made and the facts that are established during consultations do much to shape the substance and the scope of subsequent panel proceedings." *India - Patent Protection for Pharmaceutical and Agricultural Chemical Products*, adopted 16 January 1998, WT/DS50/AB/R, para. 94.

[193] As stated by the Appellate Body in a somewhat different context in *European Communities - Regime for the Importation, Sale and Distribution of Bananas,* adopted 25 September 1997, WT/DS27/AB/R, para. 142:

> "We recognize that a panel request will usually be approved automatically at the DSB meeting following the meeting at which the request first appears on the DSB's agenda. As a panel request is normally not subjected to detailed scrutiny by the DSB, it is incumbent upon a panel to examine the request for the establishment of the panel carefully to ensure its compliance with both the letter and the spirit of Article 6.2 of the DSU."

spect to a "dispute", and that a preliminary objection may properly be sustained if a party can establish that the required consultations had not been held with respect to a dispute. We do not believe, however, that either Article 4.7 of the DSU or Article 4.4 of the SCM Agreement requires a precise identity between the matter with respect to which consultations were held and that with respect to which establishment of a panel was requested.

7.11 Applying this analysis to the case at hand, we recall that Brazil and Canada consulted "regarding certain export subsidies granted under the Brazilian *Programa de Financiamento ás Exportações* (PROEX) to foreign purchasers of Brazil's EMBRAER aircraft", and that the request for establishment of a panel relates to "export subsidies under PROEX". We consider that the consultations and request for establishment relate to what is fundamentally the same "dispute", because they involve essentially the same practice, i.e., the payment of export subsidies under PROEX. Under these circumstances, and notwithstanding the fact that both the authorizing legal instrument and certain other legal instruments relating to the administration of the PROEX interest equalization regime changed or were only introduced subsequent to the last consultations, we cannot say that Canada has failed to comply with the requirements of Article 4.7 of the DSU. Accordingly, the preliminary objection of Brazil is denied.

C. *Are PROEX Interest Rate Equalization Payments Export Subsidies?*

7.12 Canada argues that PROEX payments are subsidies within the meaning of Article 1 of the SCM Agreement which are contingent upon export performance within the meaning of Article 3.1(a) of that Agreement. Specifically, Canada contends that PROEX payments are financial contributions in the form either of a direct transfer of funds (a grant) within the meaning of Article 1.1(a)(1)(i) or an "indirect financial contribution" through a funding mechanism or a private body in the sense of Article 1.1(a)(1)(iv) of the SCM Agreement. Canada further contends that this "financial contribution" confers a "benefit" within the meaning of Article 1.1(b) of the SCM Agreement in as much as it reduces the interest rate paid by purchasers of exported Brazilian regional aircraft by up to 3.8 percentage points. Finally, Canada asserts that PROEX payments are contingent upon export performance within the meaning of Article 3.1(a) of the SCM Agreement in as much as they are available only with respect to the financing of export shipments. In its first submission, Brazil stated that it "does not dispute the assertion that PROEX interest equalization payments for aircraft constitute an export subsidy."[194] In response to a question from the Panel, Brazil reaffirmed that it "has not denied that PROEX interest rate equalization payments for aircraft

[194] Brazil first submission, para. 6.1.

fulfill the definition of a subsidy within the meaning of Article 1 and are contingent upon export within the meaning of Article 3.1(a)."[195]

7.13 As noted above, the parties agree that PROEX payments are subsidies within the meaning of Article 1 of the SCM Agreement which are contingent upon exportation within the meaning of Article 3.1(a) of the Agreement, and we agree with them. Although the parties disagree about the form of the financial contribution involved - with Canada arguing that they involve a direct transfer of funds, and Brazil adopting the European Communities' view that they also involve a potential direct transfer of funds provided at an earlier moment in time - we consider that the issue presented relates to the question as to when the subsidies in question are paid and not as to whether they exist. We note that, according to Article 1:1(i) a subsidy exists if a government practice involves a direct transfer of funds or a potential direct transfer of funds and not only when a government actually effectuates such a transfer or potential transfer (otherwise the text of (i) would read: "a government directly transfers funds ... or engages in potential direct transfers of funds or liabilities"). The PROEX interest rate equalization scheme for aircraft fulfils the definition of a subsidy because there is a government practice, whether it involves a direct transfer of funds - as Canada believes - or a potential direct transfer of funds - as Brazil believes. As soon as there is such a *practice*, a subsidy exists, and the question whether the practice involves a direct transfer of funds or a potential direct transfer of funds is not relevant to the existence of a subsidy. One or the other is sufficient. If subsidies were deemed to exist only once a direct or potential direct transfer of funds had actually been effectuated, the Agreement would be rendered totally ineffective and even the typical WTO remedy (i.e. the cessation of the violation) would not be possible. We, therefore, consider that, the parties having agreed that PROEX payments are subsidies, the question of the form of financial contribution relates to the question of when the subsidy is paid, not when it comes into existence. This issue is taken up in section E.3. of these findings, where we consider whether Brazil has increased the level of its export subsidies.

7.14 For the foregoing reasons, we conclude that PROEX payments on exports of Brazilian regional aircraft are subsidies within the meaning of Article 1 of the SCM Agreement which are contingent upon export performance within the meaning of Article 3.1(a) of that Agreement.

[195] The question asked by the Panel was: "Brazil stated in its first submission (para. 6.1) that it 'does not dispute the assertion that PROEX equalization payments for aircraft constitute an export subsidy.' Without prejudice to your material advantage defense under item (k) of the Illustrative List, do you acknowledge that PROEX payments otherwise fulfill the definition of a subsidy within the meaning of Article 1 which is contingent upon export performance within the meaning of Article 3.1(a)? If not, please identify precisely all elements of Articles 1 and 3 you consider are not satisfied and a detailed explanation of your views with regard to those elements."

D. *Are PROEX Interest Rate Equalization Payments "Permitted" by Item (k) of the Illustrative List of Export Subsidies?*

7.15 We have found - and Brazil does not dispute - that PROEX payments are subsidies within the meaning of Article 1 of the SCM Agreement which are contingent upon export performance within the meaning of Article 3.1(a). Brazil does *not* concede, however, that these export subsidies are prohibited subsidies. Rather, Brazil contends that, although PROEX payments are export subsidies, they are nevertheless permitted by item (k) of the Illustrative List of Export Subsidies. Specifically, Brazil asserts that PROEX payments are the "payment by [governments] of all or part of the costs incurred by exporters or financial institutions in obtaining credits" within the meaning of item (k). Brazil further argues that, pursuant to item (k), such payments are prohibited only "in so far as they are used to secure a material advantage in the field of export credit terms", and that *a contrario* "such payments are *permitted* in so far as they are *not* used to secure a material advantage in the field of export credit terms." Finally, Brazil argues that PROEX payments are not used to secure a material advantage in the field of export credit terms, because they are merely used to offset "Brazil risk" and Canada's subsidies to Bombardier. Accordingly, Brazil concludes that PROEX payments are permitted by the SCM Agreement.

7.16 Canada contests Brazil's arguments on a number of grounds. First, Canada disputes Brazil's view that the first paragraph of item (k) may be used to establish that a measure is "permitted" by the SCM Agreement. It is Canada's view - strongly supported by the European Communities as third party - that footnote 5 to the SCM Agreement, which states that "[m]easures referred to in Annex I as not constituting export subsidies shall not be prohibited under this or any other provision of this Agreement", constitutes the only basis for arguing on the basis of the Illustrative List of Export Subsidies that a measure that does not fall within the scope of the Illustrative List is not prohibited, and Canada considers that the first paragraph of item (k) does not fall within the scope of that footnote. Second, Canada rejects Brazil's view that PROEX payments are the "payment by [governments] of all or part of the costs incurred by exporters or financial institutions in obtaining credits". Finally, Canada both disagrees with Brazil's interpretation of the "material advantage" clause in the first paragraph of item (k) and contends that PROEX payments are in fact "used to secure a material advantage" within the meaning of item (k).

7.17 In reviewing Brazil's item (k) defense, we note that in order for this Panel to rule in favour of Brazil we must find for Brazil on all of the following points. First, we must find that PROEX payments are the "payment by [governments] of all or part of the costs incurred by exporters or financial institutions in obtaining credits" within the meaning of item (k). Second, we must find that PROEX payments are not "used to secure a material advantage in the field of export credit terms" within the meaning of item (k). Finally, we must find that a "payment" within the meaning of item (k) which is not "used to secure a material advantage in the field of export credit terms" is "permitted" by the SCM Agreement even though it is a subsidy within the meaning of Article 1 of the SCM Agreement which is contingent upon export performance within the meaning of Article 3.1(a) of that Agreement. If we were to find against Brazil on any of these points, Brazil's item (k) defense would fail. Finally, we note Brazil's explicit acknowledgement that "its view of the 'material advantage' clause is that it constitutes an affirmative defense and, therefore, the burden of establishing entitlement to it is on the challenged party."[196]

7.18 It is by no means clear to us that it is permissible to use the first paragraph of item (k) as the basis for an *a contrario* argument as asserted by Brazil,[197] or that PROEX payments in fact constitute the "payment by [governments] of all or part of the costs incurred by exporters or financial institutions in obtaining credits".[198] Even assuming for the sake of argument, however, that Brazil is correct with respect to these two points, we consider Brazil's interpretation of the "material advantage" clause of item (k) is incorrect, and that, under a proper interpretation of that clause, Brazil has not demonstrated that PROEX interest rate equalization payments do not confer a material advantage in the field of

[196] Brazil answer to panel question 41. *See United States - Measure Affecting Imports of Woven Wool Shirts and Blouses from India*, WT/DS33/AB/R, DSR 1997:I, 323, at 337, adopted 23 May 1997 ("It is only reasonable that the burden of establishing [an affirmative] defence should rest on the party asserting it.").

[197] Footnote 5 to the SCM Agreement states that "[m]easures referred to in Annex I as not constituting export subsidies shall not be prohibited under [Article 3.1(a)] or any other provision of this Agreement." The only measures in the Illustrative List that are explicitly "referred to . . . as not constituting export subsidies" are export credit practices in conformity with the interest rate provisions of the Arrangement under the second paragraph of item (k). There are also a number of other cases, cited by Canada, where the Illustrative List affirmatively provides that a measure is not prohibited - at least by that item - or is permissible. The first paragraph of item (k), however, does not contain any such affirmative language, and would not appear to fall within the scope of footnote 5. Thus, a strong argument can be made that footnote 5 - together with footnote 1 - define the extent to which the Illustrative List can be used to establish that a measure is a "permitted" subsidy or, in the case of footnote 1, is not a subsidy at all. In light of our findings with respect to "material advantage", however, we need not decide this question.

[198] PROEX payments relating to export of Brazilian regional aircraft are provided in support of buyers' credits, i.e., export credits are extended to the foreign purchaser rather than to EMBRAER. Brazil's theory appears to be that lenders providing export credits must borrow funds in order to finance their lending, that the export credits so funded are provided at below the lenders' cost of borrowing, and that PROEX payments are provided to compensate the lenders for this difference. In Brazil's view, this difference between the lender's cost of borrowing and the rate it charges for the export credits extended to purchasers therefore represents a "cost incurred by . . . financial institutions in obtaining credits." In addition, Brazil seeks to demonstrate that, although EMBRAER itself does not extend export credits to its customers, EMBRAER incurred certain costs in relation to the provision of buyer's credits to purchasers of Brazilian regional aircraft. Because our findings on the issue of "material advantage" dispose of Brazil's item (k) defense, we need not decide whether Brazil's view on this issue is correct. We note in passing, however, that - assuming lenders providing export credits supported by PROEX payments are in fact providing export credits at below their cost of funds - it is highly questionable whether that represents a cost for the lenders in "*obtaining* credits" as opposed to a cost incurred in *providing* credits.

export credit terms. As noted above, Brazil's "item (k)" defense can succeed only if Brazil prevails on all three legal issues. Because we dispose of Brazil's defense on the issue of whether PROEX interest rate equalization payments have been demonstrated not to confer a "material advantage", we need not decide whether Brazil's arguments on the first two issues are correct.

7.19 It will be recalled that, under item (k) of the Illustrative List, the following is an export subsidy:

> "The grant by governments (or special institutions controlled by and/or acting under the authority of governments) of export credits at rates below those which they actually have to pay for the funds so employed . . . , *or the payment by them of all or part of the costs incurred by exporters or financial institutions in obtaining credits, in so far as they are used to secure a material advantage in the field of export credit terms.*" (emphasis added).

Assuming for the sake of argument that PROEX payments are payments within the meaning of item (k), the question presented in this dispute is the benchmark that should be used in determining whether such payments are in fact "used to secure a material advantage." In Brazil's view, the proper benchmark for determining whether PROEX payments are "used to secure a material advantage in the field of export credit terms" is to compare the export credit terms of transactions supported by PROEX payments with the export credit terms available to purchasers of *Canadian* regional aircraft. As stated in the Finan Report, "Material advantage in the field of export credit terms cannot be measured by evaluating just one country's subsidy benefits. Rather, determining material advantage requires evaluating one country's set of export credit terms relative to another country's set by applying a consistent methodology appropriate under the facts and circumstances."[199]

7.20 Brazil considers that, as a result of several factors, PROEX payments do not result in export credit terms for purchasers of *Brazilian* regional aircraft which secure a material advantage -i.e., are more favourable - than the export credit terms available for purchasers of *Canadian* regional aircraft:

> "The concept of material advantage, as noted above, includes comparison - advantage vis-à-vis someone or something. Two points of comparison are relevant to the determination in this dispute of whether PROEX is used by Brazil to secure a material advantage in the field of export credit terms: (1) Brazil risk and (2) Canada's subsidies to Bombardier. On either measure alone, PROEX provides no material advantage. When the two are con-

[199] p. 1.9.

sidered together, it is clear that it is Canada's programmes, not Brazil's, that are used to secure a material advantage."[200]

7.21 Turning to the first "point of comparison" proposed by Brazil, Brazil argues that PROEX payments do no more than offset "Brazil risk". Specifically, Brazil contends that, due to the high level of risk perceived by international markets with respect to Brazilian borrowers, the cost to EMBRAER and to Brazilian financial institutions of raising funds to finance exports of Brazilian regional aircraft is higher than the cost to Bombardier and Canadian financial institutions of raising funds to finance exports of Canadian regional aircraft. Because PROEX payments merely offset in part that higher cost of funds, allowing export credit financing for Brazilian regional aircraft on terms that are closer to, but still less favourable than, those available for competing Canadian regional aircraft, those payments are not in Brazil's view used to secure a material advantage in the field of export credit terms.

7.22 With respect to the second "point of comparison", Brazil contends that "material advantage should be determined by comparison of the total subsidy packages" available to competing regional aircraft. In support of this view, Brazil argues that "the field of export credit terms" includes not only the interest rate and duration of the financing but also the price of the aircraft being financed. Brazil contends that Canada provides a wide range of "direct and indirect subsidies" for Canadian regional aircraft, and that these subsidies reduce the price of Canadian regional aircraft, the cost of credit to purchasers or other "export credit terms." Brazil concludes that, because PROEX payments do not fully offset these subsidies, those payments are not "used to secure a material advantage in the field of export credit terms".

7.23 As can be seen from the above arguments, Brazil's material advantage defense is based upon the principle that a consideration whether an item (k) payment "is used to secure a material advantage in the field of export credit terms" involves a comparison between the export credit terms of the transaction supported by the payment and the export credit terms of potential competing transactions. We do not agree. We note the definition of "advantage" in *Webster's New International Dictionary of the English Language*, cited by Brazil, as "a more favorable or improved position". Similarly, the *Shorter Oxford English Dictionary* defines "advantage" as "superior position". Thus, we concur with Brazil that the term "advantage" involves the concept of comparison. In our view, however, nothing in the text of the first paragraph of item (k) indicates that the examination of material advantage involves a comparison *with the export credit terms available with respect to competing products from other Members*. To the contrary, we consider that, in its ordinary meaning, a payment is "used to secure a material advantage in the field of export credit terms" where the pay-

[200] Brazil first submission, para. 6.6.

ment is used to secure export credit terms that are materially more favorable than the terms that would have been available in the absence of the payment. Accordingly, we consider that an item (k) payment is "used to secure a material advantage" where the payment has resulted in the availability of export credit on terms which are more favourable than the terms that would otherwise be available in the marketplace to the purchaser with respect to the transaction in question.

7.24 Our understanding of the meaning of the "material advantage" clause is supported by its context in the SCM Agreement. Brazil's approach to determining whether an item (k) payment is used to secure a material advantage and thus represents an export subsidy differs strikingly from that applied elsewhere in the SCM Agreement with respect to determining whether a measure is a subsidy generally, or an export subsidy specifically. In this respect, the Agreement does not focus on the conditions under which a competing product from another Member is being sold and exported. Rather, the general approach of the SCM Agreement to determining whether a measure is a subsidy and thus subject to discipline is whether the measure confers a "benefit" within the meaning of Article 1. Although the concept of benefit is not defined in the SCM Agreement, its application in various circumstances suggests that one should examine objective benchmarks, whether involving a comparison of the terms of the financial contribution to a market benchmark reflecting the terms under which the beneficiary of the financial contribution would be operating in the absence of the government financial contribution (as provided for in the calculation of the amount of the subsidy in terms of benefit to the recipient in a countervailing duty context under Article 14 of the Agreement)[201] or the existence of a cost to the government in providing the financial contribution (as envisioned by Annex IV relating to the calculation of the *ad valorem* subsidization for the purposes of the presumption of serious prejudice under Article 6.1(a) of the Agreement). In no case is it suggested that whether or not a benefit exists would depend upon a comparison with advantages available to a competing product from another Member.

7.25 Nor can we find any suggestion in either Article 3.1(a) of the SCM Agreement or the Illustrative List of Export Subsidies that whether a measure is a prohibited export subsidy should depend upon whether the measure merely offsets advantages bestowed on competing products from another Member. For example, item (c) of the Illustrative List treats as an export subsidy internal transport or freight charges on export shipments "on terms more favourable than

[201] The example of loans under Article 14 is instructive. Under Article 14(b), "a loan by a government shall not be considered as conferring a benefit, unless there is a difference between the amount that the firm receiving the loan pays on the government loan and the amount the firm would pay on a comparable commercial loan which the firm could actually obtain on the market." In other words, the relevant question is whether, as a result of the government intervention, the firm receiving the loan is better off than if that same firm had been required to obtain a loan in the marketplace.

for domestic shipments", irrespective of whether those charges are higher, lower or equal to the charges paid with respect to the shipments of competing products from other Members. Item (d) of the Illustrative List treats the provision of goods or services by a government for use in the production of exported goods as a prohibited export subsidy if the terms and conditions on which the goods or services are provided are more favourable than for the provision of goods for use in the production of goods for domestic consumption and if those terms and conditions are "more favourable than those commercially available on world markets *to their exporters*" (emphasis added). This last example is instructive, as the relevant test involves a comparison of the terms and conditions of the goods or services being provided by the government with the terms and conditions that would otherwise be available *to the exporters receiving the alleged export subsidy*; the fact that a foreign competitor had access to the same goods or services on better terms than those available to the exporters in question would not be a defense. In items (e), (f), (g), (h) and (i) of the Illustrative List, all of which relate to exemptions, remissions or deferrals of taxes or import charges, there is no hint that a tax advantage would not constitute an export subsidy simply because it reduced the exporter's tax burden to a level comparable to that of foreign competitors. In short, in asking us to look at the relative position of competitors in determining the disciplines applicable to item (k) payments, Brazil is asking us to construe that "material advantage" clause in a manner which does not conform to the general approach of the SCM Agreement.

7.26 In essence, Brazil's approach to "material advantage" boils down to an argument that an admitted export subsidy should not be deemed to be prohibited if it can be demonstrated merely to offset some advantage or advantages available to the competing product of another Member. We consider that such an interpretation would produce results that would be contrary to the object and purpose of the SCM Agreement. In our view, the object and purpose of the SCM Agreement is to impose multilateral disciplines on subsidies which distort international trade. It is for this reason that the SCM Agreement prohibits two categories of subsidies - subsidies contingent upon exportation and upon the use of domestic over imported goods - that are specifically designed to affect trade. The Brazilian approach to item (k), however, would effectively allow a Member to raise the provision of export subsidies -or indeed of any subsidy - by the complaining Member as a defense justifying its own provision of export subsidies. This would entail a race to the bottom, as each WTO Member sought to justify the provision of export subsidies on the grounds that other Members were doing the same. Further, it should be recalled that under Articles 27 and 29 of the SCM Agreement certain Members are entitled to special and differential treatment and are not subject to the prohibition on export subsidies. It may be queried whether, if we were to interpret item (k) in the manner suggested by Brazil, developed country Members would in effect be authorized to match the export credit terms, however favourable, offered by developing country Members without falling afoul of the SCM Agreement's prohibition on the provision of export subsidies, with its consequent weakening of the SCM Agreement's disciplines on export subsidies. Such results certainly would not be consistent with the object and purpose of the Agreement identified above.

7.27 Finally, Brazil's interpretation of the material advantage clause would in our view generate results that are manifestly unreasonable in the context of the SCM Agreement. First, under Brazil's interpretation the determination whether an item (k) payment represented an export subsidy would require in each case an examination of the terms and conditions of the export credits available for competing products of another Member. Thus, a Member seeking to determine whether it could provide item (k) payments without violating Article 3 of the SCM Agreement would be required to first assess the terms and conditions under which export credits were available with respect to the competing products of all other Members. This might well prove impossible, given that the terms and conditions of a given export credit transaction are confidential business information not generally available to the public at large. Second, a payment could be found to be a prohibited export subsidy when challenged by one complainant yet found not to be a prohibited export subsidy when challenged by a different complainant whose exporters had access to export credit on more favourable terms, thus generating inconsistent results under the WTO dispute settlement system. Third, export subsidies that were "permitted" at a given moment might be transformed into prohibited export subsidies as a result of changes in the terms and conditions under which export credits were available in other Members.[202] We consider that an interpretation of item (k) that would make the status of a Member's measures as a possible export subsidy dependent on factors outside its knowledge and control, and that could generate such unpredictable results, is unreasonable and thus to be avoided.

7.28 Even if we were to agree with Brazil - which we do not - that in order to ascertain whether an item (k) payment secures a material advantage it is necessary to examine the export credit terms available with respect to competing products exported from other Members, we still could not agree with Brazil's interpretation of the clause "in the field of export credit terms". It will be recalled that Brazil's interpretation of that clause would include as an export credit term the price at which a product was sold, and would therefore allow Brazil to offset through item (k) payments all subsidies provided to Bombardier that could reduce the price at which regional aircraft exported by that manufacturer could be sold and thus reduce the amount of the transaction to be financed. In our view, this interpretation stretches far beyond the ordinary meaning of the phrase in question. In its ordinary meaning, the field of export credit terms would refer

[202] In response to a question from the Panel, Brazil acknowledges this, stating that "[i]t is true that under Brazil's theory, a permitted subsidy could become prohibited and vice versa depending on the action of other Members, but, Brazil submits, this is a logical consequence of the ordinary meaning of the language of item (k)."

to items directly related to export credits, such as interest rates, grace periods, transaction costs, maturities and the like. We consider that this interpretation is supported contextually by item (k) itself, which refers to a loan's "maturity and other credit terms". We see nothing in the ordinary meaning of the phrase to suggest that "the field of export credit terms" generally encompasses the price at which a product is sold. [203]

7.29 Brazil's arguments regarding the meaning of the "material advantage" clause seek to characterize its interpretation of that clause as necessary to protect the rights of developing country Members. Brazil's argument, if we understand it correctly, is that developed country Members have negotiated for themselves, in the second paragraph of item (k), a special safe haven from the export subsidy prohibition for export credit practices that conform to the interest rate provisions of the OECD Arrangement on Guidelines for Officially Supported Export Credits ("the OECD Arrangement"). Because of their high sovereign risk premiums, however, most developing country Members cannot afford to borrow on international capital markets at high rates of interest in order to engage in direct financing on terms consistent with the Arrangement. Under the first paragraph of item (k), however, developing country Members may - if Brazil's interpretation of "material advantage" is accepted - effect a reduction in the interest rates charged by financial institutions on export credits for their exports by making item (k) payments, at a lower cost than were the developing country Member to provide export credits directly at the same interest rates. Accordingly, and in Brazil's words, developing country Members "bargained . . . for the 'material advantage' language of item (k) precisely because, when Article 27's protection expires, they needed something they could afford in view of the fact that developed countries had their own self-designed exemption, which is presently in the second paragraph of item (k)."

7.30 We find Brazil's effort to characterize the interpretation of the first paragraph of item (k) as a developed/developing country issue unconvincing. First, we note that the "material advantage" clause has it origins in the Tokyo Round Subsidies Code[204] and was carried over unchanged into the SCM Agreement.

[203] We recognize that there might be cases where an item (k) payment, rather than being used to reduce the interest rate or improve some other term related to the transaction, is applied to reduce the amount of the transaction financed. In fact, evidence on the record suggests that PROEX payments are sometimes used in precisely this manner, in that the financial institution providing the export credits, rather than using the PROEX payments to reduce the interest rate charged to the purchaser of an EMBRAER regional aircraft, may also sell the NTN-1 bonds it receives from the Government of Brazil in the market and use the proceeds to provide a cash discount to the purchaser. We do not preclude that, in such a particular situation, the field of export credit terms might be deemed to include the price of the goods being financed. This is a far cry, however, from the broad argument made by Brazil.

[204] Agreement on Interpretation and Application of Articles VI, XVI and XXIII of the General Agreement on Tariffs and Trade.

Given that developing country signatories of the Code were exempted by Article 14.2 of the Code from the commitment not to grant export subsidies on products other than certain primary products, it seems unlikely that the material advantage clause was conceived at that time as a protection for developing countries. Nor has Brazil submitted any substantial support for the proposition that developing country Members sought to retain the "material advantage" clause during the Uruguay Round in order to retain the ability to offset the high sovereign risk of developing country Members through item (k) payments.[205]

7.31 Second, we believe that Brazil is incorrect in its underlying assumption that the second paragraph of item (k) provides a safe haven only with respect to direct export credit financing. The second paragraph of item (k) provides that "an export credit practice", whether of an Arrangement Participant or of a non-Arrangement WTO Member, which is in conformity with the "interest rate provisions" of the OECD Arrangement shall not be considered an export subsidy prohibited by the SCM Agreement. Chapter I:2 of the OECD Arrangement, titled "Scope of Application", provides that the Arrangement

> "shall apply to all official support for exports of goods and/or services . . . which have repayment terms of . . . two years or more . . . . regardless of whether the official support is given by means of direct credit/financing, refinancing, *interest rate support*, guarantee or insurance" (emphasis added).

Accordingly, a developing country Member could under the second paragraph of item (k) provide interest rate support to reduce the interest rates on export credits to the levels allowed by the OECD Arrangement if it considered that direct financing at those rates was too expensive.[206] Thus, Brazil's view that developing

[205] In response to a question from the Panel, Brazil argues that a proposal during the Uruguay Round by "a developed country" to modify the first paragraph of item (k) by, *inter alia,* deleting the material advantage clause was rejected by Brazil and other developing countries. The informal negotiating document submitted by Brazil in relation to this answer tells us little about the issues before this Panel, however. First, the document in question says nothing about which countries made and which countries rejected the proposal. More importantly, the proposal not only would have deleted the "material advantage" clause, but would also have changed the benchmark for when direct export financing constitutes an export subsidy from a cost of borrowing standard to a market benchmark ("terms and conditions more favourable than the terms and conditions the borrower would otherwise obtain for financing comparable transactions"). An accompanying note focuses on the latter issue, and provides no explanation as to why the proposed deletion of the "material advantage" clause was rejected.

[206] Because Brazil has not invoked the second paragraph of item (k) as a defense in this dispute, we need not consider the application of that provision to PROEX payments. However, we note that the *Finan Report's* contention that PROEX interest rate equalization would not "by definition" be permitted by the OECD Arrangement because it is "designed to offset a portion of Brazil risk" is mistaken. In support of its contention, the *Finan Report* relies on paragraph 20 of the OECD Arrangement, which provides that:

> "[t]he Participants providing official support through direct credits/financing, refinancing, export credit insurance and guarantees, shall charge no less than the

country Members cannot afford to use the safe haven of the second paragraph of item (k) and must therefore rely on the "material advantage" clause of the first paragraph of item (k), as interpreted by Brazil, is also incorrect.

7.32 Finally, not only is item (k) on its face *not* a provision relating to special and differential treatment - which provisions may be found in Article 27 of the SCM Agreement - but Brazil's interpretation of material advantage could actually undermine the value of Article 27 for developing country Members. In particular, if the Panel were to accept the interpretation of material advantage advanced by Brazil, the first paragraph of item (k) could - as noted in paragraph 7.26 above - be used by developed country Members as a justification to match, with export subsidies that would otherwise be prohibited, export subsidies provided by developing countries consistent with Article 27. Thus, while Brazil's interpretation of "material advantage" may serve the interests of one particular developing country Member with respect to its defense of one particular type of subsidy in one particular dispute, it cannot be generalized from this that Brazil's interpretation of the "material advantage" clause is necessary to protect the interests of developing country Members collectively. Rather, Brazil's interpretation would serve to benefit developing country Members only to the extent that one considers that a general lowering of the level of SCM Agreement disciplines on export subsidies applicable to all WTO Members is in the interests of developing country Members.

7.33 For the reasons discussed above, we consider that an item (k) payment is "used to secure a material advantage" and is thus a prohibited export subsidy where the payment has resulted in the availability of export credit on terms which are more favourable than the terms that would otherwise be available in the marketplace to the purchaser with respect to the transaction in question.

7.34 Applying the above standard to the case at hand, we consider it evident that PROEX payments result in the availability of export credit for Brazilian regional aircraft on terms which are more favourable than the terms that would otherwise be available with respect to the transaction in question. This follows from the very design of PROEX and the manner in which PROEX interest rate equalization operates. As characterized by Brazil, the purpose of PROEX payments is to improve the terms of export credit financing that would otherwise be available to purchasers of Brazilian regional aircraft and other Brazilian products by offsetting "Brazil risk". Thus, under the PROEX interest rate equalization scheme EMBRAER and its export customers are free to negotiate the best

---

> minimum premium benchmarks for the sovereign risk and the country credit risk, irrespective of whether the buyer/borrower is a private or a public entity."

Paragraph 20, however, excludes "interest rate support" from the categories of official support for which a minimum premium must be charged, presumably because in the case of interest rate support the government does not bear the risk of loss in the case of default. In any event, these premia relate to the risk relating to the country of the *buyer/borrower*, not that of the *lender*.

export credit terms they may obtain in the market, irrespective of whether the lender is a Brazilian or foreign financial institution. As a tool to obtain the most favourable terms possible, they may request a letter of commitment from the Government of Brazil committing Brazil to provide fixed PROEX interest rate equalization payments of 3.8 percentage points to the lender; there is no requirement to demonstrate in a particular case that a 3.8 percentage point level is necessary to compensate for the lender's higher cost of funds. The payments may be used to improve the export credit terms in one of several ways. For example, the availability of the payments may be used to negotiate lower interest rates for the export credits in question than would otherwise be available for the transaction. In the alternative, the lending bank may agree to discount the bonds and to pass the sum along to the purchaser/borrower as a cash discount. In any event, we consider that, as a matter of logic, the payments will as a natural consequence allow EMBRAER and the purchaser to negotiate more favourable export credit terms than they could otherwise achieve in the marketplace.

7.35 We recall Brazil's acknowledgement that its "material advantage" argument constitutes an affirmative defense and, therefore, the burden of establishing entitlement to it is on Brazil. In this case, not only has Brazil failed to demonstrate that PROEX payments do not allow the purchaser of Brazilian regional aircraft to obtain more favourable export credit terms than the terms that would otherwise be available to the purchaser with respect to the transaction in the market, but Brazil has conceded to the contrary. Thus, in response to a question from the Panel[207], Brazil stated that:

> "PROEX presumably would always be more favorable to the purchaser than the terms it could obtain on its own; otherwise, the purchaser would have no interest in PROEX. If the PROEX-supported export credit term is compared merely to the credit terms a particular buyer could obtain on its own, PROEX could never provide assistance and always would be at a disadvantage vis-à-vis competitors supported by an export credit agency, whether that agency's programmes were or were not consistent with WTO obligations."

[207] The question asked by the Panel was as follows: "Canada argues that the phrase 'in the field of export credit terms' as used in item (k) of Annex I of the SCM Agreement is limited to the interest rates and other transaction costs. Assuming for the sake of argument that this view is correct, what would be the appropriate benchmark for a comparison? Specifically, should the export credit terms of the transaction supported by PROEX interest rate equalization be compared to the export credit terms that would be available to the purchaser of EMBRAER aircraft on the market for the purchase of those aircraft if the PROEX interest rate equalization were not available for the transaction, or should it relate to the export credit terms available (including through official financing at OECD consensus rates by a Participant to the OECD Arrangement) to the purchaser if it purchased a competing civil aircraft?" Brazil responded that, "[w]ith regard to the two specific examples, Brazil would answer 'The latter'". The quote above followed.

Brazil makes a similar admission in the Finan Report, where it states that:

> "Brazil's PROEX programme, applied to support exports of regional aircraft, acts to reduce the cost of export financing for the aircraft buyer."[208]

Thus, we consider that as a factual matter Brazil does not argue that PROEX payments do not confer a "material advantage" as that term has been interpreted by this Panel.

7.36 Neither has Brazil asserted, much less submitted evidence supporting an assertion, that any specific transactions relating to the export of Brazilian regional aircraft supported by PROEX payments have not resulted in export credit terms that are more favourable than the terms that would otherwise have been available to the purchaser in the market with respect to those transactions. In fact, Brazil has not submitted any significant evidence regarding the specific terms and conditions, such as the interest rate, at which export credits supported by PROEX payments were provided, much less information regarding the export credit terms that would otherwise have been available with respect to the transaction in the market. Brazil did assert that, "in transactions when the lender was inside Brazil, the actual interest rate was always above LIBOR or the OECD rate in practice." But even with respect to this assertion, which in any event is not relevant in our view to the proper application of the "material advantage" clause, Brazil has not provided any supporting evidence. To the contrary, in response to a question from the Panel asking for specific information with respect to each transaction alleged by Brazil to be at or above the CIRR rate[209], Brazil responded that:

> "[t]his information requested by the Panel is not readily available to PROEX administrators. These authorities simply ensure that the bonds are issued to the agent bank and have no control, jurisdiction or access to specific details of the commercial transactions . . . ."[210]

In fact, with the respect to the one transaction supported by PROEX payments with respect to which Brazil has provided detailed information - on a Business

[208] *Finan Report*, p. 1.2.

[209] The CIRR rate is the "commercial interest reference rate" which represents the minimum interest rate to be charged on officially supported export credits under the OECD Arrangement.

[210] The question posed by the Panel was: For each sale of EMBRAER regional aircraft supported by PROEX interest rate equalization which you contend was at an interest rate at or above the CIRR rate (taking into account the interest rate equalization), please specify: (a) the purchaser; (b) the financial institution providing the financing; (c) the date of the transaction; the currency in which export financing was provided; (e) the maturity of the financing; (f) the terms of the financing, including whether the interest rate is fixed or variable and, in the latter case, how it is established; (g) the rate of interest before and after PROEX interest rate equalization is considered. Please provide any supporting documentation which you consider necessary to support your factual assertions in this regard."

Confidential basis - it is clear that the PROEX payments resulted in a very substantial improvement in the export credit terms as compared to the terms that could have been obtained in the absence of the payments.

7.37 In conclusion, we consider that an item (k) payment is "used to secure a material advantage" where the payment has resulted in the availability of export credit on terms which are more favourable than the terms that would otherwise have been be available to the purchaser with respect to the transaction in question. Even if we were to assume, as argued by Brazil, that PROEX payments are the "payment by [a government] of all or part of the costs incurred by exporters or financial institutions in obtaining credits", and that such payments can be deemed to be "permitted" by item (k) where they are not "used to secure a material advantage in the field of export credit terms" - issues we need not here decide - Brazil has failed to demonstrate the PROEX payments are not "used to secure a material advantage in the field of export credit terms". Accordingly, we reject Brazil's affirmative defense based on item (k) of the Illustrative List.

E. Is the Prohibition on Export Subsidies Inapplicable to Brazil by Reason of its Status as a Developing Country Member?

7.38 In the foregoing sections of this Report, we have found that PROEX payments are subsidies within the meaning of Article 1 of the SCM Agreement, and that those subsidies are contingent upon exportation within the meaning of Article 3.1(a) of that Agreement. Further, we have found that Brazil has not demonstrated that those subsidies are "permitted" by the first paragraph of item (k) of the SCM Agreement. In the usual case, this would be sufficient to establish that the subsidies in question are prohibited by Article 3 of the SCM Agreement. In this case, however, the parties agree that Brazil is a developing country Member within the meaning of the SCM Agreement. As such, Brazil is entitled to the extensive special and differential treatment accorded to such Members by Article 27 of the SCM Agreement. Accordingly, and as required by Article 12.11 of the DSU, we must now consider whether, under the facts of this case, Brazil is shielded from the Article 3.1(a) prohibition by reason of Article 27.

1. Is Article 27 Lex Specialis to Article 3?

7.39 Brazil argues *en passant* that Article 27 is *lex specialis* to Article 3, in that it provides special rules with regard to export subsidy programmes of developing country Members. In other words, it is Brazil's view that the specific provisions of Article 27 relating to developing country Members' export subsidies displace the general provisions of Article 3.1(a), and that it is therefore not possible for developing country Members to act in a manner inconsistent with Article 3. Because Canada has not alleged that Brazil has violated Article 27 of the

SCM Agreement, nor is any such claim within the Panel's terms of reference, Brazil considers that the Panel must deny Canada's complaint in this dispute.

7.40 Brazil has not vigorously pursued its *lex specialis* argument, and for good reason. In our view, Brazil's argument cannot be reconciled with the ordinary meaning of Article 27.2 of the SCM Agreement. It will be recalled that Article 27.2 provides that "[t]he prohibition of paragraph 1(a) of Article 3 shall not apply to . . . developing country Members [other than those referred to in Annex VII] for a period of eight years from the date of entry into force of the WTO Agreement, *subject to compliance with the provisions of paragraph 4* [of Article 27]" (emphasis added). It is evident to us from this language that Article 27 does not "displace" Article 3.1(a) of the SCM Agreement unconditionally as argued by Brazil. Rather, the prohibition of Article 3.1(a) shall not apply "subject to compliance with the provisions of paragraph 4". The exemption for developing country Members other than those referred to in Annex VII from the application of the Article 3.1(a) prohibition on export subsidies is clearly conditional on compliance with the provisions in paragraph 4 of Article 27. Thus, we consider that, where the provisions in Article 27.4 have not been complied with, the Article 3.1(a) prohibition applies to such developing country Members.

7.41 Although we have addressed Brazil's *lex specialis* argument for the sake of completeness, Brazil arguably abandoned its *lex specialis* argument during the course of the proceedings. Thus, in a question to Brazil the Panel quoted Article 27.2(b) and stated that "[i]t could be argued that, by negative implication, the prohibition *does* apply. Please comment." Brazil responded that "[t]his is true, but the central question is which party bears the burden of proof . . . ." Accordingly, it is to that question that we now turn.

2. *Article 27.4 Conditions and Burden of Proof*

7.42 As explained above, we consider that the prohibition on export subsidies applies to developing country Members other than those referred to in Annex VII[211] in the event of non-compliance with the provisions in Article 27.4. In Canada's view, Article 27.4 contains three relevant conditions. *First*, export subsidies must be phased out within the eight-year period. *Second*, the level of export subsidies must not increase during that period. *Third,* export subsidies must be eliminated within a period shorter than eight years when the use of these subsidies is not consistent with the Member's development needs. Before turning to a discussion of the specific elements of Article 27.4, however, we must consider the issue, which has been argued extensively by the parties, regarding who bears

[211] For the sake of convenience, we will generally refer to "developing country Members other than those referred to in Annex VII" simply as "developing country Members." This should not be construed as suggesting that the non-application of Article 3.1(a) to developing country Members referred to in Annex VII is conditioned on compliance with the provisions of Article 27.4.

the burden of proof with respect to compliance with the provisions of Article 27.4.

7.43 Article 27.2(b) of the SCM Agreement provides:

> 27.2 The prohibition of paragraph 1(a) of Article 3 shall not apply to:
>
> ....
>
> (b) developing country Members for a period of eight years from the date of entry into force of the WTO Agreement, subject to compliance with the provisions of paragraph 4.

Article 27.4 of the SCM Agreement reads, in relevant part:

> 27.4 Any developing country Member referred to in paragraph 2(b) shall phase out its export subsidies within the eight-year period, preferably in a progressive manner. However, a developing country Member shall not increase the level of its export subsidies[55] and shall eliminate them within a period shorter than that provided for in this paragraph when the use of such export subsidies is inconsistent with its development needs....
>
> [55]For a developing country Member not granting export subsidies as of the date of entry into force of the WTO Agreement, this paragraph shall apply on the basis of the level of export subsidies granted in 1986.

7.44 The parties are in fundamental disagreement about the legal nature of the relationship between Article 3.1(a) and the above-cited provisions of Article 27. In particular, they disagree as to whether the provisions in Article 27.4 are an integral part of Canada's claim of violation of Article 3.1(a) with respect to which Canada bears the burden of proof, or whether these provisions constitute an "exception" from, or "affirmative defense" to, the prohibition laid out in Article 3.1(a) with respect to which Brazil bears the burden of proof. Canada contends that, because Article 27 reflects special and differential treatment for developing country Members, it is an exception to the general obligations of the SCM Agreement. In Canada's view, Article 27.2(b) sets forth a "limited and conditional exception" to the prohibition in Article 3.1(a). Canada relies on the Panel Report in *Argentina - Footwear I*[212] for the proposition that "it is for the party invoking an exception or an affirmative defense to prove that the conditions contained therein are met". According to Canada, in order to benefit from

[212] *Argentina - Measures Affecting Imports of Footwear, Textiles, Apparel and Other Items*, WT/DS56/R, para. 6.35, adopted 22 April 1998.

the "exception" in Article 27.2(b), Brazil bears the burden of demonstrating that it has complied with the conditions of Article 27.4.

7.45 Brazil disputes that Article 27.2(b) can be characterized as an "exception" to the prohibition set out in Article 3.1(a), or that it bears the burden of proof with respect to compliance with that provision and with the conditions stipulated in Article 27.4. For Brazil, Article 27 consists of carefully negotiated language that reflects a carefully drawn balance of rights and obligations. Brazil points out that the text of the provision states "clearly and unequivocally" that "the prohibition of paragraph 1(a) of Article 3 shall not apply" to developing countries, subject to the conditions in Article 27.4. In Brazil's view, Canada, as the complaining party, bears the burden of establishing that Brazil has not complied with these conditions. The third parties, the European Community and the United States, support Canada's position.

7.46 There appears to be no overriding general principle to guide a panel in distinguishing between an element of a claim of violation of a provision of the WTO Agreement and an "exception" from, or "affirmative defence" to, a provision of the WTO Agreement. However, it is clear that the mere characterization of a provision as an "exception" will not necessarily determine which party bears the burden of proof with respect to establishing the elements contained in that provision. Thus, we note that, in *EC Measures Concerning Meat and Meat Products (Hormones)*, for example, the Appellate Body stated that:

> "The general rule in a dispute settlement proceeding requiring a complaining party to establish a *prima facie* case of inconsistency ... is *not* avoided by simply describing that provision as an 'exception.'"[213]

7.47 Nevertheless, it is well-established in WTO practice that a party who asserts the affirmative of a particular claim or defence bears the burden of proof with respect to that claim or defense. As the Appellate Body stated in *United States - Measure Affecting Imports of Woven Wool Shirts and Blouses from India*:

> "... it is a generally-accepted canon of evidence in civil law, common law, and in fact, most jurisdictions, that the burden of proof rests upon the party, whether complaining or defending, who asserts the affirmative of a particular claim or defence. If that party adduces evidence sufficient to raise a presumption that what is claimed is true, the burden then shifts to the other party, who will fail unless it adduces sufficient evidence to rebut the presumption."[214]

---

[213] WT/DS26/AB/R, WT/DS48/AB/R, para. 104, adopted 13 February 1998.

[214] WT/DS33/AB/R, DSR 1997:I, 323, at 335 adopted 23 May 1997.

7.48 Therefore, in determining which party bears the burden of proof in this case with respect to the compliance with the provisions of Article 27.4 of the SCM Agreement, it is necessary to consider whether that provision is in the nature of an element of a claim of violation of Article 3.1(a) where the Member complained against is a developing country Member within the meaning of Article 27.2(b), or whether it is in the nature of an affirmative defence that may be invoked by such a developing country Member in response to a claim of inconsistency with Article 3.1(a). If it is an element of a claim of inconsistency with Article 3.1(a), then, in this case, it would fall to Canada, as the complaining party, to adduce evidence sufficient to raise a presumption that Brazil was *not in compliance* with the conditions set out in Article 27.4, at which point the burden would shift to Brazil to rebut this presumption. If, on the other hand, Article 27.4 is in the nature of an affirmative defence, it would be for Brazil to adduce evidence sufficient to raise a presumption that it was *in compliance* with the provisions in Article 27.4, at which point the burden would shift to Canada to rebut this presumption.

7.49 In our view, a determination of the nature of this provision, and an examination of which party bears the burden of proof under it, must turn on the actual wording of the relevant text of the Agreement in its context, and in light of the object and purpose of the SCM Agreement. We note that Article 27.2(b) contains an explicit textual link between itself and Article 27.4, as well as between Article 3.1(a) and Article 27.4. It states:

> "The prohibition of paragraph 1(a) of Article 3 shall not apply to: ... other developing country Members for a period of eight years from the date of entry into force of the WTO Agreement, *subject to compliance with the provisions in paragraph 4*." (emphasis added)

Because of this explicit textual linkage between Article 27.2(b) and Article 27.4, we consider that these paragraphs must be read in conjunction in order to determine the legal nature of the conditions contained in Article 27.4. Due to the wording of Article 27.2(b) highlighted above, we believe this provision to be determinative for the issue of allocating the burden of proof with respect to the conditions contained in Article 27.4.

7.50 An essential element in establishing a claim of inconsistency with a provision of the WTO Agreement is to demonstrate that the particular provision *applies* to the particular Member in question and to the particular factual situation in a given dispute. Part and parcel of asserting the affirmative of a particular claim is to demonstrate that the legal provision forming the basis for that claim applies to the Member against whom that legal provision is being invoked. Naturally, there will be no inconsistency with a given provision if a Member is explicitly excluded from its scope of application or a situation is explicitly identified in the text of the Agreement as falling outside the scope of application of a particular provision. In this regard, we recall that Article 27.2(b) states that:

"The prohibition of paragraph 1(a) of Article 3 *shall not apply to*: ... other developing country Members for a period of eight years from the date of entry into force of the WTO Agreement, subject to compliance with the provisions in paragraph 4." (emphasis added) Clearly, on the basis of the plain meaning of the text of the provision, developing country Members falling within Article 27.2(b) - that is, developing country Members (other than those referred to in Annex VII) that are in compliance with the provisions of Article 27.4 - do not fall within the scope of application of the prohibition contained in Article 3.1(a) until 1 January 2003.

7.51 We consider that this interpretation is supported by the context of Article 27.2(b). Article 27 is entitled "Special and Differential Treatment of Developing Country Members" and this provision constitutes Part VIII of the SCM Agreement, entitled "Developing Country Members". Thus, the context of the provisions indicates that they extend "special and differential treatment" to developing country Members.

7.52 The context of Article 27.2(b) also includes Article 27.3 and Article 27.7 of the SCM Agreement. Article 27.7 reads:

> 27.7 The provisions of Article 4 shall not apply to a developing country Member in the case of export subsidies which are in conformity with the provisions of paragraphs 2 through 5. The relevant provisions in such a case shall be those of Article 7.

We consider that, analogous to Article 27.2(b) in relation to Article 3.1(a), this provision would exclude developing country Members from the scope of application of Article 4 in certain circumstances. The phrase "subject to compliance with the provisions in paragraph 4" contained in Article 27.2(b) can, in our view, be seen as analogous to the phrase "which are in conformity with paragraphs 2 through 5" contained in Article 27.7. This supports an interpretation of Article 27.2(b) that developing country Members are excluded from the scope of application of the substantive obligation in question provided that they comply with certain specified conditions.

7.53 Moreover, Article 27.3 states:

> 27.3 The prohibition of paragraph 1(b) of Article 3 shall not apply to developing country Members for a period of five years, and shall not apply to least-developed country Members for a period of eight years, from the date of entry into force of the WTO Agreement.

This provision reflects that developing country Members are excluded outright from the scope of application of the substantive obligation of Article 3.1(b) (the prohibition on subsidies contingent on the use of domestic over imported goods) for a stipulated period of time. As contextual for Article 27.2(b), it supports the view that the relevant provisions of Article 27, which extend "special and differential treatment to developing countries", serve to exclude, in a qualified or unqualified manner, certain developing countries from the scope of application of certain substantive obligations found elsewhere in the Agreement for specified periods of time. Moreover, in Article 27.1, Members "recognize that subsidies may play an important role in economic development programmes of developing country Members". Therefore, on the basis of the text and context of Article 27.2(b), we consider that Article 27.2(b) serves to exclude the developing country Members referred to in that provision from the scope of application of the prohibition in Article 3.1(a), subject to compliance by the developing country Member in question with the provisions in Article 27.4.

7.54 This view, derived from the text and context of Article 27.2(b), reflects a legal relationship between Article 3.1(a), Article 27.2(b) and 27.4 of the SCM Agreement that is qualitatively different from the relationship between, for instance, the substantive obligations contained in Articles I or III of the GATT 1994 and the affirmative defences set out in the "general exceptions" of Article XX of the GATT 1994. Article 27.2(b) excludes from the scope of application of Article 3.1(a) a developing country Member referred to in Article 27.2(b) for a period of eight years from the date of entry into force of the WTO Agreement. In other words, Article 27.2(b) recognizes the autonomous right of certain developing country Members to grant or maintain export subsidies during a stipulated period. According to the specific language of that provision, this right is "subject to compliance with the provisions of paragraph 4" of Article 27. Paragraph 4 of Article 27 then sets out the conditions with which a qualifying developing country Member must comply in order to be excluded from the scope of application of the prohibition in Article 3.1(a), that is, in order that the substantive obligation in Article 3.1(a) not apply to it. This contrasts markedly with a situation that could arise with respect to the affirmative defences set out in Article XI:2 or XX of the GATT 1994, where there is no dispute that the substantive obligation contained in, say, Article I or III of the GATT 1994, applies to the Member in question, but that Member argues that, while it may have acted inconsistently with a particular provision, it should be excused from the substantive obligation contained in that provision.[215]

[215] We note that the Appellate Body stated the following in *EC - Hormones* (para. 104), in relation to the relationship between Article 3.1 and Article 3.3 of the *SPS Agreement*:

> "[t]he Panel posits the existence of a "general rule - exception" relationship between Article 3.1 (the general obligation) and Article 3.3 (an exception) and applies to the *SPS Agreement* what it calls "established practice under GATT 1947 and GATT 1994" to the effect that the burden of justifying a measure under Article XX of the GATT 1994 rests on the defending party. It appears to us that the Panel has misconceived the relationship between Articles 3.1, 3.2 and 3.3, a relationship discussed below, which is qualitatively different from the relationship between, for instance, Articles I or III and Article XX of the GATT 1994. Article 3.1 of the *SPS Agreement* simply excludes from its scope of application the kinds of situations covered by Article 3.3 of that Agreement . . . ." (footnotes omitted).

7.55 We draw, from WTO practice, further support for our view that the nature of the legal relationship between Articles 3.1, 27.2(b) and 27.4 of the SCM Agreement differs qualitatively from that between, say, Article III and Article XX of the GATT 1994. We note that, in addressing the nature of Article 6 of the Agreement on Textiles and Clothing in *United States - Shirts and Blouses*, the Appellate Body stated that Articles XI and XX are "limited exceptions from obligations under certain other provisions of GATT 1994, *not positive rules establishing obligations in themselves*". (emphasis added) Although Article 27.2(b) does not, in itself, establish any obligations, Article 27.4 does impose certain obligations, i.e., the obligation on developing country Members within the meaning of Article 27.2(b) to "phase out its export subsidies within the eight-year period, preferably in a progressive manner"; to "not increase the level of its export subsidies" and "to eliminate them within a period shorter than [eight years]when the use of such export subsidies is inconsistent with its development needs". This is not to say that Article 27.4 would necessarily form the legal basis for a separate claim of violation of the SCM Agreement.[216] Rather, because of the explicit textual link found in Article 27.2(b) between Articles 3.1(a), 27.2(b) and 27.4, the requirements of Article 27.4 must be considered in conjunction with Article 3.1(a) of the SCM Agreement in order to establish a claim of violation of that provision against a Member that is a developing country Member within the meaning of Article 27.2(b).

7.56 The fundamental issue before us, therefore, is whether the prohibition in Article 3.1(a) of the SCM Agreement *applies* to the developing country Member in question, rather than whether the developing country Member, having been found to be subject to the substantive obligations of Article 3.1(a), and having been found to have acted inconsistently with these obligations, can find justifying protection by invoking Article 27.2(b) in conjunction with Article 27.4. In our view, until non-compliance with the conditions set out in Article 27.4 is demonstrated, there is also, on the part of a developing country Member within the meaning of Article 27.2(b), no inconsistency with Article 3.1(a). We recall the words of the Appellate Body in *United States - Shirts and Blouses* that "a party claiming a violation of a provision of the WTO Agreement by another Member must assert and prove its claim."[217] Applying this terminology to the case at hand, we consider that, in order to assert and prove a claim of violation of Article 3.1(a) with respect to a Member that is a developing country Member within the meaning of Article 27.2(b), the Member asserting the claim must demonstrate that the substantive obligations contained in Article 3.1(a) of the SCM Agreement apply to the Member in question. In order to do this, the Mem-

[216] Given that Canada has made no claim of a violation of Article 27.4, this is an issue we need not and do not decide in this dispute.
[217] WT/DS33/AB/R, DSR 1997:I, 323, at 337, adopted 23 May 1997.

ber asserting the claim must demonstrate that the developing country Member concerned has not complied with the conditions stipulated in Article 27.4.

7.57 Where, as here, it is agreed that the Member in question is a developing country Member within the meaning of Article 27.2(b), it is for the Member alleging a violation of Article 3.1(a) of the SCM Agreement to demonstrate that the substantive obligation in that provision - the prohibition on export subsidies - applies to the developing country Member complained against. That is, it is for the complaining Member to demonstrate that the developing country Member in question is not in compliance with at least one of the elements laid out in Article 27.4. In light of the above, we consider that, in order to determine whether Brazil has acted inconsistently with Article 3.1(a), it is for Canada to establish that Article 3.1(a), in fact, applies to Brazil at the present time. Accordingly, we find that Canada bears the burden of proving that Brazil is not in compliance with the provisions of Article 27.4.

3. Has Brazil Increased the Level of its Export Subsidies?

7.58 Having resolved the question of burden of proof, we now turn to the first element of Article 27.4 identified by Canada, whether Brazil has increased the level of its export subsidies. It will be recalled that Article 27.4 provides, in relevant part, that "a developing country Member shall not increase the level of its export subsidies[55] . . . .". Canada asserts that Brazil has increased the level of its export subsidies. Brazil asserts, on the basis of the same data, that it has not increased the level of its export subsidies. Accordingly, before turning to the undisputed factual information submitted by the parties, we must consider a number of legal issues relating to the proper interpretation of this provision.

7.59 The first issue presented is whether "the level of export subsidies" referred to in Article 27.4 means the overall level of export subsidies of a Member during a given period, the level of export subsidies with respect to some given product during that period, or some other measurement. With respect to this issue, the parties generally agree that the "level of export subsidies" relevant to the analysis in this dispute is the overall level of Brazil's export subsidies. Although we do not decide that the overall level is the *only* possible basis for an examination of this issue, we do not see any reason to conclude that an analysis of the overall level of export subsidies is not *an* appropriate measure for the purposes of Article 27.4. The parties further agree that two programmes, PROEX and BEFIEX, are the only Brazilian export subsidy programmes relevant to this analysis. There is no information in the record before us suggesting the existence of export subsidies within the meaning of Article 3.1(a) of the SCM Agreement other than those provided pursuant to PROEX and BEFIEX. Accordingly, we will in this dispute examine the overall level of export subsidies provided by Brazil, i.e., the overall level of export subsidies provided under PROEX and BEFIEX.

7.60 The parties differ in one respect with respect to this issue. Canada contends that, because agricultural export subsidies are subject to special rules and separate reduction commitments under the Agreement on Agriculture, and because Article 13(c) of that Agreement exempts agricultural export subsidies that fully conform to Part V of that Agreement from the SCM Agreement's prohibition on export subsidies, such subsidies should be excluded in calculating the level of export subsidies under Article 27.4. Brazil disagrees, noting that Article 27 itself makes no distinction between agricultural and industrial subsidies. Brazil states, however, that neither PROEX nor BEFIEX are agricultural export subsidies, nor are they granted for the benefit of agricultural products. Canada has not contested Brazil's statements in this regard. Under these circumstances, we need not and do not decide whether the level of a Member's export subsidies within the meaning of Article 27.4 includes agricultural export subsidies.

7.61 The parties disagree as to the benchmark period against which an examination as to whether a Member has increased the level of its export subsidies should be made. Brazil asserts that, in the circumstances of this dispute, the appropriate benchmark is 1991, as that is the year in which the PROEX programme was first enacted. Canada considers that the relevant benchmark is 1994, as the condition in Article 27.4 not to increase the level of one's export subsidies became effective on 1 January 1995. We agree with Canada. The WTO Agreement entered into force on 1 January 1995. Article 27.2(b) allows developing country Members to maintain export subsidies for eight years from the date of entry into force of the WTO Agreement, provided they comply with the requirement of Article 27.4 that they not increase the level of their export subsidies during that period. Thus, logic would suggest that the appropriate reference period is the level of export subsidies in the period immediately preceding the date of entry into force.

7.62 The foregoing interpretation is confirmed by footnote 55. Footnote 55 provides that, "[f]or a developing country Member not granting export subsidies *as of the date of entry into force of the WTO Agreement,* this paragraph shall apply on the basis of the level of export subsidies granted in 1986." Footnote 55 would appear to recognize that it would be inappropriate to impose on developing country Members which had before the entry into force of the WTO Agreement autonomously eliminated their export subsidies without a multilateral obligation to do so an obligation not to increase the level of its export subsidies above a zero level. Rather, it offers for such Members a ceiling level of export subsidies based on their 1986 level. Implicit in this explanation is that, absent footnote 55, a developing country Member which granted no export subsidies *as of the date of entry into force of the WTO Agreement* would be prohibited from providing any export subsidies during the eight-year transition period. Thus, footnote 55 indicates that the relevant benchmark period against which the obligation not to increase the level of export subsidies should be measured is a period immediately preceding the date of entry into force of the WTO Agreement.

7.63 Nor has Brazil offered any cogent reason why the Panel should use the year 1991 as a benchmark. We note that the sole stated basis for Brazil's view that we should look to 1991 rather than 1994 as the benchmark period is that 1991 is the year in which the PROEX programme was created. Given the agreement of the parties that the level of export subsidies in this dispute should relate to the overall level of Brazil's export subsidies, and not to the level of PROEX export subsidies alone, we fail to understand why the date on which PROEX was created should be relevant to our choice of a benchmark period. In the circumstances of this dispute, it would be equally logical - or illogical - to use the date on which BEFIEX was enacted as the benchmark period.

7.64 Brazil contends that, if the Panel chooses not to use 1991 as a benchmark period, it should at least use a weighted average of the three or four years prior to the date of entry into force as the relevant period. It argues that such a benchmark would help reduce the distortion of the impact of a single year on the volatile economies of developing country Members. Once again, however, we consider that footnote 55 gives us useful guidance by providing at least a presumptive period for use as a benchmark. Footnote 55 provides for the use of "the level of export subsidies granted in 1986" when the developing country Member was not granting export subsidies as of the date of entry into force of the WTO Agreement. In other words, footnote 55 envisions using a one-year period as a benchmark for determining a developing country Member's level of export subsidies. Under these circumstances, and in the absence of any compelling reason to deviate from the approach suggested by footnote 55, we consider that it would be most appropriate in this case to use the single calendar year 1994 for the purpose of this analysis.

7.65 The parties also disagree vigorously with respect to whether, when considering the level of export subsidies, the Panel should examine budgeted amounts or actual expenditures. Canada contends that the level of export subsidies should be assessed by reference to actual expenditures, while Brazil contends that budgeted amounts represent the appropriate basis for the calculation. We agree with Canada. In our view, the level of a Member's export subsidies in its ordinary meaning refers to the level of subsidies actually provided, not the level of subsidies which a Member planned or authorized its government to provide through its budgetary process. This reading is in our view confirmed by footnote 55, which provides that, "[f]or a developing country Member not *granting* export subsidies as of the date of entry into force of the WTO Agreement, this paragraph shall apply on the basis of the level of export subsidies *granted* in 1986."(emphasis added). The verb "grant" has been defined to mean, *inter alia*, "to bestow by a formal act"[218] and "give, bestow, confer".[219] Thus, the

[218] *Shorter Oxford English Dictionary* (third edition).
[219] *Webster's Third New International Dictionary*.

verb "grant" in its ordinary meaning implies the actual provision of a subsidy, not its mere budgeting.[220] Accordingly, the SCM Agreement envisions that the proper point of reference in determining whether a Member has increased the level of its export subsidies is expenditures rather than budgeted amounts.

7.66 Brazil argues that "budgeted amounts, rather than expenditures, are the proper basis of comparison because they are the responsibility of the Member governments of the WTO." It contends that under the expenditure approach, a Member could increase its budgetary amounts and meet the requirements of Article 27.4 if the private sector did not fully utilize the budgeted sum, or fall out of compliance if the private sector utilized a sufficiently larger share of a smaller budgeted amount. We do not find these arguments compelling. A Member should be aware of the level of its past expenditures for export subsidies. If that Member budgets a larger amount than the amount it expended on export subsidies in a prior period, it should not be surprised if the private sector utilizes that budgeted amount and as a result the Member is deemed to have increased the level of its export subsidies. On the other hand, if a Member increases the amount budgeted for export subsidies it may be that the Member intended to increase the level of its export subsidies, but that does not mean that it has actually increased the level of its export subsidies. In this respect, we agree with Canada that an expenditure-based measurement is consistent with the object and purpose of the SCM Agreement, which is to reduce economic distortions caused by subsidies. It seems to us that an increase in the level of export subsidies budgeted, which increase is not in fact actually realized, represents no more than a failed attempt by the subsidizing Member to increase the level of its export subsidies. That failed attempt in itself does not affect the interests of other Members.

7.67 As noted in paragraph 7.13 above, the parties disagree about the form of the financial contribution involved in this dispute, an issue which they consider has implications with respect to the question of when PROEX payments should be considered to have been "granted" for the purposes of calculating the level of Brazil's export subsidies in terms of expenditures. In Canada's view, PROEX payments involve a direct transfer of funds within the meaning of Article 1.1(a)(1) which occurs either when payments are made pursuant to a NTN-1 bond (i.e., where the lender redeems the bonds) or, in the alternative, when

[220] Brazil defines "grant", without citation, as meaning "to agree, consent" or "to promise, undertake (which means 'to give formal promise or pledge')". Brazil further argues that the Portuguese term "dotação orçamentária" signifies a formal, legal binding promise - not an estimate - to the Brazilian exporter or financial institution to provide funds earmarked for PROEX in the budget, on a first-come, first-served basis, until the appropriated resources are depleted. While the verb "grant" may have a variety of meanings depending the context in which it is used, it is clear to us that, in the context of the phrase "export subsidies granted in 1986", the meanings cited by Brazil are inapposite, and it cannot reasonably be contended that a subsidy is "granted" merely because the government makes a budgetary authorization.

NTN-1 bonds are issued to an agent bank. Brazil, argues, to the contrary, that PROEX interest rate equalization in the first instance involve a potential direct transfer of funds which occurs at the moment that a letter is issued by the Export Credit Committee committing PROEX to provide interest rate equalization support for a transaction, provided that it is entered into according to the terms and conditions specified in a request for approval.

7.68 We recall that Article 1.1(a)(1) of the SCM Agreement provides that there is a financial contribution where, *inter alia*:

> "a government practice involves a direct transfer of funds (e.g., grants, loans and equity infusion), potential direct transfer of funds or liabilities (e.g., loan guarantees)."

We believe that a "potential direct transfer of funds" exists only where the action in question gives rise to a benefit and thus confers a subsidy irrespective of whether any payment occurs. In arriving at this view, we have taken contextual guidance from the example of loan guarantees provided in Article 1.1(a)(1) of the SCM Agreement. Whether or not a loan guarantee confers a subsidy does not depend upon whether a payment occurs (i.e., whether the beneficiary of the guarantee defaults and the government is required to make good on the guarantee). For example, Article 14 of the SCM Agreement provides that, when examining benefit to the recipient in a countervail context, "a loan guarantee by a government shall not be considered as conferring a benefit, unless there is a difference between the amount that the firm receiving the guarantee pays on a loan guaranteed by the government and the amount that a firm would pay on a comparable commercial loan absent the government guarantee." Thus, whether or not a loan guarantee confers a benefit depends on its effects on the terms of the loan and not on whether there is a default. Similarly, whether an export credit guarantee programme is an export subsidy under item (j) of the Illustrative List of Export Subsidies depends upon the premium rates charged and not upon whether a subsequent default occurs. While loan guarantees clearly are only one example of a "potential direct transfer of funds", we consider that other measures must share this basic characteristic in order to fall within that category of financial contribution.

7.69 In our view, if the category of potential direct transfers of funds referred simply to the situation where a government may in the future make a payment, almost any direct transfer of funds could, at an earlier date, be qualified as a potential direct transfer of funds. Nor do we see any reason to believe that a possible future payment is a "potential direct transfer of funds" merely because of a high probability that a payment will actually occur. The word "potential" has been defined as "possible as opposed to actual" or "capable of coming into being".[221] If the determination whether a measure was a "potential direct transfer

[221] *Shorter Oxford English Dictionary* (third edition).

of funds" depended upon the degree of likelihood or probability that a payment would subsequently occur, then the drafters surely would have chosen an adjective more suggestive of high probability than "potential."

7.70 Applying this approach to the case at hand, we recall Brazil's view that the issuance of a letter of commitment constitutes a potential direct transfer of funds. In this case, however, it clearly is not the alleged "potential direct transfer of funds", i.e., the letter of commitment, that confers the benefit. Rather, the benefit in the PROEX interest rate equalization scheme derives from the fact that a payment, i.e., a direct transfer of funds, has been or will be made. Brazil argues a potential direct transfer of funds exists here because Brazil is legally obligated under the letter of commitment to provide PROEX interest equalization payments *if* the export transaction to which the letter of commitment relates is concluded on the terms set forth in the request letter.[222] As explained above, the existence of a "potential direct transfer of funds" does not depend upon the probability that a payment will subsequently occur. Rather, the issue of whether and to what extent Brazil has taken a legal commitment to provide PROEX payments is relevant to determining *when* Brazil can be considered to have provided a *direct transfer of funds* in the form of a PROEX payment.

7.71 At what point in time can Brazil be considered to "grant" PROEX payments in the form of "direct transfers of funds"? As noted above, the verb "grant" has been defined to mean, *inter alia*, "to bestow by formal act" and "give, bestow, confer". Arguably, therefore PROEX payments may be "granted" where the unconditional legal right of the beneficiary to receive the payments has arisen, even if the payments themselves have not yet occurred. It is clear to us, however, that PROEX payments have not yet been "granted" at the time a letter of commitment is issued. We note that the issuance of a letter of commitment, even if legally binding on the Government of Brazil in the event certain conditions are fulfilled, provides no assurance that PROEX payments will actually be made. To the contrary, at the time the letter of commitment is issued no export sales contract has been signed, and the letter of commitment expires if a contract that conforms to the request for approval is not negotiated and signed within 90 days. Even the signing of a contract within that period does not trigger the issuance of bonds; in fact, business confidential information submitted by Brazil confirms that letters of commitment are issued with respect to options as well as firm contracts, which options may never be exercised. Rather, the right to receive the PROEX payments only arises after the conditions relating to receipt of PROEX payments, and specifically the condition that the product in question actually be exported, has been fulfilled. Thus, NTN-1 bonds are only issued if and when the aircraft whose financing is being supported by the interest rate

222 Brazil submitted a legal opinion prepared by a Brazilian lawyer for the proposition that the Government of Brazil cannot under Brazilian law annul or revoke a letter of commitment, once issued. *Legal Opinion from Professor Luiz Olavo Baptista*, Brazil exhibit 17.

equalization is actually exported. Accordingly, at the time the letter of commitment is issued, no PROEX payments have been made, nor has the beneficiary earned the unconditional right to receive PROEX payments. Rather, the issuance of the letter of commitment means only that, if an export transaction is closed within a certain period of time, and if the product in question actually is exported, a right to receive PROEX payments will arise.

7.72 The question remains whether PROEX payments are "granted" when the bonds are issued or whether they are granted only when the bonds are redeemed on a semiannual basis. In our view, PROEX payments should be considered to be "granted" when bonds are issued and title to those bonds is transferred to the lender financial institution. In this respect, we note that the terms "funds" is defined as, *inter alia*, "pecuniary resources". The word "pecuniary", in turn, is defined as, *inter alia*, "of, belonging to, or having relation to money".[223] Thus, the term "funds" can be defined to mean "resources of, belonging to, or having relation to money". It is true that the bonds are not fully equivalent to money, in that they can only be redeemed at some future date. Nevertheless, we consider that the transfer of title of these bonds to the lender should be considered to be the moment that a direct transfer of funds occurs. In this respect, we note that, while the bonds cannot be immediately redeemed, they are freely negotiable.[224] The parties agree that lenders may exercise their right to sell these bonds - albeit at a discount as determined by the market - to other entities rather than waiting until maturity to redeem the bonds themselves. Thus, at the point that title to the bonds is passed to the lenders, those lenders are the holders of a property right with a market value which is immediately realizable. Accordingly, we conclude that PROEX payments are "granted" at that point, and we will calculate the Brazil's PROEX expenditures on that basis.

7.73 Finally, we note that, while the parties appear to agree that "the level of export subsidies" should be measured in US dollars in this case, they disagree as to whether the level should be expressed in constant or nominal dollars. Brazil argues that it is logical to use a constant point of comparison to measure the level of a developing country Member's export subsidies. Canada responds that there is no indication in Article 27.4 that adjustment should be made for inflation, and that in cases - such as Annex IV:5 to the SCM Agreement - where the drafters considered that an inflation adjustment was appropriate, they specifically provided for it. In our view, however, it is appropriate in this case to use constant dollars, as that will provide a more meaningful assessment as to whether Brazil has increased the level of its export subsidies. We note that, in this case, the conclusion with respect to this issue would be the same whether constant or nominal dollars are used.

[223] *Shorter Oxford English Dictionary* (third edition).

[224] Ministry Order Nos. 121/97 of 12 August 1997 and 18/98 of 27 January 1998.

7.74 In conclusion, we consider that the level of Brazil's export subsidies should be appropriately measured in this case by reference to Brazil's overall level of export subsidies, which the parties agree consist of PROEX and BEFIEX subsidies. We further consider that the proper measure of the level of Brazil's export subsidies is the level of its expenditures, not its budgeted amounts, and that the proper benchmark period against which to examine whether that level has increased is calendar year 1994. We see no reason not to measure the level in US dollars, consistent with the data submitted by both parties.

7.75 There is no factual dispute among the parties regarding the evidence submitted to the Panel regarding the level of Brazil's export subsidies. The data which are relevant in light of our legal analysis are reflected in Table 9:

TABLE 9

Brazilian Export Subsidies (PROEX and BEFIEX)

	Total Expenditures* (current US$)	**Total Expenditures (1994 constant US$)**
1994	339.6	340
1995	269.5	263
1996	286.7	275
1997	412.5	389
1998**	537.8	502

Source: *Brazil exhibit 20.*

* PROEX payments appear as expenditures in the year the bonds are issued.

** PROEX expenditures January-October.

Applying the foregoing criteria to these undisputed data, we conclude that Brazil had by 1997 increased the level of its export subsidies above that prevailing in 1994, whether the data are expressed in nominal or in constant dollars. The increase for 1998 was even more substantial than that for 1997, reflecting as it does data for only the first ten months of the year.

7.76 For the foregoing reasons, we conclude that Brazil has "increased the level of its export subsidies" within the meaning of Article 27.4 of the SCM Agreement.

4. Has Brazil Complied with the Condition that it "Phase Out its Export Subsidies within the Eight-Year Period"?

7.77 Canada contends that, under Article 27.4, a developing country Member seeking to benefit from the non-application of the Article 3.1(a) prohibition must phase out its export subsidies within eight years from the date of entry into force of the WTO Agreement. In Canada's view, this provision reflects two requirements. First, a developing country is required to "bring gradually out of use", its export subsidies during the eight-year period. Second, the developing country Member is required to terminate its export subsidies by the end of the eight-year period. In Canada's view, Brazil has failed to comply with either condition.[225]

7.78 We note, first, that there can be no question, and Brazil does not contest, that a developing country Member other than one referred to in Annex VII is as a general rule required by Articles 27.2(b) and 27.4 to eliminate its export subsidies within eight years from the date of entry into force of the WTO Agreement. We further note, however, that Article 27.4 envisions that an extension of that period may be granted on request of the developing country Member if the Committee on Subsidies and Countervailing Measures determines that an extension of the period is justified, after examining all the relevant economic, financial, and development needs of the developing country Member. We further consider it evident that any such extension granted by the Committee would effectively extend the eight-year period specified in Article 27.2(b) and would render the prohibition on export subsidies under Article 3.1(a) inapplicable for the period for which the extension was granted (assuming the developing country Member continued to comply with the other conditions found in Article 27.4).

7.79 With respect to a developing country Member's obligations during the eight-year period, Article 27.4 provides that "[a]ny developing country Member referred to in paragraph 2(b) shall phase out its export subsidies, preferably in a progressive manner." We agree with Canada that the "principal interpretive challenge" presented by this provision is the need to reconcile the *mandatory* language providing that a developing country Member "shall phase out its export subsidies" with the hortatory language in the final clause encouraging Members to perform their phase-out in a progressive manner. In its ordinary meaning, the term "phase out" means, *inter alia*, "to discontinue the practice, production or use of by phases."[226] Thus, Article 27.4 appears to require the phased elimination of export subsidies within the eight-year period. On the other hand, Article 27.4 provides that the phase out should "preferably" be performed in a progressive manner. The word "progressive" has been defined as "proceeding step by step, occurring one after another, successive".[227] Brazil argues, not without some reason, that the term "phase out" should not be interpreted to *require* the phased elimination of export subsidies when the subsequent clause indicates that phased

[225] It could also be argued that the "phase out" obligation entails a requirement not to increase the level of a Member's export subsidies. In light of our findings with respect to the explicit requirement of Article 27.4 that a Member not increase the level of its export subsidies, we need not consider this matter further.

[226] *Webster's Third International Dictionary*.

[227] *Shorter Oxford English Dictionary* (third edition).

elimination is not required but only preferred. Canada responds that the tension between these two phrases can be reconciled if the term progressive is defined, as in the context of tax rates, to mean that a Member should phase out its export subsidies "at an increasing pace". Under this interpretation, a developing country would be required to undertake a phased elimination of its export subsidies, and would be encouraged, but not required, to reduce its subsidies at an increasing rate.

7.80 The parties have in this dispute identified what could be viewed as an internal contradiction within the text of Article 27.4. Brazil suggests that the term "phase out" must be read in the context of the subsequent clause and thus not be interpreted to require phased elimination. This however requires ascribing to the term "phase out" a meaning which is more limited than its ordinary meaning. Canada on the other hand has suggested a reading of the text which would eliminate the contradiction, but which relies upon ascribing a highly particularized meaning to the word "progressive". In fact, although Canada indicates that "progressive" may mean "at an increasing rate", it cites no dictionary in support of that definition. Further, Canada has cited no logical reason why the drafters would express a non-binding preference for an end-loaded phased elimination of export subsidies by developing country Members. Rather, given that the object and purpose of the SCM Agreement is to impose multilateral disciplines on trade-distorting subsidization, one would expect that any preference would be for a front-loaded, rather than an end-loaded, phase-out. Accordingly, the Canadian interpretation would have us ascribe a special meaning to the term "progressive" without any support, either direct or circumstantial, that the drafters so intended. Thus, neither the Canadian nor the Brazilian approach is entirely satisfactory from a legal perspective.[228]

7.81 Although the issue identified above is an interesting and complex one, we do not consider that we need resolve it in the context of this dispute. In our view, even if the term "phase out" does require the phased elimination of export subsidies by a developing country Member within the eight-year period, it does not specify in how many phases the elimination should be carried out, what the time-period between these phased reductions should be, and how these phased

[228] Although neither party has referred to the Spanish or French texts, we note that they would tend to support the Brazilian interpretation. Thus, the Spanish text provides that "Los países en desarollo Miembros a que se refiere el páraffo 2 b) eliminarán sus subvenciones a la exportación dentro del mencionado período de ocho años, preferentamente de manera progressiva." The French text provides that "Tout pays en développement Membre visé au paragraphe 2 b) supprimera ses subventions à la exportation dans le délai de huit ans, de préference de façon progressive." The terms "eliminarán" and "supprimera" do not bear the suggestion of "phased elimination" suggested by the English term "phase out".

reductions should be distributed within the eight-year period.[229] We acknowledge that Brazil has not to date carried out any phased reductions in the level of its export subsidies, and that there is nothing in the record indicating that Brazil at the moment has any intention to do so. Thus, it may be said that it is possible, or even highly likely, that Brazil will not engage in phased reductions in its export subsidies within the eight-year period. Nevertheless, we cannot preclude that Brazil will engage in phased reductions between now and 31 December 2002. Accordingly, we cannot conclude on the basis of Brazil's actions in the first four years since the date of entry into force of the WTO Agreement that Brazil has failed to comply with the phase-out requirement of Article 27.4 by reason of a failure to undertake phased reductions within the eight-year transition period.[230]

7.82 The question remains whether Brazil has failed to comply with the phase-out requirement of Article 27.4 by reason of an alleged failure to eliminate its export subsidies by the end of the eight-year period. In this respect, Canada submits that PROEX does not have a termination date; that the financing period provided for regional aircraft under PROEX interest rate equalization is from ten to fifteen years; and that various purchasers have firm orders or options for aircraft to be delivered "well after 1 January 2003" on which they expect to receive PROEX payments. With respect to the latter contention, Canada cited a press report and a study indicating that at least one carrier benefiting from PROEX interest rate equalization is expected to continue taking delivery of Brazilian regional jets into the year 2004. Canada further argues that, comparing EMBRAER's current firm orders and options to its production schedule, EMBRAER must be reserving delivery slots beyond 2002 for existing customers, and that, "to the extent that these airlines expect to receive PROEX export subsidies", Brazil is not complying with its obligation to phase out its export subsidies by the end of the eight-year period.

7.83 Turning first to Canada's argument that PROEX does not have a termination date, we do not consider that the absence of a termination date for PROEX demonstrates that Brazil is not in compliance with its obligation to eliminate its

---

[229] It is instructive in this respect to compare, for example, the highly detailed provisions regarding the phased integration into GATT 1994 of textile and clothing products in Article 2 of the Agreement on Textiles and Clothing.

[230] We note that the definition of "phase out" cited by Canada is "to bring gradually . . . out of use", and that gradually has been defined as taking place "by degrees, slowly progressive, not rapid, steep or abrupt". Canada deduces from this that Brazil's obligation is not only to "bring its export subsidies out of use in a phased manner" but also to show that it "does not intend to bring its subsidies to a 'rapid, steep or abrupt end' before the end of the eight-year period." We do not consider however that in the absence of more precise requirements we can reasonably infer into the term "phase out" any more than an obligation to bring one's export subsidies out of use in a phased manner.

export subsidies by the end of the eight-year period. In this respect, we do not agree with Canada that,

> "in order to establish its conformity with the 'phase out' Brazil must, at the very least, demonstrate that it has put in place a programme or a schedule of phased reductions of its export subsidies, *with a view to elimination at the end of the grace period.*"(emphasis in original).[231]

While developing country Members certainly would be well advised to plan as far as possible in advance for the elimination of their export subsidies, their failure to do so does not in itself demonstrate that the required elimination will not occur. Nor does the fact that PROEX interest rate equalization has been provided with respect to financing extending beyond the 31 December 2002 in our view warrant a different conclusion. As discussed in paragraph 7.72, above, we consider that a PROEX interest rate equalization subsidy is granted at the moment that title to the bonds relating to the equalization is transferred to the lender financial institution. Accordingly, the relevant question in our view is not whether bonds issued before the end of the transition period may be redeemed after the end of that period, but rather whether Brazil continues to issue new bonds - and therefore to grant further subsidies - after the end of the transition period. It is to this issue that we now turn.

7.84 As noted in paragraph 7.82 above, Canada relies upon a press report[232] and estimates in a study[233], as well as calculations based on EMBRAER's order book and production schedule, for the proposition that Brazil has already committed to provide PROEX interest rate equalization with respect to regional aircraft that will be delivered after 31 December 2002.[234] The most telling evidence is the press report, which states that "Eagle expects to take delivery of its first ERJ-135 in July of next year, and continue accepting airplanes through 2004". Brazil concedes that this transaction involves PROEX interest rate equalization.[235] Further, Brazil has argued forcefully that it is legally required, as of the date that it issues a letter of commitment to EMBRAER, to issue the bonds if the terms of the letter of commitment are respected.[236] Because, under the PROEX

---

231 Canada answer to Panel question 49.

232 *See American Eagle to Replace Aging Saabs with ERJ-135s*, in *Flight International*, 1 October 1998 (Canada exhibit 71).

233 *See* Canada exhibit 64.

234 Although this evidence may be less than conclusive, we consider it sufficient to raise a presumption that Canada's factual assertion is correct, particularly in light of the fact that access to definitive information on this issue is in the sole possession of Brazil and the companies in question, and that Brazil has at no point not contested the accuracy of Canada's assertions in this regard.

235 *See* Brazil submission "Comments on Additional Information Submitted by Canada", para. 26.

236 According to a written legal opinion submitted by Brazil to the Panel, "it is our opinion that, within the validity period of the letters of commitment and provided there are no pending debts from the exporter to the GOB, it is illegal and not viable the cancellation or the revoking of the

interest rate equalization scheme, bonds relating to an export transaction are not issued until it has been confirmed that an export transaction will in fact occur,[237] this strongly suggests that Brazil will continue to issue bonds - and hence to grant new subsidies - after 31 December 2002. Accordingly, Canada has established in our view that Brazil will continue to issue bonds, and thus to grant PROEX interest rate equalization subsidies - although at a level which cannot be determined - beyond 31 December 2002.

7.85 Is the foregoing demonstration sufficient to show, in advance, that Brazil has not complied with the condition of Article 27.4 that it "phase out its export subsidies within the eight-year period"? We consider that it is. It is true, as we stated above,[238] that the Committee on Subsidies and Countervailing Measures may extend the eight-year period, and that during the period of any such extension the Article 3.1(a) prohibition on export subsidies would continue to be inapplicable to the developing country Member in question. Brazil, however, has entered into a legally binding commitment to issue bonds where certain conditions are met without having yet even requested an extension of that period. Further, we note that this commitment has had an effect on the marketplace by allowing EMBRAER to conclude export contracts for deliveries of regional aircraft to occur, and for subsidies to be granted, after the end of that period. Accordingly, we must conclude on the facts before us that Brazil has not complied with its obligation to phase out its export subsidies by the end of the transition period.

7.86 For the foregoing reasons, we find that Brazil has failed to comply with the condition of Article 27.4 relating to the phase out of its export subsidies.

5. *Are Brazil's Export Subsidies "Inconsistent with its Development Needs"?*

7.87 Canada considers that, under the second sentence of Article 27.4, a developing country Member seeking to benefit from non-application of the Article 3.1(a) prohibition on export subsidies must demonstrate that its export subsidies are consistent with its development needs. Canada considers that this is not a self-judging provision, and that it should be applied on the basis of objective standards. Although Canada "does not propose to set out these standards", it does argue that one objective standard in this case consists of the domestic content standards established by Brazil with respect to PROEX. Specifically, Can-

interest rate equalization concessions made for the referred to transactions." *Legal Opinion from Professor Luiz Olavo Baptista*, Brazil exhibit 17.

237 According to Brazil, where there is confirmation of the shipment of goods or the effective settlement of the relevant foreign exchange contract for the aircraft in question. *See* Brazil's answer to Panel question 28.

238 Paragraph 7.82.

ada argues that with respect to regional aircraft Brazil has waived the domestic content rules generally applicable under PROEX and provides interest rate equalization on the full value of the aircraft in spite of the low domestic content of those aircraft. Canada argues that another relevant standard may be foreign exchange earnings versus foreign exchange expenditure on export subsidies.

7.88 Brazil argues that Article 27 presumes that export subsidies are consistent with a developing country Member's development needs. In support of this view, it cites Article 27.1 of the SCM Agreement, which provides that "Members recognize that that subsidies may play an important role in economic development programmes of developing country Members." Brazil further argues that the language of Article 27.4, which provides that export subsidies shall be eliminated in a period shorter than eight years "when the use of subsidies is inconsistent with" a developing country Member's development needs, clearly means that the burden is on the challenging Member to demonstrate the "inconsistency". Brazil rejects Canada's view that the waiver of certain domestic content regulations in the case of PROEX interest rate equalization payments for regional aircraft is relevant: Article 27 contains no domestic content requirement, and any standards applied with respect to this issue should in Brazil's view relate to the overall needs of the developing country Member, not to one particular industry or economic sector. Finally, Brazil asserts on the basis of certain information regarding economic conditions and the importance of an open, export-oriented economy that PROEX is in fact consistent with its development needs.

7.89 In considering this issue, we note that this element of Article 27.4 is troubling from the perspective of a panel. Article 27.4 provides in relevant part that a developing country Member "shall eliminate [its export subsidies] within a period shorter than that provided for in this paragraph when the use of such export subsidies is inconsistent with its development needs." We recognize that as written this clause is mandatory, and a conclusion that this clause was not susceptible of application by a panel would be inconsistent with the principle of effective treaty interpretation. On the other hand, an examination as to whether export subsidies are inconsistent with a developing country Member's development needs is an inquiry of a peculiarly economic and political nature, and notably ill-suited to review by a panel whose function is fundamentally legal.[239] Further, the SCM Agreement provides panels with no guidance with respect to the criteria to be applied in performing this examination. We consider that it is the developing country Member itself which is best positioned to identify its development needs and to assess whether its export subsidies are consistent with

[239] It may be noted that under Article 27.14, "[t]he Committee [on Subsidies and Countervailing Measures] shall, upon request by an interested Member, undertake a review of a specific export subsidy practice of a developing country Member to examine whether the practice is in conformity with its development needs." In our view, a body such as the Committee is far better equipped to perform this type of examination than is a panel.

those needs. Thus, in applying this provision we consider that panels should give substantial deference to the views of the developing country Member in question.

7.90 As discussed above, we consider that Canada bears the burden of demonstrating that, because Brazil has not complied with the conditions set forth in Article 27.4, the Article 3.1(a) prohibition on export subsidies applies to Brazil. Further, we note that Article 27.4 does not provide that a developing country Member must eliminate its export subsidies in a period shorter than eight years *unless* the use of such export subsidies *is consistent* with its development needs. Rather, it provides that a developing country Member must eliminate its export subsidies in a period shorter than eight years *if* the use of such export subsidies is *inconsistent* with its development needs. Thus, in order to prevail on this issue Canada must present evidence and argument sufficient to raise a presumption that the use of export subsidies by Brazil is inconsistent with Brazil's development needs.

7.91 Canada argues that PROEX payments on exports of regional aircraft are inconsistent with Brazil's development needs because Brazil has waived certain domestic content rules generally applicable under PROEX in the context of the export of such regional aircraft. Specifically, Canada asserts that under PROEX regulations, exports with a domestic content index of 60 per cent or more are subject to interest rate equalization payments on 100 per cent of their value, while for goods with a domestic content index of less than 60 per cent, the percentage eligible for interest rate equalization is reduced according to a formula. Canada asserts that the ERJ-145 regional jet, for example, has a domestic content index of approximately 15 per cent, and thus should be eligible for interest rate equalization on only 55 per cent of its value, but that it in fact benefits from 100 per cent equalization. Canada further notes that the spare parts may make up as much as thirty per cent of the value of the export package, and that these spare parts could have no Brazilian content whatsoever. Brazil has not contested Canada's calculations of the Brazilian value-added of the ERJ-145, nor its characterization of PROEX domestic content rules.[240]

7.92 It is not entirely clear whether under Article 27.4 it is a particular export subsidy practice or a Member's export subsidies generally which must be shown

---

[240] Canada's calculations appear to be based on a study performed by Ernst and Young on behalf of Canada entitled *Analysis of EMBRAER's Use of the Brazilian Export Financing Program PROEX*. Although Canada did not submit this study into evidence, Brazil submitted it as exhibit 9 to support certain arguments of its own. On the basis of this study (p. 18), it appears that the domestic content figure cited by Canada in fact referred to the ERJ-135 (with an estimated Brazilian value-added of 14.8 per cent) rather than to the ERJ-145 (with an estimated Brazilian value-added of 26.1 per cent). We note however that business confidential documents submitted by Brazil indicate that in the view of the Bank of Brazil the domestic content of the ERJ-145 is substantially higher than estimated by Canada.

to be inconsistent with its development needs.[241] Even if we assume that it is appropriate to review whether a particular subsidy practice with respect to a particular product is inconsistent with a developing country Member's development needs, we do not believe that the evidence submitted by Canada is sufficient to raise a presumption that PROEX payments on regional aircraft are inconsistent with Brazil's development needs. In our view, the fact that Brazil has a generally applicable rule regarding the relationship between the domestic content of an exported product and the extent of the PROEX interest rate equalization available with respect to that product does not mean that the deviation from that rule in a particular case is necessarily inconsistent with a developing country Member's development needs. Nor do we see any basis to conclude that PROEX payments on regional aircraft are necessarily inconsistent with Brazil's development needs merely because the Brazilian value-added of the aircraft being exported is relatively low. There could be any number of reasons why the provision of export subsidies might be consistent with a Member's development needs in such a case. For example, a developing country Member might be interested in the possible technological spin-off effects from the development and production of the product in question, or the need to establish a strong market presence and reputation in foreign markets as a stepping stone to introducing products with greater national value-added. In fact, Canada has not made any meaningful effort to relate the issue of Brazilian value-added to the broader issue of Brazilian development needs.[242]

7.93 For the foregoing reasons, we conclude that Canada has failed to present evidence and argument sufficient to raise a presumption that the use of export subsidies by Brazil is inconsistent with Brazil's development needs.

VIII. CONCLUSIONS AND RECOMMENDATION

8.1 In conclusion, we find that:

(a) PROEX interest rate equalization payments on exports of Brazilian regional aircraft are subsidies within the meaning of Article 1 of the SCM Agreement which are contingent upon export performance within the meaning of Article 3.1(a) of that Agreement;

---

241 Article 27.14 envisions the review by the Committee of whether a "specific export subsidy practice" by a developing country Member is in conformity with its development needs. This language differs notably from that of Article 27.4, which refers merely to "such export subsidies", with "such" presumably referring back to the export subsidies whose level a Member is not to increase (and recalling that, in this case at least, the "level of export subsidies" is being examined in terms of the overall level of export subsidies being provided by Brazil).

242 In light of our view that the evidence submitted by Canada is insufficient to raise a presumption that PROEX payments are inconsistent with Brazil's development needs, we need not consider Brazil's response to Canada's assertions.

(b) PROEX interest rate equalization payments on exports of Brazilian regional aircraft are not "permitted" by reason of the first paragraph of item (k) of the Illustrative List of Export Subsidies;

(c) Brazil has failed to comply with certain of the conditions of Article 27.4 of the SCM Agreement and the prohibition of Article 3.1(a) of the SCM Agreement is therefore applicable to Brazil.

8.2 Accordingly, we find that payments on exports of regional aircraft under the PROEX interest rate equalization scheme are export subsidies inconsistent with Article 3 of the SCM Agreement.

8.3 Pursuant to Article 3.8 of the DSU, the finding in paragraph 8.2 also constitutes a case of *prima facie* nullification or impairment of benefits accruing to Canada under the SCM Agreement, which Brazil has not rebutted.

8.4 Canada has requested that the Panel make specific recommendations regarding implementation of these findings. We consider however that we are required to make the recommendation provided for in Article 4.7 of the SCM Agreement and are authorized to make no other. Accordingly, we recommend that Brazil withdraw the subsidies identified above without delay.

8.5 Article 4.7 further provides that "the panel shall specify in its recommendation the time-period within which the measure [i.e., the measure found to be a prohibited subsidy] must be withdrawn." Presumably, we are expected to take into account the nature of the measures and the difficulties likely to be faced in implementing the recommendation when specifying what period would represent withdrawal "without delay". We note, however, that there is no experience with respect to what steps could constitute "withdrawal" of the subsidies in various factual circumstances, and we do not consider that it is within our mandate to tell Brazil what steps are required in order to implement our recommendation. Accordingly, taking into account the nature of the measures and the procedures which may be required to implement our recommendation, on the one hand, and the requirement that Brazil withdraw its subsidies "without delay" on the other, we conclude that Brazil shall withdraw the subsidies within 90 days.

ANNEX 1

PROCEDURES GOVERNING BUSINESS CONFIDENTIAL INFORMATION AND DECLARATION OF NON-DISCLOSURE

PROCEDURES GOVERNING BUSINESS CONFIDENTIAL INFORMATION

I. BASIC PRINCIPLE

1. The treatment of information as Business Confidential under these procedures imposes a substantial burden on the Panel and the parties. The indiscriminate designation of information as Business Confidential could limit the ability of a party to fully include in its litigation team individuals who have particular knowledge and expertise relevant to presenting the party's case, impede the work of the Panel and complicate the Panel's task in formulating credible public findings and conclusions. Finally, the Panel recalls that all WTO Members are obliged under Article 25.9 of the SCM Agreement to provide information regarding the nature and extent of any subsidy "in a comprehensive manner" and with "sufficient details to enable the other Member to assess their compliance with the terms" of the SCM Agreement. Accordingly, while the Panel recognizes that the parties have a legitimate interest in protecting sensitive Business Confidential information, *the Panel expects that parties will exercise the utmost restraint in designating information as Business Confidential.*

II. DEFINITIONS

"approved person" means

- i) a Panel member;
- ii) a representative;
- iii) a Secretariat employee; or
- iv) a PGE member,

who has filed with the Chairman of the Panel a Declaration of Non-disclosure.

"conclusion of the Panel" means when, pursuant to DSU Article 16.4, the Panel report is;

- i) adopted;
- ii) not adopted; or

iii) the Panel report is appealed and the report of the Appellate Body is adopted.

"Business Confidential information" means any information that has been designated as Business Confidential by the party submitting the information, and that is not otherwise available in the public domain.

"Declaration of Non-disclosure" means a copy of the declaration set out in Annex II, signed and dated by the person making the declaration.

"designated as Business Confidential" means:

(i) for printed information, clearly marked with the notation 'BUSINESS CONFIDENTIAL INFORMATION' and with the name of the party that submitted the document;

(ii) for binary-encoded information, clearly marked with the notation 'BUSINESS CONFIDENTIAL INFORMATION' on a label on the storage medium, and clearly annotated with the notation 'BUSINESS CONFIDENTIAL INFORMATION' in the binary-encoded files; and

(iii) for uttered information, declared by the speaker to be "Business Confidential information" prior to the disclosure.

"dispute" means Canada's challenge to certain Brazilian measures under Article 4 of the WTO Agreement on Subsidies and Countervailing Measures, WT/DS46, entitled "Brazil - Export Financing Programme for Aircraft".

"DSU" means the WTO Understanding on Rules and Procedures Governing the Settlement of Disputes.

"Geneva mission" means the buildings and grounds of Brazil and Canada at Ancienne Route 17B, 1218 Grand-Saconnex and Rue du Pré-de-la-Bichette 1, 1202 Geneva, respectively.

"information" means:

i) printed information;

ii) binary-encoded information stored in computer diskettes, computer disc drives, CD roms, or other electronic media; or

iii) uttered information,

including without limiting the generality of the foregoing, offers, agreements, reports, forecasts, compilations, studies, plans, presentations, charts, graphs, pictures and drawings.

"Panel" means the WTO panel established pursuant to DSU Article 6 by the 23 July 1998 decision of the WTO Dispute Settlement Body to examine the dispute.

"Panel meeting" means a substantive meeting of the Panel with the parties or the interim review meeting of the Panel with the parties, as described in the working procedures of DSU Appendix 3.

"Panel member" means a person selected pursuant to DSU Article 8 to serve on the Panel.

"Panel process" means the process of the Panel as described in DSU Articles 12, 15 and 16, until and including the conclusion of the Panel.

"party" means Brazil or Canada.

"PGE member" means a person appointed to the Permanent Group of Experts established pursuant to SCM Agreement Article 24, and who has been requested to assist the Panel pursuant to Article 4.5 of the SCM Agreement.

"premises of the WTO" means buildings and grounds of the WTO at Centre William Rappard, Rue de Lausanne 154, Geneva, Switzerland.

"representative" means:

(i) an employee of a party;

(ii) an agent for all purposes of a party; or

(iii) a legal counsel or other advisor of a party,

who has been authorized by a party to act on behalf of such party in the course of the dispute and whose authorization has been notified to the Chairman of the Panel and to the other party, but in no circumstances shall this definition include an employee, officer or agent of a private company engaged in aircraft manufacturing.

"SCM Agreement" means the WTO Agreement on Subsidies and Countervailing Measures.

"Secretariat" means the Secretariat of the World Trade Organization.

"Secretariat employee" means a person employed or appointed by the Secretariat who has been authorized by the Secretariat to work on this dispute and whose authorization has been notified to the Chairman of the Panel, including without limiting the generality of the foregoing, translators and transcribers present at the Panel hearings.

"secure location" means a locked storage receptacle on the premises of the WTO chosen by the Secretariat to provide secure storage for Business Confidential information.

"submit" means:

(i) the filing by a party of printed or binary-encoded information at the Secretariat during the dispute;

(ii) the filing by a party of printed or binary-encoded information with the Panel during a Panel hearing; or

(iii) the uttering of information during a Panel hearing.

"third party" means a Member having notified its interest in the dispute to the DSB pursuant to DSU Article 10.

III. SCOPE

1. These procedures apply to all Business Confidential information submitted during the Panel process.

IV. OBLIGATION ON PARTIES

1. Each party shall ensure that its representatives comply with these procedures.

V. SUBMISSION BY A PARTY

1. When submitting information, a party may designate all or any part or parts of that information as Business Confidential information. Business Confidential information shall be submitted in two copies: one copy of the Business Confidential information shall be submitted to the Secretariat; the other copy of the Business Confidential information shall be submitted to the other party at its Geneva mission.

2. If, taking into the account the Basic Principle stated in Article I, the Panel considers that a party has designated as Business Confidential information which is not reasonably entitled to such treatment, the Panel may decline to consider such information. In such a case, the party submitting the information may, at its discretion:

i) withdraw the information, in which case the Panel and the other party shall promptly return the information to the party submitting it; or

ii) withdraw the designation of the information as Business Confidential.

3. When submitting printed or binary-encoded Business Confidential information, the party shall also provide:

i) a non-Business Confidential edited version, redacted in such a manner as to convey a reasonable understanding of the substance of the information;

ii) a non-Business Confidential summary in sufficient detail to convey a reasonable understanding of the substance of the information; or

iii) in exceptional circumstances, a written statement:

(a) that such a non-Business Confidential edited version or non-Business Confidential summary cannot be made, or

(b) that such a non-Business Confidential edited version or non-Business Confidential summary would disclose facts that the party has a proper reason for wishing to keep business confidential.

4. If the Panel considers that a non-Business Confidential edited version or summary does not fulfill the requirements of paragraph 3(i) or (ii), or that such exceptional circumstances as justify a statement pursuant to paragraph 3(iii) do not exist, the Panel may decline to consider the Business Confidential information in question. In such a case, the party submitting the information may, at its discretion,

i) withdraw the information, in which case the Secretariat and the other party shall promptly return the information to the party submitting it; or

ii) comply with the provisions of paragraph 3 to the satisfaction of the Panel.

5. When uttering Business Confidential information at a Panel meeting, the speaker shall also provide a brief non-Business Confidential oral statement in sufficient detail to convey a reasonable understanding of the substance of the information that will be uttered.

VI. STORAGE

1. The Secretariat shall store all Business Confidential information submitted in the secure location when not in use by an approved person.

2. Each party shall store all Business Confidential information submitted to it by the other party in a safe in a locked room at the premises of its Geneva mission, when not in use by a representative. Only a representative shall be given authority to unlock the locked room containing the safe, and the locked safe. If requested, either party may visit the other party's Geneva mission to review the proposed location of the safe, and to propose any changes. Any disagreements between the parties regarding the location of the safe, or any other aspect related to the safeguarding of the Business Confidential information will be decided by the Panel.

3. An approved person shall take all necessary precautions to safeguard Business Confidential information when in use.

VII. OBLIGATION NOT TO DISCLOSE

1. Where Business Confidential information has been submitted pursuant to these procedures, no approved person who views or hears such information shall disclose that information, or allow it to be disclosed, to any person other than another approved person, except in accordance with these procedures.

2. The Panel shall not disclose Business Confidential information in its interim and final reports, but may make statements of conclusion drawn from such information.

VIII. DISCLOSURE

1. The Secretariat shall make available for viewing or hearing only on the premises of the WTO any Business Confidential information requested by an approved person.

2. Each party shall promptly, and in a convenient manner, make available for viewing on the premises of its embassy or other diplomatic mission in the capital of the other party or, at the request of a approved person, on the premises of its embassy or other diplomatic mission at some other location, any Business Confidential information requested by an approved person.

3. Business Confidential information stored at the Geneva mission of a party may only be viewed by a representative of that party.

4. An approved person viewing or hearing Business Confidential information may take written summary notes of that information for the sole purpose of the Panel process.

5. Business Confidential information shall not be copied, distributed, or removed from the premises of the WTO, or from the premises of a party's Geneva mission, or from the premises of the embassy or other diplomatic mission referred to in paragraph 2, except as specifically provided in these Procedures.

6. Notwithstanding paragraph 5. above, a Panel member may remove a copy of Business Confidential information from the premises of the WTO. Any copies of Business Confidential information removed from the premises of the WTO by a Panel member shall be used exclusively by that Panel member for the purpose of working on the dispute, and shall be returned to the Secretariat upon conclusion of the Panel. Copies of Business Confidential information removed from the premises of the WTO by a Panel member shall be stored in a locked receptacle.

IX. DISCLOSURE AT A PANEL MEETING

1. A party that wishes to submit Business Confidential information during a Panel meeting may request the Panel to exclude persons who are not approved persons from the meeting. The Panel shall exclude such persons from the meeting for the duration of the submission of such information.

X. DISCLOSURE TO THIRD PARTIES

1. Article 10.3 of the DSU provides that "[t]hird parties shall receive the submissions of the parties to the dispute to the first meeting of the panel." Accordingly, disclosure shall be granted to representatives of third parties of Business Confidential information contained in the first submissions of the parties on the premises of the WTO, or on the premises of an embassy or other diplomatic mission of the party submitting the Business Confidential information consistent with Section VIII, paragraph 2. The provisions of these procedures shall apply *mutatis mutandis* to any such disclosure.

XI. TAPES AND TRANSCRIPTS

1. Any tapes and transcripts of Panel meetings at which Business Confidential information is uttered shall be treated as Business Confidential information under these procedures.

XII. RETURN AND DESTRUCTION

1. At the conclusion of the Panel the Secretariat and the parties shall:

   (i) return any printed or binary-encoded Business Confidential information in their possession to the party that submitted such Business Confidential, unless that party agrees otherwise; and

   (ii) destroy all tapes and transcripts of the Panel hearings that contain Business Confidential information, unless the parties mutually agree otherwise.

2. If the Panel Report is appealed, the Secretariat shall transmit any printed or binary encoded Business Confidential information, plus all tapes and transcripts of the Panel hearings that contain Business Confidential information, to the Appellate Body as part of the record of the Panel proceedings. The Secretariat shall transmit such information to the Appellate Body separately from the rest of the record and shall inform the Appellate Body of the special procedures that the Panel has applied with respect to such Business Confidential information. The parties shall comply with any directive of the Appellate Body regarding disclosure of Business Confidential information to parties or third parties as the Appellate Body may deem appropriate.

DECLARATION OF NON-DISCLOSURE

In accordance with the Procedures Governing Business Confidential information contained Annex I to the Working Procedures of the Panel on *Brazil - Export Financing Programme for Aircraft* (the Procedures), I agree to the following:

Words defined in the procedures have the same meaning in this Declaration of Non-Disclosure as in the Procedures.

1. I acknowledge having received a copy of the Procedures, a copy of which is attached.
2. I acknowledge having read and understood the Procedures.
3. I agree to be bound by, and to adhere to, the provisions of the Procedures and, accordingly, without limitation, to treat confidentially all Business Confidential information that I may view or hear from time to time in accordance with the Procedures.

Executed on this __________ day of ____________________, 1998.

BY: ____________________________

Name:

Title:

(Advisors only) Affiliation or employment:

CANADA - MEASURES AFFECTING THE EXPORT OF CIVILIAN AIRCRAFT

Report of the Appellate Body

WT/DS70/AB/R

Adopted by the Dispute Settlement Body on 20 August 1999

Canada, *Appellant/Appellee*	Present:
Brazil, *Appellant/Appellee*	Bacchus, Presiding Member
European Communities, *Third Participant*	Feliciano, Member
United States, *Third Participant*	Matsushita, Member

TABLE OF CONTENTS

I. INTRODUCTION

1. Canada and Brazil both appeal from certain issues of law and legal interpretations developed in the Panel Report, *Canada - Measures Affecting the Export of Civilian Aircraft* (the "Panel Report").[1] The Panel was established by the Dispute Settlement Body (the "DSB"), pursuant to Article 4.4 of the *Agreement on Subsidies and Countervailing Measures* (the "*SCM Agreement*") and Article 6 of the *Understanding on Rules and Procedures Governing the Settlement of Disputes* (the "DSU"), to examine certain alleged subsidies that Brazil contended Canada or its provinces had granted, inconsistently with its obligations under paragraphs 1(a) and 2 of Article 3 of the *SCM Agreement*, to support the export of civilian aircraft. A brief outline of the factual aspects of the dispute is given at paragraphs 2.1 and 2.2 of the Panel Report.

2. The Panel considered claims made by Brazil relating to the activities of the Export Development Corporation (the "EDC"); the operation of Canada Account; the Canada-Quebec Subsidiary Agreements on Industrial Development; Société de Développement Industriel du Quebec; Technology Partnerships Canada ("TPC") and the Defence Industry Productivity Programme, as well as the

[1] WT/DS70/R, 14 April 1999.

sale to Bombardier Inc. ("Bombardier"), a Canadian corporation, by the Government of Ontario (through the Ontario Aerospace Corporation) of a 49 per cent interest in de Havilland Holdings Inc. The Panel Report was circulated to the Members of the World Trade Organization (the "WTO") on 14 April 1999. The Panel found "that Canada Account debt financing since 1 January 1995 for the export of Canadian regional aircraft" and "TPC assistance to the Canadian regional aircraft industry" constitute prohibited export subsidies inconsistent with Articles 3.1(a) and 3.2 of the *SCM Agreement*.[2] The Panel rejected all of Brazil's other claims.[3] The Panel recommended that Canada withdraw the prohibited export subsidies "without delay" and, in any event, "within 90 days".[4]

3. On 3 May 1999, Canada notified the DSB of its intention to appeal legal interpretations developed by the Panel, and certain issues of law covered in the Panel Report, pursuant to paragraph 4 of Article 16 of the DSU, and filed a Notice of Appeal with the Appellate Body, pursuant to Rule 20 of the *Working Procedures for Appellate Review* (the "*Working Procedures*").

4. By joint letter of 5 May 1999, Canada and Brazil informed the Appellate Body that, pursuant to footnote 6 of Article 4 of the *SCM Agreement*, they had decided, by mutual agreement, to extend until 2 August 1999 the time-period provided in Article 4.9 of the *SCM Agreement* for the Appellate Body to issue its decision in this appeal.

5. On 13 May 1999, Canada filed its appellant's submission.[5] On 18 May 1999, pursuant to Rule 23 of the *Working Procedures*, Brazil filed its appellant's submission. On 28 May 1999, Brazil and Canada each filed their respective appellee's submissions[6], and, on the same date, the European Communities and the United States filed third participants' submissions.[7] The oral hearing, provided for in Rule 27 of the *Working Procedures*, took place on 14 June 1999.

6. As described more fully in Section III of this Report, by joint letter of 27 May 1999, Brazil and Canada requested that the Appellate Body apply, *mutatis mutandis*, the Procedures Governing Business Confidential Information (the "BCI Procedures")[8] adopted by the Panel in this case. A preliminary hearing on this issue was held on 10 June 1999, with this Division sitting jointly with the Division of the Appellate Body hearing the appeal in *Brazil - Export Financing*

---

2 Panel Report, para. 10.1.
3 *Ibid.*
4 *Ibid.*, paras. 10.3 and 10.4.
5 Pursuant to Rule 21 of the *Working Procedures*.
6 Pursuant to Rule 22 of the *Working Procedures*.
7 Pursuant to Rule 24 of the *Working Procedures*.
8 The BCI Procedures adopted by the Panel are reproduced in Annex I of the Panel Report.

Programme For Aircraft ("*Brazil - Aircraft*"),[9] and a preliminary ruling was issued by this Division on 11 June 1999.

II. ARGUMENTS OF THE PARTICIPANTS AND THE THIRD PARTICIPANTS

A. *Claims of Error by Canada - Appellant*

1. *Interpretation of "Benefit" in Article 1.1(b) of the SCM Agreement*

7. Canada argues on appeal that the Panel erred, as a matter of law, in interpreting Article 1 of the *SCM Agreement* by effectively holding that the guidelines set out in Article 14 of the *SCM Agreement* establish the criteria for the determination of "benefit" in Article 1.1. The Panel, Canada asserts, failed to apply the principles of treaty interpretation in customary international law. These principles, set out in part in the *Vienna Convention on the Law of Treaties*[10] (the "*Vienna Convention*"), require that a treaty be interpreted in accordance with the ordinary meaning of its terms, in their context and in the light of its object and purpose. However, the Panel rejected relevant context, did not take into account the object and purpose of the *SCM Agreement*, and, in effect, wrote into the *SCM Agreement* provisions that the Members of the WTO did not negotiate.

8. Canada agreed with the Panel that the ordinary meaning of the term "benefit" is "advantage". The Panel asserted, however, that the existence of a "benefit" can be determined only by assessing "*whether the financial contribution places the recipient in a more advantageous position than would have been the case but for the financial contribution.*"[11] (emphasis added) The Panel erred in concluding that the existence of a "benefit" should be determined on the basis of "the commercial benchmarks applied in Article 14."[12]

9. Canada maintains that, in interpreting Article 1.1 of the *SCM Agreement*, account must be taken of the "cost to government" of a subsidy and that, therefore, the Panel's focus on Article 14 to the exclusion of "cost to government" amounts to an error in law.

10. Canada contends the Panel erred by reading into Article 1.1 words it does not contain and by asserting that the "only logical basis" for determining the existence of a "benefit" is a commercial benchmark.[13] Canada insists that nothing in Article 1 leads to such a "logical" conclusion.

---

[9] WT/DS70/AB/R, circulated to Members of the WTO on 2 August 1999.

[10] Done at Vienna, 23 May 1969, 1155 U.N.T.S. 331; (1969) 8 International Legal Materials 679.

[11] Panel Report, para. 9.112.

[12] *Ibid.*, 9.113.

[13] *Ibid.*, para. 9.112.

11. Furthermore, Canada argues that the Panel erred by failing to give full effect to the opening clause of Article 14 ("For the purpose of Part V..."). This clause is a limiting clause that applies to the entirety of Article 14 and means that it has direct relevance only for domestic countervailing duty proceedings. Canada does not, however, dispute that Article 14 may serve as relevant context in the interpretation of Article 1.1. It is *not*, however, the only element of relevant context. Moreover, Article 14 provides only one methodology for calculating the amount of a subsidy. Nothing in the *SCM Agreement* indicates that the commercial benchmark methodology is the *sole* means of calculating the amount of "benefit" or a subsidy.

12. Canada maintains that the Panel erred in dismissing Canada's argument that Annex IV to the *SCM Agreement* is also relevant context for determining the existence of a "benefit" (or measuring a subsidy). The Panel noted that Annex IV and Article 14 differ because Article 14 explicitly refers to the calculation of "benefit", while Annex IV "refers only to the calculation of the amount of a subsidy".[14] (emphasis in original) This is a misreading of Article 14 because the heading of this provision refers to the calculation of the amount of a *subsidy*. Moreover, both Article 14 and Annex IV have an identical limiting clause ("for the purpose of"). Canada, therefore, believes that both Article 14 and Annex IV constitute relevant context in interpreting Article 1.1.

13. Canada contends that the Panel erred in concluding that incorporating the "cost to government" into Article 1 would "exclude from the definition of 'subsidy' situations explicitly identified in Article 1.1(a)(1) itself as constituting government financial contributions ... ." [15] When a private body is directed or entrusted by the government to make a financial contribution, the private body incurs a cost on behalf of the government. The private body may or may not be compensated by the government, but a cost is nevertheless incurred through government action.

14. Canada maintains that, in the absence of a definition of "benefit" in the *SCM Agreement*, the Panel should have looked to the negotiating history of the *SCM Agreement*. Had it done so, the Panel would have discovered that, during the negotiations, there was disagreement over the appropriate criteria for valuing a subsidy and measuring a "benefit". The final text of the *SCM Agreement* "did not resolve the issue."[16] The *SCM Agreement* reflects, in effect, an agreement to leave the "gaps and ambiguities ... to be decided in a future negotiation." [17] In the meantime, panels should interpret and apply the negotiated text, not write an agreement that the negotiators did not make.

[14] Panel Report, para. 9.116.
[15] *Ibid.*, para. 9.115.
[16] Canada's appellant's submission, para. 108.
[17] *Ibid.*, para.109.

2. *"Contingent in Fact Upon Export Performance"*

15. In Canada's opinion, the Panel's finding that TPC contributions were "contingent ... in fact ... upon export performance" rests on three kinds of evidence:

(a) the "export propensity" of the Canadian regional aircraft industry;

(b) evidence that this "export propensity" was one of the considerations taken into account by the TPC programme administrators and that exports were viewed, by Canadian government officials, as one of the positive achievements and objectives of TPC; and

(c) evidence that the TPC programme provides assistance for projects that were relatively near to being ready for commercial exploitation.

16. According to Canada, such evidence cannot, as a matter of law, establish that subsidies are "contingent ... in fact ... upon export performance". To establish such a contingency, a complainant must adduce evidence that the subsidy induced the recipient to distort its marketing decisions in favour of exportation over domestic sales. The fact that the recipient industry has a high "export propensity" is not sufficient to establish export contingency.

17. Canada contends that the Panel Report has the effect of converting an enormous class of actionable subsidies into prohibited export subsidies. The *SCM Agreement* makes a fundamental distinction between prohibited and non-prohibited subsidies. The drafters did not intend to prohibit all subsidies to exporters. Rather, they structured the *SCM Agreement* so that most subsidies granted to exporters would be actionable, rather than prohibited. The proper categorization of a subsidy depends on the nature and trade effect of the subsidy, not on whether the recipient is an exporter. Further, the Panel's emphasis on "export propensity" would particularly affect countries with small markets that are highly export dependent, as well as developing countries which export a high proportion of their production.

18. In Canada's view, the expression "contingent ... upon" in Article 3.1, whether *de jure* or *de facto*, is defined by reference to conditionality. The requirements of Article 3.1 are met when a complainant establishes that the subsidy in question would not have been granted but for past or future exportation. A subsidy is "contingent ... in fact ... upon export performance" when the facts and circumstances are such that the recipient will reasonably know that there is a requirement to export, or to undertake export development, for the recipient to benefit from a subsidy.

19. Canada observes that, prior to the conclusion of the *SCM Agreement*, there was no treaty provision prohibiting subsidies "contingent ... in fact ... upon export performance". The negotiating history of this provision of the *SCM Agreement* confirms that the "in fact" language was intended to prevent circumvention of the *de jure* prohibition. It was not a means of expanding the

scope of Article 3. Canada draws two conclusions from this. First, there is a single legal standard of "contingency", whether it is contingency in fact or in law. Second, application of that single legal standard requires an examination of the legal instruments or the administration of the subsidy programme as a whole, and not just of isolated subsidies granted pursuant to the programme.

20. Canada also observes that, during the negotiation of the *SCM Agreement*, the United States advocated a "quantitative" approach to the determination of whether a subsidy was export contingent as well as application of an "export propensity" test. The "export propensity" test was rejected by negotiators because it would be inequitable for small economies that are more dependent on export markets. Furthermore, the negotiators did not consider that an intent-based approach would adequately reflect the scope of the *de jure* prohibition in Article 3. Thus, the negotiating history of footnote 4 confirms that the *de facto* contingency standard is based on the conditions attached to the subsidy and not on either intent or "export propensity". In Canada's view, to satisfy the requirements of the "in fact" standard, *the subsidy must cause the recipient to prefer exports to domestic sales.*

21. Canada argues that the meaning of "anticipated exportation" in footnote 4 was a primary source of the Panel's misinterpretation of Article 3.1. In its view, "anticipated exportation" reflects nothing more than that subsidy programmes which are contingent on export performance may be tied to exports that have not yet taken place. The expression does not create a standard different from that applied to contingency in law, nor does it diminish the requirements of conditionality.

22. In the case of a subsidy to an export-oriented company, it will naturally be expected that exports will continue to be made. But, in Canada's view, absent some understanding *by the company* that it is required to export as a condition of receipt of the subsidy, the subsidy would simply be actionable. Any other understanding of "anticipated exportation" would blur the distinction between prohibited, actionable and non-actionable subsidies.

23. The Panel's misinterpretation of Article 3.1(a), Canada believes, resulted in an erroneous finding that the TPC programme provides subsidies "contingent … in fact … upon export performance". The Panel erred in two ways. First, the Panel erred in its interpretation and application of the legal standard of contingency in fact. It did so by confusing the *considerations* that TPC took into account in deciding whether to provide the subsidy with *conditions* or *contingencies*. Second, by misinterpreting what constitutes anticipated export performance, the Panel made export orientation the "effective test" of contingency.[18] The Panel did not consider evidence that, on the basis of uniform criteria, TPC made contributions to enterprises in other sectors that are not export-oriented.

[18] Canada's appellant's submission, para. 61.

This demonstrates that exportation was not a condition of receipt of TPC contributions. Canada acknowledges that Brazil only challenged TPC contributions to the regional aircraft industry. However, since the criteria applied to all TPC contributions were the same, the Panel should have assessed - but did not - contributions made under TPC as a whole.

24. Canada notes that, in terms of both objectives and contributions made, TPC provides broad support to virtually all industrial sectors. TPC administrators may consider whether a project is likely to build on an export base, sell domestically or produce import substitution. However, none of these considerations is a mandatory condition. There are no rewards or penalties for recipients depending on whether projected export sales targets are achieved. The Panel, however, found "anticipated exportation" to be a condition of the contributions on the basis of "projected export sales".[19] There is, however, no finding of fact that these projections were a condition of receiving TPC contributions. In Canada's opinion, the Panel mistakes trends and possibilities for future requirements or commitments.

25. Canada maintains that, in reaching its finding of *de facto* export contingency, the Panel relies almost exclusively on selective evidence as to the *motivation* underlying TPC contributions. But, even assuming that the motivation was export-related, that motivation is not a *condition* binding the recipient to prefer exportation over domestic sales. The Panel failed to determine whether the recipient would reasonably consider itself as being required, as a condition of receiving the contributions, to make export sales that would not otherwise be made. Canada notes that the Panel stated that "Canada has provided no evidence to ... show that the *export-related considerations*, described above, ... were not also taken into account by the TPC administrators." [20] (emphasis added) Canada insists, though, that Article 3 of the *SCM Agreement* is not concerned with "export-related *considerations*", but with whether export performance is a *condition*.

26. The Panel states that "the closer a subsidy brings a product to sale on the export market, the greater the possibility that the facts may demonstrate that the subsidy" was contingent on export performance.[21] The Panel, therefore, makes a link between "anticipated" exportation and the point in the development of a project at which a subsidy is paid. However, there is nothing in the text of Article 3, its context or its object and purpose, to justify this link. A subsidy granted for pure research could be export contingent, in the same way that a direct sales subsidy need not be. Canada notes that, in terms of Article 8 of the *SCM Agreement* support for "pre-competitive development activity" is non-

[19] Panel Report, para. 9.346.

[20] *Ibid.*, para. 9.344.

[21] *Ibid.*, para. 9.339.

actionable. To conclude that the short step from pre-competitive development subsidies to "close to the market subsidies" makes the difference between non-actionable and prohibited subsidies is to ignore the role of actionable subsidies.

B. Arguments by Brazil - Appellee

1. Interpretation of "Benefit" in Article 1.1(b) of the SCM Agreement

27. Although Article 1.1(b) of the *SCM Agreement* defines a subsidy as a government financial contribution conferring an advantage, Brazil argues that the text of that provision gives little further guidance as to the relevant benchmark against which to judge whether an advantage was conferred. Resort to the relevant context is, therefore, required.

28. Brazil notes that the ordinary meaning of the term "confer" is to "[g]ive, grant, or bestow". This verb is, therefore, not self-referential. It implies action by the grantor upon someone else and, thus, implies "benefit to the recipient" - that is, the government, in making a contribution, conferred, gave, granted or bestowed an advantage *upon someone else*. The "cost to government" standard is, by contrast, inherently self-referential. It is concerned with the effect of a government contribution *on the government itself*, rather than on the recipient of the contribution.

29. Brazil maintains that the Panel was justified in accepting Article 14 and rejecting Annex IV as relevant context in interpreting "benefit". Indeed, Brazil notes that Canada accepts that Article 14 of the *SCM Agreement* may serve as relevant context in interpreting Article 1. Although Annex IV.1 relates to the "calculation" of a *subsidy*, Article 14 relates to the calculation of "*benefit*" pursuant to Article 1.1(b). The purpose of Annex IV is to determine whether the value of a subsidy is sufficient to constitute "serious prejudice" in an actionable subsidies case. Article 14, in contrast, is concerned with the calculation of the amount of "benefit" flowing from a government financial contribution, with a view to determining whether there was a "benefit" conferred and therefore a subsidy provided in the first place.

30. Brazil asserts that the Panel's adoption of a "commercial benchmark" standard avoids the problems of both "over-inclusiveness" (that is, prohibiting commercial governmental activity), and "under-inclusiveness".[22] Commercial governmental activity will not be prohibited under the Panel's interpretation because it is not provided on terms more advantageous than those available in the marketplace. However, in Brazil's view, the "cost to government" standard proposed by Canada would be "*under-inclusive*" because it would not cover cases where a government provided funds at more than its cost of funds, but with a

[22] Brazil's appellee's submission, para. 113.

maximum projected return rate significantly below what a commercial investor would receive. The Panel's approach avoids this problem.

31. Brazil emphasizes that the Panel's rejection of Annex IV as relevant context for the purposes of interpreting the meaning of the term "benefit" under Article 1.1 does not mean that, for the purposes of determining serious prejudice under Article 6.1(a), "cost to government" is irrelevant or, even, excluded.

32. Finally, Brazil argues Canada's claim that the Panel should not fill in the "gaps" in a delicately negotiated agreement, but should let both cost to government and benefit to recipient co-exist is "rather disingenuous".[23] There is no way for both standards to co-exist since the application of one would, in reality, preclude the application of the other. If there were no "cost to government", then the existence of a "benefit" alone would not have sufficed to show the existence of a subsidy and Canada would have prevailed.

2. *"Contingent in Fact Upon Export Performance"*

33. Brazil considers that the Panel found correctly that Article 3.1(a) of the *SCM Agreement* requires conditionality between the subsidy and exportation, irrespective of whether the subsidy is *de facto* or *de jure* contingent on export performance. Footnote 4 of the *SCM Agreement* confirms that the Panel was correct in finding that in the case of a *de facto* export contingent subsidy, the element of conditionality may be between the subsidy and "anticipated" exportation. Therefore, in the view of Brazil, contrary to Canada's claim, the nature of the contingency requirement is not the same for *de jure* and *de facto* contingency.

34. The ordinary meaning of the words "actual" and "anticipated" is, respectively, "[e]xisting in act or fact; real" and "[l]ook forward to; . . . expect", "[t]ake into consideration or mention before the due time", or "[o]bserve or practise in advance of the due time". This meaning speaks to an actor's *expectation* of a future event, such as exports, and it underscores the relevance, in examining *de facto* export contingency, of statements made by the grantor that express its intent, purpose, reasons or motivation in granting the subsidy.

35. Moreover, according to Brazil, contrary to Canada's assertions, the negotiating history of footnote 4, to the extent that it is relevant at all in terms of Article 32 of the *Vienna Convention*, does not demonstrate the rejection of an intent-based approach. Although the word "intended" was removed from an early draft of footnote 4, the word "anticipated" was added. In Brazil's view, this word expressly recognizes the relevance of the grantor's reasons for extending the subsidy.

[23] Brazil's appellee's submission, para. 123.

36. With respect to Canada's arguments concerning the object and purpose of the *SCM Agreement*, Brazil recalls that the Appellate Body has stated that it is from the text, read in its context, "that the object and purpose of ... the treaty must first be sought".[24] Canada does the reverse. Rather than relying on the object and purpose of the *SCM Agreement* to confirm its interpretation of the text in its context, Canada instead bases its interpretation of the text on the object and purpose of the *SCM Agreement*. The Appellate Body has ruled previously that the object and purpose of a treaty is relevant "[w]here the meaning imparted by the text itself is equivocal or inconclusive, or where confirmation of the correctness of the reading of the text itself is desired".[25] In Brazil's view, that is not so in the case of either Article 3.1(a) or footnote 4.

37. Brazil makes specific comments on what it regards as Canada's two alternative legal tests for showing *de facto* export contingency. With respect to the first, Canada argues that a panel should determine whether the recipient believed it was required to prefer export over domestic sales or whether the recipient would reasonably have known that there was a requirement to export. Brazil considers that this involves "*subjective judgments* requiring insight into the recipient's thoughts."[26] (emphasis added) However, footnote 4 calls for a review of the "*objective expressions* of the grantor's expectations."[27] (emphasis in original) Furthermore, according to Brazil, Canada's focus on the recipient's, rather than the grantor's, intent finds no support in the text of footnote 4, which speaks directly to actions undertaken by the grantor.

38. Under Canada's second alternative test for showing *de facto* export contingency, a panel should determine whether the subsidy induced distortion of marketing decisions in favour of exportation over domestic sales or whether the recipient would reasonably consider that it was required to make export sales that would not otherwise be made. With respect to this second alternative test, Brazil repeats the observations it made regarding the first test. This second test is also a subjective test that wrongly focuses on the recipient instead of the grantor. In Brazil's view, satisfaction of this test would, in any event, require documentary evidence which Canada did not provide to the Panel.

39. Brazil contends that Canada overlooks the context of Article 3.1(a) that is most critical to this dispute, namely the distinction between *de facto* and *de jure* export contingency. Common to both *de facto* and *de jure* contingency is the requirement to prove the element of contingency. However, footnote 4 of the *SCM Agreement* describes how *de facto* export contingency should be "demon-

---

[24] *United States - Import Prohibition of Certain Shrimp and Shrimp Products* ("*United States - Shrimp*"), WT/DS58/AB/R, adopted 6 November 1998, para. 114.

[25] *United States - Import Prohibition of Certain Shrimp and Shrimp Products* ("*United States - Shrimp*"), WT/DS58/AB/R, adopted 6 November 1998, para. 114.

[26] Brazil's appellee's submission, para. 34.

[27] *Ibid.*, para. 35.

strated". According to Brazil, the Panel, mindful of the text of footnote 4, recognized the different nature of the burden imposed on claimants lodging *de facto*, as opposed to *de jure*, claims. In a *de jure* case, conditionality will be evident on the face of the relevant legal text, whereas, in a *de facto* case, the facts must demonstrate the existence of the condition.

40. Brazil explains, furthermore, that facts can demonstrate that a contribution was in fact export contingent, without any one of those facts itself being a condition. There is no qualification in the text of the treaty on what facts can be used to demonstrate the existence of *de facto* export contingency. It was, therefore, permissible for the Panel to consider the relevance of evidence such as the TPC materials, as well as statements made by government officials, that demonstrated the granting authority's expectations.

41. Brazil's observes that the Panel recognized that, under footnote 4 to the *SCM Agreement,* export orientation cannot, on its own, make a subsidy *de facto* export contingent. But the Panel found, nonetheless, that export orientation was still a relevant fact in this dispute. Brazil acknowledges that export orientation would not necessarily be relevant in all cases. Moreover, the Panel's treatment of export orientation in this dispute does not mean that *every* recipient of a financial contribution with export-oriented sales will automatically be considered to have received a prohibited export subsidy. Brazil emphasizes that, in addressing Canada's actions in this dispute, the Panel considered a range of other facts, in addition to export orientation.[28]

42. According to Brazil, preference for near-market projects may reflect a desire for greater certainty about the preferred destination for a product. The Panel determined that as an evidentiary matter, a claim of "anticipation" is stronger if the sale which would realize that anticipation is in view when the subsidy is granted. This consideration was simply additional to others that demonstrated that TPC contributions were *de facto* export contingent. Furthermore, the effect of the Panel's consideration of this additional evidentiary requirement was "to make Brazil's burden of proof more difficult to satisfy."[29]

43. Brazil observes that the Panel recognized that Brazil had challenged the "actual application" of the TPC programme itself. Therefore, the Panel would have been justified in limiting its review solely to TPC contributions to the regional aircraft industry, which was the subject of the dispute.

44. According to Brazil, the Appellate Body should not accept Canada's argument that, the fact that TPC made contributions that were not export contingent, immunized Canada from a challenge in cases where TPC contribution were indeed export contingent. If that view prevailed, only programmes mandating the grant of export subsidies would be open to challenge.

---

[28] Panel Report, paras. 9.340-9.346.

[29] Brazil's appellee's submission, para. 68.

45. Brazil argues that, contrary to Canada's claim, the Panel did consider all of the TPC materials, including the TPC Interim Reference Binder, the TPC Applications Kit, and the TPC Business Plan, and, as a factual matter, determined that this evidence contained facts demonstrating *de facto* export contingency.[30] In any event, "the Panel was not given access to detailed information regarding TPC subsidies to other industries." [31]

C. *Claims of Error by Brazil - Appellant*

1. *Drawing Adverse Inferences from Certain Facts*

46. Brazil claims on appeal that the Panel erred in law by failing to draw adverse inferences from Canada's refusal to provide information about the EDC's debt financing activities and, in particular, information about the EDC's financing of the purchase from Bombardier of regional jet aircraft by ASA Holdings Inc. and its subsidiary Atlantic Southeast Airlines ("ASA").[32] Brazil requests that the Appellate Body reverse the Panel's conclusion and determine that the evidence on the record, "together with the adverse inferences flowing from Canada's failure to satisfy its duty of collaboration and to respond to the Panel's requests for information, lead to the conclusion that the EDC's debt financing confers a 'benefit'"[33] under Article 1.1(b) of the *SCM Agreement*.

47. According to Brazil, during consultations, "Canada refused to provide to Brazil transaction-specific details of EDC activities in the regional aircraft sector".[34] This was in direct contravention of the Appellate Body's previous statement that parties be "fully forthcoming" and freely disclose facts relating to claims, "in consultations as well as in the more formal setting of panel proceedings".[35] Brazil, therefore, asked the Panel to engage in additional fact-finding and to request Canada to furnish the complete details of, *inter alia*, the EDC's operations relating to the regional aircraft industry. The Panel declined to grant Brazil's request for additional fact-finding.[36]

48. According to Brazil, despite the Panel's adoption of the BCI Procedures, Canada "repeatedly refused to provide information dealing with specific transactions".[37] The Panel rejected Canada's justification for its refusals to disclose information[38] and Brazil argues that these refusals were in direct contravention

---

30 Panel Report, para. 9.340.

31 Brazil's appellee's submission, para. 84.

32 For further details of the "ASA transaction" see Panel Report, para. 6.56.

33 Brazil's appellant's submission, para. 84.

34 *Ibid.*, para. 34.

35 *India - Patent Protection for Pharmaceutical and Agricultural Chemical Products* ("*India - Patents*"), WT/DS50/AB/R, adopted 16 January 1998, para. 94.

36 Panel Report, para. 9.53.

37 Brazil's appellant's submission, para. 38.

38 Panel Report, paras. 9.69 and 9.347, footnote 633.

of what Brazil sees as Canada's duty of collaboration under Article 3.10 of the DSU.

49. Brazil maintains that the Panel Report illustrates that Brazil made every attempt to demonstrate, first, that the EDC enjoys discretionary authority to extend financing on terms that would constitute a "benefit", and, second, that the EDC's debt financing was provided to ASA on below-market terms. Brazil could not have presented more evidence without Canada's collaboration. Therefore, Brazil satisfied its burden of production as regards the EDC's debt financing to the extent that it was possible under the circumstances to do so.

50. Brazil argues that Canada was under a legal obligation, under Article 3.10 of the DSU, "to engage in these [dispute settlement] procedures in good faith ...". Brazil notes that this "good faith" obligation places a considerable burden upon Members and it has been the object of rulings by the Appellate Body and previous panels.

51. Brazil observes that the panel in *Argentina - Measures Affecting Imports of Footwear, Textiles, Apparel and Other Items* ("*Argentina - Textiles and Apparel*") emphasized the "rule of collaboration" incumbent upon parties to WTO dispute settlement.[39] According to that panel, the rule of collaboration provides that once "the claimant has *done its best* to secure evidence and has actually produced *some prima facie* evidence in support of its case", the respondent has the obligation "to provide the tribunal with relevant documents which are in its sole possession."[40] (emphasis added) Brazil argues that it is clear from the Panel record that Brazil satisfied the threshold requirement set out in the panel report in *Argentina - Textiles and Apparel* and that Canada's duty of collaboration was, therefore, triggered.

52. Brazil asserts that in public international law, the duty of collaboration has been broadly recognized as placing an exceptional burden on parties to international disputes, and is essentially derived from two shortcomings of international litigation. First, the duty of collaboration is imposed on a respondent state to counter the obstacles facing a complainant state in gathering evidence peculiarly within the control of an uncooperative respondent. Second, the duty of collaboration is a response to the inability of international tribunals to compel the production of information.

53. Brazil considers that, because Brazil satisfied its burden of production, it was incumbent on Canada, as a matter of law, to uphold its duty of collaboration by producing all relevant information within its control. Canada expressly refused to do so.[41]

[39] Panel report, WT/DS56/R, adopted 22 April 1998, as modified by the Appellate Body Report, WT/DS56/AB/R, para. 6.40.

[40] Panel report, *Argentina - Textiles and Apparel*, *supra*, footnote 39, para. 6.40.

[41] Panel Report, para. 9.176.

54. In addition to the duty of collaboration, Brazil believes that Canada was under an obligation by virtue of Article 13.1 of the DSU to respond to the Panel's requests for information. Brazil contends that by refusing to produce documents specifically requested by the Panel under Article 13.1 of the DSU, in particular documents relating to the ASA transaction, Canada failed to fulfil its obligation to "respond" under the DSU.

55. Brazil requested the Panel to draw adverse inferences from Canada's refusal to provide information about, in particular, the EDC's financing of the ASA transaction, and to presume that the information withheld constituted inculpatory evidence of Canada's infringement of the *SCM Agreement*.

56. The Panel refused to adopt adverse inferences in connection with the ASA transaction because, it said, "Brazil ha[d] made no attempt to demonstrate that EDC debt financing was provided to ASA on below-market terms", or because Brazil had not shown that "EDC debt financing generally confers a 'benefit'."[42] In so doing, the Panel erred in law. Brazil is concerned that the Panel has provided a "simple and foolproof roadmap for recalcitrant Members to avoid liability for infringements" of the *SCM Agreement*.[43]

57. Brazil maintains that in the absence of a power to compel production of information, the only viable means of enforcing the duty of collaboration and the duty to respond is to employ adverse inferences. Nothing in the DSU or the *SCM Agreement* prohibits the application of adverse inferences. Brazil notes that the Appellate Body has, in fact, recognized the use of similar presumptions. In its recent decision in *Japan - Measures Affecting Agricultural Products* ("*Japan - Agricultural Products*"), for example, the Appellate Body stated that the failure of a responding party to produce documentary evidence, such as studies or reports, supporting a particular phytosanitary testing requirement "would have been a strong indication that there are no such studies or reports".[44]

58. Brazil concludes that the situation in this present case is precisely the type of situation in which, in the words of the International Court of Justice, "a more liberal recourse to inferences of fact" is appropriate.[45] Indeed, adopting adverse inferences to enforce a party's duty to produce evidence peculiarly within its possession is overwhelmingly the rule among those permanent and *ad hoc* international tribunals that have addressed the issue, even where the agreement underlying their jurisdiction does not specifically authorize such action.

59. In support of its position, Brazil cites numerous decisions from the International Court of Justice, the Mexican-United States Claims Commission, the

42 Panel Report, para. 9.181.

43 Brazil's appellant's submission, para. 76.

44 Appellate Body Report, WT/DS76/AB/R, adopted 19 March 1999, para. 137.

45 *The Corfu Channel Case*, 1949 ICJ 4, p. 18.

French-Venezuelan Mixed Claims Commission, and the Iran-United States Claims Tribunal.

2. *EDC Debt Financing*

60. Brazil submits that the Panel's conclusion that the EDC's debt financing does not confer a "benefit" is contrary to the facts established by the Panel and the undisputed evidence of record. Brazil emphasizes that it does not challenge the Panel's factual findings. Rather, Brazil challenges the Panel's legal characterization of those factual findings and the legal characterization of the undisputed evidence of record. The Panel's legal characterization of the facts was inconsistent with the definitions of "benefit" and "subsidy", which Brazil argues were correctly set out by the Panel.

61. In seeking to establish that the Panel's legal characterization of the facts was inconsistent with the evidence on the record, Brazil relies on evidence from three sources:

(a) an EDC Standing Board Resolution and the EDC's support to ASA

(b) statements by a former EDC President

(c) a statement by Canada made to the Panel in the course of the dispute

62. Brazil construes the EDC's constituent statute as allowing it to choose whether or not to grant subsidies within the meaning of Article 1.1 of the *SCM Agreement*. Consistent with this discretion, an EDC Standing Board Resolution provides that in appropriate cases, the EDC is authorized to offer financing terms that, in Brazil's view, are more generous than those available on the market.

63. Brazil refers to the *Arrangement on Guidelines for Officially Supported Export Credits of the Organization for Economic Cooperation and Development* (the "*OECD Arrangement*"). The prefatory language of the *OECD Arrangement* states, under the heading "Best Endeavours",

> The Arrangement sets out the most generous repayment terms and conditions that may be supported. All Participants recognize the risk that over time, these maximum repayment terms and conditions may come to be regarded as normal practice. They therefore undertake to take the necessary steps to prevent this risk from materializing.

64. In Brazil's view, as a consequence of this statement, even *meeting* the terms of the *OECD Arrangement* exceeds the outer bounds of what Participants in the *Arrangement* consider "normal" commercial practice. It, therefore, follows that if the EDC offers terms that go beyond the outer bounds of the *OECD Arrangement*, customers of Canadian exporters receive a "benefit", as that term is defined by the Panel.

65. Brazil argues that the Panel erred in concluding that Brazil did not establish that the EDC has exercised this discretionary authority by offering terms going beyond those provided in the *OECD Arrangement*. Brazil introduced uncontested evidence about the one example of the EDC's debt financing to the regional aircraft industry for which a modest amount of public information was available, namely the ASA transaction. The Panel noted that Canada did not contest the evidence regarding the factual elements of the transaction[46], which included a commitment to finance 16.5-year leases of the aircraft purchased.

66. Brazil submits that these repayment terms go beyond those included in the *OECD Arrangement*, which allows for a maximum repayment term of 10 years.[47] The repayment terms offered in the ASA transaction, therefore, go well beyond the outer bounds of "normal" commercial practice. Thus, under the Panel's market-based legal standard of "benefit" and "subsidy", the evidence demonstrates that the EDC has conferred a "benefit".

67. The former President of the EDC, Mr. Paul Labbé, stated in a publication issued by Canada's Department of Foreign Affairs and International Trade, that:

> EDC's financing support gives Canadian exporters an edge when they bid on overseas projects. ...Trade deals increasingly depend on complex and tightly negotiated financing arrangements where a few basis points in interest rates can make or break the deal. Exporters are having to bid not just on the basis of quality and price, but also on the basis of the financing package supporting the sale.[48]

68. Brazil maintains that the Panel found that it would be possible to conclude from this statement that the EDC's debt financing confers a "benefit" and constitutes a "subsidy". This conclusion is correct, as demonstrated by a review of the three underlying facts acknowledged in the statement:

- First, Canada did not dispute that the "EDC's financing support gives Canadian exporters an edge". An "edge" is an "advantage" and constitutes a subsidy.
- Second, Brazil believes that the Panel found that the "edge" stems from the EDC's "financing support" in the form of, among other things, "a few basis points". This is a subsidy.
- Third, Canada did not dispute that the EDC helps exporters compete "on the basis of the financing package supporting the sale", rather than on the two factors, quality and price", identified by Canada and other Participants in the *OECD Arrangement* as relevant to normal

46 Panel Report, para. 6.79.

47 *OECD Arrangement*, Annex III, Part 2, Chapter V, para. 21(a).

48 Panel Report, para. 6.57.

commercial competition. In looking beyond those two factors, the EDC confers a subsidy.

69. Brazil submits that the Panel, however, took the view that there was a "possibility for divergent contextual interpretations" of Mr. Labbé's statement and concluded that the EDC's debt financing does not confer a "benefit".[49] The Panel found that Mr Labbé's statement implied two, non-mutually exclusive conclusions. Brazil believes that at least one of those conclusions - that the EDC grants exporters an "edge" in the form of "a few basis points" - required the Panel to determine that the EDC's financing extends assistance at better-than-market rates.

70. Brazil notes also that Canada stated to the Panel that the EDC "does not always offer the most attractive financing package available to regional aircraft customers".[50] The Panel followed this up by asking Canada a question that correctly noted that the statement could mean that the EDC does, "sometimes", provide the most attractive financing package available.[51] If, by Canada's own admission, the EDC "sometimes" offers "the most attractive financing package available", by definition, the EDC sometimes offers terms that are better-than-market.

71. Thus, in conclusion, Brazil argues the Panel erred in its legal characterization of the facts in the record. Brazil maintains that when applied to the Panel's legal standard, those facts demonstrate that the EDC's debt financing confers a "benefit" and constitutes a "subsidy" within the meaning of Article 1.1 of the *SCM Agreement*. Accordingly, the Panel's legal conclusion on the EDC's debt financing is in error and should be reversed.

3. EDC Equity Financing of CRJ Capital

72. Brazil contends also that, contrary to the Panel's conclusion, the evidence of record concerning the EDC's equity investment, through Exinvest, in CRJ Capital, establishes that this investment confers a "benefit".

73. Brazil originally argued before the Panel that CRJ Capital leased aircraft to customers. However, in response to Canada's denial that CRJ Capital leases aircraft, Brazil emphasized that, whether the financing supports leases of aircraft or, alternatively, sales of aircraft, is irrelevant to Brazil's claim that a "benefit" is conferred by the EDC's equity investment in CRJ Capital.

74. Brazil maintains that 20% of CRJ Capital's total capital is in the form of equity provided by the EDC (10%) and Bombardier (10%), and the remaining 80% is debt from unspecified lenders. This capital structure permits CRJ Capital

[49] Panel Report, para. 9.163.

[50] Canada's second written submission to the Panel, para. 63, footnote 48.

[51] Question 10 of the Questions posed by the Panel at the second Panel meeting with the parties.

to provide financing at below-market rates. The only charge on CRJ Capital's total capital, Brazil asserts, is the charge required to service its debt, because equity holders are paid only from profits. Therefore, financing payments from aircraft purchasers, which need only cover the cost to CRJ Capital of its debt, are lower than they would be if, in the absence of the EDC's investment, CRJ Capital had to rely on debt for 100% of its underlying capital.

75. Brazil notes a statement by Richard Dixon, Industry Canada's Director of Airframe Systems, to the effect that CRJ Capital seeks to offer aircraft purchasers with a double-B credit rating financing terms ordinarily available only to double-A credit risks.[52] Canada did not contest this statement. Brazil considers that particular weight should be attached to it, given that it is by a Canadian official and is "against interest".[53] In Brazil's view, offering such preferential credit terms constitutes a "benefit".

76. Brazil requests the Appellate Body to reverse the Panel's finding on this point and determine that the EDC's equity investment in CRJ Capital constitutes a subsidy within the meaning of Article 1.1 of the *SCM Agreement*.

D. Arguments by Canada - Appellee

1. Drawing Adverse Inferences from Certain Facts

77. Canada begins with a review of some of the international law authorities cited by Brazil. According to Canada, Brazil has cited authorities incorrectly, out of context, and for propositions that they do not support. Moreover, some of the authorities cited by Brazil do not involve a tribunal drawing adverse inferences at all, but stand for the proposition that, in the absence of best evidence through no fault of the claimant, a tribunal may make inferences of fact based on the evidence of record. This is not the same as drawing adverse inferences.

78. Canada agrees that the "WTO dispute settlement process cannot function properly unless the parties to the dispute are willing to co-operate. This principle underlies the whole of the DSU."[54] However, this principle of collaboration is, in no way, meant to relieve the claimant of its burden of proof. In the absence of a *prima facie* case presented by the claimant, the respondent is under no obligation to provide any evidence and therefore the duty of collaboration does not arise. According to Kazazi, "the respondent should not be expected to provide any evidence before the claimant presents at least *prima facie* evidence in favour of its case."[55]

---

52 See Panel Report, para. 6.108.

53 Brazil's appellant's submission, para. 97.

54 Canada's appellee's submission, para. 103.

55 Mojtaba Kazazi, *Burden of Proof and Related Issues: A Study of Evidence Before International Tribunals* (Kluwer Law International, 1996), p. 138.

79. Canada acknowledges that panels have "comprehensive" authority to seek information under Article 13.1 of the DSU; but that authority is not without limits. A panel's authority under Article 13.1 is qualified by the principles of due process and the fundamental considerations that underlie any judicial system of dispute settlement. One of these considerations is the burden of proof. Canada quotes the Appellate Body in *Japan - Agricultural Products*, to the effect that a panel's authority under Article 13.1 "cannot be used by a panel to rule in favour of a complaining party which has not established a *prima facie* case of inconsistency...".[56] Moreover, information obtained through Article 13.1 cannot be used "to make the case for a complaining party".[57] Canada, therefore, argues that a panel may not engage in a fact-finding mission to assist the complaining party.

80. Canada notes that neither the DSU nor the *SCM Agreement* provides explicit authority for a panel to draw adverse inferences from a party's refusal to produce evidence requested by the panel. However, assuming that this authority may exist, the practice of international tribunals establishes that it arises only when certain requirements have been met.[58] One of the requirements identified by Kazazi is that the claimant must have made a *prima facie* case before adverse inferences can be drawn.[59] This is because in the absence of a *prima facie* case and, therefore, in the absence of the duty to collaborate, a respondent's decision not to provide information should not be perceived adversely. According to Canada, the legal authorities cited by Brazil support this view.

81. Canada argues that even if a *prima facie* case has been made, explanations provided by a respondent for not providing evidence or information should be taken into account by a tribunal. It is only unexplained refusals to produce evidence which may lead to adverse inferences being drawn. Again, Canada considers that authorities cited by Brazil support this view.

82. Canada concludes that in the absence of a *prima facie* case against the EDC's debt financing activities, the duty to collaborate did not arise and, thus, the Panel correctly decided not to draw adverse inferences against Canada. Furthermore, Canada offered two justifications for its refusal to supply information. First, Brazil had not made out a *prima facie* case and, second, the procedures adopted by the Panel for protecting sensitive business confidential information were "inadequate".[60]

83. Whereas Brazil argues that the Panel erred by failing to draw adverse inferences from Canada's refusal to provide requested information, Canada submits that the "real issue" is whether the Panel should have asked Canada to pro-

---

56 *Supra,* footnote 44, para. 129.

57 *Ibid.*

58 See Kazazi, *supra*, footnote 55, pp. 320-322.

59 *Supra*, footnote 55, pp. 321-322.

60 Canada's appellee's submission, para. 152.

vide the information requested.[61] In the absence of a *prima facie* case against the EDC's debt financing, the Panel's request that Canada provide details of the terms and conditions of the alleged EDC debt financing to ASA was "improper".[62] This request was, in effect, "an initiative by the Panel to advance Brazil's case" and, was therefore inconsistent with Article 13.1 and the rules on burden of proof.[63]

2. *EDC Debt Financing*

84. According to Canada, Brazil's argument that the EDC's debt financing of the ASA transaction goes beyond the terms of the *OECD Arrangement* is an entirely new issue that was never raised before the Panel. *At no time* did Brazil argue before the Panel that the 10-year term set out in the *OECD Arrangement* sets or exceeds the outer bounds of normal commercial practice. Likewise, *at no time* did Brazil argue that a 16.5-year lease was beyond commercial practice. Canada argues that this new argument cannot, therefore, be an issue of law covered in the panel report, as required for appeals by Article 17.6 of the DSU.

85. Furthermore, Canada maintains that, if Brazil had made these arguments before the Panel, Canada could have readily adduced evidence to demonstrate that a financing term for regional jet aircraft of more than 10 years, and even of up to 18 years, is entirely within the bounds of commercial practice. To that end, Canada cites four transactions, from 1997 and 1998, involving financing terms for aircraft of 15.25 years, 15.5 years, 16.5 years and 18.25 years.

86. Moreover, in Canada's opinion, Brazil bases its argument on the *OECD Arrangement* on the unfounded proposition that the Participants in the *Arrangement* have determined that the *Arrangement's* terms and conditions constitute "normal commercial practice". This argument is not tenable. Nothing in Article 1 of the *SCM Agreement*, or indeed in the *OECD Arrangement* itself, provides that the *Arrangement* may serve as the relevant commercial benchmark for the *SCM Agreement*. A preambular statement in the *OECD Arrangement* is not enough to read into the *SCM Agreement* a benchmark that has not been expressly provided for in that *Agreement*. Moreover, the reference in the preamble of the *OECD Arrangement* to "practice" refers to the practice of "officially supported export credits" and not to "commercial practice". Canada adds that it would, in any event, be unacceptable to define the standards of consistency with a WTO agreement by reference to criteria established by an organization outside the WTO, over which most WTO Members have no control or influence.

87. Canada also asserts that if, as the Panel said, market criteria are to serve as benchmarks for determining whether there is a "benefit", it is nonsensical to

---

[61] Canada's appellee's submission, para. 127.

[62] *Ibid.*, para. 128.

[63] *Ibid.*, para. 131.

argue that the *OECD Arrangement* is a better indicator of the market than the practice of commercial banks, because, in many instances, the market is more generous than the *OECD Arrangement*.

88. Canada is of the view that Brazil's other arguments on the EDC's debt financing are an attempt to have the Appellate Body revisit the evidentiary record that was thoroughly considered by the Panel. Brazil's real challenge, in Canada's view, is to the Panel's weighing of the evidence and to the Panel's discretion to determine what constitutes *prima facie* evidence.

89. Canada recalls that a panel's fact-finding process - the determination of the credibility and weight properly to be ascribed to evidence - is beyond appellate review, unless the panel's fact-finding is so "egregious" that it calls into question the good faith of the panel.[64] A panel's objective assessment of the facts includes the panel's determination of whether a claimant has adduced evidence sufficient to make out a *prima facie* case. It is not a legal error for a panel to accord a different weight to the evidence than that suggested by one of the parties.

90. As for the statement by Mr. Labbé concerning the "edge" provided by the EDC's debt financing, Canada argues that Brazil is challenging the Panel's assessment of the weight of that evidence, rather than its legal characterization. The issue is not whether the statement *itself* amounted to a subsidy. That is, it is not the *legal character of the statement* that Brazil challenges. The Panel considered and weighed the statement in question and found that it was not evidence sufficient to raise a presumption that what Brazil claimed was true. Canada argues that this is a factual finding and clearly outside the scope of appellate review.

91. Canada finds "particularly puzzling" Brazil's claim that a financial institution goes beyond the market by the mere fact of offering the most attractive financing package relative to other market players.[65] When a borrower seeks financing, it will look at a variety of financing options. Choosing the package offered by one lender over another does not mean that the successful lender is "below market". Indeed, if that were the definition of "market", the successful financing party *would always be below the market*. In that case, Canada contends, the financing provided by all state-owned banks and lending institutions would always be, by definition, subsidies.

---

[64] Appellate Body Report, *EC Measures Concerning Meat and Meat Products (Hormones)* ("*European Communities - Hormones*"), WT/DS26/AB/R, WT/DS48/AB/R, adopted 13 February 1998, paras. 132 and 133; Appellate Body Report, *Korea - Taxes on Alcoholic Beverages*, WT/DS75/AB/R, adopted 17 February 1999, paras. 161 and 162.

[65] Canada's appellee's submission, para. 75.

3. *EDC Equity Financing of CRJ Capital*

92. As regards the proper scope of appellate review, Canada reiterates that a panel's fact-finding process is beyond appellate review, unless the panel's fact-finding is so "egregious" that it calls into question the good faith of the Panel.

93. Canada believes that Brazil's argument on the EDC's equity infusion into CRJ Capital is without merit. The Panel carefully weighed Brazil's evidence, and found it wanting. Brazil has not challenged the Panel's assessment of the facts under Article 11 of the DSU. Accordingly, the Panel's findings of fact are not subject to appellate review. Canada recalls the Panel's finding that there is "*no factual basis*" to establish a *prima facie* case in terms of Brazil's claim.[66] (emphasis added) As Canada interprets this statement, the Panel, therefore, found that it was unable to attach *any* weight to the evidence supplied by Brazil. To entertain Brazil's appeal, the Appellate Body would have to overturn this appreciation of the evidence.

94. In any event, Canada says, CRJ Capital has only participated in the commercial financing of the sale of 17 regional aircraft for Air Canada. These are domestic sales that, therefore, fall outside of the scope of Article 3 of the *SCM Agreement*. According to Canada, "Brazil has presented no evidence that CRJ Capital has participated in the commercial financing of aircraft for *export*, as indeed it has not."[67] (emphasis added)

E. *Third Participants*

1. *European Communities*

(a) Interpretation of "Benefit" in Article 1.1(b) of the *SCM Agreement*

95. Canada argues that the notion of "benefit" in Article 1.1(b) required an element of net cost to the government as well as "benefit" to the recipient. The European Communities considers that the criterion of net cost to government is more relevant to the question of financial contribution than it is to "benefit". In this respect, the European Communities believes that the Panel should have examined the issue of cost to government more closely because the Canadian programmes that have been found to be prohibited export subsidies appear to be *self-financing* and, therefore involve no net cost to government.

96. According to the European Communities, the text of Articles 1, 14 and Annex IV of the *SCM Agreement* reflects a delicately negotiated compromise that panels and the Appellate Body should be careful not to upset. It is clear from the text of Article 1.1 that the definition of subsidy requires two elements:

---

[66] Panel Report, para. 9.200.

[67] Canada's appellee's submission, para. 89.

a financial contribution by a government and a "benefit" which is *thereby* conferred. The word "thereby" makes clear the need for a causal link between the financial contribution and the "benefit". It is only that part of the financial contribution which confers a "benefit", and only that part of the "benefit" which can be said to result from a financial contribution, that can be considered to constitute a subsidy. In other words, the notions of financial contribution and of "benefit" impart meaning to one another.

97. In the view of the European Communities, Annex IV.1 confirms that "cost to government" is the appropriate measure of "financial contribution". Annex IV.1 is, therefore, just as much part of the context of Article 1 as Article 14, and the Panel erred in finding otherwise. Annex IV and Article 14 confirm that when measuring the amount of a subsidy, both the market value of the "benefit" and the cost to the government are relevant. The Panel, therefore, should have examined the *extent* of the financial contribution, that is the cost to government, because only in that way could it have established whether a "benefit" was *thereby* conferred.

98. The European Communities believes that, as an illustrative list of what is *included* within the prohibition of export subsidies, "Annex I cannot be used for the purpose of interpreting Article 1."[68] However, if Annex I were to be accepted as relevant to the interpretation of Article 1, the European Communities would point out that the items contained in Annex I are drafted in terms of cost to the government.

99. The European Communities adds that the Panel's interpretation of Article 1 would have the effect of compromising many types of government activity which do not give rise to a net cost or are indeed profitable and which are undertaken for the "benefit" of industry in situations where government action is more efficient than action of the private sector.

(b) "Contingent in Fact Upon Export Performance"

100. The European Communities agrees with Canada that the Panel has adopted an unjustifiably broad approach to *de facto* export contingency. Like Canada, the European Communities considers that the legal nature of contingency is essentially the same for both *de jure* and *de facto* subsidies. Export performance must be a *condition* for the receipt of the subsidy, or, in other words, the subsidy would not have been granted *but for* the export performance.

101. The European Communities maintains that footnote 4 to the *SCM Agreement* provides further guidance as to the meaning of contingent in fact. As the Panel recognized, the words "tied to" in footnote 4 imply some kind of con-

---

68 European Communities' third participant's submission, para. 29.

straint. The Panel, however, used the language in footnote 4 to develop a legal standard based, not on conditionality, but rather on expectation of exportation.

102. In the European Communities' view, in the present case, the Panel should have compared the situations where TPC assistance was granted with those where it was refused, and looked at the reasons for TPC's decisions. If a consistent pattern emerged of preference being given to applicants because of their commitment to export, this would have indicated *de facto* conditionality. Instead, the Panel declined to examine the operation of the TPC programme in other sectors.

103. The European Communities is of the view that an indication of *de facto* export contingency might be found if the effect of a subsidy could be demonstrated to increase export effort at the expense of domestic sales. But, this factor should be treated with "great caution".[69] A policy of encouraging global competitiveness is not the same as export contingency, and the fact that a programme of assistance leads to increased exports, even if more rapidly than domestic sales, may be the normal economic consequence of an investment rather than the result of some artificial constraint or condition.

104. According to the European Communities, the object and purpose of the prohibition of *de facto* export contingency is to prevent circumvention of the *de jure* prohibition. The Panel should, therefore, have looked for evidence of conditions that were imposed in the contract that would *in practice* require exportation, albeit without export contingency being an express condition. For example, *de facto* export contingency might be indicated if the recipient were required, in the contract, to achieve certain minimum production and sales targets which could only be achieved through increased export effort and not through domestic sales. A government may also attempt to circumvent the *de jure* prohibition by contractually obliging a company to produce twice as much as it sells domestically. Such a condition will require increased export efforts. A panel could also consider whether the recipient's freedom to direct his sales effort to the domestic or the export market is somehow restricted.

105. The European Communities takes issue with the Panel's reliance on the closeness to export market and of the projects supported by TPC. The closeness of a subsidy to export marketing of a product has no relevance to its export contingency. A subsidy granted for research and development can just as easily be made *de facto* contingent on export performance as a subsidy granted at a later stage in product development.

[69] European Communities' third participant's submission, para. 43.

(c) Drawing Adverse Inferences from Certain Facts

106. The European Communities agrees with Brazil that there is a duty of collaboration on parties to dispute settlement proceedings to provide information that is within their control. The European Communities does not agree that the appropriate remedy for a failure to comply with this obligation is the drawing of adverse inferences, by a panel, unless there is specific legal basis in a covered agreement that empowers a panel to draw such inferences.

107. The European Communities argues that the *SCM Agreement* provides such an express power in certain circumstances, but in others requires reliance on the facts available.[70] These provisions show that where a power to draw adverse inferences was considered necessary, specific provision was made for it. In the absence of such express provision, as in the present situation, all that a panel can do is base its decision on an objective assessment of the facts available to it, as provided for in Article 11 of the DSU.

108. The European Communities believes that, under Article 11 of the DSU, a panel may draw *logical* inferences from the facts. However, drawing *adverse* inferences is different because it implies a preference for the adverse over the favourable (or simply logical) inference, as a form of "punishment" designed to enforce the duty of collaboration. In addition, the European Communities argues, under Article 11 of the DSU, inferences should be drawn from *facts*, whereas the power to draw adverse inferences applies where a responding party does *not* produce facts to rebut a mere *assertion* made against it.

109. The European Communities concludes that the Appellate Body should reject Brazil's claim that the Panel should have drawn adverse inferences and it should also take this opportunity to reverse the Panel's finding in paragraph 9.181 of the Panel Report that the Panel had the power to draw adverse inferences.

2. *United States*

(a) Interpretation of "Benefit" in Article 1.1(b) of the *SCM Agreement*

110. The United States argues that the focus of Article 1.1(b) of the *SCM Agreement* is on the advantage conferred on the recipient, and not on the cost to the subsidizing government. A beneficiary is no less advantaged by a subsidy merely because it involved no net cost to the government. Thus, the United States believes that the Panel's interpretation of Article 1.1 was correct and should be sustained.

---

70 See Articles 12.7 and 18.6 and Annex V, paras. 6, 7 and 8 of the *SCM Agreement*.

111. In the view of the United States, the Panel based its interpretation of the term "benefit" on the ordinary meaning of the term, and not on the guidelines set out in Article 14 of the *SCM Agreement*. Thus, contrary to Canada's arguments, the Panel looked to Article 14 only as contextual support for the interpretation it had already reached. Canada is also incorrect in claiming that the Panel failed to consider the object and purpose of the *SCM Agreement*. The Panel did consider it but did not agree with Canada that the object and purpose of the *SCM Agreement* was the avoidance of a net cost to the government.[71]

112. According to the United States, the fundamental error in Canada's position is its conclusion that the purported failure of the *SCM Agreement* negotiations to resolve the question of how to measure the amount of a subsidy means that there must be both a cost to the government and a "benefit" to the recipient before there can be a "benefit". The United States contends that Canada's attempt to conflate these two unrelated inquiries finds no support in the plain text of Article 1.1.

113. The United States maintains that both Article 14 and Annex IV.1 have relevance to other provisions of the *SCM Agreement*. However, it would be improper to assume that these provisions are relevant in places where, in fact, they are not. For instance, nothing in the language of Annex IV suggests that the "cost to government" standard found there is in any way relevant to determining the existence of a "benefit" under Article 1.1. Indeed, Annex IV.1 never even mentions Article 1.1. In contrast, the United States notes that the text of Article 14 makes an explicit and deliberate link between that provision and Article 1.1.

114. The United States agrees with the Panel's observation that requiring a "cost to government" as a condition for finding a "benefit" would write much of Article 1.1(a)(1)(iv) out of Article 1.1(a). Canada's argument that a private body would incur a cost on *behalf* of a government does not change the fact that there would be no cost to the government itself.

(b) "Contingent in Fact Upon Export Performance"

115. The United States takes no position on whether, as a factual matter, assistance under the TPC programme is, in fact, a prohibited export subsidy. However, the United States strongly disagrees with Canada's interpretation of what constitutes a subsidy that is "contingent ... in fact ... upon export performance" and is "in fact tied to actual or anticipated exportation or export earnings" under Article 3.1(a).

116. According to the United States, Canada's interpretation of contingent in fact upon export performance is "flawed".[72] First, contrary to Canada's assertion,

[71] See Panel Report, para. 9.119.

[72] United States' third participant's submission, para. 35.

there is no recipient "knowledge test" and a complainant is not required "to plumb the subjective understandings of subsidy recipients".[73] Instead, the question is whether the granting of a subsidy is tied to actual or anticipated exportation or export earnings. The focus is, therefore, on the grantor. The recipient's understanding of the government's motivation is irrelevant.

117. Furthermore, in the view of the United States, if the existence of a *de facto* export subsidy were dependent on the subjective understanding of the recipient and on how the recipient reacts after it receives the subsidy, there would be no way for a Member to determine in advance whether granting a particular subsidy would violate Article 3.2 of the *SCM Agreement*. This would undermine the *ex ante* character of the prohibition in Article 3.1 and would place a Member's adherence to WTO obligations in the hands of subsidy recipients.

118. Also, the United States maintains that, contrary to Canada's proposed interpretation, nothing in Article 3.1(a) suggests that a *de facto* export subsidy exists only if the subsidy induced the recipient to distort its marketing decisions in favour of exportation. There is no mention in Article 3.1(a) of the subsidy's effect on the recipient's domestic sales activities, much less any requirement that the complaining Member demonstrate that the recipient increased its exports in order to receive the subsidy.

119. In addition, the United States maintains that Canada ignores that Article 3.1(a) applies to *anticipated* exportation. The ordinary meaning of "anticipate" is to "look forward to; *colloq.* expect." Thus, a *de facto* export subsidy can exist where the granting of a subsidy is tied to *expected* exportation or export earnings. There is no requirement that exportation or export earnings have actually occurred, that penalties be imposed if expectations are not fulfilled, or that the recipient respond to the contribution in a particular way.

120. Finally, the United States argues that "the word 'anticipated' connotes a test based on intent."[74] The United States acknowledges that the final text of footnote 4 does not contain a government "knowledge test", as originally articulated by the European Communities during the negotiation of the *SCM Agreement*. However, the word "anticipated" is, nonetheless, consistent with a test that takes into account the intent of the subsidizing government.

(c) Drawing Adverse Inferences from Certain Facts

121. The United States is sympathetic to Canada's concerns about the need to protect business confidential information. It also recognizes that the dispute settlement process could be used improperly by Members to conduct "fishing ex-

[73] United States' third participant's submission, para. 35

[74] United States' third participant's submission, para. 39.

peditions" through the files of their adversaries.[75] However, if the dispute settlement process is to be effective, parties to disputes cannot be permitted to frustrate legitimate inquiries through ill-founded claims of business privilege. In this case, the Panel established BCI Procedures that it viewed as sufficient. Given this fact, "the Panel should have required parties to submit relevant information, and should not have permitted the parties to benefit from their refusal to do so".[76]

122. The Panel's approach to this issue has several negative consequences. First, permitting parties to self-select the information that they are willing to provide gives responding Members control of the course of a dispute. Second, since the complaining Member generally bears the burden of proof, responding Members, with a less transparent approach to governing, will be unfairly advantaged vis-à-vis Members with more open systems. This will encourage Members to avoid publicly disclosing their subsidy practices. Third, the overall utility of the dispute settlement provisions is likely to be undermined.

123. In the view of the United States, the Panel's actions point to the importance of establishing formal procedures for protecting business confidential information. Once these procedures are established, parties should not be permitted to refuse to provide business confidential information without consequence. This is not to say that parties will be required to submit business confidential information, "merely that the refusal to do so should entail some negative result".[77]

124. The United States takes no position on Brazil's claim that Canada violated the duty to be fully forthcoming and the duty of collaboration, nor on Brazil's discussion of the duty of collaboration in other international law contexts.

III. PRELIMINARY PROCEDURAL MATTER AND RULING

A. *Procedures Governing Business Confidential Information*

125. By joint letter of 27 May 1999, Brazil and Canada requested that we apply, *mutatis mutandis*, the BCI Procedures adopted by the Panel in this case. In their request, they also asked that certain of the BCI Procedures be applied to the third participants in this appeal; in particular, that the third participants designate authorized representatives who would be required to file declarations of non-disclosure with the Presiding Member of this Division before being allowed to view any information designated as "business confidential" or to attend portions of the oral hearing when such information may be discussed.

[75] United States' third participant's submission, para. 47.
[76] *Ibid.*, para. 48.
[77] *Ibid.*, para. 51.

126. By letter of 31 May 1999, we invited the participants to file legal memoranda in support of their request, and offered each an opportunity to respond to the legal memorandum submitted by the other. The third participants were also given an opportunity to file legal memoranda. Brazil and Canada submitted legal memoranda on 2 June 1999. On 4 June 1999, the third participants, the European Communities and the United States, also filed legal memoranda. On the same date, Brazil and Canada each filed a written response to the memorandum previously submitted by the other on 2 June 1999. A preliminary hearing on this issue was held on 10 June 1999, with this Division sitting jointly with the Division of the Appellate Body hearing the appeal in *Brazil - Aircraft*.

1. Arguments of Participants and Third Participants

(a) Canada

127. Canada considers that Article 18.2 of the DSU does not provide adequate procedural protection for confidential proprietary business information of the type that is before the Appellate Body in this case. This information is not in the public domain and would be of significant commercial interest, particularly to competitors of the enterprises that it concerns.

128. Canada observes that, in the absence of procedures to protect business confidential information at the appellate review stage, Brazil made references in its other appellant's submission and in its appellee's submission to business confidential information that Canada had submitted to the Panel under the BCI Procedures. The information submitted by Brazil was not, therefore, subject to any procedures to protect its confidentiality. Canada also argues that the Appellate Body should adopt procedures to ensure that the questions it poses at the oral hearing can be given a complete response, where necessary by reference to business confidential information included in the Panel record.

129. In adopting procedures for protecting business confidential information, Canada submits that the Appellate Body must balance two competing interests, both rooted in fairness and due process, and neither having a claim to better protection than the other. First, both the Appellate Body and the participants must be given reasonable access to the information that was introduced into evidence before the Panel. Second, however, additional procedural safeguards are necessary to provide private business interests with adequate protection for their proprietary business information when Canada or Brazil deems it necessary to refer to such evidence in support of its case. Canada, therefore, requests that, pursuant to Rule 16(1) of the *Working Procedures*, the Appellate Body adopt, *mutatis mutandis*, the Panel's BCI procedures and the "Declaration of Non-Disclosure" set out in Annexes I and II of the Panel Report.

(b) Brazil

130. Brazil states that it agreed to join in Canada's request that the Appellate Body adopt procedures for protecting business confidential information as a good faith attempt to accommodate Canada's concerns on confidentiality. Brazil notes two qualifications to its acceptance in principle of the BCI Procedures by the Appellate Body. First, the procedures should not unduly restrict the access of authorized persons to the information. Second, the procedures must be limited to business proprietary information of private parties who are not subject to the confidentiality obligations of the DSU.

131. Brazil recalls that in its submissions to the Appellate Body, it cited certain information that Canada had designated before the Panel as business confidential information. Brazil does not consider that this particular information is, in any sense, business confidential information entitled to special protection.

132. Brazil emphasizes that, in including certain information Canada had designated as "business confidential" before the Panel, in its submissions to the Appellate Body, and in serving those submissions on Canada and on the third participants in this appeal, it did not act inconsistently with either the letter or the spirit of the DSU. Brazil notes that Rule 18(2) of the *Working Procedures* required it to serve its written submissions on Canada as well as the third participants, and Brazil states that it "has no reason to doubt" that the third participants will comply with their obligations under Article VII:1 of the *Rules of Conduct for the Understanding on Rules and Procedures Governing the Settlement of Disputes* (the "*Rules of Conduct*"). Brazil maintains as well that the confidentiality provisions of Article 18.2 of the DSU also apply to the third participants.

(c) European Communities

133. The European Communities considers that the BCI Procedures are based on the administrative protective order system used in countervailing duty procedures before the administrative authorities of certain Members of the WTO. This system cannot simply be transplanted into the WTO.

134. The European Communities contends that the proposed procedures for protecting business confidential information are inconsistent with the DSU in two ways. First, the proposed procedures deprive Members of rights contained in the DSU. They are inconsistent with Article 18.1 of the DSU, which forbids *ex parte* communications with a panel or the Appellate Body. In the case of the Appellate Body, the prohibition against *ex parte* communications also extends to third participants under Rule 19(1) of the *Working Procedures*. Such procedures would deny a party to a dispute access to business confidential information if that party could not accept the procedures for protecting business confidential information developed by the panel or the Appellate Body Division. The proposed procedures for protecting business confidential information are also inconsistent with Rule 18(2) of the *Working Procedures*, which requires "every

document" filed by a participant or a third participant to be served on the other participants and third participants.

135. Second, the proposed procedures would impose new obligations on Members and create new rights for Members, contrary to Article 3.2 of the DSU. Such additional procedures would restrict access to certain documents to defined places, thereby restricting a party's ability to consider them. They would require the receiving party to permit the providing party to inspect the safe in its Mission where the information is to be stored. The European Communities argues that this is "tantamount to a waiver of the immunity enjoyed by those premises under international law". In addition, the procedures would require officials of the European Communities to sign undertakings incompatible with the "conduct of their duties".

136. The European Communities submits that Articles 14 and 18.2 of the DSU regulate the question of confidentiality in dispute settlement proceedings. If information is designated as confidential by a party to a dispute, Article 18.2 requires the other parties to take all necessary precautions according to their own administrative traditions and structures. The "bad faith" of other Members cannot be presumed. The proper place to resolve problems posed by the treatment of confidential information is in the current review of the DSU by WTO Members.

(d) United States

137. The United States argues that the need for additional procedures for protecting business confidential information is *extremely important*, "because it goes to the viability of WTO dispute settlement as a vehicle for preserving the rights and obligations of Members". In the view of the United States, "basic considerations of due process, as well as the need to preserve rights and obligations of Members, require the Appellate Body to apply such procedures". As a consequence, the United States has no objection to the joint request made by Brazil and Canada.

138. The United States makes three general arguments in support of the use of additional procedures for protecting business confidential information in WTO dispute settlement proceedings. First, the United States argues that nothing in the DSU precludes panels or the Appellate Body from adopting additional procedures for protecting business confidential information. On the contrary, Article 12.1 of the DSU explicitly allows panels to deviate from the working procedures set out in Appendix 3 of the DSU. The United States believes that the Appellate Body has authority comparable to that of panels to adopt such procedures as a result of Article 17.9 of the DSU and Article 16(1) of the *Working Procedures*.

139. Second, the United States argues that the application of procedures for protecting business confidential information promotes important objectives because Members' rights and obligations under the covered agreements can only be

preserved if due process is accorded to both the complaining party and the responding party. The United States maintains that the demands of due process are not satisfied, however, if the absence of such procedures precludes a Member from properly making its case.

140. Third, the United States maintains, contrary to the position taken by the European Communities, that a Member's national laws do not provide a basis for depriving another Member of its rights under the *WTO Agreement*. Thus, the United States asserts, the claim by the European Communities that its officials would be unable, under their staff regulations, to accept the undertakings proposed "should not be allowed".

2. *Ruling and Reasons*

141. In our preliminary ruling of 11 June 1999, we concluded that it is not necessary, under all the circumstances of this case, to adopt *additional* procedures to protect business confidential information in these appellate proceedings. Our ruling was as follows:

> Pursuant to Article 17.9 of the *Understanding on Rules and Procedures Governing the Settlement of Disputes* (the "DSU"), the Appellate Body has the authority to draw up its own Working Procedures. Under Rule 16.1 of our *Working Procedures for Appellate Review*, a Division of the Appellate Body may adopt additional procedures for the orderly conduct of a particular appeal, provided that any such additional procedures are not inconsistent with the DSU, the other covered agreements and the *Working Procedures for Appellate Review*. We have concluded, however, that it is not necessary, under all the circumstances of this case, to adopt *additional* procedures to protect "business confidential information" during these appellate proceedings.
>
> We note that, with respect to "business confidential information" submitted to the Panel that remains currently in the possession of the participants, Article XII of the Panel Procedures Governing Business Confidential Information required the parties, "[a]t the conclusion of the Panel", to "return any printed or binary-encoded Business Confidential information in their possession to the party that submitted such Business Confidential (sic)" and to "destroy all tapes and transcripts of the Panel hearings that contain Business Confidential information, unless the parties mutually agree otherwise." It thus appears that each participant has an obligation, under the Panel Procedures, to return any Business Confidential information submitted

by the other participant. The WTO Secretariat, assisting the Panel, was required, by the Panel Procedures, to "transmit any printed or binary-encoded Business Confidential information, plus all tapes and transcripts of the panel hearings that contain Business Confidential Information, to the Appellate Body as part of the record of the Panel proceedings." That information will be kept in a secure, locked cabinet in the Appellate Body Secretariat.

> We also note that *all* Members are obliged, by the provisions of the DSU, to treat these proceedings of the Appellate Body, including written submissions and other documents filed by the participants and the third participants, as confidential. We are confident that the participants and the third participants in this appeal will *fully respect* their obligations under the DSU, recognizing that a Member's obligation to maintain the confidentiality of these proceedings extends also to the individuals whom that Member selects to act as its representatives, counsel and consultants.
>
> Accordingly, we decline the request of Brazil and Canada. The reasons for this ruling will be set out more fully in the Appellate Body Report in this appeal.

142. We have no further reasons to add to the first two paragraphs of our ruling above. The following is an elaboration of the reasons in the third paragraph of our ruling. Our ruling applies only to the request for *additional* procedures to protect "business confidential information" in these appellate proceedings, and it, therefore, has no effect on the BCI Procedures adopted by the Panel. Neither the Panel's decision to adopt BCI Procedures, nor the content of those Procedures, has been appealed.

143. With respect to appellate proceedings, in particular, the provisions of the DSU impose an obligation of confidentiality which applies to WTO Members generally as well as to Appellate Body Members and staff. In this respect, Article 17.10 of the DSU states, without qualification, that "[t]he *proceedings* of the Appellate Body *shall be confidential*." (emphasis added) The word "proceeding" has been defined as follows:

> In a general sense, the form and manner of conducting juridical business before a court or judicial officer. Regular and orderly progress in form of law, *including all possible*

> *steps in an action from its commencement to the execution of judgment.*[78] (emphasis added)

More broadly, the word "proceedings" has been defined as "the business transacted by a court".[79] In its ordinary meaning, we take "proceedings" to include, in an appellate proceeding, any written submissions, legal memoranda, written responses to questions, and oral statements by the participants and the third participants; the conduct of the oral hearing before the Appellate Body, including any transcripts or tapes of that hearing; and the deliberations, the exchange of views and internal workings of the Appellate Body.

144. Article 18.2 of the DSU also contains rules protecting the confidentiality of written submissions and information submitted to the Appellate Body:

> *Written submissions to the panel or the Appellate Body shall be treated as confidential*, but shall be made available to the parties to the dispute. Nothing in this Understanding shall preclude a party to a dispute from disclosing statements of its own positions to the public. *Members shall treat as confidential information submitted by another Member to the panel or the Appellate Body* which that Member has designated as confidential. A party to a dispute shall also, upon request of a Member, provide a non-confidential summary of the information contained in its written submissions that could be disclosed to the public. (emphasis added)

145. In our view, the provisions of Articles 17.10 and 18.2 apply to all Members of the WTO, and oblige them to maintain the confidentiality of any submissions or information submitted, or received, in an Appellate Body proceeding. Moreover, those provisions oblige Members to ensure that such confidentiality is fully respected by any person that a Member selects to act as its representative, counsel or consultant. In this respect, we note, with approval, the following statement made by the panel in *Indonesia - Certain Measures Affecting the Automobile Industry:*

> We would like to emphasize that *all members of parties' delegations - whether or not they are government employees - are present as representatives of their governments, and as such are subject to the provisions of the DSU and of the standard working procedures, including Articles 18.1 and 18.2 of the DSU and paragraphs 2 and 3 of those procedures*. In particular, parties are required to treat as confidential all submissions to the Panel and all informa-

[78] *Black's Law Dictionary* (West Publishing Co. 1990), p. 1204.

[79] *The New Shorter Oxford English Dictionary*, (Clarendon Press, 1993), Vol. II, p. 2364.

> tion so designated by other Members; and, in addition, the Panel meets in closed session. Accordingly, *we expect that all delegations will fully respect those obligations and will treat these proceedings with the utmost circumspection and discretion.*[80] (emphasis added)

146. Finally, we wish to recall that Members of the Appellate Body and its staff are covered by Article VII:1 of the *Rules of Conduct*[81], which provides:

> Each covered person *shall at all times maintain the confidentiality of dispute settlement deliberations and proceedings together with any information identified by a party as confidential.* (emphasis added)

147. For these reasons, we do not consider that it is necessary, under all the circumstances of this case, to adopt *additional* procedures for the protection of business confidential information in these appellate proceedings. We, therefore, decline the request of Brazil and Canada.

IV. ISSUES RAISED IN THIS APPEAL

148. This appeal raises the following issues:

(a) whether the Panel erred in its interpretation of the term "benefit" in Article 1.1(b) of the *SCM Agreement*;

(b) whether the Panel erred in its interpretation and application of the expression "contingent ... in fact ... upon export performance" in Article 3.1(a) of the *SCM Agreement*;

(c) whether the Panel erred in declining to draw inferences from Canada's refusal to provide information about certain debt financing activities of the EDC;

(d) whether the Panel erred in finding that certain debt financing activities of the EDC in support of the Canadian regional aircraft industry do not confer a "benefit" within the meaning of Article 1.1(b) of the *SCM Agreement*; and

(e) whether the Panel erred in finding that the equity investment by the EDC in CRJ Capital does not confer a "benefit" within the meaning of Article 1.1(b) of the *SCM Agreement*.

---

80 Panel report, WT/DS54/R, WT/DS55/R, WT/DS59/R, WT/DS64/R, adopted 23 July 1998, para. 14.1.

81 The *Rules of Conduct* have been directly incorporated into the *Working Procedures* (see Rule 8 of those *Working Procedures*).

V. INTERPRETATION OF "BENEFIT" IN ARTICLE 1.1(B) OF THE *SCM AGREEMENT*

149. In interpreting the term "benefit" in Article 1.1(b) of the *SCM Agreement*, the Panel found that:

> ... the ordinary meaning of "benefit" clearly encompasses some form of advantage. ... In order to determine whether a financial contribution (in the sense of Article 1.1(a)(i)) confers a "benefit", *i.e.*, an advantage, it is necessary to determine whether the financial contribution places the *recipient* in a *more advantageous position than would have been the case but for the financial contribution*. In our view, the only logical basis for determining the position the recipient would have been in absent the financial contribution is the *market*. Accordingly, a financial contribution will only confer a "benefit", *i.e.*, an advantage, if it is *provided on terms that are more advantageous than those that would have been available to the recipient on the market*.[82] (emphasis added)

150. The Panel concluded that the notion of "cost to government" is not relevant to the interpretation and application of the term "benefit", within the meaning of Article 1.1(b) of the *SCM Agreement*.[83] The Panel found contextual support for this reading of "benefit" in Article 14 of the *SCM Agreement*. It also found that Annex IV of that Agreement does not form part of the relevant context of "benefit" in Article 1.1(b).

151. Canada appeals the Panel's legal interpretation of the term "benefit" in Article 1.1(b) of the *SCM Agreement*. In Canada's view, the Panel erred in its interpretation of "benefit" by focusing on the commercial benchmarks in Article 14 "to the exclusion of cost to government", and by rejecting Annex IV as relevant context.[84] Canada maintains that Annex IV of the *SCM Agreement* supports the view that "cost to government", which is mentioned in Annex IV, is a legitimate interpretation of the term "benefit". In its appellee's submission, Brazil agrees fully with the Panel's interpretation.

152. Under the heading "*Definition of a Subsidy*", Article 1.1 of the *SCM Agreement* provides, in relevant part:

> 1.1 For the purpose of this Agreement, a subsidy shall be deemed to exist if:

---

[82] Panel Report, para. 9.112. The Panel confirmed its interpretation in similar terms in its conclusion at para. 9.120 of the Panel Report.

[83] *Ibid.*, para. 9.112.

[84] Canada's appellant's submission, paras. 98 and 102.

> (a)(1) there is a financial contribution by a government or any public body within the territory of a Member (referred to in this Agreement as "government") ...
>
> ...
>
> and
>
> (b) *a benefit is thereby conferred.* (emphasis added)

153. In addressing this issue, we start with the ordinary meaning of "benefit". The dictionary meaning of "benefit" is "advantage", "good", "gift", "profit", or, more generally, "a favourable or helpful factor or circumstance".[85] Each of these alternative words or phrases gives flavour to the term "benefit" and helps to convey some of the essence of that term. These definitions also confirm that the Panel correctly stated that "the ordinary meaning of 'benefit' clearly encompasses some form of advantage."[86] Clearly, however, dictionary meanings leave many interpretive questions open.

154. A "benefit" does not exist in the abstract, but must be received and enjoyed by a beneficiary or a recipient. Logically, a "benefit" can be said to arise only if a person, natural or legal, or a group of persons, has in fact received something. The term "benefit", therefore, implies that there must be a recipient. This provides textual support for the view that the focus of the inquiry under Article 1.1(b) of the *SCM Agreement* should be on the recipient and not on the granting authority. The ordinary meaning of the word "confer", as used in Article 1.1(b), bears this out. "Confer" means, *inter alia*, "give", "grant" or "bestow".[87] The use of the past participle "conferred" in the passive form, in conjunction with the word "thereby", naturally calls for an inquiry into *what was conferred on the recipient*. Accordingly, we believe that Canada's argument that "cost to government" is one way of conceiving of "benefit" is at odds with the ordinary meaning of Article 1.1(b), which focuses on the *recipient* and not on the *government* providing the "financial contribution".

155. We find support for this reading of "benefit" in the context of Article 1.1(b) of the *SCM Agreement*. Article 14 sets forth guidelines for calculating the amount of a subsidy in terms of "the benefit to the recipient". Although the opening words of Article 14 state that the guidelines it establishes apply "[f]or

---

85 *The New Shorter Oxford English Dictionary*, (Clarendon Press, 1993), Vol. I, p. 214; *The Concise Oxford Dictionary*, (Clarendon Press, 1995), p. 120; *Webster's Third New International Dictionary* (unabridged), (William Benton, 1966), Vol. I, p. 204.

86 Panel Report, para. 9.112.

87 *The New Shorter Oxford English Dictionary*, (Clarendon Press, 1993) Vol. I, p. 474; *The Concise Oxford English Dictionary*, (Clarendon Press, 1995), p. 278; *Webster's Third New International Dictionary*, (William Benton, 1966), Vol. I, p. 475.

the purposes of Part V" of the *SCM Agreement*, which relates to "countervailing measures", our view is that Article 14, nonetheless, constitutes relevant context for the interpretation of "benefit" in Article 1.1(b). The guidelines set forth in Article 14 apply to the calculation of the "benefit *to the recipient* conferred *pursuant to paragraph 1 of Article 1*". (emphasis added) This explicit textual reference to Article 1.1 in Article 14 indicates to us that "benefit" is used in the same sense in Article 14 as it is in Article 1.1. Therefore, the reference to "benefit *to the recipient*" in Article 14 also implies that the word "benefit", *as used in Article 1.1*, is concerned with the "benefit *to the recipient*" and not with the "cost to government", as Canada contends.

156. The structure of Article 1.1 as a whole confirms our view that Article 1.1(b) is concerned with the "benefit" to the recipient, and not with the "cost to government". The definition of "subsidy" in Article 1.1 has two discrete elements: "a financial contribution by a government or any public body" and "a benefit is thereby conferred". The first element of this definition is concerned with whether the *government* made a "financial contribution", as that term is defined in Article 1.1(a). The focus of the first element is on the action of the government in making the "financial contribution". That being so, it seems to us logical that the second element in Article 1.1 is concerned with the "benefit... conferred" on the *recipient* by that governmental action. Thus, subparagraphs (a) and (b) of Article 1.1 define a "subsidy" by reference, first, to the action of the granting authority and, second, to what was conferred on the recipient. Therefore, Canada's argument that "cost to *government*" is relevant to the question of whether there is a "benefit" to the *recipient* under Article 1.1(b) disregards the overall structure of Article 1.1.

157. We also believe that the word "benefit", as used in Article 1.1(b), implies some kind of comparison. This must be so, for there can be no "benefit" to the recipient unless the "financial contribution" makes the recipient "better off" than it would otherwise have been, absent that contribution. In our view, the marketplace provides an appropriate basis for comparison in determining whether a "benefit" has been "conferred", because the trade-distorting potential of a "financial contribution" can be identified by determining whether the recipient has received a "financial contribution" on terms more favourable than those available to the recipient in the market.

158. Article 14, which we have said is relevant context in interpreting Article 1.1(b), supports our view that the marketplace is an appropriate basis for comparison. The guidelines set forth in Article 14 relate to equity investments, loans, loan guarantees, the provision of goods or services by a government, and the purchase of goods by a government. A "benefit" arises under each of the guidelines if the recipient has received a "financial contribution" on terms more favourable than those available to the recipient in the market.

159. Canada has argued that the Panel erred in failing to take account of paragraph 1 of Annex IV as part of the relevant context of the term "benefit". We fail

to see the relevance of this provision to the interpretation of "benefit" in Article 1.1(b) of the *SCM Agreement*. Annex IV provides a method for calculating the total *ad valorem* subsidization of a product under the "serious prejudice" provisions of Article 6 of the *SCM Agreement*, with a view to determining whether a subsidy is used in such a manner as to have "adverse effects". Annex IV, therefore, has nothing to do with whether a "*benefit*" has been conferred, nor with whether a measure constitutes a subsidy within the meaning of Article 1.1. We agree with the Panel that Annex IV is not useful context for interpreting Article 1.1(b) of the *SCM Agreement*.

160. Canada insists that the concept of "cost to government" is relevant in the interpretation of "benefit". We note that this interpretation of "benefit" would exclude from the scope of that term those situations where a "benefit" is conferred by a private body under the direction of government. These situations cannot be *excluded* from the definition of "benefit" in Article 1.1(b), given that they are specifically *included* in the definition of "financial contribution" in Article 1.1(a)(iv). We are, therefore, not persuaded by this argument of Canada.

161. In light of the foregoing, we find that the Panel has not erred in its interpretation of the word "benefit", as used in Article 1.1(b) of the *SCM Agreement*.

VI. "CONTINGENT IN FACT UPON EXPORT PERFORMANCE"

162. The Panel held that a subsidy is "contingent ... in fact ... upon export performance" under Article 3.1(a) of the *SCM Agreement* if there is a relationship of conditionality or dependence "between the grant of the subsidy and the 'anticipated exportation or export earnings'".[88] The Panel stated that it could:

> ... examine most effectively whether there exists the requisite conditionality between the grant of TPC assistance to the Canadian regional aircraft industry and anticipated exportation or export earnings, by determining whether the facts demonstrate that such TPC assistance would not have been granted to the regional aircraft industry *but for* anticipated exportation or export earnings.[89] (emphasis in original)

With respect to demonstrating *de facto* export contingency, the Panel held that:

> ... it is clear from the ordinary meaning of footnote 4 that *any* fact could be relevant, provided it "demonstrates" (either individually or in conjunction with other facts) whether or not a subsidy would have been granted but for

[88] Panel Report, para. 9.331.

[89] *Ibid*., para. 9.332.

> anticipated exportation or export earnings. We consider that this is true of the export-orientation of the recipient, or of the reason for the grant of the subsidy, just as it is true of a host of other facts potentially surrounding the grant of the subsidy in question. In any given case, the relative importance of each fact can only be determined in the context of that case, and not on the basis of generalities. [90] (emphasis in original)

The Panel also opined that:

> ... the closer a subsidy brings a product to sale on the export market, the greater the possibility that the facts may demonstrate that the subsidy would not have been granted but for anticipated exportation or export earnings. Conversely, the further removed a subsidy is from sales on the export market, the less the possibility that the facts may demonstrate that the subsidy would not have been granted but for anticipated exportation or export earnings.[91]

163. On this basis, and after examination of the facts before it, the Panel found that "TPC assistance to the Canadian regional aircraft industry is 'contingent...in fact...upon export performance' within the meaning of Article 3.1(a) of the SCM Agreement."[92]

164. Canada appeals the Panel's finding that TPC assistance is "contingent ... in fact ... upon export performance". Canada argues, *inter alia*, that a subsidy is "contingent ... in fact ... upon export performance" when "the facts and circumstances are such that the recipient will reasonably know that there is a requirement to export ... ."[93] Canada maintains that the Panel made the export orientation of the Canadian regional aircraft industry the "effective test" of *de facto* export contingency.[94] Canada also argues that the Panel erred in concluding that "the closer a subsidy brings a product to sale on the export market, the greater the possibility that the facts may demonstrate that the subsidy would not have been granted but for anticipated exportation or export earnings."[95] Canada contends further that the Panel "confus[ed]" *considerations* taken into account by TPC with *conditions* based on export performance.[96] Finally, Canada maintains that the Panel erred because it gave "no indication that ... the operation of

[90] Panel Report, para. 9.337.
[91] *Ibid.*, para. 9.339.
[92] Panel Report, para. 9.347.
[93] Canada's appellant's submission, para. 30.
[94] *Ibid.*, para. 61.
[95] Panel Report, para. 9.339.
[96] Canada's appellant's submission, para. 59.

the TPC programme as a whole" had been considered.[97] For its part, Brazil agrees fully with the Panel's interpretation and application of the expression "contingent … in fact … upon export performance".

165. Article 3.1 of the *SCM Agreement* provides, in pertinent part:

> Except as provided in the Agreement on Agriculture, the following subsidies, within the meaning of Article 1, shall be prohibited:
>
> (a) subsidies contingent, in law or in fact[4], whether solely or as one of several other conditions, upon export performance, including those illustrated in Annex I …
>
> [4] This standard is met when the facts demonstrate that the granting of a subsidy, without having been made legally contingent upon export performance, is in fact tied to actual or anticipated exportation or export earnings. The mere fact that a subsidy is granted to enterprises which export shall not for that reason alone be considered to be an export subsidy within the meaning of this provision.

Article 3.2 adds that "[a] Member shall neither grant nor maintain subsidies referred to in paragraph 1."

166. In confronting this issue, we start our interpretive task once more by examining the ordinary meaning of the treaty text. In our view, the key word in Article 3.1(a) is "contingent". As the Panel observed, the ordinary connotation of "contingent" is "conditional" or "dependent for its existence on something else".[98] This common understanding of the word "contingent" is borne out by the text of Article 3.1(a), which makes an explicit link between "contingency" and "conditionality" in stating that export contingency can be the sole or "one of several other *conditions*".

167. Article 3.1(a) prohibits *any* subsidy that is contingent upon export performance, whether that subsidy is contingent "in law or in fact". The Uruguay Round negotiators have, through the prohibition against export subsidies that are contingent *in fact* upon export performance, sought to prevent circumvention of the prohibition against subsidies contingent *in law* upon export performance.[99] In our view, the legal standard expressed by the word "contingent" is the same

[97] Canada's appellant's submission, para. 77.

[98] *The New Shorter Oxford English Dictionary*, (Clarendon Press, 1993), Vol. I, p. 494; *The Concise Oxford English Dictionary*, (Clarendon Press, 1995), p. 289. See also *Webster's Third New International Dictionary*, (William Benton, 1966), Vol. I, p. 493. See Panel Report, para. 9.331.

[99] See the submission of the European Communities during the negotiations of the *SCM Agreement*, entitled "Elements of the Negotiating Framework" (MTN.GNG/NG10/W/31), which was cited before us para. 40 of the United States' third participant's submission.

for both *de jure* or *de facto* contingency. There is a difference, however, in what evidence may be employed to prove that a subsidy is export contingent. *De jure* export contingency is demonstrated on the basis of the words of the relevant legislation, regulation or other legal instrument. Proving *de facto* export contingency is a much more difficult task. There is no single legal document which will demonstrate, on its face, that a subsidy is "contingent ...in fact ... upon export performance". Instead, the existence of this relationship of contingency, between the subsidy and export performance, must be *inferred* from the total configuration of the facts constituting and surrounding the granting of the subsidy, none of which on its own is likely to be decisive in any given case.

168. Recognizing the difficulties inherent in demonstrating *de facto* export contingency, the Uruguay Round negotiators provided a standard, in footnote 4 of the *SCM Agreement*, for determining when a subsidy is "contingent ... in fact ... upon export performance". Footnote 4 reads:

> This *standard is met* when the *facts demonstrate* that the *granting* of a subsidy, without having been made legally contingent upon export performance, is *in fact tied to actual or anticipated exportation or export earnings*. The mere fact that a subsidy is granted to enterprises which export shall not for that reason alone be considered to be an export subsidy within the meaning of this provision. (emphasis added)

169. Footnote 4 makes it clear that *de facto* export contingency must be *demonstrated* by the *facts*. We agree with the Panel that what facts *should* be taken into account in a particular case will depend on the circumstances of that case. We also agree with the Panel that there can be no general rule as to what facts or what kinds of facts *must* be taken into account. We note that satisfaction of the standard for determining *de facto* export contingency set out in footnote 4 requires proof of three different substantive elements: first, the "*granting* of a subsidy"; second, "is ... *tied to* ..."; and, third, "actual or anticipated exportation or export earnings". (emphasis added) We will examine each of these elements in turn.

170. The first element of the standard for determining *de facto* export contingency is the "*granting* of a subsidy". In our view, the initial inquiry must be on whether the *granting authority* imposed a condition based on export performance in providing the subsidy. In the words of Article 3.2 and footnote 4, the prohibition is on the "*granting* of a subsidy", and not on receiving it. The treaty obligation is imposed on the *granting* Member, and not on the recipient. Consequently, we do not agree with Canada that an analysis of "contin-

gent ... in fact ... upon export performance" should focus on the reasonable knowledge of the recipient.[100]

171. The second substantive element in footnote 4 is "tied to". The ordinary meaning of "tied to" confirms the linkage of "contingency" with "conditionality" in Article 3.1(a). Among the many meanings of the verb "tie", we believe that, in this instance, because the word "tie" is immediately followed by the word "to" in footnote 4, the relevant ordinary meaning of "tie" must be to "limit or restrict as to ... conditions".[101] This element of the standard set forth in footnote 4, therefore, emphasizes that a relationship of conditionality or dependence must be demonstrated. The second substantive element is at the very heart of the legal standard in footnote 4 and cannot be overlooked. In any given case, the facts must "demonstrate" that the granting of a subsidy is *tied to* or *contingent upon* actual or anticipated exports.[102] It does *not* suffice to demonstrate solely that a government granting a subsidy *anticipated* that exports would result. The prohibition in Article 3.1(a) applies to subsidies that are *contingent* upon export performance.

172. We turn now to the third substantive element provided in footnote 4. The dictionary meaning of the word "anticipated" is "expected".[103] The use of this word, however, does *not* transform the standard for "contingent ... in fact" into a standard merely for ascertaining "expectations" of exports on the part of the granting authority. Whether exports were anticipated or "expected" is to be gleaned from an examination of objective evidence. This examination is quite separate from, *and should not be confused with*, the examination of whether a subsidy is "tied to" actual or anticipated exports. A subsidy may well be granted in the knowledge, or with the anticipation, that exports will result. Yet, that alone is not sufficient, because that alone is not proof that the granting of the subsidy is *tied to* the anticipation of exportation.

173. There is a logical relationship between the second sentence of footnote 4 and the "tied to" requirement set forth in the first sentence of that footnote. The second sentence of footnote 4 precludes a panel from making a finding of *de*

---

[100] In finding that the knowledge of the recipient is not part of the legal standard of *de facto* export contingency, we do not suggest that relevant objective evidence relating to the recipient can never be considered by a panel.

[101] *The New Shorter Oxford English Dictionary*, (Clarendon Press, 1993), Vol. II, p. 3307. See also *The Concise Oxford English Dictionary*, (Clarendon Press, 1995), p. 1457.

[102] We note that the Panel considered that the most effective means of demonstrating whether a subsidy is contingent in fact upon export performance is to examine whether the subsidy would have been granted *but for* the anticipated exportation or export earnings (Panel Report, para. 9.332). While we consider that the Panel did not err in its overall approach to *de facto* export contingency, we, and panels as well, must interpret and apply the language actually used in the treaty (see, for instance, Appellate Body Report, *India - Patents*, *supra*, footnote 35, para. 45).

[103] *The New Shorter Oxford English Dictionary*, (Clarendon Press, 1993), Vol. I, p. 88, states that a colloquial meaning for "anticipate" is "expect". *The Concise Oxford English Dictionary*, (Clarendon Press, 1995), p. 53, identifies "expect" as a disputed meaning of "anticipate".

facto export contingency for the sole reason that the subsidy is "granted to enterprises which export". In our view, merely knowing that a recipient's sales are export-oriented does not demonstrate, without more, that the granting of a subsidy is tied to actual or anticipated exports. The second sentence of footnote 4 is, therefore, a specific expression of the requirement in the first sentence to demonstrate the "tied to" requirement. We agree with the Panel that, under the second sentence of footnote 4, the export orientation of a recipient may be taken into account as *a* relevant fact, provided that it is one of several facts which are considered and is not the only fact supporting a finding.

174. Canada argues that the Panel erred in stating that "the closer a subsidy brings a product to sale on the export market, *the greater the possibility* that the facts may demonstrate that the subsidy"[104] is "contingent ... in fact ... upon export performance". (emphasis added) We recall that the Panel added that "the further removed a subsidy is from sales on the export market, *the less the possibility* that the facts may demonstrate that the subsidy"[105] is "contingent ... in fact ... upon export performance". (emphasis added) By these statements, the Panel appears to us to apply what could be read to be a legal presumption. While we agree that this nearness-to-the-export-market factor *may*, in certain circumstances, be a relevant fact, we do not believe that it should be regarded as a legal presumption. It is, for instance, no "*less ... possible*" that the facts, taken together, may demonstrate that a pre-production subsidy for research and development is "contingent ... in fact ... upon export performance". If a panel takes this factor into account, it should treat it with considerable caution. In our opinion, the mere presence or absence of this factor in any given case does not give rise to a presumption that a subsidy is or is not *de facto* contingent upon export performance. The legal standard to be applied remains the same: it is necessary to establish each of the three substantive elements in footnote 4.

175. Having examined the legal standard set forth in footnote 4 for determining *de facto* export contingency under Article 3.1(a), we turn next to the Panel's application of that legal standard to the facts relating to assistance provided by TPC to the Canadian regional aircraft industry. The Panel set out in some detail the various facts that it took into account in concluding that TPC assistance was "contingent ... in fact ... upon export performance".[106] Indeed, the Panel took into account sixteen different factual elements, which covered a variety of matters, including: TPC's statement of its overall objectives; types of information called for in applications for TPC funding; the considerations, or eligibility criteria, employed by TPC in deciding whether to grant assistance; factors to be identified by TPC officials in making recommendations about applications for funding; TPC's record of funding in the export field, generally, and in the aero-

[104] Panel Report, para. 9.339.

[105] *Ibid.*, para. 9.339.

[106] Panel Report, para. 9.340.

space and defence sector, in particular; the nearness-to-the-export-market of the projects funded; the importance of projected export sales by applicants to TPC's funding decisions; and the export orientation of the firms or the industry supported.

176. From our scrutiny of the Panel Report, we are unable to agree with Canada that the Panel made the export orientation of the regional aircraft industry the "effective test". In keeping with the standard set forth in footnote 4, the fact of the Canadian industry's export orientation seems to us not to have been given undue emphasis by the Panel. Rather, this fact was simply one of a number of facts that, when considered together, the Panel found demonstrated that the granting of subsidies by TPC was "tied to" actual or anticipated exports.

177. We recall our finding that the Panel could be understood as having treated the nearness-to-the-export-market factor as giving rise to a legal presumption in determining whether TPC assistance was "contingent … in fact … upon export performance".[107] However, we also have said that this factor may, in certain circumstances, be a relevant factor in making such a determination. In our view, in the circumstances of this case, the Panel did not err in taking this nearness-to-the-export-market factor into consideration, together with all the other facts that the Panel considered. Moreover, in our view and in light of all the facts the Panel considered, the Panel would, in all probability, have concluded that TPC assistance to the Canadian regional export industry was "contingent … in fact … upon export performance", even if it had not taken this factor into account.

178. Canada also asserts that the Panel "confused" *considerations* - that is, the eligibility criteria set out in the TPC Handbook that TPC took into account in making its funding decisions - with *conditions* based on export performance.[108] We do not agree. The Panel did *not* find that the TPC eligibility criteria *were* conditions, but, rather, it found that those criteria helped to *demonstrate* the existence of *de facto* contingency upon export performance.[109] We consider it perfectly possible that such considerations, especially when taken together with other facts, could demonstrate that a subsidy is "contingent … in fact … upon export performance".[110] Indeed, in many cases, the eligibility criteria used by a granting authority, and their application in practice, may provide particularly good evidence of whether the granting of a subsidy is "contingent … in fact … upon export performance".

---

[107] *Supra*, para. 174.

[108] Canada's appellant's submission, para. 59.

[109] See Panel Report, paras. 9.340 and 9.341.

[110] We note that none of the considerations or eligibility criteria, by itself, amounts to an export condition because, if that were so, there would be a case of *de jure* export contingency.

179. We note, finally, that the Panel took into account a number of facts related to the TPC programme as a whole.[111] Therefore, we do not agree with Canada's assertion that "[t]here is no indication that the Panel considered the operation of the TPC programme as a whole".[112] Moreover, the fact that some of TPC's contributions, in some industry sectors, are *not* contingent upon export performance, does not necessarily mean that the same is true for all of TPC's contributions. It is enough to show that one or some of TPC's contributions do constitute subsidies "contingent ... in fact ... upon export performance".

180. For all these reasons, we uphold the Panel's legal finding that "TPC assistance to the Canadian regional aircraft industry is 'contingent...in fact...upon export performance' within the meaning of Article 3.1(a) of the SCM Agreement."[113]

VII. DRAWING ADVERSE INFERENCES FROM CERTAIN FACTS

181. We come to the issue of whether the Panel erred in law in declining to draw adverse inferences from Canada's refusal to provide information to the Panel about the EDC's debt financing activities. The Panel's ruling on this issue needs to be quoted *in extenso*:

> We note that Brazil asked us to make adverse inferences in light of Canada's refusal to provide details of the ASA transaction. In certain circumstances when direct evidence is not available, we consider that a panel may be required to make such inferences when there is sufficient basis to do so. This is especially true when direct evidence is not available because it is withheld by a party with sole possession of that evidence. In the present instance, however, we do not consider that there is sufficient basis for an inference that EDC debt financing in the Canadian regional aircraft sector confers a "benefit". In particular, Brazil has made no attempt to demonstrate that EDC debt financing was provided to ASA on below-market terms. Furthermore, Brazil has not demonstrated, on the basis of its arguments concerning statements by EDC officials and EDC's financial performance, that EDC debt financing generally con-

[111] The facts identified in the eighth, ninth, eleventh and thirteenth points of para. 9.340 of the Panel Report all relate to the TPC programme as a whole.
[112] Canada's appellant's submission, para. 77.
[113] Panel Report, para. 9.347.

> fers a "benefit". Had Brazil done so, we may have been required to make the inferences requested by Brazil.[114]

182. Brazil appeals this ruling of the Panel and claims that the Panel committed an error of law by failing to draw adverse inferences from Canada's refusal to submit information requested about the EDC's financing of the ASA transaction. Brazil believes that, in the circumstances of this case, the Panel was obliged to infer that the information Canada withheld was prejudicial to Canada's position. Brazil supports its arguments by reference to authorities cited from public international law. Brazil asks us to reverse the Panel ruling, to draw ourselves the adverse inferences which Brazil contends the Panel should have drawn, and to determine that the evidence of record, together with such adverse inferences, lead to the conclusion that the EDC's debt financing confers a "benefit" and hence fulfils that necessary element of a "subsidy". Canada maintains that the Panel did not err. Canada argues that adverse inferences may only be drawn by a panel, in the event of one party's refusal to provide information, if the other party has made out its case on a *prima facie* basis. Canada also argues that the Panel should not have requested information from it under Article 13.1 since Brazil had not yet established a *prima facie* case. The parties' arguments and counter-arguments on this issue raise a number of questions with fundamental and far-reaching implications for the entire WTO dispute settlement system. These questions relate to: first, the authority of a panel to request a party to a dispute to submit information about that dispute; second, the duty of a party to submit information requested by a panel; and, third, the authority of a panel to draw adverse inferences from the refusal by a party to provide requested information. We shall deal with these questions in that sequence.

(a) The authority of a panel to request information from a party to the dispute

183. Article 13 of the DSU reads as follows:

> 1. Each panel shall have the right to seek information and technical advice from any individual or body which it deems appropriate. However, before a panel seeks such information or advice from any individual or body within the jurisdiction of a Member it shall inform the authorities of that Member. A Member should respond promptly and fully to any request by a panel for such information as the panel considers necessary and appropriate. Confidential information which is provided shall not be revealed without

[114] Panel Report, para. 9.181.

> formal authorization from the individual, body, or authorities of the Member providing the information.
>
> 2. Panels may seek information from any relevant source and may consult experts to obtain their opinion on certain aspects of the matter. With respect to a factual issue concerning a scientific or other technical matter raised by a party to a dispute, a panel may request an advisory report in writing from an expert review group. Rules for the establishment of such a group and its procedures are set forth in Appendix 4.

184. In *Argentina - Measures Affecting Imports of Footwear, Textiles, Apparel and Other Items*, we ruled that Article 13 of the DSU made "a grant of *discretionary authority*" to panels enabling them to seek information from any relevant source.[115] (emphasis added) In *European Communities - Hormones*, we observed that Article 13 of the DSU "enable[s] panels to seek information and advice *as they deem appropriate in a particular case*."[116] (emphasis added) And, in *United States - Shrimp*, we underscored "*the comprehensive nature*" of the authority of a panel to seek information and technical advice from "any individual or body" it may consider appropriate, or from "any relevant source."[117] (emphasis added) There, we stated that:

> *It is particularly within the province and the authority of a panel to determine the need for information and advice in a specific case*, to ascertain the *acceptability* and *relevancy* of information or advice received, and to decide *what weight to ascribe to that information or advice* or to conclude that no weight at all should be given to what has been received.[118] (emphasis added)
>
> ...
>
> The thrust of Articles 12 and 13, taken together, is that *the DSU accords to a panel established by the DSB*, and engaged in a dispute settlement proceeding, *ample and extensive authority to undertake and to control the process by which it informs itself both of the relevant facts of the dispute and of the legal norms and principles applicable to such facts*. That authority, and the breadth thereof, is *indispensably necessary* to enable a panel to discharge its duty imposed by Article 11 of the DSU to "make an objective

115 Appellate Body Report, WT/DS56/AB/R, adopted 22 April 1998, para. 84.
116 *Supra*, footnote 64, para. 147.
117 *Supra*, footnote 24, para. 104.
118 *Supra*, footnote 24, para. 104.

> assessment of the matter before it, including an *objective assessment of the facts of the case* and the *applicability of and conformity with the relevant covered agreements* ... ."[119] (emphasis added)

185. It is clear from the language of Article 13 that the discretionary authority of a panel may be exercised to request and obtain information, not just "from any individual or body" within the jurisdiction of a Member of the WTO, but also from *any Member*, including *a fortiori* a Member who is a party to a dispute before a panel. This is made crystal clear by the third sentence of Article 13.1, which states: "*A Member* should respond promptly and fully to *any request by a panel for such information as the panel considers necessary and appropriate*." (emphasis added) It is equally important to stress that this discretionary authority to seek and obtain information is *not* made conditional by this, or any other provision, of the DSU upon the other party to the dispute having previously established, on a *prima facie* basis, such other party's claim or defence. Indeed, Article 13.1 imposes *no conditions* on the exercise of this discretionary authority. Canada argues that the Panel in this case had *no authority to request* the submission of information relating to the EDC's financing of the ASA transaction because Brazil had not previously established a *prima facie* case that the financial contribution offered by such financing conferred a "benefit" on ASA and therefore satisfied that other prerequisite of a prohibited export subsidy. This argument is, quite simply, bereft of any textual or logical basis. There is nothing in either the DSU or the *SCM Agreement* to sustain it. Nor can any support for this argument be derived from a consideration of the nature of the functions and responsibilities entrusted to panels in the WTO dispute settlement system - a consideration which we essay below.

(b) The duty of a Member to comply with the request of a panel to provide information

186. An important part of Brazil's appeal with respect to the issue of adverse inferences is Brazil's contention that Canada was under a duty to comply with the Panel's request to provide information relating to the EDC's financing of the ASA transaction. Canada denies that it was legally burdened with such a duty.

187. We note that Article 13.1 of the DSU provides that "A Member *should* respond promptly and fully to any request by a panel for such information as the panel considers necessary and appropriate." (emphasis added) Although the word "should" is often used colloquially to imply an exhortation, or to state a preference, it is not always used in those ways. It can also be used "to express a

[119] *Supra*, footnote 24, para. 106.

duty [or] obligation".[120] The word "should" has, for instance, previously been interpreted by us as expressing a "duty" of panels in the context of Article 11 of the DSU.[121] Similarly, we are of the view that the word "should" in the third sentence of Article 13.1 is, in the context of the whole of Article 13, used in a normative, rather than a merely exhortative, sense. Members are, in other words, under a duty and an obligation to "respond promptly and fully" to requests made by panels for information under Article 13.1 of the DSU.

188. If Members that were requested by a panel to provide information had no legal duty to "respond" by providing such information, that panel's undoubted legal "*right* to seek" information under the first sentence of Article 13.1 would be rendered meaningless. A Member party to a dispute could, at will, thwart the panel's fact-finding powers and take control itself of the information-gathering process that Articles 12 and 13 of the DSU place in the hands of the panel.[122] A Member could, in other words, prevent a panel from carrying out its task of finding the facts constituting the dispute before it and, inevitably, from going forward with the legal characterization of those facts. Article 12.7 of the DSU provides, in relevant part, that "...the report of a panel shall set out the findings of fact, the applicability of relevant provisions and the basic rationale behind any findings and recommendations that it makes." If a panel is prevented from ascertaining the real or relevant facts of a dispute, it will not be in a position to determine the applicability of the pertinent treaty provisions to those facts, and, therefore, it will be unable to make any principled findings and recommendations to the DSB.

189. The chain of potential consequences does not stop there. To hold that a Member party to a dispute is not legally bound to comply with a panel's request for information relating to that dispute, is, in effect, to declare that Member legally free to preclude a panel from carrying out its mandate and responsibility under the DSU. So to rule would be to reduce to an illusion and a vanity the fundamental right of Members to have disputes arising between them resolved through the system and proceedings for which they bargained in concluding the DSU. We are bound to reject an interpretation that promises such consequences.

190. We believe also that the duty of a Member party to a dispute to comply with a request from the panel to provide information under Article 13.1 of the DSU is but one specific manifestation of the broader duties of Members under Article 3.10 of the DSU not to consider the "use of the dispute settlement proce-

[120] *The Concise Oxford English Dictionary*, (Clarendon Press, 1995), p. 1283. See also *The Shorter Oxford English Dictionary*, (Clarendon Press, 1993), Vol. II, p. 2808, and *Black's Law Dictionary*, (West Publishing Co., 1990), p. 1379, which states that "should" "ordinarily impl[ies] duty or obligation; although usually no more than an obligation of propriety or expediency, or moral obligation, thereby distinguishing it from 'ought'."

[121] *European Communities - Hormones*, *supra*, footnote 64, para. 133.

[122] *United States - Shrimp*, *supra*, footnote 24, para. 106.

dures...as contentious acts", and, when a dispute does arise, to "engage in these procedures in good faith in an effort to resolve the dispute."

191. As noted earlier, Brazil alleges that Canada acted in disregard of its duties under Articles 13.1 and 3.10 of the DSU in refusing to comply with the Panel's request for information about the EDC's financing of the ASA transaction. Canada controverts this allegation and submits two justifications for its failure to provide the requested information. Canada's first justification is that Brazil had not, when the Panel issued its request for information on the EDC's financing for the ASA transaction, established by other evidence, a *prima facie* case that such financing constituted a prohibited export subsidy under Article 3.1(a) of the *SCM Agreement*. The second justification pleaded by Canada is that the information requested by the Panel constituted "business confidential information" and that the BCI Procedures adopted by the Panel were not adequate to ensure the protection of such information.

192. Canada's first justification rests on the assumption that a Member's duty to respond promptly and fully to a Panel's request for information arises only *after* the opposing party to the dispute has established a *prima facie* case that its complaint or defence is meritorious. A *prima facie* case, it is well to remember, is a case which, in the absence of effective refutation by the defending party (that is, in the present appeal, the Member requested to provide the information), requires a panel, as a matter of law, to rule in favour of the complaining party presenting the *prima facie* case.[123] There is, as noted earlier, nothing in either the DSU or the *SCM Agreement* to support Canada's assumption. To the contrary, a panel is vested with ample and extensive discretionary authority to determine *when* it needs information to resolve a dispute and *what* information it needs. A panel may need such information before or after a complaining or a responding Member has established its complaint or defence on a *prima facie* basis. A panel may, in fact, need the information sought in order to evaluate evidence already before it in the course of determining whether the claiming or the responding Member, as the case may be, has established a *prima facie* case or defence. Furthermore, a refusal to provide information requested on the basis that a *prima facie* case has not been made implies that the Member concerned believes that it is able to judge for itself whether the other party has made a *prima facie* case. However, no Member is free to determine for itself whether a *prima facie* case or defence has been established by the other party. That competence is necessarily vested in the panel under the DSU, and not in the Members that are parties to the dispute. We are not, therefore, persuaded by the first justification Canada gave for its refusal to provide the information requested by the Panel.

---

[123] See *European Communities - Hormones*, *supra*, footnote 64, para. 104.

193. This view is entirely consistent with our ruling in *Japan - Agricultural Products*. There, the complainant, the United States, claiming that the Japanese measure requiring varietal testing was inconsistent with Article 5.6 of the *Agreement on the Application of Sanitary and Phytosanitary Measures* (the "*SPS Agreement*"), had to show that there was an alternative measure which satisfied the three requirements of Article 5.6. The panel was not persuaded by the United States that "testing by product" was such an alternative measure. However, the panel "deduced" from statements made by experts advising it that there was another measure, the "determination of sorption levels", that met the requirements of the *SPS Agreement* - something which the United States had not even alleged or argued before the panel, let alone something on which the United States had submitted any evidence. The panel in that case proceeded to find that the Japanese measure was inconsistent with Article 5.6 of the *SPS Agreement*. In reversing this finding of the panel, we said:

> In the present case, *the Panel was correct to seek information and advice from experts to help it to understand and evaluate the evidence submitted and the arguments made by the United States and Japan* with regard to the alleged violation of Article 5.6. The Panel erred, however, when it used that expert information and advice as the basis for a finding of inconsistency with Article 5.6, since the United States did not establish a prima facie case of inconsistency with Article 5.6 based on claims relating to the "determination of sorption levels". The *United States did not even argue that the "determination of sorption levels" is an alternative measure which meets the three elements under Article 5.6.*[124] (emphasis added)

194. Thus, in *Japan - Agricultural Products*, the issue was not whether the panel there had the authority to *request* particular information from the responding Member, nor whether that responding Member was under a duty to comply with the panel's request. Nor, in that case, did any Member refuse to provide information to the panel. The issue of a panel's authority to draw adverse inferences from a party's refusal to provide requested information did not, therefore, arise. The panel in *Japan - Agricultural Products* had simply and erroneously relieved the complaining Member of the task of showing the inconsistency of the responding Member's measure with Article 5.6 of the *SPS Agreement*.

195. Canada's second justification for its refusal to comply with the Panel's request for information relates to the authority of the Panel to adopt special procedures for the additional protection of so-called business confidential informa-

[124] *Supra,* footnote 44, para. 130.

tion. Canada, with the acquiescence of Brazil, asked the Panel to adopt certain procedures, submitted by Canada, for the protection of such information. The Panel accommodated Canada's request, making only one change, at Brazil's request. We do not believe that, having requested such procedures in the first place, Canada was entitled unilaterally to reject the additional procedures adopted by the Panel and then to withhold information requested by the Panel on the ground that Canada found those procedures inadequate. Canada's position is inconsistent with the Panel's authority under the DSU to determine its own procedures. The Panel's decision to adopt the additional confidentiality procedures was in the nature of an interlocutory ruling made in the course of the proceedings before it. Canada has not appealed that interlocutory ruling and, accordingly, must be held bound by it.

196. Finally, we recall that Canada, jointly with Brazil, asked the Appellate Body to adopt *mutatis mutandis* the BCI Procedures in the course of proceedings before the Appellate Body. If Canada truly considered those procedures so inadequate as to compel it to reject the Panel's requests for information that Canada regarded as business confidential, then Canada's request that we adopt those very procedures on appeal appears to us a curious one. We find Canada's second justification for its refusal to provide requested information, just as we did its first one, less than persuasive.

(c) The drawing of adverse inferences from the refusal of a party to provide information requested by the Panel

197. We have concluded that a panel has broad legal authority to request information from a Member that is a party to a dispute, and that a party so requested has a legal duty to provide such information. The question remains: if that Member refuses to provide that information, does the panel have the authority to draw adverse inferences from that refusal?

198. We approach this question by noting once more that the mandate of a panel under the DSU requires it to determine the facts of the dispute with which it is seized, and to evaluate or characterize those facts in terms of their consistency or inconsistency with a particular provision of the *SCM Agreement* or another covered agreement. The DSU does not purport to state in what detailed circumstances inferences, adverse or otherwise, may be drawn by panels from infinitely varying combinations of facts. Yet, in all cases, in carrying out their mandate and seeking to achieve the "objective assessment of the facts" required by Article 11 of the DSU, panels routinely draw inferences from the facts placed on the record. The inferences drawn may be inferences of fact: that is, from fact A and fact B, it is reasonable to infer the existence of fact C. Or the inferences derived may be inferences of law: for example, the *ensemble* of facts found to exist warrants the characterization of a "subsidy" or a "subsidy contingent ... in fact ... upon export performance". The facts must, of course, ration-

ally support the inferences made, but inferences may be drawn whether or not the facts already on the record deserve the qualification of a *prima facie* case. The drawing of inferences is, in other words, an inherent and unavoidable aspect of a panel's basic task of finding and characterizing the facts making up a dispute. In contrast, the burden of proof is a procedural concept which speaks to the fair and orderly management and disposition of a dispute. The burden of proof is distinct from, and is not to be confused with, the drawing of inferences from facts.

199. The facts before the Panel on the issue of the EDC's debt financing may be summarized in the following terms: Brazil submitted certain evidence about the EDC's financing of the ASA transaction.[125] Canada refused to provide Brazil with information on the EDC's financing activities that Brazil requested during consultations. The Panel then requested Canada to submit transaction-specific information on the terms and conditions of the EDC's financing of the ASA transaction. Canada refused to provide the information requested by the Panel. There appears to us to be no objective reason to consider that the information requested and withheld did not exist or was not pertinent to Brazil's claim. We consider it safe to assume that the information requested by the Panel was in the possession of Canada because Canada did not indicate otherwise to the Panel. The information requested by the Panel was not publicly available. As we have explained, Canada's justifications for its refusal to provide information requested by the Panel were not accepted by the Panel.[126] On this basis, Brazil urges that the Panel erred in law by not drawing the inference that the information withheld by Canada was, in its nature or tenor, adverse to Canada and supportive of Brazil's claim that the EDC's debt financing, at least in that particular transaction, amounted to a prohibited export subsidy under Article 3.1(a) of the *SCM Agreement*.

200. We note, preliminarily, that the "adverse inference" that Brazil believes the Panel should have drawn is not appropriately regarded as a punitive inference in the sense of a "punishment" or "penalty" for Canada's withholding of information. It is merely an inference which in certain circumstances could be logically or reasonably derived by a panel from the facts before it.

201. We note also the fact that Article 4 of the *SCM Agreement*, which is applicable in respect of proceedings relating to alleged *prohibited export subsidies*, does not specifically address the matter of drawing adverse inferences from a Member's refusal to provide information. We take special note, however, of the

---

[125] The evidence presented to the Panel on the ASA transaction consisted of a Form 10-Q, filed by ASA Holdings, Inc., with the US Securities and Exchange Commission for the quarterly period ended 31 March 1997 (file No. 333-13071) and the 1997 Annual Report of ASA Holdings, Inc. (see Panel Report, para. 6.56, footnotes 200 and 201).

[126] We agree with the Panel that Canada's justifications were not legally acceptable (see paras. 192 and 196 of this Report).

fact that Annex V of the *SCM Agreement*, which deals with procedures for developing information about "serious prejudice" in cases involving *actionable subsidies* under Part III of the same Agreement, *does* address, in impressive detail, the drawing of adverse inferences under certain circumstances.[127] Annex V of the *SCM Agreement* reads, in pertinent part:

> 1. *Every Member shall cooperate in the development of evidence to be examined by a panel in procedures under paragraphs 4 through 6 of Article 7.*
>
> ...
>
> 6. *If the subsidizing and/or third-country Member fail to cooperate in the information-gathering process, the complaining Member will present its case of serious prejudice, based on evidence available to it, together with facts and circumstances of the non-cooperation of the subsidizing and/or third-country Member.* Where information is unavailable due to non-cooperation by the subsidizing and/or third-country Member, *the panel may complete the record as necessary relying on best information otherwise available.*
>
> 7. *In making its determination, the panel should draw adverse inferences from instances of non- cooperation by any party involved in the information-gathering process.*
>
> 8. In making a *determination to use either best information available or adverse inferences, the panel shall consider* the advice of the DSB representative nominated under paragraph 4 as to the *reasonableness of any requests for information and the efforts made by parties to comply with these requests in a cooperative and timely manner.*
>
> 9. *Nothing in the information-gathering process shall limit the ability of the panel to seek such additional information it deems essential to a proper resolution to the dispute, and which was not adequately sought or developed during that process.* However, ordinarily the panel should not request additional information to complete the record *where the information would support a particular party's position and the absence of that information in the record is the result of unreasonable non-cooperation by that party in the* information-gathering process. (emphases added)

[127] The provisions of Annex V of the *SCM Agreement* are identified in Appendix 2 of the DSU as "special or additional rules and procedures".

202. There is no logical reason why the Members of the WTO would, in conceiving and concluding the *SCM Agreement*, have granted panels the authority to draw inferences in cases involving actionable subsidies that *may* be illegal *if* they have certain trade effects, but not in cases that involve prohibited export subsidies for which the adverse effects are presumed. To the contrary, the appropriate inference is that the authority to draw adverse inferences from a Member's refusal to provide information belongs *a fortiori* also to panels examining claims of prohibited export subsidies. Indeed, that authority seems to us an ordinary aspect of the task of all panels to determine the relevant facts of any dispute involving any covered agreement: a view supported by the general practice and usage of international tribunals.[128]

203. Clearly, in our view, the Panel had the legal authority and the discretion to draw inferences from the facts before it - including the fact that Canada had refused to provide information sought by the Panel.[129] The Panel acknowledged that it had the authority to draw such inferences, but it declined nonetheless to draw the "inference that EDC debt financing in the Canadian regional aircraft sector confers a 'benefit'." The Panel stated that it did not believe "there is sufficient basis" for such an inference.[130] Brazil poses the issue: did the Panel err in law or abuse its discretion by declining to make that inference?

204. In confronting this issue, we note that the Panel's statement seems less than completely clear. Did the Panel, in fact, decline to take account of Canada's refusal to provide information and refuse to infer that the information withheld would support Brazil's claim? Or was the Panel saying that *all* the facts before

---

[128] See, for instance, *The Corfu Channel Case*, 1949, ICJ 4, p. 18, where the International Court of Justice stated that " ... the victim of a breach of international law is often unable to furnish direct proof of facts giving rise to responsibility. Such a State should be allowed a more liberal recourse to inferences of fact and circumstantial evidence. This indirect evidence is admitted in all systems of law, and its use is recognized by international decisions."; *Case Concerning Military and Paramilitary Activities In and Against Nicaragua*, 1986 ICJ 14, pp. 82-86, paras. 152, 154-156, where on the basis of the facts before it, the International Court of Justice found that it could "reasonably infer" that certain aid had been provided from Nicaraguan territory; the International Court of Justice also made use of inferences to conclude that the scale of this aid ceased to be significant after the early months of 1981; *Case Concerning The Barcelona Traction, Light and Power Company, Limited*, 1970 ICJ 3, p. 215, para. 97. Judge Jessup, in his separate opinion, opined that "... if a party fails to produce on demand a relevant document which is in its possession, there may be an inference that the document 'if brought, would have exposed facts unfavourable to the party ...'". The Mexican-United States General Claims Commissions stated, in *William A. Parker (U.S.A.) v. United Mexican States* (Reports of International Arbitral Awards, Vol. IV, 35, p. 39), that "[i]n any case where evidence which would probably influence its decision is peculiarly within the knowledge of the claimant or of the respondent Government, the failure to produce it, unexplained, may be taken into account by the Commission in reaching a decision." See also D.V. Sandifer, *Evidence Before International Tribunals*, Revised Edition, (University Press of Virginia, 1975), p. 153.

[129] We have summarized certain of the pertinent facts that were before the Panel in para. 199 of this Report.

[130] Panel Report, para. 9.181.

it, *including* Canada's withholding of information, did not reasonably warrant a finding that the EDC's debt financing in the Canadian regional aircraft sector confers a "benefit" and amounts to a prohibited subsidy? This appears to us to be precisely the type of situation in which a panel should examine very closely indeed whether the full *ensemble* of the facts on the record reasonably permits the inference urged by one of the parties to be drawn, because a party's refusal to collaborate has the potential to undermine the functioning of the dispute settlement system. The continued viability of that system depends, in substantial measure, on the willingness of panels to take all steps open to them to induce the parties to the dispute to comply with their duty to provide information deemed necessary for dispute settlement. In particular, a panel should be willing expressly to remind parties - during the course of dispute settlement proceedings - that a refusal to provide information requested by the panel may lead to inferences being drawn about the inculpatory character of the information withheld.

205. If we had been deciding the issue that confronted the Panel, we might well have concluded that the facts of record[131] did warrant the inference that the information Canada withheld on the ASA transaction[132] included information prejudicial to Canada's denial that the EDC had conferred a "benefit" and granted a prohibited export subsidy. Yet, we do not believe that the record provides a sufficient basis for us to hold that the Panel erred in law, or abused its discretionary authority, in concluding that Brazil had not done enough to compel the Panel to make the inferences requested by Brazil. For this reason, we let the Panel's finding of *not proven* remain, and we decline Brazil's appeal on this issue.

206. By this finding, we do not intend to suggest that Brazil is precluded from pursuing another dispute settlement complaint against Canada, under the provisions of the *SCM Agreement* and the DSU, concerning the consistency of certain of the EDC's financing measures with the provisions of the *SCM Agreement*. In that respect, we note that Brazil may request information from Canada, under Article 25.8 of the *SCM Agreement*. In the event of such a request, Article 25.9 of the *SCM Agreement* requires Canada to provide information sufficient to en-

---

[131] Certain of these facts are summarized at para. 199 of this Report.

[132] Brazil appealed the Panel's failure to draw adverse inferences from a refusal by Canada, in only one instance, to provide information requested by the Panel, that is, its refusal to provide information on the terms and conditions of the ASA transaction. However, we note that Canada also withheld, for various reasons, such as the protection of information claimed to be "business confidential" and "Cabinet" and "Ministerial" privilege, other information requested by the Panel under Article 13.1 of the DSU (the Panel records Canada's repeated refusals to provide full information to the Panel at paras. 9.188, 9.218, 9.242, 9.272, 9.293, 9.294, 9.299, 9.303, 9.313 and 9.327 of the Panel Report). We observe that the Panel "regretted" that Canada chose not to provide the Panel with certain of the information requested under Article 13.1 of the DSU (see Panel Report, paras. 9.244 and 9.314, footnote 621) and that the Panel did not accept Canada's reasons for withholding that information (see Panel Report, paras. 9.66-9.69 and 9.347, footnote 633).

able Brazil to assess the "compliance" of those measures with the *SCM Agreement*.

VIII. EDC DEBT FINANCING

207. With respect to the EDC's debt financing activities, the Panel found that "there is no *prima facie* case that EDC debt financing confers a 'benefit', and therefore constitutes a 'subsidy', within the meaning of Article 1 of the SCM Agreement."[133] In reaching this finding, the Panel reviewed evidence presented by Brazil in the form of certain statements made by officials of the EDC[134], evidence on the EDC's "financial performance" and, in particular, its net interest margin[135], and evidence on the EDC's financing of the ASA transaction.[136]

208. Brazil argues that, in making this finding, the Panel erred in its "legal characterization" of the facts.[137] In its appeal, Brazil relies on three pieces of evidence that it believes demonstrate that the "financial contribution" in the form of the EDC's debt financing "confers" a "benefit" and is, therefore, a "subsidy" within the meaning of Article 1.1 of the *SCM Agreement*: first, the EDC's provision of a 16.5-year lease period for the financing of the ASA transaction; second, a statement by the former President of the EDC, Mr. Paul Labbé, that the EDC's debt financing provides Canadian exporters with an "edge"[138]; and, third, a statement by Canada in the course of the Panel proceedings that the EDC "does not always offer the most attractive financing package".[139]

209. With respect to the ASA transaction, Brazil argues that the 16.5-year lease period constitutes a "benefit" since this lease-period exceeds the maximum 10-year lease period that governments participating in the *OECD Arrangement* are authorized to offer.[140] Canada contends that Brazil did not make this argument to the Panel and that, as a result, this argument "cannot give rise to an 'issue of law covered in the panel report'."[141]

210. During the oral hearing, we asked Brazil to identify where, in its arguments before the Panel, it had argued that the 16.5-year financing term was a "benefit" on the ground that it exceeded the terms of the *OECD Arrangement*. In a written response to our question, Brazil pointed, on the one hand, to statements it made to the Panel concerning the 16.5-year length of the ASA financing pe-

133 Panel Report, para. 9.182.
134 *Ibid.*, paras. 9.162 - 9.165.
135 *Ibid.*, paras. 9.166 - 9.174.
136 *Ibid.*, paras. 9.175 - 9.182.
137 Brazil's appellant's submission, para. 9.
138 This statement is quoted in full at para. 6.57 of the Panel Report.
139 Canada's second written submission to the Panel, para. 63, footnote 48.
140 *OECD Arrangement*, Annex III, Part 2, chapter V, para. 21(a).
141 Canada's appellee's submission, para. 10, quoting Article 17.6 of the DSU.

riod and the allegedly "concessionary *rates*"[142] offered by the EDC to ASA and, on the other hand, to arguments Brazil made to the Panel about the *OECD Arrangement* in the context of the EDC's equity financing.[143] Having examined those statements and arguments, we conclude that Brazil has not identified any submission to the Panel, oral or written, in which it brought these two distinct elements together to argue that a 16.5-year lease period is a "benefit" because it exceeds the terms of the *OECD Arrangement*. Therefore, we find that this argument was not made to the Panel and that the Panel made no finding relating to it. It was raised for the first time in this appeal.

211. In our view, this new argument raised by Brazil is beyond the scope of appellate review. Article 17.6 of the DSU provides that "[a]n appeal shall be limited to issues of law covered in the panel report and legal interpretations developed by the panel." In principle, new arguments are not *per se* excluded from the scope of appellate review, simply because they are new. However, for us to rule on Brazil's new argument, we would have to solicit, receive and review new facts that were not before the Panel, and were not considered by it. In our view, Article 17.6 of the DSU manifestly precludes us from engaging in any such enterprise. We note, furthermore, that, if complaining parties were allowed to raise new arguments of this nature on appeal, that could also undermine the due process rights of responding parties, which would not have had the opportunity to rebut such allegations by submitting evidence in response.[144]

212. The statement made by the former President of the EDC to which Brazil refers was the following:

> EDC's financing support gives Canadian exporters an *edge* when they bid on overseas projects. . . . Trade deals increasingly depend on complex and tightly negotiated financing arrangements where a few basis points in interest rates can make or break the deal. Exporters are having to bid not just on the basis of quality and price, but also on

[142] Brazil's first written submission to the Panel, para. 6.4.

[143] Brazil's reply, by letter of 15 June 1999, to our question posed at the oral hearing. Brazil referred to: its first written submission to the Panel, paras. 4.4 and 6.4; Brazil's reply to Question 11 of the Questions Posed by the Panel at the first Panel meeting with the parties; Brazil's comments of 8 January 1999 on Canada's replies to Questions 6, 10 and 28 of the Questions Posed by the Panel at the second Panel meeting with the parties; Brazil also referred to Canada's first written submission to the Panel, paras. 73, 74, 160 and 161; Canada's reply to Question 28 of the Questions Posed by the Panel at the second Panel meeting with the parties; and Canada's statement of its oral submission to the Panel at the first Panel meeting with the parties, para. 5.

[144] In that respect, we observe that Canada cites four transactions in the field of aircraft financing which it believes demonstrate that "a financing term for regional jet aircraft of greater than 10 years - as a matter of fact, up to 18 years - is entirely within the bounds of commercial practice." Canada's appellee's submission, para. 64.

the basis of the financing package supporting the sale. (emphasis added)

213. The Panel observed that, in view of Canada's explanation of this statement, "the relevant 'edge' is the ability of the EDC's officials to assemble better structured financial packages on the basis of their knowledge and expertise."[145] In light of Canada's explanation, the Panel took the view that there was a "possibility for divergent contextual interpretations" of this statement and inferred that it "provides no firm guidance as to whether the EDC provides exporters with an 'edge' through subsidization."[146] The Panel's inference from this evidence does not appear to us to be either illogical or unreasonable, and Brazil has not demonstrated that the Panel's conclusion is tainted by any error of law. Thus, we are not persuaded by Brazil's argument based on this statement.

214. The third fact on which Brazil relies in appealing this issue is Canada's statement, made in its second written submission to the Panel, that the EDC "does not always offer the most attractive financing package available to regional aircraft customers." This statement was not the subject of any factual or legal findings by the Panel. Brazil does not argue that the Panel erred in failing to make a finding relying on this statement. Rather, Brazil argues that this statement helps to show that the EDC's debt financing constitutes a "benefit".

215. Brazil has failed to demonstrate that the Panel erred in law in its consideration of this statement. We note that the Panel asked Canada for clarification as to the meaning of the statement[147], and Canada's response to the Panel indicates that this statement appears consistent with the EDC doing no more than acting as a commercial financing body.[148] We are unable, therefore, to hold that the Panel has erred in law in failing to rely on this statement.

216. For these reasons, we conclude that Brazil's arguments on appeal do not demonstrate that the Panel committed an error of law in finding that "there is no *prima facie* case that the EDC's debt financing confers a 'benefit', and therefore constitutes a 'subsidy', within the meaning of Article 1 of the SCM Agreement."[149]

---

[145] Panel Report, para. 9.163.

[146] *Ibid.*

[147] Question 10 of the Questions, dated 10 December 1998, posed by the Panel to Canada at the second Panel meeting with the parties.

[148] Canada's reply, of 21 December 1998, to Question 10 of the Questions posed by the Panel at the second Panel meeting with the parties.

[149] Panel Report, para. 9.182.

IX. EDC EQUITY FINANCING OF CRJ CAPITAL

217. Brazil contests the Panel's finding that "there is no factual basis on which to establish a *prima facie* case that the EDC has made equity infusions into CRJ Capital that have facilitated CRJ Capital's ability to lease or sell Canadian regional aircraft at a reduced price."[150] Brazil argues that the evidence on the Panel record establishes that this investment confers a "benefit", and, therefore, constitutes a "subsidy". In making this argument, Brazil relies on CRJ Capital's "total capital"[151] structure and certain statements made by Mr. Richard Dixon, an official of Industry Canada, to the effect that CRJ Capital offers borrowers with a double-B credit rating lending rates that are ordinarily available only to borrowers with a double-A credit rating.[152]

218. Brazil asserts before us, as it did before the Panel, that CRJ Capital's "total capital" structure permits CRJ Capital to provide financing of regional aircraft at lower-than-market rates. However, we see no facts in the Panel record to support this assertion. Indeed, in these appeal proceedings, Canada contested Brazil's description of CRJ Capital's capital structure, which is an essential aspect of Brazil's argument.[153] Moreover, in our view, Mr. Dixon's statements are not sufficient, on their own, to establish a finding that CRJ Capital offered preferential financing, let alone that it was the EDC's equity investment that permitted CRJ Capital to provide such financing. We note, for instance, that there is no evidence in the Panel record of any transaction in which CRJ Capital *actually offered* financing terms of the type described by Mr. Dixon.

219. We, therefore, find that Brazil's arguments on appeal do not demonstrate that the Panel erred in law by finding that "there is no factual basis on which to establish a *prima facie* case that the EDC has made equity infusions into CRJ Capital that have facilitated CRJ Capital's ability to lease or sell Canadian regional aircraft at a reduced price." [154]

X. FINDINGS AND CONCLUSIONS

220. For the reasons set out in this Report, the Appellate Body:

(a) upholds the Panel's interpretation of the term "benefit" in Article 1.1(b) of the *SCM Agreement*;

(b) upholds the Panel's interpretation and application of the expression "contingent ... in fact ... upon export performance" and the

[150] Panel Report, para. 9.200.
[151] Brazil's appellant's submission, para. 92.
[152] This statement is quoted at para. 6.136 of the Panel Report.
[153] Statement by Canada at the oral hearing.
[154] Panel Report, para. 9.200.

Panel's finding that "TPC assistance to the Canadian regional aircraft industry is 'contingent...in fact...upon export performance' within the meaning of Article 3.1(a) of the *SCM Agreement*"[155];

(c) concludes that the Panel did not err in law or abuse its discretion by declining to draw inferences from Canada's refusal to provide information requested by the Panel about certain debt financing activities of the EDC;

(d) upholds the finding of the Panel that Brazil had not established a *prima facie* case that the debt financing activities of the EDC in support of the Canadian regional aircraft industry confer a "benefit" within the meaning of Article 1.1(b) of the *SCM Agreement*; and

(e) upholds the finding of the Panel that Brazil had not established a *prima facie* case that the equity investment by the EDC in CRJ Capital confers a "benefit" within the meaning of Article 1.1(b) of the *SCM Agreement*.

221. The Appellate Body *recommends* that the DSB request that Canada bring its export subsidies found in the Panel Report, as upheld by our Report, to be inconsistent with Canada's obligations under Articles 3.1(a) and 3.2 of the *SCM Agreement* into conformity with its obligations under that Agreement. Specifically, we recall that the Panel recommended that "Canada shall withdraw the subsidies identified in sub-paragraphs (b) and (f) of [paragraph 10.1 of the Panel Report] within 90 days."[156]

155 Panel Report, para. 9.347.

156 Panel Report, para. 10.4.